ENGLISH AND WELSH
PRIESTS 1558–1800

ENGLISH AND WELSH PRIESTS 1558–1800

A Working List

edited by

DOMINIC AIDAN BELLENGER

Monk of Downside

DOWNSIDE ABBEY
BATH, ENGLAND

Downside Abbey
Stratton on the Fosse
Bath, England, BA3 4RH

British Library Cataloguing in Publication Data:

English and Welsh Priests 1558–1800
   1. Catholic Church—England—Clergy—Biography
   2. Catholic Church—England—History—Modern period, 1500–
   3. Clergy—England—Biography

I. Bellenger, Dominic Aidan
262'.14242   BX4676

ISBN   0-9502759-2-1

Cum permissu superiorum

Data capture and manipulation by Dom Charles Fitzgerald-Lombard.
Transmitted for typesetting to The Oakhill Press, Bath.
Printed and bound at Gateshead, England, by The Paradigm Press.

CONTENTS

PREFACE

English and Welsh Priests is intended to provide as complete a list as possible of Roman Catholic priests ordained between the years 1558 and 1800 who either worked on the English and Welsh Mission or who were members of English religious communities abroad. It also records, as much as information allows, foreign priests (and those from Scotland and Ireland) who worked in England and Wales together with English and Welsh priests who lived and worked abroad as members of non-English religious communities.

The work leading up to the publication of this volume began in the summer of 1982 when Miss Rosemary Rendel, the secretary of the Catholic Record Society, asked me to collate the information contained in the card index of recusant priests compiled by the late Brigadier T. B. Trappes-Lomax (1895-1962) which is kept in the Society's library at Mount Street.

What follows, however, is not merely a summary of the card index. Although the index provided a starting-point much of its information has been supplanted by material which has come to light since the Brigadier's death. Many more details have become available both in manuscript and in print, and the alphabetical list of nearly 6000 priests, which forms the core of this work, is the distillation of many sources.

New material is constantly appearing and being re-interpreted and it is hoped that the present list will encourage further research. It makes no pretence at being definitive—a task made impossible not only by the nature of surviving records but also by the secrecy and circumlocution which were characteristic features of English Catholic life, especially in the first hundred years covered by this volume. Nevertheless, the storage of historical data on the computer allows corrections and additions to be made with comparative ease, and it is hoped that later editions of the work will have the benefit of criticism and new information.

I would like to thank the following for their help in the course of the last two years: Fr Godfrey Anstruther O.P.; Fr Beda (Chronicler of the Sacro Eremo, Tuscolano); Mrs J. Brooks; Fr Isidore Carey O.D.C.; Miss Judith Champ; Mr J. M. Cleary; Fr Richard Copsey O.Carm.; Mr Jakob Cornides; Fr Francis Edwards S.J.; Mr Michael Formoso; Mr Michael Foster; Mr Stewart Foster; Br Jonathan Gell O.C.S.O.; Mr John Gray; Fr Michael B. Hackett O.S.A.; Fr Sebastian Holland O.F.M.Cap.; Fr Geoffrey Holt S.J.; Dr David Lunn; Professor F. X. Martin O.S.A.; Fr Justin McLoughlin O.F.M.; Fr W. J. Nicholson; Fr Edmund O'Gorman O.F.M.Conv.; Mr Geoffrey Parmiter; Miss Elizabeth Poyser; Dr David Rogers; Dom Geoffrey Scott; Fr Christopher Smith; Fr W. Vincent Smith; Hon. Georgina Stonor; Fr Benedict Wallis, O.Cart.; Fr Piet Wijngaard O.Carm.; Fr Michael Williams. My particular debt is to the Abbot and

1

Community of Downside who have supported this venture throughout, and especially DD. Denis Agius, Boniface Hill, Philip Jebb, Andrew Moore, Daniel Rees, Hilary Steuert and Richard Yeo. Without the close assistance and expertise of Dom Charles Fitzgerald-Lombard the book would not have seen the light of day and he is to be thanked as the most patient and helpful of collaborators.

HISTORICAL INTRODUCTION

I THE ENGLISH CATHOLICS 1558-1800

The Reformation brought to an end the unity of the medieval *Ecclesia Anglicana*. Although the majority of the population accepted the new church order of the Tudors, a minority remained faithful to the Holy See. This small community developed over the centuries a cohesive identity and ecclesiastical organisation of its own. In the survival and consolidation of that community the priests, of whom about 6000 have been traced, played a crucial part, providing through the sacraments, and especially through the mass, a focal point for what might otherwise have been a life on the margins of society.

John Bossy, in the introduction to his magisterial survey of *The English Catholic Community* argues for a clear distinction between a history of Pre-Reformation Christendom in England and a history of English Catholicism. He chooses the foundation of the seminary in Douai (1568) as the *terminus a quo* of the English Catholic Community, and the restoration of the hierarchy (1850), a moment of critical discontinuity, as the *terminus ad quem*. In general, such a demarcation seems to make sense, and I have followed it to the extent of not listing those Henrician and Marian priests who continued to adhere to 'the old religion' in Elizabeth's reign. The choice of the dates 1558-1800 has been dictated by another consideration. The accession of Elizabeth marks the end of the native education and ordination of the Roman Catholic clergy. The end of the eighteenth century, with the disruptive impact of the French Revolution on the English Catholic foundations in Europe, brings the period of exclusively foreign formation to an end. It is the English and Welsh priests who were educated abroad who form, with some exceptions, the subjects of this book.

Education abroad was made necessary by the policy of government opposition to the Catholics for most of the period 1558-1800, an opposition which became at times an active persecution. The State marked out Catholics as different. In the course of Elizabeth's reign the Catholics became known as recusants (Latin, *recusare*, to refuse) because they were unwilling to attend the worship of the Established Church, an obligation enjoined by the Act of Uniformity of 1559 and reinforced by later statutes. Recusants were liable to be prosecuted in both civil and ecclesiastical courts, and, if convicted, could find themselves not only facing financial penalties, but also expulsion from London, restriction to their own homes, and excommunication. The names of convicted recusants who had been fined by the sheriffs in each county were entered, in the early days, on the Pipe Rolls, and then, from 1592 to 1691, in a separate series of Recusant Rolls. These records listed Catholic and Protestant recusants together, but the term recusant is now generally restricted to Catholics. The failure of the Stuarts (who, under James II, had

3

attempted a Catholic revival) led to renewed legislation. In 1689, under William and Mary, those refusing the oaths of allegiance, supremacy, and the test declaration (originally imposed in 1678) were considered guilty of 'constructive recusancy' and from 1693 such people could be punished by a double land tax, an exaction rarely enforced. Under Queen Anne in 1726 'constructive recusancy' was broadened to embrace 'every Papist or Person making Profession of the Popish Religion'. In the course of the eighteenth century official attitudes to Catholicism softened, and the legislation was gradually repealed after the first Catholic Relief Act of 1778; the offence of recusancy was abolished by the Relief Act of 1791.

The priests, in addition, had particular legislation to restrict their activities. In 1585 an act was passed against Jesuits, seminary priests 'and other such like disobedient persons' which made it treasonable for any such to be found in England. Over one hundred Elizabethan priests were to die as martyrs following this legislation. Similar legislation continued to be passed in the seventeenth century and was given new teeth by an act of 1699 which was concerned with 'further preventing the growth of Popery'. This offered £100 for the apprehension of a priest, and life imprisonment for a Catholic discovered exercising episcopal or sacerdotal functions.

The draconian character of the legislation conceals from view the quiet and undisturbed lives which many English Catholics and their priests were able to live in the recusant period, especially after the reign of Elizabeth. Nevertheless, the Catholics learnt to be circumspect, and this is no more clearly demonstrated than in the organisation of what became known as 'The English Mission'.

The Catholic Church in England and Wales during the recusant period was not governed by a normal diocesan structure. On the death of the last of the Marian bishops (Thomas Goldwell of St Asaph) in 1585, the ancient hierarchy came to an end. In the fifty years that followed, no serious effort was made either to continue the line, or to organise the Catholic community in a new way. Many believed that the 'Elizabethan Settlement' would not last, and considered it best to wait until what they considered an inevitable Catholic revival took place. In the interim the English Catholics had to be content with what organisation they could muster themselves. Henry Garnet, who was Jesuit superior in England from 1586 until his arrest after the Gunpowder Plot of 1605, acted for much of that time as unofficial co-ordinator of 'the mission' as a whole, while in Rome, Cardinal William Allen, designated 'Prefect of the English Mission' in 1581, looked after English Catholic interests. In 1598 an archpriest, with twelve regional assistants, was appointed, but he never exercised wide jurisdiction, and the English Catholic clergy were much disturbed by controversies between seculars and Jesuits.

In 1623, Pope Gregory XV, who had established *Propaganda Fide* (the Roman curial department dealing with missionary countries), appointed a vicar apostolic for England. A vicar apostolic was a prelate in episcopal orders who had jurisdiction in missionary areas, but who did not have the complete authority of a diocesan bishop; he was directly answerable for all his actions to *Propaganda*. In the years 1623-1631, the Vicars Apostolic of England, encouraged by the regaining of episcopal status for the English Catholic clergy, attempted to impose their authority on the fledgling community, seeing themselves as the symbol of a church restored. The experiment in episcopal government was far from being an unqualified success, but during these years the institutions of a missionary church were established. Vicars general, archdeacons and rural deans were appointed. A chapter of a dean and eighteen canons, representing the secular clergy, gained sufficient authority to rule the mission as an oligarchy in the fifty years up to 1688 when the English Catholics were again without a bishop. By the middle of the seventeenth century the English Catholics had a more or less effective church organisation dominated on the one hand by the chapter of the secular clergy, and on the other by the effectively autonomous regulars.

In 1688 Pope Innocent XII revived the idea of the vicars apostolic, and created four districts or vicariates: the London, Midland, Northern and Western, which survived until 1840. From 1688 the secular mission, and to an increasing extent the mission as a whole, was run by four individuals operating in four large areas: the seeds of a diocesan structure were being sown.

There were no Catholic parishes as such throughout the period, and chapels were provided through three main agencies: the gentry, who built chapels in their houses for themselves, their tenants and their servants; the embassy chapels in London (supplemented for several decades in the seventeenth century by the Chapels Royal at St James's and Somerset House provided for the use of the Catholic Queens of England) which opened their doors to the metropolitan Catholic population, not all of it native; and, increasingly as time went on, 'self-financing' chapels supported by members of the major religious orders, or paid for by prosperous Catholics either singly or in groups. In some places where there was none of these supports priests were 'on circuit' living in rented rooms and finding shelter where they could.

The English Catholic Community, by the end of the eighteenth century, despite a decline in priestly vocations, had a well developed missionary structure. It was gaining in confidence and was particularly strong in Lancashire, the county which always remained the heartland of Catholic England. In general the English Catholics were distinguished by their Englishness. The list of names which follows is a striking affirmation of this, as is the absence, outside London, of large numbers of foreign priests at work on the mission. The priests, bound by a mission oath to serve in England, were as proud to be English Catholics as they were to be Roman Catholics.

II THE SECULAR CLERGY

The seculars, who formed the majority of the English Catholic clergy, were the products of the English seminaries on the continent. At Elizabeth's accession many Catholic-minded university men (mainly from Oxford, which seems always to have been a more 'Catholic' university than Cambridge) went abroad to follow their consciences. Many settled at the university of Louvain, which provided the first centre for the English Catholics in exile. The Low Countries, then under Spanish rule and easy of access to England, were to remain the chief foreign centre for the English Catholic clergy in exile throughout the period, and one town in particular, Douai, in Flanders, where a university with a theological faculty was opened in 1562, gave shelter to several English Catholic religious establishments.

The most notable of these establishments was the English College, an English

5

seminary inspired by the teaching of the Council of Trent which had decreed the setting up of special colleges where selected boys could be given a thorough religious training to provide a fruitful seed-bed (Latin, *seminarium*) for ministers of God. At the beginning the English College had about it something of the character of an Oxford College. The training of a secular priest tended to be a long process, beginning with the classical foundations essential for a church which used Latin as its official and living language, and ending in holy orders. The candidates for holy orders—some financed by their parents, others on scholarships—started their training in their early teens, and finished it in their early twenties: the three major orders of sub-deacon, deacon and priest normally being conferred at the ages of 21, 22 and 24 respectively.

The secular priest, although not bound by religious vows, passed his formative years in the quasi-monastic setting of the seminary, and these establishments provided a common background and characteristic spirituality for the clergy. The principal seminaries were:

DOUAI   The English College at Douai was opened officially on 29 September 1568. Political troubles forced its move to Rheims in March 1578. It remained there until June 1593 when it again became possible to return to Douai. Its superior, the president, was always an English secular priest, and it remained the most important of the colleges, both in influence and in numbers ordained, until its suppression in 1792.

LISBON   The College of SS Peter and Paul at Lisbon was founded in 1622, and the first priests and students arrived—from Douai—in August 1628. It survived until 1971. Its presidents, like Douai's, were always secular priests.

MADRID   St George's College, Madrid, was founded in 1611, and was suppressed in 1767 because it was under the supervision of the Jesuits.

PARIS   In 1611 Arras College in Paris was founded as a house of higher studies and as a centre of Catholic polemical writing for the English Catholics. This establishment had closed by about 1635, and St Gregory's College, which existed from 1667 to 1785, was a new foundation. It was intended to give priests or students for the priesthood the opportunity of attending the Sorbonne, with a view to obtaining a doctorate in divinity. This college was an élite establishment with few members, and in its entire life it produced only 32 doctors.

ROME   The English Pilgrim Hospice in Rome, with its medieval origins, was gradually transformed into a seminary. Students began to arrive there from Douai as early as August 1576, but the Bull of foundation was not issued until 1 May 1579 and the feast of St Thomas of Canterbury, 29 December 1580, is kept as the official foundation date. The English College Rome had a Jesuit superior until 1773, when (until its temporary closure in 1798) it was under the supervision of Italian seculars. In that last quarter century its contribution to the mission was small, but it was successfully re-established in 1818 and is still operating.

SEVILLE   The English College at Seville was founded in November 1592 by a group of priests and students from Valladolid. It was a small college, and, as it was under Jesuit management, was suppressed in 1767.

VALLADOLID The College of St Alban, Valladolid, was officially opened in September 1589. The college, which still exists, was administered firstly by Jesuits and later by seculars. Many future Benedictines received their early training at this college, but it was never a large establishment: there were never more than twenty-two students after the peak year of 1604, and the other Iberian colleges never had as many. There were no students between 1739 and 1756 when the college was being rebuilt, and there were few in the two politically troubled decades leading up to 1800.

The French Revolution and the wars which followed it threatened the existence of the English seminaries abroad. Although Lisbon, Rome and Valladolid were to continue in their old homes when peace was restored Douai remained closed. Three new colleges were quickly established in England to educate priests for the mission:

ST CUTHBERT'S (USHAW) The northern students expelled from Douai, settled first at Old Hall Green, and were then temporarily put up at a lay school at Tudhoe, five miles from Durham, in the early months of 1794. In September of the same year a move was made to Pontop Hall, and the following month to Crook Hall, both in County Durham. The first students moved into the new college at Ushaw, in the same county, in 1808.

ST EDMUND'S (OLD HALL) The school established at Old Hall Green, near Ware, in Hertfordshire, in 1769, provided accommodation for a large group of professors and students from Douai in 1793. St Edmund's College, Old Hall, was formally established on 16 November 1793, and by 1800 new and spacious college buildings were ready for use as a seminary for students from the south of England.

ST MARY'S (OSCOTT) The Vicar Apostolic of the Midland District had decided by the end of 1793 to open a seminary which would produce at least one priest a year for his district. The college was at Oscott, three or four miles from the centre of Birmingham, in Staffordshire (it is now in Warwickshire). The present St Mary's College, Oscott, on a new but nearby site, was built between 1835 and 1838. In the second half of the eighteenth century many clerical students in the Midland District began their studies at Sedgley Park School, near Wolverhampton, in Staffordshire, founded by Bishop Challoner in 1763, and transferred to Cotton Hall, in the same county, in 1873.

III THE RELIGIOUS ORDERS

The religious orders, particularly the Benedictines, Dominicans, Franciscans and Jesuits, played an active part in the life of the English Mission after the reign of Elizabeth when the seculars predominated. At a time when normal episcopal government was lacking, the organisation of the religious provided an invaluable administrative framework, and the influence of the Benedictine and Jesuit superiors, which could occasionally come into conflict with the power of vicars apostolic, was considerable. Habits were not worn on the mission (clerical or religious dress being the luxury of a tolerant society), but the Orders preserved the corporate identity and individual charisms which were inculcated in the years of preparation. Moreover, the popular names for some of the orders based on the colour of their habits persisted: thus the Benedictines were often known as Black

Monks, the Dominicans as Black Friars, the Franciscans as Grey Friars and the Carmelites as White Friars.

The formation of a religious was a more complex and lengthy process than the training of a secular. Most of the orders, with the notable exception of the Jesuits, followed a similar pattern. The aspirant to the religious life, perhaps after some time as a postulant, but more often direct from the school attached to the religious house of his choice, would receive the habit, and then spend a year under close supervision as a novice. After the novitiate, he would make his religious profession as a member of his order, and take religious vows, generally for life. According to the decree *De Regularibus et Monialibus* of the twenty-fifth session of the Council of Trent, profession could not be made before the age of sixteen nor before a complete year's probation after the reception of the habit, under penalty of invalidation. Most of the religious in the period covered by this book were professed before they reached the age of twenty, although those who received their education in the lands of the Austrian Emperor Joseph II in the middle years of the eighteenth century had their profession deferred until they reached the age of twenty-five. After profession those who were to be ordained to the priesthood followed studies similar to the seculars.

The Jesuit system was quite distinct. A period of postulancy, which tended to be short for prospective priests, was followed by a novitiate normally lasting two years. Vows of poverty, chastity and obedience were then taken. A period of study for priest students, known in England as 'the juniorate' (a term used, too, by other religious orders) was followed by three years' philosophy, university study for younger members, and 'regency'—a period of teaching in the colleges. Four years' theology came next, with ordination to the priesthood normally taking place in the third year. A year's ascetical discipline and study—the 'tertianship' or third probation—completed training. The last step was 'profession' whereby 'temporal coadjutors' (lay brothers) and 'spiritual coadjutors' (priests) made their final commitment to the religious life. There was an inner élite of Fathers who added a fourth vow of obedience to the Pope—these were then 'professed of the four vows'.

The following religious orders were represented in the recusant period:

Augustinians

The name of St Augustine of Hippo (354-430) gave prestige to the 'Augustinian Rule' which was probably drawn up by one of his disciples in the middle of the fifth century. It legislated for a common life in accordance with the ideals of the Gospel. Augustinians were far less dependent on St Augustine than the Benedictines were on St Benedict, and the Augustinian Rule provided a framework rather than a detailed pattern of observance. The Augustinians consisted of two main groups:

(1) Canons Regular

Canons regular are clerics living in community under a rule and bound by solemn vows. Houses of *canonici regulares* have existed in one form or another since the early Church: a notable experiment in this form of life was made by St Augustine himself. The formal foundation of the Augustinian or Austin Canons, however, coincided with the reform of the papacy and the 'clericalisation' of the Church associated with Pope St Gregory VII (c.1021- 1095). During 'the Gregorian Reform' the Rule of St Augustine became the normal rule for communities of 'clerks regular', and from then onwards the terms 'regular canon' and 'Augustinian canon' were almost synonymous. There was no English house of Augustinian canons in the period covered by this book, although the order survived the Reformation and is represented today most notably in the 'Canons Regular of the Lateran' whom Pope Alexander II (1061-1073) instituted in the cathedral church of Rome.

(2) Friars

The Order of Hermits of St Augustine was founded in 1256 when Pope Alexander IV (1254-1261) united several groups of hermits who followed St Augustine's Rule and placed them under a prior general. Their constitutions were similar to those of the Dominicans. There were no English communities of 'Austin Friars', as they were generally known in medieval England, between 1558 and 1800, although many Irishmen belonged to the order and a small number worked on the English Mission. In 1588 the Discalced Augustinians (also known as Augustinian Recollects) were founded as a reformed congregation of the order.

Benedictines

I.   St Benedict's Rule, which was written in the first half of the sixth century, was the foundation document for monastic life in Western Europe. The Rule legislates for a self-sufficient, patriarchal community in which complete authority is vested in an abbot elected by a vote of the whole monastic family. The centre of Benedictine life is the communal performance of the *Opus Dei* (the divine office) and to it all other activities, intellectual and manual, ideally take second place. In the earliest times Benedictine monks were not normally in priestly orders, but by the central Middle Ages ordination was the norm for 'choir monks', as distinct from the 'lay brothers'.

In the Middle Ages, the Benedictines formed the largest and richest section of the body of English religious 'orders'. In the strict sense there is no Benedictine 'order', each monastery forming, in theory, an independent unit within a broadly similar tradition. Nevertheless, communities formed groups—often determined by historic links of foundation or geography—and the Fourth Lateran Council (1215) decreed that all Benedictine monasteries were to be organised into congregations. The first general chapter of Benedictine monks in England was held at Oxford in 1218.

The dissolution of the monasteries (1536-1540) under Henry VIII brought to an end the great period of Benedictine monasticism in England, but did not kill the congregation. Under Mary Tudor, Westminster Abbey experienced a brief revival, and during the Elizabethan and Early Stuart period a trickle of English and Welsh subjects entered Benedictine monasteries in Italy and Spain. In 1607 the last of the Westminster monks, Dom Sigebert Buckley, 'aggregated' two young English monks of the Cassinese Congregation (centred on St Benedict's own monastery at Monte Cassino) to the pre-Reformation English Congregation—thus forging some kind of link between the Black Monks of the Middle Ages and the modern period. The connection was recognised by Pope Urban VIII in the Bull *Plantata* (1633) which bestowed on the congregation, which had been restored in 1619 'every privilege, grant, indulgence, faculty and other prerogative which had ever belonged to the ancient English congregation'. This same Pope also approved of the monks serving in England outside their monasteries, and taking the missionary oath.

This system of government in the English Congregation remained in force until abrogated by the apostolic letter *Religiosus Ordo* in 1890. The communities of English monks in European exile were governed by priors (in one case, Lamspring, by an abbot) and had a normal conventual structure, but in character they were as close in spirit to the English seminaries as to a traditional monastery. This is not to say that they were lax in their observance, but that most of their number spent the greater part of their lives in England. Once on the mission, the monks became part of a corporate body distinct from their monastery of profession: the missionary province. There were two of these: Canterbury and York. The Province of York comprised all the missions in the six northern counties, together with Derbyshire, Cheshire, Nottinghamshire, Lincolnshire, and, if necessary, Scotland; the Province of Canterbury embraced the rest of England and Wales.

The whole congregation was headed by a President General who was attached, for the duration of his office, neither to province nor to monastery. In matters of importance the President General had the assistance of a council of three fathers, called 'Definitors of the Regimen' who were not allowed to hold any office with jurisdiction and formed a court of appeal. All officials, including the President General, were elected for a term of four years, a quadriennium, but at the end of four years were eligible for re-election by General Chapter. General Chapter, which was the supreme legislative authority of the Congregation, consisted of the superiors with jurisdiction, the definitor of the regimen and titular dignitaries; a number of the senior fathers of the Congregation were given the title of Cathedral Prior to perpetuate the names of the Pre-Reformation Cathedral priories. The Provincials of Canterbury and York each had a small curia consisting of two 'Definitors of the Province', and a 'Procurator' to advise on business matters. Each province was sub-divided into smaller units *praepositurae*, three in the north, four in the south.

II. The monasteries described below were the continental houses of the English Benedictine congregation in the period covered by this volume:

Abbey of SS. Adrian and Denis, Lamspring.

In 1628, as a result of territorial advances made by the Emperor Ferdinand II during the Thirty Years War, a number of former Benedictine abbeys in Germany were released from Protestant hands and became available for renewed monastic use. The English Benedictines were willing to provide the manpower. An English community resided for a short time between 1632 and 1633 at Rintelin in Westphalia, but no monks were professed for the house and the English fathers were expelled (in 1633) by the Lutherans. Lamspring an ancient foundation, formerly of nuns, was 'lent' to the English Congregation in 1643 and remained the home of the community of SS. Adrian and Denis until 1803 when it was suppressed by the Prussian government, the monks being allowed to reside there on a small pension until death. An unsuccessful revival of the community was attempted at Broadway, Worcestershire, in 1834, but relinquished in 1841. Fort Augustus Abbey in Scotland, founded in 1878, received the few survivors of the only English Benedictine house of its time to have the dignity of an abbey.

Priory of St Benedict, St Malo.

This house, founded in 1611 at St Malo in Brittany, was the least successful monastery of the congregation. It was transferred to French Maurist jurisdiction in 1669.

Priory of St Edmund, King and Martyr, Paris.

This community, founded in Paris in 1615, enabled English monks to study theology at the Sorbonne. A permanent monastery was established in the rue Saint Jacques in 1642. The community's novitiate was at a separate house at Chelles outside Paris. During the French Revolution the monks remained, under restraint, in Paris, and when peace came moved to Douai to occupy the buildings vacated by St Gregory's. They remained there until 1903 when the community settled at Woolhampton in Berkshire, retaining the name of Douai Abbey.

Priory of St Gregory the Great, Douai.

A group of English monks from the Cassinese and Valladolid (Spanish) congregations gathered at Douai in the early years of the seventeenth century and formed an English community. The first novice was received in 1607. In 1611 the monks took possession of quarters provided by Dom Philip de Caverel, Abbot of St Vedast's, Arras, which remained their home until the end of the eighteenth century. St Gregory's had a school which developed into a predominantly lay school but which, nevertheless, provided many vocations for the community. In the middle years of the eighteenth century St Gregory's served as a congregational house of studies. Driven from Douai at the French Revolution, the community lived for twenty years at Acton Burnell in Shropshire before taking possession of its present home at Downside, in Somerset, in 1814.

Priory of St Laurence the Martyr, Dieulouard.

Monastic life began at St Laurence's, Dieulouard, in Lorraine, in 1608, and continued until the French Revolution. St Laurence's was without a permanent home for some years following its removal from the continent, but it settled at Ampleforth, in Yorkshire, in the years following 1802.

III.   A small group of priests working in England belonged to the Scotic group of monasteries in Germany. At the Fourth Lateran Council, a special arrangement was made for the Scotic monasteries or *Schottenklöster* at that time Irish (the Irish were known as Scoti up to the eleventh century and the name was kept), which were to be grouped according to nationality under the jurisdiction of the abbot of St James in Ratisbon. The monasteries which remained in Irish hands were taken over by the Scots in 1515, but only two survived the Reformation—Ratisbon and Erfurt. The post-Reformation Scottish monks in Ratisbon made efforts to recover other houses, and in 1595 Würzburg was restored to Scottish monks from Ratisbon with the co-operation of Julius Echter, the reforming Prince-Bishop of Würzburg. *Plantata* encouraged the Scots monks to petition Rome for a Scots congregation—with a home mission. This did not materialize, but there was a small group of Scots monks on the English mission.

The Bridgettines

The Order of the Most Holy Saviour *(Ordo Sanctissimi Salvatoris)*, whose members are commonly known as Bridgettines or Brigittines, was founded by St

Bridget of Sweden (c.1303-1373). Bridgettine communities were organised as 'double monasteries' of men and women. The abbess ruled both communities in all temporal affairs, and 'the confessor general' (the elected superior of the men) had responsibility for spiritual direction.

The only English house of the Order, the monastery 'of St Saviour, Our Lady St Mary and St Bridget of Syon', was established by King Henry V at Twickenham in 1415, and transferred to Osterley in 1426. Suppressed in 1539 it was revived by Mary Tudor and closed once again by Elizabeth I. Community life continued at various temporary homes in the Low Counties from 1559 to 1580 in which year a house was taken at Rouen. A group of the community continued to live in England, at Lyford Grange in Berkshire, at least until the 1580's. A more permanent home was found at Lisbon where the community lived from 1594 to 1861. It survives today at East Brent in Devon, but it is now exclusively a women's order. The number of English male Bridgettines was never great.

Camaldolese

The Camaldolese were founded by St Romuald (c.953-1027). He emphasized the life of the hermit within the framework of the Benedictine Rule. His ideal was an absolute minimum of community ties, and his austere regime never attracted many followers. The life at Camaldoli (Romuald's foundation in Tuscany) greatly influenced St Bruno and the Carthusians. There were no Camaldolese houses in medieval England.

Carmelites

The Carmelites claim some continuity with the pre-Christian hermits who lived on Mount Carmel and have been seen by some to be descended directly from Elijah and 'the sons of the prophets' (2 Kings 2). Founded in Palestine by St Berthold (d. c.1195) in the 1150's, the Carmelites were given a rule in 1209 by the Latin Patriarch of Jerusalem. The failure of the Crusades caused many members of the order to return to Europe, and under their English general, St Simon Stock (c.1165-1265), they were reformed as a mendicant order. The Carmelites, by the end of the sixteenth century, were divided into two branches:

(1) The Old Observance

The Friars who continued to follow what became known as the 'mitigated' rule— 'unreformed' or calced Carmelites—never had a secure foothold in England in the recusant period, but various attempts to revive the pre-Reformation order were made. One Carmelite, George Rayner (or Raynes) came to England at the end of Mary's reign, and is said to have died in 1613 having spent some time in prison. An Irishman, Bernard of St Matthew (who died in London in 1661), worked in England during the Cromwellian period. With the accession of James II there was an attempt to make the English Mission a going concern for the Carmelites. The general, Father Paul of St Ignatius, looked to France to provide suitable missionaries and the first arrived in 1688. This mission—made up of English, Irish and French Friars—was not a success, but individual Carmelites worked in England until the end of the eighteenth century.

(2) The Discalced Carmelites

St Teresa of Avila (1515-1582) began a reform of the women's branch of the Carmelite Order which was intended to restore the 'Primitive Rule'. Her disciple St John of the Cross (1542-1591) did similar work among the friars, and the 'Teresian' reform eventually won wide acceptance. A number of Discalced Carmelites served on the English Mission, many coming from the missionary priory at Louvain and, during the reign of James II, there was a London priory at Bucklesbury. In the last few years before the French Revolution, the former Jesuit College at Tongres near Liege was used as a college for the English Carmelites. The last of the English Carmelites, Fr Francis Brewster (who described himself as having 'no superior, no inferior, being the last man') died in 1849.

Carthusians

The Carthusians owed their origin to St Bruno (c.1032-1101). His form of monasticism was eremitical and austere, and was much influenced by the primitive monks of Egypt and Palestine. The Order spread from its original monastery of the Grande Chartreuse near Grenoble (from which the English words Carthusian and Charterhouse stem) throughout Europe. The Prior of the Grande Chartreuse is *ex officio* general, and each community is governed by a prior and has its own novitiate. Most of the domestic work was done by lay brothers who ensured that the choir monks had little or no contact with the outside world. The Carthusians had only nine houses in late medieval England, but their spiritual influence was considerable, and their integrity unquestioned. Under Henry VIII, the Carthusians held to the Roman allegiance and many died for their beliefs. Mary Tudor re-opened the charterhouse of Sheen in Surrey in 1555, which was dissolved in 1559. After many years of wandering, the small community of English Carthusians, often called Sheen Anglorum, settled at Nieuport in Flanders. After its suppression in 1783, the community failed to re-establish itself, and the last of its members, Dom Bruno Finch, died in 1821. The exiled French Carthusian community at Coombe Priory, in Wiltshire, does not seem to have had any English subjects. Many of those who tried their vocation at Sheen Anglorum had already been ordained as secular priests.

Cistercians

This order, a branch of the Benedictine family, takes its name from the Abbey of Citeaux in Burgundy which was established in 1098. It attempted to follow the Benedictine Rule as literally as possible. The reform of La Trappe, a French monastery of the Order, took the Cistercians towards an ever more austere way of life. A Trappist monastery was established at Lulworth in Dorset in the 1790's, and although it was originally a French community, it took some English subjects before its closure in 1817. The first to enter was Francis Stephen Hawkins in 1795. He was ordained deacon in 1796 but never ordained priest. He died in 1856. No other English subjects were ordained before 1800.

Dominicans

St Dominic Guzman (c.1170-1221), a native of Castile, founded an order of Friars Preachers dedicated to combating heresy and teaching the faith. Under St Dominic's direction, the order took definite shape at two general chapters held at

Bologna in 1220 and 1221. The Black Friars became famous for their theological learning and for their organisational skill.

The order, under the central authority of a Master General, had a sophisticated government, which was more representative than the older orders. Groups of individual priories were arranged into provinces, which had an annual provincial chapter which consisted of the prior, and one representative from each house. The provinces (which were all equal in status) sent delegates to the Chapter General, the supreme legislative body of the Order, which had, among other duties, the responsibility of choosing the Master General—who was elected for life.

The English province was founded by St Dominic at the general chapter of 1221, and the first house was at Oxford. In Mary Tudor's reign a Dominican community was settled, in 1555, in the abandoned priory of the Austin Canons in Smithfield, on the northern edge of the City of London, while the Dominicanesses (and their chaplains) were given the ancient convent at Dartford in Kent. Both houses were closed on the accession of Elizabeth, and until the middle of the seventeenth century there was never more than a handful of English Dominicans.

The revival of the province is closely related to the influence and benevolence of Cardinal Thomas Howard, during whose lifetime the English Friars Preachers were given new life. A religious house, complete with church, at Bornhem, in Flanders, came into the hands of the English Dominicans in 1657, and with its school (opened in 1660) it provided a centre for English Dominican activity and studies on the continent. It was the rule of the order during this period that a friar was affiliated not to a province but to a particular convent. Here he would pass his novitiate and make his profession before being sent to a *studium generale* to complete his training. Such higher studies were encouraged in 1675 when Cardinal Howard acquired (from Pope Clement X) the church and adjoining house of SS. John and Paul in Rome, which became a house for English Dominican students doing their theological studies in the city. In 1695, the students vacated this college, and began the move to the new college of St Thomas at Louvain which was founded with money bequeathed by the Cardinal. In the interim, in 1685, the English Province was formally re-established.

At any one time in the period covered by this book, about half the province's manpower was engaged on missionary work. Although never on the scale of the Benedictine or Jesuit missions there were, between the years of 1620 and 1800, some sixty places served at different times by Dominicans. Their only 'permanent' missions, however, were those of Weybridge and Woburn Lodge in Surrey, Leeds in Yorkshire, Leicester and Hinckley in Leicestershire, and Hexham and Stonecroft in Northumberland. The houses at Bornhem and Louvain were closed in 1794, and the establishment opened at Carshalton in Surrey to provide a home for the Bornhem community and school closed in 1810.

Franciscans

St Francis of Assisi (c.1182-1226) taught his followers, the Friars Minor, a simple rule: 'to observe the holy Gospel of Our Lord Jesus Christ, by living in obedience without property and in chastity'. Although, as the order increased in number, the Grey Friars lost something of their founder's simplicity, they always looked back to the message of St Francis as their ideal. The Franciscans arrived in England in 1224 and made foundations at once at Canterbury, Oxford and London. By the middle of the thirteenth century there were some fifty friaries and more than 1200 Franciscans in England. The medieval Franciscans, whose founder left no detailed pattern of life for his followers, developed an administrative pattern—with a minister general, provincials and guardians (the superiors of individual houses)— not dissimilar to the Dominicans. This structure was maintained through the centuries, although, by the time of the Reformation, the tensions between the original Franciscan inspiration and the practical running of a religious order had left the male Franciscans divided into three main groups or traditions:

(1) Capuchins. This Franciscan reform movement was founded by Matteo di Bassi, of Urbino (d.1552), an observant friar. Its members wear a pointed hood (*capuche*), sandals and a beard. Its Rule, drawn up in 1529, emphasised poverty and simplicity. They were the branch of Franciscans most closely associated with the Counter-Reformation.

The first Capuchins arrived in England at the close of the sixteenth century, and as early as 1608 a start was made on an organised English Capuchin mission. By 1617 the mission was a going concern. Capuchins acted as chaplains to Queen Henrietta Maria in London. The English and Scottish Capuchins, originally supervised by a superior appointed from Ireland, were eventually formed into a provincial vicariate subject to the Irish Province. Although, in the early Stuart period, there were a number of French Capuchins in London, most of the Capuchins serving on their English mission—which lasted until 1802—were English or Irish. It is not easy to distinguish between those who worked in England and those who worked in Ireland.

(2) Conventuals. The Conventuals were those Franciscans who believed that the Order could not be restricted by the absolute poverty which had prevented the early Franciscans from having settled houses. Their ideal was the ordered life of the community. The Conventual Franciscan died out in England at the Reformation, but one Scotsman, William Thompson or Thomson, is known to have joined the order and to have been ordained in Rome about 1602. He was made titular provincial of England, and having spent time imprisoned in London, became a chaplain to Henrietta Maria. He died in Rome.

(3) Recollects. The Observants attempted to follow the Franciscan ideal without laxity. The group was given ecclesiastical approval in 1415 when the Council of Constance granted their French province special superiors. In 1443 Pope Eugenius IV provided them with a separate vicar general, and in 1517 they were given complete independence from the conventuals. The most celebrated Pre-Reformation observant house was at Greenwich, a community which resisted the policies of Henry VIII and was re-established, briefly, by Mary Tudor. There is a continuous, if sometimes tenuous link between Greenwich and the modern English Friars Minor: the provincial seal has been passed down from generation to generation.

After the Reformation discipline among some of the observants was at a low ebb and another reformed group came into existence: the Recollects. The name came from 'the house of recollection' which St Francis had seen as an essential feature of Franciscan life, a house where friars would be spiritually refreshed. This is what the Recollects hoped to provide for all the friars. The first recollect house was founded in 1570, and by 1601 a special commissary had been appointed to deal with their affairs. In 1637 the Recollects, whose reform began in France and spread widely through Europe, were given their own vicar general.

The headquarters of the English Friars Minor, who adhered to the Recollect reforms, was St Bonaventure's Friary, Douai, which provided from 1618 until 1793 a flow of priests for the mission, and a base for the province, which was restored in 1629. At the time of French Revolutionary disruption—which closed St Bonaventure's—various attempts were made to establish a house of studies in England, notably at Osmotherley in Yorkshire, and at Abergavenny and Perthyr, both in Monmouthshire. None of these were really successful and the order (in common with many other religious communities within the Church) had to wait until the middle years of the nineteenth century for a revival.

A number of Irish Franciscans—belonging to the Irish province and never officially attached to the English—worked on the English mission, especially in the second half of the seventeenth century when the Irish Church in general and Friars (who were very numerous in Ireland) in particular went through a period of crisis. The two centres of the Irish Franciscans were Louvain and Rome. St Anthony's College, Louvain, was established with the patronage of Philip III of Spain and the approval of Pope Paul V, whose Bull of foundation is dated 3 April 1607. Permanent buildings were ready for use by 1627. In 1625 the Irish Franciscans established a second friary in exile, at Rome, the college of St Isidore on the Pincian Hill.

In 1667 Catherine of Braganza built a convent for the use of a group of Portuguese Franciscans to the east of the Catholic Chapel Royal at St James's. These friars were known as the Arabidoes but were a part of the Observant branch of the order. This convent, like all the Stuart Royal foundations, lasted only a short time and numbered at most 13 members.

Jesuits

I. The Society of Jesus, a religious order of clerks regular, whose members are commonly known as Jesuits (originally a derisory term, but now in general usage), was the most formidable and successful of the Counter-Reformation foundations. It owed its inspiration to St Ignatius Loyola (1491-1556), and was given formal recognition by Pope Paul III in the Bull *Regimini Militantis Ecclesiae* of 1540. The Jesuits have no rule as such, but have a body of authoritative writings called the *Institutum* (which includes the 'Jesuit Constitutions' and 'The Spiritual Exercises of St Ignatius'). The Jesuits gave more priests to the English mission than any other religious order, and their efficient organisation and high standards of education made them a strongly disciplined presence among the English clergy.

The Society, whose active character was symbolised by the lifting of the normal obligation of all religious to recite the Divine Office in choir, was organised under a general (elected for life) and provinces (under a provincial). The Society was highly centralised, and adaptable: its vocation was to work wherever and in whatever way

16

was needed, *Ad Maiorem Dei Gloriam*. The General, who was elected by a general congregation of the Society, was the only elected official; all subordinate officials, including provincials, were appointed by the General for a term of office usually not more than six years.

The English province developed gradually. After a slow start, there was a marked increase in the number of clerical students and mission priests entering the Society in the last years of the sixteenth century. In 1593 there were only forty-nine English Jesuits, of whom thirty were priests, and only nine in England. By 1620 there were 211 in the Province and 106 missioners in England. By 1641 overall numbers had risen to nearly 400 of whom 180 were on the mission. Even as late as 1773 there were 274 English Jesuits, about half of them resident in England. This sizeable body of men, formally elected into a province in 1623, was divided by county (for administrative purposes) into a number of nominal 'colleges' (for the more important areas) and 'residences' (for the others) which survived until the suppression of the Society:

The College of St Ignatius—Middlesex, Surrey, Kent, Berkshire and Hertfordshire.

The College of the Holy Apostles—Suffolk, Norfolk, Cambridge and Essex.

The College of St Aloysius—Lancashire, Cheshire, Westmorland and, until 1660, Staffordshire.

The College of the Immaculate Conception—Derbyshire, Leicestershire, Nottinghamshire and Rutland.

The College of St Francis Xavier—the whole of North (until c.1666) and South Wales and Monmouthshire, Herefordshire, Gloucestershire and Somersetshire.

The Residence of St Michael—Yorkshire.

The Residence of St John the Evangelist—Durham, Cumberland and Northumberland.

The Residence of St Dominic (which became the College of St Hugh in 1676)—Lincolnshire.

The Residence of St George—Worcester and Warwickshire.

The Residence of St Mary—Oxfordshire, Buckinghamshire, Bedfordshire and Northamptonshire.

The Residence (after 1675 College) of St Thomas of Canterbury—Hampshire, Wiltshire, Sussex and Dorset.

The Residence of St Stanislaus—Cornwall and Devonshire.

The Residence of St Chad—Staffordshire; established in 1660, it became a College c.1671.

The Residence of St Winefrid—North Wales; set up c.1666.

Not all ordained English Jesuits worked in England. Some worked in America as missionaries in Maryland and Pennsylvania. A small number worked in the far-flung Jesuit missions overseas. Others acted as confessors at Rome, and elsewhere, and as convent chaplains. Some were much occupied in official business in the principal cities of Catholic Europe. A few acted as tutors to the sons of English families travelling on the continent, or served as military chaplains. A larger number were employed as professors in English seminaries in Europe, and some taught in the early years of the eighteenth century, at the episcopal seminary at Liege.

II.   Almost all English Jesuits, after the province had been formally established, made their novitiate at Watten, their ecclesiastical studies at Liege, their tertianship at Ghent, and some taught, before ordination, at St Omers College. In periods of financial crisis, as in the 1740's, some young Jesuits were sent to study theology at other colleges of the Society in France or Germany. Before the suppression of the Society, the European houses of the English province were at:

Ghent. The tertians studied at the house there, and the novices also lived there from 1765 until the suppression.

Liege. This was the principal house of studies for the scholastics. In 1773 it became the Liege Academy—a school and a seminary for the training of priests conducted by the ex-Jesuits. In 1794 it migrated to Stonyhurst in Lancashire.

St Omers. St Omers College was a boarding school founded by the Society in 1593 for boys from England and Wales. When the College was seized by the French government, the school moved in 1762 to Bruges, and in 1773 to Liege. In the course of the eighteenth century, the English Jesuits had, in addition, preparatory schools at Boulogne (1742-1752), Watten (1752-1765) and Bruges (1765-1773).

Watten. The original novitiate for the English Jesuits was at St John's, Louvain. In 1614 it was moved to Liege, and in 1625 to Watten, where it remained until 1765.

III.   In the second half of the eighteenth century the Society met with increasing opposition in 'enlightened' Europe. In 1759 the Jesuits were expelled from Portugal. In 1764 they were expelled from France, and in 1767, 6000 were deported from Spain. In 1773 Pope Clement XIV, under pressure from these states, as well as from many of the Italian principalities, issued the Bull *Dominus ac Redemptor* suppressing the Society.

The Jesuits, however, were not so easily destroyed. They were tolerated in Austria, in Prussia and in Russia. Gradually they re-established themselves and in 1814 the Society was officially restored by the Bull *Sollicitudo Omnium Ecclesiarum*. During the years of papal ban, a trickle of recruits continued to enter the English province of the ex-Jesuits, and by 1803 the English Jesuits began to re-admit members. A few of those ordained for the Jesuits in these twilight years never formally entered the Society.

Minims

The Order of Minims was one of the last religious orders to be founded before the Council of Trent. Their founder was St Francis of Paola (1416-1507), and their particular mark was humility: they regarded themselves as the least of all religious. Their life, which owed much to the inspiration of St Francis of Assisi, was most austere, and included the taking of a fourth vow of 'perpetual lent' which involved abstinence not only from meat and fish, but also from eggs, cheese, butter and milk.

The superiors of the Minims are called 'correctors', the 'corrector-general' being elected for six years, the 'corrector-provincial' for three. The Roman headquarters of the Minims was the old Scots church of S.Andrea delle Fratte, and there were more Scots members of the Order than English.

Oratorians

The Congregation of the Oratory was founded by St Philip Neri (1515-1595). The Congregation, approved in 1575, consists of priests sharing a common life, but not bound by vows nor by renunciation of property. Each house of the Congregation is independent and elects its superior for three years. The Oratorians were to be introduced into England by Cardinal Newman in the nineteenth century. There had been an earlier Oratorian presence during the Stuart period when French Oratorians served as chaplains to Queen Henrietta Maria. The first French oratory had been established at Cotignac as early as 1592, but in 1611 Cardinal Pierre de Bérulle began the process of creating a centralised and specifically French congregation. The French Oratory is distinct from the Institute of the Oratory of St Philip Neri. There is a common novitiate, and members move from one community to another. The French Oratory was suppressed in 1790 and did not revive until 1852.

Theatines

This congregation was founded in 1524 at Rome as the 'Clerks Regular of the Divine Providence' by St Cajetan (1480-1547) and Gian Pietro Caraffa (1476-1589). Caraffa went on to become Pope Paul III, but when the Theatines were established he was bishop of Chieti (Latin, *Theate*), hence the name. The Theatines had ideals very similar to the Oratorians and the Society of Jesus and were one of the élite groups of the Counter-Reformation. No English member has been traced, but a number of French Theatines accompanied Queen Henrietta Maria to England and served her chapel.

TECHNICAL INTRODUCTION

Aliases

In the Elizabethan period most students entering the English Colleges in Europe adopted an alias. These were used for reasons of security, and some priests were known by their aliases all their lives: in a few cases it is almost impossible to disentangle aliases from real names. The custom of taking aliases persisted until the end of the period, but as time passed, they were retained for reasons of pietas rather than necessity. Aliases are rarely fanciful, and can often help in the identification of a priest: mother's maiden names were often used. In many cases the alias retained the priest's real Christian name. In those instances where the Christian name was changed, shortage of space has not allowed us to include it. Literary aliases have not, in general, been included, and the alias list can claim only to provide a selection of aliases rather than a comprehensive list.

Apostates

Many priests at one time or another experienced doubts about their vocation, and a small number gave up their active ministry. These men are difficult to trace as their memory has often been expunged from official records. An even smaller number formally apostasized—recanting their beliefs publicly—and became members of other churches. A few of these continued their ministry in their new communions, generally as clergymen of the Church of England. I have counted both categories under the heading 'apostate'. Some religious who left their institutes continued to exercise their priestly function. Those who were eventually 'repentant' have not been classified as apostates.

Bishops, see Titles

Converts

It is not always easy to isolate the converts. Catholicism was often secretly practised, especially in the reign of Elizabeth, and many who considered themselves Catholics were prepared to come to an accommodation with the Established Church. 'Converts' often came from such backgrounds. In this survey I have restricted the definition of convert to those who abandoned one form or another of Christianity and were formally 'converted' or 'reconciled' to Catholicism. Graduates of the two universities can, from Elizabeth's reign onwards, be assumed to be 'converts' (even if they were baptized under a Catholic dispensation), although here again there is much ambiguity. The number of future priests who attended Oxford and Cambridge grew smaller as religious tests grew stronger. The Inns of Court in London, however, especially the Inner and Middle Temples, harboured many notable recusants although few were called to the bar. In the first half of the seventeenth century, in particular, studying at the Inns was regarded as a part of a good general education.

Counties

The Local Government Act of 1972 re-organised local government in England and Wales by creating a new county structure which retained many historic names but few traditional boundaries. Until 1972, despite small changes in status and some major innovations like the formation of a new county of London, the counties had remained comparatively stable since medieval times. The counties of origin indicated here are those historic English and Welsh counties: a full list appears with the abbreviations. Those who were born in London, including the Cities of London and Westminster, are included under Middlesex. Irish and Scottish counties are not indicated. Birthplace takes precedence over normal family residence if there is a conflict. In the cases where a priest's diocese of origin but not his county is known (and generally indicated in a footnote) guesses have not been attempted: the dioceses of the Church of England were not co-terminous with the counties. The division for much of the period, together with the abbreviations used in the general notes, is as follows:

Bangor (Bg) Anglesey; nearly all Caernarvonshire; part of Merioneth, Denbigh, Montgomery.

Bath & Wells (Ba) All of Somerset.

Bristol (Bs) City of Bristol; part of Gloucestershire; all of Dorset.

Canterbury (Ca) Part of Kent, Buckinghamshire, Essex, Middlesex, Oxfordshire, Suffolk, Surrey, Sussex.

Carlisle (Ce) Most of Cumberland and Westmorland.

Chester (Ch) All Cheshire and Lancashire; part of Cumberland, Westmorland, Yorkshire, Flint and Denbigh.

Chichester (Cr) Almost all of Sussex.

Durham (Dh) All of Durham and Northumberland; part of Cumberland.

Ely (Ey) Nearly all of Cambridgeshire.

Exeter (Er) All of Devon and Cornwall.

Gloucester (Gl) Nearly all Gloucestershire; part of Wiltshire.

Hereford (Hr) Part of Herefordshire, Shropshire, Worcestershire, Montgomery, Monmouth, Radnor.

Lichfield (Lh) All Derbyshire; part of Staffordshire, Warwickshire and Shropshire.

Lincoln (Ln) Lincolnshire, Leicestershire, Huntingdonshire, Bedfordshire; part of Buckinghamshire, Hertfordshire, Northamptonshire, Oxfordshire & Rutland.

Llandaff (Lf) Most of Glamorgan and Monmouthshire.

London (Lo) Most of Middlesex; part of Essex, Hertfordshire and Buckinghamshire.

Norwich (Nr) All of Norfolk; part of Suffolk and Cambridgeshire.

Oxford (Ox) Nearly all of Oxfordshire.

Peterborough (Pb) Nearly all of Northamptonshire and Rutland.

Rochester (Ro) City of Rochester; town of Chatham, one parish in Suffolk and Cambridgeshire.

Saint Asaph (Sa) Part of Flint, Merioneth, Montgomery, Denbigh, Caernarvonshire and Shropshire.

Saint Davids (Sd) All of Pembrokeshire, Cardigan, Carmarthenshire and Glamorgan; part of Radnor, Herefordshire, Monmouthshire and Montgomery.

Salisbury (Sb) All of Berkshire; part of Wiltshire.

Winchester (Wi) Hampshire and part of Surrey.

Worcester (Wr) Part of Worcestershire and Warwickshire; two parishes in Staffordshire.

York (Yo) Most of Yorkshire; all Nottinghamshire.

Dating

The year has been made to begin on 1 January, although, until the eighteenth century, the year officially began, in England and Wales, on 25 March following. This reflected the existence of two parallel calendars, the Julian (or 'Old Style') and the Gregorian (or 'New Style'). The Gregorian Calendar, introduced into much of Catholic Europe in 1582, failed to obtain early acceptance in England; it was too closely associated with the Papacy. It was not until 1752 that the change came officially. In that year, by which time the difference between the New and Old Style calendars amounted to 11 days, the day after 2 September 1752 was declared to be 14 September 1752. Approximate dates on the list sometimes stem from the confusion between the two styles—both used, at different times and places by the English Catholics—especially in the crucial months of January, February and March.

Approximate dates are also indicated if there is any doubt about the certainty of a particular date. Every effort has been made to exclude dates which are not based on convincing evidence. If no date is available, the century in which the priest 'flourished' has been indicated.

District

The four districts or vicariates form a convenient geographical division of the country. Those listed as working in a particular district are either those who spent most of their priestly life in one vicariate or (as is the case for many foreign clergy) those who worked in one place only as far as our evidence suggests. Seculars were gradually becoming attached to a single district. A similar trend seems to be true of the regulars on the mission, although this is less easy to pinpoint because their own administrative divisions did not correspond to the districts. Nevertheless, many priests continued to work at different stages of their careers in several parts of the country and some in all four.

22

Education

The place of ecclesiastical training indicated on the list is the principal place of priestly study in each case. If, as happened on some occasions, a student attended more than one college, it is the college which he was attending at the time of his ordination that is noted. If a priest entered a religious order after his ordination, his place of priestly training, not his house of religious formation, is shown. The three major English foundations at Douai: the English College, St Bonaventure's Friary and St Gregory's Priory, are separately indicated, as is the English College at Rheims. Most of those educated at Rome were members of the English College, but a number were students at other colleges and religious houses—these have all been grouped together. Members of the Society of Jesus who followed the usual pattern of training, even those whose education had slight variations, are designated under one heading. Priest-monks of the Benedictine Order have been listed as being trained at their house of profession unless they were ordained as seculars in which case their seminary is indicated. A similar division has been applied to Carthusians and members of other religious orders.

Foreign Priests

Many of the priests who were born abroad came from families of English (or partly-English) origin who lived in exile on the continent especially in the Low Countries and Northern France. Many of the towns which the English chose to settle in (including Douai) were, in the sixteenth and seventeenth centuries, under Spanish rule, coming under French authority during the wars of Louis XIV. Thus, those born in Douai (which fell to the French in 1677) and neighbouring towns were born in what is described here as the Low Countries and after Louis XIV in France.

Some French Jesuits who came to England, or who joined the English Province when the Society was suppressed in France, are listed here, but the great body of exiled clergy who fled France after the Revolution of 1789—several thousands in total—will be examined in a further volume.

Scotland, for most of this period, was ecclesiastically independent of England and Wales, but many Scots clergy passed through England, and it is sometimes difficult to decide whether they qualify for the list or not: the policy for foreign priests is to include only those who probably did pastoral work on the mission. Thus I have excluded George Con, the Scottish clerical diplomat, Bishop George Hay whose visits, although frequent, were on official business, and Placid Fleming who visited London several times between 1685 and 1688 to play his part in mission strategy, but who did not stay for an extended period. I have included, however, R. A. Hay, who may originally have come to England to revive the Augustinian canons: he was probably in England as an apostate 'layman', but I have given him the benefit of the doubt. I have also included Bishop Alexander MacDonell who was in England from time to time with the Glengarry Regiment. The most cohesive group of Scots working in England were the Benedictines from the German Schottenklöster. They seem to have done most of their ministry in 'the Borders' area.

The number of Irish priests working on the mission grew gradually over the period, and by 1800 there were a considerable number, especially in London. Some were colourful characters escaping from ecclesiastical censure and church discipline in Ireland. Others were the pioneers of the great band of Irish priests who have done so much over the last two centuries to minister to the Catholics of England and Wales. The Irish had almost thirty colleges and religious houses on the continent, and as with the Scots priests, I feel that I have just skimmed the surface as far as information is concerned.

English-America, despite its anti-Catholic laws and generally hostile attitude to 'papists', had its Catholic minority. This was centred in Maryland, but there were pockets in Pennsylvania, Virginia, New York and New Jersey. Maryland was the birthplace of a number of priests who were very much part of the English Mission. Most of them were Jesuits: the first to enter was Robert Brooke in 1684, and before the dissolution of the Society 41 entered, but not all persisted. The largest number of priests working in the combined Maryland-Pennsylvania region (all Jesuits) was 23, the figure for 1773. The first English-American bishop, John Carroll, was consecrated by Bishop Charles Walmesley at Lulworth Castle Chapel, Dorset, in 1790.

A few priests came from other parts of the Empire into the English Mission. They included clergy both from the West Indies and the Indian sub-continent.

Martyrs

Those who were executed for their religion are marked as martyrs. Those who were executed for other reasons are not. The martyrs include the majority of the Forty Martyrs canonised by Pope Paul VI on 25 October 1970 (though not those who died in the Henrician persecution or the lay martyrs) and a significant proportion of those beatified in 1886, 1895 and 1929. Those who have been canonised or beatified are indicated, as are those whose cause is pending and who have the title venerable.

Names

The spelling of personal names became consistent slowly, and in some cases spellings have been regularised. Where there are two common spellings of a name, or various alternative spellings these have been cross-referenced where possible. Some names have been translated from the Latin or anglicised from the Welsh. Those surnames with 'de' as prefix have been listed under their surname proper unless the prefix has become part of the name. Christian names too, are liable to variable spelling and the following conventions have been observed: Angelus not Angel, Anthony not Antony, Augustine not Austin, Dominic not Dominick, Edmund not Edmond, Lawrence not Laurence, Louis not Lewis, Stephen not Steven.

It is the custom in many religious orders to take a new Christian name on entering. On the mission these names were sometimes used and sometimes not. In a few cases the religious name alone has come down to us. Where a religious name is known it is included in brackets, and if it appears to be a religious name it is listed as such. Names in religion tended to be more characteristically 'Catholic' than their baptismal counterparts. Converts often took similarly 'Catholic names' at their confirmation and were often known by them. In some cases it has been necessary to abbreviate the more elaborate forms of religious name—'X of St Y'—for reasons of space.

Ordination

Evidence for the year of ordination, especially for alumni of the colleges of Lisbon and Seville and for most religious, is not always available. Estimated dates have been avoided. In some cases it is possible that an unordained student has been admitted to the list; if there is a strong probability of ordination, individuals have been included.

Peers, see Titles

Prison

A number of priests spent some of their working life in prison. No attempt has been made to list these 'Confessors of the Faith'. Those known to have died in prison are so marked.

Profession

The date of religious profession is indicated where possible although in some cases this date may refer to clothing. The 'profession' date of members of the Society of Jesus given here is not that of their final profession but of their entry into the Society.

Religious Names, see Names

Titles

Ecclesiastical titles other than episcopal and cardinalatial ones have not been included. The details of bishops' careers are indicated in the footnotes. English secular titles of nobility (much confused by the legal complications of recusancy), baronetcies and knighthoods have been shown, but not foreign titles. Degrees and diplomas, fellowships of learned societies, and other honours have been omitted.

Training, see Education

SOURCES

It is unfortunate that owing to lack of printing space (it would have doubled the size of the book), I have been unable to cite individual references for each entry. In general, the technique of reaching the final version was as follows. The first stage was the summarising and collating of the Trappes-Lomax Index which lacks cross-references and is full of duplications and variable spellings. Each name was checked against standard histories and specialised studies, supplemented, where possible, by primary sources, unpublished material and personal information. This section of the introduction indicates the 'sources' for each of the main 'groups' in the volume. A full list of works consulted is provided in the bibliography at the end of the book which should also suggest further reading.

THE TRAPPES-LOMAX INDEX

The wide variety of sources used in the Trappes-Lomax index, which includes a number of Marian priests as well as clergy ordained after 1800, are listed in one of the thirteen boxes in which the index is stored. These sources include many county histories, monographs, published official records and Catholic periodicals. More importantly, the index draws on many unpublished registers and family papers. Registers consulted include both those of the Established Church and the Catholic community. Among the Catholic registers examined were the following: Bonham, Brailes, Britwell, Brooms, Bury St Edmunds, East Hendred, Fernyhalgh, Husbands Bosworth, King's Lynn, Little Malvern, Marnhull, Shefford, Stonor, Warkworth and Wigan. Family papers include: Arundell (Wardour), Bedingfeld (Oxburgh), Berkeley (Spetchley), Blount (Mapledurham), Blundell (Crosby), Eyston (Hendred), Fitzherbert (Swynnerton), Howard (Arundel), Huddleston (Sawston), Jerningham (Costessey), Rookwood (Coldham), Tempest (Broughton), Throckmorton (Coughton), Vaughan (Courtfield) and Weld (Lulworth).

THE SECULARS

The work of Father Godfrey Anstruther on the secular clergy which was published in the four volumes of *The Seminary Priests* is the essential starting-point for all studies of the English and Welsh priests in the period covered by this book. Without Anstruther many avoidable inaccuracies would have been made in this present volume. I have had access to the MS corrections and additions to Anstruther made by Fr W. V. Smith, and to the annotated copy kept in the archives at Archbishop's House, Westminster. Some details of Irish secular clergy working in England and Wales have come to light in CRS 12 and, overall, the CRS volumes have been invaluable in checking details. The publications of the various local Catholic History Societies (listed by *Williams 1983*, 442) have yielded some useful corrections. *Cleary 1958* clarifies some confusing Welsh details.

AUGUSTINIANS

There is no major history of the Post-Reformation Augustinians in England in print, but well documented articles have been written by *de Mejer*. Further information is given by *Martin* in two published papers (1956 and 1976).

BENEDICTINES

Birt, despite its inaccuracies, remains the starting point for Benedictine biographies. There is a copy at Downside, annotated by Dom Hugh Connolly (who was partly responsible for CRS 33), Dom Philip Jebb (who is preparing a revision of *Birt*) and Dr David Lunn, which corrects many errors. The lists compiled by *Moore, Scott* and *Whelan* provide much of interest, as does *Allanson* which is frank in its treatment of 'apostates' not included in *Birt*. *Lunn* has updated much earlier material and lists the many early English Benedictines who were students at Valladolid and those who before the English Benedictine Congregation was revived were professed at Benedictine houses on the continent. *Dilworth 1958-1974* shows the contribution of the Scottish monks to the English Mission. Several of his articles appeared in the *Downside Review* which continues to publish many important studies of monastic history.

BRIDGETTINES

Fletcher, the only existing English study of this order, contains little information. There is a great need for a new study of Syon Abbey.

CAMALDOLESE

The *Acti Capitolari* in the Camaldolese Archives have been consulted to discover, without success, more details about the one Englishman (HARD26) who seems to have joined the order. *Lugano* provides some information, but it seems that the Camaldolese are among the most elusive of religious orders.

CARMELITES

McGreal provides a useful introduction to the small Calced Carmelite mission to England, while *Smet* makes full use of the rich primary sources to fill out the account and to present it 'warts and all'. *Zimmerman*, badly in need of a revised edition (it was published in 1899), remains the only accessible study of the Discalced Carmelites in England.

CARTHUSIANS

Hendriks, especially in chapter 6, provides historical background and some names. The two works by *de Grauwe* have transformed the study of the English Carthusians, especially if used in conjunction with *Anstruther. De Grauwe 1976*, in particular, made somewhat difficult to use by the listing of the Carthusians under their religious names, has proved of great value and is based on a thorough reading of manuscript material including J. Long's *Notitia Cartusianorum Anglorum* which is preserved at the Grande Chartreuse.

CISTERCIANS

Lekai is a very wide-ranging account of the Cistercians throughout their history and is particularly useful on the Cistercian 'revival' of the late eighteenth and early nineteenth centuries. *Bellenger 1980* and *Gell* fill in some telling details.

DOMINICANS

Gumbley is the standard work on the members of the English Dominican Province and contains a thorough historical introduction. These obituary notices depend heavily on *Palmer* as well as on the Provincial Archives. Further details were gathered from *Anstruther 1958*, CRS 24, and *Mould* which contains, as an appendix, a brief list of the Irish Dominicans who were known to have worked in England.

FRANCISCANS

Thaddeus contains a biographical summary of the 'Members of the Second English Franciscan Province', but his claim that 'it is morally certain that the names of all the fathers will be found here' cannot be sustained. Much more detail can be obtained from CRS 24, especially from the necrology, pp.259-314, which is now kept at Forest Gate, where the English Provincial Archives are a well-organised and potentially very important resource. *Gillespie* improved the information on Welsh Franciscans, while *Millett* has a useful discussion of 'Irish Franciscans in England' as one of his appendices.

The Capuchins are not so well covered. The *English Capuchin Ordo*, which was last published in 1963, contains a summary history of the English Province (in Latin) and a necrology with bald biographical details. A full account of some individuals is given by *Cuthbert* and *Reel*. *Gamache* provides a contemporary account of the French Capuchins in the Stuart Chapels Royal who are also discussed by *Barnes*.

Anderson provides a comprehensive survey of the life and career of the Conventual, William Thompson or Thomson.

JESUITS

The weighty survey by *Foley* remains of great interest. CRS 70 provides much new information as well as many amendments to *Foley* for the period from 1650-1829. For the earlier period, the working copy of *Foley* (annotated by the editor and others) kept at Mount Street prevented some duplications, while *Edwards 1981* filled some gaps.

MINIMS

Whitmore is a good general introduction to the order at the height of its influence. Individual Minims are considered by *Durkan* and *Giblin* in a series of articles in the *Innes Review*, by *Rogers 1970* and by *Roberti*.

ORATORIANS

Addington introduces the Oratorian ethos, while *Leherpeur* gives a succinct survey of the French Oratory. *Ingold* contains much biographical material.

ABBREVIATIONS

REGULAR AND SECULAR CLERGY—*Column heading: 'Reg'*

S	SECULAR	CRT	CARTHUSIAN
OSB	BENEDICTINE	OP	DOMINICAN
OFM	FRANCISCAN (RECOLLECT)	OSS	BRIDGETTINE
CAP	FRANCISCAN (CAPUCHIN)	MIN	MINIMS
CON	FRANCISCAN (CONVENTUAL)	SJ	SOCIETY OF JESUS
OSA	AUGUSTINIAN FRIAR	CRL	AUGUSTINIAN CANON
ORA	ORATORIAN	CAR	CARMELITE (CALCED)
CAM	CAMALDOLESE	ODC	CARMELITE (DISCALCED)

ECCLESIASTICAL DISTRICTS (VICARIATES APOSTOLIC)—*Column heading: 'D'*

L	LONDON DISTRICT	M	MIDLAND DISTRICT
N	NORTHERN DISTRICT	W	WESTERN DISTRICT

COUNTIES OR COUNTRIES OF ORIGIN—*Column heading: 'Co'*

AY	ANGLESEY	GS	GERMAN STATES
BD	BEDFORDSHIRE	HA	HAMPSHIRE
BK	BERKSHIRE	HR	HEREFORDSHIRE
BR	BRECKNOCKSHIRE	HT	HERTFORDSHIRE
BU	BUCKINGHAMSHIRE	HU	HUNTINGDONSHIRE
CB	CAMBRIDGESHIRE	IR	IRELAND
CD	CUMBERLAND	IT	ITALIAN STATES
CH	CHESHIRE	KT	KENT
CL	CORNWALL	LA	LANCASHIRE
CM	CARMARTHENSHIRE	LC	LOW COUNTRIES
CN	CAERNARVONSHIRE	LE	LEICESTERSHIRE
DB	DENBIGHSHIRE	LN	LINCOLNSHIRE
DE	DERBYSHIRE	MD	MARYLAND
DH	DURHAM	MH	MERIONETHSHIRE
DT	DORSET	MI	ISLE OF MAN
DV	DEVONSHIRE	MO	MONMOUTHSHIRE
ES	SPAIN	MT	MONTGOMERYSHIRE
EX	ESSEX	MX	MIDDLESEX
FR	FRANCE	ND	NORTHUMBERLAND
FT	FLINTSHIRE	NK	NORFOLK
GL	GLOUCESTERSHIRE	NN	NORTHAMPTONSHIRE
GM	GLAMORGANSHIRE	NT	NOTTINGHAMSHIRE

OX	OXFORDSHIRE		ST	STAFFORDSHIRE
PB	PEMBROKESHIRE		SX	SUSSEX
PL	PORTUGAL		SY	SURREY
RN	RADNORSHIRE		WD	WESTMORLAND
RT	RUTLAND		WK	WARWICKSHIRE
SC	SCOTLAND		WR	WORCESTERSHIRE
SK	SUFFOLK		WT	WILTSHIRE
SM	SOMERSET		YO	YORKSHIRE
SP	SHROPSHIRE		ZZ	ELSEWHERE

PLACES OF TRAINING—*Column heading: 'T'*

A	ANTWERP
B	BRUSSELS
C	NIEUPORT
D	ENGLISH COLLEGE, DOUAI
E	ST EDMUND'S, PARIS
F	ST BONAVENTURE'S, DOUAI
G	ST GREGORY'S, DOUAI
J	SCHOTTENKLOSTER
L	LISBON
M	MALTA
N	LOUVAIN
P	PARIS (excl St Edmund's)
Q	RHEIMS
R	ROME
S	SEVILLE
T	OLD HALL, WARE
U	USHAW, Co DURHAM
V	VALLADOLID
W	ST LAWRENCE'S, DIEULOUARD
X	LAMSPRING
Y	JESUIT FORMATION (Liege etc)
Z	ELSEWHERE

SYMBOLS USED IN THE LIST—*Column heading: 'Notes'*

#	SEE ALIAS INDEX		‡	OXFORD
+	MARTYR		†	CAMBRIDGE
x	DIED IN PRISON		§	CONVERT
*	SEE GENERAL NOTES		=	INNS OF COURT
1	YEAR OF BIRTH UNCERTAIN		°	APOSTATE
2	YEAR OF PROFESSION UNCERTAIN		Bt	BARONET
3	YEAR OF ORDINATION UNCERTAIN		Kt	KNIGHT
4	YEAR OF DEATH UNCERTAIN		Ld	PEER
6	XVI CENTURY			
7	XVII CENTURY			
8	XVIII CENTURY			

31

ALPHABETICAL LIST OF PRIESTS

Name	Reg	D	Co	T	Notes	Born	Prof	Ordn	Died	Code
ABATHELL Nicholas	S		FR	N	†3	..	..	1571	..	ABAT02
ABBOT John Austin	OSS	L	MX	D	#*‡24	1588	1614	1612	1650	ABBO02
ABERCROMBIE John	S	L	MX	R	#3	1742	..	1770	1779	ABER02
ABERCROMBIE Robert	SJ	L	SC		#1	1532	..	..	1613	ABER04
ABITHEL see ABATHELL										
ABRED see ALDRED										
ACTON Francis (Augustine)	OSB	N	MX	G		1660	1681	..	1695	ACTO02
ACTON John (Placid)	OSB	N	MX	G	1	1667	1685	..	1727	ACTO04
ACTON Thomas	SJ		WR	Y	#	1640	1662	1675	1721	ACTO05
ADAMS James	SJ	M		Y	#*3	1737	1756	1767	1802	ADAM00
ADAMS John VEN.	S	W	DT	Q	#+‡1	1546	..	1580	1586	ADAM02
ADAMS John	S	L	ST	R		1709	..	1735	1737	ADAM03
ADAMS (Pacificus of S.Giles)	OFM		MO	F	123	1669	1686	1691	1701	ADAM04
ADAMS Roland	S			L	*3	..	..	1694	..	ADAM08
ADAMS Thomas	S	M	ST			..	..	..	1733	ADAM09
ADAMS Thos. (Peter Alcantara)	OFM	N		F	#°3	..	..	1725	1737	ADAM10
ADAMSON John	S	N	LA	V	3	1580	..	1604	..	ADAM11
ADDIS Joseph	S	L	HR	V		1742	..	1771	1821	ADDI02
ADDISON Thomas ?John	SJ	N	YO	V	#x3	1634	1668	1660	1685	ADDI03
ADDISON William	S	N	YO	D	#13	1662	..	1690	1736	ADDI04
ADDY Bartholomew (Bede)	OSB	N	DH	X		..	1655	..	1705	ADDY02
ADELHAM John (Placid)	OSB	L	WT	E	x	..	1652	..	1679	ADEL01
AERTS Philip	OP	L	LC		*7	..	..	..	..	AERT02
AIERY James (Alban S.Agatha)	OFM		MX	F	123	1649	1667	1673	1705	AIER02
(Aimé of Beauvais)	CAP	L	FR		2	..	1612	..	1652	AIME01
AINSCOMB Thomas	SJ					..	..	..	1674	AINS04
AINSCOUGH Edward	S		LA	R	1	1675	..	1701	..	AINS06
AINSWORTH John	S	L	MX	D	#†	1577	..	1603	..	AINS07
AINSWORTH (Ralph)	OSB	W	LA	W		1763	1784	1788	1814	AINS08
AISLEY Edward (Onuphrius)	ODC	L	DH		2	1661	1682	..	1711	AISL01
AKERS James	S	L	HA	L	#°	1763	..	1788	1820	AKER02
ALBERONI John (Francis)	OSB		MX	Z	*	..	1652	..	1693	ALBE02
ALBERY William	S	L	MX	D	#	..	..	1624	1675	ALBE04
ALBIN Robert or Richard	SJ		LA	Y		1630	1651	1660	1667	ALBI02
ALCOCK John	SJ	M	BU	Y	#1	1615	1635	..	1703	ALCO02
ALCOCK William (Jerome)	OSB		LA	X		1775	1792	..	1817	ALCO04
ALDINGTON Thomas	SJ	M		D	#*2	1579	1621	1611	1649	ALDI02
ALDRED Christopher	CRT			C		..	1583	..	1607	ALDR01
ALDRED John	S			R		..	..	1570	..	ALDR02
ALDRED Robert	SJ	N		Y	#*1	1673	1697	1703	1728	ALDR04
ALDRED Thomas	S		NK	R	#1	1670	..	1694	..	ALDR06
ALDRINGTON see ALDINGTON										
ALEWORTH see AYLWORTH										
ALFIELD Thomas BL.	S	L	GL	D	#+†	1552	..	1581	1585	ALFI02
ALLAM William (Ambrose)	OSB	M	MX	G	2	1749	1768	..	1812	ALLA02
ALLAN see ALLEN										
ALLANSON Matthew (Paul)	OSB	M	YO	X	1	1692	1713	..	1768	ALLA06
ALLEN Gregory	SJ					..	..	..	1646	ALLE02
ALLEN Henry	S	N	YO	D		1681	..	1704	1733	ALLE04
ALLEN Jerome	S	L	MX	L		1730	..	1756	1815	ALLE05
ALLEN John	OSB		MX	G		..	1624	..	1635	ALLE06
ALLEN Peter	S			S		..	..	1617	..	ALLE07
ALLEN Peter	S	L	MX	D	13	1635	..	1666	..	ALLE08
ALLEN Ralph	SJ		MX	D		..	1577	1574	1587	ALLE10

Name	Reg	D	Co	T	Notes	Born	Prof	Ordn	Died	Code
ALLEN Roger or William	S	L		D	*	..	..	1578	..	ALLE11
ALLEN William CARD.	S		LA	N	‡*	1532	..	1565	1594	ALLE12
ALLEN William	S			S	3	..	..	1608	..	ALLE13
ALLEN William	SJ	L	YO	Y	#13	1732	1750	1757	1814	ALLE14
ALLERTON Matthew	S			S		..	..	1677	..	ALLE15
ALLERTON Matthew (Denis)	OSB	N	LA	X		1754	1771	..	1829	ALLE16
ALLIBON Job	S	L	YO	D	#13	1638	..	1661	1709	ALLI02
ALLOT William	S	M	LN	N	†13	1540	..	1570	1587	ALLO02
ALLOWAY John James	SJ	N	OX	R		1743	1766	1769	1808	ALLO04
ALMEIDA Paul d'		L	PL		*7	..	..	..	..	ALME02
ALMOND James	S	N	LA	R		1646	..	1669	1719	ALMO02
ALMOND John ST.	S	L	LA	R	#+	1567	..	1601	1612	ALMO06
ALMOND Oliver	S	M	OX	R	#‡	1561	..	1587	..	ALMO08
ALRED see ALDRED										
AMBLER George	S			Q	*	..	..	1588	..	AMBL02
(Ambrose of St Angelus)	ODC	L				..	..	..	1743	AMBR01
AMIAS John BL.	S	N	YO	Q	#+	..	..	1581	1589	AMIA02
ANDERSON Lionel (Albert)	OP	L	LN		#13	1620	1659	1665	1710	ANDE08
ANDERSON Patrick	SJ	L	SC	R		1575	1597	..	1624	ANDE10
ANDERSON William	SJ	M	LN	Y	#3	1689	1721	1729	1764	ANDE12
ANDERSON William	S	N	DH	V	*1	1710	..	1733	1759	ANDE13
ANDERSON Beuno	S	N	LA	R	#	1643	..	1668	1723	ANDE14
ANDERTON Christopher	OSB		LA	G	#	1607	1624	..	1653	ANDE18
ANDERTON Christopher	SJ		LA	Y		1615	1636	1645	1695	ANDE19
ANDERTON Edward	S	N	LA	R	#	1623	..	1648	1683	ANDE20
ANDERTON Francis	SJ	N	LA	R	3	1665	1685	1694	1723	ANDE22
ANDERTON Francis (Bede)	OSB	M	LA	G		1740	1757	..	1779	ANDE24
ANDERTON James	OSB	N	LA	G	4	1600	1623	..	1646	ANDE28
ANDERTON John	S		LA	R	#	1618	..	1642	..	ANDE32
ANDERTON John (Michael)	OSB		LA	X	°	1690	1709	1715	1742	ANDE33
ANDERTON Lawrence	SJ	N	LA	R	#†	1577	1604	..	1643	ANDE34
ANDERTON Robert BL.	S		MI	Q	+‡	1560	..	1584	1586	ANDE38
ANDERTON Robert	S	L	LA	R	#	1625	..	1651	1685	ANDE40
ANDERTON Robert (Celestine)	OSB	N	LA	D	2	1619	1650	1646	1697	ANDE44
ANDERTON Robert (John Ev.)	OFM	L	MX	F	1	1725	1746	1752	1795	ANDE46
ANDERTON Robert (Placid)	OSB		LA	E	#4	..	1635	1639	1677	ANDE47
ANDERTON Roger	S	N	LA	R	#	1621	..	1645	1696	ANDE48
ANDERTON Thomas	OSB	N	LA	E		1611	1630	1636	1671	ANDE52
ANDERTON Thomas	S			S		..	..	1686	..	ANDE53
ANDERTON Thomas	S	N	LA	R		1675	..	1702	1741	ANDE54
ANDERTON Thurstan	S	N	LA		3	..	..	1678	1697	ANDE56
ANDERTON William	S	L	LA	V	x	..	..	1637	..	ANDE58
ANDERTON William	SJ	W	LA	Y		1754	1806	1780	1823	ANDE60
ANDERTON William (Placid)	OSB	M	LA	E		1673	1696	..	1718	ANDE62
ANDERTON (William of S.Ant'y)	OFM	N	LA	F	12	1601	1628	1634	1672	ANDE64
ANDLEBY William BL.	S	N	YO	D	+†1	1552	..	1577	1597	ANDL02
ANDRE Philip	OFM		FR	F		..	..	1728	1772	ANDR01
ANDREWS William (Bernardine)	OFM		MO	F	123	1636	1658	1663	1679	ANDR02
ANDREWS Thomas	S	W				..	..	..	1679	ANDR06
ANGEL James	S	L	EX	R		1720	..	1745	1775	ANGE02
(Angelus of Raconisio)	CAP	L	FR		2	..	1595	..	1637	ANGE04
(Angelus of Soissons)	CAP	L	FR		2	..	1615	..	1646	ANGE06
ANGIER Francis	S			V		..	..	1637	..	ANGI01
ANGIER Robert (Hyacinth)	OP	M	MX	N		1762	1787	1788	1850	ANGI02
ANGIER Thomas	SJ	M	NK	Y		1730	1752	1760	1788	ANGI04
ANGIER Thomas	SJ	M	NK	Y		1754	1772	1780	1837	ANGI06
ANLABY see ANDLEBY										
ANNE George	SJ	N	YO	R	x	1595	1623	1620	1660	ANNE02
(Anselm of S.Simon Stock)	CAR	L	IR		*8	..	..	..	..	ANSE02
ANSLEY Henry	S		OX	R		..	..	1584	..	ANSL02
ANSON Joseph	S	L	MX	D	3	1753	..	1780	1827	ANSO02
ANSTEAD William	S	L	MX	R		1737	..	1762	1791	ANST02
ANTROBUS Ralph (Francis)	OSB	M	CH	Z	*‡	1576	1606	..	1626	ANTR02
ANTROBUS Richard	S	L	CH	D	#	1735	..	1773	1800	ANTR04
APEDAILE George	S	M	DH	D	3	1738	..	1762	1799	APED02
(Apollinaris of Paris)	CAP	L	FR			..	..	..	1665	APOL02

Name	Reg	D	Co	T	Notes	Born	Prof	Ordn	Died	Code
APPLEBY James	S	L	MX	V		..	..	1790	1799	APPL01
APPLEBY Robert (Paulinus)	OSB	N	YO		#*2	1580	1604	..	1645	APPL02
APPLEBY William	SJ	L	YO	S	#3	1591	1629	1629	1671	APPL04
APPLETON Henry	OFM	N		F	124	1675	1695	1699	1738	APPL06
APPLETON James	S	M	NK	D	#3	1742	..	1769	1813	APPL10
APPLETON John (Henry)	OFM	M	WK	F	#3	..	1738	1746	1766	APPL13
APPLETON ?Roger (Lawrence)	OSB		EX	G	4	..	1635	..	1661	APPL16
APPLETON Thomas	SJ	L	KT	R	#	1596	1622	1622	1662	APPL18
APPLETON Thomas (Anselm)	OSB	N	LA	W		1766	1788	1790	1842	APPL19
APPLETREE John	S	L	OX	Q	#‡1	1555	..	1579	..	APPL20
APRICE (Joseph)	OSB	L	MX	W		1650	1667	..	1703	APRI02
APRICE Thomas (Ildephonsus)	OB	L	MX	W		..	1668	..	1712	APRI04
APRICE see also PRICE										
ARAY Martin	S	L		N	#*14	1550	..	1577	1620	ARAY02
(Archangelus of Beauvais)	CAP	L	FR		2	..	1655	..	1706	ARCH01
ARCHBOLD Richard	SJ		IR	Y	°23	1713	1731	1739	..	ARCH02
ARCHDEACON Robert	S	L	MX	R	#	1746	..	1769	1814	ARCH04
ARCHER Giles	S		OX	Q		..	..	1587	1602	ARCH06
ARCHER James	S	L	MX	D		1751	..	1780	1834	ARCH08
ARCHER John	SJ					..	..	..	1580	ARCH10
ARCHER John	SJ	W	MO	Y	#12	1627	1650	1657	1674	ARCH12
ARCHER Philip	S		MO	R	#4	1624	..	1650	1651	ARCH14
ARCHER Robert	S			S	3	..	..	1616	..	ARCH16
ARDEN Henry	S		SX	R	#14	1578	..	1602	1602	ARDE04
ARDEN Robert	SJ		SX			..	1567	..	..	ARDE06
ARDENSON James	SJ					..	..	..	1694	ARDE08
ARMOUR (Luke)	OP	L	IR		*	..	..	..	1764	ARMO02
ARMSTRONG Daniel	SJ	N	NT	V	#3	1643	1675	1667	1684	ARMS06
ARMSTRONG John	SJ	N	ND	R	#	1591	1621	1616	1660	ARMS08
ARMSTRONG (Peter of S.Mary)	OFM	L		F	4	..	..	1663	1697	ARMS10
ARMSTRONG Robert	OP	N	ND	R	#	1603	1626	..	1663	ARMS12
ARMSTRONG Thomas	OP	N	ND	R	#	1607	1632	..	1662	ARMS14
ARNOLD Adam	SJ	W			14	1565	..	..	1621	ARNO02
ARNOLD John	CRT					..	1576	..	1589	ARNO06
ARNOLD Richard	S		ST	R	#	1586	..	1610	..	ARNO08
ARNOLD Richard (Joachim)	OFM	N	WK	F	134	1724	1743	1749	1778	ARNO10
ARROWSMITH Edmund	S		LA	Q	4	1563	..	1587	1601	ARRO01
ARROWSMITH Edmund Brian ST.	SJ	N	LA	D	#+	1585	1624	1612	1628	ARRO02
ARTHUR (James)	OP	L	IR		*7	..	..	..	..	ARTH02
ARTON William	S	M	CB	V	4	1576	..	1603	1610	ARTO02
ASCOUGH see ASKEW										
ASHE Edward	OSB	L	MX		*	..	1605	..	1629	ASHE02
ASHMALL Ferdinand	S	N	DH	R		1650	..	1674	1712	ASHM01
ASHMALL Ferdinand	S	N	DH	L		1696	..	1720	1798	ASHM02
ASHMALL John	S	N	DH	R	4	1653	..	1676	1706	ASHM06
ASHTON Arthur (Alban)	OSB		LA	E		1680	1699	..	1748	ASHT02
ASHTON Charles	S		CH	L	3	..	..	1792	1797	ASHT04
ASHTON John	S				7	..	..	..	..	ASHT06
ASHTON John	S			D	3	..	..	1688	..	ASHT07
ASHTON John	SJ		IR	Y	3	1742	1759	1765	1815	ASHT08
ASHTON Nicholas	S		ST	V	#34	..	..	1595	1605	ASHT10
ASHTON Richard (Joseph)	OSB		LA	G		1667	1688	..	1700	ASHT12
ASHTON Richard or Jn (Placid)	OSB	M	LA	E		1708	1725	..	1761	ASHT14
ASHTON Thomas	SJ			Y	#*1	1662	1684	1689	1707	ASHT16
ASKEW George	S		MX	R	‡	1575	..	1600	..	ASKE02
ASKEW John	S			D	*3	1545	..	1577	1586	ASKE04
ASKEW Robert	S		YO	D	#	..	..	1602	..	ASKE06
ASLOAN Audomarus John	OSB	N	SC	J	12	1595	1624	..	1661	ASLO02
ASLOAN George (Benedict)	OSB	N	SC	R	34	..	1639	1619	1661	ASLO04
ASPINALL Edward	SJ	M	LA	Y	#°3	1678	1696	1705	1732	ASPI02
ASPINALL Henry	SJ	M	LA	Y	#3	1715	1734	1747	1784	ASPI04
ASPINALL John	OSB	L	YO	E		..	1714	..	1762	ASPI05
ASPINALL Joseph	SJ		LA	Y	#3	1726	1745	1752	1763	ASPI06
ASPINALL Thomas	SJ		LA	Y	#3	1719	1740	1747	1773	ASPI08
ASTLEY Edward	SJ		MX	R	#1	1584	1608	..	1646	ASTL02
ASTON Philip (Placid)	OFM	W	MX	F	*23	1709	1726	1735	1755	ASTO02

Name	Reg	D	Co	T	Notes	Born	Prof	Ordn	Died	Code
ASTON William	SJ		MX	Y		1735	1751	..	1800	ASTO06
ASTON see also ASHTON										
ATCHISON see ATKINSON										
(Athanasius of S.Maurice)	CAR	L			8	..	..	..	..	ATHA02
ATHERTON Christopher	S			R	*1	1555	..	1585	..	ATHE02
ATHERTON Thomas	S	M	LA	D	#	1706	..	1732	1758	ATHE04
ATKINS Francis	SJ		ZZ	Z	*	1733	1752	..	1778	ATKI01
ATKINS William	SJ	M	CB	S	x23	1601	1635	1628	1681	ATKI02
ATKINS William (Maurus)	OSB		NK	G		..	1614	..	1635	ATKI04
ATKINSON James or John	SJ			R	*3	1687	1708	1723	1763	ATKI10
ATKINSON John	S		SM	R		1709	..	1746	1750	ATKI11
ATKINSON John	OSB	N	LA	E		1759	1781	..	1822	ATKI12
ATKINSON John (Benedict)	OP	L		N	#	1757	1782	1784	1826	ATKI13
ATKINSON Matthew (Paul)	OFM	L	YO	F	x13	1655	1673	1679	1729	ATKI14
ATKINSON (Peter of S.Ber'dne)	OFM	N	YO	F	123	1654	1672	1680	1686	ATKI16
ATKINSON Thomas VEN.	S	N	YO	Q	+1	1546	..	1588	1616	ATKI18
ATKINSON Thomas	S		YO	D		1700	..	1724	1728	ATKI19
ATKINSON William	S		YO	N	3	..	..	1570	..	ATKI20
ATKINSON William	S	L	LA	V	°3	..	..	1596	..	ATKI22
ATSLOW see ASTLEY										
ATWOOD John (Peter)	OP	L	WK	N	#	1643	1664	1669	1712	ATWO02
ATWOOD Peter	SJ		WR	Y	3	1682	1703	1711	1734	ATWO04
AUBEIL Francis, or Marcus d'	SJ	L	FR		*7	..	..	..	..	AUBE02
AUDLEY John	S				7	..	..	..	..	AUDL02
(Augustine of Dublin)	CAP		IR		4	..	..	..	1748	AUGU02
(Augustine of Presentation)	ODC	L			*8	..	..	..	..	AUGU04
AYLMER William (Augustine)	OFM			F	°3	..	..	1695	..	AYLM02
AYLWARD James	S			L	*8	..	..	..	..	AYLW04
AYLWORTH Matthew	S		MO	L	#	..	..	1641	..	AYLW05
AYLWORTH William	SJ	M	MO	Y	#	1625	1641	..	1679	AYLW06
AYRAY see AIERY										
AYROLI John Baptist	SJ		IT	Y	#3	1652	1670	1682	..	AYRO02
BABE James (Bruno)	OFM		MT	F	#13	1716	1737	1743	1784	BABE02
BABINGTON William	S				7	..	..	..	..	BABI02
BABTHORPE Albert	SJ	N	LC	Y	1	1646	1664	1674	1720	BABT02
BABTHORPE Ralph	SJ	N	YO	N	#124	1594	1615	..	1628	BABT04
BABTHORPE Richard	SJ	M	YO	R	1	1618	1651	1645	1681	BABT06
BABTHORPE Robert (Mellitus)	OSB	N	YO	W	#1	1584	1609	..	1654	BABT08
BABTHORPE Thomas	SJ		YO	R	#12	1598	1618	..	1656	BABT10
BABTHORPE Thomas	SJ		YO	R	#1	1613	1635	..	1655	BABT12
BABTHORPE William	S		YO		#	1613	..	..	..	BABT14
BACKHOUSE Richard	S	M	ST	D	#	1589	..	1615	..	BACK02
BACON George (Gregory)	OSB	M	NK	V	#2	1594	1622	1618	1663	BACO02
BACON John	SJ		NK	Y	#°	1597	..	..	1667	BACO04
BACON Nathaniel	SJ		NK	R	#	1599	..	1622	1676	BACO06
BACON Thomas	SJ		NK	R	#	1592	1613	..	1647	BACO08
BADDULEY Robert	SJ		ST		#1	1598	1618	..	1642	BADD02
BADDULEY William	SJ		ST	V	1	1597	1622	..	..	BADD04
BAGNAL (Placid)	OSB			W		..	1693	..	1708	BAGN02
BAGSHAWE Christopher	S	L	ST	Q	‡4	1552	..	1583	1625	BAGS02
BAGSHAWE Robert (Sigebert)	OSB		ST	Q		..	1613	1586	1633	BAGS04
BAGSHAWE Thomas	S	N	ST	D	#	..	..	1616	..	BAGS06
BAILEY Andrew (Gabriel)	OP	L	YO	R	°24	..	1592	..	1610	BAIL02
BAILLIE William (Placid)	OSB		SC	J	#3	1633	..	1660	1674	BAIL06
BAINES John	S		LA	R		1626	..	1662	..	BAIN04
BAINES John	S	N	LA	R	#	1653	..	1678	1727	BAIN06
BAINES Richard	S			Q		..	..	1581	..	BAIN08
BAKER Alexander	SJ	L	NK	S	2	1582	1610	..	1638	BAKE04
BAKER Arthur (Pacificus)	OFM	L		F	13	1694	..	1725	1774	BAKE06
BAKER Bernard	SJ	L	IR	Y	#34	1698	1721	1734	1773	BAKE08
BAKER David (Augustine)	OSB	L	MO		‡=	1575	1607	1613	1641	BAKE10
BAKER John	SJ		ES	Y	1	1644	1670	1678	1719	BAKE12
BAKER Richard	CRT			C	4	..	..	..	1623	BAKE18
BALDI Angelus Dominic	SJ	L	IT	Y		..	..	1683	..	BALD02
BALDWIN George	S	W	SM	V		1749	..	1775	1818	BALD03
BALDWIN John	S	L		Q	*x4	..	..	1584	1588	BALD04

35

Name	Reg	D	Co	T	Notes	Born	Prof	Ordn	Died	Code
BALDWIN William	SJ		CL	R		1563	1590	1588	1632	BALD08
BALES Christopher BL.	S	L	DH	Q	#+1	1564	..	1587	1590	BALE02
BALFOUR de	ORA	L			*7	..	..	..		BALF02
BALL Edward	S	L	LA	D	#	1717	..	1741	1789	BALL02
BALL George	S	N	LA	R		1678	..	1704	1734	BALL06
BALL George	S	N	LA	D	#	1704	..	1729	1748	BALL08
BALL John	S	M	LA	D	#	1723	..	1746	1781	BALL10
BALLANTYNE see BALLENDEN										
BALLARD John	S	L	CB	Q	#*†	..	..	1581	1586	BALL12
BALLENDEN William	S		SC	R	*3	1616	..	1641	1661	BALL14
BALLYMAN John (Gregory)	OSB		DV	X		1734	1754	..	1811	BALL16
BALLYMAN Thomas	OSB	M	DV	X		1737	1756	..	1795	BALL18
BAMBER Edward VEN.	S	N	LA	S	#+1	1602	..	1626	1646	BAMB02
BAMBER John	S	N	LA	D		1712	..	1740	1780	BAMB04
BAMBER William	S	M	LA	D	#4	1604	..	1628	1636	BAMB06
BAMFIELD George	SJ		WK	Y	#1	1589	1613	..	1657	BAMF02
BANISTER Henry	S	N	LA	D	#3	1755	..	1781	1838	BANI04
BANISTER Robert	S	N	LA	D		1725	..	1750	1812	BANI08
BANISTER William	OSB	W	LA	G		..	1688	..	1726	BANI10
BANKS Christopher	S	N	YO	R	#†1	1615	..	1647	1678	BANK02
BANKS Richard	SJ		MX	R	#1	1569	1597	1592	1643	BANK06
BARBER Christopher (Maurus)	OSB	N	MX	G		..	1683	..	1728	BARB06
BARBER Francis	S		MO	D	14	1593	..	1618	1633	BARB10
BARBER James (Lawrence)	OP					1700	1730	1731	1752	BARB16
BARCROFT Thomas	S	N	LA	R		1566	..	1589	..	BARC02
BARDWELL James	SJ		NK	Y	#†=12	1583	1610	..	1633	BARD02
BARGE John	SJ				4	..	..	..	1594	BARG02
BARKER Alexader	S	N	LA	D	#	1606	..	1631	1665	BARK01
BARKER Charles	OSB	M	ST	W		..	1688	..	1703	BARK02
BARKER Edmund (Leo)	OFM			F	123	1708	1726	1732	1752	BARK03
BARKER Edward	S			D	#*	..	..	1647	1658	BARK04
BARKER Edward	S			L	†	..	..	..	1684	BARK05
BARKER Edward (Bernard)	OFM		MX	F	134	1728	1746	1755	1776	BARK07
BARKER John	SJ	M	EX	Y	1	1640	1662	1670	1705	BARK08
BARKER Thomas	OSB	M	CB	G	3	1768	1790	1797	1798	BARK10
BARKER Thomas	S	L		S	3	..	..	1630	1673	BARK12
BARKER Thomas (Giles S.Ambr.)	OFM		MX	F	12	1602	1625	..	1660	BARK13
BARKER William	S		YO	R	‡	1562	..	1588	..	BARK14
BARKWORTH Mark BL.	OSB	L	LN	V	#+*‡	1572	1601	1599	1601	BARK18
BARLEY John	S			S	3	..	..	1602	..	BARL02
BARLOW Edward (Ambrose) ST.	OSB	N	LA	G	#+	1585	1616	1617	1641	BARL04
BARLOW Edward	S	N	LA	D	#	1694	..	1721	1736	BARL08
BARLOW John	S	N	HA	R		1687	..	1712	1748	BARL10
BARLOW Louis	S	M	PB	D	*=1	1550	..	1574	1610	BARL12
BARLOW William (Archangelus)	CAP	L	PB	P		..	1587	..	1632	BARL14
BARLOW William (Rudesind)	OSB	L	LA		#*	1584	1606	1608	1656	BARL16
BARNABY Francis	S	L	YO	R	‡=°	1573	..	1598	..	BARN02
BARNABY Thomas	S	M	MX	D	#3	1727	..	1752	1783	BARN04
BARNARD Francis	CRT			C		..	1579	..	1594	BARN05
BARNARD James	S	L	MX	S		1733	..	1757	1803	BARN06
BARNARD Martin (Adrian)	OSB		LA	X		..	1690	..	1699	BARN10
BARNES John	S			Q	*	..	..	1578	..	BARN14
BARNES John	OSB		NK	V	†1	1581	1605	1608	1661	BARN16
BARNES John (Lawrence)	OSB	N	DT	G		1748	1768	..	1803	BARN18
BARNES Joseph	S	N		D	*	1713	..	1739	1761	BARN20
BARNES Louis (John)	OSB	L	MX	E		1731	1746	..	1775	BARN22
BARNES Stephen	S			R	*	1576	..	1601	1653	BARN24
BARNES William	S	M	WT	R	13	1764	..	1793	1845	BARN26
BARNEWALL Anthony	S		IR			..	..	..	1778	BARN27
BARNEWALL John	S	L	IR			..	..	..	1782	BARN28
BARNEWALL John (Cyprian)	OSB		MX	X		1761	1783	..	1788	BARN29
BARNEWALL Joseph	S	L		V	#3	..	..	1763	1765	BARN30
BARNEWALL Patrick	SJ	N	IR	Z		1709	..	..	1762	BARN32
BARNEY see BARNES										
BARNSLEY Henry	S	M	WR	D	#4	1604	..	1628	1678	BARN40
BARON John	SJ		LA	R	#2	1605	1632	1630	1638	BARO02

Name	Reg	D	Co	T	Notes	Born	Prof	Ordn	Died	Code
BARR Thomas (Bernard)	OSB	M	HA	G		1740	1757	..	1823	BARR04
BARRARD Richard	SJ		LA	Y	#	1661	1690	1698	1740	BARR06
BARRASS (Bernardine)	OFM		YO	F	4	1659	1686	1687	1696	BARR08
BARRASS Nicholas	OSS		DH	Q		..	1585	1584	1621	BARR10
BARRETT Andrew (Edward)	OFM	L		F	123	1685	1709	1711	1745	BARR22
BARRETT Edward	S	N	LA	D	3	1741	..	1765	1829	BARR24
BARRETT George	S	M	WK	L	#	1638	..	1661	1699	BARR26
BARRETT Richard	S		WK	R	#‡	1544	..	1580	1599	BARR27
BARRETT Richard (Maurus)	OSB	W	LA	W		1736	1751	..	1794	BARR28
BARRETT Thomas	S	L	SK	V	#†3	..	..	1613	1631	BARR29
BARREYS see BARWISE										
BARRISTER Thomas	S			S	3	..	..	1645	..	BARR32
BARROW Edward	SJ		LA	Y	#3	1660	1683	1690	1721	BARR34
BARROW James	S	N	LA	R		1726	..	1751	1800	BARR36
BARROW John	S	N	LA	R		1735	..	1766	1811	BARR38
BARROW John	S	N	LA	D		1751	..	1777	1811	BARR40
BARROW Joseph	SJ	N	LA	Y		1740	1758	1765	1813	BARR42
BARROW Richard	SJ	N	LA	Y	3	1738	1755	1763	1799	BARR44
BARROW Thomas	SJ	N	LA	Y	3	1747	1764	1772	1814	BARR46
BARROW William BL.	SJ	L	LA	Y	#+	1608	1632	..	1679	BARR48
BARROWS Christopher	S			D	#*	..	..	1621	..	BARR50
BARTER John	OSB	L		G		1599	1654	..	1667	BART02
BARTLETT Edward	S	M	WR	D		1702	..	1727	1782	BART04
BARTLETT Felix	SJ	M	WR	Y		1708	1726	1734	1777	BART06
BARTLETT Richard	S	M	WR	D	#3	1684	..	1709	1734	BART10
BARTLETT Richard	SJ		WR	R	#	1577	1616	1612	1645	BART12
BARTLETT Richard (Bernard)	OSB	N	WR	G		1669	1692	..	1735	BART13
BARTON James	S			S	7	..	..	..	..	BART15
BARTON James	S			V	3	..	..	1707	..	BART16
BARTON John	S				7	..	..	..	..	BART17
BARTON John	S		LA	R	#°	1679	..	1703	..	BART18
BARTON Richard (Bede)	OSB		LA	E		1739	1757	..	1790	BART22
BARTON William	S	N	LA	R	#	1649	..	1673	1728	BART24
BARWICK John				N	*3	..	..	1570	..	BARW01
BARWISE Robert	S			Q	#*	1563	..	1589	..	BARW02
(Basil of Rheims)	CAP		FR		2	..	1612	..	1655	BASI02
(Basil of Soissons)	CAP	L	FR		2	..	1634	..	1698	BASI04
BASKERVILLE (Bonavent.S.Mary)	OFM		RN	F	123	1666	1682	1691	1705	BASK02
BASKERVILLE William (Bernard)	OFM	W	RN	F	234	1655	1671	1679	1727	BASK04
BASTARD Robert	SJ		NK	D		1571	1608	1602	1633	BAST02
BATCHELOR William (Edmund)	OSB	L	YO	E		1709	1726	..	1737	BATC02
BATES John	S			D	#	..	..	1619	..	BATE02
BATES Reginald	S	M	LA	R	#	1569	..	1594	..	BATE04
BATESON George (Richard)	ODC	L	MX		1	1657	..	..	1694	BATE06
BATESON John (Ildephonsus)	ODC		MX		24	1669	1686	..	1746	BATE08
BATT Edward	S			S	3	..	..	1608	..	BATT02
BATT William	S	W	WT	D	#	..	..	1604	..	BATT04
BATT William (Anthony)	OSB		WT	W		..	1616	..	1651	BATT06
BATTIN (Adam of S.Michael)	OFM		BK	F	12	1623	1642	..	1675	BATT08
BAVANT John	S			R	*‡34	..	..	1577	1598	BAVA02
BAWDEN see BALDWIN										
BAXTER Benedict	CRT			C		..	..	..	1648	BAXT02
BAYAERT William	S		MX	D	#‡	1597	..	1625	1651	BAYA02
BAYLES see BALES										
BAYNHAM George (Athanasius)	OFM	L	SY	F	13	1738	1754	1761	1803	BAYN08
BAYNHAM John	SJ	M	WR	Y	#3	1720	1740	1746	1796	BAYN10
BAZIER Matthieu	SJ		FR		#x12	1608	1633	..	1650	BAZI02
BEADNALL James	SJ		ND	Y	#3	1718	1739	1746	1772	BEAD04
BEAKE John	S	L	KT	D	*	..	..	1587	..	BEAK02
BEAR Matthew	S		DV	P		1688	..	1721	1743	BEAR02
BEARE George	OSB			G		..	1660	..	1695	BEAR04
BEAUCHAMP William	S	L	MX	T		..	..	1795	1812	BEAU02
BEAUMONT Edward	S	M	DE	D		1732	..	1757	1820	BEAU06
BEAUMONT Francis	SJ	N	MO	Y	#	1682	1702	1711	1738	BEAU07
BEAUMONT Henry	SJ		LE	Y	#1	1610	1630	..	1673	BEAU08
BEAUMONT John (Baptist)	OFM	W	SM	F	13	1697	..	1725	1774	BEAU14

Name	Reg	D	Co	T	Notes	Born	Prof	Ordn	Died	Code
BEAUMONT Joseph	SJ	N	SM	Y	3	1702	1723	1730	1773	BEAU16
BEAUMONT William	SJ	W	SM	Y	3	1697	1718	1727	1764	BEAU24
BEBB see BABE										
BECKET Nicholas	OSB	M	ST		*2	1583	1604	..	1618	BECK04
BECKET Thomas	S			S	3	..	..	1631	..	BECK06
BECKINSALL Thomas	S				7	..	..	..	..	BECK08
BEDFORD William	S	W	HR	D	#3	1659	..	1694	1719	BEDF02
BEDINGFELD Anthony	SJ		SK	Y	3	1697	1714	1723	1752	BEDI04
BEDINGFELD Chas.(Bonaventure)	OFM		NK	F	§23	1698	1725	1731	1782	BEDI06
BEDINGFELD Edmund	S		NK	S		1615	..	1644	1680	BEDI08
BEDINGFELD Edward	SJ	M	SK	Y	#1	1595	1617	..	1659	BEDI10
BEDINGFELD Henry	SJ	L	SK	R	1	1582	1602	..	1659	BEDI12
BEDINGFELD John	SJ				4	..	..	..	1618	BEDI14
BEDINGFELD John	S	M			7	..	..	..	..	BEDI15
BEDINGFELD Thomas	SJ		SK	S	#34	1612	1635	1635	1649	BEDI16
BEECH Robert (Anselm)	OSB		LA	Q	*14	1568	1596	1594	1634	BEEC02
BEECHAM see BEAUCHAMP										
BEEN (John)	OP					..	..	..	1690	BEEN02
BERE Anthony	S		OX	R	#§	1624	..	1648	..	BEER02
BEESLEY George VEN.	S	L	LA	Q	#+	1562	..	1587	1591	BEES04
BEESLEY John	SJ	M	YO	S	#	1593	1622	1620	1670	BEES06
BEESLEY John	S	N	LA	D	#3	1609	..	1634	1674	BEES08
BEESLEY Richard	S	N	LA	Q		1570	..	1595	..	BEES10
BEESTON Francis	SJ			Y	4	1751	..	..	1810	BEES11
BEESTON George	S	M	LN	D	3	1737	..	1762	1797	BEES12
BEESTON Peter	S	M	LN	D	3	1727	..	1752	1767	BEES14
BEESTON Robert	SJ		LN	Y	#3	1659	1680	1688	1732	BEES15
BEESTON Robert	S	M	LN	D	3	1743	..	1768	1832	BEES16
BEESTON see also BESTON										
BELASYSE Chas.Ld.Fauconberg	S	L	IT	P		1750	..	1775	1815	BELA02
BELFIELD Henry	SJ	L	HA	R	#§	1578	1613	1608	1632	BELF02
BELFIELD John	S	L	HA	D	#§	..	..	1603	..	BELF04
BELL Arthur (Francis) VEN.	OFM		WR	V	+	1591	1618	1618	1643	BELL02
BELL Henry	SJ		DE		24	1563	1596	1589	1597	BELL06
BELL John	S	N	YO	D		1767	..	1794	1854	BELL10
BELL Thomas	S	N	YO	R	§°3	1551	..	1579	..	BELL12
BELLASS Isaac	S	L		D	*3	1761	..	1786	1817	BELL14
BENLOS Peter	SJ		WD	R	#†	1568	1613	..	1636	BENL02
BENNET Alexius	OSB			W	§2	..	1620	..	1636	BENN02
BENNET Edward	S	L	FT	R	#	1569	..	1594	1637	BENN04
BENNET George or John	CRT			C		..	1576	..	1579	BENN05
BENNET John	SJ	W	FT	D	#1	1548	1586	1578	1625	BENN06
BENNET John	S	W	FT	V	#13	1570	..	1597	1623	BENN08
BENNET John	SJ		MX	Y	#	1692	1710	1719	1751	BENN09
BENNET John (Placid)	OSB	N	LA	W		1741	1758	..	1795	BENN10
BENNET Robert	SJ			R	*	1560	1587	1583	1590	BENN12
BENNET Thomas	S	L	LA	R	#1	1656	..	1681	..	BENN14
BENNET Thomas (Bede)	OSB	L	LA	G		1723	1741	..	1800	BENN16
BENNET William	CRT					..	..	..	1574	BENN18
BENSON Robert	S		NK	R	#	1571	..	1597	..	BENS02
BENSON (Thomas of S.Anne)	OFM	L	BU	F	123	1622	1652	1655	1705	BENS04
BENSTEAD Thomas VEN.	S	M	NK	S	#+	1574	..	..	1600	BENS06
BENTLEY Christopher	S	M	LN	V	3	..	..	1683	1694	BENT04
BENTLEY Edward	SJ	W	DE	R	#1	1588	1609	..	1656	BENT08
BENTLEY Henry	SJ		DE	R	#14	1583	1610	1609	1628	BENT12
BENTLEY Hugh	S		CH	V	‡3	..	..	1593	..	BENT13
BENTLEY John	SJ		DE	R	#12	1590	1611	..	1663	BENT14
BENTNEY William	SJ		CH	Y	#x2	1609	1630	..	1692	BENT16
BENWELL Francis	S	L		L	#7	..	..	..	..	BENW02
BENYON Thomas	S		LA	R		1715	..	1739	1756	BENY02
BERESFORD William	SJ	M	LN	Y	#	1670	1692	1697	1726	BERE02
BERINGTON Charles BP.	S	M	EX	P	*	1748	..	1775	1798	BERI02
BERINGTON George	OSB	W	HR	V	12	1576	..	..	1664	BERI04
BERINGTON John	SJ	N	HR	Y	#3	1673	1691	1699	1743	BERI06
BERINGTON John (Bernard)	OSB		HR	S	23	..	1607	1593	1639	BERI08
BERINGTON Joseph	S	L	HR	D		1743	..	1770	1827	BERI10

Name	Reg	D	Co	T	Notes	Born	Prof	Ordn	Died	Code
BERINGTON Simon	S	L	HR	D	#3	1680	..	1706	1755	BERI12
BERINGTON Thomas	S	L	SP	D	3	1673	..	1698	1755	BERI14
BERINGTON Thomas	S	L	EX	D	3	1740	..	1768	1805	BERI16
BERMINGHAM Nicholas	SJ		IR		#	1721	1740	..	..	BERM02
BERMINGHAM William	SJ		FR	Y	#1	1692	1711	1721	..	BERM04
(Bernard of S. Matthew)	CAR	L	IR	Z		..	..	..	1661	BERN01
BERNARD Richard	S			N	‡34	..	..	1570	1596	BERN04
BERNARD see also BARNARD										
BERNEY (Robert of S. Francis)	OFM		YO	F	12	1593	1634	..	1659	BERN06
BERRIMAN (Alban)	OSB	L	SM	E		..	1661	..	1715	BERR02
BERRIMAN Joseph	OSB	W	SM	G		..	1654	..	1715	BERR04
BERRY James (Augustine)	OSB	N	ND	E		1758	1779	..	1786	BERR06
BERRY John (Jerome)	OSB		LA	W	#	1714	1731	..	1792	BERR08
BERRY Robert	S	L	HA	R	#	1686	..	1711	1736	BERR10
BERRY Thomas	S		CH	D		1635	..	1661	1684	BERR12
BERRY Thomas	S	N	LA	D		1766	..	1797	1851	BERR14
BERTIE Jerome	SJ		LN	Y		1673	1693	1701	1739	BERT02
BERTRAM William (Michael)	OP	N	ND	Z	*13	1643	1666	1675	1691	BERT04
BERULLE Pierre de CARD.	ORA	L	FR	P	*2	1575	1611	1599	1629	BERU02
BESTON John	S			S	3	..	..	1637	..	BEST04
BESTON see also BEESTON										
BESTUNICUS Nicholas	S		YO	D	*	..	..	1618	..	BEST06
BESWICK Edward	SJ	M	MX	Y	#1	1615	1639	..	1680	BESW02
BESWICK Francis	OSB		LA	G	x	1765	1786	..	1793	BESW04
BETENSON Edward (Placid)	OSB		EX	G		1630	1649	..	1689	BETE02
BETHAM James	SJ	L	ST	Y	1	1604	1624	..	1669	BETH01
BETHAM John	S		WK	D	#3	1642	..	1667	1709	BETH02
BETHAM William	S		WK	D	#1	1597	..	1628	..	BETH04
BETTS James (Joseph)	CRT		MX	D	1	1665	1711	1691	1729	BETT04
BETTS John	S		MX	L		..	..	1676	..	BETT06
BETTS John (Philip)	S	L	HA	D		..	..	1726	1770	BETT08
BEVAN John	SJ		FR	Y	1	1702	1726	1724	1728	BEVA02
BEVANS Francis (Ambrose)	OFM		BR	F	14	1620	..	..	1686	BEVA04
BEVERIDGE Thomas	S		DE	R		1619	..	1644	..	BEVE02
BEVERIDGE Jerome	OFM			F	3	..	..	1713	1765	BEVE04
BEVERIDGE John	SJ		DE	Y		1615	1636	1646	1646	BEVE06
BEVERIDGE Thomas	SJ		DE	Y	#12	1583	1604	..	1658	BEVE08
BEW John	S	M	MX	P		1755	..	1784	1829	BEWA02
BEWES William	S			D	#*	..	..	1612	..	BEWE02
BEWLY Robert	S			D	*	..	..	1623	1623	BEWL02
BIAR John	S			Q	*	..	..	1579	..	BIAR02
BICKLEY Ralph	SJ		HA	R	‡1	1557	1597	1580	1619	BICK02
BIDDLECOMB Martin	S	W	DT	L	#	..	..	1633	1678	BIDD02
BIDDULPH Andrew	S		ST	V	#3	1605	..	1629	1661	BIDD04
BIDDULPH Francis	SJ		ST	Y	#1	1595	1615	..	1673	BIDD06
BIDDULPH Peter	S		ST	R	#	1602	..	1625	1657	BIDD08
BIFIELD see BYFIELD										
BILCLIFFE Peter	S		LN	V	#	..	..	..	1632	BILC02
BILCLIFFE Peter	CRT		YO	C		..	1661	..	1693	BILC04
BILCLIFFE Thomas	CRT			C		..	1673	..	1692	BILC06
BILLINGE Charles	SJ	M	LA	Y	°3	1735	1753	1763	1805	BILL02
BILLINGE Richard	SJ	N	LA	Y	1	1674	1698	1706	1733	BILL04
BILLINGE Richard Lawrence	SJ	L	LA	V	#	1713	1739	1739	1769	BILL06
BILLINGE Thomas	S	L	LA	R	#	1654	..	1682	1740	BILL08
BILLINGTON John	S	N	LA	L	3	1763	..	1784	1845	BILL10
BILLINGTON Richard	S	N	LA	D	3	1757	..	1781	1830	BILL12
BILLINGTON William	S	N	LA	V		1747	..	1775	1811	BILL14
BINANS de, see DEBENHAM										
BING Edward	OP	L		B	§3	1625	1663	1669	1701	BING02
BING John	S	N	YO	Q		..	..	1594	..	BING04
BIRCH Henry	S			V	3	..	..	1708	1708	BIRC04
BIRD Christopher	S		MX	L	#34	..	..	1689	1710	BIRD02
BIRKBECK Edward	SJ		WD	Y	#	1667	1690	1699	1722	BIRK02
BIRKBECK Gervase	S		WD	R	#1	1671	..	1710	1733	BIRK04
BIRKBECK William	S		DH	Q	†	..	..	1581	..	BIRK06
BIRKET George	S	L	DH	D	#	1549	..	1577	1614	BIRK08

39

Name	Reg	D	Co	T	Notes	Born	Prof	Ordn	Died	Code
BIRTWISTLE James	CRT			C	#	..	..	..	1684	BIRT02
BIRTWISTLE John	S	N	LA	V	*3	..	..	1600	1620	BIRT04
BIRTWISTLE John	S	N				..	..	..	1680	BIRT06
BIRTWISTLE Richard	S	N	LA	L	#	1713	..	1737	1743	BIRT08
BISHOP Bartholomew (Denis)	OSB	L	OX	X		..	1682	..	1725	BISH02
BISHOP Francis	S	M	WR	D		1757	..	1783	1821	BISH04
BISHOP George	S	M	WK	P	3	1695	..	1723	1768	BISH06
BISHOP Henry	OFM	M	WK	F	3	1726	1749	1755	1811	BISH08
BISHOP John	S		ST	D	#‡	1580	..	1602	..	BISH12
BISHOP John	S	L		D	#§°	1692	..	1719	..	BISH14
BISHOP William BP.	S	L	WK	R	*‡3	1553	..	1581	1624	BISH18
BISHOP William	S			Q		..	..	1583	..	BISH20
BITHEL Peter	S				7	..	..	..	..	BITH02
BIX (Angelus of S.Agnes)	OFM	L	MX	F	1234	1646	1666	1672	1695	BIXA02
BIX (John Ev of S.Hubert)	OFM		KT	F	1234	1658	1676	1685	1703	BIXA04
BIX Nicholas	S			L	3	..	..	1697	..	BIXA06
BLACKBURN Edward	S	N	LA	R	#	1634	..	1661	1709	BLAC04
BLACKBURN John	S	N	LA	R		1654	..	1679	1728	BLAC06
BLACKBURN Lancelot	S			Q	*	..	..	1575	..	BLAC08
BLACKFAN John	SJ		SX	V	#†3	1560	1594	1593	1641	BLAC10
BLACKFAN Thomas	SJ	W	SX	Y	#4	1601	1624	..	1663	BLAC12
BLACKISTON Francis	OSB		DH	G		..	1626	..	1650	BLAC13
BLACKISTON Francis	SJ		DH	Y	3	1617	1637	1646	1693	BLAC14
BLACKISTON Francis	SJ	M	LN	Y	#12	1635	1657	1667	1701	BLAC16
BLACKISTON Michael	OSB		DH	G		..	1625	..	1632	BLAC17
BLACKISTON William John	SJ		ND	V	#3	1698	1723	1723	1768	BLAC18
BLACKLOW see BLACOE										
BLACKWELL George	S		MX	D	x‡	1547	..	1575	1612	BLAC20
BLACKWELL William	SJ		HA	Y	1	1613	1640	..	1699	BLAC22
BLACOE Joseph	S	L	LA	L	#3	..	..	1697	1740	BLAC24
BLACOE Robert	S	N	LA	D		1767	..	1794	1823	BLAC26
BLACOE William	S	N	LA	R		1732	..	1756	1815	BLAC28
BLAIR James	SJ		MX	V	3	1693	1713	1722	1759	BLAI02
BLAKE James	SJ	L		S	#13	1649	1675	1674	1728	BLAK02
BLAKESTON see BLACKISTON										
BLAKEY Philip	OSB		ND	X		..	1690	..	1707	BLAK08
BLAKEY William (Anselm)	OSB	L	ND	X	4	..	1682	..	1723	BLAK10
BLANDY (Boniface)	OSB		BK		*	..	1606	..	1634	BLAN02
BLAY Edward	S			D	*°	1672	..	1697	..	BLAY02
BLECHINDER Thomas	CRT			C		..	1596	..	1606	BLEC02
BLENKINSOP Francis	S		WD	D		..	..	1612	..	BLEN02
BLEVIN (Aloysius)	CRT		LA	C		..	1730	..	1761	BLEV01
BLEVIN James	S		MX	L		1732	..	..	..	BLEV02
BLEVIN William	S	L	MX	D	3	1735	..	1762	1788	BLEV04
BLINKHORNE John	S			D	*	..	..	1579	..	BLIN02
BLOODSWORTH Thomas	S	N	HU	V		1757	..	1781	1815	BLOO02
BLOOMER Edward (Lawrence)	OFM		NK	F	12	1602	1626	..	1672	BLOO03
BLOUNT Charles	S	M	WR	D	3	1735	..	1761	1810	BLOU02
BLOUNT Francis	S		HR	R	#§	1612	..	1639	..	BLOU04
BLOUNT Gilbert	S		SP	L		1621	..	1645	..	BLOU06
BLOUNT Henry Tichborne	S	M	OX	D	#	1723	..	1748	1810	BLOU08
BLOUNT James Walter (Jerome)	OSS		ST	L	#	1622	..	1649	1694	BLOU10
BLOUNT Richard	SJ		LE	R	#‡	1563	1596	1589	1638	BLOU11
BLOUNT Richard (Godric)	OSB		BK	G		1617	1649	..	1667	BLOU12
BLOUNT Thomas	S	M	SP	L	x1	1616	..	1641	1647	BLOU14
BLUETT John	SJ	L	ST	Y	#	1602	1628	..	1678	BLUE04
BLUETT Thomas	S		MO	D	§°4	1539	..	1578	1604	BLUE06
BLUNDELL Francis	S	N	LA	D		1753	..	1779	1792	BLUN02
BLUNDELL James	SJ				1	1581	1607	..	1609	BLUN04
BLUNDELL James	S	N	LA	L	3	1768	..	1792	1839	BLUN06
BLUNDELL Joseph	SJ	N	LA	Y		1686	1703	1712	1759	BLUN12
BLUNDELL Nicholas	SJ		LA	Y	3	1640	1662	1670	1680	BLUN14
BLUNDELL Robert Francis	SJ	N	LA	N	3	1717	1738	1745	1779	BLUN16
BLUNDELL Thomas	SJ	N	LA	Y		1648	1667	1678	1702	BLUN18
BLUNDELL William	S		LA	R		1568	..	1594	1596	BLUN20
BLUNDESTON Daniel or Robert	S	N	NT	D	#4	1596	..	1622	1657	BLUN22

Name	Reg	D	Co	T	Notes	Born	Prof	Ordn	Died	Code
BLUNDESTON Lawrence	S		NT	R	#§	1592	..	1620	..	BLUN24
BLUNDEVILLE James	S		MX	D	#1	1603	..	1630	1658	BLUN26
BLUNT see BLOUNT										
BLYDE Ignatius	SJ		YO	Y	13	1720	1756	1762	1788	BLYD02
BLYTH Francis (Simon Stock)	ODC	L		M	#§1	1704	..	..	1772	BLYT01
BOARMAN John	SJ		MD	Y		1743	1762	1769	1797	BOAR02
BOARMAN Sylvester	SJ		MD	Y	4	1746	1765	1772	1812	BOAR04
BODENHAM Hugh	S		ST	R		1645	..	1676	..	BODE02
BODENHAM John	SJ	W	HR	Y	#13	1689	1709	1714	1750	BODE04
BODENHAM William	S		HR	L	#3	1630	..	1654	..	BODE06
BODWIN see BALDWIN										
BOELMANS Lambert	SJ	L	LC	Y		1649	1672	1678	1690	BOEL02
BOLAND see BOWLAND										
BOLAS Bernard (Benedict)	OSB	N	SP	X		..	1744	..	1773	BOLA02
BOLAS Thomas (Anselm)	OSB	N	SP	X		1732	1751	..	1797	BOLA04
BOLBET Roger	SJ		ST		2	..	1559	..	1572	BOLB02
BOLD Thomas	S			S	3	..	..	1650	1650	BOLD02
BOLE (Nicholas)	OFM			F	123	1680	1697	1705	1726	BOLE02
BOLNEY Robert	S		DH	L	3	1679	..	1705	1716	BOLN02
BOLT Clement	S		NK	R	#†	1659	..	1692	..	BOLT02
BOLT Henry	S			L	*	1556	..	..	..	BOLT04
BOLT Henry	SJ		WK	Y	#3	1670	1691	1699	1743	BOLT05
BOLT John	S		DV	Y	#§	1563	..	1605	1640	BOLT06
BOLTON Cuthbert or John	S			R		1579	..	1616	..	BOLT08
BOLTON John	S		LA	R	4	1560	..	1584	1630	BOLT10
BOLTON John	SJ			Y	3	1742	1761	1769	1809	BOLT12
BOLTON John (Anselm)	OSB	N	LA	W		1736	1751	..	1805	BOLT14
BOLTON Joseph	S	L	LA	D	3	1736	..	1764	1783	BOLT16
BOND John	S			S	#3	..	..	1600	..	BOND02
BONHAM (Joachim)	CAP	L			8					BONH02
BONVILLE Anthony	SJ		DT	R	#§	1621	1647	1647	1676	BONV02
BONVILLE Francis	S		DT	L	3	..	..	1682	..	BONV04
BOON Edward	SJ	N	MD	Y	3	1734	1756	1764	1785	BOON04
BOON John	SJ	N	MD	Y	3	1735	1756	1762	1795	BOON06
BOON Joseph	SJ		MD	Y		..	..	..	1779	BOON08
BOOTH Charles	SJ	W	FR	Y	#3	1707	1724	1731	1797	BOOT02
BOOTH Edward	S	N	LA	L	#	1638	..	1663	1719	BOOT04
BOOTH Francis	S	L	FR	V		..	..	1733	..	BOOT06
BOOTH John	S	N	YO	L		..	..	1696	1722	BOOT08
BOOTH Ralph	SJ		FR	Y	#3	1721	1737	1747	1780	BOOT10
BOOTH Robert (Ambrose)	OSB			W		..	1673	..	1679	BOOT12
BOOTHBY George	S	M		D	#*3	..	..	1680	..	BOOT14
BORDLEY Simon George	S	N	LA	D	§	1709	..	1734	1799	BORD02
BOSGRAVE James	SJ		DT	R	1	1547	1564	1572	1623	BOSG02
BOSTE John ST.	S	N	WD	Q	#‡+1	1543	..	1581	1594	BOST02
BOSTE John	S	N			7	..	..	..	..	BOST03
BOSTOCK George	S		DB	R	#	1664	..	1688	1727	BOST04
BOSTOCK George	S	N	LA	R	#	1672	..	1700	1728	BOST06
BOSVILLE John	S		KT	V	#134	1567	..	1592	1631	BOSV02
BOSVILLE John	S	W	MO	D	#	1716	..	1743	1779	BOSV04
BOUCHER Richard	SJ	W	MX	Y	3	1696	1713	1727	1760	BOUC02
BOUCHER Robert (Ambrose)	OSB		MX	X		1726	1744	..	1766	BOUC04
BOUCHER William	SJ				1	1682	..	..	1757	BOUC06
BOULT see BOLT										
BOURGEOIS James Philip	SJ	W	FR	Y	#3	1738	1760	1767	1811	BOUR02
BOURNE Jonas	S	N	SM	R	#3	1690	..	1715	1738	BOUR04
BOURNE Samuel	S		ST	D	#§3	1682	..	1711	1711	BOUR06
BOVILLE see BONVILLE										
BOWER Archibald	SJ		SC	R	°	1686	1706	..	1766	BOWE02
BOWER William	S		NT	D	3	1735	..	1766	1773	BOWE04
BOWES Robert	S	W	SX	D	#3	1673	..	1697	1735	BOWE06
BOWES Stanislaus	S		SX	R		1680	..	1709	1710	BOWE08
BOWES Stephen	S		SX	D		1676	..	..	1713	BOWE10
BOWKER Alexander	S		NN	D	#§*°	1608	..	1608	1618	BOWK02
BOWLAND James	S	N	YO	R		1564	..	1586	..	BOWL01
BOWLAND John Francis	S	L		D	*1	1770	..	1795	1857	BOWL02

41

Name	Reg	D	Co	T	Notes	Born	Prof	Ordn	Died	Code
BOWYER James (Vincent)	OP	L				1756	1780	1780	1807	BOWY02
BOYCE George	S	N	YO	D	#§	1590	..	1615	..	BOYC02
BOYLAN Bartholomew	S			S	3	..	..	1739	..	BOYL02
BRABANT Ellis or Elias	S				#4	..	..	..	1643	BRAB02
BRACEY Edmund	SJ	M	WR	Y	4	1709	1730	1738	1783	BRAC02
BRADDOCK Edmund	S		NK	R		..	..	1583	..	BRAD02
BRADDOCK Henry	S		NK	Q		..	..	1583	..	BRAD04
BRADILL Edward	S	N	LA	Q	#	..	..	1587	..	BRAD06
BRADLEY Richard	SJ	N	LA	Y	x2	1605	1622	..	1645	BRAD10
BRADSHAIGH see also BRADSHAW										
BRADSHAIGH Edward (Elias)	ODC	L	IR	B	#	..	1619	1621	1652	BRAD12
BRADSHAIGH Edward	S		LA	R	#4	1603	..	1628	1681	BRAD14
BRADSHAIGH Peter	SJ	N	LA	Y	#	1609	1631	..	1676	BRAD16
BRADSHAIGH Richard	SJ		LA	R	#	1601	1625	..	1669	BRAD18
BRADSHAIGH Robert	SJ		LA	S	#3	1589	1614	1612	1617	BRAD20
BRADSHAIGH Thomas	SJ	L	LA	R	#	1606	1631	1631	1663	BRAD22
BRADSHAW Anselm (Bernard)	OSB		SP	X	#	..	1723	..	1774	BRAD24
BRADSHAW Bernard (Anselm)	OSB	N	DH	X		1742	1760	..	1799	BRAD26
BRADSHAW Francis (Basil)	OSB		DH	X		..	1762	..	1770	BRAD28
BRADSHAW John	S	N	LA	R	1	1742	..	1766	1790	BRAD32
BRADSHAW Robert	S		LA	D	#†4	1572	..	1602	1610	BRAD34
BRADSHAW Thomas (Augustine)	OSB	M	WR	V	#	1576	1600	1600	1618	BRAD36
BRADSHAW see also BRADSHAIGH										
BRADSHEET John	S	M		V	#1	1634	..	1658	1689	BRAD38
BRAILSFORD Peter	S	L		L	3	..	..	1697	1734	BRAI02
BRAITHWAITE (Richard of Magd)	OFM		WD	F		1626	1653	1655	1695	BRAI06
BRAITHWAITE Robert	S		WD	D	#1	1623	..	1650	..	BRAI08
BRAMLY George	S	N	YO	D	#	..	..	1577	..	BRAM02
BRAMSTON James Yorke BP.	S	L	NN	L	*§=	1763	..	1799	1836	BRAM04
BRAMSTON Thomas	S		KT	Q	‡	1540	..	1585	1606	BRAM06
BRAND John	S	M	MX	D	#3	1675	..	1706	1750	BRAN02
BRAY Richard	SJ				4	..	..	..	1594	BRAY02
BRECON see BRYCHAN										
BREERS Lawrence	S	L	LA	D	13	1667	..	1691	1744	BREE02
BREERS William	S	N	LA	L	#1	1690	..	1725	1741	BREE06
BRENNAN John ? (James)	OP	L	IR		#*	..	..	..	1748	BREN00
BRENNAN Luke	S		IR	S		..	..	1772	..	BREN01
BRENNAN Thomas	SJ	M	IR	R	1	1708	1726	..	1773	BREN02
BRENT James	SJ					..	..	..	1657	BREN06
BRENT Richard (George)	OSB		WR	X		..	1696	..	1716	BREN10
BRETT John Bede	ODC		HR		1	1667	..	..	1711	BRET01
BRETT Robert	SJ	W	SM	Y	3	1636	1657	1667	1678	BRET04
BRETT Robert (Gabriel)	OSB	L	SM	Z	1*	1597	1615	1627	1665	BRET06
BRETTON see BRITTON										
BREVAL Francis Durant de	CAP	L	FR		°	..	.‑.	..	1707	BREV02
BREWER John	SJ	W	LA	Y	3	1732	1752	1761	1797	BREW04
BREWER John (Bede)	OSB	N	LA	W	1	1742	1758	..	1822	BREW06
BREWER Thomas	SJ	W	LA	Y	3	1743	1761	1771	1787	BREW08
BREWER see also BREERS										
BREWSTER Francis Willoughby	ODC	M	LN			1770	..	..	1849	BREW10
BREWSTER William	SJ	M	MX	Y		1700	1724	1730	1758	BREW12
BREYLE Anthony	S			S	3	..	..	1688	..	BREY02
BRIAN John	S			D	*	..	..	1602	..	BRIA02
BRIAN John	S	W		R	#*4	1647	..	1672	1694	BRIA04
BRIAN see also BRYON										
BRIANT Alexander ST.	SJ	W	SM	D	*+‡	1556	1581	1578	1581	BRIA06
BRIANT Edward	S			S		..	..	1651	..	BRIA08
BRIANT Henry	SJ	M	SK		1	1599	..	..	1658	BRIA10
BRIANT see also O'BRIEN										
BRICKNELL Gaspar George	S	M	BK	V		1768	..	1793	1833	BRIC04
BRIDE (Ambrose)	OSB			G		..	1657	..	1669	BRID02
BRIDE William	S				7	..	..	..	..	BRID03
BRIDGES Richard	S	L	HR	R	#	1608	..	1632	1685	BRID04
BRIDGEWOOD Thomas	S	M			#	..	..	..	1732	BRID06
BRIGHAM Henry (Augustine)	OSB		YO	G		..	1731	..	1738	BRIG02
BRIGHAM Peter	CRT			C		..	..	..	1679	BRIG04

Name	Reg	D	Co	T	Notes	Born	Prof	Ordn	Died	Code
BRINDLE John (Basil)	OSB	W	LA	W		1746	1765	..	1802	BRIN02
BRINDLEY James (Bonaventure)	OFM			F	12	1615	1642	..	1653	BRIN03
BRINKWORTH Robert (Bede)	ODC	L				1702	1724	..	..	BRIN04
BRISCOE Bernard	CRT			C		..	1727	..	1748	BRIS01
BRISCOE Thomas	S		YO	V	‡3	1553	..	1594	..	BRIS02
BRISTOW Richard	S	L	WR	D	‡x	1538	..	1573	1581	BRIS04
BRITTAIN Thomas (Louis)	OP	W	CH	N	§3	1745	1767	1771	1827	BRIT02
BRITTON Matthew	S	N	YO	R	#4	1564	..	1590	1643	BRIT04
BRITTON Richard	S		YO	S	3	..	..	1610	..	BRIT06
BROCKHOLES Charles	SJ	N	LA	Y	3	1684	1705	1713	1759	BROC02
BROCKHOLES Roger	S	N	LA	L	3	1658	..	1684	1700	BROC04
BROCKHOLES Roger	S	N	LA	R	1	1682	..	1708	1742	BROC06
BROCKHOLES Thomas	S	N	LA	D	3	1655	..	1680	1738	BROC08
BROCKHOLES Thomas	S	M	LA	D		1683	..	1706	1758	BROC10
BRODERICK Richard	S	L	MX	T		1771	..	1798	1831	BROD02
BROME John	S		HR	Q		..	..	1584	..	BROM02
BROME see also BROWN										
BROMLEY Thomas (Anselm)	OSB		LA	W		1749	1766	..	1779	BROM07
BROMWICH Andrew	S	M	ST	L	3	..	..	1672	1702	BROM08
BROOKE Adam	SJ		MX	R	‡	1542	1564	..	1605	BROO02
BROOKE Charles (Joseph)	CRT		MD	C		1735	1769	..	1784	BROO05
BROOKE Ignatius	SJ		MD	V		1671	1699	1696	1751	BROO08
BROOKE Ignatius	SJ		MD	Y	4	1751	1770	..	1815	BROO09
BROOKE Leonard	SJ	W	MD	Y		1750	1769	..	1813	BROO10
BROOKE Matthew	SJ		MD	V		1672	1699	1697	1702	BROO12
BROOKE Ralph	CRT			C	2	..	1579	..	1621	BROO13
BROOKE Robert	SJ		MD	Y	3	1663	1684	1692	1714	BROO14
BROOKE Thomas	SJ	M	SX	V	13	1678	1701	1701	1761	BROO16
BROOKE Thomas	S		DV	L	§	1727	..	1751	1756	BROO18
BROOKE William	S			Q	*	..	..	1581	..	BROO20
BROOKES see BROOKE										
BROOMHEAD Roland	S	N	YO	R		1751	..	1775	1820	BROO22
BROUGHTON Richard	S	M	HU	Q	#†	1561	..	1592	1635	BROU02
BROWN (Adam of S.Michael)	OFM			F	3	..	..	1650	1675	BROW00
BROWN Alexander (Bernardine)	OFM	M	SC	D	#13	1723	1745	1746	1757	BROW01
BROWN Alexander (Macarius)	OSB	N	SC	J		1639	1660	..	1697	BROW02
BROWN (Anselm)	OSB		OX	W		..	1688	..	1706	BROW04
BROWN (Bernard)	OFM			F	1	1605	..	..	1640	BROW05
BROWN Christopher	S		IR		8	..	..	..	..	BROW08
BROWN Edward	SJ		ZZ	Y	*3	1743	1767	1770	1770	BROW09
BROWN Francis	SJ	L	DH	Y	4	1590	1623	..	1625	BROW10
BROWN (Francis Joseph)	CAP	L	IR			..	..	..	1675	BROW12
BROWN George	OSB		EX	Z	#*2	..	1604	..	1628	BROW13
BROWN George	SJ	N	LA	Y	#	1670	1688	1696	1735	BROW14
BROWN Ignatius	SJ		IR			..	..	..	1679	BROW18
BROWN James or Joseph	S	N	MX	D		1707	..	1740	..	BROW20
BROWN John	S				7	..	..	..	..	BROW22
BROWN (John)	MIN	L	SC		12	1568	1595	..	1643	BROW23
BROWN Levinius	SJ		NK	R		1671	1698	1696	1764	BROW24
BROWN (Mark)	OFM		IR		*7	..	..	..	..	BROW25
BROWN Peter	S	L	ES	D	13	1730	..	1754	1794	BROW26
BROWN Peter	S		KT	P		1730	..	1757	..	BROW28
BROWN (Peter)	CAR	L			*8	..	..	..	..	BROW29
BROWN Thomas	S	L		D	#*	..	..	1578	..	BROW30
BROWN Thomas	S	L	YO	D	#3	1662	..	1686	1728	BROW31
BROWN Thomas	S			D	#*	1665	..	1696	1748	BROW32
BROWN Thomas Lont (Hyacinth)	OP		MX	N	#3	1754	1779	1779	1826	BROW36
BROWN William	S		SP	R	4	1609	..	1632	1663	BROW38
BROWN William	S	M				..	..	..	1750	BROW40
BROWN William (Ambrose)	OSB		WD	G		1670	1700	1706	1755	BROW42
BRUCE Robert (Pius)	OP			N		1688	1715	1717	1768	BRUC02
BRUERTON John	SJ		SP	Y	#	1633	1651	..	1684	BRUE02
BRULLAGHAN Patrick BP.	OP	L	IR	R	#*13	1705	..	1730	1760	BRUL02
BRUNEAU Joseph	SJ		FR	P	4	1704	1721	..	1774	BRUN04
BRUNETTI Joseph	SJ		MX	Y		1671	1689	1698	1715	BRUN06
BRUNING Anthony	SJ	L	HA	Y	#	1636	1660	1668	1704	BRUN08

Name	Reg	D	Co	T	Notes	Born	Prof	Ordn	Died	Code
BRUNING Anthony	SJ	L	HA	Y	3	1716	1733	1741	1776	BRUN10
BRUNING Francis	SJ	M	HA	Y	#1	1620	1641	..	1680	BRUN12
BRUNING Francis	SJ	N	HA	Y	#	1648	1670	1678	1714	BRUN14
BRUNING Francis	OSB	M	BK	X		1675	1699	..	1748	BRUN16
BRUNING George	SJ	L	HA	Y	3	1738	1756	1763	1802	BRUN18
BRUNING Richard (Placid)	OSB	W	HA	E		..	1663	..	1719	BRUN20
BRUNING Thomas	OSB	W	HA	E		1674	1696	..	1719	BRUN22
BRUNO see BROME, BROWN										
BRUSHFORD John	S		CL	R	x	1559	..	1584	1593	BRUS02
BRYCHAN Eleyson (Benedict)	OSB	L	BR	G	#	1610	1625	..	1676	BRYC02
BRYERLEY Anthony	S			L	34	..	..	1698	1719	BRYE02
BRYON Francis	SJ		SX	Y	#°3	1725	1742	1749	..	BRYO02
BRYON see also BRIAN, BRIANT										
BUCK John	SJ	N	MX	Y	#3	1715	1736	1741	1770	BUCK02
BUCK Robert	SJ		CB	D		1573	1612	1600	1648	BUCK04
BUCKLAND Ralph	S	W	SM	R	‡	1564	..	1588	1611	BUCK06
BUCKLEY James	OSB	L	MX	E		..	1708	..	1749	BUCK10
BUCKLEY James BP.	S	L	MX	L	*	1770	..	1794	1828	BUCK12
BUCKLEY John	S			V		..	..	1635	1639	BUCK14
BUCKLEY John (Maurus)	OSB	N	YO	G		..	1714	..	1729	BUCK16
BUCKLEY Robert	SJ			Y	1	1619	1640	..	1680	BUCK18
BUFFLE Leopold	S	L			*8	..	..	..	..	BUFF02
BULLAKER Thomas (Jn Bp.) VEN.	OFM	L	SX	V	+123	1604	1624	1628	1642	BULL02
BULLEN (Michael of Magdalen)	OFM			F	123	1638	1656	1660	1707	BULL03
BULLEN Robert	S	N	LA	R		1740	..	1764	1792	BULL04
BULLER John	SJ	N	LA	Y	3	1746	1768	1771	1811	BULL06
BULLOCK Charles	OP		YO	N	13	1752	1769	1777	1794	BULL08
BULLOCK John (Raymund)	OP	L	YO	N		1750	1767	1773	1819	BULL10
BULLOCK William (Joseph)	OP	N		N		1699	1721	1725	1730	BULL12
BULLY John	S	L	DT	R	#	1627	..	1654	1687	BULL14
BULMER Bertram (Edward)	OSB	N	YO	X		..	1685	..	1745	BULM02
BULMER Bertram (Maurus)	OSB	N	YO	W		1704	1724	..	1788	BULM04
BULMER John (Denis)	OSB		MX	X		..	1732	1736	1741	BULM06
BULSTRODE James	S		FR	R		1724	..	1748	..	BULS02
BURDEN Edward VEN.	S		YO	Q	+‡	..	..	1584	1588	BURD02
BURDETT Anthony	SJ	N	YO	D	1	1610	1642	..	1657	BURD06
BURGAIGNE George	OFM			F	4	..	..	..	1634	BURG00
BURGESS Edward (Ambrose)	OP	L		N	§1	1674	1697	1700	1747	BURG01
BURGESS James (Bede)	OSB	N	LA	W		1768	1789	1792	1837	BURG02
BURGESS Matthew	S		MX	D		1752	..	1777	1786	BURG04
BURGH Robert	S				7	..	..	..	..	BURG05
BURGIS see BURGESS										
BURKE Charles	SJ	L	MX	Y	#3	1713	1733	1747	1787	BURK02
BURKE Jeffrey MacHugho	S	L	IR		*8	..	..	..	..	BURK04
BURKE (Theobald)	OFM	L	IR		*7	..	..	..	..	BURK06
BURKE William	SJ		IR	Y	3	1711	1731	1739	1746	BURK08
BURNELL Francis	SJ		LN	Y	x14	1656	1676	1685	1689	BURN02
BURNETT Thomas	SJ	N	YO	Y	1	1659	1681	1689	1727	BURN04
BURON James	S			S	3	..	..	1643	..	BURO02
BURROUGHS see BARROWS										
BURSCOUGH Richard	S	N	LA	R	#	1651	..	1677	1731	BURS02
BURSCOUGH Richard	S		LA	V	3	..	..	1700	..	BURS04
BURSCOUGH William	S			S	3	..	..	1669	..	BURS06
BURT William	S		SM	D	#	..	..	1603	..	BURT02
BURTON (Augustine of Bern'dn)	OFM		YO	F	123	1679	1696	1705	1706	BURT03
BURTON Christopher	SJ	N	SK	Y	13	1671	1693	1703	1744	BURT04
BURTON Thomas (Lambert)	ODC	L			#12	1695	1722	..	..	BURT06
BURY Anthony	S			S	*3	..	..	1612	..	BURY02
BUSBY George	SJ		LC	Y	#	1638	1656	1667	1695	BUSB01
BUSBY John	SJ	W	OX	Y	#	1679	1699	1708	1743	BUSB02
BUSBY John	S		LC	V	1	1640	..	..	..	BUSB04
BUSBY John	S	M		D	*	1715	..	1738	1794	BUSB06
BUSBY John	S	L	KT	D	°	1762	..	1786	..	BUSB08
BUSBY Richard	SJ	N	YO	Y		1595	1623	1627	1648	BUSB10
BUSBY Thomas	SJ	M	BK	Y	#	1656	1675	1683	1750	BUSB12
BUSBY William	SJ	M	BK	Y		1646	1667	1675	1692	BUSB14

Name	Reg	D	Co	T	Notes	Born	Prof	Ordn	Died	Code
BUSCA John James (Charles)	ODC	L	LC			1632	1652	..	1688	BUSC01
BUSINO Orazio	S	L	IT		*7	..	..	..	..	BUS102
BUSTARD John	SJ		OX		‡12	1550	1570	..	1576	BUST02
BUTLER Alban	S		NN	D	#	1709	..	1734	1773	BUTL02
BUTLER George	S		WK	Q	#	1553	..	1592	..	BUTL06
BUTLER (James)	OP	L	IR		*8	..	..	..	..	BUTL07
BUTLER John	S			Q	#*	..	..	1588	..	BUTL08
BUTLER John	S		LA	D	#4	..	..	1625	1672	BUTL10
BUTLER John	S			V		..	..	1638	..	BUTL12
BUTLER John, Ld. Caher	SJ	W	IR	Y	#*3	1727	1745	1753	1786	BUTL13
BUTLER Philip	S	N	A	D		1724	..	1750	1777	BUTL14
BUTLER Richard (Ambrose)	OP			Z	*	..	1719	..	1733	BUTL15
BUTLER Richard (Bernard)	OSB	N	LA	G		1748	1776	..	1825	BUTL16
BUTLER Thomas	S				*34	..	..	1589	1590	BUTL18
BUTLER Thomas	S	M		D	*	..	..	1600	..	BUTL20
BUTLER Thomas, Hon.	SJ	M	LA	Y	#3	1718	1739	1746	1779	BUTL22
BUTLER Thomas	S	N	LA	D		1734	..	1761	1795	BUTL24
BUTTON Richard	S		ST	R	#4	..	..	1594	1643	BUTT04
BUXTON Christopher BL.	S		DE	R	+§	1562	..	1586	1588	BUXT02
BUXTON George	S		NN	R	#§1	1686	..	1713	1759	BUXT04
BYERLEY Charles	SJ		LE	Y	3	1718	1738	1744	1796	BYER02
BYERLEY William	S		DH	R		1669	..	1702	..	BYER04
BYERLEY William (Ildephonsus)	OSB	M	LE	G	4	..	1708	1711	1753	BYER06
BYERLEY see also BRYERLEY										
BYFIELD William (Raphael)	OSB			R	*4	1570	1596	1594	1607	BYFI02
BYFLEET John (Edward)	OSB	W	SM	G	#	1607	1624	..	1701	BYFL02
BYFLEET Robert	S		SM	D	#	1616	..	1642	..	BYFL04
BYFLEET William	S	W	SM	D	#3	1613	..	1640	1703	BYFL06
BYRNE Denis	OFM	W	IR	N		..	..	1743	1779	BYRN02
BYRNE Edmund	OSA		IR		*7	..	..	..	..	BYRN04
BYRON Thomas	S			L	#1	1660	..	1684	..	BYRO02
CABLEY John	S			Q	*	..	..	1586	..	CABL02
CADWALLADOR Charles	S	W	MT	D	#‡	1591	..	1628	1650	CADW02
CADWALLADOR Roger VEN.	S	W	HR	V	#+1	1567	..	1593	1610	CADW04
CAESTRYCK Charles (Benedict)	OP	M	LC	Z	*	1762	1785	..	1844	CAES02
CAHER see BUTLER										CAHI02
CAHILL John	S	L	IR	Z	*8	..	..	..	..	CALD02
CALDERBANK (James)	OSB	W	LA	W		1770	1792	1793	1821	CALD04
CALDWELL John BL.	SJ	L	DH	Y	#+§	1628	1656	1664	1679	CALD06
CALDWELL William	SJ		ST	R	#‡4	1580	1609	1606	1609	CALD08
CALDWELL William (Augustine)	OSB	L	LA	G	#	1735	1757	..	1815	CALE02
CALEY James (Anthony S.Jo'ph)	OFM	M	LN	F	13	1756	1776	1779	1800	CALL02
CALLAGHAN Richard	SJ		IR	S	1	1728	..	..	1807	CALL04
CALLANAN (Hugh)	OP	L	IR		*7	..	..	..	..	CALV02
CALVERLEY Edmund	S		YO	R	1	1563	..	1585	..	CALV04
CALVERT Charles	SJ		LA	R	#	1620	1647	1644	1657	CALV06
CALVERT William	S	N	YO	V		..	..	1689	1735	CAME02
CAMERON Alexander	SJ		SC		x	1701	1734	..	1746	CAMP02
CAMPBELL (John Chrysostom)	CAP					..	..	..	1627	CAMP04
CAMPION Edmund ST.	SJ		MX	D	#+‡	1540	1573	1578	1581	CAMP06
CAMPION Francis	S			S	7	..	..	..	..	CAND02
CANDALO John	S			S		..	..	1617	..	CANE02
CANES Thomas (Jn Bpt Vincent)	OFM	L	LE	F	#†1	1609	..	..	1672	
CANES see also KEYNES										
CANFIELD see FITCH										
CANNELL James	SJ	N	MI	Y		1649	1671	1678	1722	CANN02
CANNING John	OP		WK	N	1	1641	1658	1665	1676	CANN04
CANNING William	S		WK	D	#	..	..	1643	..	CANN06
CANNON Edmund	S		EX	S	x34	1578	..	1602	1649	CANN08
CANSFIELD Brian VEN.	SJ		LA	R	#+x§	1580	1604	..	1645	CANS02
CANSFIELD Charles	S	L	LA	R	#	1613	..	1643	1693	CANS04
CANTRILL (Bruno)	OFM	L		F	123	1675	1695	1699	1759	CANT02
CAPE (Francis)	OSB		SX	G		1608	1620	..	1668	CAPE02
CAPE Joseph (Anth'y of S.Jos)	OFM		SX	F	124	1600	1620	..	1669	CAPE04
CAPE Luke (Benedict)	OSB		SX	G	4	..	1615	..	1620	CAPE06
CAPE (Michael)	OSB	N	SX	E		1609	1628	1638	1668	CAPE08

45

Name	Reg	D	Co	T	Notes	Born	Prof	Ordn	Died	Code
CAPE (Peter of S.Augustine)	OFM		MX	F	12	1607	1628	..	1668	CAPE09
CAPES John (Augustine)	OSB		SM	R	#§	1585	..	1612	1628	CAPE10
CARDWELL John	S	N	LA	R		1675	..	1701	1728	CARD06
CAREW (Henry of S.Mary)	OFM		HA	F	12	1640	1661	..	1683	CARE02
CAREW see also CARY										
CAREY see CARY										
CARLETON John	S	M	NK	R	#1	1595	..	1618	1671	CARL02
CARLETON Philip	SJ	M	CB	Y	#	1606	1625	..	1658	CARL03
CARLETON Robert(of S.Barbara)	OSS								1693	CARL04
CARLETON Thomas	SJ		CB	V	#	1592	1617	1617	1666	CARL05
CARLETON William	SJ		OX			1577	1617	..	1622	CARL06
CARLOS William	SJ	L	ST	Y	#3	1631	1656	1667	1679	CARL08
CARNABY Rbert	S			D	*3	..		1667	..	CARN02
CARNE Charles	S		GM	D	§3	1639	..	1663	1712	CARN04
CARNE Francis	SJ	N	SM	Y	3	1686	1704	1713	1715	CARN06
CARON Redmond or Raymond	OFM		IR	N		1605	..	..	1666	CARO04
CARPENTER Hermengild	SJ	M	LC	Y		1703	1721	1729	1770	CARP02
CARPENTER Richard Francis	S		NN	R	#*§°	1606	..	1635	1670	CARP06
CARPENTER Sebastian	S			D	*°	..	..	1597	..	CARP08
CARPENTER William	S		HR	R	#°	1604	..	1630	..	CARP10
CARPUE Joseph Francis	S	L	MX	D	3	1766	..	1791	1849	CARP12
CARRINGTON see SMITH										
CARROLL Anthony	SJ		IR	Y		1722	1744	1754	1794	CARR02
CARROLL James	S			S		..	..	1713	..	CARR03
CARROLL James	SJ		IR	Y	3	1717	1741	1747	1756	CARR04
CARROLL John ARCHBP.	SJ	W	MD	Y	*	1735	1753	1761	1815	CARR06
CARROLL William	OSA		IR		*7	..	..	..	..	CARR08
CARTER George (Anselm)	OSB	N	WR	G	1	1648	1670	..	1727	CART02
CARTER Henry	S	N	LA	D	3	1761	..	1785	1826	CART04
CARTER James	S	N	LA	D	#3	1736	..	1762	1814	CART06
CARTER John	S	N	LA	L		1711	..	1736	1789	CART08
CARTER John	S	M	LA	D		1750	..	1776	1803	CART10
CARTERET Edward	SJ		MX	Y	#13	1689	1709	1719	1753	CART14
CARTERET Francis (Joseph)	OSB	L	MX	G		..	1723	..	1783	CART16
CARTERET Jean Frederick Cyr	S		MX		*8	..	..	..	..	CART18
CARTERET Philip	SJ	M	MX	Y	3	1694	1709	1721	1756	CART20
CARTWRIGHT (Gervase of S.Fra)	OFM		NT	F	123	1628	1647	1651	1691	CART22
CARY Edward	S	W	SK	R		..	..	1651	1711	CARY04
CARY Francis	SJ		DV	S		1610	1647	..	1665	CARY06
CARY Henry (Placid), Hon.	OSB		IR	E	*°13	1618	1641	1643	1653	CARY08
CARY John	SJ		SK	Y		1618	..	..	1682	CARY10
CARY Richard	SJ					..	..	..	1696	CARY14
CARY Thomas	SJ		SK	Y		1621	1639	..	1672	CARY16
CARYLL Charles	SJ	W	SX	Y	#3	1685	1704	1713	1745	CARY18
CARYLL Peter (Alexius)	OSB	L	SX	G		1631	1654	..	1686	CARY20
CARYLL Richard, Hon.	SJ	W	SX	Y	#3	1692	1711	1720	1751	CARY22
CASE Henry	S		HR	R	#	1609	..	1632	1633	CASE02
CASE James	SJ		LA	Y	3	1691	1712	1721	1731	CASE04
CASE William	S	L	DT	V	#	1585	..	1613	..	CASE06
CASE William	SJ	M	LA	Y	#13	1689	1711	1720	1747	CASE08
CASEMORE William (Ignatius)	OFM		BK	F	3	1751	1777	1779	1824	CASE10
CASEY Matthew	S	L	IR			1732	..	..	1808	CASE12
CASSE (Lawrence)	OSB	N	YO	E		..	1689	..	1732	CASS02
CASSEY (Anselm)	OSB	W	HR	G		1610	1626	..	1671	CASS04
CASTELL John	SJ		CL		=	..	1574	..	1580	CAST02
CATCHER Edward	SJ		MX	R	#§123	1584	1609	1619	1624	CATC02
CATCHMAY George (Thomas)	OP	L			3	1598	1624	1626	1669	CATC04
CATER Francis	SJ	M	LN	Y	#	1598	1621	..	1656	CATE02
CATHERICK see CATTERICK										
CATON Thomas	S	N	LA	L		1756	..	1780	1826	CATO02
CATON William	S	N	LA	R		1675	..	1699	1749	CATO04
CATROW Charles	S	W		D	*	1753	..	1777	1804	CATR02
CATTAWAY Henry	SJ	M	SK	Y		1675	1693	1701	1718	CATT02
CATTERALL Alexander (Bene'ct)	OSB	N	LA	E		1725	1743	..	1791	CATT04
CATTERALL Edward (Bernard)	OSB	N	LA	W		..	1725	..	1781	CATT06
CATTERALL John (Stephen)	OP	N	ND	Z	*	1702	1719	1726	1765	CATT10

Name	Reg	D	Co	T	Notes	Born	Prof	Ordn	Died	Code
CATTERALL Thomas	S	N		V		..	..	1644	..	CATT12
CATTERICK Edmund BL.	S	N	YO	D	#+3	1605	..	1630	1642	CATT14
CATTERICK George	S	N	YO	D	#1	1595	..	1621	1667	CATT16
CATTERICK George	S			S	3	..	..	1645	..	CATT18
CAVERLEY (James)	OFM	M	IR		*7	..	..	..	..	CAVE02
CAWSER Thomas (Benedict)	OSB		LA	E	x	1747	1764	..	1795	CAWS02
CAYNES see KEYNES										
CECIL John	S			WR	R	#‡	1558	..	1584	1626	CECl02
CELOSSE see SELOSSE										
CHADDERTON Henry	S	L	HA	R	#	1552	..	1601	..	CHAD02
CHADDOCK William	S		LA	R	1	1561	..	1586	..	CHAD04
CHADWICK John	S	N	LA		4	..	..	..	1645	CHAD05
CHADWICK John	S	N	LA	D		1728	..	1752	1802	CHAD06
CHALLONER Henry	SJ		LA	Y	#1	1639	1660	..	1673	CHAL02
CHALLONER John	S	N	LA	D		..	..	1605	..	CHAL04
CHALLONER Richard BP.	S	L	SX	D	#*	1691	..	1716	1781	CHAL06
CHALLONER William	SJ		LA	V	#	..	1659	1656	1665	CHAL08
CHAMBERLAIN Francis	S			V		..	..	1642	1667	CHAM02
CHAMBERLAIN George BP.	S		LC	R	*	1576	..	1600	1634	CHAM04
CHAMBERLAIN George	S	L	NK	D	†	1739	..	1783	1815	CHAM05
CHAMBERLAIN James	SJ		LA	Y	3	1739	1759	1765	1779	CHAM06
CHAMBERLAIN John Joseph	SJ	N	LA	R		1727	1752	1751	1796	CHAM08
CHAMBERS Matthew	S	N	MX	D	†	1623	..	1653	1698	CHAM12
CHAMBERS Oswald	S	N	YO	Q		..	..	1579	..	CHAM14
CHAMBERS Peter	S			D	#*°4	..	..	1605	1609	CHAM16
CHAMBERS Robert	S			R	*4	1571	..	1597	1624	CHAM18
CHAMBERS Robert	S	N	MX	D	†	1624	..	1653	1689	CHAM20
CHAMBERS Sabine	SJ	L	LE		‡1	1560	1587	..	1633	CHAM22
CHAMBERS Thomas	S	N		D	*	1698	..	1725	1759	CHAM24
CHAMBERS William (Cyril)	CRT			C	2	..	1603	..	1629	CHAM25
CHAMPION John	SJ	M	CL	Y	3	1695	1713	1723	1776	CHAM26
CHAMPNEY Anthony	S	L	YO	R	#	1569	..	1596	1644	CHAM28
CHAMPNEY (William)	OSB	N	YO	W	4	..	..	1712	1740	CHAM30
CHAMPNEY William (Lawrence)	OSB	N	MX	W		1667	1684	..	1732	CHAM32
CHANDLER (Boniface)	OSB			W		..	1620	..	1658	CHAN02
CHANDLER Richard (Paul)	OSB		MD	G		1685	1705	1710	1712	CHAN04
CHANTRELL William	S	N	CH	R		1708	..	1731	1753	CHAN06
CHAPLIN James (Maurus)	OSB	N	NK	X		1745	1763	..	1808	CHAP10
CHAPLIN Michael (Anselm)	OSB	N	MX	X		1754	1771	..	1784	CHAP12
CHAPLIN Roch	S	L	EX	R	1	1558	..	1584	..	CHAP13
CHAPLIN William	S			Q	*x4	..	..	1581	1583	CHAP14
CHAPMAN Edward	S	L	DT	D		1539	..	1595	..	CHAP16
CHAPMAN Francis (Athanasius)	OFM		WK	F	3	1704	1728	1729	1749	CHAP18
CHAPMAN James	SJ		MX	Y	#°3	1694	1711	1720	..	CHAP19
CHAPMAN John	S			Q	*‡	..	..	1581	..	CHAP20
CHAPMAN John	SJ	L	KT	Y	#	1670	1692	1703	1729	CHAP22
CHAPMAN Richard	S	L		D	*	..	..	1576	..	CHAP24
CHAPMAN (Romanus)	OFM	L		F	34	..	..	1743	1794	CHAP26
CHAPMAN Stephen	SJ					..	..	..	1602	CHAP28
CHAPPELL Henry (Francis X.)	OP	M	MX	N		1749	1775	1776	1825	CHAP30
(Charles of Beauvais)	CAP	L	FR		2	..	1616	..	1669	CHAR00
(Charles Francis Abbeville)	CAP	L	FR			..	..	..	1665	CHAR01
CHARLTON John	OSB	N	ND	G		1717	1736	..	1786	CHAR02
CHARNLEY James	S	N	LA	D	#	1668	..	1695	..	CHAR04
CHARNOCK John	SJ	N	LA	Y	#	1744	1763	..	1804	CHAR06
CHARNOCK Robert	S	L	MX	R	‡=13	1561	..	1586	..	CHAR08
CHARNOCK Robert	S	N	LA	L	#	1615	..	1639	1671	CHAR10
CHATTERTON Thomas	S			S	7	..	..	..	..	CHAT02
CHENEY Charles	S	L	HA	R	#1	1604	..	1636	..	CHEN02
CHENEY Philip	S	L	LC		7	..	..	..	..	CHEN04
CHERFOMONT Stanislaus	SJ			Y		1749	1771	..	1773	CHER02
CHERITON (Basil)	OSB		OX	E		..	1651	..	1662	CHER04
CHERITON Matthew	OSB	N	OX	W		..	1656	..	1670	CHER06
(Cherubimus of Amiens)	CAP	L	FR		2	..	1609	..	1653	CHER08
CHESTERMAN James	S	L	BK	R	#	1698	..	1724	1777	CHES02
CHETWIN Ralph	SJ		ST	Y	#	1641	1665	1673	1719	CHET02

Name	Reg	D	Co	T	Notes	Born	Prof	Ordn	Died	Code
CHETWYND see CHETWIN										
CHEW William (Alexius)	OSB	N	LA	W		1771	1792	1795	1832	CHEW02
CHILTON Philip Jos.(Vincent)	OP		ND	R	3	1664	1682	1688	1722	CHIL02
CHORLEY Edward (John)	OSB	N	LA	G		..	1698	1704	1718	CHOR02
CHORLEY Thomas	SJ		LA	Y		1688	1705	1713	1718	CHOR04
CHRISTMAS Emmanuel	S			D	*	1679	..	1710	1748	CHRI06
CHRISTMAS John	S		SK	D	†3	..	..	1693	1743	CHRI08
CHURCH Edward	SJ	N		Y	*3	1728	1748	1760	1820	CHUR02
CHURCHER John	S	L	HA	V	34	..	..	1647	1692	CHUR04
CHURCHILL Thomas	S	L	MX	D	#	1628	..	1653	1705	CHUR06
CLAMPET Philip	S	L	BK	D		..	..	1624	1665	CLAM02
CLARE John	SJ	W	WT	V	#1	1581	1605	1603	1628	CLAR02
CLARGENET William	S		YO	Q		..	..	1585	..	CLAR04
CLARK Anthony	S		YO	Q	°3	1565	..	1590	..	CLAR06
CLARK Anthony	S	L	SY	D	3	..	..	1687	..	CLAR08
CLARK Christopher	S	W	HR	V	#1	1607	..	1642	1677	CLAR10
CLARK Edward	S		HR	R	#	1606	..	1633	..	CLAR12
CLARK Francis	S		NK	V	#§3	1576	..	1600	..	CLAR14
CLARK Francis	SJ			Y	#*	1619	..	..	1657	CLAR15
CLARK Gabriel	S		KT	R	#4	1610	..	1635	1644	CLAR17
CLARK Henry	SJ	L	DH	Y	1	1669	1690	1699	1729	CLAR18
CLARK Hubert	OFM			F	3	..	..	1695	..	CLAR19
CLARK James (Francis)	OFM		MX	F	13	1750	1767	1776	1782	CLAR20
CLARK John	SJ		EX	S	3	1604	1632	1630	1672	CLAR21
CLARK John	SJ		IR	Y	1	1662	1681	1689	1723	CLAR22
CLARK John (Anthony of S.Jn.)	OFM		HR	F	12	1593	1618	..	1673	CLAR23
CLARK Robert	S	L	MX	R	#	1628	..	1653	1685	CLAR24
CLARK (Samuel of S.Henry)	OFM	M		F	12	1630	1648	..	1706	CLAR26
CLARK Thomas	S		KT	Q	°4	1555	..	1590	1610	CLAR28
CLARK Thomas (Bonaventure)	OFM			F	12	1601	1620	..	1667	CLAR29
CLARK Thomas	CRT			C	°8	..	..	..	..	CLAR32
CLARK William	S		ST	R	*1	1568	..	1592	1603	CLAR34
CLARK William	SJ	W	MX	Y	3	1669	1687	1696	1734	CLAR40
CLARKE see CLARK										
CLARKSON Edward (Alban)	OSB	N	LA	X		1766	1787	..	1815	CLAR42
CLARKSON George	SJ	N	LA	Y	3	1738	1758	1765	1813	CLAR44
CLARKSON James (Augustine)	OFM	M	LA	F	134	1723	1746	1752	1776	CLAR45
CLARKSON John	OP	M		N		1697	1716	1721	1763	CLAR46
CLARKSON John	S	L	LA	T	*	1773	..	1798	1823	CLAR48
CLARKSON Thomas	S	N	YO	D		..	..	1600	..	CLAR50
CLARKSON William Peter	ODC				4	..	..	..	1820	CLAR54
CLAVERING Nicholas Matthew	S	N	ND	D	#	1728	..`	1752	1805	CLAV02
CLAVERING Ralph	S		ND	R	4	1655	..	1686	1718	CLAV04
CLAVERING Thomas	S		ND	R	#§14	1628	..	1654	1695	CLAV06
CLAXTON James BL.	S		YO	Q	#+	..	..	1582	1588	CLAX02
CLAXTON Ralph	S		DH	D	#	..	..	1612	..	CLAX04
CLAY (Daniel of S.Francis)	OFM	L	IR		*4	..	..	..	1681	CLAY02
CLAY Roger	S	N			7 .	..	..	..	..	CLAY03
CLAYBROOK William	S		SM		#*‡	1603	..	..	..	CLAY04
CLAYTON Francis	S	N	DE	R		1565	..	1589	1596	CLAY08
CLAYTON James	S	M	YO	Q	§	..	..	1584	1589	CLAY10
CLAYTON John	S	M	WK		#4	..	..	..	1656	CLAY12
CLAYTON John	SJ		LA	Y		1611	1629	..	1663	CLAY14
CLAYTON Ralph	S	L	SP	D	#3	..	..	1686	1743	CLAY16
CLAYTON Thomas	S				7	..	..	..	..	CLAY17
CLAYTON Thomas	S		WK	R	#	1616	..	1641	..	CLAY18
CLAYTON Thomas	S	M	SP	D	#	1672	..	1699	1746	CLAY20
CLEMENT Caesar	S		LC	R		1561	..	1586	1626	CLEM02
CLEMENTS Charles	S	M	OX	V		1765	..	1790	1797	CLEM04
CLENNOCK Morgan	S	W	CN	R		1558	..	1582	1620	CLEN02
CLIBBURN Gerard	S			Q	*	..	..	1587	..	CLIB02
CLIFFE Francis Adam	S	N	LA	D		1728	..	1756	1799	CLIF02
CLIFFE Henry (Ildephonsus)	OSB		MX	R	#*	1585	1615	1609	1657	CLIF04
CLIFFORD Thomas	SJ	N	LA	Y		1614	1635	..	1692	CLIF06
CLIFFORD William Ld.Cumberld.	S		LN	V	#*3	1594	..	1619	1670	CLIF08
CLIFTON Cuthbert	SJ	N	LA	Y	#	1611	1630	..	1675	CLIF10

Name	Reg	D	Co	T	Notes	Born	Prof	Ordn	Died	Code
CLIFTON Francis	S	N	LA	R	‡	1682	..	1706	..	CLIF14
CLIFTON Francis	SJ		NT	Y	3	1702	1719	1732	1757	CLIF16
CLIFTON James	SJ	N	LA	Y	3	1698	1719	1728	1750	CLIF18
CLIFTON James (Bernardine)	OFM	L		F	123	1680	1699	1706	1738	CLIF20
CLIFTON (Lambert)	OSB	N	LA		*4	..	..		1631	CLIF22
CLIFTON Thomas	S	L		Q	*x	..	..	1579	1593	CLIF24
CLIFTON Thomas	SJ	M	LA	Y		1700	1718	1730	1777	CLIF28
CLIFTON William	SJ	N	LA	Y		1678	1699	1708	1749	CLIF30
CLINCH Henry	S	M	OX	Q		..	..	1581	..	CLIN02
CLINCH John	S	N	OX	Q		..	..	1590	..	CLIN04
CLITHEROW Henry	OP		YO	R		1572	..			CLIT02
CLITHEROW William	CRT		YO	Q		1542	1589	1582	..	CLIT04
CLITHEROW William	S	N	YO	D	1	1563	..	1608	1636	CLIT06
CLOPTON Cuthbert	S	L	WK	R	#	1607	..	1636	1644	CLOP02
CLOSETTE Joseph	SJ	W	LC	Y		1752	1771	1776	1781	CLOS02
CLOUGH Anthony	S	M	SP	D		1729	..	1753	1793	CLOU02
CLOUGH Richard	SJ	M	SP	Y	#3	1728	1744	1757	1777	CLOU06
CLOUGH Robert	S	M	ST	R	#	1616	..	1641	..	CLOU08
CLYNNOG see CLENNOCK										
COATES John	S	N	ND	D		1700	..	1725	1794	COAT02
COCK see COOK										
COCKETT (Constantine)	OSB		MX		*	..	1634	..	..	COCK06
COCKETT Thomas	CRL		NK	R		..	1626	..	..	COCK08
CODNER David	OSB	L			#*4	..	1606	..	1647	CODN02
CODRINGTON (Anthony)	OFM		WT	F	123	1693	1711	1719	1729	CODR02
CODRINGTON (Bonaventure)	S	L	WT	D		..	..		1727	CODR04
CODRINGTON Thomas	S		WT	D	#	..	..	1676	1694	CODR06
COEN Michael	S	L	IR	P		..	..		1810	COEN02
COFFIN Edward	SJ		DV	R	§	1570	1598	1593	1626	COFF02
COFFIN Peter	S		FR	V	3	1583	..	1607	..	COFF04
COFFIN Thomas	S	N	WR	R	#	1568	..	1591	..	COFF06
COFFIN Thomas	SJ		MX	Y	4	..	..		1628	COFF08
COGHLAN James (Peter)	OFM		MX	F	1	1761	1783	1785	1798	COGH02
COGHLAN William Augustine	S	N	MX	V		1768	..	1791	1836	COGH04
COKE Thomas	SJ		MX	R	#§	1589	1614	1614	1670	COKE02
COKE William	S		KT	R	#	1600	..	1624	..	COKE04
COKE see also COOK										
COLE (Anthony)	OFM	L	IR		#*7	..	..			COLE01
COLE Edmund	S	L	BK	V	#‡	..	..	1624	..	COLE02
COLE Edward	S	L		R	*	1564	..	1589	..	COLE04
COLE Edward	S		MD	V	3	..	..	1763	1763	COLE06
COLE Henry	SJ		MD	Y	3	1727	1747	1762	1763	COLE08
COLE Joseph	SJ	L	MD	Y	3	1732	1752	1760	1812	COLE10
COLE Robert	S	L	WR	R	#§	1596	..	1620	..	COLE12
COLE Thomas	ODC		IR		4	..	..	..	1755	COLE14
COLEMAN (Columbanus)	ODC		IR		8	..	..	..	..	COLE16
COLEMAN Nicholas	OFM	L	ST	F	#x123	1600	1626	1634	1645	COLE20
COLEMAN Walter (Christopher)	SJ	M	FR		1	1717	1734		1768	COLG02
COLGRAVE Andrew	S	L	SM	D	#‡	1548	..	1576	1635	COLL02
COLLETON John	S		KT	D	°	..	..	1606	..	COLL04
COLLIER Edward William	OFM			F		..	..	1734	1764	COLL06
COLLINGRIDGE (Matthew)	OFM	W	OX	F	*3	1757	1780	1784	1829	COLL08
COLLINGRIDGE Peter(Ber'dn) BP	OFM			F	1234	1684	1698	1718	1732	COLL09
COLLINGRIDGE Richard	S	N	OX	Y		1771	..	..	1854	COLL10
COLLINGRIDGE Thomas	SJ	M	ND	Y		1664	1688	1691	1719	COLL12
COLLINGWOOD Charles	S		DH	R		1676	..	1698	1734	COLL14
COLLINGWOOD George	S			D	*	..	..	1725	..	COLL16
COLLINGWOOD John	SJ	M	ND	Y		1657	1677	1686	1741	COLL18
COLLINGWOOD Robert	OSB	N	ND	X	x	..	1663	..	1679	COLL20
COLLINGWOOD Roger (Anselm)	S	N	ND	V	3	..	..	1631	..	COLL22
COLLINGWOOD Thomas	SJ	N	ND	Y	#1	1631	1652	1661	1680	COLL24
COLLINGWOOD Thomas	SJ	N	DH	Y	#	1651	1676	1685	1725	COLL26
COLLINGWOOD Thomas	S		DV	D	#	..	..	1601	..	COLL28
COLLINS John	S		ST	V	#3	1601	..	1627	1678	COLL30
COLLINS John	S			V	#3	1608	..	1633	..	COLL32
COLLINS Nicholas	CRT			C	2	..	1755	..	..	COLL33
COLLINS Paul										

49

Name	Reg	D	Co	T	Notes	Born	Prof	Ordn	Died	Code
COLLINS William	OP	L	IR		2	1622	1649	..	1699	COLL34
COLLINS William	SJ	M	KT	Y		1650	1669	1678	1704	COLL36
COLLINS William	SJ	M	MX	Y	13	1683	1704	1713	1745	COLL38
COLLINS William (Joseph)	OSB	N	MX	X		1758	1783	..	1803	COLL40
COLLINS see also COWLING										
COLLINSON George	S	L		Q	*†	..	..	1582	..	COLL42
COLOSSE see SELOSSE										
COLSTON Nicholas	OSB		DH	X		..	1673	..	1702	COLS02
COLSTON William	S	L	MX	L		..	..	1678	1695	COLS04
COLUMB John	SJ		DV	N	‡1	1546	1572	..	1582	COLU02
COMBERFORD Gerard	SJ	M	IR	Y		1632	1651	1657	..	COMB02
COMPTON George	S		SC	D	3	..	..	1662	..	COMP02
COMPTON James (Bernard)	OSB		WT	Y	*°3	1748	1775	1773	..	COMP03
COMPTON Philip	S	W	SM	D		1734	..	1763	1803	COMP04
COMPTON Richard	S	L	LN	R	†	1651	..	1701	1726	COMP06
COMPTON William	S	L			7	..	..	..	..	COMP08
CONIERS see CONYERS										
CONNELL Michael	SJ		IR	Y	3	1688	1707	1715	1726	CONN02
CONRY (Maurice)	OFM		IR	R	*4	..	..	..	1669	CONR02
CONSTABLE David (Benedict)	OSB	N	YO	X	x	..	1669	..	1683	CONS04
CONSTABLE (Francis)	OSB	L		W		..	1614	..	1655	CONS06
CONSTABLE Henry	S		YO	R	#†1	1587	..	1618	1623	CONS10
CONSTABLE Ignatius	SJ	M		Y	#*	1666	1709	1714	1727	CONS12
CONSTABLE John	S		LN	D	#	1605	..	1631	..	CONS14
CONSTABLE John	SJ	M	LN	Y	#13	1676	1695	1704	1743	CONS15
CONSTABLE John (Philip)	OSB	N	YO	G		..	1660	..	..	CONS16
CONSTABLE Marmaduke or Joseph	SJ		LN	Y	1	1672	1690	1699	1750	CONS18
CONSTABLE Michael	SJ		YO	Y	1	1648	1668	1681	1707	CONS20
CONSTABLE Philip (Wilfrid)	OSB	M	YO	E		1707	1725	..	1764	CONS22
CONSTABLE Robert	SJ		YO	R	#	1597	1619	..	1678	CONS24
CONSTABLE Robert	SJ		YO	Y	13	1673	1711	1716	1739	CONS26
CONSTABLE Robert	SJ	W	YO	R		1705	1729	1728	1770	CONS28
CONSTABLE Thomas (Augustine)	OSB	L	LN	G		..	1649	..	1712	CONS30
CONWAY William	SJ		FT	Y	#3	1659	1679	1688	1689	CONW02
CONWAY William	SJ		FT	Y	#3	1683	1702	1710	1741	CONW04
CONYERS (Augustine)	OSB		YO	G	4	..	1638	..	1682	CONY02
CONYERS Christopher	SJ	L	KT	Y		1669	1688	1697	1730	CONY04
CONYERS George	SJ	N	YO	R	1	1575	1604	1602	1652	CONY06
CONYERS George	SJ	L	KT	Y	1	1644	1665	1676	1711	CONY08
CONYERS John	SJ		KT	R	#134	1675	1694	1708	1724	CONY10
CONYERS Leonard or Louis	SJ	L	KT	Y	1	1671	1690	1699	1745	CONY12
CONYERS Samuel	S		YO	Q		..	..	1582	1587	CONY14
CONYERS Thomas	SJ		YO		1	1562	1584	..	1639	CONY16
CONYERS Thomas	SJ		KT	Y	#13	1664	1685	1694	1721	CONY18
CONYERS Thomas	SJ	N		Y	*3	1715	1734	1741	1780	CONY20
COOK Anthony	S	L			7	..	..	..	..	COOK02
COOK Henry	S			D	*	..	..	1577	..	COOK03
COOK Thomas	S		SK	R	#	..	..	1631	..	COOK04
COOK Thomas	S		SP	D	3	..	..	1690	..	COOK06
COOK see also COKE										
COOMBES William	S	W	SM	D	3	1743	..	1777	1822	COOM02
COOMBES William Henry	S	W	SM	D		1767	..	1791	1850	COOM04
COOPE James	S	N		Q	*	..	..	1585	..	COOP02
COOPER James	S		LN	V		1579	..	1603	..	COOP04
COOPER John	S			Q	*	..	..	1592	..	COOP06
COOPER John	S		LA	V	3	..	..	1676	..	COOP10
COOPER John	SJ		HA	Y		1610	1630	..	1646	COOP12
COOPER Louis (Francis)	OSB		LA	W		1771	1792	1795	1850	COOP14
COOPER Richard	S	N		Q	*	..	..	1582	..	COOP16
COOPER Richard	S			D	#*	..	..	1608	..	COOP18
COOPER William	S			S	3	..	..	1642	..	COOP20
COOPER see also COWPER										
COPE Alan	S			N	*†	..	..	..	1578	COPE02
COPELAND John	S	N	LA	D	#	..	..	1648	..	COPE04
COPLEY Charles (Anselm)	OFM			F	34	..	..	1735	1778	COPL01
COPLEY Henry	S		FR	R		1705	..	1728	..	COPL02

Name	Reg	D	Co	T	Notes	Born	Prof	Ordn	Died	Code
COPLEY John	S	L	LC	R	#°1	1577	..	1602	1662	COPL04
COPLEY Peter	SJ		SM	Q		..	1586	1581	1587	COPL06
COPLEY (Richard)	OFM		SX	F	123	1666	1684	1690	1702	COPL07
COPLEY Thomas	SJ	L	ES	Y	#14	1595	1616	..	1652	COPL08
COPLEY William	SJ	M	SY	Y	13	1668	1686	1695	1727	COPL10
COPPINGER Henry	SJ	M	SK	R	#†2	1580	1615	1613	1652	COPP02
CORBALLY Robert	S			S		..	..	1725	..	CORB04
CORBETT Christopher	S	L	MX	R	#	1674	..	1706	..	CORB06
CORBINGTON see CORBY										
CORBISHLEY Samuel	S	M	LA	L		1759	..	1789	1830	CORB10
CORBUSIER John	SJ	L	LC	Y	#	1707	1726	1738	1765	CORB12
CORBY Ambrose	SJ		DH	Y	#	1604	1627	..	1649	CORB14
CORBY Henry	SJ		SX	Y	3	1700	1722	1730	1765	CORB16
CORBY Ralph BL.	SJ	N	IR	V	#+	1598	1625	..	1644	CORB18
CORBY Robert	SJ		IR	S	#3	1596	1626	1624	1637	CORB20
CORDELL Charles	S	N	MX	D		1720	..	1744	1791	CORD02
CORHAM Robert	OSB		LC	G		..	1643	..	1665	CORH02
CORKER James (Maurus)	OSB	L	YO	X	§	1636	1656	..	1715	CORK02
CORNE Charles	S		ST	D	§3	1716	..	1757	1777	CORN02
CORNE James	S	M	ST	D	3	1745	..	1773	1817	CORN04
CORNE John	S	M	ST	D		1749	..	1776	1816	CORN06
CORNELISON James	SJ		LC	Y	1	1644	1664	1672	..	CORN07
CORNELIUS John BL.	S	W	CL	R	#*+‡1	1554	..	1583	1594	CORN08
CORNFORTH Lawrence	CRT			C		..	1753	..	1764	CORN09
CORNFORTH Thomas	SJ			R	#*	1570	1600	1597	1649	CORN10
CORNFORTH Thomas	S	N	YO	D	134	1648	..	1672	1720	CORN14
CORNFORTH Thomas	S	W	ST	D	3	1679	..	1708	1748	CORN15
CORNTHWAITE Richard	S	M	LA	D	3	1736	..	1765	1803	CORN16
CORNWALLIS Richard	S		NK	R	†	1568	..	1599	..	CORN20
CORNWALLIS William	S		NK	Q	14	1527	..	1580	1600	CORN22
COSIN John	S	L	DH	R	#†	1633	..	1658	1675	COSI02
COSTER Francis	SJ					..	..	..	1619	COST02
COTTAM John	S	N	SM	D	3	1646	..	1670	..	COTT02
COTTAM Lawrence (Thomas)	OP			R		1658	..	1681	1693	COTT04
COTTAM Thomas BL.	S		LA	D	*+‡3	1549	..	1580	1582	COTT06
COTTAM Thomas	S			V	*	..	..	..	1597	COTT08
COTTON Francis VEN.	SJ	W	HA	Y	#x	1595	1616	..	1679	COTT16
COTTON George	SJ	L	MX	R	#	1636	1653	..	1697	COTT18
COTTON John	SJ	W	NK	Y	#23	1724	1741	1749	1769	COTT20
COTTON Richard	SJ	M	MX	Y	#	1665	1681	1693	1740	COTT22
COTTRELL Benjamin (Thomas)	OFM		WK	F	134	1739	1759	1767	1817	COTT26
COUCHE John	SJ	L	CL	Y	3	1744	1762	1770	1813	COUC02
COULSON William	OSA				*7	..	..	..	..	COUL02
COUPE Abraham (Maurus)	OSB		LA	E		..	1731	..	1753	COUP02
COUPE Thomas Jerome	OSB	N	LA	W		1754	1775	..	1827	COUP06
COURTNEY George	S			S		..	..	1743	..	COUR02
COVERT George	S			S	3	..	..	1608	..	COVE02
COWBAN John	S	N	LA	D	#	1701	..	1728	1777	COWB02
COWBAN William	S		LA	R	#	1611	..	1636	..	COWB04
COWLEY John	S		LA	R	#	..	..	1634	1662	COWL02
COWLEY John	S	N	LA	R	#	1643	..	1666	..	COWL04
COWLEY Thomas	S		LA	R	#	..	..	1631	1663	COWL06
COWLEY William	S			D	#*3	..	..	1678	1728	COWL08
COWLEY William (Gregory)	OSB	N	LA	W		1732	1749	..	1799	COWL10
COWLING John	S	N	LA	R		1712	..	1736	1768	COWL12
COWLING Richard	SJ		YO	R	#	1562	1588	1587	1617	COWL14
COWLING William	S		YO	R		1557	..	1582	1592	COWL16
COWPER Thomas (Vincent Hyac.)	OP		NK	R	†	1629	1667	1659	1690	COWP02
COX Conrad	SJ		GS			1597	1619	..	1636	COXA03
COX David (Edmund)	OSB		MX	E		1662	1698	..	1748	COXA04
COX Edward (Charles Mary)	ODC	L			134	1699	..	1724	1758	COXA08
COX James (Boniface)	OFM		MO	F	13	1736	1752	1761	1764	COXA11
COX Robert	SJ	M	WK	Y	1	1579	1623	..	1648	COXA12
COX Robert (Benedict)	OSB	L		W	x24	..	1620	..	1650	COXA14
COX Thomas (Felix)	OFM	L	MO	F	13	1726	1742	1749	1788	COXA16
COXIE William	S		CH	Q	#	..	..	1587	..	COXI02

51

Name	Reg	D	Co	T	Notes	Born	Prof	Ordn	Died	Code
COXON John	S		LN	R	#4	1639	..	1670	1688	COXO02
COXON Thomas	SJ	L	DH	Y		1654	1676	1687	1735	COXO04
COYNEY Edward	S	M	ST	D	#3	1646	..	1670	1722	COYN02
CRAFT Vincent (Peter Martyr)	OP				3	..	..	1627	..	CRAF02
CRANE William	SJ	L	NK	R	#	1650	1676	1674	1709	CRAN04
CRATHORNE Francis	OSB	M	YO	G	*	1575	1621	..	1667	CRAT02
CRATHORNE Francis	S	N	YO	V		1762	..	1787	1822	CRAT04
CRATHORNE John	SJ	M	YO	Y		1590	1611	..	1656	CRAT06
CRATHORNE Ralph	S		YO	P	3	1667	..	1693	1698	CRAT08
CRATHORNE Thomas (Anselm)	OSB		YO	X		..	1703	..	1746	CRAT10
CRATHORNE William	S	L	YO	D	#	1670	..	1697	1740	CRAT12
CRAVEN Vincent	OSB		LA	W		..	1686	..	1704	CRAV02
CRAYFORD Cuthbert	S	N		Q	*†	..	..	1581	..	CRAY02
CRESWELL John	S			S		..	..	1652	1655	CRES02
CRESSY Hugh P'linus (Serenus)	OSB	L	YO	G	#‡13	1605	1649	1651	1674	CRES04
CRESWELL Arthur	SJ		MX	R	14	1556	1583	..	1588	CRES06
CRESWELL Joseph	SJ		MX	R	#4	1557	1583	..	1622	CRES08
CRICHLOW Oliver	S	N	LA	R	#	1607	..	1634	1671	CRIC02
CRICHLOW Richard	S	N	LA	R	#1	1610	..	1634	..	CRIC04
CRICHLOW William	S	N	LA	R	#1	1600	..	1631	1669	CRIC06
CRISP	S			S	#°3	1602	..	1626	..	CRIS02
CRISP (Benedict of S.Joseph)	OFM			F	°3	..	..	1653	..	CRIS04
CRISP Thomas	S			S	3	..	..	1599	..	CRIS08
CRISP Thomas	ODC	L			#	1701	1723	..	1736	CRIS10
CRITCHLEY see CRICHLOW										
CROCKETT Ralph BL.	S	L	CH	Q	+†‡	1552	..	1585	1588	CROC02
CROOK George	S	N	LA	D		..	..	1661	1709	CROO02
CROOK George (James)	OSB		LA	E		..	1739	..	1770	CROO04
CROOK George (Joseph)	OSB	N	LA	X	#	1753	1771	..	1800	CROO06
CROSBY George	S		LA	D	#	1703	..	1729	1729	CROS02
CROSBY James	S	L	MX	V		1757	..	1781	1819	CROS04
CROSBY John	SJ	N	WR	Y	#13	1637	1664	1672	1709	CROS06
CROSBY Roland (Wulstan)	OSB		WR	R	#	1640	1660	1666	1713	CROS08
CROSKELL William	S	N	LA	D	1	1767	..	1795	1838	CROS10
CROSLAND Charles	SJ		YO	Y	3	1655	1677	1686	1724	CROS14
CROSLAND George	S	N	YO	R		1667	..	1705	1731	CROS16
CROSLAND Henry (Thomas)	OP	N	YO			1670	1692	1693	1719	CROS18
CROSS Bernard	SJ	W	ZZ	Y	*	1715	1737	1744	1785	CROS20
CROSS John	S	M	LA	Y		1767	..	..	1835	CROS22
CROSS Joseph	SJ		LA	Y	#	1766	1803	1791	1843	CROS24
CROSS (Nicholas of Hly Cross)	OFM	L	DE	F	1234	1615	1639	1640	1698	CROS26
CROSS Richard	S		LA	R	‡	..	..	1648	..	CROS28
CROSS Robert	S		LA	D	7	..	..	..	..	CROS30
CROSS Thomas	SJ	M	LA	Y	3	1739	1758	1765	1813	CROS32
CROUCHER Christopher	S		SX	L		1713	..	1757	1765	CROU02
CROW Alexander VEN.	S	N	YO	Q	+1	1551	..	1583	1587	CROW02
CROWTHER Arthur (Anselm)	OSB	L	MT	G	#	1588	1611	..	1666	CROW04
CROWTHER John (Mark)	OSB	W	SP	V	#3	1584	1609	1608	1658	CROW06
CROWTHER Thomas	S		SP	D	x‡1	1546	..	1575	1585	CROW08
CRUMP John	S		SX	D	*3	1654	..	1688	..	CRUM02
CUDWORTH (Anthony of S.Mary)	OFM		YO	F	12	1624	1653	..	1681	CUDW02
CUERDON John (Hyacinth)	ODC		LA			1696	1715	1720	1761	CUER02
CUERDON Thomas	SJ	N	LA	Y	3	1718	1737	1745	1793	CUER04
CUFFAUD Alexander	SJ	W	HA	Y	#12	1602	1624	..	1674	CUFF02
CUFFAUD Edward	SJ	L	HA	Y		1620	1641	..	1695	CUFF04
CUFFAUD Godfrey	SJ	M	HA	R	#14	1608	1639	1633	1676	CUFF06
CUFFAUD John	SJ	N	HA	Y	#	1668	1688	1697	1716	CUFF10
CULCHETH Charles	SJ		LA	Y	#	1631	1652	1665	1667	CULC02
CULCHETH Thomas	SJ	L	LA	Y	#3	1654	1674	1686	1730	CULC04
CULCHETH Thomas	SJ	W	LA	Y	3	1741	1763	1765	1809	CULC06
CULCHETH William	SJ	M	LA	Y	#	1637	..	..	1684	CULC08
CULLAM see COLUMB										
CULSHAW John	OSB		LA	G	°	1767	1788	..	..	CULS02
CUMBERLAND see CLIFFORD										
CUMBERLEGE John (Benedict)	OSB		ST	X		..	1703	..	1730	CUMB02
CURRE John (Maurus)	OSB		BK	G		..	1614	..	1635	CURR02

Name	Reg	D	Co	T	Notes	Born	Prof	Ordn	Died	Code
CURRE (Nicholas)	OSB	M	BK	W	2	..	1615	..	1649	CURR04
CURRY John	SJ	L	CL	D	#124	1550	1583	1577	1598	CURR06
CURTIS John	SJ	N	HA	D		1573	1612	1605	1651	CURT02
CURTIS Peter	S	L	HA	R	#§	1595	..	1625	1673	CURT04
CURTIS Peter	S	L	HA	D	3	1655	..	1681	1729	CURT06
CURTIS Thomas	SJ	L	HA	D	#	1576	1605	1600	1657	CURT08
CURWEN Patrick	OSB			W		..	1668	..	1707	CURW02
CURZON Peter, Bt.	SJ	L	OX	Y	#13	1686	1705	1715	1766	CURZ02
(Cyprien of Gamaches)	CAP	L	FR		2	..	1620	..	1679	CYPR02
DAKINS Edward	S		YO	Q	#†	1554	..	1582	..	DAKI02
DAKINS John	OSB	W	LE	E		1668	1688	1695	1710	DAKI04
DALBY Robert BL.	S	N	YO	Q	+§	..	..	1588	1589	DALB02
DALLAS Ignatius	SJ		FR	Y	#4	1733	1761	1761	1773	DALL02
DALRYMPLE George (Robert)	CAP		SC			1567	..	..	1603	DALR02
DALTON James	S	N	YO	R	#	1597	..	1631	1672	DALT02
DALTON Marmaduke	S	N	YO	D	#†3	1637	..	1670	1695	DALT04
DALTON Robert	CRT			C		..	..	..	1636	DALT06
DALYSON Edmund or Joseph	S			S	13	1658	..	1681	..	DALY01
DALYSON (Gregory)	OSB	L	LN	X		..	1670	..	1710	DALY02
DALYSON (Nicholas of S.Mary)	OFM		LN	F	123	1639	1675	1677	1707	DALY04
DAMFORD John	S		CH	V		1576	..	1600	1601	DAMF02
(Damian of Touraine)	CAR	L	FR		*8	..	..	..	..	DAMI02
DANBY John	S	N	YO	L	†1	1661	..	1689	1719	DANB02
DANBY Thomas (George)	OFM		YO	F	12	1645	1665	..	1673	DANB04
DANIEL Edward	S	N	LA	D	#	1709	..	1733	1765	DANI02
DANIEL Edward	S	N	LA	D		1749	..	1775	1819	DANI04
DANIEL John	S		LA	D	3	1745	..	1771	1823	DANI08
DANIEL John	S	N	LA	D		1755	..	1779	1802	DANI10
DANIEL Richard	S		LA	R		1687	..	1710	1753	DANI12
DANIEL Robert	OSB	N	LA	W		1717	1735	..	1781	DANI14
DANIEL Thomas	S				7	..	..	..	..	DANI15
DANIEL Thomas	S	N	LA	D		1714	..	1739	1770	DANI16
DANIEL Thomas	SJ	N	SC	Y	#13	1716	1751	1757	1779	DANI18
DANIEL William	S		LA	D		1713	..	1741	1761	DANI20
DANIEL William	S	N	LA	D	#	1725	..	1750	1777	DANI22
DANSON William	S	N	LA	R	#	1730	..	1754	1806	DANS02
DANVERS William (Romuald)	OSB		SK	D	†	..	1620	1619	1634	DANV02
DARBYSHIRE James (Dominic)	OP	W		N	3	1690	1714	1717	1757	DARB02
DARBYSHIRE Robert	CRT	L		Q	#*‡	..	1593	1582	1612	DARB04
DARCY Anthony	S			S	3	..	..	1646	..	DARC02
DARCY Arthur	S		NN	R	#	1605	..	1630	..	DARC04
DARCY John	CAP	L			*8	..	..	..	..	DARC06
DARELL James	SJ	L	KT	Y	3	1707	1723	1731	1785	DARE02
DARELL John	S		SX	V	#3	1586	..	1610	..	DARE03
DARELL John	SJ	N	KT	Y	3	1705	1722	1731	1768	DARE04
DARELL Richard	SJ		SX	Y	#	1596	1616	..	1628	DARE06
DARELL William	SJ		BK	Y	3	1651	1671	1680	1721	DARE08
DARRAGH William	S	M	LA	V		1759	..	1783	1816	DARR02
DARREL John	S		SX	V	#3	1586	..	1610	..	DARR04
DAVENPORT Christophr(Francis)	OFM	L	WK	F	#§1	1590	1618	1620	1680	DAVE02
DAVENPORT (Ignatius of Magd.)	OFM		CH	F	12	1626	1652	..	1679	DAVE04
DAVIES Charles or Samuel	S	W	MT	R		1679	..	1704	1761	DAVI02
DAVIES James	S		MT	R		1667	..	1694	..	DAVI04
DAVIES John	S			D	3	..	..	1625	..	DAVI06
DAVIES John	S	L		V	3	..	..	1707	1753	DAVI07
DAVIES John (Bernard)	OSB		MX	X	#	1714	1733	1738	1789	DAVI08
DAVIES John (Leander)	OSB	L	MX	X		1670	1689	..	1734	DAVI09
DAVIES Miles	S	M	FT	R	#1	1662	..	1688	..	DAVI10
DAVIES Peter	SJ		MX	Y	13	1690	1711	1720	1759	DAVI11
DAVIES Richard	S	L		Q	*3	1551	..	1578	1623	DAVI12
DAVIES Robert (Ambrose)	OSB	N	MX	E		..	1688	1697	1654	DAVI13
DAVIES Roger	S	W		Q	*	..	..	1587	..	DAVI14
DAVIES Rowland	S	M	MX	D	§	1740	..	1772	1797	DAVI16
DAVIES William VEN.	S	W	MO	Q	+‡1	1558	..	1585	1593	DAVI18
DAVIES William	S		SP	V	3	1538	..	1595	..	DAVI20
DAVIES William	S		CH	D	1	1556	..	1604	..	DAVI22

Name	Reg	D	Co	T	Notes	Born	Prof	Ordn	Died	Code
DAVIES William	S	W	MO	D	3	1767	..	1794	1814	DAVI34
DAVIES William (Maurus)	OSB	N	FT	E	#	..	1642	..	1663	DAVI36
DAVIS see DAVIES										
DAVISON see DAWSON										
DAWBENY Thomas	S			D	*	..	..	1594	..	DAWB02
DAWBER John	OSB	M	LA	W		1769	1791	..	1810	DAWB04
DAWNEY Obed (Alban)	OSB		LA	X	§	1654	1683	..	1737	DAWN02
DAWSON Edward	SJ		MX		124	1576	1606	..	1624	DAWS02
DAWSON Miles	S		YO	V	†1	1566	..	1594	..	DAWS04
DAWSON Thomas (Simon Stock)	ODC	L	LN	R	#1	1574	1613	1610	1652	DAWS06
DAWSON William	S			S	3	..	..	1631	..	DAWS10
DAY John (Nicholas)	OFM	M	OX		12	1575	1601	..	1655	DAYA02
DAY William	S		MX	D	#	1608	..	1636	1639	DAYA04
DE see under surname										
DEAKINS John	CRT			Q	*	..	..	1587	1618	DEAK02
DEAKINS John	CRT					..	..	..	1618	DEAK04
DEAN Michael	SJ		FR	Y	13	1695	1714	1724	1760	DEAN02
DEAN Thomas	SJ		ES	Y	#	1693	1709	1719	1719	DEAN03
DEAN William BL.	S	L	YO	Q	+†1	1557	..	1581	1588	DEAN04
DEASE Robert	S			S		..	..	1644	..	DEAS02
DEBENHAM Samuel (Jn. Francis)	MIN		EX		†1	1565	1586	..	1613	DEBE02
DEBORD John	S	N	DH	D	#	1715	..	1739	1774	DEBO02
DEDAY James (Benedict)	OSB	M	NK	G		1773	1794	1800	1845	DEDA02
DELANEY (Dominic)	OP	L	IR		*	..	..	..	1763	DELA01
DELANEY James	S	L	IR	T	1	1768	..	1798	1847	DELA02
DELATTRE Anthony (Charles)	OSB		MX	X		1683	1711	1715	1731	DELA10
DELATTRE Edward (Augustine)	OSB		MX	R		1676	1706	1701	1733	DELA12
DELEAU see L'EAU										
DENNETT Henry	S	N	LA	D	3	1754	..	1780	1803	DENN02
DENNETT James	SJ	M	LA	Y	3	1702	1720	1728	1789	DENN04
DENNETT James	S	N	LA	L		1767	..	1794	1850	DENN06
DENNIS John	S			S	3	..	..	1630	..	DENN08
DENTIERS Philip	SJ		LC		4	1580	1598	..	1621	DENT02
DENTON William	S	L	YO	Q	1	1530	..	1581	..	DENT04
DEVEREUX John	S	L	IR	T	1	1764	..	1796	1838	DEVE02
DEVOIS (Theodoric of S.René)	CAR	L	FR			1665	1681	..	1728	DEVO02
DIAS SANTOS Emanuel Thomas	S	L	MX	L	*	1765	..	1799	1834	DIAS02
DIAZ Emmanuel		L	PL		*7	..	..	..	..	DIAZ02
DIBDALE Robert VEN.	S	L	WK	Q	#+	..	..	1584	1586	DIBD02
DICCONSON Edward BP.	S	N	LA	D	#*	1670	..	1701	1752	DICC02
DICCONSON Ignatius	SJ	M	LN	Y	°1	1663	1685	1693	..	DICC03
DICCONSON Robert	SJ	M	LN	Y		1642	1663	1672	1693	DICC04
DICCONSON Thomas	SJ	N	LA	Y		1651	1672	1681	1704	DICC06
DICCONSON see also DICKENSON										
DICHFIELD Edward	S	N	LA	D		..	..	1618	..	DICH02
DICKENSON Francis BL.	S		YO	Q	#+	1565	..	1589	1590	DICK02
DICKENSON John Francis	S				7	..	..	..	..	DICK04
DICKENSON Matthew	OFM	M	ND	F	134	1725	1741	1749	1767	DICK05
DICKENSON Roger BL.	S		LN	Q	#+	..	..	1583	1591	DICK06
DICKENSON (Theodore S.Barb'a)	OFM	L		F	123	1650	1667	1675	1719	DICK08
DIDERICH John Baptist	SJ				#*	1726	1745	..	1793	DIDE02
DIGBY John (Bartholomew)	ODC				°13	1598	..	1630	..	DIGB02
DIGBY John, Hon.	S		DT		*	1617	..	..	1664	DIGB04
DIGBY Joseph	S		RT	D	13	1662	..	1693	1708	DIGB06
DIGBY William (Jerome)	OSB	N	MX	G		1744	1761	..	1825	DIGB08
DIGGES Francis	SJ	N	MD	Y	3	1712	1733	1741	1781	DIGG02
DIGGES John	SJ		MD	Y	3	1712	1734	1741	1746	DIGG04
DIGGES John Dudley	S		MD	R	#	1689	..	1715	1771	DIGG06
DIGGES Thomas	SJ		MD	Y	3	1711	1729	1737	1805	DIGG10
DIGNAM Thomas	S				8	..	..	..	..	DIGN02
DILLON (George) Hon.	OFM	L	IR		*7	..	..	..	..	DILL01
DILLON Gerald (Vincent)	OP	N	IR		x	..	..	..	1651	DILL02
DILLON (James)	OP	L	IR		*8	..	..	..	..	DILL03
DILLON Richard	S	L	IR	S		..	..	1742	1780	DILL04
DIMMOCK see DYMOCK										
DINMORE William	S	N	YO	R	§4	1650	..	1676	1716	DINM02

Name	Reg	D	Co	T	Notes	Born	Prof	Ordn	Died	Code
DIRDO James	S		DT	D	3	..	..	1660	..	DIRD02
DITCHFIELD see DICHFIELD										
DIXON Christopher	OSA					..	..	..	1616	DIXO04
DIXON Henry (Thomas)	OFM		WR	F	134	1729	1746	1755	1776	DIXO05
DIXON James	S	N	LA	D		1720	..	1745	1759	DIXO06
DIXON (Jerome)	OFM			F	1234	1728	1744	1751	1755	DIXO07
DIXON Nicholas (Ambrose)	OP	N		N		1746	1770	..	1782	DIXO08
DIXON (Paul)	OFM	L		F	3	..	..	1734	..	DIXO09
DOBSON Gabriel	S			Q	*‡	..	..	1581	..	DOBS02
DOBSON Robert (Elphege)	OSB		KT	X		..	1709	..	1750	DOBS04
DODD Francis	S		ST	L	3	..	..	1698	1734	DODD02
DODD (Francis)	OFM	M		F	12	1673	1694	1697	1747	DODD04
DODD James	S	L	ST	V	#	..	..	1683	1738	DODD06
DODSWORTH Christopher	S	L	YO	D	4	..	..	1612	1613	DODS02
DOLMAN Peter	CRT			C		..	1622	..	1671	DOLM02
DOLMAN Robert	S	N	YO	R	1	1634	..	1658	..	DOLM04
DOMINIS Marco Antonio de, ABP	SJ		ZZ		*x°2	1560	1596	..	1624	DOMI02
DONCKER John Bapt de (Gaspar)	ODC		LC			1633	1657	..	1694	DONC02
DONELLAN Patrick	OP	L	IR			..	..	..	1794	DONE02
DONING John	S			S	#	..	..	1644	..	DONI02
DONZE Francis	SJ		FR			..	1761	..	..	DONZ02
DORMER Charles, 6th Ld.	SJ		BK	Y	3	1690	1709	1718	1761	DORM02
DORMER Francis, Hon.	SJ	W	HA	Y	3	1717	1734	1743	1770	DORM04
DORMER John Baptist, Hon.	SJ		HA	Y	3	1716	1734	1741	1743	DORM06
DORMER Robert, Hon.	SJ	W	BK	Y	3	1726	1743	1751	1792	DORM08
DORMER William, Hon.	SJ	W	HA	Y		1696	1714	1723	1758	DORM10
DORMER William	SJ	L	MX	Y	#°13	1710	1728	1736	..	DORM12
DORNAN (Hugh)	OFM		IR		*7	..	..	..	..	DORN02
DORREL Joseph	S			D		..	..	1661	..	DORR02
DORRINGTON Andrew	S	M	SP	R	#3	1567	..	1597	..	DORR04
DORRINGTON Francis	S		SP	R	#	1608	..	1638	..	DORR06
DORRINGTON Robert	S			S		..	..	1638	..	DORR08
DOUGLASS John BP.	S	L	YO	D	*3	1743	..	1768	1812	DOUG02
DOWDALL (James)	OP	L	IR		*8	..	..	..	..	DOWD01
DOWDALL (Jn.Bp.of Glaspistle)	CAP	L	IR		x12	1625	1648	..	1710	DOWD02
DOWDALL John	OSA		IR		*	..	..	..	1739	DOWD03
DOWDALL (Lawrence)	CAP	L				..	..	..	..	DOWD04
DOWNES Edmund	SJ		NK	R	#	1578	1625	1621	1637	DOWN02
DOWNES Thomas VEN.	SJ	L	NK	Y	#x1	1617	1639	..	1678	DOWN04
DOWNING John	S		SX	D	3	..	..	1646	..	DOWN06
DOWSE (Francis Dominic)	OP		IR		23	1688	1708	1713	1755	DOWS02
DOYLE William	SJ	N	IR		12	1716	1734	..	1785	DOYL04
DOYLY James	S			D	*°34	1676	..	1701	1746	DOYL06
DOYNE Joseph	SJ	N	MD	Y	3	1734	1758	1764	1803	DOYN02
DRAPER Thomas	S			S	3	..	..	1620	..	DRAP04
DRURY Edward	S				7	..	..	..	..	DRUR01
DRURY John	SJ		MX	Y	12	1600	1626	..	1663	DRUR02
DRURY Robert VEN.	S	L	BU	V	+3	1567	..	1592	1607	DRUR04
DRURY Robert	SJ	L	EX	R	#1	1587	1608	..	1623	DRUR06
DRURY William	S		EX	R	#	1584	..	1610	..	DRUR08
DRURY William	S		NK	R	1	1645	..	1670	..	DRUR10
DRYDEN Erasmus (Thomas), Bt.	OP	M		R	§	1669	1692	1694	1710	DRYD02
DRYLAND Christopher	SJ		KT	D	#2	..	1603	1582	..	DRYL02
DU see under surname										
DUCKETT George (Edmund)	OSB		LA	E		1741	1760	..	1792	DUCK00
DUCKETT Henry	S	N	LA	R		1729	..	1754	1755	DUCK02
DUCKETT James	S	N		D	*	..	..	1623	..	DUCK04
DUCKETT John	CRT		MX	D		1588	1629	1615	1647	DUCK06
DUCKETT John BL.	S	N	YO	D	#+§	1614	..	1639	1644	DUCK08
DUCKETT John	S			V		..	..	1659	..	DUCK10
DUCKETT Robert	S		WD	D	#	1598	..	1627	1656	DUCK12
DUCKETT William	S	N				..	..	..	1673	DUCK14
DUCLOS Anthony	SJ	L	FR		4	..	..	..	1764	DUCL02
DUDDELL William (Odo)	OSB		MX	X		1670	1689	..	1738	DUDD02
DUDLEY Richard	S	N	WD	R	#=	1563	..	1588	..	DUDL02
DUFF (Matthew)	OFM		IR		#*7	..	..	..	..	DUFF01

Name	Reg	D	Co	T	Notes	Born	Prof	Ordn	Died	Code
DUFFIELD Thomas	S	N	YO	D	#	..	..	1646	..	DUFF02
DUKE Edmund VEN.	S	N	KT	R	+§	1563	..	1589	1590	DUKE02
DUNCOMB William	S	M			7	..	..	..	..	DUNC02
DUNGAN Joseph	S	L	IR		3	1748	..	1772	1797	DUNG02
DUNN Francis	S	L	ND	D		1722	..	1748	1757	DUNN02
DUNN John	S	N	ND	D	#	1692	..	1717	1741	DUNN04
DUNN John	S	L	LA	D		1718	..	1743	1778	DUNN06
DUNN Lawrence	S	L	IR		8	..	..	..	..	DUNN08
DUNN Peter	S	M				..	..	..	1724	DUNN10
DUNN Roland (William)	OSB	N	SC	J	4	1644	1660	..	1678	DUNN12
DUNN William	S	N	YO	P	#1	1749	..	1780	1805	DUNN14
DUNSCOMBE Simon (Augustine)	OSB		DV			1702	1722	..	1736	DUNS02
DUNTON (Robert of S.Francis)	OFM			F	123	1667	1687	1691	1699	DUNT02
DUPERRON Jacques BP.	S	L	FR		*	..	..	..	1649	DUPE02
DUPUY Louis	S		MX	R		1721	..	1743	1743	DUPU02
DURAND Thomas	SJ		RT	Y	12	1597	1620	..	1633	DURA02
DURET Pierre (Remigius)	ODC	L	FR			1661	1683	..	1728	DURE02
DURHAM John	SJ	N	SC			1616	..	..	1674	DURH02
DUTTON Edmund	CRT		LA	D	#§	..	1649	1627	1652	DUTT02
DUVAL Edward	S	L		L	#	1720	..	1744	1778	DUVA02
DUVIVIERS James (Placid)	OSB	W	MX	G	#	1740	1757	..	1808	DUVI02
DYMOCK Charles	OSS					..	1619	..	1659	DYMO02
DYMOCK James	S	L	NK		4	..	..	..	1718	DYMO04
EARLE John	S	L	MX	D		1749	..	1779	1818	EARL02
EARPE Joseph	SJ	N	LA		#	1746	1764	1771	1827	EARP02
EAST Alban	S		HT	V	#3	1595	..	1618	1671	EAST00
EAST Francis	SJ		HT	Y	#	1606	1626	..	1658	EAST01
EAST George	S		BU	Q		..	..	1581	..	EAST02
EAST Louis (Augustine)	OFM			F	2	..	1634	..	1680	EAST04
EAST Richard	S		HT	D	#	1605	..	1631	..	EAST08
EASTERN see EYSTON										
EASTGATE Ambrose	OSB			W		..	1715	..	1725	EAST10
EASTGATE William	S	N	NK	D	#3	1646	..	1671	1687	EAST12
EASTHAM Evan (Anselm)	OSB	N	LA	E		1703	1731	..	1774	EAST14
EATON Reginald	SJ	W		Q	#*2	1559	1610	1587	1641	EATO02
EATON William	SJ		DE	Q	24	..	1583	1582	1614	EATO04
EAVES (Oswald)	OSB	N	LA	W		1738	1753	..	1793	EAVE02
EAVES Thomas	OSB		LA	W		1659	1688	..	1747	EAVE04
EBERSON Thomas	SJ		LE	Y	#3	1660	1679	1689	1733	EBER02
ECCLES Edward (Thos of S.Edw)	OFM	W	LA	F	3	..	1740	1746	1767	ECCL02
ECCLES (Lawrence)	OFM			F	3	..	..	1758	1810	ECCL03
ECCLESTON Thomas	SJ	N	LA	Y	#	1643	1668	1677	1698	ECCL04
ECCLESTON Thomas	S	N	LA	D	3	..	..	1661	1700	ECCL06
ECCLESTON Thomas	SJ	N	LA	Y	#3	1659	1697	1703	1743	ECCL08
ECCOP Charles	SJ	L	FR	Y	3	1697	1715	1724	1735	ECCO02
EDEN James (John)	CRT		DH	R	#*	1663	1698	1690	1707	EDEN02
EDISFORD John	SJ		YO	Y		1656	1675	1684	1720	EDIS04
EDISFORD John	SJ		YO	Y	#3	1700	1720	1729	1750	EDIS06
EDISFORD John	SJ	W	LA	Y	#3	1738	1760	1767	1789	EDIS08
EDISFORD William	S	N	YO	R	4	1673	..	1697	1700	EDIS10
EDMONDSON Henry	S	N	LA	D		1723	..	1747	1785	EDMO02
EDMONDSON Hugh	S	N	LA	D		1715	..	1743	1755	EDMO04
EDMONDSON Richard	S	N	LA	D	3	1754	..	1779	1812	EDMO06
(Edmund of St Thomas)	ODC				2	..	1693	..	..	EDMU04
EDMUNDS (Bernard)	OSB		KT	W		..	1614	..	1636	EDMU06
EDMUNDS Robert	OSB				*124	1572	1604	..	1614	EDMU08
EDMUNDS Robert	S	L	DB	V	*x134	1583	..	1609	1615	EDMU10
EDNER Louis (Justus)	OSB	M	MX	V	#2	1585	1604	..	1635	EDNE02
(Edward of S.Joseph)	ODC	W				..	..	..	1727	EDWA02
(Edward of S.Theresa)	ODC				1	1662	..	..	1725	EDWA04
EDWARDS Francis	S	L	DB	Q	†°	1557	..	1584	..	EDWA06
EDWARDS Gerard or Edward BL.	S		SP	Q	#+‡1	1552	..	1587	1588	EDWA08
EDWARDS Henry	S			S	#3	..	..	1665	..	EDWA10
EDWARDS Humphrey	SJ				‡	..	..	..	1587	EDWA12
EDWARDS Joseph	OP	L	LE	N	#§	1725	1754	..	1781	EDWA14
EDWARDS Robert	S	W				..	..	..	1685	EDWA18

56

Name	Reg	D	Co	T	Notes	Born	Prof	Ordn	Died	Code
EDWARDS Robert	S	W	DB	L	§	..	..	1664	1677	EDWA19
EGERTON John	S		CH	D	#	..	..	1613	..	EGER02
EGERTON John	S	N		L	34	..	..	1675	1719	EGER04
EGLIONBY see INGLEBY										
EGMOND John	SJ					..	..	..	1660	EGMO02
ELIOT see ELLIOT										
ELLERRER Thomas	SJ	N	DH	Y	3	1738	1755	1762	1795	ELLE02
ELIOT Edward (Ambrose)	OSB	M	SP	G		1699	1719	..	1773	ELLI02
ELLIOT John	S				7	..	..	..	..	ELLI03
ELLIOT Nathaniel	SJ	M	SP	Y	#3	1705	1723	1736	1780	ELLI04
ELLIOT William	S	W	HR	R	#	1610	..	1636	1678	ELLI06
ELLIS (Angelus)	OFM			F	123	1703	1721	1728	1736	ELLI07
ELLIS Griffen	S	W		R		1556	..	1582	..	ELLI08
ELLIS John	S				7	..	..	..	..	ELLI09
ELLIS Philip (Michael) BP.	OSB	L	BU	G	*§	1653	1670	..	1726	ELLI10
ELLIS William	S			R	#*	1559	..	1596	..	ELLI12
ELLIS William	SJ	N	BU		#1	1590	..	..	1640	ELLI14
ELMER Felix (Jocelin)	OSB		WR	W	23	..	1613	1617	1651	ELME02
ELRINGTON Edward	S	M	YO	V	#†3	1599	..	1624	1652	ELRI02
ELRINGTON Edward	S		MX	D	#3	1638	..	1661	1713	ELRI03
ELRINGTON Henry	S		YO	D	3	1637	..	1667	..	ELRI04
ELSTON see EYSTON										
ELY Humphrey	S			Q	#*‡	1539	..	1582	1604	ELYA02
EMERSON Ralph	SJ	N	MX	S	3	1609	1635	1633	1684	EMER02
EMERSON Thomas	OSB		YO		#*§1	1579	1604	..	1630	EMER04
EMITH see SMITH										
EMMOTT Joseph	SJ	N	MX	Y	3	1734	1753	1761	1816	EMMO02
ENGHAM Richard	SJ			R	*3	1555	1582	1580	1583	ENGH02
ENGHAM see also INGHAM										
ENGLEFIELD Charles (Felix)	OFM	W	BK	F	23	..	1731	1731	1767	ENGL02
ENGLEFIELD (Felix of S.Mary)	OFM		BK	F	12	1669	1689	1697	1703	ENGL04
ENGLEFIELD John	SJ	W	BK	Y	#3	1676	1696	1705	1733	ENGL06
ENGLISH Giles	SJ					..	..	..	1571	ENGL08
ENGLISH Robert	S	M	SK	Q	†#	..	..	1580	..	ENGL10
ENGLISH Thomas	S			R	*3	..	..	1560	..	ENGL12
ERRINGTON Anthony	S		ND		4	..	..	..	1719	ERRI02
ERRINGTON Charles	S		YO	R	#	1640	..	1664	1666	ERRI04
ERRINGTON George	S			S	3	..	..	1637	..	ERRI06
ERRINGTON William	S	N	YO	L		..	..	1693	1733	ERRI08
ERRINGTON William	S	L	WT	D		1716	..	1747	1768	ERRI10
EURE Francis	SJ	M	YO	Y	#	1630	1647	..	1698	EURE02
EURE Thomas	SJ	M	LN	Y	#	1607	1630	..	1645	EURE04
EURE William	SJ	M	LN	Y	#	1648	1669	1678	1698	EURE06
EUSTACE John Chetwode	S	M	IR	Z	*13	1764	..	1795	1815	EUST02
EVANS Charles	SJ	L	CN	Y	3	1640	1661	1672	1680	EVAN02
EVANS (Charles of S.Jn.Ev.)	OFM			F	123	1690	1723	1725	1751	EVAN03
EVANS Edward	S			S	3	..	..	1605	..	EVAN04
EVANS Francis	S			D	*	..	..	1672	..	EVAN06
EVANS Francis	SJ	W	MO	Y	#	1659	1679	1688	1727	EVAN08
EVANS Humphrey	SJ	W	CN	R	#‡	1599	1625	1623	1679	EVAN10
EVANS John	S		CN	S		1576	..	..	..	EVAN12
EVANS John	S		BR	D	#3	1629	..	1658	1669	EVAN14
EVANS John	S		MX	R	#	1688	..	1718	..	EVAN16
EVANS Philip ST.	SJ	W	MO	Y	+	1645	1665	1674	1679	EVAN18
EVANS Thomas	SJ		EX	R		1558	1585	1585	1587	EVAN20
EVANS Thomas	S		CN	V	‡1	1570	..	1599	..	EVAN24
EVANS William	S		CN	V	#	1578	..	1603	..	EVAN26
EVANS William	S		CH	R	#§	1679	..	1712	..	EVAN28
EVELEIGH Amesius	S			S	#3	..	..	1627	..	EVEL02
EVERARD (Bernardine)	CAP		IR		8	..	..	..	..	EVER02
EVERARD (Dunstan)	OSB	L	SK	G		..	1616	..	1650	EVER04
EVERARD James	S	M		V	3	1604	..	1628	1675	EVER06
EVERARD John	SJ		NN		#†	1584	..	..	1649	EVER08
EVERARD John (Bernardine)	OFM	L	IR		*7	..	..	..	..	EVER09
EVERARD Lambert	SJ					..	..	..	1680	EVER10
EVERARD Patrick ARCHBP.	S	N	IR	Z	*	1753	..	1783	1820	EVER12

Name	Reg	D	Co	T	Notes	Born	Prof	Ordn	Died	Code
EVERARD Thomas	SJ	L	SK	Q	†	1560	1593	1592	1633	EVER14
EVERARD Thomas	S		WT	R	#‡=	1570	..	1601	..	EVER16
EVERARD William	SJ					..	..	..	1590	EVER18
EVERARD William	S		SK	S	#§3	1590	..	1615	..	EVER20
EVERINGHAM (Peter of S.Mary)	OFM	L		F	#	1615	1638	1641	1686	EVER22
EVISON John Alexander	SJ	L	MX	Y	#1	1577	1599	..	1651	EVIS02
EWEN Maurice	SJ	L	SM	R	#	1611	1636	1634	1687	EWEN02
EXLEY John	S	L	YO	D	#	1716	..	1748	1778	EXLE02
EYRE Anthony	S			S	3	..	..	1689	..	EYRE02
EYRE Edward	S	M	DE	D		1745	..	1772	1834	EYRE04
EYRE John	S		DE	V	#*	1582	..	1607	..	EYRE06
EYRE John	S	N	DE	P		1747	..	1772	1790	EYRE08
EYRE Thomas	SJ		LE	Y	1	1669	1687	1696	1715	EYRE10
EYRE Thomas	S	N	DE	D	3	1748	..	1772	1810	EYRE12
EYRE William	SJ	N	LE	Y	#	1638	1658	1667	1675	EYRE16
EYRE William	SJ	M		Y	*3	1678	1698	1707	1724	EYRE18
EYSTON (Basil)	OSB		BK	G		1711	1733	..	1785	EYST02
EYSTON Charles (Jn.Capistran)	OFM	L	BK	F	123	1675	1693	1700	1732	EYST03
EYSTON George	SJ		BK	Y	13	1667	1688	1710	1745	EYST04
EYSTON John (Bernardine)	OFM		BK	F	123	1627	1644	1651	1709	EYST06
EYSTON Robert	S		BK	S	13	1590	..	1612	..	EYST10
EYSTON Robert	SJ	L	BK	Y	1	1729	1751	1757	1766	EYST12
EYSTON William (Joseph)	OP	L	BK	F	*	1674	1729	1697	1758	EYST14
EYTON see EATON										
EYVES see EAVES										
FAIRBURN George	S	L	NT	S	x3	..	..	1608	1615	FAIR01
FAIRCHILD Thomas	SJ	N		Y	#*3	1715	1736	1750	1764	FAIR02
FAIRCLOUGH Alexander	SJ	M	MX	V	#23	1575	1605	1602	1645	FAIR04
FAIRFAX Thomas	SJ		YO	Y	#1	1655	1675	1683	1716	FAIR08
FALCONER see FAULKNER										
FALKNER see FAULKNER										
FALLON Thomas (James)	OP	L	IR		1	1752	..	..	1800	FALL02
FALLOWFIELD Richard	S	N			4	..	..	..	1668	FALL04
FANNING Dominic	SJ	L	MX	Y	#3	1742	1762	1773	1812	FANN02
FARLEY Elliot	SJ		WR	R	#‡1	1600	1632	1629	1650	FARL02
FARMER Gregory	S	M			#x	..	..	..	1685	FARM01
FARMER John	S	L	NN	D		..	..	1605	1660	FARM02
FARMER Thomas	SJ	L	BU	R	#1	1594	1621	1620	1683	FARM04
FARMER see also FERMOR										
FARNWORTH John (Jerome)	OSB	N	LA	E		..	1696	..	1711	FARN02
FARNWORTH Ralph (Cuthbert)	OSB	N	LA	W	#	1680	1700	..	1754	FARN04
FARRAR James	SJ	N	LA	Y	3	1707	1725	1734	1763	FARR02
FARRELL Patrick	S			S		..	..	1740	1741	FARR04
FARRELL (Patrick)	OP	L	IR		*	..	..	..	1764	FARR05
FARRINGTON John	SJ		LA	Y		1615	1637	..	1656	FARR06
FARRINGTON Thomas	SJ	N	LA	Y		1611	1631	..	1678	FARR08
FATHERING Hugh	S				7	..	..	..	..	FATH01
FATHERS Thomas	S	L	SM	D	#	1591	..	1622	1663	FATH02
FAUCONBERG see BELASYSE										
FAULKNER John	SJ	W	DT	R	#‡	1577	1604	1603	1657	FAUL02
FAULKNER John	S		WT	R	§3	1600	..	1623	1664	FAUL04
FAULKNER Ralph	S	L	MD	R		1736	..	1761	..	FAUL06
FAULKNER Stephen	SJ	N	KT	S	3	1621	1650	1647	1670	FAUL08
FAULKNER Thomas	SJ	M	LA	Z	*§	1707	1732	..	1784	FAUL10
FAUNT Lawrence Arthur	SJ		LE	R	‡	1554	1570	..	1591	FAUN02
FAZAKERLEY Thomas	S	N	LA	R	#	1611	..	1635	1665	FAZA02
FEATHERSTONE Anthony	OFM			F	8	..	..	..	..	FEAT02
FEATHERSTONE John	S	M		V	3	..	..	1604	..	FEAT04
FEATHERSTONE Thomas	SJ			Y	*	1671	1690	1702	1724	FEAT06
FECK Thomas	SJ		MX	R		1573	1601	1601	1647	FECK02
FELTON Francis	S			S	*3	1576	..	1603	..	FELT02
FENN James BL.	S	W	SM	Q	+‡1	1540	..	1580	1584	FENN02
FENN John	S		SM	L	‡3	1535	..	1574	1614	FENN04
FENN Robert	S		SM		‡1	1536	..	..	1587	FENN06
FENNELL Edmund	S				7	..	..	..	..	FENN08
FENNELL Simon	S	L	SX	Q	‡	..	..	1583	..	FENN10

Name	Reg	D	Co	T	Notes	Born	Prof	Ordn	Died	Code
FENWICK Edward (Dominic) BP.	OP	L	MD		*	1768	1790	1792	1832	FENW02
FENWICK Francis	OSB	L	MX	E		1645	1664	..	1694	FENW04
FENWICK John (Ceslaus)	OP	L	MD		1	1759	1783	1785	1815	FENW06
FENWICK Louis (Lawrence)	OSB	L	ND	G		..	1685	..	1746	FENW08
FENWICK William (Augustine)	OSB	N	ND	G		..	1693	1694	1726	FENW10
FENWICK William (Didacus)	OFM			F	124	1620	1637	..	1647	FENW12
FERBY Thomas	S	N	YO	R		1740	..	1763	1823	FERB02
FEREIRA James	S	L	PL		*8	..	..	..	..	FERE02
FERLAMAN James	OP		ND	N	3	1740	1759	1762	1796	FERL02
FERMOR Henry	SJ	M	OX	Y	#3	1637	1656	1665	1680	FERM02
FERMOR Henry	S		IT	R		1756	..	..	1825	FERM04
FERMOR James	OP		IT	R		1757	1780	..	1833	FERM06
FERMOR Thomas	SJ	L	OX	Y		1649	1667	1676	1710	FERM08
FERMOR see also FARMER										
FERNANDEZ Antonio	SJ	L	PL			..	..	..	1674	FERN02
FERRERS Joseph	ODC	L	WK			1725	1745	1749	1797	FERR02
FERREYRA James Roiz	OSB	L	PL	W		..	1676	..	1712	FERR04
FESARD Giles	SJ				6	..	..	..	..	FESA02
FETTIPLACE Edward	CRT		BK	D	#3	1607	1646	1634	1659	FETT02
FIDDEN John (Thomas)	OP	L		Z	*13	1625	1656	1659	1679	FIDD02
FIELD John	S				7	..	..	..	..	FIEL01
FIELDESEND Robert	S			D	*	..	..	1597	..	FIEL02
FIELDING John	S			V		..	..	1647	..	FIEL03
FIELDING Nicholas	S			S	3	..	..	1609	..	FIEL04
FILBY John	S	M	OX	D	#‡	..	..	1578	..	FILB02
FILBY William BL.	S	L	OX	Q	+‡1	1555	..	1581	1582	FILB04
FILCH see FITCH										
FILCOCK Roger VEN.	SJ		KT	V	#+3	..	1600	1597	1601	FILC02
FILIALL John	S		SX	D	7	..	..	..	..	FILI02
FINCH James (Bruno)	CRT	N	LA	C		1748	1770	1772	1821	FINC02
FINCH Thomas	S		KT	S	°3	..	..	1605	..	FINC04
FINCH Richard	S		CB	R	#4	1635	..	1660	1689	FINC06
FINGLAS Robert	SJ	N	IR		#	1606	1647	..	1663	FING02
FINGLEY John BL.	S	N	YO	Q	+†	1553	..	1581	1586	FING04
FINN (James)	CAR	L	IR		*8	..	..	..	..	FINN01
FINN John	S		IR	S		..	..	1744	..	FINN02
FIRBY see FERBY										
FIRTH Anthony (Richard)	ODC		YO			1719	1738	..	1792	FIRT02
FISHER Clement	S	L	YO	V		1743	..	1775	..	FISH02
FISHER Daniel	S	L	MX	L	§3	1646	..	1670	1686	FISH04
FISHER George	S	L	NN	R	#§1	1580	..	1606	1645	FISH06
FISHER John	SJ	M	YO	Y	1	1608	1628	..	1654	FISH08
FISHER John	OSB	N	LA	W		1710	1726	..	1793	FISH10
FISHER Ralph	S		YO	D		..	..	1598	..	FISH14
FISHER Richard (Edward)	OSB	N	LA	W		1748	1766	1772	1824	FISH16
FISHER Thomas	S		LN	D	#	1578	..	1603	1667	FISH22
FISHER Thomas (Wilfrid)	OSB	N	ST	X	3	1767	1787	1791	1847	FISH24
FISHER William	S	N	LA	L		..	..	1760	1813	FISH26
FISHWICK Richard	S	M	HA	D		1736	..	1773	1803	FISH28
FITCH William (Benet)	CAP		EX	P	#§	1561	1588	..	1611	FITC02
FITTER Daniel	S	M	ST	L	#	1628	..	1651	1700	FITT02
FITTER Francis	S	M	ST	L	#	1622	..	1645	1710	FITT04
FITTON Francis	S			D	#*	..	..	1600	..	FITT06
FITZGERALD (Francis)	OFM		IR		*4	..	..	..	1666	FITZ00
FITZGERALD (John)	OFM	L	IR		*7	..	..	..	..	FITZ01
FITZHERBERT Anthony	S		DE	R		1649	..	..	..	FITZ02
FITZHERBERT (Francis)	CAP		DE		7	..	..	..	..	FITZ03
FITZHERBERT Francis	SJ		DE	Y	#	1613	1634	..	1687	FITZ04
FITZHERBERT John	S	M	DE	R	#1	1607	..	1632	1673	FITZ06
FITZHERBERT Robert	S	M	DE	L	#	1629	..	1652	1701	FITZ08
FITZHERBERT Thomas	SJ		ST	R	‡	1552	1613	1602	1640	FITZ10
FITZJAMES Nicholas	OSB	W	SM	D	‡1	1564	1608	1601	1652	FITZ12
FITZJAMES Thomas	S		SM	R	3	1668	..	1694	..	FITZ14
FITZMORRIS (James S.Joseph)	CAR	L	IR	Z	8	..	..	..	..	FITZ15
FITZMORRIS (Thomas S.Elias)	CAR	L	IR	Z	8	..	..	..	..	FITZ16
FITZSIMON Henry	SJ		IR	N	‡34	1566	1592	1597	1645	FITZ17

Name	Reg	D	Co	T	Notes	Born	Prof	Ordn	Died	Code
FITZSIMON Patrick Lawrence	S	L	MX	S		..	..	1735	..	FITZ18
FITZWILLIAM George	S	N	LN	R		1649	..	1673	1678	FITZ20
FITZWILLIAM John	SJ		LN	Y	#	1635	1654	1663	1665	FITZ21
FITZWILLIAM William Ignatius	S			V	3	..	..	1724	..	FITZ22
FITZWILLIAMS Charles	S	M	MX	R	#	1700	..	1729	1750	FITZ24
FITZWILLIAMS George	OSB	N	LA	G		..	1695	..	1725	FITZ26
FIXER John	S		HA	Q	‡	1562	..	1587	..	FIXE02
FLACK William	SJ		SK	V	†	1561	1585	1591	1637	FLAC02
FLATHERS Matthew or Major VEN	S	N	YO	D	+‡1	1560	..	1606	1608	FLAT02
FLECK see FLACK										
FLECKNOE Richard	S	L	MX	Y	§4	1600	..	1636	1678	FLEC02
FLECKNOE William	SJ	W	OX	D	#2	1575	1611	1600	1632	FLEC04
FLEET John (Bernardine)	OFM	M	DT	F	1	1740	1759	..	1815	FLEE02
FLEETWOOD Francis or Jn Waltr	SJ	L	MX	V	#3	1699	1735	1724	1774	FLEE04
FLEETWOOD John	SJ	N	MX	Y	3	1703	1723	1728	1734	FLEE06
FLEETWOOD John (Ignatius)	ODC	M	ST	Z	1	1662	1681	..	1733	FLEE08
FLEMING (Bruno)	CRT	N	SC	C		..	1732	..	1761	FLEM02
FLEMING (Jerome)	OFM	M		F	123	1702	1722	1728	1746	FLEM04
FLETCHER Anthony	SJ	L	WD	R	#	1564	1612	1610	1624	FLET02
FLETCHER John	S	L	LA	D		1766	..	1795	1845	FLET04
FLETCHER Owen	S		OX	Q	‡	..	..	1592	..	FLET06
FLETCHER Peter	S	N		R	*	1563	..	1587	..	FLET08
FLETCHER Richard	S	N	LA	D	#3	..	..	1650	1701	FLET09
FLETCHER Robert	S		LA	D	#	1609	..	..	..	FLET10
FLETCHER Thomas	S	L	SX	R	#	1590	..	1616	..	FLET12
FLETCHER William	S	N	LA	D	#	1722	..	1746	1803	FLET14
FLETCHER William	S	N	LA	D		1752	..	1776	1812	FLET16
FLEURY Charles	SJ	W	FR		#	1739	1756	..	1825	FLEU02
FLEUTOT (Maurus)	OSB		FR	W		1610	1630	..	1669	FLEU04
FLEXNEY see FLECKNOE										
FLINT Thomas	SJ	M	WK	R		1576	1621	1600	1638	FLIN02
FLORECKEN (Benedict)	OSB	L	GS	Z	*	..	..	..	1697	FLOR02
FLORENCE Bartholomew	CRT			Z	*23	..	1585	1575	1607	FLOR04
FLOYD Charles	SJ		AY	R	24	1562	1611	1596	1620	FLOY02
FLOYD Francis	SJ			Y		1692	1710	1719	1729	FLOY04
FLOYD Griffin or Griffith	SJ		CN	R	°	1569	1593	1593	..	FLOY06
FLOYD Henry	SJ	L	CB	V	#13	1563	1599	1592	1641	FLOY08
FLOYD Henry	SJ	M	CH	Y	#	1621	1643	..	1687	FLOY10
FLOYD John	SJ		CB	R	#	1572	1592	..	1649	FLOY16
FLOYD John	SJ	W		Y	#	1606	1625	..	1670	FLOY17
FLOYD Owen	S		AY	D	‡1	1545	..	1578	1591	FLOY18
FLOYD Thomas	S	L		Q	*4	..	..	1582	1594	FLOY20
FLUDD see FLOYD										
FLYNN Thomas	S	M	IR		1	1720	..	..	1797	FLYN02
FLYNN Thomas	OFM	W	IR		8	..	..	..	..	FLYN04
FOLERE see FOWLER										
FOLLIOT John	S		WR	D	#	..	..	1607	..	FOLL02
FONTAINE John Baptist de la	SJ		FR	Y	3	1739	1757	1767	1821	FONT02
FONTAINE Wm. (Placid) de la	OSB		NN	G		..	1731	..	1780	FONT04
FOOTHEAD John	S		MX	R		1763	..	..	1788	FOOT04
FORBES James	OP				4	..	..	..	1640	FORB02
FORBES John, Ld.(Archangelus)	CAP		SC		§	1570	1593	..	1606	FORB04
FORBES Wm. (Archangelus) Hon.	CAP		SC			1563	1589	..	1592	FORB06
FORCER Francis	SJ	N	DH		1	1583	1604	..	1655	FORC02
FORCER John	SJ	N	DH	R	#	1580	1605	1604	1630	FORC04
FORD Francis	S	N				..	..	..	1689	FORD01
FORD Thomas BL.	S	L	DV	D	+‡	..	..	1573	1582	FORD02
FORD see also FORTH										
FORMAN Robert	S			R		..	..	1573	..	FORM01
FORMBY (Macarius)	CRT		LA	C		..	1734	..	1771	FORM02
FORSHAW John (Lawrence)	OSB	N	LA	X	3	1769	1788	1795	1815	FORS04
FORSTER (Bede)	OSB	N		Z	#*	..	1634	..	1694	FORS06
FORSTER Charles	SJ		MX	Y		1623	1643	..	1680	FORS07
FORSTER John	SJ		HT	Y		1618	1637	..	1693	FORS08
FORSTER see also FOSTER										
FORSYTE	OP	L	SC	R	*°7	..	..	..	..	FORS16

60

Name	Reg	D	Co	T	Notes	Born	Prof	Ordn	Died	Code
FORTESCUE	S			S	3	..	..	1603	..	FORT02
FORTESCUE Adrian	SJ		BU	R	#124	1601	1624	..	1653	FORT04
FORTESCUE (Angelus of S.Mary)	OFM		WR	F	123	1658	1675	1683	1718	FORT06
FORTESCUE (Anthony)	OSB			W	2	..	1620	..	..	FORT08
FORTESCUE (Bonaventure)	OFM			F	1234	1659	1673	1681	1720	FORT09
FORTH James	S	N	LA	Q	#	..	..	1584	..	FORT10
FORTIN James	CAR				7	..	..	..	..	FORT12
FOSTER Bartholomew	SJ		SK	R	#12	1592	1616	1616	1617	FOST02
FOSTER Francis	SJ	M	MX	V	2	1601	1622	..	1653	FOST04
FOSTER Francis (Thomas)	OSB	M	SP	D	#2	1572	1611	1598	1631	FOST06
FOSTER George (Thomas)	OP			R	*‡	1562	1586	1590	..	FOST08
FOSTER Henry	S			S	3	..	..	1637	..	FOST10
FOSTER James	S	M	LA	R	#	1635	..	1661	..	FOST12
FOSTER James	S	N	LA	D		1747	..	1775	1824	FOST14
FOSTER John	S				7	..	..	..	..	FOST15
FOSTER (Joseph)	OSB		YO	W		..	1630	..	1636	FOST16
FOSTER Matthew	S	N	YO	D	#	1658	..	..	1723	FOST18
FOSTER Michael	SJ		SK	Y	#3	1642	1660	1667	1684	FOST20
FOSTER Richard	SJ	N	LA	Y		1672	1692	1701	1707	FOST22
FOSTER Robert	SJ	L	SK	Z	#*	1588	1609	..	1641	FOST23
FOSTER Seth	OSS		YO	R		1557	1584	1581	1628	FOST24
FOSTER Thomas	SJ	M	YO	R	#	1590	1617	1614	1648	FOST26
FOSTER William	SJ		SK		#§1	1588	1609	..	1657	FOST28
FOSTER William	S	N	LA	D	4	1707	..	1730	1754	FOST30
FOTHERING see FATHERING										
FOULKES Jerome	SJ	M			*	1575	1609	..	1645	FOUL02
FOURNIERS Nicholas	SJ	N	MT	Y	#	1708	1725	1733	1779	FOUR02
FOWLER Andrew	MIN		GL	Q		..	1587	1581	1594	FOWL02
FOWLER Francis	SJ	M	MX	Y	12	1609	1631	..	1659	FOWL04
FOWLER Francis (William)	OP	M	FT		#2	1591	1610	..	1662	FOWL05
FOWLER John	S		ST	R	#‡3	1569	..	1610	..	FOWL06
FOX Nicholas	S	M	EX	Q	x‡	1533	..	1581	1592	FOXA02
FOXE James	SJ		YO	Y	#3	1685	1707	1715	1760	FOXE01
FOXE James	SJ	N	SP	Y		1729	1749	1755	1795	FOXE02
FRAINE George	S		MX	D	#	1768	..	1792	1805	FRAI02
FRAMBACK Augustine	SJ		GS			1723	1744	..	1795	FRAM02
FRANCIS Alban (Placid)	OSB	M	MX	X		..	1670	..	1715	FRAN02
FRANCIS John	S		SX	D	#	1672	..	1706	1729	FRAN04
(Francis Mary of Paris)	CAP		FR		2	..	1621	..	1652	FRAN05
FRANCIS Thomas (Leo)	OFM		WK	F	13	1726	1742	1749	1774	FRAN06
FRANKISH Nicholas	S	N		Q	*	..	..	1587	..	FRAN07
FRANKLAND Hugh	OSB	N	YO	G		1671	1700	1705	1755	FRAN08
FRANKS Richard	S	N	YO	V	#3	1601	..	1632	..	FRAN12
FRANKS Richard	S	N	YO	V		1630	..	1655	1696	FRAN14
FREEMAN John	S		WK	R	#	1594	..	1620	..	FREE02
FREEMAN John	SJ		YO	V		..	1632	..	..	FREE04
FREEMAN Michael	SJ	N	YO	R		1578	1608	1603	1642	FREE06
FREEMAN Thomas	S		LE	Q		..	..	1581	..	FREE08
FREEMAN William BL.	S	M	YO	Q	#+‡	..	..	1587	1595	FREE10
FRENCH (Anthony)	OFM			F	3	..	..	1743	..	FREN02
FRENCH James (Thomas)	OP	L	IR		*8	..	..	..	..	FREN04
FRERE Joseph	OSB		EX	G		1598	1620	1629	1694	FRER02
FRERE (Placid)	OSB		EX	G	1	1602	1624	1631	1632	FRER04
FRITH see FIRTH										
FRIZELLE Francis	S			S		..	..	1652	..	FRIZ02
FRIZELLE George	S			S		..	..	1652	..	FRIZ04
FROMOND Gregory	S		SY	V	#	1592	..	1618	..	FROM02
FROMOND William	S	L			1	1618	..	..	1678	FROM04
FROST James (Peter)	OFM	M	ST	F	3	1731	1749	1755	1785	FROS02
FRYER Charles	S		SM	D	#	1738	..	1771	1811	FRYE04
FRYER William	S		SM	D		1739	..	1770	1805	FRYE06
FRYER William Victor	S	L	SM	L		1768	..	..	1844	FRYE08
FUENTE Diego de la	OP	L	ES		*	..	1601	..	1630	FUEN02
FULLART (Bonaventure)	OFM			F	13	1610	..	1647	1651	FULL02
FULLER Henry	S	L	NK	L	3	..	..	1690	1713	FULL04
FULLER John	S	L	MX	D	3	1729	..	1754	1792	FULL06

Name	Reg	D	Co	T	Notes	Born	Prof	Ordn	Died	Code
FULLER Zachary (Alban)	OSB		NK	W		..	1674	..	1691	FULL08
FULWOOD Hugh	S		ST	R	#	1602	..	1627	..	FULW02
FULWOOD Thomas (Damasus)	CAR	L	MX		#§°12	1654	1674	..	..	FULW04
FURLONG Pierce	OP		IR		*7	..	..	..	..	FURL02
FURSDON John (Cuthbert)	OSB	L	DV	G	#1	1604	1620	..	1638	FURS02
FURSDON (Cuthbert)	OSB		DV	W		1585	1620	..	1677	FURS04
GABB Thomas	S	L	MX	D	#	1742	..	1772	1817	GABB02
(Gabriel of S.Eliseus)	ODC					..	..	..	1725	GABR02
GADBURY John	SJ		MX	Y	#12	1599	1620	..	1668	GADB02
GAFFEY Daniel	OFM	L	IR	N		..	..	1773	1815	GAFF02
GAGE Charles	SJ	M	LC	Y	#°1	1655	1675	1683	..	GAGE02
GAGE Francis	S	M	MX	P	#	1621	..	1646	1682	GAGE04
GAGE George	S		SX		*	..	..	1614	..	GAGE06
GAGE George	S		SY	D	#x	..	..	1626	1652	GAGE08
GAGE James (Ambrose)	OP	L	SK	N		1723	1745	1747	1796	GAGE10
GAGE John	S		MX	D	#	1619	..	1646	..	GAGE12
GAGE John	SJ	M	SK	Y	#	1651	1670	1679	1728	GAGE14
GAGE John	SJ	M	SK	Y	3	1720	1740	1744	1790	GAGE16
GAGE Thomas	OP		SY		°14	1604	..	..	1656	GAGE18
GAGE William	SJ	M	MX	Y	#	1599	1619	..	1683	GAGE20
GAGNIER John	CRL		FR	P	*°1	1670	..	..	1740	GAGN02
GAHAN William	OSA		IR	N		1732	1748	1755	1804	GAHA02
GAILE (Bede)	OSB	N	YO	G	#	..	1620	..	1629	GAIL02
GAIRE Gregory (George)	OSB	L		W	2	..	1614	..	1634	GAIR02
GALICANUS John	S			S		..	..	1618	..	GALI02
GALLI Anthony	SJ	L	IT		#12	1623	1645	..	1703	GALL02
GALLOP Giles	SJ				‡	..	1575	..	1580	GALL04
GALLOWAY Edward	SJ	L	MX	Y		1706	1724	1735	1799	GALL06
GAMACHES see Cyprien of Gama.										
GANDY James	S	N	WD	D	#3	1698	..	1726	1761	GAND02
GANT see GAUNT										
GANTLET Anthony	SJ					..	..	..	..	GANT04
GARDEN James	SJ		SC		1	1718	..	..	1793	GARD02
GARDINER Bernard	S	L	NK	R		1563	..	1592	..	GARD04
GARDINER James	S	N	LA	Q		..	..	1582	..	GARD06
GARDINER James	S	N	ND	D	#3	1669	..	1699	1750	GARD08
GARDINER John	SJ		DT	Y		1588	1618	..	1652	GARD10
GARDINER John	S		CH	R	#	1606	..	1632	..	GARD12
GARDINER John	S			D	*3	1660	..	1689	..	GARD14
GARDINER John	SJ	M	LA	Y		1659	1680	1687	1727	GARD16
GARDINER Luke	S	N	ND	P	#	1683	..	1713	1740	GARD18
GARDINER Michael	S		OX	D		..	..	1603	..	GARD20
GARDINER William	SJ	N	LA	Y	#	1651	1673	1681	1725	GARD22
GARGRAVE George	S	N	DH	V	§13	1598	..	1628	..	GARG02
GARLICK Nicholas VEN.	S	M	DE	Q	+‡1	1554	..	1582	1588	GARL02
GARNER Thomas (Benedict)	OSB		LA	X		1736	1758	..	1796	GARN02
GARNET Charles	S			S		..	..	1660	..	GARN04
GARNET Edmund	S		LA	V		..	..	1674	..	GARN06
GARNET Henry	SJ		DE	R	#*§3	1555	1575	1582	1606	GARN08
GARNET James	S			S	3	..	..	1633	..	GARN10
GARNET John	S			V		..	..	1653	..	GARN12
GARNET John	CRT					..	..	..	1693	GARN14
GARNET Paul	S			V		..	..	1638	..	GARN16
GARNET Richard	S		LA	R	#†	1580	..	1606	..	GARN18
GARNET Stephen	S		p	Q	*	..	..	1581	..	GARN20
GARNET Thomas ST.	SJ	M	SY	V	#+3	1574	1604	1599	1608	GARN22
GARNET William	S			S		..	..	1676	1670	GARN24
GARSTANG William (Dunstan)	OSB	L	LA	E		1736	1753	..	1814	GARS02
GARTER George (John S.Mary)	OFM				123	1590	1646	1648	1675	GART01
GARTER John	OSB		NN	E		..	1639	1643	1650	GART02
GARTH Richard	S			S	*	..	..	1593	..	GART06
GASCOIGNE Francis	S	N	YO	D	#3	1605	..	1636	1676	GASC02
GASCOIGNE Henry	SJ	M	BU	Y	1	1595	1617	..	1676	GASC04
GASCOIGNE John (Placid)	OSB	N	YO	W	#2	1599	1615	1623	1681	GASC06
GASCOIGNE Michael	OSB	N	YO	G		..	1622	..	1657	GASC08
GASCOIGNE Thomas	SJ	N	YO	Y		1605	1630	..	1669	GASC10

Name	Reg	D	Co	T	Notes	Born	Prof	Ordn	Died	Code
GASCOIGNE William	CRT		YO	B	1	1557	1579	..	1588	GASC12
GASCOIGNE William	S	N	YO	D	#3	1631	..	1655	1690	GASC14
GASKINS see GASCOIGNE										
GATENBY Richard	S	N	YO	V	#	..	..	1645	1677	GATE02
GATTI	S	L	IT		*7	..	..	..	..	GATT02
GAULTIER Francois	S		FR		*8	..	..	..	..	GAUL02
GAUNT James	S		LA	R	#	1580	..	1607	..	GAUN02
GAUNT James	S	N	LA	D		..	..	..	1734	GAUN04
GAUNT Thomas	S	N	LA	R	#	1587	..	1613	..	GAUN06
GAUNT William	S	N	LA	D	1	1721	..	1747	1773	GAUN08
GAVAN see GAWEN										
GAVIN Antonio	S		ES		*°8	..	..	..	..	GAVI02
GAWEN Edward	S			S	#3	..	..	1615	..	GAWE02
GAWEN Henry	SJ		MX	Y	3	1668	1685	1693	1701	GAWE04
GAWEN John BL.	SJ	M	MX	R	#+	1640	1660	1670	1679	GAWE06
GAWEN Thomas	SJ	M	MX	R	13	1646	1668	1677	1712	GAWE08
GAWEN William (Ambrose)	OSB	N	MX	X		..	1690	..	1737	GAWE10
GEARNON (Anthony)	OFM	L	IR		*7	..	..	..	..	GEAR01
GEARY John (Anselm)	OSB	L	MX	X		1714	1732	1739	1795	GEAR02
GEDDES Alexander	S	L	SC	P		1737	..	1764	1802	GEDD02
GEISSLER Luke	SJ		GS			1737	1755	..	1786	GEIS02
GENNINGS Edmund ST.	S	L	ST	Q	#+§	1567	..	1590	1591	GENN02
GENNINGS John (Thomas)	OFM		ST	R	§2	1576	1616	1600	1660	GENN04
GENNINGS see also JENNINGS										
GENNISON see JENISON										
GEOFFREY see JEFFREY										
GEORGE Thomas	S	W			7	..	..	..	..	GEOR02
GERARD Alexander	S	N	LA	Q	#	..	..	1586	..	GERA02
GERARD Caryl or Charles	S		LA	R	#	1695	..	1720	1779	GERA04
GERARD Gilbert	SJ	L	LA	R	1	1569	1602	1593	1606	GERA06
GERARD Gilbert	SJ		LA	R	#	1614	1642	1640	1645	GERA08
GERARD James	S	N	LA	R	x4	1677	..	1702	1715	GERA10
GERARD John	SJ		LA	R	#‡	1564	1588	1588	1637	GERA12
GERARD Miles BL.	S		LA	Q	#+	1549	..	1583	1590	GERA16
GERARD Philip, 7th Ld.	SJ	W	ST	Y	#	1665	1684	1693	1733	GERA18
GERARD Ralph	S		LA	D	#3	1669	..	1698	1699	GERA20
GERARD Thomas	SJ	L	EX	R	#=	1605	1629	1631	1665	GERA22
GERARD Thomas	SJ	N	LA	Y	#3	1640	1675	1678	1682	GERA24
GERARD Thomas	CRT			C		..	..	..	1667	GERA25
GERARD Thomas	SJ	N	LA	Y	#	1667	1686	1696	1715	GERA26
GERARD Thomas	SJ	M	LA	Y	13	1692	1714	1724	1761	GERA28
GERARD William	S	N	LA	V	1	1613	..	..	1673	GERA32
GERARD William	SJ		ST	Y	#3	1662	1683	1688	1706	GERA34
GERARD William	SJ		LA	Y	3	1687	1707	1716	1731	GERA36
GERARD William	S		DT	D		1754	..	..	1830	GERA38
GERVASE George BL.	OSB		SX	D	*+2	1569	1608	1603	1608	GERV02
GERVASE John	S		ST	V		..	..	1599	1599	GERV04
GIBBON (Benedict)	OSB	L	KT	X		..	1673	..	1723	GIBB02
GIBBON Henry	OSA	L	IR		*7	..	..	..	..	GIBB03
GIBBONS Andrew	S		SM	R		..	..	1581	1583	GIBB04
GIBBONS John	SJ		SM	R	‡3	1544	1578	1576	1589	GIBB06
GIBBONS John	S		DV	R	#§	1652	..	1677	..	GIBB08
GIBBONS Richard	SJ		SM		3	1549	1572	1575	1632	GIBB10
GIBBONS Tobias	S	L	ZZ	L	*3	..	..	1696	1737	GIBB12
GIBLET William	S			N	*‡3	1535	..	1563	1590	GIBL02
GIBSON (Dunstan)	OSB		YO	E		..	1629	1634	..	GIBS02
GIBSON Francis	SJ	M	WK	Y	13	1668	1687	1695	1738	GIBS04
GIBSON George	S	N	ND	D		1726	..	1750	1778	GIBS06
GIBSON George (Thomas)	OP	N	ND			..	1673	..	1696	GIBS08
GIBSON Isaac	SJ	M	WK	Y	2	1674	1693	1702	1738	GIBS10
GIBSON (John Baptist)	OFM			F	123	1678	1696	1703	1757	GIBS12
GIBSON Matthew BP.	S	N	ND	D	*3	1734	..	1758	1790	GIBS14
GIBSON Richard	S	M	ND	D	3	1739	..	1763	1801	GIBS16
GIBSON Thomas	S	N	ND	D	#3	1688	..	1716	1765	GIBS18
GIBSON William BP.	S	N	ND	D	*3	1738	..	1765	1821	GIBS20
GIBSON William (Thomas)	OP	N	ND	R		1668	1687	1692	1724	GIBS22

Name	Reg	D	Co	T	Notes	Born	Prof	Ordn	Died	Code
GICOU Francis	OSB		FR	E		1585	1617	..	1648	GICO02
GIFFARD Andrew	S	L	ST	D	#*13	1646	..	1674	1714	GIFF02
GIFFARD Augustine	S	M	ST			..	..	..	1721	GIFF04
GIFFARD Bonaventure BP.	S	L	ST	D	#*13	1643	..	1667	1734	GIFF06
GIFFARD Edward	SJ	N	ST	R	#1	1598	1621	..	1640	GIFF10
GIFFARD John	SJ	N	MX	Y	13	1683	1705	1713	1757	GIFF14
GIFFARD Joseph	SJ	M	ST	Y	#	1620	1640	..	1673	GIFF16
GIFFARD Peter or Richard	SJ	L	ST	Y	#	1613	1633	1642	1697	GIFF18
GIFFARD Peter	S	N	SP	L		1629	..	1653	1689	GIFF20
GIFFARD Thomas	S		BK	R	#§1	1600	..	1631	1632	GIFF22
GIFFORD Gilbert	S			Q	#*x°	1560	..	1587	1590	GIFF23
GIFFORD Maurice	OP	L	MX		2	..	1659	..	1699	GIFF24
GIFFORD Wm.(Gabriel) ARCHBP.	OSB		HA	R	*‡	1558	1581	1581	1629	GIFF26
GILBERT William	SJ	M	SM	Y		1607	1627	..	1677	GILB02
GILDART George Thomas	S	W	MX	V		1764	..	1787	1827	GILD02
GILDON John	S	L	DT	L	#1	1637	..	1661	1700	GILD04
GILDON Joseph	S	L	SM	L	3	..	..	1707	1736	GILD06
GILDON Robert	S		DT	D	#3	..	..	1656	1667	GILD08
GILDON William	S	W	DT	D	#3	1680	..	1703	1743	GILD10
GILFORD see GUILDFORD										
GILLIBRAND Richard	SJ		LA	Y	3	1717	1735	1744	1774	GILL02
GILLIBRAND William	SJ	N	LA	Y	#3	1662	1682	1690	1722	GILL04
GILLIBRAND William	SJ	N	LA	Y	3	1716	1735	1743	1779	GILL06
GILLOW John	S	N	LA	D		1753	..	1779	1828	GILL10
GILLOW Thomas	S	N	LA	U	*	1769	..	1797	1857	GILL12
GILMORE Robert (Paul)	OSB	N	WT	X		..	1685	..	1748	GILM02
GILPIN Arthur	CRT		WD	D	#	..	..	1612	1630	GILP02
GILPIN Edward	S	N		D	#*3	..	..	1693	1725	GILP04
GILPIN Thomas	S	N	YO	D	#	1646	..	1668	1717	GILP06
GIRLINGTON John	S	N	YO	L	13	1657	..	1684	1729	GIRL02
GIRLINGTON John	OSB	N	LA	E	#	..	1653	..	..	GIRL04
GISLER see GEISSLER										
GITTINS Joseph	SJ	M		Y	#	1744	1762	1769	1797	GITT02
GLEWE Henry	S		SM	D	‡	..	..	1643	..	GLEW02
GLOSTER Edward	OSB		EX	E	#	..	1640	..	1652	GLOS02
GLOVER Joseph	S		LA	L		1739	..	1764	1818	GLOV02
GLYN Cadwallador or John	S		CN	R	1	1660	..	1690	..	GLYN02
GODBERY see GADBURY										
GODFREY Arthur (Michael)	OSB		SK	Z	#*4	..	1611	..	1626	GODF02
GODSALF George	S	M	SM		‡4	..	..	1576	1592	GODS02
GODSALF John	S		SM		‡	1553	..	1584	..	GODS04
GODSON Henry	SJ				4	1564	1601	..	1620	GODS06
GODWIN see GOODWIN										
GOFFE see GOUGH										
GOLDEN Richard	S		LA	R	#	1568	..	1597	..	GOLD02
GOLDING Edward, Bt.	CAP		SK		124	1599	1655	..	1666	GOLD04
GOLDING (Edward of S.Anne)	OFM	L	NT	F	123	1627	1653	1657	1688	GOLD06
GOLDING (George of S.Barbara)	OFM		NT	F	123	1630	1650	1656	1701	GOLD08
GOLDSMITH Peter	S		HA	D	#	..	..	1609	..	GOLD12
GOLTY Samuel	S	L	SK	L	#†3	..	..	1689	1725	GOLT02
GONEUTTE James	SJ		FR			1653	1688	..	1698	GONE02
GOOCH Edmund	S				7	..	..	..	..	GOOC01
GOOCH Thomas	S	L	SK	V	#†	1578	..	1603	..	GOOC02
GOOD Edward (Francis S.Peter)	OFM			F	12	1602	1624	..	1661	GOOD01
GOOD John	S		WK	R	#†	1584	..	1612	..	GOOD02
GOOD John	S		MX	L	#3	..	..	1698	..	GOOD04
GOOD Thomas	S	M	MO	L		..	..	1689	1732	GOOD06
GOODEN James	SJ			Y	*	1670	1689	1702	1730	GOOD08
GOODEN Peter	S	N	LA	L	3	1643	..	1670	1694	GOOD10
GOODEN Richard	S		DB			1668	..	..	..	GOOD12
GOODLAD (James of Holy Cross)	OP			Z	*	1641	1661	1666	1684	GOOD14
GOODMAN John VEN.	S	L	DB	D	†x4	1592	..	1631	1645	GOOD16
GOODRICK Thomas	S	N	YO	D	4	1600	..	1630	1678	GOOD18
GOODWIN James (Ignatius)	SJ	L	SM	V	#12	1601	1623	..	1667	GOOD20
GOODYEAR George (Hugh)	OFM		MX	V	12	1643	1664	..	1677	GOOD22
GOOLDE Robert	OSB	L	MX	E		1734	1755	..	1798	GOOL02

64

Name	Reg	D	Co	T	Notes	Born	Prof	Ordn	Died	Code
GORDON (Andrew)	OSB	L	SC	J		..	1755	..	..	GORD02
GORDON James (Mary of S.Mrgt)	ODC	M	SC			1702	..	..	..	GORD04
GORDON Rbt. (Peter Alcantara)	OFM		SC	F	1234	1668	1696	1700	1748	GORD06
GORDON William	OSB	N	SC	J	12	1560	1609	..	1638	GORD08
GORMLEY Patrick	OP		IR		4	..	..	..	1722	GORM02
GORSUCH George	S		LA	V	#3	1580	..	1624	..	GORS02
GORSUCH James	S	N	LA	D	#3	1683	..	1710	1739	GORS04
GOTHER John	S	L	HA	L	#1	1654	..	1676	1704	GOTH02
GOUGH John Baptist	S		FR	D	3	..	..	1730	..	GOUG02
GOUGH Stephen	ORA		SX	P	3	1605	1652	1652	1682	GOUG04
GOULDING Fortescue	S		LA	V	#	..	..	..	1676	GOUL02
GOVAERDT Christian	OSB		LC	G		..	1624	..	..	GOVA02
GOWER Henry	S	M		D	#*	1593	..	1628	1667	GOWE02
GOWER John	S		YO	R	#	1547	..	1580	..	GOWE06
GOWER William	S			D	3	..	..	1664	..	GOWE08
GRACE Patrick	S	L	IR	S	#	..	..	1722	1778	GRAC02
GRADWELL Christopher	S	N	LA	D		1709	..	1734	1758	GRAD02
GRADWELL John	S	N	CH	D		..	..	1617	..	GRAD04
GRADWELL Thomas	S	N	LA	D	#	..	..	1646	1672	GRAD06
GRAFTON Thomas (Stephen)	OFM	W	WK	F	3	1764	1780	1788	1847	GRAF02
GRAHAM (Archangelus)	CAP				6	..	..	..	..	GRAH02
GRAHAM see also GRYMES										
GRAIN Robert	CAR			D	*	..	1632	1628	1675	GRAI02
GRANGE George (Gregory)	OSB	N	YO	G	#	1598	1624	..	1673	GRAN02
GRANGE Gregory	S		YO	D	#13	1658	..	1688	1736	GRAN04
GRANGE Thomas	S	L	YO	D	#3	1648	..	1676	1722	GRAN06
GRANGE William (Gregory)	OSB	L	YO	V	#§2	1579	1603	..	1619	GRAN08
GRANHAM Edward	S	M			4	..	..	..	1760	GRAN10
GRANT James	SJ		SC			1721	1743	1752	1769	GRAN12
GRANT Robert	SJ		YO	Y	#14	1594	1618	..	1655	GRAN14
GRANT William (Killian)	OSB		SC	J		1700	1726	1724	1765	GRAN16
GRANVILLE Etienne	ODC	L			*	..	..	..	1740	GRAN18
GRATLEY Edward	S			R	#x°	1555	..	1580	..	GRAT02
GRAVENOR John	SJ		WK		#	1589	1623	..	1640	GRAV02
GRAVENOR John	S		SP	D	#	..	..	1606	..	GRAV04
GRAVENOR Walter	S		SP	V	1	1576	..	1602	..	GRAV06
GRAVENOR see also GROSVENOR										
GRAY George	SJ	M	LA	Y	1	1608	1629	..	1686	GRAY02
GRAY (Gervase)	OSB	N		Z	*	..	1611	..	1641	GRAY04
GRAY John	SJ			Y	#*1	1657	1677	1685	1705	GRAY06
GRAY (Philip of S.Clare)	OFM		ND	F		1616	1636	1642	1698	GRAY08
GRAY Robert	S		ND	R	#°	1562	..	1586	..	GRAY10
GREATON James or Joseph	SJ		MX	V	3	1679	1708	1708	1753	GREA02
GREAVES Francis	S	L	YO	D	#	..	..	1611	1673	GREA04
GREAVES John	SJ		SM	R	‡	1574	1601	1599	1652	GREA06
GREAVES Joseph (Bernard)	OSB	N	ND	G		..	1676	..	1720	GREA08
GREEN Adam	S	M	WK	Q	‡	..	..	1591	..	GREE02
GREEN Charles	S			S	3	..	..	1635	..	GREE04
GREEN Charles (Dominic)	OSB		BK	E	§	1665	1688	..	1699	GREE06
GREEN Christopher	SJ		IR	R		1629	1658	1653	1697	GREE08
GREEN Edmund	S	M	YO	D	#	1606	..	1633	1685	GREE10
GREEN Edward	SJ	L	MX	Y	#3	1647	1668	1678	1727	GREE12
GREEN Francis	S			S	34	..	..	1654	1716	GREE14
GREEN Francis	SJ	M	LA	Y	1	1744	1764	1772	1775	GREE16
GREEN Francis (Leander)	OSB	N	MO	X		..	1660	..	1704	GREE18
GREEN Henry	S	N	YO	D		1584	..	1628	..	GREE20
GREEN Hugh BL.	S	W	MX	D	#+†1	1585	..	1612	1642	GREE22
GREEN James	S		MX	D	#	1725	..	1749	1803	GREE24
GREEN John	S		ST	Q		1561	..	1585	..	GREE26
GREEN John	S			S	3	..	..	1620	..	GREE28
GREEN John (Joseph)	OP	N	LA	P	#1	1702	1721	..	1750	GREE29
GREEN John (Raymund)	OP			Z	*‡	1655	1675	1679	1741	GREE30
GREEN Martin	SJ		IR	Y		1616	1637	..	1667	GREE31
GREEN Paul	S		DE	S	#3	..	..	1602	..	GREE32
GREEN Richard	S		EX	R		..	..	1582	1590	GREE34
GREEN Richard	SJ			S	#	..	1603	..	..	GREE36

65

Name	Reg	D	Co	T	Notes	Born	Prof	Ordn	Died	Code
GREEN Richard	S	L	WR	L		1683	..	..	1750	GREE38
GREEN Stanislaus	SJ	N	MX	Y		1662	1682	1691	1720	GREE40
GREEN Stephen	S	L		R	§	1772	..	1797	1815	GREE42
GREEN Thomas	OSB			V	#*2	..	1604	..	1624	GREE44
GREEN Thomas	SJ		KT	Y		1608	1627	..	1636	GREE46
GREEN Thomas	S	L	NK	V	#1	1600	..	..	1657	GREE48
GREEN Thomas	S		LN	Q	†=	..	..	..	1591	GREE50
GREEN Thomas	CRT			C		..	..	..	1631	GREE51
GREEN Thomas BL.	S	L	OX	S	#+	1579	..	1602	1642	GREE52
GREEN Thomas	S		WR	R	#‡	1639	..	1665	1666	GREE54
GREEN William	S	L	ST	L		..	..	..	1727	GREE58
GREENHAM John	S	L	MX	V		1752	..	1775	1817	GREE66
GREENWAY Anthony	SJ	N	BU	R	#‡	1575	1611	1608	1644	GREE68
GREENWAY John	S	W	DV	V		1752	..	1777	1800	GREE70
GREENWAY Robert	S		SM	R	#	1655	..	1690	1694	GREE72
GREENWELL John Baptist	S	L	MX	D		1750	..	1777	1802	GREE74
GREENWELL Thomas	S	N	DH	L		..	..	1735	1753	GREE76
GREENWOOD Christopher	SJ	L	EX	Y	1	1584	1605	..	1651	GREE78
GREENWOOD (Gabriel)	OFM		OX	F	4	1669	1699	1706	1709	GREE79
GREENWOOD (Gregory)	OSB	M	OX	G		1670	1688	..	1744	GREE80
GREENWOOD Henry (Paulinus)	OSB		EX	G	#	1586	1612	..	1645	GREE82
GREGG John	S	L	SY	D		1760	..	1784	1811	GREG02
GREGSON (Augustine)	OSB		LA	W		..	1728	..	1779	GREG04
GREGSON Richard (Vincent)	OSB	N	LA	W		1721	1741	..	1800	GREG06
GREGSON William (Bernard)	OSB	L	LA	W		1650	1668	..	1711	GREG08
GREGSON William (Gregory)	OSB	L	LA	E		1728	1751	..	1800	GREG10
GRENE see GREEN										
GRESWOLD Thomas (Andrew)	OFM	L		F	3	..	..	1734	1770	GRES02
GREY see GRAY										
GRIFFETH Hugh	S			R		1555	..	..	1600	GRIF02
GRIFFETH John	S			D	*	..	..	1578	..	GRIF04
GRIFFETH John	S	L	MX	D		1753	..	1779	1815	GRIF06
GRIFFETH Louis	S	W	CN	S		1571	..	1595	..	GRIF08
GRIFFETH see also GRIFFITH										
GRIFFIN George	OSS		WK	L	1	1621	..	..	1695	GRIF12
GRIFFIN Nicholas	SJ	M	WK	Y	4	1672	1691	1700	1720	GRIF14
GRIFFIN Richard	S			D	*1	1574	..	1598	..	GRIF16
GRIFFIN Richard (Raymund)	OP			N		1723	1741	1747	1752	GRIF18
GRIFFITH George	SJ	W	FT	Y	13	1668	1688	1695	1718	GRIF20
GRIFFITH James	S	M	WR	L	3	..	..	1688	1735	GRIF22
GRIFFITH Michael	SJ	M	MX	N	#	1587	1607	..	1652	GRIF24
GRIFFITH Richard	SJ			R	#*	1576	1594	..	1607	GRIF26
GRIFFITH Robert	SJ		SY	R	#§	1582	1611	1607	1640	GRIF27
GRIFFITH Thomas	S	N	CH	D	#3	1665	..	1690	..	GRIF28
GRIFFITH see also GRIFFETH										
GRIFFITHS see GRIFFETH										
GRIFFITHS see also GRIFFITH										
GRIMBALDSTONE Joseph (Paul)	OSB		LA	X		1756	1777	..	1807	GRIM00
GRIMBALDSTONE (Louis)	OFM			F	1234	1657	1675	1681	1737	GRIM01
GRIMBALDSTONE Thomas Emir	S	N	LA	D		1715	..	1739	1786	GRIM02
GRIMBALDSTONE William	S	N	LA	D		1708	..	1735	1770	GRIM08
GRIMBALDSTONE Wm. (Clement)	OSB	N	LA	X		1752	1774	..	1824	GRIM10
GRIME John Edward (Cuthbert)	OSB		EX	G		1743	1764	1784	1786	GRIM12
GRIMSHAW John	S	L	IR		*8	..	..	..	..	GRIM14
GRIMSTON John	SJ	W	OX	Y	#	1576	1620	..	1649	GRIM18
GRIMSTON (Martin of St Chas.)	OFM		YO	F	123	1657	1675	1682	1729	GRIM20
GRISOLD George	S		WK	V	*	1579	..	1602	..	GRIS02
GRISOLD Richard	S			Q	*	..	..	1586	..	GRIS04
GROSSE John	SJ	M	NK	R	#†	1580	1610	1606	1645	GROS02
GROSSIER William (Romanus)	OSB		FR	E	*	..	1620	..	..	GROS03
GROSVENOR Richard	S		ST	D	#3	1646	..	1675	1726	GROS04
GROSVENOR Robert	SJ	M	YO	R	#=	1582	1620	1616	1668	GROS06
GROSVENOR see also GRAVENOR										
GROVE (Dunstan)	OSB			E	#	..	1632	..	..	GROV02
GROVE John	S	L		V	#	..	..	1691	1741	GROV04
GRYMES Richard (Ambrose Thos)	OP	L		Z	*	1647	1666	1670	1719	GRYM02

66

Name	Reg	D	Co	T	Notes	Born	Prof	Ordn	Died	Code
GRYMES see also GRAHAM										
GUILDFORD Henry	SJ	L	SX	Y	#13	1603	1625	1630	1638	GUIL02
GUILICK Nicholas	SJ		FR	Y	12	1647	1668	1674	1694	GUIL04
GUILLET Rupert	OSB				*	1595	1618	..	1629	GUIL06
GUILLIAM David	OSB		MO	E		..	1652	..	1669	GUIL08
GUILLIAM John	CRT			C		..	..	..	1672	GUIL10
GUNSTON John	S	L	MX	R	#†	1693	..	1719	1736	GUNS02
GUNTER William BL.	S	L	MO	Q	+1	1560	..	1587	1588	GUNT02
GURNAL Thomas (Adrian)	OSB	N	MX	X		1724	1763	1767	1811	GURN02
GWILLIMS see WILLIAMS										
GWINN see GWYN										
GWYN Charles	SJ	W	CN	R	#§	1582	1620	1613	1647	GWYN02
GWYN Robert	S	W	CN	D	‡	..	..	1575	..	GWYN04
GWYN Roger	S	W	CN	V		1577	..	1602	..	GWYN06
GWYN Thomas	S		CN	R		1604	..	1631	..	GWYN08
GWYN William	S	W	MO	R	‡	1576	..	1602	1640	GWYN10
HABERLEY Thomas	S			Q	*‡	..	..	1580	..	HABE02
HABERLEY Thomas	S			V	3	..	..	1620	..	HABE04
HACKET James	S		FT	L		1692	..	1715	1718	HACK01
HACKSHOTT John	S		MX	D	#	1601	..	1625	1663	HACK02
HACON Hubert	SJ		NK	Y	#3	1677	1698	1707	1751	HACO02
HADDOCK see HAYDOCK										
HADDON (Leo)	OFM			F	3	..	..	1779	..	HADD06
HADLEY John (Edmund)	OSB	N	MX	G		1744	1761	..	1807	HADL02
HADLEY Joseph (Lawrence)	OSB	N	MX	G		1739	1757	..	1805	HADL04
HAGGER William	S					..	..	..	1677	HAGG02
HAGGERSTON (Francis S.Clare)	OFM		ND	F	12	1665	1686	..	1704	HAGG03
HAGGERSTON Francis (Placid)	OSB		ND	G		1680	1701	1708	1716	HAGG04
HAGGERSTON Henry	SJ	N	ND	Y	#3	1658	1679	1688	1714	HAGG06
HAGGERSTON John	SJ	N	ND	Y	#	1661	1680	1689	1726	HAGG08
HAIME John (Hyacinth)	OP				3	1771	1793	1798	1823	HAIM02
HALDENBY Francis	S	M	YO	L		1654	..	1678	..	HALD02
HALE John	S			D	*	..	..	1613	..	HALE02
HALFORD John	S	W	MX	D	3	1753	..	1788	1806	HALF02
HALING William	S			S	#1	1600	..	..	..	HALI02
HALL Francis	S		MX	R	#	1662	..	1685	1728	HALL04
HALL Henry	S		GL	R		1672	..	1700	1748	HALL06
HALL John	S			V	*	1574	..	1599	..	HALL10
HALL John	SJ		MX	Y		1664	1683	1691	1703	HALL12
HALL John	S	W	HR	R	#§	1636	..	1662	..	HALL14
HALL Richard	S			N	†3	..	..	1570	1604	HALL18
HALL Roger (Boniface)	OSB	W	LA	X		1737	1756	..	1803	HALL20
HALL Thomas	S			Q	*	..	..	1595	..	HALL22
HALL Thomas	S		MX	D	1	1660	..	1689	1719	HALL24
HALL Thomas (Lawrence)	OFM	M		F	#3	..	..	1720	1783	HALL25
HALL William	CRT	L	MX	L	3	1658	1693	1684	1718	HALL26
HALLAM Andrew	S	M	DE	D		..	..	1617	..	HALL28
HALLEY Charles	S					..	..	..	1660	HALL29
HALLOWELL Oliver	S		LA	R	4	1556	..	1582	1600	HALL30
HALLOWES Thomas	CRT			C		..	..	..	1644	HALL32
HALSALL Arthur (Bede)	OSB		ND	G		..	1687	..	1739	HALS01
HALSALL George	SJ	M	LA	R	1	1714	1739	1738	1744	HALS02
HALSEY George	S	L	HR	R		1751	..	1775	1834	HALS04
HALSWORTH see HOLDSWORTH										
HAMBLEY John VEN.	S	W	CL	Q	#+§	..	..	1584	1587	HAMB02
HAMEL Maurice de	SJ	L	FR		*7	..	..	..	..	HAME01
HAMELYN John	S		SX	S	#1	1619	..	1644	..	HAME02
HAMERTON Gervase	SJ	N	YO	Y	23	1668	1686	1695	1708	HAME04
HAMERTON Henry	SJ		YO	Y	3	1644	1669	1678	1718	HAME06
HAMERTON Peter	SJ	M	YO	Y	#13	1637	1661	1669	1714	HAME08
HAMERTON William	SJ			Y	34	..	..	1686	1687	HAME10
HAMES (Maurus of the Cross)	OSB			Z	*	..	1630	..	1657	HAME12
HAMILTON James (Placid)	OSB	L	SC	J	1	1699	1719	..	1786	HAMI02
HAMMON Lawrence	S			S	*	1575	..	..	..	HAMM04
HANCOCK (Alexius)	OFM			F	123	1646	1675	1675	1721	HANC02
HANDS Edward	S		LE	D	#4	..	..	1612	1625	HAND04

Name	Reg	D	Co	T	Notes	Born	Prof	Ordn	Died	Code
HANDS Robert	S			D	#*	..	..	1607	..	HAND06
HANKIN John	S	N	ND	D		1706	..	1731	1782	HANK02
HANMER Francis	SJ	L	LE	Y	12	1593	1610	..	1666	HANM02
HANMER Humphrey	S	W	FT	Q	=	1546	..	1584	..	HANM04
HANMER John	SJ	L	SP	Y	#1	1663	1691	1697	1716	HANM06
HANNE Charles	SJ	N	CL	Y		1711	1731	1739	1799	HANN02
HANNES see HANDS										
HANSBIE Morgan (Joseph)	OP	L	YO	N		1663	1696	1698	1750	HANS02
HANSE Everard BL.	S	L	NN	Q	+†	..	..	1581	1581	HANS04
HANSE William	S	M	NN	Q	#	..	..	1579	..	HANS06
HASLEPP Roger	S	W	GL	D	#3	1642	..	1675	..	HANS08
HANSOM John (Anselm)	ODC	L	NK		1	1603	1625	..	1679	HANS10
HANSON William (Ildephonsus)	OSB	N	LA	S	#	..	1615	..	1644	HANS12
HARCOURT Francis	S		ST	R	#	1632	..	1657	1657	HARC02
HARCOURT Henry	SJ		LE	Y	#1	1610	1630	..	1673	HARC04
HARCOURT Valentine	S	M	ST	R	#4	1611	..	1633	1691	HARC06
HARCOURT William	S			S	3	..	..	1643	..	HARC08
HARDCASTLE Robert (John)	OSB	L	YO	W		..	1692	..	1741	HARD02
HARDCASTLE William	S	N		V	#3	..	..	1670	..	HARD04
HARDEN see HAWARDEN										
HARDESTY John	SJ		YO	Y	#	1681	1699	1711	1752	HARD10
HARDESTY Thomas (Adrian)	OSB		YO	X	#	1686	1703	..	1761	HARD12
HARDESTY William	S		YO	R	°	1559	..	1586	..	HARD14
HARDESTY William (Lawrence)	OSB	N	MX	X		1714	1732	1738	1787	HARD16
HARDING Anthony	S		WR	V	#	..	..	1621	..	HARD18
HARDING James	S		MX	V	#	..	..	1621	..	HARD20
HARDING John	OP				°7	..	..	..	..	HARD21
HARDING Robert, Jn or Richard	SJ		NT	Y	3	1701	1722	1731	1772	HARD22
HARDWICK Francis (Jn Bened't)	CAM	L	YO	R	#*2	1644	1679	1669	..	HARD26
HARDWICK George Wm Francis	S	M		D	*	1712	..	1741	1787	HARD28
HARDWICK John	S	N		Q	*	..	..	1581	..	HARD30
HARDWICK John	S	N		D		..	..	..	1678	HARD32
HARDWICK William (Francis)	OFM		YO	F	123	1649	1671	1677	1705	HARD34
HAREWELL William	S	L	SK	D	#4	..	..	1615	1640	HARE02
HAREWOOD Edmund	SJ			R		..	..	..	1597	HARE04
HARGOT Edmund	S			N	3	..	..	1570	..	HARG01
HARGRAVE James	S	N	LA	V	§	1585	..	1609	..	HARG02
HARGRAVE John	S			R	*3	1560	..	1583	1590	HARG04
HARGRAVE William	S		LA	R	#	1597	..	1622	1661	HARG06
HARGREAVES see HARGRAVE										
HARLAY Achille de BP.	ORA	L	FR		*	1581	..	..	1646	HARL02
HARLEY Thomas	S			Q	*	..	..	1592	..	HARL04
HARNAGE Henry	S	M	SP	L		1650	..	..	1737	HARN02
HARNAGE Thomas	S	L	SP	D	#	1664	..	..	1719	HARN04
HARPER (John of S.Emilian)	OSB	L		Z	*2	..	1604	..	1639	HARP02
HARPER William	S		HR	D	#	1572	..	1604	..	HARP04
HARRINGTON Mark	S	L	YO	D	#	1592	..	1616	1657	HARR02
HARRINGTON (Martin)	OFM			F		..	..	..	1624	HARR03
HARRINGTON Nicholas	SJ			S		1586	1613	..	1614	HARR04
HARRINGTON William BL.	S	L	YO	Q	+	1566	..	1592	1594	HARR06
HARRIS Anthony	S	L		D		..	..	1656	1672	HARR08
HARRIS Charles	SJ			Y		1612	1632	..	1662	HARR10
HARRIS Francis	S	L	HA	Q	°	1601	..	1625	..	HARR12
HARRIS John	S			R	*	..	..	1569	..	HARR14
HARRIS Richard (Swithun)	OSB	L	HA	E		1731	1755	..	1810	HARR16
HARRIS Thomas or John	SJ	W	MO	Y	14	1595	1619	..	1676	HARR18
HARRIS William	S	L		N	*‡3	1546	..	1575	1602	HARR20
HARRIS William	S		CB	D	#3	1647	..	1676	..	HARR22
HARRIS William	S	M	MX	R		..	..	1795	1823	HARR24
HARRISON Edmund	SJ	L	LA	Y	1	1727	1746	1755	1801	HARR28
HARRISON Edward	S	N		D	#*	..	..	1609	..	HARR30
HARRISON Henry	SJ		LC	Y		1652	1673	1682	1701	HARR32
HARRISON Henry	SJ		LA	Y	#3	1676	1698	1704	1739	HARR33
HARRISON James VEN.	S	N	DE	Q	+	..	..	1583	1602	HARR34
HARRISON James	S			Q	*	..	..	1585	..	HARR36
HARRISON John	S			Q	*x	..	..	1585	1586	HARR40

Name	Reg	D	Co	T	Notes	Born	Prof	Ordn	Died	Code
HARRISON John	S	M			7	..	..	..	..	HARR41
HARRISON John	SJ		WR	Y		1615	1636	1645	1678	HARR42
HARRISON John	SJ	L	FR	Y	#	1690	1708	1718	1725	HARR44
HARRISON John	S	N	LA	D		1714	..	1741	1780	HARR46
HARRISON John (Augustine)	OSB		YO	G		1773	1792	1800	1846	HARR48
HARRISON Matthew	S	N		D	#*4		..	1597	1599	HARR50
HARRISON Matthew or Matthias	S	N	LA	R		1638	..	1665	..	HARR51
HARRISON (Paschal)	OFM			F	3	..	..	1785	1830	HARR52
HARRISON Philip	SJ		OX			..	..	..	1578	HARR53
HARRISON Philip	SJ				#	..	1586	..	1606	HARR54
HARRISON Richard (Maurus)	OSB	N	YO	G		..	1701	1707	1717	HARR56
HARRISON William	S			R	*1	1553	..	1579	1621	HARR58
HARRISON William	S			Q	*	..	..	1581	..	HARR60
HARSNIP Thomas (Placid)	OSB		LA	X		1753	1770	1777	1807	HARS02
HART John	SJ		OX	D		..	1583	1578	1586	HART02
HART John	SJ				#4	..	..	..	1621	HART04
HART John	S	M	KT	R	#§	1627	..	1654	1695	HART06
HART Joseph (John)	OFM		LA	F	13	1760	1782	1784	1803	HART08
HART Nicholas	SJ	W	KT	R	#‡=12	1579	1604	1603	1650	HART12
HART William BL.	S	N	SM	R	+‡	1558	..	1581	1583	HART14
HART William	SJ	L	DV	Y	#34	1594	1616	1620	1624	HART16
HART William	SJ		MX	Y	#1	1640	1660	1667	1667	HART18
HARTBURN John or Rbt.(Placid)	OSB	N	DH	D	#	..	1617	1609	1655	HART20
HARTBURN Martin (Cuthbert)	OSB	N	DH	G	#4	..	1614	..	1646	HART22
HARTBURN Bernard	S	N		Q	*	..	..	1591	..	HART24
HARTLEY George	S	M	OX	L		1769	..	1794	1806	HART26
HARTLEY John	S	N			7	..	..	..	..	HART27
HARTLEY John Evangelist	SJ		MX	V	3	1716	1739	1739	1760	HART28
HARTLEY Thomas	S	M	WK	R		1740	..	1764	1781	HART30
HARTLEY William BL.	S	M	DE	Q	+‡	1551	..	1580	1588	HART32
HARTLEY William	S	M	WK	R		1742	..	1766	1794	HART34
HARTWELL Bernard	SJ		BU	Y		1607	1626	..	1646	HART36
HARVEY George	SJ		LC		7	..	..	..	..	HARV02
HARVEY John	SJ	M		Y	'#*	1632	1651	1661	1705	HARV04
HARVEY Monox	S		SK	R	#§	1699	..	1728	1756	HARV06
HARVEY Robert	S	L		V	§4	..	..	1647	1695	HARV08
HARVEY Thomas	SJ			Y	#*1	1632	1653	1662	1696	HARV10
HARWOOD Edmund	SJ		MX	R		1554	1578	..	1597	HARW02
HASELHURST Peter	S		NT	R	#†	1585	..	1615	..	HASE02
HASELWOOD James	S		NT	D	#4	1602	..	1625	1679	HASE04
HASKETT Richard	S	L	MX	R	#	1694	..	1719	1774	HASK02
HASSALL William	S	M	SP	D		1706	..	1730	1741	HASS02
HASSELS Walter	S		ST	D		1574	..	1599	..	HASS04
HATCH Thomas	S				7	..	..	..	..	HATC02
HATHERLEY John	S			D	#*34	1682	..	1710	1732	HATH02
HATHERSTY Joseph	SJ			Y	*1	1735	1753	1761	1771	HATH04
HATHORNTHWAITE Robert	S	N		L		..	..	..	1684	HATH06
HATTERSKEY see HATHERSTY										
HATTON Clare (Augustine)	OSB		NK	X		1738	1758	..	1823	HATT04
HATTON Edward (Antoninus)	OP	N				1704	1722	..	1783	HATT06
HATTON Francis	S			S	3	..	..	1620	..	HATT08
HATTON John	S			S		..	..	1617	..	HATT10
HAUGHTON Edward	SJ		LA	V	#	1602	1641	1629	1651	HAUG02
HAUGHTON Robert	CRT		MX	D	#2	1603	1631	1628	1675	HAUG04
HAUGHTON William	S		LA	D	#	1597	..	1623	..	HAUG06
HAVARD Louis	S	L	BR	T		1774	..	1800	1858	HAVA02
HAVERS John (Bartholomew)	OSB		NK	G		..	1729	..	1735	HAVE04
HAVERS Thomas	SJ		NK	Y	1	1668	1688	1696	1737	HAVE06
HAVET Louis	SJ					..	..	..	1703	HAVE08
HAWARDEN Charles	S		LA	D	#	1677	..	..	..	HAWA02
HAWARDEN Edward	S		LA	D	#	1662	..	1686	1735	HAWA04
HAWARDEN Edward	S	N	LA	D		1732	..	1758	1793	HAWA06
HAWARDEN John	S	N	LA	D		1724	..	1749	1770	HAWA08
HAWARDEN Joseph (Bernard)	OSB	W	LA	G	°3	1771	1792	1800	1851	HAWA10
HAWARDEN Michael	OFM			F	123	1664	1681	1688	1738	HAWA11
HAWARDEN Thomas	S	N	LA	D		1693	..	1719	1746	HAWA12

Name	Reg	D	Co	T	Notes	Born	Prof	Ordn	Died	Code
HAWARDEN William	S	N	LA	D	#3	1666	..	1693	1727	HAWA14
HAWETT Edmund	OSB	N	LA	E		..	1683	..	1688	HAWE02
HAWKER John	S		OX	R	#	1650	..	1673	1707	HAWK02
HAWKER John	SJ	M	MX	Y	#3	1687	1704	1713	1764	HAWK04
HAWKESWORTH Robert	S		YO	R	°	1567	..	1593	..	HAWK06
HAWKINS Francis	SJ		MX	Y		1628	1649	..	1681	HAWK08
HAWKINS Henry	SJ	L	MX	R	#	1577	1615	1614	1646	HAWK10
HAWKINS James	OSB		GL	X		..	1705	..	1752	HAWK12
HAWKINS John (Augustine)	OSB		KT	G	°	1745	1761	..	1804	HAWK14
HAWKINS Thomas	SJ	M	SX	R	#	1722	1747	1747	1785	HAWK16
HAWLET see HOWLETT										
HAWLEY James (Lawrence S.Jn.)	OFM	M	WK	F	13	1752	1769	1779	1833	HAWL04
HAWORTH Joseph (of S.Mary)	OSB		LA	W		..	1609	..	1624	HAWO02
HAY Alexander	S		SC	D		..	..	1603	..	HAYA02
HAY Richard (Augustine)	CRL	L	SC		*§4	1661	1678	1685	1736	HAYA06
HAYDOCK Cuthbert	S	M	LA	D	3	1684	..	1710	1763	HAYD02
HAYDOCK Ewan or Evan	S	N	LA	D		..	..	1575	1581	HAYD04
HAYDOCK George VEN.	S	L	LA	Q	+1	1556	..	1581	1584	HAYD06
HAYDOCK George Leo	S	N	LA	U		1774	..	1798	1849	HAYD08
HAYDOCK Gilbert	S		LA	D	3	1682	..	1709	1749	HAYD10
HAYDOCK (James)	OFM		LA	F	12	1671	1689	1697	1718	HAYD12
HAYDOCK James	S	N	LA	D		1765	..	1792	1809	HAYD13
HAYDOCK Richard	S	N	LA	D	1	1551	..	1577	1605	HAYD14
HAYDOCK Robert	OSB	N	LA	V	#1	1582	1603	..	1650	HAYD16
HAYDOCK see also HADDOCK										
HAYDON John	SJ	L	MX	Y		1603	1629	..	1663	HAYD18
HAYES John or Timothy	SJ	N	DT	D	#	1584	1617	1609	1646	HAYE02
HAYES Thomas	SJ	N	LA	Y		1746	1765	1772	1774	HAYE03
HAYES William	S	M	MX	V		1775	..	1799	1855	HAYE04
HAYMAN Richard	SJ	W	CL	Y	#1	1668	1687	1696	1756	HAYM02
HAYNES Joseph	S		EX	V	#†3	1581	..	1609	1629	HAYN02
HAYWARD (Gregory)	OSB		OX	G	1	1602	1621	1628	1632	HAYW02
HAYWOOD John	S		OX	Q		..	..	1586	..	HAYW04
HAZLE John	SJ		MX	Y	#	1621	1636	..	1649	HAZL02
HEADLAM John	S			D	#	..	..	1619	..	HEAD02
HEALEY Richard (Bonaventure)	OFM	L	MX	F	#3	1726	1744	1749	1777	HEAL02
HEARTLEY see HARTLEY										
HEATH (Augustine)	OSB		HA	W	2	..	1620	..	1631	HEAT02
HEATH Henry (Paul) VEN.	OFM		CB	F	+†2	1600	1625	..	1643	HEAT04
HEATHCOTE John	SJ		DE	R	#§	1590	1615	1614	1657	HEAT06
HEATLEY Hugh (Jerome)	OSB	W	LA	X		1757	1777	..	1792	HEAT08
HEATLEY James	SJ	N	LA	Y		1715	1735	1744	1782	HEAT10
HEATLEY John (Louis)	OSB		LA	X		1752	1776	..	1805	HEAT12
HEATLEY William (Maurus)	OSB	L	LA	X		1722	1740	1746	1802	HEAT14
HEATON Henry or John	SJ	M	LA	R	#§1	1601	1626	1625	1683	HEAT16
HEBB Edward	S	L	MX	R	1	1668	..	1692	1741	HEBB02
HEBBURN Anthony	S	L		R	#*	1567	..	1592	..	HEBB04
HEDDON George Henry	S	N		D	*	1708	..	1733	1764	HEDD02
HEIGHAM John	S		LC	R	#1	1617	..	1646	..	HEIG02
HEIGHINGTON William	S		YO	R		1563	..	1585	..	HEIG04
HELME (Gregory)	OSB	N	LA	W		..	1686	..	1696	HELM02
HELME Hugh (Bede)	OSB	N	LA	Z	#*1	1580	1604	..	1636	HELM04
HELME Richard	OSB	N	LA	G		..	1676	..	1717	HELM06
HELME Thomas (Wilfrid)	OSB	N	LA	E		..	1699	..	1742	HELM08
HELMES Edward	S	N	LA	D		1725	..	1748	1773	HELM10
HELMES see also HOLMES										
HEMERFORD Thomas BL.	S		DT	R	+‡	1554	..	1583	1584	HEME02
HEMISS John	S		ST	D	#1	1579	..	1621	..	HEMI02
HEMSWORTH George (Benedict)	OSB	N		G		..	1657	..	1702	HEMS02
HEMSWORTH John	S	N	YO	R		..	..	1579	..	HEMS04
HENRION Nicholas(Constantius)	OFM		FR	F	3	1733	1766	1779	1824	HENR02
HENSON Thomas	S			R		..	..	..	1733	HENS02
HEREDIA Martin de (Gratian)	ODC	L	PL		1	1610	1641	..	1667	HERE02
HESKETH Bartholomew (Gregory)	OSB	N	LA	W		..	1653	..	1695	HESK02
HESKETH George	S		LA	R	#§1	1598	..	1626	..	HESK04
HESKETH George	S		LA	L		1641	..	1665	1666	HESK06

70

Name	Reg	D	Co	T	Notes	Born	Prof	Ordn	Died	Code
HESKETH (Mellitus)	OSB	N	LA	W	2	1644	1664	..	1674	HESK12
HESKETH Nicholas	OSB	N	LA	W		..	1668	..	1688	HESK14
HESKETH Roger	S		LA	L	3	1643	..	1667	1715	HESK16
HESKETH (Jerome)	OSB		LA	G	#	..	1643	..	1693	HESK18
HESKETH Roger (Joseph)	OSB		LA	G		..	1681	..	1703	HESK20
HESKETH Thomas	S		LA		#3	..	..	1591	..	HESK22
HESKETH Thomas	OSB		LA	E		1655	1673	..	1694	HESK24
HESKETH Thomas	SJ		LA	Y	13	1668	..	1701	1712	HESK26
HESKETH Thomas	S		LA	L		1696	..	1720	1730	HESK28
HEVENINGHAM John	SJ		ST	Y	#	1642	1667	1673	1708	HEVE02
HEWETT John BL.	S		YO	Q	#+†	..	..	1585	1588	HEWE02
HEWETT Martin	SJ	M	DE	Y	#	1606	1627	..	1661	HEWE04
HEWLETT William	OSB	N	HA	E		..	1699	..	1747	HEWL02
HEYDON Robert	S	L	GL	P	#	1683	..	1708	1718	HEYD02
HEYLIN John Francis	S	L	DT	D	#	1715	..	1739	1753	HEYL02
HEYWOOD see HAYWOOD										
HICCOCKS John (Bede)	ODC	L	MX	N	#§	1588	1612	..	1647	HICC02
HICHIN Philip	S	M	WK	R		1670	..	1696	1736	HICH02
HICHIN William	S	M	WK	R		1635	..	1675	..	HICH04
HICKENS, HICKIN see HICHIN										
HICKFORD see HUGFORD										
HICKINS (Augustine)	OFM	W		F	3	..	..	1734	1774	HICK06
HICKINS Joseph	OFM			F	34	..	..	1728	1773	HICK08
HICKINS see also HIGGINS										
HIDE see HYDE										
HIGGINS Adam	SJ		MX		4	..	..	..	1615	HIGG04
HIGGINS (Augustine)	OFM		WR	F	123	1660	1678	1685	1707	HIGG06
HIGGINS Christopher	S	L		V	3	..	..	1708	1740	HIGG08
HIGGINS Isaac	S		MX	Q	°	1560	..	1584	..	HIGG09
HIGGINSON James	OSB	N	LA	G		1764	1785	..	1835	HIGG10
HIGGINSON Joseph	S	N	LA	D		1758	..	1783	1846	HIGG12
HIGGINSON Thomas	S		WK	R		1667	..	1690	..	HIGG14
HIGGS Charles	S	W	MX	L	3	1675	..	1702	1736	HIGG16
HILDESLEY Francis	SJ	M	OX	Y	1	1655	1675	1683	1719	HILD02
HILDRETH John	SJ		ND	Y	1	1654	1677	1690	1702	HILD04
HILDRETH William	S		DH	V	#§	1585	..	..	..	HILD06
HILDRETH William	S	N	YO	D	§	..	..	1691	1736	HILD08
HILDYARD Thomas	SJ	W	MX	Y	3	1690	1707	1716	1746	HILD10
HILL (Augustine of S.Monica)	OFM		HA	F	#123	1635	1652	1657	1702	HILL02
HILL John	S	L	MX	L	3	..	..	1703	1723	HILL04
HILL John	SJ	L	MT	Y		1683	1704	1712	1751	HILL06
HILL Richard VEN.	S	N	YO	Q	+	..	..	1589	1590	HILL08
HILL Robert	S	W	DV	R	#§4	1635	..	1661	1709	HILL10
HILL Thomas (of S.Gregory)	OSB	L	SM	R	#	1564	1613	1594	1644	HILL12
HILL William	S				7	..	..	..	..	HILL14
HILLIARD see HILDYARD										
HILLS Henry	CRT			C		..	1690	..	1730	HILL17
HILLS Robert	S	L	MX	D	#	1671	..	..	1746	HILL18
HILTON Thomas (Placid)	OSB	L	CD	D	#	1583	1610	1609	1626	HILT02
HIMSWORTH Robert	S	N	YO	D	3	1761	..	1788	1811	HIMS02
HINDE Brian	S	M	ST	D	#3	..	..	1682	1724	HIND02
HINDE Francis	S	M	LN	P	1	1716	..	1749	1810	HIND04
HINDE George	S		HT	D	#3	1684	..	1710	1752	HIND06
HIRD (Paulinus)	OSB	N	YO	G	#	..	1631	..	1645	HIRD02
HISLOP (Clement of S.Andrew)	OFM		SC	F	12	1670	1698	1703	1723	HISL02
HITCHCOCK William	OSB		BU	R	#	1625	1654	1649	1711	HITC02
HITCHMOUTH Richard	S		LA	R	#°4	1676	..	1702	1727	HITC04
HOBART (Basil of S.Catherine)	OFM			F	3	..	..	1668	1697	HOBA02
HODGES Joseph	S			Z	*	..	..	..	1747	HODG02
HODGKINSON Charles	SJ	N	LA	R	#	1700	1729	1726	1770	HODG04
HODGSON Charles	SJ		LA	Y		1742	1760	1771	1805	HODG06
HODGSON Christopher	S	N	YO	L		1729	..	1753	1765	HODG08
HODGSON Edmund	S		DH	R	#1	1608	..	1636	..	HODG10
HODGSON Francis	S	N		D	*13	1650	..	1676	1726	HODG12
HODGSON Francis	S		YO	D	#3	1682	..	1707	1733	HODG14
HODGSON George	S	N	YO		14	1632	..	..	1679	HODG16

Name	Reg	D	Co	T	Notes	Born	Prof	Ordn	Died	Code
HODGSON James	S	M	NK	D		1709	..	1736	1750	HODG18
HODGSON James	S					1742	..	..	1808	HODG20
HODGSON John	S	N	DH	D	#14	1603	..	1631	1649	HODG22
HODGSON John	SJ	N	LA	Y	13	1750	1769	1776	1807	HODG24
HODGSON Joseph	S	L	MX	D		1756	..	..	1821	HODG26
HODGSON Matthew Francis(Bede)	ODC		OX	R	#	1630	1656	1654	1667	HODG28
HODGSON (Richard of S.John)	OSB		YO	G	4	..	1614		1624	HODG30
HODGSON Samuel	S	L	YO	L		..	..	1760	1766	HODG32
HODGSON Stephen	OSB	N	DH	W		1763	1784	1788	1816	HODG34
HODGSON Thomas	SJ	N	ST	R	‡	1562	1601	1601	1646	HODG36
HODGSON Thomas	S		ST	V	#§3	1601	..	1628	..	HODG38
HODGSON Thomas	SJ		YO	Y		1682	1703	1711	1726	HODG40
HODGSON see also HODSON										
HODSKINSON see HODGKINSON										
HODSON Christopher	S		LA	R		..	..	1583	..	HODS04
HODSON John	S	N		Q	*	..	..	1584	..	HODS06
HODSON Thomas	S		YO	Q		..	..	1578	..	HODS08
HODSON Thomas	S		YO	V		1566	..	1597	..	HODS10
HODSON William	S	L		Q	*	..	..	1580	..	HODS12
HODSON see also HODGSON										
HOGG Gregory	S		YO	D		1631	..	..	..	HOGG02
HOGG John VEN.	S	N	YO	Q	+	..	..	1589	1590	HOGG04
HOGHTON see HOUGHTON										
HOLDEN Henry	S		LA	D	#4	1597	..	1622	1662	HOLD02
HOLDEN Henry	S	N	LA	D		..	..	..	1688	HOLD04
HOLDEN John	D	N			7	..	..	..	..	HOLD06
HOLDEN Joseph	S	N	LA	P		..	..	1728	1767	HOLD08
HOLDERNESS Peter (Dunstan)	OSB	N		W		1720	1741	..	1782	HOLD10
HOLDSWORTH Daniel	S		YO	R		1558	..	1583	1596	HOLD14
HOLFORD Peter	S		CH	L	#²†1	1690		1712	1722	HOLF02
HOLFORD Thomas BL.	S	L	CH	Q	#+§	1541	..	1583	1588	HOLF04
HOLFORD Thomas Francis	S			P	#	..	..	1730	1770	HOLF06
HOLIDAY Richard or John VEN.	S	N	YO	Q	+	..	..	1589	1590	HOLI02
HOLLAND Alexander	SJ	N	LA	V		1623	1651	1649	1677	HOLL02
HOLLAND George	S			S	3	..	..	1620	..	HOLL04
HOLLAND Guy	SJ	M	LN	V	#†	1587	1615	1613	1660	HOLL06
HOLLAND Henry	S		NN	Q	‡	1550	..	1580	1625	HOLL08
HOLLAND Henry	SJ	N	CH	R		1577	1609	1603	1656	HOLL10
HOLLAND John	S		LE	R		1569	..	1603	..	HOLL12
HOLLAND Joseph or Richard	SJ	W	LA	Y	1	1676	1697	1709	1740	HOLL14
HOLLAND Thomas BL.	SJ	L	LA	Y	#+13	1601	1620	1624	1642	HOLL16
HOLLAR John	SJ		MX	Y		1674	1696	1708	1712	HOLL18
HOLLOWOOD see HOLYWOOD										
HOLME Edward	SJ	N	LA	Y	#3	1740	1759	1767	1809	HOLM02
HOLME Francis	SJ	N	LA	Y	#	1724	1740	1752	1802	HOLM04
HOLME John	SJ		LA	Y	#3	1718	1737	1750	1783	HOLM06
HOLME John	S	M	LA	Y	#	1764	..	..	1826	HOLM08
HOLME Richard	S	N	LA	R	#§	1604	..	1630	1634	HOLM10
HOLMES (Germain)	OFM	N	LA	F	x123	1711	1728	1735	1746	HOLM12
HOLMES John (Edward of Cross)	OFM		EX	F	°1	1733	1758	..	..	HOLM13
HOLMES Matthew	S	W	DT	S	7	..	..	..	..	HOLM14
HOLMES Robert	S	L		Q	#*x	..	..	1580	1584	HOLM16
HOLMES Thomas	S	N	LA	S	§	1577	..	..	..	HOLM18
HOLMES Thomas	OFM	M		F	34	..	..	1713	1773	HOLM20
HOLMES see also HELME										
HOLT Alexander	S	L	LA	R	#	1629	..	1656	1680	HOLT02
HOLT Gilbert	SJ		LA	Y	13	1688	1710	1718	1725	HOLT04
HOLT William	SJ		LA	D	#‡	1548	1578	1576	1599	HOLT06
HOLTBY George	SJ		YO	R	#	1591	1617	1616	1669	HOLT08
HOLTBY John	SJ				4	..	..	..	1593	HOLT10
HOLTBY Richard	SJ	N	YO	D	#†‡	1552	1583	1578	1640	HOLT12
HOLTBY Robert	S	L	YO	R	#4	1596	..	1621	1659	HOLT14
HOLYWOOD Christopher	SJ		IR		2	1559	1582	..	1626	HOLY02
HONNACOTT Abraham	SJ		DV	R	#*	1585	1612	1610	1612	HONN02
HOOKER Thomas	S		HA	V	#	1572	..	1609	..	HOOK02
HOPE Edward	SJ		ZZ		#*	1737	1751	..	1812	HOPE02

72

Name	Reg	D	Co	T	Notes	Born	Prof	Ordn	Died	Code
HORMASA Raymond	SJ	N	ES		#	1741	1756	..	1789	HORM02
HORNBY Francis	S		BK	R	#	1633	..	1659	..	HORN04
HORNBY Robert	SJ	L	LA	Y	3	1646	1668	1676	1694	HORN06
HORNE Henry	S	L	MX	R	#	1732	..	1755	1769	HORN08
HORNE James	S	L	MX	R	#	1725	..	1750	1802	HORN10
HORNE William	SJ		GS	Y	#	1736	1753	1762	1799	HORN12
HORNER Richard VEN.	S	N	YO	D	+	..	..	1595	1598	HORN14
HORNER William	S			Q	*	..	..	1579	..	HORN16
HORNYOLD John Joseph BP.	S	M	WR	D	*	1706	..	1736	1778	HORN18
HORNYOLD Ralph	SJ	N	WR	Y	#	1674	1693	1702	1740	HORN20
HORNYOLD Thomas	S		WR	D		1664	..	..	..	HORN22
HORRABIN Thomas	S	L	LA	V		1747	..	1775	1801	HORR02
HORSLEY Thomas (Cuthbert)	OSB			W		1597	1626	..	1677	HORS02
HORSMAN James (Adrian)	OSB		YO	X		1765	1787	..	1799	HORS04
HOSKINS Anthony	SJ		HR			1568	1593	..	1615	HOSK02
HOSKINS Ralph	SJ	N	MD	Y	3	1729	1749	1764	1794	HOSK04
HOTHERSALL George	OSB	N	LA	V	#234	1560	1614	1593	1633	HOTH02
HOTHERSALL William	SJ	M	LA	Y	3	1725	1742	1751	1803	HOTH04
HOUGHTON Charles	S	N	LA	D	3	1749	..	1775	1799	HOUG02
HOUGHTON Henry	SJ	L	CH	V	#	1710	1733	1733	1750	HOUG04
HOUGHTON Richard (Bede)	OSB	N	LA	E	#	..	1642	1644	1687	HOUG06
HOUGHTON Robert (Edward)	OSB	N	LA	W		..	1710	1720	1751	HOUG07
HOUGHTON William (Hyacinth)	OP	N	LA	N		1736	1754	1760	1823	HOUG08
HOUGHTON see also HAUGHTON										
HOUNSHILL (Martin)	S	L	HA	L		1720	..	1742	1783	HOUN02
HOUSE Joseph (James S.N'olas)	OFM	M	MX	F	13	1747	1763	1773	1822	HOUS02
HOUSE William	S	L	BU	S	1	1573	..	1595	..	HOUS04
HOUSEMAN Christopher	SJ		DH	Y	#1	1726	1744	1751	1769	HOUS06
HOWARD Bernard	S	M	DE	D		1711	..	1735	1745	HOWA02
HOWARD Charles	S	L	DE	P		1717	..	1742	1792	HOWA04
HOWARD Charles	S	N	LA	P	#	1740	..	1765	1821	HOWA06
HOWARD Francis	OSB	M		W		..	1708	..	1755	HOWA08
HOWARD Henry, Hon.	S	L	NT	D	*	1684	..	1709	1720	HOWA10
HOWARD John (Placid)	OSB	L	CD	G		1698	1719	..	1766	HOWA14
HOWARD Philip (Thomas) CARD.	OP	L	MX	Z	*	1629	1646	1652	1694	HOWA16
HOWARD Richard, Hon.	S		NT	R	3	1687	..	1708	1722	HOWA18
HOWARD Rbt.(Louis of Naz'eth)	OFM		CD	F	3	1597	..	1634	1676	HOWA19
HOWARD Thomas	S			S	7	..	..	..	..	HOWA20
HOWARD Thomas	S		DE	D		..	..	1743	1746	HOWA22
HOWARD Thomas (Augustine)	OSB	L	CD	G		1644	1662	1668	1718	HOWA24
HOWARD William	SJ	N	LA	V	#	1687	1713	1713	1770	HOWA26
HOWARD William (Joseph)	OSB	M	CD	G		..	1712	..	1733	HOWA28
HOWARDEN see HAWARDEN										
HOWARTH John	S	L		D	#*	1707	..	1740	1761	HOWA30
HOWARTH see also HAWORTH										
HOWE George	S	M	ST	L		1771	..	1795	1837	HOWE02
HOWE Joseph	SJ	N	SP	Y	#3	1711	1729	1737	1792	HOWE04
HOWE William	SJ	M	SP	Y	#3	1701	1722	1731	1746	HOWE06
HOWELL John	S	W	ST	V		1765	..	1789	1810	HOWE08
HOWES John	S	N	LA	L	34	..	..	1674	1704	HOWE10
HOWES Matthew	S	W			7	..	..	..	..	HOWE12
HOWLETT John	SJ		RT	D	#‡	1545	1571	..	1589	HOWL02
HOWSE see HOUSE										
HUBBARD see HOBART										
HUDD John	SJ	M	DH		x2	1571	1620	..	1649	HUDD02
HUDDLESTON Brian	S		CD	S	6	..	..	..	..	HUDD03
HUDDLESTON John	SJ	M	MX	R	#	1597	1624	1621	1661	HUDD04
HUDDLESTON John	S	M	CB	R		1693	..	1717	1773	HUDD08
HUDDLESTON John	SJ	L	EX		#3	1636	1656	1669	1700	HUDD10
HUDDLESTON John (Denis)	OSB	L	LA	R	#2	1608	1653	1637	1698	HUDD11
HUDDLESTON Richard	OSB	N	LA	D	#2	1583	1612	1607	1655	HUDD12
HUDDLESTON William	S	N	LA	S	3	1578	..	1602	..	HUDD14
HUDDLESTON William (Denis)	OSB	N	CB	X	°	1684	1701	..	1743	HUDD16
HUDSON John (Augustine)	OSB	M	LA	W		..	1686	..	1732	HUDS04
HUDSON Joseph Augustine	S		MX	V	3	1775	..	1797	..	HUDS06
HUGFORD Henry	S	M	WR	D	4	1666	..	..	1739	HUGF02

Name	Reg	D	Co	T	Notes	Born	Prof	Ordn	Died	Code
HUGHES Edward	S	W		D	*	1546	..	1578	..	HUGH02
HUGHES Edward	S			S	*3	..	..	1602	..	HUGH04
HUGHES Edward	S	L	DV	R	#	1601	..	1631	1672	HUGH06
HUGHES Humphrey	S	W	DB	R	#4	1572	..	1599	1652	HUGH08
HUGHES John	S			D	*	..	..	1602	..	HUGH10
HUGHES John	SJ	N	MX	Y		1754	1770	1778	1828	HUGH12
HUGHES Louis	S			Q	*	..	..	1582	1596	HUGH14
HUGHES Robert	S	W		V	*4	1589	..	..	1631	HUGH16
HUGHES Stephen	S				7	..	..	..	..	HUGH18
HULL (Francis of S.Mary)	OSB		DV	W	2	..	1616	..	1645	HULL02
HULL William	S	N	LA	D	3	1751	..	1779	1835	HULL04
HULME see HELME										
HUMBERSTON Edward	SJ	L	NK	R	#1	1635	1667	1663	1707	HUMB02
HUMBERSTON Henry	SJ	M	NK	Y	#	1638	1658	1669	1708	HUMB04
HUMPHREY John	S		OX	D		..	..	1597	..	HUMP02
HUMPHREY Richard	S		CL	S		1578	..	..	..	HUMP04
HUMPHRIES John	SJ			Y		1610	1639	..	1676	HUMP06
HUNGATE Robert (Gregory)	OSB	N	YO	G		..	1610	..	1657	HUNG02
HUNGATE (Augustine)	OSB	N	YO	Z	*12	1584	1607	..	1672	HUNG04
HUNT Edward	S	L	BD	D	#3	..	..	1679	1726	HUNT02
HUNT Gilbert	SJ	M	YO	D	2	1576	1622	1605	1647	HUNT06
HUNT Joseph	S	W	SM	D	#	1762	..	1790	1838	HUNT07
HUNT Joseph	S	L	MX	D	3	1765	..	1792	1841	HUNT08
HUNT (Louis of S.Francis)	OFM			F	x1	1595	..	..	1620	HUNT09
HUNT (Peter of S.Gregory)	OSB			W		..	1616	..	1669	HUNT10
HUNT Simon	SJ					..	1578	..	1585	HUNT12
HUNT Thurstan VEN.	S	N	YO	Q	#+	..	..	1585	1601	HUNT14
HUNT Thomas	SJ	M	LN		=24	1552	1582	..	1628	HUNT16
HUNT William	S	N	YO	L	3	..	..	1707	1733	HUNT18
HUNT see also LE HUNT										
HUNTER Anthony	SJ	L	YO		#x13	1606	1649	1649	1684	HUNT20
HUNTER George	CRT		ND	V		..	1694	..	1727	HUNT22
HUNTER George	SJ		ND	Y	3	1713	1730	1744	1779	HUNT24
HUNTER Thomas	SJ	N	ND	Y	3	1666	1684	1696	1725	HUNT26
HUNTER (Thomas)	OP	L	LA	N	12	1679	1700	..	1723	HUNT28
HUNTER Thomas	SJ	N	ND	Y	#3	1718	1735	1744	1773	HUNT30
HUNTER William	SJ			Y	*	1661	1679	..	1723	HUNT32
HURST John	S	M	LA	D	3	1735	..	1761	1792	HURS02
HURST Thomas	S		LA	L	3	1774	..	1798	155	HURS04
HURST William	S		LA	D	x	1737	..	1762	1793	HURS06
HURST William	S	L	LA	L		1776	..	1800	1823	HURS08
HUSBAND William	S	L		D	#*3	..	..	1680	1725	HUSB02
HUSBAND William	S	N	YO	D	3	1743	..	1768	1779	HUSB04
HUSSEY Edward	OSB	W	DT	G		1712	1731	..	1786	HUSS02
HUSSEY James	S	W	ZZ	Y	*	1765	..	..	1810	HUSS04
HUSSEY Thomas	S		DT	R	#	1697	..	1729	1739	HUSS06
HUSSEY Thomas BP.	S	L	IR	Z	*1	1745	..	1769	1803	HUSS08
HUTCHINSON Anthony (Cuthbert)	OSB	N	YO	G		..	1723	..	1760	HUTC02
HUTCHINSON (Bonaventure)	OFM	N		F	#123	1690	1708	1714	1750	HUTC04
HUTCHINSON Joseph (Wilfrid)	OSB	N	ND	X		..	1679	..	1717	HUTC06
HUTCHINSON Matthew (Dunstan)	OSB		ND	X		..	1685	..	1730	HUTC08
HUTTON John	CRT			C		..	..	..	1651	HUTT02
HUTTON Robert	SJ		WR	R	#13	1628	1656	1653	1692	HUTT08
HUTTON Thomas (John)	OSB	N	YO	S	3	1573	1600	1598	1642	HUTT09
HUTTON Thomas (Placid)	OSB	N	DH	X		..	1714	1720	1755	HUTT10
HUTTON William (Bede)	OSB	N	DH	X		..	1713	1720	1756	HUTT12
HUTTON William (Cuthbert)	OSB	N	DH	G	#	..	1685	..	1702	HUTT14
HUXLEY George	S		CH	V	34	1581	..	1607	1607	HUXL02
HUYATH Edward	S			S	3	..	..	1608	..	HUYA02
HYDE Charles	S	L	BK	R		1683	..	1707	1745	HYDE02
HYDE Humphrey	S	L	BK	R	#	1579	..	1604	..	HYDE04
HYDE Leonard	S		BK	D		1550	..	1577	1608	HYDE05
HYDE Richard	SJ		BK	R	°12	1628	1646	..	1662	HYDE06
HYDE Richard	SJ		BK	Y	3	1687	1706	1715	1744	HYDE08
IMMES see YEMS										
INGHAM Richard (Wulstan)	OSB			E	#	..	1630	1634	1638	INGH04

Name	Reg	D	Co	T	Notes	Born	Prof	Ordn	Died	Code
INGHAM Walter	S		KT	Q		..	..	1591	..	INGH06
INGHAM see also ENGHAM										
INGLEBY Augustine	SJ	L	YO	Y		1602	1624	..	1657	INGL02
INGLEBY Charles	S	N	YO	R		1694	..	1718	1743	INGL04
INGLEBY Francis VEN.	S	N	YO	Q	+‡=	..	..	1583	1586	INGL06
INGLEBY Francis	S			V	#3	..	..	1691	..	INGL08
INGLEBY George	CRT			C		..	1597	..	1627	INGL09
INGLEBY Peter	SJ	M		Y	*13	1691	1712	1721	1741	INGL10
INGLEBY Robert	OSB		YO	W		..	1626	..	1636	INGL12
INGLEBY Thomas	S		YO	V	=	1595	..	1636	..	INGL14
INGLEBY Thomas	S	N	YO	D	3	1635	..	1664	..	INGL16
INGLEBY Thomas	SJ	W	YO	Y		1684	1703	1712	1729	INGL18
INGLEFIELD see ENGLEFIELD										
INGLETON John	S		YO	P	3	1658	..	1688	1739	INGL20
INGRAM Christopher	S		WR	Q	†4	..	..	1582	1594	INGR04
INGRAM George (Joachim or Jn)	OFM			F	34	..	..	1734	1779	INGR06
INGRAM John BL.	S	N	HR	R	#+	1565	..	1589	1594	INGR08
INGRAM John (Angelus)	OFM		WK	F	134	1742	1761	1767	1794	INGR09
INGRAM Thomas (Joachim)	OFM		WK	F	134	1737	1755	1761	1803	INGR10
IPSLEY Thomas	SJ		WT			1580	1603	..	1642	IPSL02
IRELAND Alexander	SJ	N	LA	R	#‡	1604	1638	1632	1652	IREL02
IRELAND Andrew	OFM				3	..	..	1710	1719	IREL04
IRELAND Lawrence	SJ	N	LA	Y	#	1634	1664	1672	1673	IREL06
IRELAND Richard	S		MX	P	‡	1571	..	1612	1637	IREL08
IRELAND William BL.	SJ	L	LN	Y	#+	1636	1655	1667	1679	IREL10
IRVING William	S	N	LA	V	#	1776	..	1800	1822	IRVI02
ISHAM William	S		SM	V		1578	..	1602	..	ISHA02
ISHERWOOD John (Richard)	OSB	W	LA	X	#	..	1685	..	1745	ISHE02
ITHELL John	S			Q	*	..	..	1581	..	ITHE02
ITHELL Ralph	S	L	EX	R	*†°3	1547	..	1577	1618	ITHE04
IVISON see EVISON										
JACKSON Ambrose	SJ	N	YO	Y	#	1685	1704	1712	1746	JACK02
JACKSON Anthony	S	N	YO	D	1	1666	..	..	1741	JACK04
JACKSON Bernard	S		YO	D		..	..	1604	..	JACK06
JACKSON (Bonaventure)	OFM				23	..	1618	1618	..	JACK08
JACKSON (Constantine)	OFM	N		F	123	1647	1678	1680	1717	JACK10
JACKSON	S			Q	*	..	..	1585	..	JACK12
JACKSON Francis	SJ	N	YO	D	#	1579	1608	1605	1645	JACK14
JACKSON (Gregory)	OFM	L		F	13	1666	..	1691	1731	JACK16
JACKSON John	S	L		D	#*x4	1573	..	1598	1651	JACK18
JACKSON John	SJ		MX	Y	#3	1698	1719	1728	1752	JACK22
JACKSON John	S				#	..	..	..	1732	JACK24
JACKSON (Michael)	OFM	N	LA	F	123	1653	1670	1677	1709	JACK26
JACKSON Robert	S	L	DH	R		1741	..	1766	1814	JACK28
JACKSON Thomas	SJ			Q	#*24	1564	1593	1588	1621	JACK30
JACOBSON William	SJ		FR	Y		1692	1714	1721	1764	JACO02
JAKEMAN Francis	S	M	ST	R	#§	1698	..	1725	1778	JAKE02
JAKEMAN George	S	M	ST	R	#§3	1700	..	1730	1740	JAKE04
JAMES Bartholomew	SJ					..	..	..	..	JAME02
JAMES Edward BL.	S	L	DE	R	+‡1	1559	..	1583	1588	JAME04
JAMESON Richard	S	N	LA	D	#3	..	..	1695	1734	JAME08
JAMESON Thomas	S		LA	D		1667	..	1696	..	JAME10
JANION George	SJ	N	LA	Y	#	1646	1668	1677	1698	JANI02
JANION William	SJ		LA	Y		1652	1672	1678	1685	JANI04
JANSON Richard	S		S		3	..	..	1608	..	JANS02
JANSON William	S		S		3	..	..	1620	..	JANS04
JEANES Robert	S	W	SM	D		..	..	1606	..	JEAN02
JEFFERSON Philip	OSB	N	ND	E		1732	1750	..	1776	JEFF02
JEFFERSON Robert	S	N	YO	D	3	1667	..	1695	1735	JEFF04
JEFFREY Owen	SJ	W	CN	S	#†	1591	1620	1617	1654	JEFF08
JEFFREY Thomas	SJ					1591	1620	..	1654	JEFF09
JEFFREY Thomas	SJ		MX	Y	#3	1703	1721	1730	1730	JEFF10
JEFFRIES see JEFFREY										
JENNINGS see JENNINGS										
JENISON Augustine	S	N	DH	D	#	1674	..	1701	..	JENI04
JENISON Augustine	SJ	W	DH	Y	#34	1735	1755	1762	1794	JENI06

Name	Reg	D	Co	T	Notes	Born	Prof	Ordn	Died	Code
JENISON James	SJ	W	DH	Y	3	1737	1755	1765	1799	JEN108
JENISON John	SJ	W	DH	Y	#	1729	1745	1756	1793	JEN110
JENISON Michael	SJ		LA	Y	#	1603	1622	..	1648	JEN112
JENISON Michael	S		DH	R	#	1628	..	1653		JEN114
JENISON Michael	SJ	L	DH	Y	#1	1655	1675	1683	1735	JEN116
JENISON Ralph	SJ	N	DH	Y	#1	1635	1656	1669	1719	JEN118
JENISON Robert	SJ		DH	Y	#2	1590	1617	..	1656	JEN120
JENISON Thomas	S		DH	R	#	1603	..	1637	..	JEN122
JENISON Thomas	SJ	M	ND	Y	#x§3	1643	1663	1672	1679	JEN124
JENISON Thomas	SJ		DH		#	1643	1664	1674	1701	JEN126
JENISON Thomas (Ambrose)	OFM			F	12	1686	1707		1734	JEN128
JENISON William	SJ		DH	Y	3	1653	1675	1680	1683	JEN130
JENISON see also JANION										
JENKIN (John)	OP		KT		§	1637	1660	1662	1663	JENK02
JENKINS (Augustine)	SJ		MD	Y	3	1742	1766	1773	1800	JENK04
JENKINS Peter	SJ	M	SY	Y	3	1735	1753	1762	1818	JENK08
JENKINSON Christopher	S	N	LA	L	3	..	..	1701	1723	JENK10
JENKS Silvester	S	L	WR	D	#*	1656	..	1684	1714	JENK12
JENNINGS Charles	S		EX	D	#	1628	..	1654	1677	JENN04
JENNINGS Jerome	S	M	EX	L	4	1621	..	1649	1681	JENN06
JENNINGS John	S			D	*	1577	..	1607	..	JENN08
JENNINGS John	S	L	EX	S	#3	..	..	1637	1678	JENN10
JENNINGS John (Bruno)	OSB		MX	G	#	..	1668	..	1701	JENN12
JENNINGS Michael	S	M	NN	R	*	1597	..	1628	1667	JENN14
JENNINGS Richard	SJ	M	EX	S	#3	1613	1637	1636	1643	JENN15
JENNINGS see also GENNINGS										
JENNINGTON Philip	SJ					..	..	..	1704	JENN17
JENNYNS see JENNINGS										
JERNINGHAM Francis	SJ	M	NK	Y	3	1688	1707	1714	1739	JERN02
JERNINGHAM Francis	SJ		MX	Y	3	1721	1738	1745	1752	JERN04
JERNINGHAM Hugh (Jo'ph S.Mgt)	OFM		MX	F	1	1730	1750	..	1793	JERN06
JERNINGHAM Richard	S			V	#	..	..	1629	..	JERN10
JETTER George	S	L	SK	Q	4	..	..	1581	1609	JETT02
(John Chrysostom II)	CAP		SC			..	..	..	1688	JOHN00
(John Louis d'Avancy-Danglas)	CAP				2	..	1620	..	1676	JOHN01
(John Mary of Trélon)	CAP		FR		2	..	1620	..	1647	JOHN02
(John of S.Augustine)	OSA		IR		*7	..	..	..	..	JOHN03
JOHNS Edward	S	L			7	..	..	..	..	JOHN04
JOHNSON Cuthbert	S	N	DH	Q	#	..	..	1583	..	JOHN05
JOHNSON Edward	OSB		MX	R	#	1623	1663	1650	1683	JOHN06
JOHNSON Emmanuel	S		SP	R	#	1559	..	1603	..	JOHN08
JOHNSON George	OSB	M	WK	G		1748	1768	..	1803	JOHN10
JOHNSON James	S	N	LA	D	3	1745	..	1771	1790	JOHN12
JOHNSON John	SJ	M				..	..	..	1614	JOHN14
JOHNSON John	S	M	YO	D	3	1657	..	1689	1739	JOHN16
JOHNSON Joseph	SJ	M		Y		1737	1758	1764	1817	JOHN18
JOHNSON Lawrence BL.	S	N	LA	D	#+‡	..	..	1577	1582	JOHN20
JOHNSON (Placid)	OSB		YO	W		..	1652	..	1668	JOHN24
JOHNSON Richard	S		YO	D	#§	1562	..	1603	..	JOHN26
JOHNSON Robert BL.	S	L	SP	D	*+	..	..	1576	1582	JOHN28
JOHNSON Robert	S	N	DH	D	3	1724	..	1753	1799	JOHN30
JOHNSON Robert	SJ	N	LA	Y		1745	1764	1771	1823	JOHN32
JOHNSON Thomas	S	N		V	#3	..	..	1708	1750	JOHN34
JOHNSON William	SJ			V	*2	..	1596	1596	1614	JOHN36
JOHNSON William	OSB	L	DH	Z	#1	1580	1600	..	1663	JOHN38
JOHNSON William	S	N	DH	V	°3	..	..	1603	..	JOHN39
JOHNSON see also JACKSON										
JOHNSON see also JENISON										
JOHNSTON (Dominic Thomas)	OP		SC		*3	..	1670	1645	1685	JOHN42
JOHNSTON Henry (Joseph)	OSB	L	YO	E	§	..	1675	..	1723	JOHN43
JOHNSTON James (Oswald)	OSB	N	LA	X		1750	1772	..	1818	JOHN44
JOLLEY (Alexius)	OFM	W		F	#123	1678	1695	1702	1757	JOLL02
JOLLEY (Andrew)	OFM			F	1234	1676	1688	1696	1730	JOLL04
JONES Edward BL.	S	L		Q	*+§	..	..	1588	1590	JONF02
JONES Edward	S		ST	L		1669	..	1691	1738	JONF04
JONES Edward	S	W	MO	D	3	1747	..	1774	1799	JONF06

Name	Reg	D	Co	T	Notes	Born	Prof	Ordn	Died	Code
JONES George	S		MO	D	#1	1657	..	..	..	JONE08
JONES (Gregory)	OFM	N		F	#123	1652	1669	1676	1724	JONE10
JONES James	SJ		WR	D	#	1573	1623	1612	1636	JONE12
JONES James Augustine	S		MX	R	§	1690	..	1719	1737	JONE14
JONES John	SJ	N		Y	*3	1683	1709	1718	1748	JONE16
JONES John	SJ	L	MO	Y	3	1721	1739	1752	1803	JONE18
JONES John	S	N	LA	D	13	1733	..	1760	1786	JONE20
JONES John	S		MX	D	§3	1760	..	1787	1840	JONE22
JONES John (Alexius)	OSB	M	MX	G		1679	1699	1705	1755	JONE24
JONES John (Francis Mary)	CAP		MX		1	1724	..	..	1799	JONE25
JONES Jn (Godfrey Maurice) ST	OFM	L	CN		#*+	1559	1591	..	1598	JONE26
JONES John (Albert)	OFM		HA	F	123	1747	1764	1772	1793	JONE27
JONES John (Leander)	OSB	L	BR	Z	#*‡	1575	1600	..	1635	JONE28
JONES Joseph	S		MX	R		1714	..	1740	1760	JONE30
JONES Lawrence	S	W		V	#1	1620	..	1646	1679	JONE32
JONES Peter	OFM	M		F	#13	1759	..	1795	1827	JONE36
JONES Philip	S	W	MO	D	#	1722	..	1746	1800	JONE40
JONES Robert	SJ	W	DB	R	#	1564	1583	..	1615	JONE42
JONES Robert	S	L	FT	D	#	1646	..	1672	1714	JONE44
JONES Walter	S		MO	V	3	..	..	1647	..	JONE45
JONES William	S	W		D	*	..	..	1603	..	JONE46
JONES William (Benedict)	OSB	L	MX	D	#§2	..	1604	1598	1639	JONE48
JONES William Constantine	S			D	#*	1697	..	1723	1735	JONE50
JORIS Henry John	SJ	W	MX		#	1733	1752	..	1796	JORI02
JORIS Peter Andrew	SJ		MX			1735	1753	..	..	JORI04
(Joseph of the Assumption)	ODC	M			8	..	..	..	..	JOSE02
(Joseph of S.John Bpt)	ODC				4	..	..	..	1731	JOSE04
JOSSAER Bernard	SJ	N	FR	Y	#	1712	1731	1739	1775	JOSS02
JOSSAER Michael	SJ		FR	Y	13	1708	1727	1736	1759	JOSS04
JOWSEY Andrew	S	N	YO	D	1	1646	..	1674	..	JOWS02
JOWSEY John	S	N	YO	D		..	..	1647	1678	JOWS04
JOY Matthew	SJ	N		Y	*	1742	1761	..	1798	JOYA02
JOYEUSE Henri (Angelus) de	CAP		FR	P	*	1563	1587	..	1608	JOYE02
JUKES John	SJ	M	SP	R	#°23	1580	1624	1616	..	JUKE02
JULIAENS Peter (Charles)	OFM	L	LC	F	3	1735	1757	1764	1807	JULI02
(Julian of Garneston)	CAP		SC			..	..	..	1641	JULI04
JUMP Gilbert	CRT		LA	C		1705	1726	..	1772	JUMP02
JUMP Richard	SJ		CH	Y	#3	1714	1736	1743	1755	JUMP04
KAYE James (Ambrose)	OSB	N	LA	W		1717	1735	..	1777	KAYE02
KAYE Thomas	S	N	YO	L	3	1768	..	1795	1838	KAYE06
KAYE see also KEYS										
KEARNEY (Christopher Cashel)	CAP		IR			1582	..	..	1656	KEAR01
KEARNEY Francis	OFM		IR	N	12	1667	1689	1694	1747	KEAR02
KEARNEY George	S		MX	R		1676	..	1701	..	KEAR04
KEARTON John	OP	L		N		1733	1754	..	1800	KEAR08
KEATING (Ambrose)	OFM	L			*8	..	..	..	..	KEAT02
KEEL Thomas	SJ		BU			1577	1617	..	1651	KEEL02
KEELING Thomas	S		ST	D	#	..	..	1601	..	KEEL04
KEIGHTLEY William	S		HT	D	3	1667	..	1692	1696	KEIG02
KELLAM (Joachim)	OFM		LC	F	123	1657	1676	1686	1703	KELL02
KELLET Henry	S	N	LA	V		1763	..	1787	1808	KELL06
KELLET Robert (Augustine)	OSB		LA	E		1731	1751	..	1809	KELL08
KELLISON Matthew	S		NN	R	#	1561	..	1587	1641	KELL10
KELLY (Dominic)	OP	L	IR		*7	..	..	..	..	KELL11
KELLY Francis	OSA		IR		*7	..	..	..	..	KELL14
KELLY John Jseph	SJ	N	IR	Y	#°3	1743	1762	1769	1808	KELL16
KELLY John (Louis S.Dominic)	OFM	M	MX	F	13	1748	1766	1779	1808	KELL18
KEMBLE Francis (Simon Stock)	ODC		HR	R	13	1652	1671	1676	1720	KEMB02
KEMBLE George (Francis)	ODC		HR	R	1	1633	1652	..	1711	KEMB04
KEMBLE John ST.	S	W	HR	D	#+	1599	..	1625	1679	KEMB06
KEMBLE Roger (John Joseph)	ODC		HR		°	1640	1659	..	..	KEMB08
KEMBLE Walter (William)	OSB	W	HR	G		..	1620	..	1633	KEMB10
KEMBLE William (Augustine)	OFM	M	HR	F	13	1745	1761	1770	1801	KEMB12
KEMELE (Peter of S.Joseph)	OFM		LC	F	124	1624	1648	..	1653	KEME02
KEMP David	OSS		CL	Q	#2	..	1588	1581	1615	KEMP02
KEMP Francis	S			V	*3	..	..	1598	1598	KEMP04

Name	Reg	D	Co	T	Notes	Born	Prof	Ordn	Died	Code
KEMP Francis (Boniface)	OSB	N	MX	Z	*4	1578	1604	..	1644	KEMP06
KEMP George	S	L	MX	R	#	1626	..	1651	1698	KEMP08
KEMP Henry	SJ	M	SX	Y	#	1672	1692	1700	1737	KEMP10
KEMPER Herman	SJ	N	GS	Y		1745	1766	1774	1811	KEMP12
KEMYS David (Joseph)	OP	L	MO	R	x	..	..	..	1680	KEMY01
KEMYS John	S	W	MT	R	#	1635	..	1658	1709	KEMY02
KEMYS Thomas	OSB		SM	R	#‡2	1575	1612	1603	..	KEMY04
KENDALL George	S	N	LA	D		1698	..	1722	1766	KEND02
KENDALL Henry	S	N	LA	D		1689	..	1716	1752	KEND04
KENDALL Hugh	S	M	LA	D		1708	..	1736	1781	KEND06
KENDALL Richard	S	L	LA	D		1709	..	1735	1780	KEND08
KENDALL Richard	S	L	LA	D	3	1685	..	1710	1748	KEND10
KENDALL Richard (Peter)	OSB	M	SM	G		1758	1779	1782	1814	KEND12
KENDALL Robert	S	N	LA	D		1700		1724	1746	KEND14
KENDALL Thomas	SJ		DV	Y		1612	1635	..	1672	KEND16
KENNEDY Francis	S		MX	D		1723	..	1748	1791	KENN02
KENNEDY William (Joseph), Bt.	OSB		IR	E	§	1661	1692	1694	1738	KENN04
KENNET Brian	S	L	DH	D	#3	..	..	1680	1724	KENN06
KENNET Charles	SJ	L	DH	Y	1	1660	1681	1689	1728	KENN08
KENNET Francis (Joseph)	OSB	N		W		..	1685	..	1709	KENN10
KENNET Henry	S	N	DH	D	3	1667	..	1691	1743	KENN12
KENNET Samuel (Bartholomew)	OSB		KT	R	#§4	1563	1603	1589	1635	KENN14
KENNET Samuel (Joseph)	OP				4	1659	1681	..	1694	KENN16
KENSINGTON Thomas	SJ			S	3	..	1629	1618		KENS02
KENT Robert	S		LN	R	#§	1643	..	1667	1687	KENT02
KENYON Edward	S	W	LA	V	3	..	..	1599	..	KENY02
KENYON Edward	S	N	LA	D		1761	..	1789	1837	KENY04
KENYON Thomas (Anselm)	OSB	M	LA	X		1770	1787	1794	1850	KENY06
KEOGH (Thaddeus)	OP				*7	..	..	..	..	KEOG02
KERKE see KIRK										
KETTLEBEATER (Louis)	ODC	L			7	..	..	..	..	KETT02
KEYNES Alexander	SJ		SM	R	#	1642	1669	1665	1713	KEYN02
KEYNES Charles	SJ		SM		#3	..	1663	1671	1673	KEYN04
KEYNES Edward	SJ	N	SM	Y	12	1608	1627	..	1665	KEYN06
KEYNES George	SJ		SM		‡	1553	1593	..	1611	KEYN08
KEYNES George	SJ		SM	R	#	1628	1649	1654	1659	KEYN10
KEYNES John	SJ	L	SM		1	1624	1645	..	1697	KEYN12
KEYNES Maurice	SJ		SM		1	1591	1616	..	1654	KEYN16
KEYNES Maximilian	SJ		MX	Y	#	1652	1674	1683	1720	KEYN18
KEYS Peter	S		LA	L	3	..	..	1693	..	KEYS02
KIERNAN William	S			S	*3	..	..	1720	..	KIER02
KIGHLEY Thomas	S	L	EX	V	#=3	1577	..	1611	..	KIGH02
KILLINGBECK Robert	OSB	N	YO	X		1630	1653	..	1710	KILL02
KILLINGHAM Thomas	S			S	3	..	..	1617	..	KILL04
KIMBER Thomas	SJ	W	OX	Y		1688	1706	1716	1742	KIMB02
KIMBERLY John (Thomas)	OP	L				1734	1762	..	1792	KIMB04
KINASTON see KYNASTON										
KINDER (Augustine)	OSB	W	NT	G		1596	1621	..	1676	KIND02
KING Ernest	SJ					1714	..	..	1762	KING01
KING Richard	OSB	W	BD	E	#	..	1639	1639	1664	KING02
KING William	S			S	3	..	..	1605	..	KING06
KINGDON Abraham	SJ		MX	Y	3	1718	1737	1745	1782	KING08
KINGDON John	SJ		SM	Y		1716	1735	1743	1761	KING10
KINGSLEY Ignatius George	SJ		CH	R	#3	1701	1720	1735	1787	KING12
KINGSLEY Owen Joseph	SJ	M	CH	Y	13	1697	1716	1725	1739	KING14
KINGSLEY Thomas	SJ	L	KT	Y	#‡4	1650	1676	1684	1696	KING16
KINGSLEY Thomas	SJ	L	CH	Y	3	1705	1723	1732	1781	KING18
KINGSLEY William	SJ	N	MX	Y	3	1696	1713	1721	1734	KING20
KINGTON Thomas (Pacificus)	OFM	W	WK	F	13	1754	1770	1779	1827	KING22
KINN Edward	S	M	GL	D	#§	1625	..	1653	1711	KINN02
KINN John	S	M	GL	D	#§	..	..	1643	1683	KINN04
KINSMAN Bernard	SJ	M	MX	Y		1611	1626	..	1668	KINS02
KINSMAN Edward	S		MX	D		..	..	1627	..	KINS04
KINSMAN Michael	SJ	M	MX	Y		1614	1631	..	1694	KINS06
KIRBY George	S	L	MX	R		1739	..	1763	1784	KIRB02
KIRBY Henry	S	M	FR	R		1712	..	1735	1767	KIRB04

78

Name	Reg	D	Co	T	Notes	Born	Prof	Ordn	Died	Code
KIRBY Lawrence	OSB	N	LA	W		..	1715	..	1743	KIRB06
KIRBY Luke ST.	S		YO	D	+	1548	..	1577	1582	KIRB08
KIRBY Peter	S				7	..	..	..	..	KIRB10
KIRK Francis	S	N		V	#	..	..	1669	1721	KIRK02
KIRK James	S			S	3	..	..	1631	..	KIRK04
KIRK John	S		SP	R		1760	..	1784	1851	KIRK06
KIRK Thomas	SJ	M		Y	*1	1665	1689	1696	1718	KIRK08
KIRKHAM Henry	SJ	N		R	#*	1575	1605	1601	1646	KIRK10
KIRKHAM Richard	SJ		LA	Y	#	1671	1691	1700	1708	KIRK12
KIRKMAN Richard BL.	S	N	YO	Q	+	..	..	1579	1582	KIRK14
KIRSOPP William (Peter)	OP		ND	R		1670	1687	1694	1705	KIRS02
KIRWAN Walter Black	S	L	IR	N	*°	..	..	1775	1805	KIRW02
KITCHEN Edward	S	N	LA	D	#3	..	..	1675	..	KITC01
KITCHEN Edward	S		LA	D	1	1705	..	1731	1732	KITC02
KITCHEN Edward	S	N	LA	D	#	1747	..	1771	1793	KITC04
KITCHEN John	S	N	LA	D	3	1741	..	1770	1793	KITC06
KNAPP Joseph	S	L	HA	D		1747	..	1775	1817	KNAP02
KNARESBOROUGH Ch'pher or Rchd	S	L	YO	S	3	..	..	1603	..	KNAR02
KNARESBOROUGH John	S	N	YO	D	3	1672	..	1699	1722	KNAR04
KNATCHBULL John	SJ		KT	S	#34	1571	1618	1602	1631	KNAT02
KNATCHBULL Robert	SJ	N	MD	Y		1716	1735	1742	1782	KNAT04
KNIGHT Christopher	S	N		R	*	1565	..	1591	..	KNIG02
KNIGHT Francis (Benedict)	OSB		LN	X		1716	1733	..	1743	KNIG04
KNIGHT George	SJ	W	SM	Y		1733	1754	1761	1790	KNIG06
KNIGHT James	S					..	..	..	1667	KNIG07
KNIGHT James (Dunstan)	OSB	M	LN	X		1714	1732	..	1787	KNIG08
KNIGHT John	S		BU	D	#	..	..	1601	..	KNIG10
KNIGHT John	S		WK	R	#‡	1633	..	1657	1657	KNIG12
KNIGHT Nicholas	S			Q	*	..	..	1584	..	KNIG14
KNIGHT Richard	SJ	M	LN	Y	#3	1720	1739	1746	1793	KNIG16
KNIGHT William (Nicholas)	OFM		SM	F	3	1730	1750	1758	1806	KNIG18
KNIGHTLEY Andrew	S	L	WK			..	..	..	1660	KNIG20
KNIGHTLEY John (Maurus)	OSB	L	WK	X		..	1670	..	1708	KNIG22
KNIPE William	S		WT	D	3	1643	..	1667	..	KNIP02
KNOWLES Gilbert	OSB	N	HA	G		1667	1692	1700	1734	KNOW02
KNOWLES John	SJ		ST	Y		1607	1624	..	1637	KNOW04
KORSACK Norbert	SJ	N	ZZ	Z	*2	1773	1787	..	1846	KORS02
KYNASTON Roger	S	W	SP	R		1649	..	1675	1712	KYNA02
KYNNE see KINN										
LABROSSE Joseph (Angelus)	ODC	L	FR		23	1636	1655	1660	1697	LABR02
LACEY Francis	S	L	MX	R	#3	1686	..	1712	1774	LACE01
LACEY William BL.	S	N	YO	R	+1	1531	..	1581	1582	LACE02
LA COLOMBIERE Claude de BL.	SJ	L	FR	P	3	1641	1659	1670	1682	LACO02
LACON Edward	S	L	SP	R	#	1615	..	1641	1679	LACO04
LACON John	S		SP	R	#	1610	..	1635	..	LACO06
LACON Richard	S		SP	R		1640	..	1666	..	LACO08
LACON Rowland (Michael)	OSB	N	SP	G		1744	1761	..	1807	LACO10
LA CROIX Stephen	SJ		FR		4	1706	..	..	1761	LACR02
LA FONTAINE see FONTAINE										
LA FUENTE see FUENTE										
LAITHWAIT Edward	SJ	W	LA	R	#§	1584	1615	1612	1643	LAIT02
LAITHWAIT Francis	SJ		LA		#24	1589	1607	..	1624	LAIT04
LAITHWAIT Thomas	SJ	L	LA	S	#3	1577	1607	1604	1655	LAIT06
LAKE James Louis	OP			N	1	1709	1736	1738	1748	LAKE02
LALART John Bapt.	SJ	L	FR	Y	#3	1693	1715	1723	1743	LALA02
LAMB Anthony	SJ		HA	R	#	1592	1617	1617	1668	LAMB01
LAMB John Augustine	S	M	MX	R	#	1742	..	1765	1809	LAMB02
(Lambert of Fliscour)	CAP	L	FR		2	..	1619	..	1654	LAMB03
LAMBERT (Alexander)	OFM		YO	F	1234	1658	1670	1682	1707	LAMB04
LAMBERT (Anthony of S.Marg't)	OFM		YO	F	12	1671	1688	1697	1714	LAMB05
LAMBERT John	S		LA	R	#	1600	..	1628	1631	LAMB06
LAMBTON Joseph VEN.	S	N	YO	R	+	1568	..	1592	1592	LAMB08
LA MOTTE DU PLESSIS Daniel BP	S	L	FR		*	..	..	..	1628	LAMO02
LANCASTER Francis	S	M		D	#4	..	..	1604	1656	LANC02
LANCASTER Francis (Anthony)	OFM		LA	F	13	1728	1746	1751	1758	LANC03
LANCASTER George	OFM	M		F	3	..	..	1722	1766	LANC04

Name	Reg	D	Co	T	Notes	Born	Prof	Ordn	Died	Code
LANCASTER George (Oswald)	OFM		LA	F	134	1734	1760	1767	1784	LANC06
LANCASTER James	S	N	LA	D		1768	..	1793	1827	LANC08
LANCASTER Oswald	S		LA	D		1715	..	1741	1753	LANC10
LANCASTER Roger	S		SM	Q		..	..	1584	1598	LANC12
LANCASTER Thomas	S	N	LA	R		1690	..	1717	1752	LANC14
LAND Thomas	SJ		SK	Y	12	1582	1612	..	1632	LAND02
LANE Bonaventure	SJ	N	HA	Y	13	1684	1706	1717	1750	LANE02
LANE George	S		NT	D	34	1669	..	1702	1702	LANE04
LANE James	SJ	M	WR	Y		1737	1758	1769	1821	LANE06
LANE Richard	S	L	SX	V	#3	1585	..	1608	1656	LANE08
LANE Thomas	S	M	BU	V	#‡3	1582	..	1609	..	LANE10
LANE William	SJ	L	NK	V	1	1671	1699	1696	1752	LANE12
LANE see also LAND										
LANGDALE Jordan (Maurus)	OSB		YO	G		1733	1751	..	1760	LANG02
LANGDALE Marmaduke	SJ	N	LA	Y		1748	1766	1776	1786	LANG04
LANGDALE Thomas	SJ				°	..	1562	..	..	LANG06
LANGDON William	S		SM	Q		..	..	1582	..	LANG08
LANGHORN Benjamin	S			D	*	1566	..	1603	..	LANG10
LANGHORN Charles	S	L	MX	V	#	1660	..	1683	1723	LANG12
LANGHORN Francis	S	L	MX	V	#	..	..	1682	1709	LANG14
LANGLEY John	S			S		..	..	1660	..	LANG16
LANGTON John (Ambrose)	OSB		MX	W	24	..	1615	..	1620	LANG18
LANGTON John (Bonaventure)	OFM		LA	F	1234	1602	1630	1633	1634	LANG19
LANGTON Thomas	S		LA	R	#	1642	..	1669	1710	LANG20
LANGTREE Richard	S	N			7	..	..	..	..	LANG21
LANGWORTH Anthony	CRT			C	2	..	1626	..	1639	LANG22
LANGWORTH Anthony (Bern'dine)	OFM	N	LA	F	123	1643	1666	1671	1702	LANG23
LANGWORTH Basil	SJ		LN	V	#	1632	1661	1657	1683	LANG24
LANMAN Henry	SJ		SK	R	#§	1573	1606	1603	1614	LANM02
LANSANCH (Peter John) de	OFM		LC	F	12	1644	1675	..	1691	LANS02
LA POLE see POLE										
LASCELLES Christopher	S	N	YO	Q		..	..	1588	..	LASC02
LASCELLES John	S	N	YO	D	#4	1600	..	1625	1663	LASC04
LASCELLES Ralph	S		YO	D	#3	1612	..	1641	..	LASC06
LASCELLES Richard	S		YO	D	#	1603	..	1632	1668	LASC08
LASCELLES Thomas	S	N	YO	D	#	1599	..	1624	..	LASC10
LATHAM Christopher	S	N		D	3	..	..	1679	..	LATH02
LATHAM Frederick (Alexius)	OSB		GS	X		..	1743	..	1761	LATH04
LATHAM (Gabriel)	OSB		LA	E		..	1622	1627	1635	LATH06
LATHAM George (Joseph)	OSB	W	LA	D		..	1617	1615	1646	LATH08
LATHAM Henry (Augustine)	OSB	L	LA	E		1619	1640	1642	1677	LATH10
LATHAM John	S	N		V	#3	..	..	1629	..	LATH12
LATHAM Thomas (Torquatus)	OSB		LA	Z	*	..	1606	..	1624	LATH14
LATHAM (Vincent)	OSB		LA	G		..	1622	..	1640	LATH16
LATHAM William (Swithbert)	OSB	N	LA	D		..	1614	1612	1640	LATH18
LATHOT Henry	S		LA	R	#3	1626	..	1650	..	LATH20
LAUGHTON John	S				7	..	..	..	..	LAUG02
L'AUNAY Alambert	SJ		FR			..	..	..	1789	LAUN02
LAURENSON James	S	N	LA	D	3	1752	..	1780	1828	LAUR04
LAURENSON John	SJ	N	EX	Y	3	1760	1803	1788	1834	LAUR06
LAURENZO Augustine	SJ	L	PL		7	..	..	..	..	LAUR08
LAW John	S	L		T	*	1768	..	1794	1832	LAWA04
(Lawrence of St Thomas)	ODC	L			7	..	..	..	..	LAWR02
LAWRENCE John	S	L			7	..	..	..	..	LAWR04
LAWRENCE Thomas	CRT			C		..	1570	..	1589	LAWR05
LAWRENSON see LAURENSON										
LAWSON Christopher	S	N		D		..	..	..	1675	LAWS02
LAWSON Francis	OSB	N	YO	G		..	1650	..	1712	LAWS04
LAWSON Henry	SJ	N	ND	Y	#x§	1628	1656	1662	1679	LAWS06
LAWSON Henry	OSB	N	YO	G		1763	1785	1788	1829	LAWS07
LAWSON Peter	S				7	..	..	..	..	LAWS08
LAWSON (Richard of Magdalen)	OFM			F		..	..	..	1696	LAWS09
LAWSON Thomas	SJ	N	YO	Y	#	1666	1684	1691	1750	LAWS10
LAWSON Thomas	SJ	L	YO	Y	3	1720	1736	1744	1807	LAWS12
LAWSON Thomas (Augustine)	OSB	N	YO	G		1758	1779	1783	1830	LAWS14
LAWSON William (Benedict)	OSB		YO	X		..	1685	..	1737	LAWS16

Name	Reg	D	Co	T	Notes	Born	Prof	Ordn	Died	Code
LAYFIELD Christopher	S	M	LA	D		1713	..	1742	1761	LAYF02
LAYFIELD James	S	M	LA	R		1701	..	1726	1756	LAYF04
LAYTON John	SJ	N	YO	R	#1	1588	1614	1611	1624	LAYT02
LAYTON John	S			S	3	..	..	1617	..	LAYT04
LAYTON John	S	N		S	3	..	..	1642	..	LAYT06
LAYTON Thomas	SJ		DE	Y	#1	1592	1614	..	1661	LAYT08
LAYTON William	S	N	MX	L	#	1638	..	1661	1689	LAYT10
LAZENBY John	SJ	L	OX	Y	#	1655	1675	1683	1724	LAZE02
LEADBITTER Edward	OP	N	ND	N	#	1747	1770	..	1788	LEAD02
LEADBITTER Jasper (Dalmatius)	OP	N	ND	N	3	1749	1772	1775	1830	LEAD04
LEADBITTER (John)	OP	N	ND	N	3	1740	1767	1769	1811	LEAD06
LEADBITTER (Matthew)	OP		ND	N		1702	1724	1726	1735	LEAD08
LEADBITTER Nicholas(Hyacinth)	OP	N	ND	N		1722	1743	1745	1768	LEAD10
L'EAU Louis de	OFM		LC	F	123	1685	1706	1722	1757	LEAU02
LE BRETON (Germain)	CAR	L	FR			1645	1664	..	..	LEBR02
LECHMERE Edmund	S		HR	D	#‡1	1586	..	1622	1640	LECH02
LECKONBY Richard	SJ	N	LA	Y	3	1699	1720	1729	1771	LECK02
LECKONBY Thomas	SJ		LA	Y	3	1707	1721	1730	1734	LECK04
LECKONBY Thomas	SJ	N	LA	Y	3	1717	1736	1744	1778	LECK06
LE COURAYER Pierre Francois	S	L	FR		*3	1681	..	1706	1776	LECO02
LE DIEU (Peter)	OFM			F	123	1684	1706	1712	1730	LEDI02
LEE Augustine	OSB	L	SY	S	#3	..	1624	1603	1640	LEEA02
LEE Benjamin Charles	CRT		MX	D	#	1674	1714	1716	1740	LEEA04
LEE Edward	S			S	3	..	..	1614	..	LEEA06
LEE Francis	S	L	ST	D		1759	..	1785	1830	LEEA08
LEE George (John Bapt)	CRT			C		1749	1769	..	..	LEEA10
LEE John	SJ	W	KT	Y		1657	1678	1686	1687	LEEA12
LEE John	S	L		D	*3	1739	..	1762	1821	LEEA14
LEE John	S	L	MX	D		1768	..	1793	1839	LEEA16
LEE Joseph	S	W	MX	D		1765	..	1789	1840	LEEA18
LEE Roger	SJ		BU		#	1568	1600	..	1615	LEEA22
LEE Stephen	S	M	ST	D	#	..	..	1622	1671	LEEA24
LEE William	S			D	*	..	..	1613	..	LEEA26
LEE William	S		MX	R	#	1671	..	1696	..	LEEA28
LEE see also LEIGH										
LEECH Humphrey	SJ	N	SP	R	#‡	1571	1618	1612	1629	LEEC02
LEEDES Edward	SJ	L	SX	R	#1	1598	1621	..	1677	LEED02
LEEDES Thomas	SJ		SX	R	#‡	1594	1618	1618	1668	LEED04
LEEK Gilbert	S	W		V	#	..	..	1629	..	LEEK02
LEEK Thomas	S	L	ST	V	#‡	1565	..	1596	1638	LEEK04
LE FEVRE George	SJ	L	SC		#	..	..	..	1703	LEFE02
LEGATT (Amatus)	OSB		DT	G	4	..	1625	..	1633	LEGA06
LEGATT John	SJ		WT	Y	#	1615	1635	..	1672	LEGA08
LEGGE William	S	L	HA	Q	#	1561	..	1587	..	LEGG02
LE GRAND (Anthony of Padua)	OFM	M	LC	F	123	1628	1648	1653	1699	LEGR02
LE GRAND James (Joseph)	OSB	N	MX	R	#§	1711	1737	1734	1772	LEGR04
LE HUNT Edward	S	M	RT	R	#	1641	..	1667	..	LEHU02
LE HUNT John	SJ	N	HU	Y	#	1675	1693	1703	1759	LEHU04
LE HUNT William	S	L	MX	R		1668	..	1696	..	LEHU06
LEIGH Alexander	SJ	N	LA	Y	#	1681	1700	1710	1748	LEIG02
LEIGH Christopher (Francis)	ODC	L		N	*x1	1600	1621	..	1641	LEIG04
LEIGH Edward	S		CH	R	3	1553	..	1595	..	LEIG06
LEIGH John	SJ		LA	Y	#3	1639	1660	1671	1703	LEIG08
LEIGH Philip	SJ	N	LA	R	#1	1650	1678	1675	1717	LEIG10
LEIGH Richard BL.	S	L	MX	R	#+	1561	..	1586	1588	LEIG12
LEIGH Roger	SJ	N	LA	Y		1708	1728	1753	1781	LEIG14
LEIGH William	SJ		ST			1598	1621	..	..	LEIG16
LEIGH see also LEE										
LEIGHTON see LAYTON										
LEITH Gall (Robert)	OSB	W	SC	J		1706	1726	..	1775	LEIT02
LE MAITRE Charles	SJ	L	FR	Y	#1	1672	1693	1702	1737	LEMA02
LEMANS (Martial)	OFM		LC		14	1717	1744	..	1776	LEMA04
LEMOS Benedict de	SJ	L	PL		7	..	..	..	..	LEMO02
LE MOTTE James	SJ		LA	R	#3	1712	1734	1735	1772	LEMO04
LENNOX, Duke of, see STUA04										
LEONARD Frederic or Ferdinand	SJ		GS			1728	1747	..	1764	LEON02

Name	Reg	D	Co	T	Notes	Born	Prof	Ordn	Died	Code
(Leonard of Paris)	CAP	L	FR		2	..	1586	..	1641	LEON04
LEONARD (Leonard of S.Fr'cis)	OFM		LC	F	123	1663	1687	1691	1699	LEON06
LESLIE Alexander, Hon.	SJ	L	SC			1693	1712	..	1760	LESL02
LESLIE Charles, Hon.	SJ	M	SC	Y	#1	1745	1764	..	1806	LESL04
LESLIE George (Archangelus)	CAP		SC	R	1	1587	..	1608	1637	LESL05
LESLIE James, Hon.	SJ	M	SC			1741	1760	..	1816	LESL06
LEUSON see LEVESON										
LEVENTHORP Henry	S			D	#*	..	..	1603	..	LEVE02
LEVESON Edward	SJ	M	ST	R		1642	1669	1667	1720	LEVE04
LEVESON Francis (Ignatius)VEN	OFM		ST	F	x1234	1646	1664	1674	1680	LEVE06
LEVESON Richard	SJ		ST	Y		1649	1670	1679	1715	LEVE08
LEVESON William (John Bapt)	OFM		ST	F	123	1648	1666	1673	1709	LEVE10
LEVINGE Richard	SJ	M		Y	3	1687	1705	1718	1745	LEV102
LEVISON see LEVESON										
LEWGAR John	S				*‡	1602	..		1665	LEWG02
LEWIS David ST.	SJ	W	MO	R	#+§=	1616	1645	1642	1679	LEW102
LEWIS David	SJ		MO	R	#34	1671	1691	1705	1741	LEW104
LEWIS Edward	S			S	3	..	..	1602	..	LEW106
LEWIS Francis	S		SP	R	#§	1608	..	1634	1641	LEW108
LEWIS James	SJ		MX	Y		1731	1748	1756	1776	LEW110
LEWIS John	SJ	W	MO	Y	#	1610	1631	..	1648	LEW112
LEWIS John	SJ	L	NN	Y	#3	1721	1740	1747	1788	LEW114
LEWIS Louis	OFM	W		F	3	..	..	1695	1732	LEW116
LEWIS Michael George	OSB	N	HR	G	°14	1735	1752	..	1804	LEW118
LEWIS Owen BP.	S		AY		*‡	1533	..	..	1595	LEW119
LEWIS Peter	S			S		..	..	1660	..	LEW120
LEWIS Philip	S	M	MO		*	..	..	..	1710	LEW122
LEWIS Philip	S		MO	R		1688	..	1713	..	LEW124
LEWIS Theodore	SJ	L	HA	Y	#§13	1633	1654	1663	1707	LEW126
LEWIS Thomas	SJ		YO	Y		1613	1628	1638	1644	LEW128
LEWIS William Thomas	S			Q	*	..	..	1580	..	LEW130
LEWKNER Edmund	S		SX	Q	†	..	..	1580	..	LEWK02
LEWKNER Edmund	OSB		MX	G	#	..	1680	..	1714	LEWK04
LEWKNER Thomas William	SJ				#1	1588	..	..	1645	LEWK06
LEY see LEE										
LEYBURN George	S	L	WD	D	#	1600	..	1625	1677	LEYB02
LEYBURN George	S	M	LA	D	3	1673	..	1699	1737	LEYB04
LEYBURN John BP.	S	L	WD	P	*	1620	..	1646	1702	LEYB06
LEYBURN Nicholas	S		WD	D	#1	1626	..	1661	1701	LEYB08
LEYBURN Nicholas	S	N	LA	P		1674	..	1700	1739	LEYB10
LEYBURN Roger	S		WD	D	#3	1641	..	1668	..	LEYB12
LEYBURN William	S		WD	D	#3	1644	..	1668	..	LEYB14
LIBBY Christopher	S			Q	#*	..	..	1583	..	LIBB02
LICHFIELD Edward	SJ			R	#†	1583	1616	1614	1627	LICH02
LIDDELL Thomas	S	N	DH	L	3	..	..	1698	1724	LIDD02
LIDDELL Thomas	S		YO	L		1718	..	1743	1775	LIDD04
LIDIATE William	SJ	N	LA	Y		1650	1673	1681	1690	LID102
LIGER Thomas	S			S	3	..	..	1609	..	LIGE02
LINDLEY (Ambrose)	OSB		YO	X		..	1670	..	1699	LIND02
LINDOW John	S	L	LA	D	3	1729	..	1764	1806	LIND04
LINDSAY (Epiphanius)	CAP		SC		6	..	..	..	..	LIND06
LINE Francis	SJ	L	MX	Y	#	1595	1623	1628	1675	LINE02
LINE George	S			R	#*	1649	..	1675	1715	LINE04
LINGARD John	S	N	HA	D		1771	..	1795	1851	LING02
LINGEN (Francis of the Cross)	OFM		RN	F	123	1665	1681	1689	1693	LING04
LINGHAM John	S	M			7	..	..	..	..	LING06
LINGHAM Richard	S			S	3	..	..	1612	..	LING08
LISTER Christopher	S	M	LA	S	3	..	..	1605	..	LIST02
LISTER John	S	N	LA	Q		..	..	1584	..	LIST04
LISTER Thomas	SJ		LA		#	1559	1583	..	1628	LIST06
LISTER Thomas	S	N			7	..	..	..	..	LIST07
LISTER William	OP		HA	R	#	1561	1595	..	..	LIST08
LITCHFIELD see LICHFIELD										
LITTLETON Gervase (Pius)	OP	N			#	1649	1675	..	1723	LITT02
LIVERS Arnold	SJ		MD	Y	3	1705	1724	1733	1767	LIVE02
LIVESEY Thomas	S	N	LA	D	#	1764	..	1789	1857	LIVE04

82

Name	Reg	D	Co	T	Notes	Born	Prof	Ordn	Died	Code
LLEWELLYN Edward (Augustine)	OSB	W	HU	E	†1	1621	1658	..	1711	LLEW02
LLOYD David	S		CN	R	#§14	1601	..	1626	1650	LLOY02
LLOYD John ST.	S	W	BR	V	+	..	..	1653	1679	LLOY04
LLOYD John or Nicholas	S		CM	L	#	1682	..	1707	1724	LLOY06
LLOYD Sylvester Louis	OFM			F	°8	..	..	..		LLOY10
LLOYD Thomas	S	W				..	..	..	1704	LLOY12
LLOYD William	S		CM	L	x	1614	..	1639	1679	LLOY14
LLOYD see also FLOYD										
LOADER (Placid)	OSB		MX	G	#	..	1620	1624	1646	LOAD02
LOBB Emmanuel	SJ	L	HA	Y	#1	1593	1619	..	1671	LOBB02
LOCK Richard	S		DV	L	‡	1695	..	1725	..	LOCK02
LOCKETT John	S		DT	R	§1	1640	..	1666	..	LOCK04
LOCKHART Thomas	SJ		HR	Y		1672	1693	1702	1744	LOCK06
LOCKIER John	S			S	3	..	..	1604	..	LOCK07
LOCKIER (Wm. of S.Francis)	OFM			F	123	1658	1677	1685	1721	LOCK08
LOCKWOOD Francis	S		YO	Q	4	..	..	1587	1632	LOCK10
LOCKWOOD John BL.	S	N	YO	R	#+	1561	..	1597	1642	LOCK12
LOCKWOOD Thomas	S	N	YO	D	#3	..	..	1676	1686	LOCK14
LODGE John	S	N	YO	D	#34	1648	..	1676	1731	LODG02
LODGE John	S	N	YO	D	3	1681	..	1706	1741	LODG04
LODGE John	S	N	YO	D		1722	..	1746	1795	LODG06
LODGE Miles	S	N	YO	D	13	1653	..	1680	1749	LODG08
LODGE Thomas	SJ	W	YO	Y	3	1726	1744	1751	1764	LODG10
LOLLI James	S		MX	D	#*x°	1728	..	1754	1779	LOLL02
LOMAX James	S			R	*x†	..	..	1582	1584	LOMA02
LOMAX John	S	M	SK	V		..	..	1697	1732	LOMA04
LONE John	OSB		KT	G		1599	1620	..	1641	LONE02
LONG Henry	S	N	LA	R	#	1637	..	1663	1677	LONG02
LONG James	CRT			C	3	..	1716	1718	1759	LONG04
LONG John	S	L		Q	*‡	..	..	1580	..	LONG06
LONGDALL see LANGDALE										
LONGDON Nicholas	S			S	3	..	..	1618	..	LONG08
LONGUEVILLE Henry	S			S	3	..	..	1617	..	LONG10
LONGUEVILLE Thomas	S	L	BU	R		1598	..	1622	..	LONG12
LONGSTAFF Robert	S	N	YO	D	#3	1736	..	1763	1798	LONG14
LONGSTAFF Valentine or M'duke	S	N	YO	D	#	1731	..	1758	1823	LONG16
LONGWORTH see LANGWORTH										
LONSDALE John	S	N	LA	D	3	1736	..	1765	1802	LONS02
LOOE see LOWE										
LOOP George (Edmund)	ODC	L	HR	R		1648	1667	..	1716	LOOP02
LOPES William	S			D	*	..	..	1597	..	LOPE02
LORRAINE (Lawrence of S.Mary)	OFM	N	ND	F	123	1651	1670	1676	1718	LORR02
LORRAINE (Philip)	OFM			F		..	1722	..	1766	LORR04
LORYMER Francis	S	W	MO	R		1708	..	1733	1765	LORY02
LORYMER Michael (Anselm)	OSB	L	MO	G		1751	1768	..	1832	LORY04
LOTHBURY Jasper	S		MX	D		1564	..	1599	..	LOTH02
(Louis of Cambridge)	OFM				4	..	..	..	1634	LOUI01
(Louis of S.Alfonso)	OP				*7	..	..	..	..	LOUI02
LOVELACE Thomas	S		KT	R		1561	..	1586	1589	LOVE02
LOVELL Charles	S			V		..	..	1638	..	LOVE04
LOVELL Francis	S	M		D	3	..	..	1676	1715	LOVE06
LOVELL George	SJ		OX	Y		1650	1669	1678	1720	LOVE08
LOVELL John	SJ	M	OX	Y	1	1604	1629	..	1683	LOVE10
LOVELL Samuel	S	M		D	3	..	..	1601	..	LOVE12
LOVETT George	SJ	L	NN		#12	1576	1611	..	1640	LOVE14
LOVETT Richard (Albert)	OP	W			2	..	1695	..	1742	LOVE16
LOWBURY see LOTHBURY										
LOWE Anthony	S		MX	R		1734	..	1758	1794	LOWE02
LOWE John	S	N	LA	Q		..	..	1579	..	LOWE03
LOWE John VEN.	S	L	MX	R	+	1553	..	1582	1586	LOWE04
LOWE John	S	L	LC	D		..	..	1604	..	LOWE06
LOWE Joseph (of S.Edmund)	ODC				1	1747	..	1789	1816	LOWE08
LOWE Nicholas	S		LC	D		1584	..	1606	1624	LOWE10
LOWE William	S	L	LC	D		..	..	1616	..	LOWE12
LOWE William	SJ		MX	Y	3	1704	1722	1731	1744	LOWE14
LOWICK (Lawrence)	OSB	M	YO	W		..	1620	..	1633	LOWI02

Name	Reg	D	Co	T	Notes	Born	Prof	Ordn	Died	Code
LOWICK Henry (Bernard)	OSB	L	YO	E		..	1673	..	1720	LOWI04
LUCAS Anthony	SJ		DH			1633	1662	..	1693	LUCA02
LUCAS John or Bernard	SJ			Y	#	1740	1763	1767	1795	LUCA04
LUCAS Simon	S	L	WR	V		1745	..	1775	1801	LUCA06
LUDDINGTON Walter (Gervase)	ODC	M	WR	N	#‡1	1600	1630	..	1658	LUDD02
LUDLAM Robert VEN.	S	M	DE	Q	+‡1	1551	..	1581	1588	LUDL02
LUGAR see LEWGAR										
LUMLEY John	OSB		YO	W		..	1656	..	1703	LUML02
LUMSDEN Alexander	OP	L	SC		4	1622	..	..	1700	LUMS02
LUND Anthony	S	N	LA	D	1	1734	..	1760	1811	LUND02
LUND John	S	N	LA	D		1733	..	1759	1812	LUND04
LUPTON Thomas	S	N	LA	U		1776	..	1800	1843	LUPT02
LUSHER Edward	SJ	L	NK	Y	#	..	..	..	1665	LUSH02
LUSHER Edward	S		MX	R	#	1628	..	1659	..	LUSH04
LUSHER Nicholas	SJ		MX		2	1589	1624	..	1653	LUSH06
LUSHER Thomas	S		NK	V		1575	..	1599	..	LUSH08
LUTLEY Humphrey	S	M	SP		1	1599	..	..	..	LUTL02
LUTLEY Philip	S	M	SP	R	#	1601	..	1624	1684	LUTL04
LUYNES (Archangelus) de	CAP		FR			..	..	..	1649	LUYN02
LYCETT Francis	S	M	IT	T		1776	..	1800	1853	LYCE02
LYNCH Francis (Anselm)	OSB		MX	G		1693	1714	..	1777	LYNC02
LYNCH (William)	OFM	L	IR		*7	..	..	..	..	LYNC04
LYNDE see LINE										
LYNN Richard	S		NK	D		..	..	1607	..	LYNN02
MacCALL Adam ,	OSB	N	SC	J		..	..	..	1640	MACC01
MacCARLY James or Charles	S	L	MX	R	°1	1698	..	1724	1742	MACC02
MacCARTHY Charles	S	L	MX	D		1751	..	1776	1799	MACC04
MacCARTHY Daniel	S	L	IR		7	..	..	..	..	MACC06
MacCARTHY James	OSA	L	IR		*7	..	..	..	..	MACC07
McCORRY (Cyprian of Armagh)	CAP		IR		8	..	..	..	..	MACC08
MacDONALD Archibald(Benedict)	OSB	N	SC	G		1739	1757	..	1814	MACD02
MacDONELL Alexander BP.	S	L	SC	V	*	1760	..	1787	1840	MACD04
MacDONELL Charles (Francis)	OFM	L	IR	F	1234	1770	1790	1800	1843	MACD06
McEVOY Christopher	S	M			8	..	..	..	..	MACE02
MacGEOGHEGAN Arthur	OP	L	IR		+3	..	..	1624	1633	MACG02
MacGEOGHEGAN (Peter)	OFM	L	IR		*7	..	..	..	..	MACG03
McGRATH (Bernard)	CAP				8	..	..	..	..	MACG04
MacKENZIE Alexander	SJ	W	SC	Y	#	1730	1749	1758	1800	MACK04
MABBS James (Lawrence)	OSB	L	LE	G	x†	1589	1620	..	1641	MACZ01
MACEDO (Francis of S.Aug'ine)	OFM	L	PL		*7	..	..	..	..	MACZ02
MACHADO (Antonio of S.B'dine)	OFM	L	PL		*7	..	..	..	..	MACZ03
MACHELL George	S		WD	D	#	1587	..	1618	..	MACZ04
MACKAY John (Gregory)	OSB	N	ND	G		1704	1724	..	1778	MACZ06
MACKWORTH Thomas	S	M	MX	R		1692	..	1716	1734	MACZ08
MADDEN John	OSA		IR		7*	..	..	..	..	MADD01
MADDISON Edward	S		LN	D	#*	1589	..	1615	..	MADD02
MADDOCK James (Bernardine)	OFM			F	124	1601	1625	..	1654	MADD03
MADDOCK John	S		CH	S	3	..	..	1610	..	MADD04
MADEW Edward	OFM			F	1	1703	..	..	1782	MADE02
MADGEWORTH Christopher	SJ	N	LA	Y	#1	1658	1679	1685	1692	MADG02
MAGEE David	SJ	W	IR	Y	#3	1737	1755	1762	1768	MAGE02
MAGEE	S			S	3	..	..	1612	..	MAGE04
MAGELLAN Jean Hyacinthe de	OSA	L	PL		*°2	1723	1755	..	1790	MAGE06
MAGINN Patrick	S	L	IR		*7	..	..	..	..	MAGI02
MAGRUAIRK (Francis)	OFM		IR	R	°4	..	..	..	1665	MAGR02
MAGUIRE (Dominic) ARCHBP.	OP	L	ES	Z	*	..	..	..	1708	MAGU02
MAHON Thomas	OFM	L	IR		8	..	..	..	..	MAHO02
MAINI Dominic Joseph	S	N	LA	U	13	1775	..	1798	1854	MAIN02
MAINWARING Edward	SJ	N	LA	R	#3	1604	1628	1628	1664	MAIN04
MAINWARING George	SJ				#	1590	1612	..	1631	MAIN06
MAINWARING George	S	M			7	..	..	..	..	MAIN07
MAINWARING Joseph	S			D	3	..	..	1674	..	MAIN08
MAINWARING Thomas Lionel	S	M	CH	R	#§°	1681	..	1710	1740	MAIN10
MAIRE Anthony	CRT			C		..	..	..	1700	MAIR01
MAIRE Christopher	SJ		DH	Y	3	1697	1715	1727	1767	MAIR02
MAIRE Edward	SJ		DH	Y	#3	1725	1742	1749	1797	MAIR04

84

Name	Reg	D	Co	T	Notes	Born	Prof	Ordn	Died	Code
MAIRE George	SJ	M	DH	Y	3	1738	1754	1762	1796	MAIR06
MAIRE Henry	S	N	DH	D		1714	..	1738	1775	MAIR08
MAIRE James	SJ	M	DH	Y		1705	1726	1733	1746	MAIR10
MAIRE Peter	SJ	N	DH	Y	3	1707	1726	1734	1763	MAIR12
MAIRE Thomas	SJ		DH	Y	3	1703	1720	1729	1752	MAIR14
MAIRE William	S	N	DH	D	#3	1659	..	1687	1740	MAIR15
MAIRE William	S	N	DH	D		1699	..	1723	1733	MAIR16
MAIRE William BP.	S	N	YO	D	*	1704	..	1730	1769	MAIR18
MAITLAND John (Francis)	MIN	L	SC		#4	1597	..	..	1642	MAIT02
MAJOR Anthony	S			Q	*§°	1565	..	1590	..	MAJO02
MALLET Francis	S		ST	S	3	..	..	1619	..	MALL04
MALLET George	S			R	#	..	..	1612	..	MALL06
MALLET John (Gregory)	OSB	M	YO	W	#	1604	1625	1627	1681	MALL08
MALLORY Charles (Robert)	CRT			C	2	..	1613	..	1620	MALL10
MALLORY John	S			V	*	..	..	1634	..	MALL12
MALONE John Baptist	S	L	IR		8	..	..	..	..	MALO02
MALONE John (Columban)	OSB		LA	G		..	1609	..	1623	MALO04
MALTON John	S			S		..	..	1685	..	MALT01
MALTON Thomas	S	M	LC	D	#	..	..	1642	1684	MALT02
MAMBRECHT John	SJ	L	SC		#	..	..	..	1679	MAMB02
MANBY Thomas	SJ		NN	R	#§14	1588	1611	..	1620	MANB02
MANDIN see PAZZI MANDIN										
MANFIELD see MANSFIELD										
MANGER Thomas	S	W	DT	Q	4	1566	..	1592	1643	MANG02
MANLEY William or Robert	S			V		..	..	1649	1694	MANL02
MANN Wm Theodore (Augustine)	CRT		YO	C	*§	1735	1759	1760	1809	MANN02
MANNERS John	SJ		MX	Y	#1	1609	1631	..	1695	MANN04
MANNERS Oliver, Hon., Kt.	S		LE	R	†=1	1580	..	1611	1613	MANN06
MANNING Edward	S				7	..	..	..	..	MANN07
MANNING John	S	M	MX	R		1731	..	1756	1783	MANN08
MANNING Robert	S	L	LC	P	3	1655	..	1690	1732	MANN10
MANNOCK Francis	SJ	N	MX	R	#	1670	1686	1696	1748	MANN12
MANNOCK George, Bt.	SJ	M	SK	Y	3	1724	1741	1749	1787	MANN14
MANNOCK Henry	S	M	SK	D	#1	1587	..	1612	..	MANN16
MANNOCK John	SJ	L	HA	Y	#=34	1588	1624	1621	1651	MANN18
MANNOCK John (Anselm)	OSB	M	SK	G	1	1677	1700	..	1764	MANN20
MANNOCK William	S		SK	D	#§	1580	..	1605	..	MANN22
MANNOCK William	S		SK	R	3	1677	..	1700	1749	MANN24
MANRIQUE Sebastiano	OSA	L	PL		*1	1595	..	..	1669	MANR02
MANSELL (Michael)	OFM		IR	R	*7	..	..	..	..	MANS01
MANSELL Thomas	SJ		OX	Y	#3	1668	1686	1695	1724	MANS02
MANSELL William	SJ		OX	Y	#13	1669	1686	1694	1720	MANS04
MANSFIELD Robert	SJ			R	*	1652	1669	1680	1708	MANS06
MANSUETE	CAP	L			*7	..	..	..	..	MANS08
MANWARING see MAINWARING										
MARE see MAIRE										
MARK John	OSS		DV	Y	*	1621	1663	..	1697	MARK02
MARK	S	N			7	..	..	..	..	MARK03
MARKHAM (Bernardine of S.Jn.)	OFM			F	1234	1717	1733	1741	1743	MARK04
MARKLAND Alexander	S		LA	Q		1561	..	1584	..	MARK06
MARKS see MARK										
MARLEY John	S	N	DH	R		1574	..	1598	..	MARL02
MARSDEN William BL.	S		LA	Q	+‡13	1560	..	1585	1586	MARS02
MARSH Anthony	S			V		..	..	1647	..	MARS06
MARSH James	S	N	LA	V		1762	..	1787	1811	MARS08
MARSH John	OSS			Q	*2	..	1586	1579	1601	MARS09
MARSH John	S			V	1	1636	..	..	1694	MARS10
MARSH Richard	OSB	N	LA	W		1762	1783	1786	1843	MARS12
MARSH Thomas (Jerome)	OSB	N	LA	W		1743	1761	..	1798	MARS14
MARSH William	SJ	L	LC	Y	1	1615	1632	1641	1688	MARS16
MARSH William or John	SJ	M	LA	Y		1637	1658	1666	1681	MARS18
MARSHALL John	S		WR	N	‡3	..	..	1570	1597	MARS20
MARSHALL Joseph	SJ	W	GL	N		1683	1708	1715	1739	MARS22
MARSHALL Nicholas	S		LA	R		1649	..	1673	..	MARS26
MARSHALL Peter	SJ	M	DE	S	#2	1591	1620	..	1655	MARS27
MARSHALL Robert	CRT			C		..	..	..	1572	MARS28

Name	Reg	D	Co	T	Notes	Born	Prof	Ordn	Died	Code
MARSHALL Robert	OSS			S	3	..	1621	1621	..	MARS29
MARSHALL Thomas	SJ			N	*	..	1575	..	1589	MARS30
MARSLAND John	S	L	LA	D		1738	..	1763	1817	MARS32
MARTIN (Alexius)	OFM			F	123	1706	1724	1730	1755	MART02
MARTIN Anthony (Athanasius)	OSB		DT	R	#‡4	1565	1594	1591	1626	MART04
MARTIN Edward	OP		SK			1673	1695	1697	1753	MART06
MARTIN Francis	S		HA	D	#	1589	..	1614	..	MART10
MARTIN Francis	OSA		IR			1652	..	..	1722	MART11
MARTIN Gregory	S		SX	D	‡	..	..	1573	1582	MART12
MARTIN (Gregory)	OFM			F	3	..	..	1725	1773	MART14
MARTIN Henry	SJ	L	SK	Y		1642	1662	1672	1672	MART16
MARTIN John	SJ		SK	Y		1645	1667	1672	1717	MART18
MARTIN John	OP	M	SK	N		1677	1697	1700	1761	MART20
MARTIN John	S	L	YO	D		1734	..	1772	1788	MART22
MARTIN Joseph	OSB	L	MX	G	2	..	1652	..	1662	MART24
MARTIN Joseph	S	M	SK	D	#	1688	..	1716	1729	MART26
MARTIN Joseph (Bonaventure)	OFM					..	..	1800	1834	MART27
MARTIN Peter	S	W		V	*3	..	..	1597	..	MART28
MARTIN Thomas	S		DT	D	§34	1610	..	1633	1691	MART30
MARTIN Thomas	S		DT	D	‡4	1570	..	1594	1643	MART32
MARTIN William (John)	OSB		SM	G	3	..	1661	1672	1672	MART34
MARTINASH John	SJ		MX	Y	#3	1679	1699	1707	1725	MART36
MARTINDALE John	SJ		LA	Y	#	1666	1690	1698	1734	MART38
MARTINEZ John	S			S	3	..	..	1636	..	MART40
MARTINEZ Robert	S			S	3	..	..	1666	..	MART42
MARTYN see MARTIN										
MASCY see MASSEY										
MASHTER Francis	SJ	M	LA	Y	13	1678	1701	1711	1723	MASH02
MASON Francis	SJ	N	DH	R	#1	1593	1623	1619	1681	MASO02
MASON Richard (Angelus)	OFM	W	WT		123	1599	1630	1624	1678	MASO04
MASON (Stephen of S.Aug'stne)	CAR	L			*8	..	..	..	..	MASO05
MASON Thomas	S	N	LA	L		1719	..	1745	1751	MASO06
MASSER Nicholas	SJ		GS			1583	1619	..	..	MASS02
MASSEY Edward	S		CH	D	#	..	..	1611	..	MASS04
MASSEY George	S			D	3	..	..	1676	..	MASS06
MASSEY James	S				3	..	..	1602	..	MASS07
MASSEY John	S		SM	D	‡	1655	..	1693	1715	MASS08
MASSEY John	SJ	W	MX	Y	#3	1698	1717	1725	1760	MASS10
MASSEY (Masseus of S.Barbara)	OFM	L	LA	F	123	1628	1653	1658	1702	MASS12
MASSEY Thomas	S	L	LA	R	#	1622	..	1647	1676	MASS14
MASSEY see also STANLEY										
MASTERS John	S		HA	L	#§	1680	..	1702	1755	MAST02
MASTERS see also MASHTER										
MATAGON Francis	SJ	L	LC	Y	#12	1614	1632	..	1667	MATA02
MATHER (Augustine)	OSB	N	LA	W		..	1666	..	1687	MATH02
MATHER James	OSB	L	LA	W		..	1668	..	1724	MATH04
MATHER James	S	N	DH	P	4	1718	..	1746	1801	MATH06
MATHER James (Cyril)	OSB		LA	X		1769	1790	..	1812	MATH08
MATHEW Tobie, Kt.	S		WT		*§	1577	..	1614	1655	MATH10
MATHEWS see MATTHEWS										
(Matthew of S.Quentin)	CAP	L	FR		2	..	1640	..	1675	MATT01
MATTHEW John	S		CB	V	#†3	1572	..	1603	..	MATT02
MATTHEWS Anthony	CRT			C		..	1704	..	1752	MATT04
MATTHEWS (Basil)	OFM			F	123	1705	1721	1729	1758	MATT05
MATTHEWS Edward	S		HA	R	#§4	1704	..	1730	1782	MATT06
MATTHEWS Ignatius	SJ		MD	V	3	1730	1763	1763	1790	MATT08
MATTHEWS John	SJ		MX	Y		1658	1677	1685	1695	MATT10
MATTHEWS John	S	L	HA	D	#3	1659	..	1685	1744	MATT12
MATTHEWS (Patrick)	OP		IR		*7	..	..	..	..	MATT13
MATTHEWS Peter	SJ	N	MX	Y	#3	1692	1711	1722	1752	MATT14
MATTHEWS (Peter of Alcantara)	OFM	M		F		..	..	..	1676	MATT15
MATTHEWS Richard	S			S		..	..	1676	..	MATT16
MATTHEWS Thomas	S	N		V		..	..	1651	1707	MATT18
MATTHEWS William	S	L	HA	D	3	1629	..	1663	1695	MATT20
MATTINGLEY John	SJ		MD	Y		1745	1766	1770	1807	MATT22
MAWDESLEY Henry	S	W	LA	L	34	..	..	1680	1698	MAWD02

Name	Reg	D	Co	T	Notes	Born	Prof	Ordn	Died	Code
MAWDESLEY Richard	S		LA	L	34	..	..	1680	1686	MAWD04
MAWDESLEY William	S		LA	L	4	..	..	1696	1733	MAWD06
MAXEY John	S	L	MX	L	x§	..	..	..	1617	MAXE02
MAXFIELD Thomas BL.	S	L	ST	D	#+1	1585	..	1614	1616	MAXF02
MAXFIELD William	S			V	*3		..	1593	..	MAXF04
MAXWELL Albert or Herbert	SJ		SC		1	1653	1675	..	1729	MAXW02
MAXWELL James	S	M	SC	D	#1	1700	..	1722	1778	MAXW04
MAY John	S	N	YO	V	#	..	..	1649	..	MAYA02
MAYES Lawrence	S		YO	D		1673	..	1697	1749	MAYE02
MAYHEW Cuthbert	S		WT	V	3	1580	..	1603	..	MAYH02
MAYHEW Edward	OSB		WT	R		1569	1607	1594	1625	MAYH04
MAYHEW Henry	S		WT	V	3	..	..	1592	1616	MAYH06
MAYHEW John	S			S	3		..	1612	..	MAYH08
MAYLER Henry	S	L	EX		#13	1576	..	1612	..	MAYL02
MAYNE Cuthbert ST.	S	W	DV	D	+‡	1544	..	1575	1577	MAYN02
MAYNE Henry	S		BU	R	#	1609	..	1636	1689	MAYN04
MAYO see MAYHEW										
MEADE John	SJ		MX		#	1572	1592	1602	1653	MEAD02
MEALS John	S		WR	D	#3	1687	..	1712	1756	MEAL02
MEARA George	SJ		BK	Y	#	1675	1694	1703	1730	MEAR02
MEARA John	S	L	BK	R	#	1676	..	1703	1733	MEAR04
MEARA William	SJ		BK	Y	#3	1677	1698	1707	1728	MEAR06
MEASE Henry (Stephen)	OSS					1593	1621	..	1662	MEAS02
MEDCALF see METCALFE										
MEDFORD see METCALFE										
MEEHAN Charles VEN.	OFM		IR		#+1	1639	..	..	1679	MEEH02
MEERING see MERYING										
MELLIERE (Alexis) de la	CAR	L	FR		8	..	..	..	..	MELL01
MELLING Edward	S	N	LA	D	3	1683	..	1708	1733	MELL02
MELLING James	S	N		D	*	1748	..	1774	1806	MELL04
MELLING John	S	N	LA	D	#	..	..	1612	1633	MELL06
MELLING John	S		LA	D		1689	..	1713	1745	MELL08
MELLING Ralph	S	N	LA	D	1	1601	..	1629	1660	MELL10
MELLING Richard	S	N		D	*	..	..	1620	..	MELL12
MELLING Thomas	S			S		..	..	1681	..	MELL14
MELLO Emmanuel de		L	PL		*7	..	..	..	..	MELL16
MENDOZA Christopher de	SJ	N	MX		#	1641	1657	..	..	MEND02
MEPNESYN Biemigro dos		L	PL		*7	..	..	..	..	MEPN02
MERCER William	SJ		LA	Y	1	1738	1755	1763	1777	MERC02
MEREDITH Jonas	S		SM	D	#‡	1547	..	1576	..	MERE02
MEREDITH Richard	SJ		MX	D	#	1696	1716	1725	1754	MERE04
MERIDALE Humphrey	S			D	#	..	..	1603	..	MERI02
MERIDALE John	S			V		1607	..	1633	..	MERI04
MERRIMAN Michael	S	N	DH	D	#	..	..	1631	1673	MERR02
MERRIMAN Thomas (Bede)	OSB		DH	W	#1	1585	1610	..	1614	MERR04
MERYING Robert (Benedict)	OSB		WR	X	14	1598	1658	..	1666	MERY02
MESSENGER John	SJ	N	YO	Y	1	1688	1708	1716	1752	MESS02
METCALFE Anthony	S	N			4	..	..	..	1605	METC02
METCALFE Barnaby	S				*3	..	..	1640	..	METC04
METCALFE (Bernardine)	OFM	N		F	123	1671	1687	1695	1738	METC05
METCALFE Brian	S	N			4	..	..	..	1664	METC06
METCALFE John	S	N	YO	R	#	1615	..	1641	1673	METC08
METCALFE John	S	L	YO	R	#	1663	..	1687	1729	METC10
METCALFE John (Gregory)	OSB		LN	X		1724	1740	..	1752	METC12
METCALFE Joseph	S	N	YO	D	#	1633	..	1661	1695	METC14
METCALFE Joseph	SJ	N	WR	Y	#1	1670	1692	1701	1703	METC15
METCALFE Nicholas	S	N	DH	L	#3	1648	..	1674	1695	METC16
METCALFE Peter	S	L	YO	L	#	1603	..	1633	1671	METC18
METCALFE Thomas	S		YO	D	#3	1586	..	1613	1651	METC20
METCALFE Thomas	S	L		D	#*	..	..	1622	1651	METC22
METCALFE William	OSB	N	YO	G		1672	1690	1698	1738	METC24
METCALFE William	SJ		LA	S	34	..	1599	1597	1604	METC26
METCALFE William (Placid)	OSB	L	LN	X		1723	1740	..	1780	METC28
METHAM Anthony	S	N	YO	D	#3	1642	..	1670	1694	METH02
METHAM Francis	SJ		YO	Y	#	..	1645	..	1681	METH04
METHAM Philip (Sylvester)	OSB	N	YO	G		..	1683	..	1715	METH06

87

Name	Reg	D	Co	T	Notes	Born	Prof	Ordn	Died	Code
METHAM Thomas	SJ		YO	N	x‡	1532	1579	..	1592	METH08
MEYNELL James	S	N	YO	D	14	1685	..	..	1731	MEYN04
MEYNELL James	SJ	N	YO	Y		1689	1708	1713	1746	MEYN06
MEYNELL Robert	S		YO	R	#§	1608	..	1640	..	MEYN08
MEYNELL Thomas	SJ	L	YO	Y	3	1737	1756	1762	1804	MEYN10
MEYNELL William	S	N	YO	D	#	1618	..	1645	1683	MEYN12
MEYNELL William	SJ	N	YO	Y	3	1744	1761	1773	1826	MEYN14
MICHAELIS (Reginald)	OP				2	..	1626	..	..	MICH01
MICHELL John	S	N		D	*‡	..	..	1577	..	MICH02
MICO Edward VEN.	SJ	L	EX	Y	#x1	1628	1650	1657	1678	MICO02
MICO Walter	SJ		SM	R	#§	1594	1620	1620	1647	MICO04
MIDDLEHURST James	SJ		LA	V	#3	1714	1739	1738	1767	MIDD02
MIDDLEHURST Thomas	S	N	LA	R	#	1732	..	1754	1817	MIDD04
MIDDLEMORE Humphrey	SJ		SP	R	#2	1594	1624	1619	1629	MIDD06
MIDDLEMORE (Louis)	OFM			F	123	1702	1720	1726	1746	MIDD08
MIDDLETON Anthony BL.	S	L	YO	Q	+	..	..	1586	1590	MIDD10
MIDDLETON Charles	SJ		GL	Y	#§3	1660	1687	1692	1743	MIDD12
MIDDLETON Edward	S				7	..	..	..	..	MIDD13
MIDDLETON George	S	L		V	3	..	..	1636	1682	MIDD14
MIDDLETON John	S			S	*3	..	..	1596	..	MIDD16
MIDDLETON Michael	OSB			G	4	..	..	..	1646	MIDD18
MIDDLETON (Paul of S.Bernard)	OFM			F	12	1640	1664	..	1679	MIDD19
MIDDLETON Peter	SJ	M	HA	S	#4	1601	1629	1629	1665	MIDD20
MIDDLETON Robert BL.	S	N	YO	R	*+§	1570	..	1598	1601	MIDD22
MIDDLETON Thomas	OP	L			#3	..	..	1609	1662	MIDD24
MIDDLETON Thomas (Cuthbert)	OSB		YO	G		..	1643	..	1678	MIDD26
MIDDLETON William	SJ		LC	A		..	1622	1619	1625	MIDD28
MIDDLETON William	OSB		DE	Z	#*x24	..	1604	..	1644	MIDD30
MIHAN see MEEHAN										
MILBURN James	S		HR	D	3	1641	..	1667	..	MILB02
MILDMAY Francis	OSB	W	OX	X		..	1674	..	1720	MILD02
MILDMAY George	OP		OX			1638	1663	1665	1668	MILD04
MILDMAY Matthew	SJ	W	OX	Y	#13	1640	1664	1672	1713	MILD06
MILES Edward (of S.Anthony)	OFM		HA	F	13	1721	1738	1744	1751	MILE01
MILES Francis	SJ	L	MX	R	§2	1590	1619	1616	1653	MILE02
MILES Francis	SJ	M	MX	Y	1	1650	1672	1682	1693	MILE04
MILES John	S		PL	P	3	..	..	1645	..	MILE06
MILES Thomas	S		HA	S	3	..	..	1603	..	MILE08
MILESON Richard	SJ	M	YO	Y	#†	1607	1643	..	1668	MILE10
MILLER John	S	M			#*	..	..	..	1730	MILL02
MILLINGTON Edward	S	N		R	*	1570	..	1596	..	MILL04
MILLINGTON George (Bernard)	OSB	W	LA	W		1627	1651	..	1667	MILL06
MILLS James	S			D	*3	1734	..	1758	1760	MILL08
MILLS James	S					..	..	..	1791	MILL10
MILLS see also MILES										
MILNER John	S	L		L	*	..	..	1749	1782	MILN02
MILNER John BP.	S	M	MX	D	*	1752	..	1776	1826	MILN04
MILWARD Isaac (Anselm)	OFM		WR	F	12	1757	1778	1782	1813	MILW02
MINSHULL Randal	S	N	CH	R	#§	..	..	1634	1685	MINS02
MINSHULL Thomas	OSB	W	CH	D	2	..	1609	1608	1617	MINS04
MITCHELL Samuel (Augustine)	OSB	M		W		1767	1788	1791	1816	MITC02
MITCHELL see also MICHELL										
MITFORD Roger	S	N	ND	D		..	..	..	1697	MITF02
MOLIEN Edward	SJ		FR	N	3	1701	1720	1728	1761	MOLI02
MOLIEN Jean Baptiste	SJ	L	FR	N	4	1703	1721	1730	1775	MOLI04
MOLINS Francis	S			D	#*3	1670	..	1697	1742	MOLI06
MOLINS see also MULLINS										
MOLONEY John Baptist	S	L	IR		8	..	..	..	..	MOLO02
MOLSHO see MULSHO										
MOLYNEUX Edward	S	N	LA	D	#13	1640	..	1666	1704	MOLY02
MOLYNEUX Edward	S	N	LA	D	#	1700	..	1727	1739	MOLY04
MOLYNEUX Henry	SJ	L	MX	Y	3	1693	1713	1722	1771	MOLY06
MOLYNEUX Joseph	SJ		LA	Y	#	1732	1752	1763	1778	MOLY08
MOLYNEUX Mathias or Matthew	S	M	SP	R		1689	..	1712	1759	MOLY10
MOLYNEUX Richard	SJ	W	MX	Y	3	1696	1715	1723	1766	MOLY12
MOLYNEUX Richard	SJ	W		Y	#*3	1700	1722	1729	1769	MOLY14

88

Name	Reg	D	Co	T	Notes	Born	Prof	Ordn	Died	Code
MOLYNEUX Robert	SJ		LA	Y	3	1738	1757	1767	1808	MOLY16
MOLYNEUX (Thomas)	OP		KT			1630	1658	1661	1708	MOLY18
MOLYNEUX William, Visc., Bt.	SJ	N	LA	Y	3	1685	1704	1713	1759	MOLY20
MOLYNEUX William	SJ	N	LA	Y		1726	1748	1756	1789	MOLY22
MONACIO John	S			S	3	..	..	1614	..	MONA02
MOND Charles	S	N	MX	R	#§	1627	..	1655	1680	MOND02
MONINGTON Thomas	OSB	W	HR	G		..	1610	..	1642	MONI02
MONK Richard	S	N		Q	*	..	..	1591	..	MONK02
MONK Richard (Gregory)	OSB	N	CD	D	#*2	..	1622	1633	1655	MONK04
MONSON Richard (Angelus)	OFM		LN	F	1234	1665	1686	1689	1713	MONS01
MONSON (George)	OFM		LN	F	123	1678	1696	1705	1718	MONS02
MONSON	S			S	3	..	..	1605	..	MONS04
MONTAGU Walter, Hon.	S	L	MX	R	*§1	1603	..	1636	1677	MONT02
MONTEITH William	SJ	L	SC	Y		1619	1637	..	1663	MONT04
MONTFORT Francis	S	M	NK	R		1566	..	1591	..	MONT08
MONTFORT Francois	CAP	L			*8	..	..	..	..	MONT10
MONTFORT Thomas	S	M	NK	S	3	1577	..	1600	..	MONT14
MONTFORT see also MUMFORD										
MOORE Benjamin (Bede)	OSB		MX	E		..	1681	..	1735	MOOR02
MOORE James (Augustine)	OSB		BK	G		1722	1740	..	1775	MOOR04
MOORE (John of the Hly Cross)	OFM		NK	F	#123	1629	1647	1653	1689	MOOR05
MOORE John (Francis)	OSB	L	BK	E	°	..	1698	1711	1741	MOOR06
MOORE Richard	SJ		WK	Y		1672	1693	1702	1753	MOOR10
MOORE Thomas	OP	L	IR			..	..	..	1778	MOOR12
MOORE see also MORE										
MORAN (James)	OP	L	IR		*8	..	..	..	..	MORA02
MORCOT Robert or William	S	M		Q	*	..	..	1579	..	MORC02
MORDAUNT George (Ben'dct) Hon	OSB		MX	X	°1	1676	1696	..	1728	MORD02
MORE Christopher	SJ		YO	Y	3	1729	1746	1754	1781	MORE02
MORE Francis	SJ		SM	Y		1698	1718	1727	1727	MORE03
MORE Henry	MIN					..	1585	..	1587	MORE04
MORE Henry	SJ	L	EX	Y	#	1586	1607	..	1661	MORE05
MORE Henry or Francis	SJ	L	LC	Y	#	1666	1684	1691	1730	MORE06
MORE John	S	N	LA	D	1	1703	..	1731	1783	MORE10
MORE Thomas	S	L	YO	R	#3	1565	..	1591	1625	MORE12
MORE Thomas	SJ		CB	R		1586	1611	1609	1623	MORE14
MORE Thomas	SJ	L	YO	Y	3	1722	1752	1760	1795	MORE16
MORE William	SJ	M		Y	#*	1590	1613	..	1645	MORE18
MOREY Blaise	S	M	SX	V		1744	..	1775	1823	MORE20
MORGAN (David of S. Wilfrid)	OFM		MO	F	123	1637	1657	1663	1702	MORG01
MORGAN David	S	L	PB	L		1721	..	1742	1758	MORG02
MORGAN Edward VEN.	S		FT	Z	#*+§	1584	..	1618	1642	MORG04
MORGAN Francis	OSB	L	WK	G		1602	1623	..	1669	MORG08
MORGAN Francis	S		MO		7	..	..	..	..	MORG09
MORGAN George	SJ		MO		#124	1584	1609	..	1620	MORG10
MORGAN George	SJ	L	WR	Y	3	1636	1657	1671	1674	MORG12
MORGAN James	S		MO	D	#3	1647	..	1676	..	MORG14
MORGAN John	S		MX	D	#x	1627	..	1654	1680	MORG16
MORGAN John	S	M	MO	D	3	1639	..	1663	..	MORG18
MORGAN John	S	W	MH	D	#3	1660	..	1690	1719	MORG20
MORGAN Joseph	S			D	#*3	..	..	1676	..	MORG22
MORGAN Philip	S			V		..	..	1653	..	MORG24
MORGAN Polydore (Constantine)	CAP			R	1	1556	1585	1579	1616	MORG28
MORGAN Richard	SJ	N	GL	Y		1746	1766	1770	1814	MORG30
MORGAN Roger	S				3	..	..	1632	..	MORG31
MORGAN Roland	S		GM	Q	‡°	..	..	1583	..	MORG32
MORGAN Walter	SJ		MO	S	2	..	1607	..	..	MORG36
MORGAN William	SJ	W	FT	R	†	1623	1651	1657	1689	MORG38
MORGAN William	SJ	L	MO	Y	#	1648	1669	1678	1710	MORG40
MORIN Jean	ORA	L	FR	P	§	1591	1618	1619	1659	MORI02
MORLEY George	SJ		HA			1585	1610	..	1665	MORL02
MORLEY Henry	S	L	LA	R	#§4	1602	..	1626	1684	MORL04
MORPHY see MURPHY										
MORRIS (Andrew)	OP		IR		*8	..	..	..	..	MORR01
MORRIS Christopher	SJ			Y		1603	1626	..	1667	MORR02
MORRIS David	S		MO	R	#	1630	..	1654	1710	MORR04

89

Name	Reg	D	Co	T	Notes	Born	Prof	Ordn	Died	Code
MORRIS James	S	W		D	*	..	..	1600	..	MORR06
MORRIS James	S			V	*	..	..	1609	..	MORR08
MORRIS James	SJ	L	IR	Y	#	1674	1699	1708	1715	MORR10
MORRIS John	S	M	LA	Y	3	1770	..	1797	1830	MORR12
MORRIS Peter	SJ			Y		1743	1760	1767	1783	MORR14
MORRIS Roger or William	S			Q	*‡4	..	..	1582	1586	MORR16
MORRIS-NANNY David	S		SP	V	#§3	1580	..	1613	..	MORR18
MORRISON William	S		ND	R	#	1674	..	1697	..	MORR20
MORSE Henry ST.	SJ	L	NK	R	#+†=3	1595	1625	1620	1645	MORS02
MORSE William	SJ		NK	D	#§2	1591	1620	1617	1649	MORS04
MORTON Richard	S			D	*	..	..	1600	1619	MORT02
MORTON Robert BL.	S	L	YO	Q	+	1548	..	1587	1588	MORT04
MORTON see also NORTON										
MOSELEY Joseph	SJ		LN	Y	3	1731	1748	1755	1787	MOSE02
MOSELEY Michael	SJ	W	LN	Y	#3	1720	1739	1746	1777	MOSE04
MOSELEY see also MAWDESLEY										
MOSSOCK Richard	S	N	LA	D	#	1626	..	..	1674	MOSS02
MOSTYN Andrew	SJ		FT	P		1663	1691	1692	1709	MOST02
MOSTYN John	SJ	N	FT	Y	#	1657	1693	..	1721	MOST04
MOSTYN Piers, Bt.	SJ	N	FT	Y	3	1687	1707	1715	1735	MOST06
MOTET Ferdinand	SJ		LC	V	3	1658	1684	1684	1691	MOTE02
MOTTRAM John	S		LN	S	†°	..	..	1713	..	MOTT02
MOUNDEFORD see MUMFORD										
MOYLEN William	SJ		MX	Y	14	1746	1767	..	1800	MOYL02
MUDDLE (Angelus)	CAP	L	MX		1	1585	..	..	1638	MUDD02
MULLINS John	S			S	3	..	..	1612	..	MULL02
MULLINS see also MOLINS										
MULSHO John	SJ		NN	D	#§4	1584	1616	1608	1661	MULS02
MUMFORD Gervase	SJ		NT	Y		1635	1658	1669	1684	MUMF02
MUMFORD James	SJ	M	NK	Y		1606	1626	..	1666	MUMF04
MUMFORD John	OSB		NK	G	#	..	1614	..	1646	MUMF05
MUMFORD William	SJ		MX	Y	1	1628	1647	..	1712	MUMF06
MUNDAY Francis	S		CL	R	#‡	1628	..	1655	1657	MUND02
MUNDEN John BL.	S		DT	R	+‡	1543	..	1582	1584	MUND04
MUNSON see MONSON										
MURPHY Cornelius	SJ		LC	Y		1696	1711	1720	1766	MURP02
MURPHY John	SJ	N	LC	Y		1657	1678	1687	..	MURP04
MURPHY Melchior	SJ		LC	Y	1	1664	1684	1693	1736	MURP06
MURPHY Michael	SJ		ZZ	Y	*1	1725	1745	1752	1759	MURP08
MURPHY Richard	SJ	W	MX	Y	#3	1716	1734	1741	1794	MURP10
MURPHY Timothy (Vincent)	OP	L			1	1698	1717	1724	1726	MURP12
MUSGRAVE Christopher	CRT			C	7	..	..	..	..	MUSG02
MUSH John	S	N		R	#*34	1552	..	1582	1613	MUSH02
MUSH John	S				7	..	..	..	..	MUSH03
MUSH William	S	N		Q	*	..	..	1590	..	MUSH04
MUSSON John	SJ	L	MX	Y		1680	1699	1708	1755	MUSS02
MUSSON Samuel	SJ		MX	Y	#3	1686	1705	1713	1769	MUSS04
MUTTLEBURY Francis	OSB	L	SM	D	#1	1610	1658	1635	1697	MUTT02
MUTTLEBURY John (Placid)	OSB	W	SM	D	#12	1563	1610	1601	1632	MUTT04
NANCONAN Peter	S		DV	D	#	..	..	1609	..	NANC02
NANDYKE Thomas	SJ	N	YO	Y		1726	1745	1752	1793	NAND02
NAPIER see NAPPER										
NAPPER (Basil)	OFM			F	3	..	..	1700	1732	NAPP00
NAPPER Charles (Francis)	OFM		OX	F	12	1623	1653	..	1679	NAPP01
NAPPER George BL.	S	M	OX	D	+‡	1550	..	1596	1610	NAPP02
NAPPER William (Marianus)	OFM		OX	F	#123	1615	1639	1648	1693	NAPP04
NARY Cornelius	S		IR		*	1660	..	1682	1738	NARY02
NASH (Anthony)	OFM		IR		*7	..	..	..	..	NASH02
NASSAU John	S	L	PL	N		1767	..	..	1807	NASS02
NATHAL see NUTTAL										
NAYLOR Anthony	CRT			C		..	..	..	1659	NAYL01
NAYLOR George	S		MX	V	#§	..	..	1603	..	NAYL02
NAYLOR Henry	S			Q	*	..	..	1586	..	NAYL04
NAYLOR John (Ambrose)	OSB	N	LA	G		1739	1757	1764	1821	NAYL06
NAYLOR John (Placid)	OSB	L	LA	W		1724	1741	..	1795	NAYL08
NAYLOR William	S				7	..	..	..	..	NAYL09

Name	Reg	D	Co	T	Notes	Born	Prof	Ordn	Died	Code
NAYLOR William (Placid)	OSB	N	LA	W		..	1711	..	1772	NAYL10
NEALE Benedict	SJ		MD	Y	3	1709	1728	1741	1787	NEAL02
NEALE Charles	SJ		MD	Y		1751	1771	..	1823	NEAL04
NEALE Henry	SJ		MD	Y		1702	1724	1738	1748	NEAL08
NEALE John or Cornelius	S		CL	R	‡	1532	..	1579	..	NEAL10
NEALE Leonard ARCHBP.	SJ		MD	Y	*	1747	1767	1773	1817	NEAL12
NEALE Robert	SJ	M	LN	S	#3	1600	1629	1626	1688	NEAL14
NEALE William	SJ	N	MD	Y	3	1743	1760	1767	1799	NEAL16
NECHILLS William (Bernard)	OSB		MX	E		1712	1729	..	1792	NECH02
NEEDHAM (Bonaventure)	OFM			F	1234	1718	1735	1741	1743	NEED02
NEEDHAM Charles	S	W	MO	D		1716	..	1741	1802	NEED04
NEEDHAM Daniel	SJ	M	LA	Y	#	1721	1741	1749	1783	NEED06
NEEDHAM John Turberville	S	L	MX	D		1713	..	1738	1781	NEED08
NEEDHAM Joseph	OFM			F	123	1713	1733	1741	1791	NEED10
NEEDHAM Nicholas	S		NT	D	#	..	..	1600	..	NEED12
NEEDHAM Oswald	S		DE	D		..	..	1597	..	NEED14
NEEDHAM Sebastian	SJ	L	MO	Y	#1	1671	1691	1700	1743	NEED16
NEIL John	SJ	W	FR	V	#3	1716	1740	1739	1760	NEIL02
NEIL William	SJ		FR	Y	#3	1714	1732	1739	1770	NEIL04
NELSON Edward	S			D	*3	..	..	1701	..	NELS04
NELSON Francis	SJ	L	LC	Y	1	1632	1650	1660	1675	NELS06
NELSON Henry (Anselm)	OSB	N	LA	E		..	1683	..	1717	NELS07
NELSON John BL.	S		YO	D	+	1534	..	1576	1578	NELS08
NELSON John	SJ		LA	R	#	1562	..	1588	1596	NELS10
NELSON Martin	S	W	YO	D		..	..	1574	1625	NELS14
NELSON (Maurus)	OSB		LA	E		..	1681	..	1690	NELS16
NELSON Ralph (James)	OSB		LA	E		1638	1660	..	1707	NELS18
NELSON Richard (Placid)	OSB		LA	E		..	1679	..	1742	NELS20
NELSON Thomas	S		YO	D	†	..	..	1577	1625	NELL22
NELSON Thomas	OSB		LA	G		1684	1703	1707	1738	NELS24
NELSON William	S		LA	Q	‡	..	..	1587	1588	NELS26
NELSON William (Benedict)	OSB		LA	E		1618	1640	..	1699	NELS28
NELSTROP William	S	L			7	..	..	..	..	NELS30
NESFIELD John	S	L	YO	D		1726	..	1751	1777	NESF02
NEVILLE Charles	SJ	W	LE	Y	#3	1746	1763	1771	1792	NEVI02
NEVILLE Edmund	SJ	N	YO	R	#	1563	1609	1608	1646	NEVI04
NEVILLE Fulke	S		WK	D	#§	..	..	1600	..	NEVI06
NEVILLE (Lawrence)	OSB			W	4	..	1630	..	1658	NEVI08
NEVILLE Michael	SJ				#	..	..	..	1640	NEVI10
NEWBY Augustine	SJ	L	LA	Y		1616	1637	..	1669	NEWB02
NEWBY	S	N			7	..	..	..	..	NEWB04
NEWLIN Robert	S			S		..	..	1683	1696	NEWL02
NEWMAN Andrew	S			D	*	..	..	1606	..	NEWM01
NEWMAN William	S		ST	S	#	1577	..	1606	1640	NEWM02
NEWPORT Charles	S		NN	D	#	..	..	1601	..	NEWP02
NEWPORT Richard BL.	S		NN	R	#+§	1572	..	1599	1612	NEWP04
NEWSHAM Andrew	S	N	LA	D	#	1597	..	1625	1647	NEWS02
NEWSHAM James	S	L	LA	D		1743	..	1767	1825	NEWS04
NEWTON Edward John Bapt.	SJ	M	LN	Y	#3	1720	1737	1746	1788	NEWT02
NEWTON James	SJ	M	MX	Y	#3	1736	1754	1763	1803	NEWT04
NEWTON Lancelot (Bede)	OSB	N	ND	X		1714	1732	1737	1777	NEWT06
NEWTON Robert	S	M	LN	L	#	1723	..	1747	1800	NEWT08
NEWTON William	SJ	L	LN	Y	#13	1683	1702	1712	1756	NEWT10
NEWTON William	SJ	M	LN	Y	3	1718	1736	1744	1755	NEWT12
NICHOLAS James	S	L	MX	D	3	1740	..	1766	1777	NICH02
NICHOLAS William	S	W			7	..	..	..	..	NICH03
NICHOLAS George VEN.	S	M	OX	Q	+‡	..	..	1583	1589	NICH04
NICHOLS Henry	S	L		L		1724	..	1748	1774	NICH06
NICHOLS James	S			L	3	..	..	1692	..	NICH07
NICHOLS John (Thomas)	OP		HA	N		1754	1772	1775	1785	NICH08
NICHOLS Richard	S	L	KT	P	†	..	..	1650	..	NICH10
NICHOLS see also NICHOLAS										
NICHOLSON Richard	S		YO	D	13	1650	..	1676	..	NICH12
NICHOLSON William	S			D	*	..	..	1577	..	NICH16
NIFFO (Augustine)	OFM		LC		123	1605	1633	1635	1665	NIFF02
NIGHTINGALE James	S		LA	Q		..	..	1584	..	NIGH02

Name	Reg	D	Co	T	Notes	Born	Prof	Ordn	Died	Code
NIGHTINGALE Richard	S		Y	R	#†°4	1585	..	1610	1641	NIGH04
NIHILL Edward	SJ	W	ZZ	Y	*	1752	1769	1776	1806	NIH102
NIHILL John	SJ		ZZ	Y	*	1750	1768	..	..	NIH104
NIXON Edward or Edmund	SJ	N	MX	Y	#	1675	1694	1703	1728	NIXO02
NIXON Thomas	SJ	N	LA	Y	3	1735	1756	1761	1793	NIXO04
NOEL John (Augustine)	OP	N		N	3	1739	1762	1767	1812	NOEL02
NOLAN James	S	L	IR	P	1	1723	..	..	1779	NOLA02
NORDEN John	S			Q	*	..	..	1583	1597	NORD02
NORMANTON Thomas (Leander)	OSB		SK	G	#§	1615	1649	..	1665	NORM02
NORMICOTE William	S			Q	*‡	..	..	1580	..	NORM04
NORMINGTON see NORMANTON										
NORRICE see NORRIS										
NORRIS Andrew	SJ	M	LA	R	#3	1654	1676	1685	1722	NORR02
NORRIS Augustine (Ignatius)	CRT		KT	C		1740	1766	1767	1783	NORR04
NORRIS Charles	CRT			C		..	1627	..	..	NORR05
NORRIS Charles	SJ	L	LA	R		1646	1682	1670	1690	NORR06
NORRIS John	SJ	L	MX	R	13	1671	1692	1706	1754	NORR08
NORRIS Richard	S	L	SM	Q	‡	1579	..	..	1590	NORR10
NORRIS Richard	S			S		..	..	1660	..	NORR12
NORRIS Richard	SJ		LA		#3	1658	1680	1686	1717	NORR14
NORRIS Robert or John	S		SM	D	°3	1764	..	1786	..	NORR16
NORRIS Sebastian	S	W	LA	R	#	1722	..	1746	1757	NORR18
NORRIS Silvester	SJ		SM	R	#12	1570	1606	1595	1630	NORR20
NORRIS	S			S	3	..	..	1612	..	NORR22
NORTH Andrew	S	N		D	3	..	..	1630	..	NORT02
NORTH John	S	N	LA	D	#	1603	..	1631	1669	NORT04
NORTHALL John	OSB		SP	G	#	..	1626	..	1666	NORT06
NORTHALL Richard (Clement)	OSB	L	SP	G	#	..	1645	..	1686	NORT08
NORTON Basil or John	S	L	YO	D	#	1595	..	1621	1662	NORT10
NORTON Benjamin	S	L	HA	R	4	1567	..	1591	1643	NORT12
NORTON (Edward)	OFM					..	..	..	1663	NORT14
NORTON Henry (Louis of Mary)	OFM				1	1586	..	..	1637	NORT15
NORTON John	OSB		SX	G		..	1624	..	1631	NORT16
NORTON Matthew (Thomas)	OP	M	YO	N	§	1732	1754	1757	1800	NORT18
NORTON Richard	S			Q	3	..	..	1589	1619	NORT20
NOTTLE (Joseph)	OP		MX	Z	#*	1654	1682	..	1696	NOTT02
NUGENT (Anthony)	CAP					..	..	..	..	NUGE02
NUGENT (Francis)	CAP				7	..	..	..	..	NUGE04
NUGENT Lavalin (Francis)	CAP		IR			1569	1592	1595	1635	NUGE06
NUGENT (Luke of Bracklyn)	CAP					1605	..	..	1673	NUGE08
NUGENT (Luke of Meath)	CAP		IR			..	..	..	1724	NUGE10
NUGENT (Peter of Meath)	CAP		IR			..	..	..	1691	NUGE12
NUTSHAW George or John	S			Q	*	..	..	1583	..	NUTS02
NUTT John (Pacificus)	OFM	M	WK	F	13	1738	1754	1761	1799	NUTT02
NUTTAL Edward (Constantius)	OSB	M	SK	W	#2	..	1610	..	1659	NUTT04
NUTTER Ellis	S			R	*	1569	..	1601	..	NUTT06
NUTTER John BL.	S		LA	Q	+†	..	..	1582	1584	NUTT08
NUTTER Robert VEN.	OP		LA	Q	#+‡12	1556	1587	1581	1600	NUTT10
OADCOCK see WOODCOCK										
OAKLEY Francis	SJ	N	WR	Y	#3	1694	1715	1729	1755	OAKL02
O'BRIEN (Francis of S.B'nard)	OFM		MX	F	13	1681	..	1702	1711	OBRI01
O'BRIEN Peter	SJ		IR	Y	3	1735	1754	1759	1807	OBRI02
O'CONNELL (Terence)	OP	L	IR		*	..	..	..	1668	OCON01
O'CONOR Charles	S	L	IR	R	3	1764	..	1791	1828	OCON04
O'DALY Daniel (Chris'er) ABP.	OP	L	IR		*3	1595	..	1627	1662	ODAL02
O'FARRELL (Bernardine)	CAP		IR			..	..	..	1669	OFAR02
O'FARREL (Lawrence)	OP		IR		*8	..	..	..	..	OFAR04
O'FINN see FINN										
OGDEN John	S				†7	..	..	..	..	OGDE02
OGILBY (Patrick)	OP			R	13	1643	1679	1685	1685	OGIL02
OGLE (Ambrose)	OFM		YO	F	123	1675	1695	1699	1728	OGLE01
OGLE William	S	N	ND	Q		..	..	1598	..	OGLE02
OGLE William	S		ND	L	#3	..	..	1644	..	OGLE04
OGNATE John (Joseph) d'	OSB	N	LC	E		..	1700	..	1740	OGNA02
O'GRADY (Patrick of Cork)	CAP	L	IR			..	..	..	1691	OGRA02
O'HEYN (Cornelius)	OP	L	IR	R	4	..	..	..	1686	OHEY02

Name	Reg	D	Co	T	Notes	Born	Prof	Ordn	Died	Code
OLDCORNE Edward BL.	SJ	M	YO	R	#+2	1561	1588	1587	1606	OLDC02
O'LEARY Arthur	CAP	L	IR	Z	*3	1729	..	1756	1802	OLEA02
OLIVER Andrew	S	M	SC			..	..	..	1823	OLIV02
OLIVER (Bertin)	CRT			C		..	..	..	1627	OLIV03
OLIVER Charles	SJ					..	..	..	1683	OLIV04
O'NEIL see NEIL										
ONION Thomas	S	M	ST	R	#	1740	..	1766	1814	ONIO02
O'PHELAN James	OP	L	IR		*	..	..	..	1705	OPHE02
ORD Ralph (Anthony)	OSB	N	ND	G		..	1685	..	1725	ORDA02
ORGAIN (Benedict of S.John)d'	OSB		FR	W	2	..	1611	..	1636	ORGA02
ORMACA see HORMASA										
ORME John	S	L	MX	R		1719	..	1744	1792	ORME02
ORRELL Brian	S	N	LA	D	#13	1664	..	1692	1739	ORRE02
ORRELL John	S	N	LA	D		1745	..	1770	1810	ORRE04
ORRELL Joseph	S	N	LA	D		1747	..	1773	1820	ORRE06
OSBALDESTON Edward VEN.	S	N	LA	Q	+	..	1585	1594		OSBA02
OSBALDESTON (Francis of Magd)	OFM			F	123	1605	1621	1646	1686	OSBA03
OSBALDESTON John	SJ	N	LA	Y		1655	1674	1683	1690	OSBA04
OSBORNE Edward	S	L	NN	Q	†4	1555	..	1581	1600	OSBO02
OSBOSTON see OSBALDESTON										
OSTCLIFFE George	S	N		Q	*	..	..	1579	..	OSTC02
OSTE (Augustine)	OSA		IR		*7	..	..	..	..	OSTE02
O'SULLIVAN (John Baptist)	OP	L	IR		*7	..	..	..	..	OSUL02
OTWAY George	S				*3	..	..	1577	..	OTWA02
OUDART (William of S.B'vent)	OFM		LC	F	123	1623	1649	1650	1665	OUDA02
OUDEN William	S	N			7	..	..	..	..	OUDE02
OVEN see OWEN										
OVERTON Edward	S		LN	V	#§	1580	..	1608	..	OVER02
OVINGTON (John)	OP					1654	1675	1678	1696	OVIN02
OWEN Hugh or John	SJ	W	AY	R	#§	1615	1648	1641	1689	OWEN02
OWEN Hugh	S	M	MI	R		1669	..	1692	1741	OWEN03
OWEN John	S	L	OX	Q	#‡°	1560	..	1584	..	OWEN04
OWEN John	S	W	OX	S	#	1593	..	..	..	OWEN05
OWEN John	S	W	GM	R		1676	..	1711	1760	OWEN06
OWEN John Francis	S		MX	D	3	1649	..	1676	..	OWEN07
OWEN Richard (Augustine)	OSB			D	*	..	1616	1599	1621	OWEN08
OWEN Robert	S		CN	D	3	..	..	1570	..	OWEN10
OWEN Robert (John)	OSB	L		V	#*†3	1584	1620	1610	1654	OWEN12
OWEN Thomas	SJ		HA		1	1557	1579	..	1618	OWEN14
OWEN Thomas	SJ				4	1614	1635	1644	1649	OWEN16
OWEN Walter	S		OX	Q	3	..	..	1591	1591	OWEN24
OWEN William	S				*6	..	..	..	..	OWEN26
OWENS see OWEN										
OWST Thomas	CRT			C		..	..	..	1679	OWST02
OXENBRIDGE Henry	SJ	L	HA	R	#=	1575	1605	1604	..	OXEN02
PAGE Alexander	SJ	L	DE	Y		1609	1631	..	1662	PAGE02
PAGE Anthony VEN.	S	N	MX	Q	+‡	..	..	1591	1593	PAGE04
PAGE Francis BL.	S	L	LC	D	#*+2	..	1602	1600	1602	PAGE06
PAGE Richard	S	L	NN	D	#	..	..	1610	1653	PAGE08
PAGES (Modestus of B.Trinity)	CAR		FR	Z	1	1650	1667	..	..	PAGE10
PAINE (Ambrose)	OFM			F	4	..	..	1743	1773	PAIN01
PAINE John ST.	S	L	NN	D	+§	..	..	1576	1582	PAIN04
PAINE (Placid)	OFM			F	#3	..	..	1754	1771	PAIN06
PAINE Thos.(Anselm S.Anthony)	OFM		MX	F	13	1736	1754	1761	1782	PAIN07
PAINTER Robert	OFM	N		F	34	..	..	1731	1770	PAIN08
PALASER Thomas VEN.	S	N	YO	V	+3	..	..	1595	1600	PALA02
PALGRAVE (Augustine of S.Ann)	OFM		NK	F	12	1608	1630	..	1679	PALG02
PALIN Richard	S	M	ST	D	3	1670	..	1698	1751	PALI02
PALIN Vincent	OSB		ST	W		..	1711	..	1735	PALI04
PALLISER see PALASER										
PALMER (Angelus)	CAP					..	..	..	1633	PALM01
PALMER Christopher	S		DV	R		..	..	1612	..	PALM02
PALMER Edward	ODC				1	1681	..	..	1727	PALM04
PALMER George	SJ	N	MX	Y	3	1692	1713	1722	1758	PALM06
PALMER John (Richard)	CAP					..	..	..	1644	PALM07
PALMER Ralph	SJ	M	YO	Y		1610	1638	..	1649	PALM08

Name	Reg	D	Co	T	Notes	Born	Prof	Ordn	Died	Code
PALMER William	OSB	L		Z	*	1575	1611	..	1655	PALM10
PALMES George	SJ	N	YO	D	#2	1576	1608	1607	1621	PALM14
PALMES George (Bernard)	OSB		YO	S	#3	1618	1643	1642	1663	PALM15
PALMES William	SJ	N	YO	R	#	1595	1618	1618	1670	PALM16
PAMEL see PALMER										
PANSFORD John	SJ		HA	V	#3	1592	1621	1620	1668	PANS02
PANTING John	SJ	W	MX	Y		1732	1749	1757	1783	PANT02
PARK Archibald	S		YO	R		1688	..	1718	..	PARK02
PARKER Bernard	OFM	M		F	#°3	..	..	1725	..	PARK04
PARKER (Cuthbert)	OSB	L	LA	E		..	1673	..	1705	PARK06
PARKER Francis	SJ		LA	Y		1606	1626	..	1679	PARK08
PARKER Francis	S	M	WR	P		1738	..	1763	1779	PARK10
PARKER (Gilbert)	OP			R	1	1667	1690	1693	1707	PARK12
PARKER Henry	OSB		LA	E		1752	1773	..	1817	PARK14
PARKER James	SJ	N	LA	S		1597	1623	1620	1657	PARK16
PARKER James	SJ	W	LA	Y	3	1747	1766	1771	1822	PARK18
PARKER John	SJ	W	ST	Y		1611	1630	..	1684	PARK20
PARKER Philip	S			Q	*	..	..	1583	..	PARK24
PARKER Richard	S	N	YO	D	#*	..	..	1577	..	PARK26
PARKER Thomas	SJ	M	LA	V	#3	1739	1763	1763	1820	PARK28
PARKINS Francis	S	L	HA	D	3	1667	..	1693	1760	PARK30
PARKINSON (Ant'y of S.B'vent)	OFM			F	34	1701	1729	1735	1750	PARK32
PARKINSON (Anthony)	OFM			F		..	..	..	1767	PARK34
PARKINSON (Bernardine)	OFM			F	1234	1677	1714	1716	1737	PARK36
PARKINSON Cuthbert	S		LA	D	3	1680	..	1710	1711	PARK38
PARKINSON Cuthbert (Anthony)	OFM	L		F	1234	1668	1686	1693	1728	PARK40
PARKINSON Edward	S	N	LA	D	#13	1664	..	1688	1735	PARK42
PARKINSON Edward	S			L	°3	..	..	1686	..	PARK44
PARKINSON Henry	S	N	LA	L		1772	..	1795	1832	PARK46
PARKINSON James	S	N	LA	D	#	1716	..	1740	1766	PARK48
PARKINSON James	S	N	LA	L		..	..	1758	1766	PARK50
PARKINSON Richard	SJ		YO	R		1681	1704	..	1748	PARK52
PARKINSON Robert	S			N	*‡3	..	..	1575	1607	PARK54
PARKINSON Thomas	S	N	LA	D	#	1713	..	1740	1751	PARK58
PARKINSON Thomas or James	S	N	LA	L		1741	..	1768	1821	PARK60
PARLOR John (Leo of M.Magdn.)	OFM		HR	F	123	1664	1684	1688	1692	PARL02
PARRY (Bonaventure of S.Anne)	OFM			F	123	1647	1662	1671	1720	PARR02
PARRY Charles	S				4	..	..	..	1684	PARR04
PARRY Edward	S	W		L	3	..	..	1670	..	PARR06
PARRY Hugh	S	W	FT	L	#	..	..	1640	..	PARR08
PARRY (Jerome of S.James)	OFM		MO	F	#1234	1653	1670	1677	1714	PARR10
PARRY John	SJ				4	1575	1604	..	1621	PARR12
PARRY John	S	W	DB	L	4	1622	..	1646	1694	PARR14
PARRY Philip	S	W	MO	L	#1	1605	..	1638	1678	PARR16
PARRY Pierce	S	M	DB	L	#	1716	..	1742	1792	PARR18
PARRY Thomas	S			D		..	..	1675	..	PARR20
PARRY William	S			D	#*34	..	..	1586	1626	PARR22
PARSLEY William	S			R	#*	1652	..	1676	1676	PARS02
PARSONS John	CRT		SM	V	2	..	1615	1594	1639	PARS04
PARSONS John	S		CH	R		1639	..	1664	..	PARS06
PARSONS Richard	SJ		MX	Y	23	1597	1627	1636	..	PARS08
PARSONS Robert	SJ		SM	R	‡	1546	1575	1578	1610	PARS10
PARSONS Robert	SJ	W	SM	R	#§3	1588	1628	1619	1658	PARS12
PARSONS Robert	SJ			R	*3	1648	1665	1678	1680	PARS14
PASTON Clement	OSB		NK	E		1663	1683	..	1724	PAST02
PASTON Edward	S		NK	D	#	1641	..	1666	1714	PAST04
PATENSON Bernard	S	N		Q	*†	..	..	1585	..	PATE02
PATENSON William BL.	S			Q	*+	..	..	1587	1592	PATE04
PATERSON George	SJ	L	SC		#	1621	1641	..	1703	PATE06
PATERSON James	S	N	LA	R	#1	1600	..	1627	..	PATE07
PATERSON John	S	M				..	..	..	1806	PATE08
PATERSON Thomas	SJ		MX			1625	1646	..	1699	PATE10
PATIENT Robert (Vincent)	OP	L		N		1730	1759	1761	1802	PATI02
PATOUILLET Nicolas	SJ	L	FR			1622	..	..	1710	PATO02
(Patrick of S.Brigit)	ODC	L	IR		*7	..	..	..	..	PATR02
(Patrick of S.Columba)	ODC	L	IR			..	..	..	1657	PATR04

Name	Reg	D	Co	T	Notes	Born	Prof	Ordn	Died	Code
(Patrick of St Columba)	OFM	L	IR		*1	1606	..	..	..	PATR06
PATTEN Thomas	OSB	N	LA	G		1727	1746	..	1787	PATT02
(Paul of London)	OP		MX		*3	..	..	1597	..	PAUL01
PAULET George	S			S		..	..	1625	..	PAUL02
(Paulinode la Estrella)	OFM	L	PL		*7	..	..	..	..	PAUL04
PAVIER Francis	S		YO	L	#	1602	..	1633	1644	PAVI02
PAYNE see PAINE										
PAYTON Thomas	SJ		LN	Y		1607	1630	..	1660	PAYT02
PAZZI MANDIN (James) de	CAR		FR		1	1656	1674	..	..	PAZZ02
PEACH Edward	S	M	GL	T		1770	..	1795	1839	PEAC02
PEACH Henry	S	L	GL	D	3	1732	..	1759	1781	PEAC04
PEARCE James	SJ		SM	Y	#°	1692	1713	1720	..	PEAR02
PEARCE Martin	S	W	CL	R	#4	1654	..	1679	1716	PEAR04
PEARCE Philip	S		DV	R	#	1613	..	1637	..	PEAR06
PEARCE Thomas	SJ		DV			1607	1639	..	1685	PEAR08
PEARCE see also PIERCE										
PEARSON John	S	N	YO	L		..	..	1689	..	PEAR10
PEARSON Thomas	SJ	N		Y	*	1646	1667	..	1732	PEAR12
PEARSON William	S	N	YO	R	#4	1632	..	1656	1669	PEAR14
PEASLEY Francis	S			S		..	..	1675	..	PEAS02
PECKHAM Robert	SJ	M	BU	V	#3	1586	1613	1608	1621	PECK02
PEDLY (Henry of S. Mary)	OFM		NT	F	123	1630	1651	1655	1693	PEDL02
PEDLY (Joseph)	OFM			F	3	..	..	1691	..	PEDL04
PEEL Robert	S			Q	*	..	..	1592	..	PEEL02
PEGGE Henry (Dominic)	OP		DE	R		1657	1677	1680	1691	PEGG02
PEGGE William	S	M	DE	D	#3	1637	..	1666	1711	PEGG04
PELCON Peter	SJ		MX	Y	#§13	1631	1656	1663	1669	PELC02
PELHAM William	SJ		SK	Y	1	1623	1643	..	1671	PELH02
PELLENTZ James	SJ		GS			1727	1744	..	1800	PELL02
PEMBERTON John William	SJ	N	LA	V	#13	1705	1733	1733	1763	PEMB02
PEMBRIDGE Michael (Benedict)	OSB	W	MX	G		1724	1741	..	1806	PEMB04
PENDRIL Richard	SJ		SP	Y	#*°	1710	1730	1738	..	PEND01
PENDRIL William	SJ	N	SP	V	#	1682	1708	1708	1748	PEND02
PENDRYCK William (Eliseus)	ODC	L	SC	R	§	1583	1613	..	1650	PEND04
PENKETH Charles	S	N	LA	S	#3	..	..	1684	..	PENK02
PENKETH John	SJ	N	LA	R	#1	1627	1663	1656	1701	PENK04
PENKETH John	S		LA	R	#*	1681	..	1710	..	PENK06
PENKETH John	S	L	LA	D	13	1732	..	1761	1813	PENK08
PENKETH Richard	S	N	LA	V	#3	1647	..	1677	1721	PENK10
PENKETH William	S	N	LA	R	#	1679	..	1704	1762	PENK12
PENKEVELL Mark	SJ		CL	R	°4	1571	1600	1599	1621	PENK14
PENNANT George	S	W	FT	D	3	..	..	1665	..	PENN02
PENNANT Thomas	SJ	W	FT	R	#§	1579	1613	1608	1638	PENN04
PENNANT Thomas	S	W	FT	D	#	1599	..	1625	..	PENN06
PENNE (Robert)	OFM			F	123	1651	1673	1677	1722	PENN07
PENNINGTON (Alan)	OP		LA			1670	1695	1696	1728	PENN08
PENNINGTON (Edmund)	OSB	N	LA	W	3	1757	1778	1782	1794	PENN10
PENNINGTON Francis	SJ		WR	Y		1644	1664	1674	1699	PENN12
PENNINGTON John	SJ		MX	Y		1647	1665	1674	1685	PENN14
PENNINGTON William	SJ		LA	Y	3	1661	1681	1689	1736	PENN16
PENNINGTON William	S	N	LA	D		1718	..	1744	1793	PENN18
PENNY (Francis of S.Mary)	OFM		DT	F		1643	..	..	1672	PENN20
PENRICE Charles	S	M	WR	L	3	..	..	1679	..	PENR02
PENSWICK Thomas	S	N	LA	R		1717	..	1743	1791	PENS02
PENSWICK Thomas BP.	S	N	LA	U	*	1772	..	1797	1836	PENS04
PENTRETH Richard	S		CL	V		1579	..	1600	..	PENT02
PERCON see PELCON										
PERCY Charles	SJ	M	YO	Y	3	1665	1685	1694	1735	PERC02
PERCY Francis	S			S	3	..	..	1650	..	PERC04
PERCY George	S		LA	Q		..	..	1587	..	PERC06
PERCY John	SJ	L	DH	R	#§	1568	1594	1593	1641	PERC08
PERCY Philip	SJ	N	YO	Y	13	1660	1683	1694	1724	PERC12
PERCY Robert	SJ	M	YO	Y	#1	1652	1674	1682	1715	PERC14
PERCY Thomas	SJ		SP	Y	3	1648	1667	1677	1685	PERC16
PERCY Walter	SJ		SP	Y	*	1651	1674	1682	..	PERC18
PERCY William	S		YO	D		..	..	1578	..	PERC20

Name	Reg	D	Co	T	Notes	Born	Prof	Ordn	Died	Code
PERCY see also PEARCE										
PEREIRA Manoel		L	PL		*7	..	..	..	1666	PERE02
PERISON William	SJ		YO	Y		1611	1631	..	1666	PERI02
PERKINS Christopher, Kt.	SJ		BK	R	°1	1547	1566	..	1622	PERK02
PERKINS James	S			D	3	..	..	1674	..	PERK04
PERKINS Richard	S	W	MO	D	#	1602	..	1627	1672	PERK06
PERROTT (George of S.William)	OFM		WR	F	12	1601	1623	..	1670	PERR02
PERROTT John	S	L	WR	L	#1	1629	..	1653	1714	PERR04
PERRY John Placidus	S	M	ST	D	3	1741	..	1770	1819	PERR06
PERRY Philip Mark	S	M	ST	P		1720	..	1751	1774	PERR08
PERSALL see also PURCELL										
PERSONS see PARSONS										
(Peter of the Mother of God)	ODC		LC		12	1635	1652	..	1705	PETE02
PETERS Charles	S	L		D	*3	1760	..	1786	1833	PETE04
PETERS James or John	S	L		D	*3	1763	..	1789	1848	PETE06
PETIT Cyriac or Charles	SJ		KT	Y	#3	1672	1697	1704	1710	PETI02
PETO Humphrey (Placid)	OSB		WK	Z	#*x24	..	1604	..	1643	PETO02
PETRE Benjamin BP.	S	L	EX	D	#*3	1672	..	1697	1758	PETR02
PETRE Charles	SJ	L	MX	Y	#	1646	1667	1673	1712	PETR04
PETRE Edward, Bt.	SJ	L	MX	Y	*	1633	1653	1662	1699	PETR06
PETRE Francis	S		EX	L		..	..	1689	1699	PETR08
PETRE Francis BP.	S	N	EX	D	#*	1692	..	1720	1775	PETR10
PETRE (Francis of S.John)	OFM		MX	F	1234	1638	1677	1679	1694	PETR11
PETRE John	SJ	M	EX	Y	#	1661	1680	1689	1738	PETR12
PETRE Philip	S		EX	D	3	1668	..	1693	..	PETR14
PETRE Richard	SJ		EX	Y	#	1634	1654	1661	1692	PETR16
PETRE Robert	SJ	L	EX	Y	#	1632	1654	1663	1713	PETR18
PETRE Robert	SJ		EX	Y	#13	1667	..	1695	1727	PETR20
PETRE Robert	SJ	N	EX	Y	3	1700	1719	1727	1766	PETR22
PETRE Thomas	SJ	N	EX	Y	13	1662	1679	1688	1729	PETR24
PETRE William	SJ			Y	#*	1650	1670	1679	1722	PETR26
PETT Henry	S		KT	R	#‡1	1570	..	1598	..	PETT02
PETT Robert	S		KT	R		..	..	1601	..	PETT04
PETINGER John (Dunstan)	OSB	L		W	#*	1586	1614	..	1665	PETT06
PEW see PUGH										
PHELAN William	S		IR	D		..	..	1779	..	PHEL02
PHELPS see PHILIPS										
PHILIP Robert	ORA				*7	..	..	..	..	PHIL01
PHILIPS (Aldhelm)	OSB		HR	W		..	1620	..	1636	PHIL02
PHILIPS Charles	S			V		..	..	1647	..	PHIL06
PHILIPS (Dominic)	OP	N	ND	N		1742	1759	1764	1783	PHIL08
PHILIPS Hugh	S	W		D	#*	..	..	1602	..	PHIL10
PHILIPS John	S	N	LA	R	#	1678	..	1703	1738	PHIL12
PHILIPS John (Columban)	OSB		PB	E		1613	1632	1639	1699	PHIL14
PHILIPS Peter	S				*13	1560	..	1611	1628	PHIL16
PHILIPS Peter	S	N	WR		#	1710	..	..	1761	PHIL18
PHILIPS Robert	ORA	L	SC		13	1585	..	1612	1647	PHIL20
PHILIPS Thomas	SJ	M	BU			1708	1726	..	1774	PHIL22
PHILIPS Vincent	SJ		WR	Y	#3	1698	1717	1726	1760	PHIL24
PHILIPS William	SJ		SM		1	1544	1569	1574	1584	PHIL26
PHILIPS William	S		HR	D	#°	..	..	1610	..	PHIL28
PHILIPS William	S	W	MO	V	#	1597	..	1622	1655	PHIL30
PHILIPS William	S			S	3	..	..	1628	..	PHIL32
PHILIPS William	OSB	L	WR	G	#	..	1682	..	1739	PHIL34
PHILIPS (William of S.Aug'ne)	OFM			F	14	1598	..	..	1634	PHIL36
PHILIPSON John	OSB		BK	G	1	1658	1676	..	1739	PHIL38
PHILIPSON William	OSB	N	BK	E		..	1684	..	1720	PHIL40
PHILLIPS see PHILIPS										
PHILMOT Philip	SJ	M	ST	Y	1	1652	1674	1683	1725	PHIL42
PHILPOTS William	S			S	3	..	..	1679	..	PHIL44
PIATT John	SJ	N	YO	Y	13	1686	1706	1715	1743	PIAT02
PIAZZA Hieronymo Bartolomeo	OP		IT		*°	..	..	..	1741	PIAZ02
PIAZZI Giuseppe	CRT		IT		*	1746	..	..	1826	PIAZ04
PIBUSH John BL.	S	L	YO	Q	#+	1557	..	1587	1601	PIBU02
PICKARD Ralph	S			R	*	..	..	1590	1590	PICK02
PICKERING Lancelot	S	N	WD	R		1681	..	1706	1763	PICK04

96

Name	Reg	D	Co	T	Notes	Born	Prof	Ordn	Died	Code
PICKERING Robert	SJ		BD	Y		1606	1622	1632	1636	PICK06
PICKERING Thomas	ODC	M	SP		1	i703	..	..	1789	PICK08
PICKFORD Edward	S		CL	D	#	1601	..	1627	1657	PICK10
PICKFORD John (Jerome)	OFM		CL	D	#24	1588	1619	1618	1665	PICK12
PICKFORD Thomas	SJ	M	CL	Y	#1	1608	1629	..	1676	PICK14
PIERCE William	S			S		..	..	1685	1687	PIER02
PIERCE see also PEARCE										
PIERCEY see PERCY										
PIERPOINT Thomas	S		OX	Q	3	..	..	1591	1591	PIER06
PIERPOINT William	S	L	LA	D	#	1753	..	1779	1828	PIER08
PIERSON see PEARSON										
PIGOTT Adam	SJ		MX	Y	#1	1673	1694	1702	1751	PIGO02
PIGOTT Christopher	S	L	MX	R		1675	..	1697	1735	PIGO04
PIGOTT Edward (Gregory)	OSB		OX	G		1692	1711	..	1749	PIGO06
PIGOTT Francis (Dunstan)	OSB		MX	G		1704	1727	..	1751	PIGO08
PIGOTT Thomas	S			S		..	..	1610	..	PIGO10
PILCHARD Thomas VEN.	S		SX	Q	#+‡1	1557	..	1583	1587	PILC02
PILE Henry	SJ	N	MD	Y	3	1743	1761	1768	1814	PILE02
PILKINGTON Robert	S		LA	Q		..	..	1583	..	PILK02
PILLING John (Bonaventure)	OFM		LA	F	1	1736	1752	1759	1801	PILL02
PILLING William (Leo S.Bonre)	OFM		LA	F	1	1746	1764	..	1801	PILL04
PINCKARD Robert	S	L	MX	D	#1	1704	..	1727	1766	PINC02
PINKNEY Miles	S		DH	D	#§	1599	..	1625	1674	PINK02
PIPPARD Luke	SJ		MX	Y	#3	1716	1733	1742	1761	PIPP02
PITCHFORD Thomas Edward	S	N	NK	T		..	..	1800	1808	PITC02
PITTS Arthur	S	M	OX	R	‡4	1557	..	1580	1635	PITT02
PITTS Henry	SJ	M	WK	Y	1	1638	1659	1668	1690	PITT04
PITTS John	S		HA	R	‡	1560	..	1586	1616	PITT06
PITTS Robert	S	M	OX	D	‡4	..	..	1576	1592	PITT08
PITTS Robert	S		DT	D	#3	1620	..	1650	1682	PITT10
PITTS Thomas (Walter)	CRT		OX	C	2	..	1575	..	1611	PITT12
PITTS William	S		HA	Q		..	..	1585	..	PITT14
PLASDEN Polydore ST.	S	L	MX	R	#+	1563	..	1586	1591	PLAS02
PLATT Francis	S		BK	R	#	1599	..	1623	..	PLAT04
PLATT Lawrence	S	L	BK	D	#	..	..	1626	1663	PLAT06
PLATT Ralph	S	N	LA	D	3	1758	..	1786	1837	PLAT08
PLEASINGTON John or Wm ST.	S	N	LA	V	#+1	1637	..	1662	1679	PLEA02
PLEASINGTON Joseph	SJ	N	LA	Y	#	1715	1737	1742	1781	PLEA04
PLEDGER Thomas	S				7	..	..	..	..	PLED02
PLETZIUS see PLOTTS										
PLOMERDEN see PLUMERDEN										
PLOTHO Delphine	SJ		LC	Y	1	1668	1687	1693	1747	PLOT02
PLOTTS John	SJ		ST	Y	#	1614	1634	..	1688	PLOT04
PLOWDEN Charles	SJ	N	SP	R	#	1743	1759	1770	1821	PLOW02
PLOWDEN Edmund	SJ			Y	#*3	1665	1682	1694	1740	PLOW04
PLOWDEN Francis	SJ		OX	Y	#1	1661	1682	1689	1736	PLOW06
PLOWDEN Francis	S		SP	P	3	..	..	1732	1788	PLOW08
PLOWDEN George	S		OX	R	*	1651	..	1676	1694	PLOW10
PLOWDEN Joseph	SJ		OX	Y		1655	1676	1685	1692	PLOW12
PLOWDEN Percy	SJ			Y	*	1672	1693	1703	1745	PLOW14
PLOWDEN Richard	SJ	L		Y	#*	1663	1679	1690	1729	PLOW16
PLOWDEN Robert	SJ	W	SP	Y	3	1740	1756	1764	1823	PLOW18
PLOWDEN Thomas	SJ	L	OX	Y	#	1594	1617	..	1664	PLOW20
PLUMMERDEN Robert	S		MX	R	#	1664	..	1688	1751	PLUM02
PLUMMERDEN Thomas	S		MX	D	#°3	1674	..	1703	..	PLUM04
PLUNKETT Gerard (Albert)	OP	N	MX	N	#1	1744	1762	1769	1814	PLUN01
PLUNKETT Oliver ARCHBP. ST.	S	L	IR	R	*+	1629	..	1654	1681	PLUN02
PLUNKETT (Oliver of Dublin)	CAP	L	IR			..	..	..	1748	PLUN03
PLUNKETT Richard	S	L	MX	R	#	1743	..	1768	1808	PLUN04
PLUNKETT Robert	SJ		MX	D	*	1752	1769	1779	1815	PLUN06
PLUNKETT Thomas (Anthony)	OP	N	MX	N		1750	1767	1774	1810	PLUN08
POLE Anthony	SJ		MX	Y	#§°13	1593	1614	1621	..	POLE02
POLE Anthony	SJ		DE	R	12	1627	1658	1658	1692	POLE04
POLE Charles de la	SJ	L	LC	Y		1669	1688	1697	1740	POLE06
POLE Edward	S	L	WK	Q	x	..	..	1580	1584	POLE08
POLE Francis	SJ	M	DE	V		1624	1653	1649	1684	POLE10

Name	Reg	D	Co	T	Notes	Born	Prof	Ordn	Died	Code
POLE Francis	SJ	M	LA	Y		1711	1728	1736	1767	POLE12
POLE George	SJ	N	DE	V		1628	1656	1653	1669	POLE14
POLE Germain	SJ	M	DE	S	23	1578	1619	1608	1648	POLE16
POLE Gervase	SJ	M	DE	R		1572	1608	1598	1641	POLE18
POLE Henry	S	N	DE	R		1670	..	1694	..	POLE20
POLE John	SJ		DE		4	1574	1598	..	1604	POLE24
POLE John	SJ	N	YO	V		1621	1660	1647	1666	POLE26
POLE Michael	SJ	W	YO	Y	3	1687	1707	1716	1748	POLE28
POLE Peter	SJ	L				1728	1748	..	1793	POLE30
POLE Toussaint de la	SJ		LC	Y		1673	1694	1703	1710	POLE32
POLE William	SJ	N		Y	3	1752	1771	1778	1828	POLE34
POLEHAMPTON Edward (Peter)	OP					1709	1729	1732	1740	POLE36
POLLEN see PULLEN										
POLTON see POULTON										
POOLE see POLE										
POPE Edward (Alexius)	OSB	W	LA	W	#	1732	1749	..	1777	POPE02
POPE James (Alexius)	OSB	N	LA	W		1755	1776	..	1837	POPE04
POPE Richard	OSB	N	LA	W		1760	1781	..	1828	POPE06
PORA (Charles)	OFM		LC	F	#123	1629	1649	1653	1693	PORA02
PORDAGE William	SJ	M	KT	Y	#1	1651	1671	1680	1736	PORD02
PORMORT Thomas VEN.	S	L	LN	R	#+†	..	..	1587	1592	PORM02
PORRET George	OFM			F	123	1599	1627	1625	1635	PORR02
PORTER Francis	OSB	N	DH	X		..	1658	..	1689	PORT04
PORTER George (Alban)	OSB	N	CD	X		..	1664	..	1693	PORT06
PORTER James	SJ		LC	Y	3	1733	1752	1759	1810	PORT08
PORTER (Jerome)	OSB		CD	G	#	..	1622	..	1632	PORT10
PORTER John	S			D	#*	..	..	1621	..	PORT12
PORTER John (Peter)	OP		DH			1725	1744	1749	1759	PORT14
PORTER Joseph Thomas	S		IT	R	°	1772	..	1795	..	PORT16
PORTER Nicholas	SJ		ES	Y	3	1724	1741	1748	1802	PORT18
PORTER Simon	S		WK	D	#	..	..	1612	..	PORT20
PORTMAN John	S	N	MX	R	#§°	1651	..	1675	..	PORT24
POSS Nicholas (Maurus)	OSB	L		G	#	..	1650	..	1699	POSS02
POSTGATE Nicholas VEN.	S	N	YO	D	#+1	1598	..	1628	1679	POST02
POSTGATE Ralph	SJ	M	OX	R		1648	1674	1674	1718	POST04
POSTLETHWAITE James	S	N	LA	D		1723	..	1748	1781	POST06
POSTLETHWAITE John	S	N	LA	D	3	1727	..	1754	1785	POST08
POSTLETHWAITE Thomas	S		LA	L		..	..	1763	1776	POST10
POTIER John	S	L	HT	D	#	1758	..	1783	1823	POTI02
POTIER Peter Philip (Pius)	OP	L	MX	N		1756	1782	1782	1846	POTI04
POTTINGER Simon	S		HA	D	#‡	..	..	1599	..	POTT02
POTTER see PORTER										
POTTS Henry Joseph	S		ND	L		1772	..	..	1800	POTT06
POTTS John (Bede)	OSB	N	ND	X		1674	1691	..	1744	POTT08
POTTS Luke	S	N	ND	D	#	1717	..	1744	1787	POTT10
POTTS Thomas	S	M	ST	D		1754	..	1778	1819	POTT12
POULTON Andrew	SJ	L	NN	Y		1654	1674	1685	1710	POUL02
POULTON Charles	SJ		NN	Y	#x	1616	1637	..	1690	POUL04
POULTON Ferdinand	SJ	L	BU	R	#§1	1584	1615	..	..	POUL06
POULTON Ferdinand	SJ	N	NN		#	1605	1625	..	1666	POUL08
POULTON Ferdinand John	SJ		BU	R	#12	1600	1621	..	1641	POUL10
POULTON George	SJ		NN	Y	3	1689	1707	1732	1739	POUL12
POULTON Giles	SJ		NN	Y	#1	1600	1622	..	1666	POUL14
POULTON Giles	SJ		NN	R	#	1694	1721	1719	1752	POUL16
POULTON Henry	SJ		NN	V	3	1583	..	1612	..	POUL18
POULTON Henry	SJ		NN	Y	#	1679	1700	..	1712	POUL20
POULTON John	SJ		NN	R	#	1610	1650	1636	1656	POUL22
POULTON John (Joseph of Jn.B)	OFM	L	NN	F	3	1682	1701	1707	1748	POUL26
POULTON Thomas	SJ		BU	R	#§	1577	1613	1617	1637	POUL28
POULTON Thomas	SJ		NN	Y	3	1668	1685	1694	1725	POUL30
POULTON Thomas	SJ		NN	Y	3	1697	1717	1724	1749	POUL32
POULTON William	SJ		NN		4	..	..	..	1596	POUL34
POULTON William	S	L	NN	R	#	1616	..	1655	1672	POUL36
POULTON William	S	M	WR	R		1676	..	1703	1726	POUL38
POUND John	S		HA		=3	..	..	1574	..	POUN02
POUND Thomas	SJ				4	1574	1594	..	1621	POUN04

Name	Reg	D	Co	T	Notes	Born	Prof	Ordn	Died	Code
POWELL Charles	SJ	N		Y	*3	1660	1679	1687	1738	POWE02
POWELL David (Gregory)	OFM	W	BR	F		..	..	..	1781	POWE04
POWELL Francis	SJ	L	EX	Y	#1	1658	1677	1689	1733	POWE06
POWELL George	S		MO	R	#	1609	..	1632	..	POWE08
POWELL James	S	W		Q	*	..	..	1583	..	POWE10
POWELL John	S	W	HR	D	#	1614	..	..	1667	POWE12
POWELL John	S			V		..	..	1656	..	POWE14
POWELL (Mansuetus)	OSB		IR	Z	*	..	1621	..	1664	POWE16
POWELL Richard	SJ	M	EX	Y	1	1610	1629	..	1653	POWE18
POWELL Roger (Philip) BL.	OSB	W	BR	N	#+=13	1594	1620	1618	1646	POWE20
POWELL Thomas	S	W	MO	L	#	1615	..	1639	1700	POWE22
POWELL Thomas	S			V		..	..	1704	..	POWE24
POWELL William	CRT			C		..	1566	..	1581	POWE25
POWELL William	SJ	W			*4	1563	1587	..	1610	POWE26
POWER Edmund	SJ	M	IR	Y	34	1736	1754	1761	1779	POWE28
POWER James	SJ	L	IR		2	1725	1741	..	1788	POWE30
POYNTER William BP.	S	L	HA	D	*	1762	..	1786	1827	POYN02
POYNTZ Francis (James)	OSB	L	NN	E	§	1661	1688	..	1718	POYN04
POYNTZ John	SJ		GL		#	1602	1625	..	1671	POYN06
POYNTZ John	SJ	L	DV	Y	#3	1709	1732	1739	1789	POYN08
POYNTZ Newdigate	S		MX	R	*	1680	..	1706	1723	POYN10
PRACID Jeremiah or John	SJ	N	YO	Y	#§	1639	1675	1665	1686	PRAC02
PRANCE Charles	S		CB	D	#	1646	..	1672	..	PRAN02
PRANCE Thomas	S	M	CB	V	#	..	..	1655	..	PRAN04
PRATER Joseph	OSB		SM	S		..	1600	1603	1631	PRAT02
PRATER Richard	S		SM	D		..	..	1604	..	PRAT04
PRATT Henry (Felix)	OSB		NN	D	#	..	1614	1606	1634	PRAT06
PRENDERGAST Peter	S	L	IR			..	..	..	1792	PREN02
PRESCOT Joseph Richard	S	L		D	*3	1737	..	1764	1783	PRES02
PRESTON (Bernard)	OSB			Z	*	..	1627	..	1649	PRES04
PRESTON Henry	S	L	LA	L	3	..	..	1692	1733	PRES08
PRESTON John	S		MX	L	§	1712	..	1736	1780	PRES10
PRESTON Roland (Thomas)	OSB	L	SP	R	x	1566	1592	1590	1647	PRES12
PRESTON William	SJ	L	NN	R	#	1637	1662	1661	1702	PRES14
PRETTY Henry	S	M		D	#*	..	..	1620	..	PRET02
PRETTY William	S	M		D	#*	..	..	1616	..	PRET04
PRICE (Bernard)	OFM			F	1234	1668	1686	1691	1730	PRIC00
PRICE (Bruno)	OFM		MT	F	8	..	..	..	..	PRIC01
PRICE (Felix)	OFM			F	34	..	..	1678	1700	PRIC02
PRICE Humphrey	S	W	MT	L	#	1611	..	1636	..	PRIC03
PRICE Ignatius (Walter)	SJ			Y	#1	1609	1634	..	1679	PRIC04
PRICE James	S	L	HR	D	3	..	..	1667	1697	PRIC06
PRICE James (Bernard)	OSB	N	LA	W		1719	1737	..	1766	PRIC08
PRICE John	SJ	M	CH	S		1576	1601	..	1645	PRIC10
PRICE John	S	N	HR	R		1681	..	1708	1738	PRIC12
PRICE John	SJ	N	CL	Y		1739	1758	1765	1813	PRIC13
PRICE Philip (Pacificus)	OFM		HR	F	123	1643	1663	1671	1706	PRIC14
PRICE Thomas	SJ		CH	V		1571	1601	1599	1625	PRIC16
PRICE Thomas	S		HA	R	#§	1603	..	1634	1635	PRIC18
PRICE Thomas	S	M	HR	V		1763	..	1787	1831	PRIC20
PRICE Thomas (Andrew)	ODC	L			14	1676	1693	..	1735	PRIC22
PRICE William	S			D		..	..	1598	..	PRIC24
PRICE William	S			D	*	..	..	1607	..	PRIC26
PRICE William (Louis)	ODC		CM		2	1657	1682	..	..	PRIC28
PRICE see also RICE, APRICE										
PRICHARD Charles	SJ	W	MO			1637	1662	..	1680	PRIC30
PRICHARD James	S		MO	D	3	1639	..	1663	1697	PRIC34
PRICHARD James	S		MO	R	#	1651	..	1677	..	PRIC35
PRICHARD John	S				#§	1700	..	..	..	PRIC36
PRICHARD (Leander)	OSB		MO	G	4	..	1623	..	1685	PRIC38
PRICHARD Matthew BP.	OFM	W	MO	F	*123	1669	1687	1693	1750	PRIC40
PRICHARD Nicholas (Maurus)	OSB		MO	G		1602	1620	..	1657	PRIC42
PRICHARD William	S		MO	R	#	1662	..	1687	..	PRIC44
PRICHARD William	S		HR	L	3	..	..	1734	1734	PRIC46
PRIFORD see PICKFORD										
PRINCE James	S	L	BD	D	#	1602	..	1628	..	PRIN02

Name	Reg	D	Co	T	Notes	Born	Prof	Ordn	Died	Code
PRINCE Richard	SJ		OX	Y	#x	1648	1668	1677	1680	PRIN04
PRISTOE James (Angelus)	OFM		LA	F		1622	1641	..	1662	PRIS02
PRITCHARD see PRICHARD										
PROBERT Edward	S	L	LA	D	#	..	..	1612	..	PROB02
PROBERT Hugh or John	S		HR	R		1546	..	1581	..	PROB04
PROBIN Edward	S	M	CH	D	#	..	..	1616	..	PROB06
PROSSER Philip	S	L	HR	R	#	1635	..	1670	..	PROS02
PRYNNE Jerome	S			L		..	..	..	1708	PRYN02
PUDSEY Stephen	S		YO	D	#34	1610	..	1636	1649	PUDS02
PUGH Henry	S		FT	R	*	..	..	1591	1592	PUGH02
PUGH John	S		CN	R	#	1621	..	1645	1645	PUGH04
PUGH John	S	W	DB	L	3	1641	..	1666	1673	PUGH06
PUGH Maurice	S	W		L	#34	..	..	1686	1719	PUGH08
PUGH Robert	S		CN	V	*x1	1610	..	1633	1679	PUGH10
PUGH Stephen	S	W			7	..	..	..	..	PUGH11
PUGH William	S	W	CN	V		..	..	1676	..	PUGH12
PUGH William (Charles)	OSB	W	FT	E	#	..	1660	..	1680	PUGH14
PULLEN see PULLEYN										
PULLEYN Gregory	S				7	..	..	..	..	PULL01
PULLEYN Joshua	SJ	L	YO	D		1543	1594	1578	1607	PULL02
PULLEYN Michael	OSB		YO	G		1653	1672	..	1723	PULL04
PULLEYN William	S		YO	Q	‡	..	..	1583	..	PULL06
PULTNEY William	S				7	..	..	..	..	PULT02
PULTON see POULTON										
PURCELL John	SJ	L	ST	R	#	1633	1653	1666	1701	PURC01
PURCELL Philip	S	L	SP	L	3	..	..	1699	..	PURC02
PURCELL Walter	S	M	ST	R	#	1627	..	1651	1679	PURC04
PURCELL Walter Chetwynd	S	M	SP	D	13	1654	..	1680	1720	PURC06
PURCELL William (Joseph)	OFM			F	3	..	..	1788	1820	PURC08
PURCELL see also PERSALL										
PURNELL William	S			S	7	..	..	..	..	PURN02
PYATT see PIATT										
QUATERMAIN William	S	W	YO	V	#3	..	..	1676	1720	QUAT02
QUIMPER (Ant'y of Corisopito)	CAP	L	FR		2	..	1655	..	1688	QUIM02
QUIN Charles	SJ	L				..	..	..	..	QUIN02
QUIN James	SJ		MX	Y	3	1698	1717	1725	1745	QUIN04
QUIN John	S	W			7	..	..	..	..	QUIN05
QUINTIN George	S	L	MX	R	#	1619	..	1647	1685	QUIN06
QUINTIN Robert	S			D	#*	..	..	1642	1674	QUIN08
QUYNEO (Bernard)	OSB		MX	W		..	1693	..	1731	QUYN02
RABAN see RATHBONE										
RADCLIFFE Fortunatus (Felix)	OFM		LA	F	124	1632	1658	..	1673	RADC01
RADCLIFFE Francis (Ildeph'us)	OSB		ND	X		..	1669	..	1689	RADC02
RADFORD John or Thomas	SJ	M		Q	#*	1561	1608	1587	1630	RADF02
RADFORD Joseph	SJ		MX	Y	°1	1646	1677	1685	..	RADF04
RAFFA Anthony (Leander)	OSB	N	MX	G		..	1733	..	1758	RAFF02
RAGWAY Thomas	S		MX	R		1674	..	1696	1698	RAGW02
RAMSEY (Dominic of S.Clare)	OFM			F	3	..	..	1668	..	RAMS02
RAND Thomas	SJ	M	OX		124	1577	1600	..	1657	RAND02
RANDOLPH (Leo of St M.Magd.)	OFM	M	WK	F	1234	1631	1652	1656	1700	RAND04
RASTELL John	SJ		GL	N	13	1533	1568	1566	..	RAST02
RATHBONE William	S		LA	D		..	..	1607	1626	RATH02
RAVENHILL John	S	W	HR	R	#1	1625	..	1652	..	RAVE02
RAVENHILL Richard (Angelus)	OFM		HR	F	134	1726	1743	1752	1791	RAVE04
RAVENHILL Thos.(Anth'y S.Jos)	OFM			F	*7	..	..	..	..	RAVE06
RAVENSCROFT James	S	M	LN	D		1635	..	1659	1703	RAVE08
RAWDON Roger	S			Q	*	..	..	1591	..	RAWD02
RAWLINS Alexander BL.	S	N	OX	Q	#+‡	1560	..	1590	1595	RAWL02
RAWLINS Henry	S		WR	R		1659	..	1686	..	RAWL04
RAWLINSON John	S	L		D	#*	..	..	1642	..	RAWL06
RAYMENT Benedict	S	N	WR	D		1764	..	1788	1842	RAYM02
RAYMOND Charles	SJ		ES	V	3	1665	1686	1694	1725	RAYM04
RAYNES Edward	S	N		D	*	..	..	1600	..	RAYN06
RAYNES Thomas (of Jesus)	ODC	L			1	1756	..	..	1810	RAYN08
RAYNOR see REYNER										
READ Francis	S		ND	R		1628	..	1652	..	READ02

Name	Reg	D	Co	T	Notes	Born	Prof	Ordn	Died	Code
READ Robert	S	L	MX	R	§	1744	..	1768	1770	READ04
READ Thomas	S	L	HA	D	‡	1606	..	1649	1669	READ06
READING Henry	SJ					..	..		1682	READ07
READING Thomas	S	N	DH	R	#§	1597	..	1638	1672	READ08
REDFORD Sebastian	SJ			Y	#*3	1701	1719	1729	1763	REDF02
REDING see READING										
REDMAN John	S	N	LA	R		1567	..	1591	1645	REDM02
REDMAN John	S			D	*	..	..	1594	1617	REDM04
REDMAN William	S		YO	D		1581		1610	..	REDM06
REES William	S		GM	R	#§	1605	..	1630		REES02
REEVE John Austin	S	M	MX	D		1758	..	1783	1813	REEV02
REEVE Joseph	SJ	W	WK	Y	#3	1733	1752	1765	1820	REEV04
REEVE Richard	SJ	N	WK	Y	#3	1740	1757	1765	1816	REEV06
REEVE Thomas	SJ	L	WR	Y	#	1752	1770	..	1826	REEV08
RENOULT Romanus	SJ		FR			1703	1722	..	1776	RENO02
REVELL (Hyacinth)	OP		LC	N	4	..	..	..	1668	REVE02
REVELL Thomas	S		YO	L	3	..	..	1697	..	REVE04
REYNER Clement (Lawrence)	OSB		YO	D	#	1587	1609	..	1664	REYN04
REYNER Wilfrid (Clement)	OSB		YO	D	#	..	1610	1602	1651	REYN05
REYNER William	S			R	*3	..	..	1592	..	REYN06
REYNOLDS William	S		DV	D	‡	1543	..	1580	1594	REYN07
REYNOLDS William	S	M	OX	L	3	1648	..	1675	1718	REYN08
REYNOLDSON John	SJ		MX	Y	3	1655	1673	1681	1686	REYN10
RHEES see REES										
RHODES Alexander	SJ				7	..	..	..	..	RHOD02
RIBE Lawrence	S			S	3	..	..	1603	..	RIBE02
RIBERTIERRE Bernard	OSB		FR	G	*	..	1621	..	1664	RIBE04
RICE Joseph	S	L	MX	R		1744	..	1768	1810	RICE02
RICE see also PRICE, APRICE										
RICH Francis	OSB	N	KT	G		1670	1692	1698	1740	RICH02
RICHARD see RICHARDS										
RICHARDS Aloysius	SJ					..	..	..	1681	RICH04
RICHARDS Henry	S	L	DT	R		1649	..	1676	1682	RICH06
RICHARDS John	S		DV	R		1561	..	1587	..	RICH08
RICHARDS John	SJ			Y	3	..	..	1768	..	RICH09
RICHARDS Edward	S		HA	V	#	1601	..	1627	..	RICH10
RICHARDSON Francis or Richard	S	W	BD	R	1	1644	..	1669	..	RICH14
RICHARDSON George	S	N			#§	..	..	..	1672	RICH15
RICHARDSON James	SJ	W		Y	*4	1650	1669	1678	1727	RICH16
RICHARDSON John	S				7	..	..	..	..	RICH17
RICHARDSON John	S		MX	R	#14	1639	..	1664	1667	RICH18
RICHARDSON John	SJ	N	LA	Y	#	1662	1684	1691	1728	RICH20
RICHARDSON John	SJ	N	LA	Y	3	1734	1755	1762	1782	RICH22
RICHARDSON John (Augustine)	OSB		SM	G	4	..	1618	..	1626	RICH24
RICHARDSON John (Nicholas)	OSB		LA	W		1715	1737	..	1762	RICH26
RICHARDSON Joseph	SJ	M	WK	Y		1606	1637	..	1670	RICH28
RICHARDSON Richard	SJ	N	LA	Y	1	1669	1690	1699	1738	RICH30
RICHARDSON Robert	SJ		MX	Y	#3	1671	1688	1698	1737	RICH32
RICHARDSON Sylvester	S	N	LA	D	3	1741	..	1768	1776	RICH34
RICHARDSON William BL.	S	L	YO	S	#+3	1572	..	1600	1603	RICH36
RICHARDSON William	SJ	N	DH	Y	#	1652	1674	1679	1689	RICH38
RICHART see RICHARDS										
RICHMOND William	S	N	DH	Q	#	..	..	1581	..	RICH40
RICKABY John	S	N	YO	U		..	..	1798	1821	RICK02
RIDDELL Edward (Joseph)	OSB		ND	X		..	1719	..	1736	RIDD02
RIDDELL George (Gregory)	OSB	L	ND	X		..	1688	..	1730	RIDD04
RIDDELL Peter	SJ		ND	Y	4	1636	1656	1664	1668	RIDD06
RIDDELL Robert	S	N	ND	R	#4	1644	..	1668	1702	RIDD08
RIDDELL Robert (Thomas)	OSB		ND	X		1698	1715	..	1740	RIDD10
RIDDELL Thomas	S	N	YO	D	#	..	..	1608	..	RIDD11
RIDDELL William	SJ	N	ND	Y	13	1669	1687	1695	1711	RIDD12
RIDER Anthony	S			Q	*3	..	..	1578	..	RIDE00
RIDER Francis	S	M	ST	D	1	1622	..	1650	..	RIDE01
RIDER Nicholas (Joseph)	ODC		IR		12	1600	1631	..	1682	RIDE02
RIDER Simon	S	L	ST	P	3	1668	..	1693	1730	RIDE04
RIDGLEY John (John Baptist)	ODC		MX	R	#§2	1587	1634	1612	1669	RIDG02

101

Name	Reg	D	Co	T	Notes	Born	Prof	Ordn	Died	Code
RIDLEY Roger (Bartholomew)	OSB		OX	D	‡124	1563	1610	1600	1616	RIDL02
RIGBY Alexander (Sixtus)	OP			R	*2	1561	1585	..	..	RIGB02
RIGBY James	S		LA	D	#3	1671	..	1699	1731	RIGB04
RIGBY James	S	M	LA	R		1705	..	1730	1751	RIGB06
RIGBY John	S		OX	D	#	1600	..	1632	1684	RIGB08
RIGBY John	SJ	N	LA	Y	3	1712	1732	1738	1758	RIGB10
RIGBY John	SJ		LA	Y	1	1737	1758	1765	1767	RIGB12
RIGBY John	S	N	LA	P		1733	..	1782	1818	RIGB14
RIGBY John (Bede)	OSB		LA	X		1774	1798	..	1837	RIGB16
RIGBY John (Placid)	OSB		LA	W		..	1728	..	1764	RIGB18
RIGBY Lawrence	S	N	LA	D		1675	..	1703	1731	RIGB20
RIGBY Roger	SJ		LA	Y	#	1608	1629	1639	1646	RIGB22
RIGBY Thomas	S	L	LA	P		1747	..	1776	1815	RIGB24
RIGLY see RIDGLEY										
RIGMAIDEN John	SJ	N	LA	Y	#	1710	1732	1739	1782	RIGM02
RIGMAIDEN John (Maurus)	OSB	M	LA	W	#	1672	1695	..	1759	RIGM04
RIGMAIDEN Simeon (Benedict)	OSB	W	LA	W	#	..	1708	..	1749	RIGM06
RILEY John	SJ	N	YO	R	#§	1610	1640	1635	1667	RILE02
RIMMER Richard	S	N	LA	D		1754	..	1779	1828	RIMM02
RISDON Edward	CRT			C		..	1570	..	1578	RISD01
RISDON Thomas	SJ	W	DV	Y	#3	1662	1682	1694	1744	RISD02
RISDON Thomas (Cuthbert)	OSB		DV	E		..	1640	..	1652	RISD04
RISDON William	SJ		DV			..	..	..	1644	RISD06
RISDON see also RISHTON										
RISHTON Edward	S	L	LA	D	‡	1550	..	1577	1585	RISH02
RISHTON Edward	S		LA	R	#	1614	..	1639	..	RISH04
RISHTON Ralph	S		LA	R	#	1612	..	1637	..	RISH06
RISHTON see RISDON										
RISHWORTH William	S		LN	D	#	..	..	1615	1637	RISH08
RISLEY William	S	N	BU	V	=§	1594	..	1637	..	RISL04
RITTER John Bapt. de	SJ				4	..	..	..	1787	RITT02
RIVERS Anthony	SJ	L			#4	..	..	..	1621	RIVE02
RIVERS Charles	S			S	3	..	..	1715	..	RIVE04
RIVERS Richard	SJ	M	LN	Y		1607	1648	..	1679	RIVE06
RIVERS William	SJ	W		Y		1605	1632	..	1642	RIVE08
ROABES (Gabriel of S.Mary)	OFM		MX	F	12	1616	1639	..	1678	ROAB02
ROAN (Basil)	OSB			G		..	1654	..	1673	ROAN02
(Robert of Paris)	CAP	L	FR		2	..	1640	..	1683	ROBE01
ROBERTS Francis	SJ		HR	Y		1611	1637	..	1652	ROBE02
ROBERTS (Gregory of S.Jn.Bpt)	OFM		BK	F	123	1683	1700	1707	1710	ROBE04
ROBERTS James	S		MT	R		1687	..	1709	1709	ROBE06
ROBERTS John	S		NN	R	†	1560	..	1587	..	ROBE08
ROBERTS John ST.	OSB	L	MH	V	+‡=1	1576	1600	1602	1610	ROBE10
ROBERTS John	S	W	FT	R		1673	..	1708	1753	ROBE12
ROBERTS Peter Anthony	SJ					..	..	..	1588	ROBE14
ROBERTS Thomas or Roderick	SJ	W	CN	Y	1	1642	1666	1670	1721	ROBE16
ROBERTS Thomas	SJ	W	AY	Y	3	1673	1696	1705	1727	ROBE18
ROBERTS William (Augustine)	OFM		MO	F	1	1763	1785	1789	1827	ROBE20
ROBERTSON see ROBINSON										
ROBEY James	S	N	LA	D	3	1762	..	1788	1841	ROBE24
ROBINS William	S		CN	V	1	1574	..	1602	..	ROBI02
ROBINSON Andrew	SJ	M	YO	Y	3	1741	1763	1769	1826	ROBI04
ROBINSON Christopher VEN.	S	N	CD	Q	+	..	..	1592	1597	ROBI06
ROBINSON Christopher	SJ	N	CD	R	§	1586	1616	1610	1677	ROBI08
ROBINSON Edward	SJ		MX	R	#	1592	1621	1618	1636	ROBI12
ROBINSON Francis	S	N	YO	R		1569	..	1597	..	ROBI14
ROBINSON George (Placid)	OSB		YO	X	#	..	1701	..	1739	ROBI16
ROBINSON George (Robert)	OSB		MX	X		..	1722	..	1762	ROBI18
ROBINSON Gerard	S	L	IR	S		1729	..	1754	1799	ROBI20
ROBINSON (Gregory)	OSB			W		1710	1730	..	1749	ROBI22
ROBINSON John BL.	S	M	YO	Q	+	..	..	1585	1588	ROBI24
ROBINSON John	SJ		CD			1588	1628	..	1669	ROBI26
ROBINSON John	SJ	N	YO		#1	1598	1620	..	1675	ROBI28
ROBINSON John	S	N	LA	L	1	1615	..	1640	1676	ROBI30
ROBINSON John	SJ	N	MX	Y	#3	1699	1718	1727	1742	ROBI32
ROBINSON John (Bernard)	OSB	N	LA	W		1767	1788	1791	1851	ROBI34

Name	Reg	D	Co	T	Notes	Born	Prof	Ordn	Died	Code
ROBINSON (Lawrence)	OFM			F	123	1693	1726	1729	1761	ROBI36
ROBINSON (Maurus)	OSB		YO	E		..	1653	..	1662	ROBI38
ROBINSON Michael	S	N	YO	D	#	1598	..	1624	..	ROBI40
ROBINSON Reginald	S	N		Q	*	..	..	1591	..	ROBI42
ROBINSON Richard	S	N	LA	D		..	..	1612	1634	ROBI44
ROBINSON Richard	OSS					..	..	..	1660	ROBI46
ROBINSON Robert (Paul)	OSB	L		W	§=1	1601	1625	..	1667	ROBI48
ROBINSON Thomas	SJ		LN	D	4	..	1575	1573	1593	ROBI50
ROBINSON Thomas	S	N	LA	R	#	1651	..	1677	..	ROBI52
ROBSON Christopher	SJ		IR	Y	#	1619	1647	1657	1685	ROBS02
ROBSON Robert (Peter)	OP			N		1743	1767	..	1788	ROBS04
ROCHE (Philip)	OFM	L	IR		*7	..	..	..	..	ROCH02
ROCK Samuel	S	M	ST	D	3	1762	..	1787	1839	ROCK02
ROCKLEY Francis	SJ		YO	Y	#4	1656	!675	1683	1725	ROCK04
RODEN see RAWDON										
ROE Bartholomew (Alban) ST.	OSB	L	SK	W	#+†	1583	1612	1615	1642	ROEA02
ROE James (Maurus)	OSB		SK	W	#§	..	1626	..	1657	ROEA04
ROE John	S	M		D	*	1757	..	1784	1838	ROEA06
ROGE Joseph	SJ		MX	Y	#	1681	1704	1712	1763	ROGE02
ROGERS Edward (Dunstan)	OSB	N	DB	E		..	1714	..	1746	ROGE06
ROGERS Francis	SJ		NK	Y		1599	1623	..	1660	ROGE08
ROGERS John	SJ	L	SM	R	#‡	1585	1611	1610	1657	ROGE10
ROGERS John	S	L		V	#	..	..	1658	1703	ROGE12
ROGERS Philip	SJ	N	DB	Y	#3	1691	1717	1727	1761	ROGE14
ROGERS Thomas	SJ	N	CB	R	#x§1	1596	1620	1620	1657	ROGE16
ROGERSON (James)	OFM		LA	F	3	..	1738	1746	1790	ROGE18
ROKEBY George (Joseph)	OSB		MX	X		1688	1703	..	1761	ROKE02
ROLAND Robert	S			S	3	..	..	1668	..	ROLA02
ROLLS Francis	S	N		D	#*	..	..	1642	1689	ROLL02
ROLSTON Francis	S	N	YO	D	1	1588	..	..	..	ROLS02
ROMSEY Benedict	S	M		R	#	1655	..	1679	1719	ROMS02
RONE Jerome	S	M	SP	R	#	1614	..	1639	..	RONE02
ROOK Henry	S		OX	Q		..	..	1589	..	ROOK02
ROOKWOOD Francis	OSB	M	SK	G		1660	1680	..	1750	ROOK04
ROOKWOOD Henry	SJ	M	SK	Y	13	1658	1681	1690	1730	ROOK06
ROOKWOOD (John)	OFM			F	#123	1666	1686	1695	1746	ROOK08
ROOKWOOD Robert	S	L	SK	R	#	1582	..	1604	..	ROOK12
ROOKWOOD Robert	S		SK	R	#	1588	..	1621	1668	ROOK14
ROOKWOOD Robert	CRT			C	#°2	..	1650	1653	1673	ROOK16
ROOTES Henry	S	L		S	#	..	..	1674	..	ROOT02
ROOTES John	S	W	SX	D	#	..	..	1661	..	ROOT04
ROOTES John	S	L		D	*	1665	..	1690	..	ROOT06
ROPER Thomas	SJ	M	KT	Y		1655	1673	1683	1716	ROPE02
ROSE Christopher	SJ	N		Y	3	1741	1763	1769	1826	ROSE02
ROSIER James	S		SK	R	#†	1576	..	1609	1609	ROSI02
ROSS Edward	SJ		EX	V	§	1585	1618	..	1665	ROSS02
ROSS George	S			S	3	..	..	1647	..	ROSS04
ROSS John	S	L	HR	R		1647	..	1680	1689	ROSS06
ROTTON Roger (Serenus)	OSB		ST	G		..	1679	..	1697	ROTT02
ROUGHT Walter	S	L	HA	D	#‡3	1608	..	1664	1688	ROUG02
ROUSE Anthony	S		SK	D	§=	..	..	1592	..	ROUS01
ROUSE John	OSB		MX	W		..	1711	..	1720	ROUS02
ROUSHAM see ROWSHAM										
ROUSSE Charles	SJ		LC	Y	#3	1690	1710	1718	1764	ROUS08
ROUSSE Louis	SJ		LC	Y	#3	1732	1753	1761	1794	ROUS10
ROUT see ROOTES or ROUGHT										
ROWE see ROE										
ROWLEY Thomas	S			Q	*	..	..	1583	..	ROWL02
ROWNTREE Leonard	S		YO	D	§°	..	..	1611	..	ROWN02
ROWSHAM Stephen VEN.	S	M	OX	Q	#+‡	..	..	1581	1587	ROWS02
ROY Pierre (Placid) du	ODC	L	FR		14	1682	1701	..	1739	ROYA01
ROYALL John	SJ		ZZ	Y	*	1729	1747	1755	1770	ROYA02
ROYDON Thomas	S	N	YO	D	#14	1630	..	1653	1700	ROYD02
ROYDON Thomas	S	N	YO	D	#3	1662	..	1686	1741	ROYD04
ROYDON Thomas	S	N	YO	D		1705	..	1730	1764	ROYD06
RUDGE William (Constantine)	ODC		DV	R	#	1623	1649	1647	1664	RUDG02

Name	Reg	D	Co	T	Notes	Born	Prof	Ordn	Died	Code
RUDGELEY see RIDGLEY										
RUFFET John	S		NK	V	#3	1567	..	1597	..	RUFF02
RUGA Bartholomew	SJ	L	IT		#2	1634	1650	..	1715	RUGA02
RUSSELL Alexander	SJ		SC		#	1669	1691	..	1742	RUSS01
RUSSELL Anthony	S			S		..	..	1674	..	RUSS02
RUSSELL George	S		YO	D		..	..	1644	..	RUSS04
RUSSELL James	S			L	*	..	..	1693	..	RUSS06
RUSSELL (Martin)	OP	M	WR			1632	1657	1658	1711	RUSS08
RUSSELL Richard BP.	S		BK	D	*	1629	..	1653	\1693	RUSS12
RUSSELL Thomas	SJ	M	WR	Y	4	1655	1676	1685	1724	RUSS14
RUSSELL William	CRT			C		..	1583	..	1587	RUSS15
RUSSELL William	OSS			S		..	..	..	1646	RUSS16
RYAN (Bernard)	CAP					..	..	..	..	RYAN02
RYCAUT Andrew	OSB		MX	E		..	1664	..	..	RYCA02
RYDER see RIDER										
RYDING Andrew (Bernard)	OSB	N	LA	G		1752	1769	1776	1841	RYDI02
RYSDEN see RISDON										
RYTHER Thomas	SJ		YO	Y		1663	1683	1691	1733	RYTH02
SABRAN Louis de	SJ	L	MX	Y	#	1652	1670	1679	1732	SABR02
SACHEVERELL John (William)	OP		LE	R	°	1568	..	1590	1625	SACH02
SACHMORTER Philip	SJ	L	FR	N	#3	1720	1738	1745	1795	SACH04
SADLEIR see SADLER										
SADLER Albert	SJ		BK	Y		1590	1616	..	1672	SADL04
SADLER Edward	SJ	L	MX	Y	1	1663	1690	1699	1751	SADL06
SADLER John	SJ	M	MX	Y	1	1664	1683	1691	1699	SADL08
SADLER Thomas (Philip S.Anne)	OFM			F	123	1665	1685	1690	1733	SADL12
SADLER Thomas Vinc. (Faustus)	OSB	L	WK	W		1604	1622	..	1681	SADL14
SADLER Walter Robt (Vincent)	OSB	L	WK	Q	§1	1563	1607	1592	1621	SADL16
SADLER William	SJ		EX	Y		1609	1630	..	1674	SADL18
SAGER Stephen	S	N	LA	P	#1	1601	..	1625	..	SAGE02
ST GEORGE William	S	N	CB	D	#†	1585	..	1614	..	SAIN02
ST GERMAIN Peter de	SJ	L			*7	..	..	..	..	SAIN04
ST PAUL (Joseph) de	CAP	L	FR		2	..	1621	..	1662	SAIN05
ST VALLIER Jean Baptiste	S					1653	..	..	1727	SAIN06
SALE Edmund	SJ		LA	Y	#124	1604	1626	..	1648	SALE02
SALE John	S	N	LA	D	#4	1601	..	1625	1664	SALE04
SALE John	SJ	N	LA	Y		1722	1741	1748	1791	SALE06
SALE Joseph	S		IR	D	#	1706	..	1736	1750	SALE08
SALE Richard	S	N	LA	R	#4	..	..	1668	1700	SALE10
SALISBURY Edward	OSB	W	DV	X	1	1685	1703	..	1725	SALI02
SALISBURY John	SJ	W	MO	V	#§	1575	1604	1600	1625	SALI04
SALISBURY William	SJ	W		Y	4	1610	1630	..	1639	SALI06
SALKELD Francis	S	N	DH	R	#	1625	..	1652	1671	SALK02
SALKELD George (Bernard)	OSB		CD	G	2	..	1650	..	1658	SALK04
SALKELD Henry	S		WD	S	°3	1584	..	1610	..	SALK06
SALKELD John	S		CD	S	°3	..	..	1608	1659	SALK08
SALKELD John	S		DH	R	#	1620	..	1647	1648	SALK10
SALKELD Thomas	S	N	DH	R	#	1624	..	1652	1691	SALK12
SALKELD Thomas	S			L	34	1666	..	1694	1718	SALK14
SALL (Nicholas)	OFM	L	IR		*7	..	..	..	..	SALL01
SALL see also SALE										
SALLINS see SALE										
SALTHOUSE Arthur	S	N	YO	D	#§13	1604	..	1637	..	SALT02
SALTMARSH Edward	SJ		YO	Y	#	1656	1678	1687	1737	SALT04
SALTMARSH Gerard	S		YO	R	#§	1652	..	1676	1733	SALT06
SALTMARSH Peter	S	L	YO	R	#1	1658	..	1686	1725	SALT08
SALTMARSH see also SALTHOUSE										
(Salvador of the Holy Spirit)	OFM	L	PL		*7	..	..	..	..	SALV01
SALVIN Peter	OSB	W	DH	G		1605	1632	..	1675	SALV02
SALVIN Ralph	SJ		DH	R	#	1600	1625	1624	1627	SALV04
SALWAY Thomas	S		WR	Q		..	..	1588	..	SALW02
SAMPSON Christopher	SJ	N	YO	R	#	1605	1634	1629	1674	SAMP02
SANCKEY see SANKEY										
SANDER Nicholas	S		SY	R	‡=3	1530	..	1560	1581	SAND01
SANDERS Charles	S	N	WK	R	#	1686	..	1712	1737	SAND02
SANDERS Erasmus	S		PB	R	*	1575	..	1600	..	SAND04

Name	Reg	D	Co	T	Notes	Born	Prof	Ordn	Died	Code
SANDERS Francis	SJ		WR	R	#	1648	1674	1672	1710	SAND06
SANDERS Nicholas	S			S	3	..	..	1620	..	SAND08
SANDERS Thomas	SJ	M	WK	Y	3	1724	1744	1751	1790	SAND10
SANDERS William	SJ	N	YO	Y	3	1638	1657	1662	1676	SAND12
SANDERS see also SANDYS										
SANDERSON (Bernard)	OSB		FR	X		..	1663	..	1669	SAND16
SANDERSON (Denis)	OSB		ND	X		..	1664	..	1670	SAND18
SANDERSON John	S		LA	R	†3	..	..	1580	1602	SAND20
SANDERSON John	S	M		Y		..	..	..	1813	SAND22
SANDERSON Nicholas	S	N	LA	R	#	1648	..	1670	..	SAND24
SANDERSON Nicholas	SJ	N	LA	Y	#	1731	1750	1756	1790	SAND26
SANDERSON Robert	SJ	N	LA	Y	3	1715	1738	1747	1781	SAND28
SANDERSON Thomas	S	N	LA	D	3	1761	..	1790	1826	SAND30
SANDFORD Matthew	OSB		SP	D	2	1588	1614	..	1644	SAND32
SANDFORD Michael	CRT		SP	D	#	1589	..	1613	..	SAND34
SADYS John VEN.	S	W	LA	Q	+‡4	..	..	1584	1586	SAND36
SANDYS see also SANDERS										
SANKEY Francis	SJ	M	LA	Y		1604	1633	..	1663	SANK02
SANKEY Lawrence	SJ		LA	Y	1	1606	1636	..	1657	SANK04
SANKEY William	SJ	L	LA	Y	#1	1609	1628	..	1680	SANK06
SANTOS see DIOS SANTOS										
SATERFORD John	S		LE	D		1566	..	1595	..	SATE02
SAUL Charles	S	N	YO	U		1767	..	1794	1813	SAUL02
SAUL see also SALE										
SAULWAY see SALWAY										
SAUNDERS see SANDERS										
SAVAGE John 5th Visc.	S	N	CH	D	#*3	1665	..	1700	1737	SAVA02
SAVAGE Paul	S			S		..	..	1690	..	SAVA04
SAVORY John (Robert)	OSB	M	OX	G		..	1687	..	1726	SAVO02
SAYER Christopher	S				7	..	..	..	..	SAYE02
SAYER Richard	SJ			V	#23	..	1624	1624	..	SAYE04
SAYER Robert (Gregory)	OSB		SK	R	†	1560	1589	1585	1602	SAYE06
SAYES see SEYES										
SAYLES Samuel	S	N	YO	R	3	1752	..	1776	1818	SAYL02
SCAMELL John	SJ	M	WT	S	3	1585	1610	1610	1624	SCAM02
SCANDRETT (Paul of S.Agnes)	OFM			F	123	1687	1705	1711	1724	SCAN02
SCARISBRICK Edward	SJ	N	LA	Y		1639	1659	1672	1709	SCAR02
SCARISBRICK Edward	SJ		LA	Y	#3	1664	1682	1690	1735	SCAR04
SCARISBRICK Edward	SJ		LA	Y	#3	1698	1716	1725	1778	SCAR06
SCARISBRICK Francis	SJ		LA	Y	#	1643	1663	1676	1713	SCAR08
SCARISBRICK Francis	SJ		LA	Y	#	1703	1722	1735	1789	SCAR10
SCARISBRICK Henry	SJ	N	LA	Y	#3	1641	1661	1670	1701	SCAR12
SCARISBRICK John	S			V		..	..	1642	..	SCAR14
SCARISBRICK Joseph or Thomas	SJ		LA	Y	#3	1673	1692	1701	1729	SCAR16
SCARISBRICK Thomas	SJ	N	LA	Y	#13	1642	1663	1672	1673	SCAR18
SCHNEIDER Theodore	SJ		GS			1703	1721	..	1764	SCHN02
SCHONDONCK Giles	SJ		LC	Y	#	1556	1576	..	1617	SCHO02
SCOBLE John	S		DV	R	#	1600	..	1624	1626	SCOB02
SCOLES Erasmus	SJ					..	..	..	1684	SCOL04
SCOREY Thomas	SJ	N	YO	Y		1681	1703	1710	1720	SCOR02
SCOTT Clement	S	L	EX	D		1692	..	1717	1731	SCOT02
SCOTT John	S			S	3	..	..	1603	..	SCOT04
SCOTT Joseph (Dunstan)	OSB	M	ND	X		1741	1760	..	1826	SCOT06
SCOTT Montford VEN.	S	M	SK	D	+†	..	..	1577	1591	SCOT08
SCOTT Nicholas	S	M	SX	V	#3	1599	..	1624	..	SCOT10
SCOTT Robert (Bede)	OSB		ND	X		1743	1763	..	1789	SCOT12
SCOTT William	S		LN	D	#	1696	..	1730	1770	SCOT14
SCOTT William (Maurus) BL.	OSB	L	EX		#*+†1	1578	1605	1610	1612	SCOT16
SCRIMSHAW William	S	W	LN	R	#1	1711	..	1734	1800	SCR102
SCRIVENER Hugh	SJ		HR		4	..	..	..	1593	SCR104
SCROGGS John (Maurus)	OSB	W	SX	G		1617	1634	..	162	SCRO02
SCROGGS (Placid)	OSB	L	BK	G	#1	1615	1634	..	1692	SCRO04
SCUDAMORE Benedict	S	M	HR	D	#	1599	..	1624	..	SCUD02
SCUDAMORE (George S.Francis)	OFM	L		F	#13	1670	..	1695	1723	SCUD04
SCUDAMORE John	S		HR	R	°1	1563	..	1592	..	SCUD06
SCUDAMORE John	SJ	W	MO	Y	#3	1696	1718	1727	1778	SCUD08

Name	Reg	D	Co	T	Notes	Born	Prof	Ordn	Died	Code
SCUDAMORE John (Placid)	OSB	L	MX	X		1659	1695	..	1704	SCUD10
SCUPHOLME John	S	N	MX	R	#†1	1643	..	1670	..	SCUP02
SEARE see SAYER										
(Sebastian of Bar sur Seine)	CAP		FR		2	..	1619	..	1667	SEBA02
SEBERN George	S			S	3	..	..	1608	..	SEBE02
SEBORNE William	S		HR	Q	=	..	..	1583	..	SEBO02
SEEL Peter (Mary of S.Teresa)	ODC	N	LA	Z	#	1705	..	..	1752	SEEL02
SEFTON John	S	N			7	..	..	..	..	SEFT02
SEFTON Thomas	SJ		LA	Y	#	1719	1738	1745	1748	SEFT04
SEISON John	S		MX	D	#	1683	..	1712	1749	SEIS02
SELBY (Daniel of S.Francis)	OFM		ND	F	123	1650	1669	1674	1715	SELB02
SELBY Edward (Gregory)	OSB	N	ND	X		..	1726	..	1759	SELB04
SELBY John	S	N	ND			1627	..	..	..	SELB06
SELBY John	S	L	ND	D		1757	..	..	1821	SELB08
SELBY Richard (Wilfrid)	OSB		DH	G	#	..	1620	..	1659	SELB10
SELOSSE Anthony	SJ		LC			1621	1658	..	1687	SELO02
SELOSSE Anthony	SJ	L	LC	Y		1653	1671	1680	1696	SELO04
SEMMES Joseph	SJ	N	MD	Y	3	1743	1761	1767	1809	SEMM02
SEMPILL see SEMPLE										
SEMPLE Hugh	SJ		SC		3	1701	1717	1728	..	SEMP04
SEPHTON see SEFTON										
(Seraphinus of Compiègne)	CAP		FR			..	1613	..	1655	SERA02
SERGEANT Francis	S		MX	R	§	1651	..	1678	..	SERG02
SERGEANT John	S	L	LN	L	#†	1623	..	1649	1707	SERG04
SERGEANT John	S	N	LA	D		1715	..	1744	1795	SERG06
SERGEANT Richard VEN.	S		GL	Q	#+‡	..	..	1583	1586	SERF08
SEWALL Charles	SJ		MD	Y	3	1744	1764	1771	1806	SEWA02
SEWALL Nicholas	SJ	N	MD	Y		1745	1766	1772	1834	SEWA04
SEWALL see also SHEWELL										
SEWELL Edward	S			R	*	1575	..	1599	..	SEWE02
SEWELL Hugh	S	N		Q	*‡	..	..	1590	..	SEWE04
SEYES Roger	OFM		GM	R	#§2	1599	1623	1622	..	SEYE02
SHACKLETON William	SJ	N	LA	R	#‡1	1584	1612	1610	1655	SHAC02
SHAFTOE (Celestine)	OSB	W	ND	X		..	1672	..	1722	SHAF02
SHAFTOE John	S		ND	Q	#3	..	..	1582	..	SHAF04
SHAFTOE (Placid)	OSB	N	DH	X		1634	1655	1659	1681	SHAF06
SHAFTOE William (Benedict)	OSB		ND	E		..	1715	..	1742	SHAF08
SHARP James	SJ	M	YO	V	#‡	1578	1607	1604	1630	SHAR02
SHARP James (Vincent)	OP	M	MX	N		1752	1772	1775	1801	SHAR04
SHARP Matthew	S	N	YO	D	3	1756	..	1784	1826	SHAR06
SHARP Richard	S	N			7	..	..	..	..	SHAR08
SHARP Robert	S	L		S		..	..	1660	1684	SHAR10
SHARROCK James (Jerome)	OSB	M	LA	G		1750	1768	..	1808	SHAR12
SHARROCK John (Dunstan)	OSB	N	LA	W		1754	1775	..	1831	SHAR14
SHARROCK William (Gregory) BP	OSB	W	LA	G	*	1742	1758	1766	1809	SHAR16
SHAW Edward (Richard S.Edwd.)	ODC	M			8	..	..	..	..	SHAW02
SHAW Francis	S			Q	#*4	..	..	1584	1609	SHAW04
SHAW Gerard	S	L	IR	S		..	..	..	1780	SHAW06
SHAW Henry	S			D	*‡4	..	..	1576	1608	SHAW08
SHAW James	S	L	MX	R	#	1710	..	1733	..	SHAW10
SHAW John	SJ	N	LA	Y	3	1739	1759	1765	1808	SHAW12
SHAW Patrick	S	L	IR			..	..	..	1742	SHAW14
SHAW Ralph (Maurus)	OSB		ND	E		1729	1757	..	1814	SHAW16
SHAW Richard	S	N		D	#*	..	..	1620	..	SHAW18
SHEADLEY see SHIRLEY										
SHELBURN John	S			Q	*	..	..	1582	..	SHEL02
SHELDON Edward	OSB		WK	G		1624	1644	..	1685	SHEL04
SHELDON Edward	SJ		WK	Y	°3	1716	1733	1741	..	SHEL06
SHELDON Henry	SJ		OX	Y		1652	1670	1679	1714	SHEL08
SHELDON Henry	SJ		WR	Y	3	1686	1705	1718	1756	SHEL10
SHELDON Lionel	OSB	L	WR	G		1633	1653	1657	1678	SHEL12
SHELDON Ralph	SJ		OX	Y	#3	1681	1700	1709	1741	SHEL14
SHELDON Richard	S		ST	R	°	1570	..	1593	..	SHEL16
SHELDON William	S		ST	R	‡	1564	..	1591	..	SHEL18
SHELLEY Anthony	S	L	SX	D		1601	..	1628	..	SHEL20
SHELLEY Cyprian	S		SX	R	4	1592	..	1616	1624	SHEL22

Name	Reg	D	Co	T	Notes	Born	Prof	Ordn	Died	Code
SHELLEY Edward	S		SX	D	#§	1588	..	1612	..	SHEL24
SHELLEY Owen	SJ		SX	R	#	1585	1615	1610	1666	SHEL26
SHELLEY Thomas	SJ		SX	R	13	1586	1620	1610	1651	SHEL28
SHELLEY Thomas	S	M	ST	D	3	1737	..	1763	1807	SHEL30
SHELLEY Waltyer	SJ		MX	Y	3	1701	1717	1725	1750	SHEL32
SHELLEY William	S	L	SX	V	34	1583	..	1606	1643	SHEL34
SHEPHERD John	S	L	LA	L	3	1678	..	1706	1761	SHEP02
SHEPHERD John	S	L	MX	L	3	1714	..	1737	1789	SHEP04
SHEPHERD John (Wm of S.Mary)	OFM	N	LA	F	12	1624	1657	..	1679	SHEP06
SHEPHERD Joseph	S		LA	D		1738	..	1764	1796	SHEP08
SHEPHERD Joseph	S	N	LA	V	#	1767	..	1791	1825	SHEP10
SHEPHERD Thomas	S	N	LA	D		1720	..	1745	1774	SHEP12
SHEPHERD Thomas (Alexius)	OSB		WK	G		..	1721	..	1755	SHEP14
SHEPPARD see SHEPHERD										
SHEPPEY (Nicholas of S.Clare)	OFM			F	3	..	..	1666	..	SHEP18
SHEPREVE see SHEPREY										
SHEPREY William	S				*‡	..	..	1574	1598	SHEP22
SHERBORNE see SHERBURN										
SHERBURN Charles	SJ		LA	Y		1684	1702	1715	1745	SHER04
SHERBURN Edward	OSB	N	EX	E		..	1699	..	1745	SHER06
SHERBURN Joseph	OSB		LA	E		1628	1652	..	1697	SHER08
SHERBURN Matthew	S	N	LA	D	#	1600	..	1623	1668	SHER10
SHERBURN Richard	S	N	LA	D	#	..	..	1622	..	SHER12
SHERBURN Thomas (James)	OSB	N	LA	G	#4	1594	1614	..	1657	SHER14
SHERIFF Thomas	S	L	MX	R		1720	..	1745	1758	SHER16
SHERLOCK Anthony	S	M			*‡°3	..	..	1586	..	SHER18
SHERRAT Henry	S		LA	S		1558	..	1593	1602	SHER20
SHERSON Martin	S	L	YO	Q	x‡	1563	..	1586	1588	SHER22
SHERT John BL.	S	L	CH	R	#+‡3	..	..	1578	1582	SHER24
SHERWIN Ralph ST.	S	L	DE	R	+ ‡	1549	..	1577	1581	SHER26
SHERWOOD Henry	S	L	MX	Q		..	..	1588	..	SHER28
SHERWOOD John	S		MX	Q		..	..	1583	1593	SHER30
SHERWOOD John	S				7	..	..	..	..	SHER32
SHERWOOD (Joseph)	OSB		LC	X		..	1653	..	1690	SHER34
SHERWOOD Philip	S	N	YO		3	..	..	1570	..	SHER36
SHERWOOD Richard	S		MX	Q	#	..	..	1584	..	SHER38
SHERWOOD Robert	OSB	M	SM	G	#	1588	1613	..	1665	SHER40
SHERWOOD Thomas	S		SM	R	#*§=	1583	..	1610	1610	SHER42
SHERWOOD William (Elphege)	OSB		SM	W		..	1626	..	1663	SHER44
SHEWELL Robert	S	M		Q	*	..	..	1580	..	SHEW02
SHEWELL Robert	S	N		Q	*	..	..	1595	..	SHEW04
SHEWELL see also SEWALL										
SHILTON William	S			S	3	..	..	1620	..	SHIL02
SHIMELL Charles	S	W	DV	D	3	1735	..	1763	1764	SHIM02
SHIMELL Richard	S	W	SP	L	#§	1692	..	1716	1763	SHIM04
SHIMELL Thomas	S		SP	D		1716	..	1741	1779	SHIM06
SHIPP Francis	CRT				8	..	..	..	..	SHIP02
SHIREBURNE see SHERBURN										
SHIRLEY Andrew	OSB	N	LA	V		1577	1604	1603	1609	SHIR04
SHIRLEY Anthony	S		OX	Q	‡	..	..	1583	..	SHIR06
SHIRLEY Henry	S		MX	S	#3	..	..	1630	..	SHIR08
SHORT Francis	SJ	L	SK	Y	#13	1718	1737	1746	1755	SHOR02
SHORT John (Jordan)	OP		SK	N		1685	1719	1721	1754	SHOR04
SHORT Thomas	S		SK	L	#†	1616	..	1641	..	SHOR06
SHORT William (Benedict)	OP	L	SK	N	3	1723	1741	1746	1800	SHOR08
SHORT see also SHERT										
SHUTTLEWORTH Edmund (Wolstan)	OSB	N	LA	E	#	..	1640	..	1677	SHUT02
SHUTTLEWORTH George	S	M	NT	D	#	1718	..	1744	1791	SHUT04
SHUTTLEWORTH John	S	M	NT	D	#3	1680	..	1711	1739	SHUT06
SHUTTLEWORTH John	SJ	M	LA	Y	#3	1708	1730	1743	1765	SHUT08
SHUTTLEWORTH John	S	N	LA	D	3	1756	..	1784	1839	SHUT10
SHUTTLEWORTH John (Stephen)	OP	L		N		1676	1699	1702	1710	SHUT12
SHUTTLEWORTH Thomas (Benedct)	OSB	N	MX	X		..	1723	.	1774	SHUT14
SICKLEMORE Humphrey	S	N	MX	R		1570	..	1596	..	SICK02
SIDGREAVES John (Bernard)	CRT				*2	1569	1590	..	1643	SIDG02
SIES Jerome (Benedict)	OSB		LC	X		..	1689	..	1697	SIES02

Name	Reg	D	Co	T	Notes	Born	Prof	Ordn	Died	Code
SILVER Ferdinand	S	M	GL	P	3	1668	..	1696	1728	SILV02
SIMEON Edward	SJ		MX	Y	#	1632	1656	1661	1701	SIME02
SIMEON Walter	SJ					..	..	..	1691	SIME04
SIMEON William	SJ					..	..	..	1698	SIME06
SIMON see SIMEON										
SIMONS Nicholas	S	M	MX	L	#3	1675	..	1702	1714	SIMO04
SIMPSON Charles (Benedict)	OFM		LN	F	34	..	1764	1776	1784	SIMP02
SIMPSON John (Benedict)	OSB		LA	W	#	1713	1736	..	1775	SIMP04
SIMPSON John (Cuthbert)	OSB	M	LA	E		1725	1746	..	1785	SIMP06
SIMPSON Joseph	SJ		DH	Y	3	1629	1656	1665	1667	SIMP08
SIMPSON Joseph (Boniface)	OFM			F	3	..	..	1743	1776	SIMP10
SIMPSON Richard VEN.	S	N	YO	D	+‡	..	..	1577	1588	SIMP12
SIMPSON Richard (Benedict)	OSB	N	LA	W		1728	1751	..	1801	SIMP14
SIMPSON Thomas	S		EX	Q	#°1	1548	..	1585	..	SIMP16
SIMPSON Thomas	OSB	N	LA	W		1718	1737	..	1764	SIMP18
SIMPSON William (Andrew)	OSB		YO	E	#1	1612	1642	..	1652	SIMP20
SIMPSON William	S	N	YO	V	14	1690	..	1713	1730	SIMP22
SIMPSON see also SAMPSON										
SINGLETON John	S	L	MX	V		1775	..	1800	1839	SING02
SINGLETON Michael William	S		LA	R		1741	..	1767	1783	SING04
SINGLETON Richard	SJ		LA	Y	2	1566	1584	..	1602	SING06
SINGLETON Robert	S		LA	D	#13	1612	..	1636	..	SING08
SINGLETON Thomas	SJ	L			1	1570	..	..	..	SING10
SINGLETON William	S			Q	*§	..	..	1587	1620	SING12
SITTENSPERGER Matthias	SJ		GS		#	1719	1737	..	1775	SITT02
SIX see SIES										
SKELTON James	S	N	CD	L	1	1690	..	1714	1760	SKEL02
SKELTON John (Elphege)	OSB	N	CD	X		..	1688	..	1705	SKEL04
SKELTON John (Gregory)	OSB	N	CD	G		..	1681	1686	1721	SKEL06
SKELTON Nicholas	S	N	CD	D		1691	..	1718	1766	SKEL08
SKELTON Simon	S	N	CD	D		..	..	1620	..	SKEL10
SKERRETT John	OSA	L	IR		14	1620	..	..	1688	SKER02
SKIDMORE see SCUDAMORE										
SKINNER Andrew	S		WK	D	#1	1610	..	1648	1672	SKIN02
SKINNER Anthony (Basil)	OSB	N	YO	G	4	..	1657	..	1685	SKIN04
SKINNER James	S	L	WK	D	#3	1608	..	1634	..	SKIN06
SKINNER James (Placid)	OSB		YO	G		..	1662	..	1697	SKIN08
SKINNER John	S	M	OX	L	#	1611	..	1636	1674	SKIN10
SKINNER John	S	M	WK	L	#3	..	..	1658	1685	SKIN12
SKINNER John	SJ	N	DE	Y	3	1662	1679	1690	1708	SKIN14
SKINNER William	S	W	WK	D	#3	..	..	1661	1694	SKIN16
SKOOPHAM see SCUPHOLME										
SLACK Richard or William	S		DE	Q		..	..	1579	..	SLAC02
SLADE Joseph	CRT			C		..	1576	..	1616	SLAD02
SLADE William	S		SP	D	‡*	..	1582	1578	..	SLAD04
SLATER Edward (Bede) BP.	OSB	N	LA	W	*	1774	1794	1798	1832	SLAT02
SLATER John (Bernard)	OSB	N	LA	W		1744	1761	..	1810	SLAT04
SLATER Thomas (Benet)	OSB	N	LA	W		1756	1777	..	1801	SLAT06
SLATER see also SLAUGHTER										
SLAUGHTER Edward	SJ		HR	Y		1655	1673	1682	1729	SLAU02
SLAUGHTER George	S		HR	L		..	..	1689	1741	SLAU04
SLAUGHTER James	S	M	HR	D		1712	..	1741	1781	SLAU06
SLINGSBY Francis	SJ		IR	R	#‡	1612	1641	1641	1642	SLIN02
SLOAN see ASLOAN										
SMAITHWAITE William	S		DH	R		1682	..	1705	..	SMAI02
SMALL Christopher	S	N	CL	Q	‡4	..	..	1579	1593	SMAL02
SMALLWOOD Joseph (Alexius)	OFM			F	123	1694	1715	1719	1756	SMAL04
SMARTHWAITE Cuthbert	S		YO	D		..	..	1601	..	SMAR02
SMARTHWAITE Thomas	S		YO	Q		..	..	1582	..	SMAR04
SMEATON John (Basil)	OSB	N	CD	X		..	1664	..	1705	SMEA02
SMITH Anthony	S			S	3	..	..	1617	..	SMIT02
SMITH Anthony	S	L	HA	L	#13	1620	..	1644	1685	SMIT03
SMITH Benjamin	S		EX	L		1769	..	1794	1795	SMIT05
SMITH (Bernardine)	OFM			F	123	1656	1673	1680	1742	SMIT06
SMITH Christopher	S	N	YO	V	#3	1602	..	1628	..	SMIT07
SMITH Clement	SJ	N	NK	Y		1657	1678	1687	1696	SMIT08

Name	Reg	D	Co	T	Notes	Born	Prof	Ordn	Died	Code
SMITH Edmund	S		OX	R	#‡	1577	..	1603	1605	SMIT09
SMITH Edmund	SJ	N	WK	Y	#	1666	1690	1698	1727	SMIT12
SMITH Edmund (Augustine)	OSB		LA	R	†	1565	1592	1591	..	SMIT13
SMITH Edward (Benedict)	OSB		LA	S	#3	1585	1617	1616	1637	SMIT14
SMITH Francis	S	M	EX	R	#1	1608	..	1632	1672	SMIT15
SMITH Francis	S	W	WK	L	3	..	..	1692	1748	SMIT16
SMITH George	S			R	*○	..	..	1589	..	SMIT17
SMITH George	SJ		DH	Y		1611	1631	..	1671	SMIT18
SMITH George	S		SX	V	‡	1602	..	1645	..	SMIT19
SMITH Gregory	S		BK	R	#§	1600	..	1625	1629	SMIT21
SMITH Gregory	OSA		IR		*7	..	..	..	..	SMIT22
SMITH Henry	S		LA	R	#	1608	..	1632	..	SMIT23
SMITH Henry	S			V		..	..	1644	..	SMIT24
SMITH Henry	SJ	N	ND	V	3	1699	1724	1724	1756	SMIT25
SMITH James BP.	S	N	HA	D	#*	1645	..	1677	1711	SMIT26
SMITH James	S	L		L	§°4	1732	..	1756	1780	SMIT27
SMITH James	S	N	LA	V		1775	..	1800	1827	SMIT28
SMITH John	S		LE	R	#‡	1580	..	1604	1604	SMIT29
SMITH John	SJ	N	YO		#x§3	..	1622	1622	1651	SMIT32
SMITH John	SJ	N	LA	Y	#	1615	1637	..	1650	SMIT33
SMITH John	SJ		SK	Y		1620	1640	..	1661	SMIT34
SMITH John	SJ	N		D	#	1616	1659	..	1674	SMIT35
SMITH John	S				7	..	..	..	..	SMIT36
SMITH John, Hon.	SJ		SX	Y	#1	1632	1663	1671	1689	SMIT37
SMITH John	S	L	DT	L	#3	..	..	1681	1714	SMIT38
SMITH John	S	M	NK	R	#	1656	..	1681	..	SMIT39
SMITH John	SJ	L	WK	Y	3	1669	1688	1695	1754	SMIT42
SMITH John	S		YO	D	3	1735	..	1759	1764	SMIT43
SMITH John	S	L	NK	R	§	1739	..	1766	1817	SMIT44
SMITH John (Bernard)	OP	M		N		1750	1772	1774	1804	SMIT45
SMITH Joseph	SJ	N	LE	Y	3	1725	1746	1760	1768	SMIT46
SMITH Joseph (Augustine)	OP	N	YO		4	1760	1784	1785	1811	SMIT47
SMITH Lawrence	S			R		1608	..	1632	..	SMIT48
SMITH (Maurus)	OSB		MX	G		..	1625	..	1633	SMIT49
SMITH Nicholas	SJ	L	MX	Q	#*2	1558	1578	1583	1630	SMIT52
SMITH Richard	S			D	*	..	..	1576	..	SMIT53
SMITH Richard	S			Q	*	..	..	1581	..	SMIT54
SMITH Richard	S			Q	#*	..	..	1587	..	SMIT55
SMITH Richard BP.	S	L	LN	R	#‡*	1567	..	1592	1655	SMIT56
SMITH Richard	S		HR	D	#§	..	..	1624	..	SMIT57
SMITH Richard	SJ		SX	Y	#13	1660	1680	1687	1735	SMIT58
SMITH Richard	S	L	MX	R		1725	..	1750	1808	SMIT59
SMITH Robert	S			Q	*	..	..	1581	..	SMIT62
SMITH Robert	S		DT	L	#	..	..	1681	1729	SMIT63
SMITH Sampson or Samuel	S					..	..	..	1663	SMIT64
SMITH Thomas	S	L		D	#*	..	..	1576	..	SMIT65
SMITH Thomas	S	L	LN	D	#	1603	..	1629	1656	SMIT66
SMITH Thomas	SJ	N	LA	V	1	1631	1662	1659	1681	SMIT67
SMITH Thomas	S	N	LA	D	3	1674	..	1701	1755	SMIT68
SMITH Thomas	SJ	N	DH	Y	#3	1674	1691	1700	1721	SMIT69
SMITH Thomas BP.	S	N	DH	D	*	1763	..	1787	1831	SMIT72
SMITH Thomas (Bernardine)	OFM		LA	F	124	1613	1634	..	1666	SMIT73
SMITH William	S	N	YO	R	#	1556	..	1581	..	SMIT74
SMITH William	OSS		YO			1597	..	..	1647	SMIT75
SMITH William	S	L	WK	R	#	1648	..	1672	1722	SMIT76
SMITH William	S	L		Z	*	1704	..	..	1776	SMIT77
SMITH William (Christopher)	ODC	M			13	1701	..	1725	..	SMIT78
SMITHERS (Oswald)	OSB	M	MX	X		..	1694	..	1725	SMIT79
SMITHERS William	SJ		FR	Y		1656	1675	1682	1685	SMIT82
SMITHSON Augustine	S	N	YO	D		..	..	1656	1717	SMIT83
SMITHSON John	S		YO	V	1	1567	..	1594	1596	SMIT84
SMITHSON John	SJ	N	YO	Y		1612	1637	..	1684	SMIT85
SMITHSON John (Alphonsus)	OFM		YO	F	12	1623	1644	..	1672	SMIT86
SMYTHE Charles	OSB		MX	G		1727	1746	..	1780	SMYT02
SMYTHE see also SMITH										
SNAPE George	S	L		Q	*○	..	..	1582	..	SNAP02

109

Name	Reg	D	Co	T	Notes	Born	Prof	Ordn	Died	Code
SNOD Peter	S	W	DT	D		1595	..	1622	..	SNOD02
SNOW Peter VEN.	S	N	YO	Q	+	..	..	1591	1598	SNOW02
SOM Henry del	SJ		LC			..	..	..	1613	SOMA02
SOMERS Thomas BL.	S	L	WD	D	#+	..	..	1606	1610	SOME02
SOMERSET Charles	S		GL	D	3	..	..	1655	..	SOME04
SOMERSET Henry	S		HR	D	#3	1671	..	1697	..	SOME06
SOMERSET Thomas, Hon.	S		GL	R	34	..	..	1645	1670	SOME08
SOMERSET Thomas	S		GL	D	#4	..	..	1659	1670	SOME10
SOMES Francis	SJ				4	..	..	..	1593	SOME12
SOUCH de la see LANSANCH										
SOUTHCOTE Edward	SJ	L	EX	Y	3	1697	1719	1727	1780	SOUT02
SOUTHCOTE Francis (Augustine)	OSB	L	EX	G		1691	1708	..	1774	SOUT04
SOUTHCOTE John	S	L	EX	#		1587	..	1612	1637	SOUT06
SOUTHCOTE John (Augustine)	OSB		EX	E		..	1689	..	1730	SOUT08
SOUTHCOTE Robert (Amandus)	OSB	W	DV	G		..	1624	..	1653	SOUT10
SOUTHCOTE Thomas	OSB	L	EX	G		1670	1688	..	1748	SOUT12
SOUTHERN William VEN.	S	N	DH	D	+3	1579	..	1601	1618	SOUT14
SOUTHERN William	SJ	M	ST	V	#3	1594	1625	1625	1658	SOUT16
SOUTHWELL John	SJ		HA	Y		1631	1649	..	..	SOUT18
SOUTHWELL John	S	L		D		..	..	1659	1688	SOUT20
SOUTHWELL Robert ST.	SJ	L	NK	R	#+	1561	1578	1584	1595	SOUT22
SOUTHWORTH Christopher	S		LA	R	#	1556	..	1583	..	SOUT24
SOUTHWORTH John ST.	S	L	LA	D	#+1	1592	..	1618	1654	SOUT26
SOUTHWORTH Ralph	S	W	LA	D		1747	..	1771	1810	SOUT28
SOUTHWORTH Richard	S	L	LA	D	#	1743	..	1768	1817	SOUT30
SOUTHWORTH Thomas	S	M	LA	D	#	1749	..	1776	1816	SOUT32
SOUTHWORTH William	S	M	LA	D	#	1752	..	1777	1814	SOUT34
SOVIGO Octavian	S		MX	R	3	..	..	1592	..	SOVI02
SPARCHFORD John	S		SP	S		1567	..	1593	..	SPAR02
SPENCE Paul	S	W		D	*	..	..	1576	..	SPEN02
SPENCER Daniel	OSB	N	LA	E		1767	1788	..	1794	SPEN04
SPENCER John	SJ	M	LN	Y	#†2	1601	1627	1632	1671	SPEN06
SPENCER William VEN.	S	N	YO	Q	+‡	..	..	1583	1589	SPEN08
SPROTT Thomas VEN.	S	M	WD	D	#+	1571	..	1596	1600	SPRO02
SQUIBB Francis	S		MX	D	#	1691	..	1716	1762	SQUI02
STABLE Francis	S			V		..	..	1658	..	STAB02
STAFFERTON Francis	S	N	BK	Q		..	..	1584	..	STAF02
STAFFERTON William	S	N	BK	R	#‡4	1557	..	1584	1594	STAF04
STAFFORD Bernard	SJ	M	IR	Y	#13	1713	1735	1741	1788	STAF06
STAFFORD Charles	SJ		SK	Y	#	1653	1676	1684	1732	STAF08
STAFFORD Henry	SJ		ST	Y		1606	1624	1632	1657	STAF10
STAFFORD Ignatius	SJ		ST	Y	#	1599	1618	..	1642	STAF11
STAFFORD Ignatius	SJ		ST	Y	#	1652	1672	1682	1720	STAF12
STAFFORD John	SJ	M	ST	Y	1	1603	1623	..	1667	STAF14
STAFFORD Nathaniel	SJ	M	SK	Y	#13	1634	1656	1665	1697	STAF16
STAFFORD William	S			S	3	..	..	1642	..	STAF18
STAMFORD Ralph	S			Q	*‡	..	..	1584	..	STAM02
STAMP Thomas	S	L	DE	N	3	..	..	1575	..	STAM04
STANDISH George	S	W	HR	V	#3	..	..	1661	..	STAN02
STANDISH James	S	L	LA	Q	‡4	..	..	1588	1621	STAN04
STANDISH Lawrence	SJ	M	LA	Y	#14	1604	1626	..	1671	STAN06
STANFIELD Robert	SJ		YO	Y	3	1668	1687	1695	1751	STAN08
STANFORD Edmund (of S.Martin)	ODC	L	WK	B		..	..	..	1635	STAN10
STANFORD John	S	M	WK	R		1654	..	1677	1737	STAN14
STANFORD Robert	SJ		ST	R	#	1593	1617	1617	1659	STAN16
STANFORD see also STAMFORD										
STANLEY Edward	SJ		ST	R	12	1564	1619	1611	1639	STAN20
STANLEY Edward	S			D		..	..	1615	..	STAN22
STANLEY Henry	SJ		LA	Y	#3	1688	1706	1714	1753	STAN24
STANLEY Henry	SJ	N	CH	Y		1713	1732	1739	1786	STAN26
STANLEY John	S		NT	D		1720	..	1744	1770	STAN28
STANLEY John	S	W	MX	V		1759	..	1785	1828	STAN29
STANLEY-MASSEY Thomas	SJ	W	CH	Y	#3	1716	1732	1746	1805	STAN30
STANNEY Thomas	SJ	L	DT	R		1558	1597	1585	1617	STAN32
STANNEY (William)	OFM			F		..	..	..	1626	STAN34
STANTON Henry Anthony or John	SJ		GL	R	#‡	1586	1616	1611	1635	STAN36

Name	Reg	D	Co	T	Notes	Born	Prof	Ordn	Died	Code
STAPLETON Brian	S	N		Q	*	..	..	1587	..	STAP02
STAPLETON Brian	S			D	*	..	..	1599	1599	STAP04
STAPLETON Gregory BP.	S	L	YO	D	*3	1748	..	1771	1802	STAP06
STAPLETON Gregory (Benedict)	OSB	L	YO	G		1623	1643	1647	1680	STAP08
STAPLETON Henry	CRT			C		..	..	..	1647	STAP09
STAPLETON Thomas	S		SX	N		..	..	1563	1598	STAP11
STAPLETON Thomas	SJ		LN	Y		1632	1651	1664	1685	STAP12
STAPLETON Thomas	S	L	YO	D	1	1713	..	1736	1754	STAP14
STARKEY Henry (Hugh)	OSB	L	CH	L	#	1612	1649	1638	1688	STAR02
STARKEY John	S		CH	R	#§	1570	..	1602	..	STAR04
STARKEY Joseph	OSB		MX	G	#	1676	1703	..	1754	STAR06
STARKEY see also SANKEY										
STAVERTON see STAFFERTON										
STEARE Robert (Benedict)	OSB	N	MX	G		1702	1720	..	1780	STEA02
STEEL William	S		YO	D		1715	..	1739	1764	STEE02
STEEN (Elijah Mt.Cml.) van de	CAR	L	LC			1656	1674	1680	1701	STEE04
STELLING Robert (Augustine)	OSB		DH	E		..	1676	..	1727	STEL02
STEPHAN see STEPHENS										
STEPHENS Francis	SJ		CL	R	#§	1597	1624	1621	1648	STEP04
STEPHENS Henry Robert	SJ		LC	Y	3	1665	1683	1688	1723	STEP06
STEPHENS John	S	W	NK	R	#	1578	..	1602	..	STEP08
STEPHENS Richard	S		WT	R	§	1631	..	1655	1657	STEP10
STEPHENS Thomas	SJ			R	#*	1549	1578	..	1619	STEP12
STEPHENSON Anthony	S			D		..	..	1655	..	STEP14
STEPHENSON Christopher	S			D	*§	..	..	1575	..	STEP16
STEPHENSON Cyprian	S		MX	R	#	1600	..	1624	1626	STEP18
STEPHENSON John	SJ	N	DE	Y		1641	1663	1672	1692	STEP20
STEPHENSON Paul	S	N	YO	D	13	1648	..	1673	..	STEP22
STEPHENSON Thomas Richard	SJ		DH	Q	#	1552	1585	1581	1624	STEP24
STERIL Stephen (a S.Cruce)	OFM			F	12	1607	1634	..	1640	STER02
STEVENS see STEPHENS										
STEVENSON see STEPHENSON										
STEWART see STUART										
STEYNMEYER Ferdinand	SJ		GS		#	1720	1743	..	1786	STEY02
STILLLINGTON Thomas	S		YO	R		1558	..	1582	1597	STIL04
STILLINGTON William	SJ	N	YO	Y	12	1596	1622	..	1654	STIL06
STILLINGTON	S			S	3	..	..	1635	..	STIL08
STITCH James	S	M	ST	L	#	1720	..	1744	1764	STIT02
STOCKER Thomas (Augustine)	OSB		LC	G	#	1598	1621	..	1668	STOC02
STOCKTON Edward	S		CH	R	#§	..	..	1677	..	STOC04
STOKER see STOCKER										
STOKES Walter	S			D	*	..	..	1577	..	STOK04
STONE Benjamin	S	M	ST	D	3	1742	..	1770	1819	STON02
STONE John	S	L				..	..	..	1754	STON04
STONE Marmaduke	SJ	N	ST	Y		1748	1767	1775	1834	STON06
STONE Thomas	S	M	ST	D		1746	..	1770	1797	STON08
STONEHOUSE Andrew	SJ	N	YO	R	#	1597	1634	1631	1663	STON10
STONOR Christopher	S	M	OX	P		1716	..	1743	1795	STON12
STONOR John					*	1571	..	..	1610	STON13
STONOR John	S				*	1580	..	..	1626	STON14
STONOR John	S	M	OX	D	#	1738	..	1764	1765	STON15
STONOR John Talbot BP.	S	M	OX	P	*	1678	..	1711	1746	STON16
STONOR Thomas	S					1659	..	..	1701	STON18
STOREY Arthur	S	N	ND	P		1742	..	1767	1825	STOR02
STOREY George	S			N	*3	..	..	1570	..	STOR03
STOREY John (Joseph)	OSB	N	ND	X		..	1751	..	1799	STOR04
STOREY Richard	SJ		GL		2	..	1574	..	1600	STOR06
STOREY Thomas	S			R	*	1561	..	1585	..	STOR08
STOREY Thomas	S	N	ND	D	3	1738	..	1766	1795	STOR10
STOURTON John, Hon.	OSB	N	WT	G		1674	1693	1699	1748	STOU02
STOURTON Thomas, Hon.	OSB		WT	G		..	1645	..	1684	STOU04
STOUT Thomas	S	N		D	*3	1767	..	1793	1828	STOU06
STRANGE Richard	SJ		ND	Y		1611	1631	..	1682	STRA02
STRANGE Thomas	SJ		GL	R	#§123	1577	1600	1603	1639	STRA04
STRANGUISH Philip	S		LA	Q	#x	..	..	1583	1598	STRA06
STRANSHAM Edward BL.	S	L	Ox	Q	#+‡	1555	..	1580	1586	STRA08

111

Name	Reg	D	Co	T	Notes	Born	Prof	Ordn	Died	Code
STRANSHAM George	S		KT	Q	#†=	..	..	1585	..	STRA10
STRANSHAM Thomas	S		OX	D		..	..	1578	..	STRA12
STRATFORD Arthur	S		GL	R		1557	..	1586	..	STRA14
STREET Anthony	S			D	*3	..	..	1681	..	STRE02
STREET Thomas	S	W	HR	D	#	1599	..	1624	1670	STRE04
STRICKLAND John	S		MX	D	#	1723	..	1747	1802	STRI02
STRICKLAND Joseph	S	M	MX	P		1724	..	1748	1790	STRI04
STRICKLAND Nicholas	S		WD	D	#34	1609	..	1634	1645	STRI06
STRICKLAND Roger	S	N	WD	D	4	..	..	1595	1643	STRI08
STRICKLAND Simon James	S	N	YO	D	#	1739	..	..	1782	STRI10
STRICKLAND Thomas John F BP.	S		WD	P	*13	1679	..	1712	1740	STRI12
STRICKLAND William	SJ	L	WD	Y		1731	1748	1756	1819	STRI14
STRUTT John (Wilfrid)	OSB	W	MX	R	#	1713	1743	1738	1782	STRU02
STRUTT Richard	S		NT	V	§3	1577	..	1608	1608	STRU04
STUART Charles	OFM	L	SC	F	#134	1724	1744	1752	1800	STUA00
STUART Henry Benedict CARD.	S		IT	R	*	1725	..	1748	1807	STUA01
STUART William	SJ	N	MX	R	#	..	1640	..	1677	STUA02
STUART d'AUBIGNY Ludovick,Dke	S		MX	P	*	1619	..	1652	1665	STUA04
STUKELEY Augustine	S		DV	S	1	1575	..	..	..	STUK02
STUKELEY John	S				#1	1595	..	..	..	STUK04
STUTTARD Richard	S		MX	L	#3°	1769	..	1795	..	STUT02
STYCHE see STITCH										
SUDALL Henry	S			Q	*	..	..	1582	..	SUDA02
SUDALL John	S	L		D	*3	1732	..	1764	1789	SUDA04
SUDBURY Henry (Peter of Alc.)	OFM		NT	F	123	1600	1624	1624	1676	SUDB02
SUERTIS John	CRT			C		..	1572	..	1620	SUER02
SUFFIELD Roger	S			Q		..	..	1581	..	SUFF02
SUFFREN Jean	SJ	L	FR			1571	1586	..	..	SUFF04
SUGAR John VEN.	S	M	ST	D	#+‡	1562	..	1601	1604	SUGA02
SULYARD Andrew	SJ	M	SK	Y	#	1605	1628	..	1673	SULY02
SULYARD Francis (Augustine)	OSB		SK	W		1686	1709	..	1768	SULY04
SULYARD John	S	M	SK	R	3	1634	..	1658	..	SULY06
SUMNER Richard (Anthony)	OFM		LA	R		1775	1791	1799	1822	SUMN02
SUMNER James (Leo)	OFM	M	LA	R		1775	1791	1799	1822	SUMN04
SUMPNER Charles	OSB		SX	G	§	1645	1672	..	1702	SUMP02
SURMONT James	SJ					..	..	..	1700	SURM02
SUTCLIFF (Thomas)	OFM		YO	F	#1234	1647	1672	1675	1721	SUTC02
SUTEUX Gregory	CRT			C		..	..	1660	1689	SUTE02
SUTTON Abraham	S	N	ST	D	‡	1551	..	1578	..	SUTT02
SUTTON (Angelus)	CAP					..	..	..	..	SUTT03
SUTTON Robert VEN.	S	M	ST	D	+‡	1544	..	1578	1588	SUTT04
SUTTON Robert	S	N	YO	L	#	1641	..	1662	1675	SUTT06
SUTTON Thomas	S	N		D		1601	..	..	..	SUTT08
SUTTON Thomas	S	L	YO	L	#3	1643	..	1670	1674	SUTT10
SUTTON Thomas	S	M				..	..	..	1766	SUTT12
SUTTON William	SJ	L	ST	D	‡	..	1582	1577	1590	SUTT14
SUTTON William	OSS		YO	L	#	1632	..	1655	1690	SUTT16
SWALE Lawrence	OSB		YO	X		..	1670	..	1718	SWAL02
SWARBRICK James	S	N	LA	R	#x	1654	..	1678	1716	SWAR02
SWARBRICK John	S	N	LA	R		1679	..	1703	1729	SWAR04
SWARBRICK Joseph	S		LA	V		1775	..	1800	1804	SWAR06
SWARBRICK Robert	S	N	LA	R	#	1675	..	1700	1737	SWAR08
SWARBRICK Robert	S	N	LA	D		1746	..	1776	1815	SWAR10
SWEET John	SJ		DV	R	1	1570	1609	1608	1632	SWEE02
SWEETMAN John	SJ		NN	V	#	1579	1606	1606	1622	SWEE04
SWETNAM see SWEETMAN										
SWINBURNE Godric (Joachim)	OSB		DH	X		1754	1776	..	1797	SWIN02
SWINBURNE John	SJ	N	DE	Y	#3	1660	1680	1688	1716	SWIN04
SWINBURNE Joseph	S	N	ND	U		1774	..	1800	1845	SWIN06
SWINBURNE Robert	S		HU	Q	†	..	..	1583	..	SWIN08
SWINBURNE Simon	SJ		YO	R		1561	1586	1586	1638	SWIN10
SWINBURNE Thomas	OSB		ND	G		1607	1625	..	1667	SWIN12
SWINBURNE William	SJ		ND	Y		1617	1636	..	1669	SWIN14
SWINDALL Stephen	SJ		MX	Y	#3	1677	1695	1703	1758	SWIN16
SYKES Edmund VEN.	S	N	YO	Q	+	..	..	1581	1587	SYKE02
SYLVESTER Thomas	SJ				7	..	..	..	..	SYLV02

Name	Reg	D	Co	T	Notes	Born	Prof	Ordn	Died	Code
SYRES Josepx	S	L	LA	D		1738	..	1762	1807	SYRE02
TALBOT George Trentham	S	L	YO	R		1685	..	1712	1752	TALB02
TALBOT Gilbert	SJ					..	..	..	1682	TALB04
TALBOT Gilbert, Earl of S'bry	SJ		ST	Y	#*1	1672	1694	1700	1743	TALB06
TALBOT Gilbert	S	N	ND	R		1681	..	1711	1748	TALB08
TALBOT James (Oswald)	OSB	N	LA	W		1768	1789	1792	1847	TALB10
TALBOT James Robert, BP.	S	L	OX	D	*	1726	..	1750	1790	TALB12
TALBOT John (Thomas)	OFM			S	23	..	1638	1635	1668	TALB14
TALBOT John	SJ	N	LA	Y	#3	1708	1728	1739	1799	TALB16
TALBOT John	S		OX	D		1724	..	1749	1751	TALB18
TALBOT John	SJ		LA	Y	3	1737	1757	1764	1801	TALB20
TALBOT Peter, ARCHBP.	S	N	IR	R	*x	1620	..	..	1680	TALB22
TALBOT Richard	S	N	LA	R		1738	..	1762	1823	TALB24
TALBOT Thomas	SJ		LA	R		1572	1598	1597	1652	TALB26
TALBOT (Thomas)	OFM	L	IR		*7	..	..	..	..	TALB27
TALBOT Thomas	SJ	L	LA	Y	#3	1717	1735	1750	1799	TALB28
TALBOT Thomas	S		LA	R		1736	..	1762	1818	TALB30
TALBOT Thomas Joseph, BP.	S	M	OX	D	*	1727	..	1752	1795	TALB32
TALBOT William	SJ		LA	N	12	1596	1618	..	1660	TALB34
TALENTIRE Richard	S			Q		..	..	1582	..	TALE02
TANCARD Charles	SJ		YO	Z		1563	1584	..	1599	TANC02
TANCARD Richard	SJ		YO	Z	#12	1556	1578	..	1596	TANC04
TANCRED see TANCARD										
TANGHE (Urban)	OFM	M	LC		7	..	..	..	..	TANG02
TANKE John (Stanislaus)	OSB		PB	G		..	1625	..	1639	TANK02
TANKE Thomas	OSB		PB	G	4	..	1623	..	1668	TANK04
TAPRELL John	S	M	MX	D	°	1718	..	1748	..	TAPR02
TARLETON John	S			S	3	..	..	1674	..	TARL02
TARLETON William (Dunstan)	OSB	N	LA	W		1772	1794	..	1816	TARL04
TASBURGH Henry	SJ	N	SK	Y	#1	1641	1664	1671	1718	TASB02
TASBURGH Richard	SJ	M	HA	Y	3	1693	1710	1723	1735	TASB04
TASBURGH Richard (Felix)	OSB	L	SK	E	1	1660	1682	..	1731	TASB06
TASBURGH Thomas	SJ	L	NK	Y	#1	1672	1691	1700	1727	TASB08
TASKER James	S	M		D	*	1751	..	1777	1815	TASK02
TATE John (Joseph)	OFM		YO	F	13	1747	1774	1779	1815	TATE02
TATHAM James (Cuthbert)	OSB		YO	G		..	1678	..	1718	TATH02
TATHAM John (Bede)	OSB		YO	G	#°	1642	1657	..	1700	TATH04
TATLOCK Henry	SJ	N	LA	Y	#	1709	1729	1736	1771	TATL02
TATLOCK John	S	N	LA	Z	#3	..	..	1649	..	TATL06
TATLOCK John	SJ	L	ST	Y	#3	1709	1729	1736	1756	TATL08
TAVERNER Edward	S	L		V	#	..	..	1690	1745	TAVE02
TAYLARD John (Bede)	OSB	N		W		1593	1622	1630	1682	TAYL02
TAYLER see TAYLOR										
TAYLOR Alexander	S	M	LA	P	°	..	..	1749	..	TAYL06
TAYLOR Augustine	S	L	HR	R		1644	..	1669	1694	TAYL08
TAYLOR (Bruno)	OFM			F	°3	..	..	1696	..	TAYL10
TAYLOR Charles (Boniface)	OSB	N	LA	X		1752	1772	..	1812	TAYL12
TAYLOR Christopher	S	L	YO	R	#	1730	..	1760	1812	TAYL14
TAYLOR Edmund	OSB		MX	G		..	1680	..	1714	TAYL16
TAYLOR Henry	S		LC		3	1602	..	1639	..	TAYL18
TAYLOR Hugh VEN.	S	N		Q	*+	..	..	1584	1585	TAYL20
TAYLOR James	S			Q	*	..	..	1580	..	TAYL22
TAYLOR James	S	N	YO	R		1730	..	1758	1774	TAYL24
TAYLOR James	S	L	MX	D	3	1761	..	1788	1806	TAYL26
TAYLOR John	S	N		D	*3	1732	..	1759	1804	TAYL28
TAYLOR John (Boniface)	OSB		LA	X		1775	1792	..	1805	TAYL30
TAYLOR Ralph	SJ	N	MX	R	#	1678	1706	1704	1727	TAYL32
TAYLOR Richard	S	N	CD	D	3	1565	..	1594	..	TAYL34
TAYLOR Richard	S	N	LA	L	#3	1657	..	1685	1726	TAYL36
TAYLOR Robert	S	N		D	*	..	..	1596	..	TAYL38
TAYLOR Robert	S		LA	L		1743	..	1768	1769	TAYL40
TAYLOR Stephen (Joseph)	OP	L	IR		*8	..	..	..	..	TAYL41
TAYLOR Thomas	S	L	LC	R		1604	..	1628	1635	TAYL42
TAYLOR Thomas	SJ	L	LA	R		1674	1702	1701	1726	TAYL44
TAYLOR Thomas	S	L	MX	V		1763	..	1787	1808	TAYL46
TAYLOR Thomas	S	N	DH	D	3	1765	..	1788	1818	TAYL48

Name	Reg	D	Co	T	Notes	Born	Prof	Ordn	Died	Code
TAYLOR William (Maurus)	OSB		CB	R	#‡†4	1576	1603	1602	1612	TAYL50
TAYLOR	S			S	3	..	..	1638	..	TAYL52
TAYLOR see also TAYLARD										
TEASDALE John (Vincent)	OP	N		N		1703	1723	1727	1790	TEAS02
TEBAY James (Louis)	OP			N		1696	1716	1721	1727	TEBA02
TEBBITT see TIPPET										
TEDDER William	S	L		R	*°4	1557	..	1582	1619	TEDD02
TEMPEST Charles	SJ		YO	V		1699	1724	1724	1768	TEMP02
TEMPEST Edward	S		DH	Q		1568	..	1594	..	TEMP04
TEMPEST Francis (Augustine)	OSB	N	YO	X		..	1664	..	1729	TEMP06
TEMPEST John	OSB		YO	X		1639	1661	..	1711	TEMP08
TEMPEST John	SJ	L	YO	R		1694	1712	1727	1737	TEMP10
TEMPEST Michael (Edward)	OSB		MX	X		..	1719	..	1773	TEMP12
TEMPEST Nicholas	S		BK	D	#3	..	..	1652	..	TEMP14
TEMPEST Nicholas	SJ	N	LA	Y	x1	1631	1652	1661	1679	TEMP16
TEMPEST Robert	S		DH	Q	14	1542	..	1584	1625	TEMP18
TEMPEST Robert	SJ	L	DH	Q		1566	1624	1591	1640	TEMP20
TEMPEST William	S	N	CB	D	3	1683	..	1710	1766	TEMP22
TEMPEST William (Bartholomew)	OFM		OX	F	12	1620	1637	..	1647	TEMP24
TEMPLE Thomas	S			S	3	..	..	1617	..	TEMP26
TERRET see TYRWHIT										
TESIMOND Oswald	SJ	M	ND	R	#1	1563	1584	..	1635	TESI02
TEVERS Peter	S		LC	R		..	..	1634	..	TEVE02
THERALL see THOROLD										
THEWLIS see THULES										
THIMELBY Edward	S		LN	R	#	1615	..	..	1676	THIM02
THIMELBY Francis	CRT			C		..	1622	..	1647	THIM03
THIMELBY John	S	L	LN	R		1675	..	1699	..	THIM04
THIMELBY Matthew	S		YO	R	#	..	..	1643	..	THIM06
THIMELBY Richard	SJ	M	LN	Y	#	1614	1632	..	1680	THIM08
THIRKELD Richard BL.	S	N	DH	D	+‡	..	..	1579	1583	THIR02
THIRWELL Robert	OSS					..	..	..	1662	THIR04
THOMAS Hugh	S	W	MO	D		1605	..	..	..	THOM02
THOMAS Hugh Benedict	S	L	MX	R	#§	1704	..	1736	1770	THOM04
THOMAS John	S	N	GM	R	#	1702	..	1730	1754	THOM06
THOMAS Morgan	S			Q	*	..	..	1582	..	THOM08
THOMAS Richard	SJ	N	MX	Y	#3	1685	1704	1713	1735	THOM10
THOMPSON Charles	SJ		MX	Y	#12	1607	1625	..	1673	THOM12
THOMPSON Charles	SJ		MD	Y	#	1746	1766	1771	1795	THOM14
THOMPSON Christopher	S			Q	*	..	..	1577	..	THOM16
THOMPSON Edward	S		FR	V		1586	..	..	..	THOM18
THOMPSON Francis	SJ	W	OX	R	#	1577	1606	1603	1614	THOM20
THOMPSON Francis	CRT			C		1672	1711	..	1727	THOM21
THOMPSON James BL.	S	N	YO	Q	#+	..	..	1581	1582	THOM22
THOMPSON John	SJ		KT	V		..	1598	1598	1616	THOM24
THOMPSON John	S	N	YO		#x	..	..	..	1642	THOM26
THOMPSON Lancelot	S		DH	P	#3	1677	..	1701	1729	THOM28
THOMPSON Peter (Antoninus)	OP	N	LC	N		1675	1696	1702	1760	THOM30
THOMPSON Richard	SJ	M	DE	Y	#14	1600	1621	..	1644	THOM32
THOMPSON Richard	S	N	LA	U		1772	..	1797	1841	THOM34
THOMPSON Richard (Leander)	OSB		DH	G	#	..	1635	..	1669	THOM36
THOMPSON Robert	S		ND	R	#1	1613	..	1638	..	THOM38
THOMPSON Roger	CRT			C		..	1566	..	1582	THOM39
THOMPSON Thomas	S	M	LN		7	..	..	..	..	THOM40
THOMPSON Thomas	S			S	3	..	..	1642	..	THOM42
THOMPSON Thomas	SJ		KT	Y	#	1614	1632	..	1680	THOM44
THOMPSON William VEN.	S	L	LA	Q	#+	..	..	1584	1586	THOM46
THOMPSON William	CON	L	SC	R	3	..	..	1602	..	THOM48
THOMPSON William	S	M	NK	D	#13	1667	..	1712	1726	THOM50
THOMSON see THOMPSON										
THORN Richard	S			V	*	..	..	1593	1597	THOR02
THORNBURGH William	S	N	WD	D		1701	..	1724	1750	THOR04
THORNELL Edmund	S			R	*	1560	..	1587	1617	THOR06
THORNTON James	SJ		LA	Y	#13	1678	1700	1711	1752	THOR08
THORNTON Nicholas	CRT			C		..	1569	..	1608	THOR09
THORNTON Robert	SJ		YO	Y	#	1658	1678	1683	1704	THOR10

Name	Reg	D	Co	T	Notes	Born	Prof	Ordn	Died	Code
THORNTON William (Bede)	OSB		ND	G	#	..	1634	..	1694	THOR12
THOROLD Alexander	SJ	M	LN	Y		1631	1655	1663	1681	THOR14
THOROLD Edmund	SJ	W	BK	Y		1657	1677	1686	1715	THOR16
THOROLD Edmund Epiphanius	SJ	M	LN	Y	#13	1669	1687	1695	1732	THOR18
THOROLD Francis	OSS		LN	D	#	..	1646	..		THOR20
THOROLD George	SJ	N	BK	Y		1670	1691	1698	1742	THOR22
THOROLD Thomas	SJ	L	LN	R	#	1600	1633	1633	1664	THOR24
THOROLD Thomas	CRT			C	°4	..	1686	..	1740	THOR26
THOROUGHGOOD James	S	L	EX	R	#	1607	..	1631	1671	THOR28
THOROWOOD see THOROUGHGOOD										
THORPE Andrew	SJ	N	MX	Y	3	1741	1758	1765	1799	THOR32
THORPE John	SJ		YO	R	3	1726	1747	1759	1792	THOR34
THORPE Robert VEN.	S	N	YO	Q	#+	..	..	1585	1591	THOR36
THREEL Maurice	S		SX	D	#	..	..	1655	..	THRE02
THROCKMORTON Fer'nd(Aemilian)	OSB		LC	E		..	1623	1627	1656	THRO02
THROCKMORTON John				Y	14	1612	1633	..	1681	THRO04
THROGMORTON see THROCKMORTON										
THULES Christopher	S		LA	R	#	1560	..	1584	..	THUL02
THULES John VEN.	S	N	LA	R	+	1568	..	1592	1616	THUL04
THULES Robert	S		LA	V	3	1572	..	1599	1602	THUL06
THUNDER Henry	SJ		KT	R	12	1575	1599	..	1638	THUN02
THURSBY Alexander (Louis)	OP	L		N		1651	1667	1674	1726	THUR02
THURSBY Charles	SJ	N	DH	D	2	1573	1606	1603	1639	THUR04
THURSBY Thomas	S		YO	D		..	..	1600	..	THUR06
THWAITES Francis	S	L	LE	R	#	..	..	1664	1723	THWA02
THWAITES (Lawrence)	OP	L		B		1642	1659	1665	1670	THWA04
THWING Edward VEN.	S	N	YO	Q	+	1565	..	1590	1600	THWI02
THWING Ralph	S	N	YO	D	#4	1644	..	..	1691	THWI04
THWING Robert	SJ		YO	R	#§	1606	1627	..	1658	THWI06
THWING Thomas	S	N	YO	R	#	1609	..	1634	..	THWI08
THWING Thomas BL.	S	N	YO	D	+	1635	..	1665	1680	THWI10
TIAS see TYAS										
TICHBORNE Francis	S	L	HA	V	3	1584	..	1608	..	TICH02
TICHBORNE Henry	SJ		HA		1	1570	1587	..	1606	TICH04
TICHBORNE John	SJ	L	HA	Y	3	1694	1712	1725	1772	TICH06
TICHBORNE John Hermengild, Bt.	SJ	L	HA	R	#	1679	1700	1711	1748	TICH08
TICHBORNE Michael	SJ	N	HA	Y		1692	1712	1720	1751	TICH10
TICHBORNE Michael	S	L	HA	R		1725	..	1759	1767	TICH12
TICHBORNE Thomas VEN.	S	L	HA	R	+	1567	..	1592	1602	TICH14
TICKLE William	S	N			7					TICK02
TIDDER Edward	SJ		SK	Y	#	1630	1652	1661	1699	TIDD02
TIDYMAN Michael	S	N	ND	V		1762	..	1785	1832	TIDY02
TIGHE Charles	CRT			C		..	1748	..	..	TIGH02
TIGNEIO John	S			S	3	..	..	1610	..	TIGN02
TILSEN Thomas	S	L	KT	L	#†	1622	..	1649	1688	TILD02
TILLETSON Francis	S		YO	Q	°	..	..	1585	..	TILL02
TILLINGHAM Charles	S	L	EX	L	#4	1653	..	..	1719	TILL04
TIMCOCK Anthony (Francis)	OSB		NN	V	#†3	1581	1609	1609	1668	TIMC02
TIMINGS Charles	S	W	MX	V		1757	..	1781	1832	TIMI02
TIMPERLEY Henry (Gregory)	OSB	M	SK	E		1631	1677	..	1709	TIMP02
TINDALL Edmund	S		SX	D	#	1584	..	1608	..	TIND02
TINDALL Robert	S		ND	R		1740	..	1767	1811	TIND04
TINDALL William	S		YO	S	3	..	..	1614	..	TIND06
TIPPET John	S		SM	D		..	..	1577	..	TIPP02
TIPPET John	CRT		CL	R	§	1560	..	1584	1593	TIPP04
TIRELL see TYRELL										
TOCKETS Alexius	SJ	N	DH	V	#	1665	1689	1689	1731	TOCK02
TODD Anthony	S		DH	D	#13	1648	..	1676	1698	TODD02
TODD Anthony	S		DH	D	#	1671	..	1703	1746	TODD04
TODD Christopher	S	N	DH	D	#3	1683	..	1709	1713	TODD06
TODD Henry	SJ	W	KT	Y	13	1666	1687	1696	1712	TODD08
TODKILL Richard	S	M	OX	D	#4	1607	..	1632	1657	TODK02
TOMLINSON James	S		LA	R	#	1673	..	1697	..	TOML02
TOMMINS Robert	S	L	MX	R		1741	..	1764	1810	TOMM02
TOOL Lawrence	OSA				*7	..	..	..	..	TOOL02
TOOTELL (Charles)	OFM	N		F	3	..	..	1734	1772	TOOT02

Name	Reg	D	Co	T	Notes	Born	Prof	Ordn	Died	Code
TOOTELL Christopher	S	N	LA	L	#3	..	..	1686	1727	TOOT04
TOOTELL Hugh	S	M	LA	D	#	1671	..	1698	1743	TOOT06
TOOTELL (John Ev.)	OFM			F	123	1677	1696	1702	1758	TOOT08
TORBET John	S	N	YO	V	#13	1663	..	1684	1727	TORB02
TORRE Vincent	OP	L	LN			1631	1652	1654	1687	TORR02
TOTTY Christopher	S	N		D	*	..	..	1603	..	TOTT02
TOUCHET George (Anselm), Hon.	OSB	L	DT	G	4	..	1643	..	1689	TOUC02
TOULOTT Matthew	SJ	L	LC	Y	3	1639	1660	1666	1677	TOUL02
TOURNER see TURNER										
TOWERS Francis	S	L	MX	R	#4	1645	..	1668	1733	TOWE02
TOWNELEY Richard (Columban)	CRT		LA	C		1664	1700	..	1729	TOWN02
TOWNELEY Thomas	S	N	LA	P	3	..	..	1694	1737	TOWN04
TOWNESHEND (Theodore)	OFM			F	1	1610	1633	..	1647	TOWN05
TOWNSEND Thomas	S	M			7	..	..	..	..	TOWN06
TOWNSON John	OSB	N	LA	X		..	1674	..	1718	TOWN08
TOWNSON Thomas (Augustine)	OSB	N	LA	X		..	1688	..	1722	TOWN10
TRAFFORD Henry	S	N	LA	D	#s	1633	..	1658	1664	TRAF02
TRANSHAM see STRANSHAM										
TRANT see TRENT										
TRAPPES (Joseph of S.Nic'las)	OFM			F	123	1644	1665	1669	1699	TRAP02
TRAPPES Nicholas	S	L	SX	R	#	1647	..	1675	..	TRAP04
TRAPPES (Richard)	OFM		SX	F	123	1654	1670	1678	1694	TRAP06
TRAPPS see TRAPPES										
TRAVERS George (Lucian)	ODC	L	DV	Z	*x§	1642	..	..	1691	TRAV02
TRAVERS John	SJ		DV	S	#§°23	1616	1645	1642	..	TRAV04
TRAVERS Walter Joseph (Bede)	ODC	L	DV	R		1619	1648	..	1696	TRAV06
TREMBY John (Celestine)	OSB			G		1591	1614	..	1629	TREM02
TRENT (Henry of S.Teresa)	CAR	L	IR		°4	1652	1669	..	1701	TREN01
TRENTHAM Roger	S		ST	D	#3	..	..	1686	1742	TREN02
TRESHAM Francis	OFM		NN	G	*3	1592	1649	1643	1660	TRES02
TRESHAM Thomas	SJ		DT	Y	23	1637	1663	1670	1671	TRES04
TREVENNIAN Charles	SJ	L	MX	Y	#13	1667	1685	1694	1737	TREV02
TREVORS William	S		DB	D		..	..	1603	..	TREV04
TRIM John	S		DT	D		..	..	1597	..	TRIM02
TRIM Richard	S	L	DT	S	#	1590	..	1613	..	TRIM04
TRISTRAM Joseph	SJ		LA	Y	#	1766	1803	1791	1843	TRIS02
TROLLOPE Cuthbert	S	N	DH	R	#	1573	..	1596	..	TROL02
TRYER see TYRER										
TUCHINER Anthony	S	M	WT	D	‡4	..	..	1600	1643	TUCH02
TUCKER James	SJ		SM	Y	#3	1710	1728	1735	..	TUCK02
TUER Daniel	CRT			C		..	..	..	1623	TUER02
TUITE Francis	S	L	MX	D	3	1768	..	1791	1838	TUIT02
TUITE William (Raymund)	OP	L	MX	N		1766	1790	1792	1833	TUIT04
TUNSTALL Anthony	S			S	3	..	..	1637	..	TUNS02
TUNSTALL Lawrence	S			S	3	..	..	1646	..	TUNS04
TUNSTALL Peter Brian	S	N	YO	D	#3	1673	..	1696	1742	TUNS06
TUNSTALL Ralph	S			S		..	..	1638	..	TUNS08
TUNSTALL Thomas BL.	S	M	WD	D	#*+	..	..	1609	1616	TUNS10
TUNSTALL Thomas	SJ		YO	Y		1635	1655	1664	1665	TUNS12
TUNSTALL William	SJ		YO	Y	1	1611	1631	..	1681	TUNS14
TURBERVILLE Anthony	OSB		GM	E		..	1664	..	1721	TURB02
TURBERVILLE Edward	S	L				..	..	..	1723	TURB04
TURBERVILLE Henry	S		ST	D	#13	1607	..	1635	1678	TURB06
TURBERVILLE Humphrey (Anselm)	OSB	W	GM	Z	#*2	1579	1604	..	1645	TURB08
TURBERVILLE John	SJ	L	BK	Y	#	1663	1683	1691	1735	TURB10
TURBERVILLE see also TURVILLE										
TURCK Augustus (Lawrence)	OSB		GS	X		..	1751	..	1769	TURC02
TURNER Anthony BL.	SJ	M	LE	R	#+†1	1628	1653	..	1679	TURN02
TURNER Bernard	S	L	SX	D	#	1693	..	1720	1735	TURN04
TURNER Christopher	S					..	..	..	1709	TURN06
TURNER Edward	SJ		LE	Y	#x†3	1625	1658	1658	1681	TURN08
TURNER Francis	SJ	M	OX	Y		1612	1635	..	1659	TURN10
TURNER Francis	S		FR	D		1646	..	..	1675	TURN12
TURNER George	OSB		LA	G		1770	1790	1800	1851	TURN14
TURNER John	SJ		OX	Y		1604	1623	1635	1681	TURN16
TURNER John	SJ		MO	Y	#12	1640	1662	..	1672	TURN18

Name	Reg	D	Co	T	Notes	Born	Prof	Ordn	Died	Code
TURNER John	S			R	*	1640	..	1670	..	TURN20
TURNER John	OSB	N	LA	E		1765	1786	1790	1844	TURN22
TURNER John (Thomas)	OSB	N	LA	W		1743	1759	..	1802	TURN24
TURNER Richard	S		SP	L		..	..	1696	1744	TURN28
TURNER Robert	S		DV	D		..	..	1574	1599	TURN30
TURNER Robert	SJ		LA	Y	#	1677	1701	1712	1734	TURN32
TURNER Robert (Augustine)	OSB	N	LA	X		1721	1740	..	1757	TURN34
TURVILLE Charles	SJ		LE	Y	#3	1681	1700	1708	1757	TURV02
TURVILLE Henry	SJ		LE	Y		1674	1693	1701	1714	TURV04
TURVILLE William	S	W	LE	R		1692	..	1719	1765	TURV06
TURVILLE see also TURBERVILLE										
TWYFORD Samuel	S	L		Q	*	..	..	1579	..	TWYF02
TYAS George	S	L	YO	D		..	..	1597	..	TYAS02
TYAS George	CRT	L	EX	D	#	1604	..	1628	1668	TYAS04
TYDDER see TIDDER										
TYFFE Lambert de	SJ		LC		1	1603	1634	..	1672	TYFF02
TYLDESLEY (Anthony)	OFM	M	LA	F	123	1686	1703	1710	1718	TYLD02
TYRER James	S	N	LA	D		1741	..	1766	1784	TYRE02
TYRER Joseph	SJ	W	LA	Y	3	1734	1753	1762	1798	TYRE04
TYRRELL Anthony	S		EX	R	3	1552	..	1580	1615	TYRR02
TYRWHIT Henry	SJ		MX	Z	#*	1672	1692	1702	1742	TYRW02
TYRWHIT Nicholas	S	M		D	*	..	..	1577	1604	TYRW04
UMFREVILLE Charles	S	L		P	#	1687	..	1713	1763	UMFR02
UNDERHILL James	S		ST	L	#3	..	..	1681	..	UNDE02
UNDERHILL John	S	L		D	*	1736	..	1767	1769	UNDE04
UNDERWOOD Francis	OP			N		1701	1719	1725	1761	UNDE06
URMESTON John	S	N	LA	S	7	..	..	..	..	URME02
VALENTINE Joseph	S	M	IT	R		1713	..	1736	1761	VALE02
VALENTINE William (Anselm)	CAP					..	..	..	1641	VALE03
(Valentine of Mother of God)	ODC				*	..	..	..	1634	VALE04
VALINGER Henry	S			S	3	..	..	1610	..	VALI02
VANCAM John	S	L		R	#*	1693	..	1716	1756	VANC02
VANDERBERG	CAR	L	IR		7	..	..	..	..	VAND02
VANE John	S	L		L	#§	..	..	1693	1733	VANE02
VAN ERP Cornelius (Sigismund)	ODC	L	LC			1646	1669	..	1721	VANE04
VAN ERP James (Luke)	ODC	L	LC			1643	1666	..	1721	VANE06
VANSTRATER Paschasius	SJ		LC		4	1587	1612	..	1621	VANS02
VANTELET Robert de	CAP	L	FR		2	..	1611	..	1659	VANT02
VAN VALCKENISSE Peter(Crucis)	ODC	L	LC			1603	1624	..	1671	VANV02
VARDER John	S	L	MX	R	#	1580	..	1606	..	VARD02
VARLEY Thomas	S	L		D	*3	1728	..	1765	1806	VARL02
VAUDREY John	SJ		SX	Y	#3	1658	1677	1686	1725	VAUD02
VAUGHAN Arthur	S	M	MX	D		1725	..	1749	1792	VAUG02
VAUGHAN Dominic	S			R	3	..	..	1576	..	VAUG04
VAUGHAN John	OFM		DB	F	#	..	1601	..	..	VAUG06
VAUGHAN Richard	SJ		MO	Y		1675	1690	1699	1727	VAUG08
VAUGHAN Roger	S	W			7	..	..	..	..	VAUG10
VAUGHAN Thomas	SJ	W	HR	D	x	1606	1632	1627	1675	VAUG12
VAUGHAN Walter (Dominic)	OFM		MO	F	123	1624	1647	1653	1661	VAUG14
VAUGHAN Walter	S		MO	R		1662	..	1696	1696	VAUG16
VAUGHAN William	S			S		..	..	1677	..	VAUG18
VAUGHAN William	SJ	W	BR	Y		1644	1672	1677	1687	VAUG20
VAUX Cuthbert	S				*‡34	..	..	1574	1588	VAUX02
VAVASOUR Francis	OFM	N	YO	F	124	1607	1626	..	1652	VAVA02
VAVASOUR Henry	S		YO	D	#	1597	..	1625	1660	VAVA04
VAVASOUR James	S		YO	R		1561	..	1586	1593	VAVA06
VAVASOUR Walter, Bt.	SJ	N	YO	Y		1662	1681	1689	1740	VAVA08
VAVASOUR William	SJ		YO	Y	#3	1618	1665	1668	1683	VAVA10
VEAL Edward	OSS		LA	V		..	..	1635	..	VEAL02
VENISE Roger	S			Z	*	..	..	1559	..	VENI02
VENNER Robert (Amandus)	OSB		DV	D	#	..	1614	1609	1628	VENN02
VERE Henry (Joseph)	OP		MX	D		..	1661	1653	1683	VERE02
VERHUYCK John	S	L	MX	R	#	1688	..	1715	1738	VERH02
VEZZOSI James	S		IT	R	#	1717	..	1740	1774	VEZZ02
VEZZOSI Joseph	SJ		IT	R	#	1720	1743	1743	1772	VEZZ04
VEZZOSI Stephen	S	L	IT	R	#	1716	..	1744	1781	VEZZ06

Name	Reg	D	Co	T	Notes	Born	Prof	Ordn	Died	Code
VICK John	SJ				‡	..	1563	..	1588	VICK02
VICTOR Francis	S	W	CL	L	#	1612	..	1636	1683	VICT04
(Victor of Paris)	CAP	L	FR		2	..	1622	..	1652	VICT06
(Victor of S.Cecily)	CAR	L	FR			..	..	..	1723	VICT08
VIETTE	ORA		FR		*7	..	..	..	..	VIET02
VINCENT Nicholas	OP		LN	R	#24	..	1596	..	1616	VINC02
VINCENT William	S		KT	V	§1	1576	..	1602	1660	VINC04
(Vincent of Beauvais)	CAP	L	FR		2	..	1597	..	1652	VINC06
VINES Henry	S		OX	R	#§	1587	..	1613	..	VINE02
VINTER Robert	S	N	HU	D	#†134	1637	..	1674	1706	VINT02
VINTER see also WINTER										
VISCONTI Hermes Mary	SJ		IT	Y		1650	1665	1678	..	VISC02
VIVIAN Ignatius	S			S	3	..	1668	..		VIVI02
VIVIAN John	OSS		CL	Q	‡2	..	1587	1579	1624	VIVI04
WADDINGTON John	S	L	LA	D	#	..	..	1645	1689	WADD02
WAFER (Simon)	OFM	L	IR		*7	..	..	..	..	WAFE01
WAFERER Andrew	S	L	HU	V	#x§=4	1576	..	1603	1648	WAFE02
WAFERER Francis	SJ		MX	Q	=1	1540	1585	1585	1588	WAFE04
WAGSTAFFE James	S	N	LA	L		1762	..	1788	1847	WAGS02
WAINMAN Christopher	S	L			7	..	..	..	..	WAIN02
WAITE James	SJ	N	YO	Y		1617	1640	..	1679	WAIT02
WAKE John (Hilarion)	OSB		DH	G	#	..	1639	..	1657	WAKE02
WAKE Richard	S		LC	R		1607	..	1634	..	WAKE04
WAKEMAN Edward	S		GL	R	#	1628	..	1660	..	WAKE06
WAKEMAN John	S		ST	R	#	1594	..	1620	..	WAKE08
WAKEMAN Joseph	SJ		GL	Y		1647	1665	1675	1720	WAKE10
WAKEMAN Roger	S			D	*x	..	..	1576	1582	WAKE12
WAKEMAN Thomas	SJ		ST	R	#	1599	1632	1630	1636	WAKE14
WALDEGRAVE Charles	SJ		EX	Y	#	1592	1616	..	1655	WALD02
WALDEGRAVE Charles	S	M	NK	L	#3	1627	..	1650	..	WALD04
WALDEGRAVE Francis	SJ	N	WT	R	#	1626	1655	1651	1701	WALD06
WALDEGRAVE Nicholas	S		NK	L	1	1666	..	1689	1734	WALD08
WALDEGRAVE William	OSB	M	EX	V	#§	1588	1650	1618	1665	WALD10
WALFRID Thomas	S		CN	V	#†	..	..	1624	..	WALF02
WALGRAVE see WALDEGRAVE										
WALKEDEN John	SJ		MX	R	#3	1663	1682	1694	1718	WALK02
WALKER Edward	S					..	..	..	1661	WALK04
WALKER (George)	CAR	L	MX		4	..	..	..	1720	WALK05
WALKER George (Augustine)	OSB	N	LA	E	x	1721	1743	..	1794	WALK06
WALKER Richard	S			L	3	..	..	1609	..	WALK08
WALKER Robert	S	N	YO	D	1	1585	..	1620	..	WALK10
WALKER Robert	S		ND	R		..	..	1601	..	WALK12
WALKER Thomas	S	N	LC	R	#	1598	..	1621	..	WALK14
WALKER Thomas	ODC		YO		2	..	1736	..	..	WALK16
WALL John (Alexius)	OSB		HA	X		..	1715	..	1730	WALL02
WALL John (Joachim) ST.	OFM	M	LA	R	#+	1620	1651	1645	1679	WALL04
WALL William (Cuthbert)	OSB	L	LA	R	#	1625	1668	1649	1704	WALL06
WALL see also WHALL, WHALLEY										
WALLACE William	SJ					1615	..	..	1682	WALL10
WALLACE see also WALLIS										
WALLEIS see WALLIS										
WALLER E.	S	W			7	..	..	..	..	WALL16
WALLET Louis Albert	S	L	MX	D	3	1735	..	1759	1812	WALL18
WALLEY Robert	S			Q	*†	..	..	1582	1587	WALL20
WALLIS (Edmund)	OFM			F		..	..	..	1642	WALL22
WALLIS Francis	SJ		SY	Y		1589	1613	..	1656	WALL24
WALLIS John (of S.Mary)	OFM		LC	F	12	1605	1638	..	1647	WALL26
WALMESLEY Charles BP.	OSB	W	LA	E	*	1722	1739	..	1797	WALM02
WALMESLEY Christopher	SJ		LA	V	#3	1684	1708	1707	1734	WALM04
WALMESLEY Francis	OSB		LA	W		1718	1735	..	1747	WALM06
WALMESLEY (Mellitus)	OSB		LA	W		..	1679	..	1689	WALM08
WALMESLEY Richard	S	N	LA	V	#3	1709	..	1733	1744	WALM10
WALMESLEY Richard (Anselm)	OSB	N	LA	W		..	1709	..	1735	WALM12
WALMESLEY Richard (Peter)	OSB		LA	G	#	1717	1736	..	1790	WALM14
WALMESLEY Thomas	SJ		LA	Y	3	1716	1737	1744	1792	WALM16
WALMESLEY William	S	M	LA	D	#	..	..	1644	..	WALM18

Name	Reg	D	Co	T	Notes	Born	Prof	Ordn	Died	Code
WALMESLEY William	SJ	M	LA	Y	3	1712	1732	1740	1769	WALM20
WALPOLE Christopher	SJ		NK	R	†	1568	1592	..	1606	WALP02
WALPOLE Christopher	SJ		NK	R	#2	1598	1624	1622	1664	WALP04
WALPOLE Edward	SJ		NK	R	#†1	1560	1593	1592	1637	WALP06
WALPOLE Henry ST.	SJ	N	NK	R	+†=	1558	1584	1588	1595	WALP08
WALPOLE Michael	SJ		NK	R	#4	1570	1593	..	1620	WALP10
WALPOLE Richard	SJ		NK	R	#†2	1564	1593	1589	1607	WALP12
WALSH Edward	SJ	N	FR	Y		1739	1756	1767	1822	WALS02
WALSH John	SJ	N	IR	Y	3	1700	1720	1728	1773	WALS04
WALSH (Peter)	OFM	L	IR	N	13	1614	..	1639	1688	WALS06
WALSH Thomas	S		FR	D		1752	..	1777	1817	WALS08
WALSINGHAM Francis	SJ	M	ND	R	#‡=	1576	1609	1608	1647	WALS10
WALSINGHAM	S					..	..	1660	1663	WALS12
WALTERS Thomas	SJ	M	WK	Y		1619	1640	..	1647	WALT02
WALTON James	S	N	LA	R	#	1609	..	1633	1671	WALT04
WALTON James	SJ		LA	Y	3	1736	1757	1765	1803	WALT06
WALTON John	SJ		LA	Y	#	1624	1642	..	1677	WALT08
WALTON Thomas	SJ	M	LA	Y	3	1740	1757	1765	1797	WALT10
WALTON William	SJ		LA	Y	3	1651	1671	1684	1706	WALT12
WALTON William BP.	S	N	LA	D	*	1715	..	1741	1780	WALT14
WAMBEKE Adrian van	SJ		LC			1630	1666	..	1687	WAMB02
WAPPELER Wilhelm	SJ	N	GS			1711	1728	1739	1781	WAPP02
WARCOP Thomas	SJ		CD	R	§	1560	1587	1584	1589	WARC02
WARD Francis	S		SX	R	4	1597	..	1621	1623	WARD02
WARD George	SJ		YO	Y	#1	1596	1619	..	1654	WARD04
WARD Henry	CRT			C		..	1570	..	1578	WARD05
WARR Lawrence	S		YO	D	#	1677	..	..	1741	WARD06
WARD Robert	S	N	DH	V	13	1660	..	1684	..	WARD08
WARD William	S	L	YO	R	#4	1592	..	1618	1645	WARD10
WARD William	SJ	M	ST	Y	°	1708	1727	1735	..	WARD12
WAREHAM John (Denis)	OSB		MX	X	#	..	1744	..	1763	WARE02
WAREING see WARING										
WARFORD William	SJ		SM	R	#‡	1560	1594	1584	1608	WARF02
WARHAM George	S	W	DT	D	#	1586	..	1612	1676	WARH02
WARHAM George	S		DT	D	#	1607	..	1633	..	WARH04
WARHAM James	S	N		P	*3	..	..	1739	1763	WARH06
WARHAM John	S	W	DT	D	#	1582	..	1610	..	WARH08
WARHAM Philip	S		IR	D		1722	..	1747	1748	WARH10
WARHAM see also WAREHAM										
WARINER Richard	S		WD	D	3	..	..	1607	..	WARI02
WARING (Ambrose)	OSB	N	LA	W		1734	1761	..	1776	WARI06
WARING Humphrey	S	L	WK	L		1605	..	1635	1676	WARI08
WARING John (Henry)	OFM		LA	F	34	1745	1763	1770	1816	WARI10
WARING Peter	S		LA	D	°	1712	..	1740	1773	WARI12
WARING Robert (Bruno)	OFM		LA	F	13	1726	1746	1755	1779	WARI13
WARING William	S	M	WK	L	#	1604	..	1633	1652	WARI14
WARING see also WAREING										
WARMINGTON William	S		DT	Q	#	1556	..	1580	..	WARM02
WARMOLL John (Bernard)	OSB	M	NK	G		1719	1737	..	1807	WARM04
WARNER John	SJ	L	WK	D		1628	1662	1653	1692	WARN02
WARNER John, Bt.	SJ		SK	Y	#§	1640	1665	1670	1705	WARN04
WARNER Vincent	S			Q		..	..	1582	..	WARN06
WARNFORD Peter	S		HA	V	#*3	1582	..	1610	1657	WARN08
WARREN Bernard	OSB		CH	E		..	1648	1649	1650	WARR10
WARREN Henry	SJ	M	KT	Y	#	1635	1652	1661	1702	WARR12
WARREN John	S			S	3	..	..	1645	..	WARR14
WARREN John	S			S	#8	..	..	..	..	WARR16
WARREN Thomas	S	N	MX	R	#§	1631	..	1658	..	WARR18
WARREN William	S		KT	R	#§	1631	..	1656	1701	WARR20
WARRILOW Joseph	S	L	ST	D	#1	1675	..	1712	1765	WARR22
WARRILOW William	SJ	N	MX	Y	3	1738	1760	1766	1807	WARR24
WARWICK George	S	N	YO	Z	#	1585	..	1609	1658	WARW02
WARWICK Thomas (Basil)	OSB	N	CD	G		..	1698	..	1732	WARW04
WATERHOUSE George	S	N	YO	R	#	1712	..	1735	1778	WATE02
WATERSON Edward BL.	S	N	MX	Q	+§	..	..	1592	1593	WATE04
WATERTON Charles	SJ		YO	Y		1744	1762	1771	1773	WATE06

Name	Reg	D	Co	T	Notes	Born	Prof	Ordn	Died	Code
WATERTON Thomas	SJ	N	YO	Y	3	1701	1721	1729	1766	WATE08
WATKINS (Charles)	OFM	W		F	#	1665	1683	1689	1737	WATK02
WATKINS Lawrence	S	W	MO	R	#4	1627	..	1653	1679	WATK04
WATKINS Walter (Gregory)	OFM	W	MO	F	13	1739	..	1770	1810	WATK06
WATKINS William	S	W		V		..	..	..	1683	WATK08
WATKINSON John (Gregory)	OSB	N	MX	G		1727	1746	..	1792	WATK10
WATKINSON Matthias	S		MX	L		1634	..	1658	1710	WATK12
WATKINSON Robert BL.	S	L	YO	D	#+	1579	..	1602	1602	WATK14
WATMOUGH Arthur (Francis)	OSB		LA	W		1665	1684	..	1733	WATM02
WATSON	OP				*7	..	..	..	..	WATS01
WATSON Ignatius	SJ	W	MX	R	#4	1586	1615	1612	1625	WATS02
WATSON James	S	N	YO	R	#‡	1699	..	1723	1772	WATS04
WATSON Walter	S		KT	R	#	1621	..	1649	..	WATS06
WATSON William	S	L	DH	Q	#‡=1	1558	..	1586	1603	WATS08
WATTS John	S	L	WK	D	#‡	1616	..	1653	1675	WATT02
WATTS William	S			D	*4	..	..	1578	1583	WATT04
WAY William BL.	S	L	DV	Q	#+	1565	..	1586	1588	WAYA02
WEARDEN John (Vincent)	OSB	N	LA	X		1769	1787	..	1801	WEAR02
WEATHERBY Peter	S	N	LA	D	#	1600	..	1624	1667	WEAT02
WEBB Edward	SJ		SK	R	§	1575	1609	1605	1622	WEBB02
WEBB George	SJ		MX	Y		1653	1672	1681	1725	WEBB04
WEBB James	S	L	MX	D	3	1726	..	1754	1781	WEBB06
WEBB Michael	SJ	N	MX	Y		1623	1642	..	1665	WEBB08
WEBB Thomas	SJ	W	GL	Y		1575	1619	..	1658	WEBB10
WEBB William Henry (Dunstan)	OSB	N	WK	X		1764	1784	1789	1848	WEBB14
WEBSTER Thomas	S	L	MX	L		1757	..	1783	1828	WEBS02
WEBSTER William BL.	S	L	WD	D	#+1	1565	..	1608	1641	WEBS04
WEEBLE see WHEBLE										
WEEDON John	S	L		S	3	..	..	1668	1694	WEED04
WEEDON Thomas	S	N	WR	R	#4	1637	..	1661	1719	WEED06
WEEDON William	S		OX	V	#°	..	..	1698	..	WEED08
WEETMAN Edward (Andrew)	OFM	W	WK	F	3	1765	..	1790	1843	WEET02
WEETMAN Francis (Andrew)	OFM	W	WK	F	13	1742	1759	1767	1795	WEET04
WELCH Thomas	OSB	N	LA	E		1726	1744	..	1790	WELC02
WELD see WELLS										
WELDON Charles or James	SJ		ND	V	#34	1716	1739	1738	1803	WELD04
WELDON (Innocent)	CAP					1640	..	..	1707	WELD05
WELDON Matthew	S			D	*3	1753	..	1782	1785	WELD06
WELDON Thomas or Fenwick	SJ	N	ND	Y	#3	1705	1723	1731	1786	WELD08
WELDON Thomas	SJ	N	IR		#3	1714	1731	..	1776	WELD10
WELDON Thomas	S	N	IR	D	°	1761	..	1788	..	WELD12
WELDON William	SJ	N	ND	Y	#3	1711	1732	1739	1761	WELD14
WELLS Ambrose	S		MX	V	#*3	..	..	1724	..	WELL02
WELLS Charles	SJ	L	HA	Y		1702	1720	1733	1757	WELL04
WELLS Edward	OSS		LA	V	#	..	1637	1635	1647	WELL06
WELLS Gilbert	SJ		HA	Y	#1	1713	1731	1739	1777	WELL08
WELSH see WALSH										
WELTON see WELDON										
WENDON Nicholas	S			R	*†	..	..	1578	..	WEND02
WESCOTTE (Francis)	OFM			F	12	1617	1636	..	1645	WESC02
WESLEY Peter	CAP	L			*8	..	..	..	..	WESL02
WEST James	S			D	*	..	..	1597	..	WEST04
WESTBROOKE William (Maurus)	OSB		KT	X	#	..	1726	..	1774	WEST06
WESTBY (Anthony of S. Francis)	OFM		LA	F	123	1670	1697	1703	1713	WEST08
WESTBY Peter	SJ		LA	Y	#	1727	1749	1757	1788	WEST10
WESTBY Thomas	SJ	L	LA	Y	3	1703	1724	1733	1736	WEST12
WESTHEAD Henry	S		MX	R	#	1698	..	1723	1772	WEST14
WESTON Edward	S	N	MX	R	‡4	1565	..	1589	1635	WEST16
WESTON John	SJ	M	SK		#1	1589	1620	..	1649	WEST18
WESTON Roger	S	N		S	*3	1578	..	1604	..	WEST20
WESTON William	SJ	L	KT	R	#‡	1550	1575	..	1615	WEST22
WESTON William (John Baptist)	OFM			F	123	1655	1673	1679	1729	WEST24
WHALE see WHALL & WALL										
WHALL Charles	S		NK	D	3	1639	..	1663	..	WHAL06
WHALL Edward	S		NK	D	#	1612	..	1653	..	WHAL10
WHALL George	OSB		NK	W		..	1666	..	1709	WHAL12

Name	Reg	D	Co	T	Notes	Born	Prof	Ordn	Died	Code
WHALL Thomas	S		NK	D	#	..	..	1632	..	WHAL14
WHALL Thomas	CRT			C		..	..	..	1692	WHAL15
WHALL William	S		NK	D	#14	1608	..	..	1640	WHAL16
WHALL William	S	M	NK	D	#	..	..	1659	1671	WHAL18
WHALL see also WALL, WHALLEY										
WHALLEY Richard (Alexius)	OFM		LA	F	#13	1739	1757	1764	1811	WHAL20
WHALLEY Thomas	S	M	LA	R	#	1675	..	1701	1730	WHAL22
WHARTON Charles (Christopher)	ODC	L	MX		2	1663	1686	..	..	WHAR02
WHARTON Charles	SJ	M	MD	Y	°3	1748	1766	1772	1833	WHAR04
WHARTON Christopher VEN.	S	N	YO	Q	+‡	..	..	1584	1600	WHAR06
WHARTON Michael	S	N	WD	L		1733	..	1760	1809	WHAR08
WHEATMAN see WEETMAN										
WHEBLE James	SJ	W	WT	Y	#3	1725	1743	1750	1788	WHEB02
WHEELER James	S	N	HA	P	3	1765	..	1789	1838	WHEE02
WHEELER John	S	M	WR	R		..	..	1696	..	WHEE04
WHEELER (John)	OFM			F	34	..	..	1740	1773	WHEE06
WHESTON see WESTON										
WHETENHALL Henry	SJ		KT	Y	3	1694	1713	1722	1745	WHET02
WHETENHALL James	S		KT	R		1702	..	1726	1773	WHET04
WHICHCOTT William	SJ		LN	Y	#12	1580	1606	..	1654	WHIC02
WHILDON see WELDON										
WHITAKER George	S	L		L	#§	1701	..	1726	1752	WHIT02
WHITAKER Humphrey	S		LA	R	#	1613	..	1638	1653	WHIT04
WHITAKER Nicholas	S		LA	V	4	..	..	1646	1653	WHIT06
WHITAKER Thomas VEN.	S	N	LA	V	#+	1611	..	1638	1646	WHIT08
WHITAKER Thomas	S	L	MX	R	#§	1702	..	1729	1778	WHIT10
WHITBREAD John	S			D	#*	1594	..	1625	..	WHIT12
WHITBREAD Thomas BL.	SJ	M	EX	Y	#+	1618	1635	..	1679	WHIT14
WHITBREAD William	S	L				..	..	..	1699	WHIT16
WHITE Andrew	SJ		MX	S	3	1579	1607	1606	1656	WHIT20
WHITE (Dominic)	CAP					..	..	..	1713	WHIT23
WHITE Edward	S	L	WR	D	1	1731	..	1759	1762	WHIT24
WHITE Eustace ST.	S	W	LN	R	+1	1560	..	1588	1591	WHIT26
WHITE Francis	SJ	L	IR		2	1610	1630	..	1697	WHIT28
WHITE Henry	SJ	L	MX	Y	#	1662	1680	1689	1693	WHIT30
WHITE James (Anselm)	OFM	M	MX	F	134	1712	1740	1746	1778	WHIT31
WHITE Jerome	S	M	EX	D	#3	..	..	1628	..	WHIT32
WHITE John	S		ES	V	#3	..	..	1648	..	WHIT34
WHITE John	S	N	LA	R	#	1710	..	1733	1778	WHIT36
WHITE John	SJ	L	LA	Y	3	1744	1768	1769	1771	WHIT38
WHITE Luke	S	N	LA	R	#	1708	..	1731	1765	WHIT40
WHITE Philip	S		BK	L		1748	..	1772	1777	WHIT42
WHITE Richard	S	M	OX	Q		..	..	1581	..	WHIT44
WHITE Richard	S	L	HA	Q		..	..	1587	..	WHIT46
WHITE Richard	S		HA	D	‡34	1539	..	1600	1612	WHIT48
WHITE Richard	S		HA	D	#	1603	..	1630	1687	WHIT50
WHITE Robert	SJ		ND	Y	#4	1622	1641	..	1678	WHIT52
WHITE Thomas	S	L	EX	D	#	1593	..	1617	1676	WHIT54
WHITE Thomas	S		WR	R	†	1643	..	1666	1670	WHIT56
WHITE Thomas	OP		HA	R	#	..	..	..	1694	WHIT58
WHITE Thomas	S	L	MX	D	3	1764	..	1791	1826	WHIT60
WHITE William	SJ	N	WT	S	3	1584	1617	1609	1624	WHIT62
WHITE William	S		HA			..	..	..	1640	WHIT64
WHITE William	SJ	W	CN	R	#1	1631	1658	1657	1688	WHIT66
WHITE William (Claude)	OSB		DB	Z	#*23	1583	1605	1609	1655	WHIT68
WHITEHAIR Anthony	S	M	SX	V	#4	1594	..	1620	1672	WHIT70
WHITEHALL Andrew	S	M	DE	D	#3	..	..	1653	1682	WHIT72
WHITFIELD Andrew	OSB		ND	G		..	1638	..	1688	WHIT74
WHITFIELD Thomas Hugh John	SJ		DH	Y		1615	1639	..	1686	WHIT76
WHITGREAVE James Abel	SJ	M	ST	Y	13	1689	1715	1724	1750	WHIT78
WHITGREAVE Thomas	SJ	M	ST	Y	1	1696	1718	1726	1757	WHIT80
WHITLEY Richard	SJ		EX	V	12	1583	1611	1611	1651	WHIT82
WHITMORE Richard	SJ		CH	Y	#2	1577	1614	..	1649	WHIT84
WHITOLF Hugh	S			D	*	1571	..	1599	..	WHIT86
WHITTAKER see WHITAKER										
WHITTELL Roger (Joseph)	OSB		MX	E		1707	1726	..	1786	WHIT90

Name	Reg	D	Co	T	Notes	Born	Prof	Ordn	Died	Code
WHITTINGHAM Thomas	S	M	ST	P		1738	..	1763	1783	WHIT92
WHITTINGHAM William Edward	SJ	L	YO	Y	#	1590	1611	..	1620	WHIT94
WHOLY see WHALLEY										
WHYTE see WHITE										
WIART (Gregory of S.Mary)	OFM		LC	F	1234	1625	1648	1652	1692	WIAR02
WICK see VICK										
WICKET (Hubert)	OFM			F		..	..	1686	1720	WICK04
WICKSTED (Polycarp)	OFM			F	3	..	..	1674	1725	WICK06
WIDDRINGTON Anthony, Hon.	SJ	N		Y	*3	1644	1665	1670	1682	WIDD02
WIDDRINGTON Henry (Paul)	OFM		ND	F	12	1627	1646	..	1685	WIDD04
WIDDRINGTON Henry, Hon.	SJ	N	ND	Y		1667	1687	1696	1729	WIDD06
WIDDRINGTON Robert, Hon.	SJ	N	ND	Y	#34	1660	1679	1688	1742	WIDD08
WIGGS William	S		MX	R	‡4	..	..	1582	1602	WIGG02
WIGMORE Richard	SJ	W	HR	Y	#1	1593	1617	..	1677	WIGM02
WIGMORE William	SJ		HR	Y	#	1599	1624	..	1665	WIGM04
WIGNAL Francis	SJ		MX	Y	#1	1678	1697	1706	1728	WIGN02
WILCOCK Charles (Peter Alcan)	OFM	N	LA	F	1	1749	1767	1773	1802	WILC02
WILCOCK Peter	OSB		LA	W		1715	1737	..	1776	WILC04
WILCOCKS see WILCOX										
WILCOX Hugh	S		SM	Q		..	..	1582	..	WILC08
WILCOX Peter	OSB			Z	*24	..	1607	..	1619	WILC10
WILCOX Robert BL.	S	L	CH	Q	+	1558	..	1585	1588	WILC12
WILCOX see also WILCOCK										
WILDS William	S	L		D	#*3	1766	..	1792	1854	WILD02
WILFORD Hugh ,	S			S	3	..	..	1616	..	WILF02
WILFORD Humphrey	S		MX	V	#3	..	..	1604	..	WILF04
WILFORD Peter (Boniface)	OSB	L	MX	V	#x	1584	1609	1607	1646	WILF06
WILFORD William	S			S		..	..	1662	..	WILF08
WILKES John	S		YO		#x	..	..	..	1642	WILK02
WILKES see also WILKS										
WILKINSON Anthony	S		YO	Q		..	..	1580	..	WILK06
WILKINSON Charles	SJ		MX	Y	#	1622	1643	..	1686	WILK08
WILKINSON Henry	SJ		NN	Y	1	1594	1617	..	1673	WILK10
WILKINSON John	S	N	WD	R	#	1670	..	1698	1734	WILK12
WILKINSON John Paul	S		LA	D		1703	..	..	1771	WILK14
WILKINSON Thomas	SJ	N	LA	V	#x	1638	1667	1662	1681	WILK16
WILKS Joseph (Cuthbert)	OSB		WK	E		1748	1764	1772	1829	WILK18
WILLACY James	S	L	LA	D	3	1738	..	1761	1805	WILL02
WILLACY Robert	CRT			C		..	..	..	1693	WILL03
WILLAN Thomas	OSS					..	..	..	1583	WILL04
WILLEMART James	OSA	L	LC	D	*2	1626	1644	..	..	WILL05
WILLIAMS (Anselm)	OSB	W		Z	*	..	1657	..	1694	WILL06
WILLIAMS Aurelius	S	W		D	*	..	..	1680	..	WILL08
WILLIAMS Charles	S		MO	L		1627	..	1651	1667	WILL10
WILLIAMS Edward	SJ			Y		1619	1640	..	1652	WILL12
WILLIAMS Edward	S	W	FT	R		1707	..	1731	1776	WILL14
WILLIAMS Edward (Dominic)	OP	L	MO	A		1643	1665	..	1688	WILL16
WILLIAMS Francis	SJ		CH	Y	#†1	1622	1659	1664	1681	WILL18
WILLIAMS George	S	N		Q	*°	..	..	1588	..	WILL20
WILLIAMS John	S	W		D	*§	..	..	1601	..	WILL22
WILLIAMS John	S		MO	L	#	..	..	1653	1674	WILL24
WILLIAMS John	SJ	W	CN	Y	1	1656	1678	1693	..	WILL26
WILLIAMS John	SJ	W	MO	Y	13	1691	1712	1723	1761	WILL28
WILLIAMS John	S		BR	L		1696	..	1723	1763	WILL30
WILLIAMS John	S	W	GM	L	§	1712	..	1735	1793	WILL32
WILLIAMS John	SJ	M	FT	Y	#3	1730	1750	1755	1801	WILL34
WILLIAMS John Morgan	S	W	FT	D	3	1761	..	1788	1816	WILL36
WILLIAMS Joseph (Francis)	CRT	M	FT	C		1729	1759	1760	1797	WILL38
WILLIAMS Louis	S	W	MO	D	§	1585	..	1610	1661	WILL40
WILLIAMS Morris	S			Q	*	..	..	1585	..	WILL42
WILLIAMS Nicholas	S		MO	D	#3	1665	..	1693	1737	WILL44
WILLIAMS (Pacificus of S.Fra)	OFM	W	HR	F	123	1618	1638	1642	1705	WILL46
WILLIAMS (Pacificus of S.Jn)	OFM		HR	F	12	1658	1676	..	1706	WILL48
WILLIAMS Peter	SJ	L	FT	Y	3	1689	1710	1719	1755	WILL50
WILLIAMS Peter	SJ	N	FT	Y	3	1717	1736	1744	1753	WILL52
WILLIAMS Reginald	S	W	MO	R	#	1658	..	1682	1737	WILL54

Name	Reg	D	Co	T	Notes	Born	Prof	Ordn	Died	Code
WILLIAMS Thomas	SJ		OX	R	‡	1539	1557	..	1613	WILL56
WILLIAMS Thomas	S		GL	V	3	1577	..	1610		WILL58
WILLIAMS Thomas (Anselm)	OSB			W		..	1622	..	1636	WILL60
WILLIAMS Thomas (Dominic) BP.	OP	N	MO	Z	*	1668	1686	1692	1740	WILL62
WILLAYS see WALLIS										
WILLIAMSON (Ambrose)	OFM		ND	F	123	1663	1684	1688	1701	WILL66
WILLIAMSON Edward	SJ	L	LA	R		1580	1617	1605	1649	WILL68
WILLIAMSON George	SJ	L	YO	Y	3	1695	1718	1725	1741	WILL70
WILLIAMSON Richard	SJ	L	LN	Y	12	1605	1626	..	1649	WILL72
WILLIAMSON William	SJ	M	NN	R	#‡	1577	1617	1611	1626	WILL74
WILLIS Thomas	S		MX	R		1722	..	1746	1768	WILL76
WILLOUGHBY Amatus (I'phonsus)	OSB			G	#	..	1667	..	1677	WILL80
WILLIUGHBY Edward	ODC	M	MX		#°2	1766	1783	..	..	WILL82
WILLOUGHBY (Giles of S.Ambr)	OFM			F	#	..	..	..	1660	WILL84
WILLOUGHBY William	S				6	..	..	..	..	WILL86
WILLS William	S			N	‡	..	..	1563	..	WILL88
WILSON Charles	SJ		MX	Y	1	1660	1680	1689	1730	WILS02
WILSON James	S	N	LA	D	#	1726	..	1753	1808	WILS04
WILSON John	S	N		D	#	..	..	1595	..	WILS06
WILSON John	S		ST	R		1576	..	1605	..	WILS08
WILSON John	SJ		YO	Y	3	1637	1658	1663	1666	WILS10
WILSON John (Benedict)	OSB	N	DH	G		..	1678	..	1725	WILS12
WILSON John (Jerome)	OSB		YO	G		..	1685	..	1700	WILS14
WILSON Matthew or Edward	SJ		ND	R	#§	1581	1606	1606	1656	WILS16
WILSON Nicholas	S	L			7	..	..	..	..	WILS18
WILSON Ralph	SJ	M	YO	Y		1743	1763	1770	1770	WILS20
WILSON Ralph (Jerome)	OSB	N	YO	G		1652	1668	1677	1719	WILS22
WILSON Ralph (Maurus)	OSB	M	DH	X		..	1688	..	1723	WILS24
WILSON Samuel (Thomas)	OP	L		N		1761	1783	1786	1824	WILS26
WILSON Simon	SJ		ST	R	1	1623	1692	1649	1695	WILS28
WILSON Thomas	OSB		YO	G		..	1667	..	1712	WILS30
WILSON Thomas	S	M	LA	R		1690	..	1713	1766	WILS34
WILSON Thomas	S	M	ST	D	#	1712	..	1737	1779	WILS36
WILSON William	S			S	*	1571	..	1595	..	WILS38
WILSON William	SJ	N	NK	Y		1615	1635	..	1679	WILS40
WILSON William (Willibrord)	OSB		DH	X		..	1684	..	1692	WILS42
WILTON John	S	N	YO	Q		..	..	1591	..	WILT02
WINDHAM see WYNDHAM										
WINDSOR John	S	L	KT	R		1590	..	1616	..	WIND06
WINN see WYNNE										
WINSTANLEY Edmund	S	M	LA	D	3	1735	..	1758	1783	WINS02
WINSTANLEY Edmund	S		DE	L		1772	..	1796	1852	WINS04
WINTER Andrew	OP		BR	N		1691	1712	1715	1754	WINT00
WINTER (Jerome)	OFM		BR	F	123	1677	1695	1701	1742	WINT01
WINTER William	S	N	DH	R		1738	..	1763	1796	WINT02
WINTER William (Benedict)	OSB		HU	G		..	1692	1707	1736	WINT04
WINTERFIELD Christopher	SJ					..	..	..	..	WINT08
WINTON James	OSB		MX	X	#	1672	1690	..	1712	WINT10
WISE George	SJ	L	LC	V	#3	1643	1670	1670	1704	WISE02
WISEMAN Francis Ignatius	S		EX	R	#	1602	..	1637	..	WISE04
WITHAM Anthony	S	M	YO	P	3	..	..	1709	1763	WITH02
WITHAM Christopher	S	N	YO	D	#3	1659	..	1683	1734	WITH04
WITHAM George BP.	S		YO	P	#*3	1655	..	1688	1725	WITH06
WITHAM George	S		DH	D	3	1750	..	1774	1829	WITH08
WITHAM James (Wilfrid)	OSB	N	YO	X		..	1715	..	1764	WITH10
WITHAM Robert	S	N	YO	D	#3	1667	..	1691	1738	WITH12
WITHAM Roger (Michael)	OSB		YO	G		..	1636	..	1657	WITH14
WITHAM Thomas	S	N	YO	P		..	..	..	1727	WITH16
WITHAM Thomas	OSB	N	YO	G		..	1685	..	1729	WITH18
WITHY Edward	SJ		CB	Y	3	1689	1707	1721	1769	WITH20
WITHY John (Edward)	OSB	L	CB	G		1691	1708	1716	1743	WITH22

Name	Reg	D	Co	T	Notes	Born	Prof	Ordn	Died	Code
WIVELL Henry	S	N	YO	D	#	1603	..	1634	..	WIVE02
WODISON see WOODSON										
WOLFALL John	SJ		LA	Y	#	1682	1702	1711	1742	WOLF02
WOLFALL Thomas	S	N	LA	R	#	1675	..	1699	1720	WOLF04
WOLFE Francis	SJ			Y	*	1647	1668	1677	1720	WOLF06
WOLFE William	SJ	M	YO	Y	#‡	1587	1611	..	1673	WOLF08
WOLFE see also WOOLFE										
WOLLEY George	S	N		R	*	1567	..	1596	..	WOLL02
WOLSELEY Edward	OSB	M	ST	G		..	1632	..	1669	WOLS02
WOLSELEY John	S		ST	Q		..	..	1586	..	WOLS04
WOLSTONHOLME Richard	S		LA	D	§	1539	..	1603	..	WOLS06
WOOD (Bernardine of S.Clare)	OFM			F	34	..	..	1647	1666	WOOD02
WOOD Edward	SJ		ST	Y	4	1663	1683	1695	1726	WOOD04
WOOD Michael	S			D	*§°	..	..	1596	..	WOOD08
WOOD William	SJ		SY	Y	#	1671	1689	1698	1720	WOOD12
WOODBERRY Gerard	S		HA	P	#	1715	..	1739	1783	WOOD14
WOODCOCK John (Martin) VEN.	OFM	N	LA	R	#+1	1602	1631	1637	1646	WOOD16
WOODCOCK John	S	N	LA	D		1766	..	1793	1837	WOOD18
WOODCOCK William	SJ		LA	Y	#13	1659	1682	1690	1717	WOOD20
WOODFEN Nicholas VEN.	S	L	HR	Q	#+	..	..	1581	1586	WOOD22
WOODFIELD John	S			V		..	..	1647	..	WOOD24
WOODFORD Gabriel	SJ		BD	Y		1599	1629	..	1663	WOOD26
WOODHOPE John	S		HR	R	#§	1607	..	1634	..	WOOD30
WOODHOPE (Thomas)	OSB	M	WR	G	#4	..	1622	..	1654	WOOD31
WOODRUFFE Robert	S	N	LA	R		1552	..	1581	..	WOOD32
WOODRUFFE Robert	S		DV	R	#	1579	..	1606	..	WOOD34
WOODRUFFE Robert	S	M	ST	L		..	..	1680	..	WOOD36
WOODS John (Ambrose)	OP		MX	N		1766	1790	1792	1842	WOOD38
WOODS see also WOOD										
WOODSON Felix	SJ		WT	Y		1584	1612	..	..	WOOD42
WOODSON Leonard	SJ		HA	S	12	1591	1630	1612	1651	WOOD46
WOODWARD Humphrey	SJ		WR	R	1	1552	1577	..	1587	WOOD48
WOODWARD John	S	N	WT	D	#3	..	..	1641	1677	WOOD50
WOODWARD (Joseph of S.Mary)	OFM		LA	F	1234	1657	1676	1681	1701	WOOD52
WOODWARD Lionel	S		SK	Q	4	..	..	1592	1609	WOOD54
WOODWARD (Matthias)	OFM		LA	F	123	1672	1693	1697	1720	WOOD56
WOODWARD Philip	S	L	SK	R	†	1558	..	1583	1610	WOOD58
WOODWARD Thomas	S		NN	D	#	..	..	1624	1662	WOOD60
WOOLFE John	S		WR	L	#	..	..	1674	1735	WOOL02
WOOLFE (Lawrence)	OSB		SP	E		1632	1656	..	1697	WOOL04
WOOLFE see also WOLFE										
WOOLMER (Massaeus of S.Jo'ph)	OFM			F	123	1651	1670	1676	1718	WOOL08
WOOLMER Thomas (Joseph)	OFM			F	12	1631	1651	..	1665	WOOL10
WOOLS Thomas	S	L	MX	R		1744	..	1769	1788	WOOL12
WOOTON see WOTTON										
WORSLEY Edward	SJ		LA	Y	‡1	1605	1626	..	1676	WORS02
WORSLEY Lawrence	SJ		SM	Y		1613	1633	..	1676	WORS04
WORSLEY Thomas	S		LA	S	#3	1572	..	1595	..	WORS06
WORSLEY Thomas	SJ	L	LC	Y	#	1597	1614	..	1671	WORS08
WORSLEY William	S		LC	V	#	1594		1618	..	WORS10
WORSWICK James	S	N	LA	D		1771	..	1795	1843	WORS12
WORSWICK John	S	N	LA	D		1761	..	1786	1809	WORS14
WORSWICK John (Dunstan)	OSB		LA	W		1743	1758	..	1770	WORS16
WORSWICK Robert	S	N	LA	P	#	1714	..	1744	1752	WORS18
WORSWICK Thomas	S		LA	D	#	1716	..	1740	1748	WORS20
WORTHINALL Richard	S		CL	D	#	..	..	1615	1615	WORT02
WORTHINGTON James	S		LA	R		1587	..	1610	..	WORT04
WORTHINGTON John	SJ	N	LA	R		1573	1598	1597	1652	WORT06
WORTHINGTON John	S	N	LA	D		..	..	1609	1622	WORT08
WORTHINGTON John	S			V		..	..	1649	..	WORT10
WORTHINGTON John	SJ	N	LA	Y	#3	1713	1735	1742	1777	WORT12
WORTHINGTON Lawrence	SJ		LA	Y	#124	1575	1598	..	1637	WORT14
WORTHINGTON Peter	SJ		LA	R		1581	1602	..	1613	WORT16
WORTHINGTON Richard	S	L	LC	R		1606	..	1631	1667	WORT18
WORTHINGTON Thomas	S		LA	D	*‡14	1548	..	1577	1626	WORT20
WORTHINGTON Thomas	S		LA	D		..	..	1625	..	WORT22

Name	Reg	D	Co	T	Notes	Born	Prof	Ordn	Died	Code
WORTHINGTON Thomas	SJ	L	LC	Y	#	1616	1633	..	1670	WORT24
WORTHINGTON Thomas	OP	N	LA	R		1671	1692	1695	1754	WORT26
WORTHINGTON William	SJ		LA	D	4	1584	..	1609	1621	WORT28
WORTLEY Francis	S		MX	L		..	..	1691	..	WORT30
WOTTON Robert	S			D	*4	..	..	1578	1592	WOTT02
WRENCH Anthony	S			Q	*1	1545	..	1581	1584	WREN02
WRENCH Bernard	S	L	MX	D	#	1602	..	1627	1629	WREN04
WREST Thomas (Louis of S.Aug)	OFM		KT	F	12	1596	1631	..	1669	WRES02
WRIGHT Bernard	S					..	..	..	1801	WRIG02
WRIGHT Charles	SJ	N	EX	Y	3	1752	1769	1775	1827	WRIG04
WRIGHT Christopher	S	W		Y		..	..	..	1799	WRIG06
WRIGHT Edward	SJ	W	SY	Y	3	1752	1768	1776	1826	WRIG08
WRIGHT Francis	S		OX	D	#1	1593	..	1621	..	WRIG10
WRIGHT John	S	M	LN	D		1754	..	1781	1797	WRIG14
WRIGHT Joseph	SJ		PL	Y	13	1698	1720	1727	1760	WRIG16
WRIGHT Matthew	SJ		ES	Y	#	1647	1668	1678	1711	WRIG18
WRIGHT Peter BL.	SJ		NN	Y	#+§1	1603	1629	..	1651	WRIG20
WRIGHT Peter	S		EX	R		1669	..	1693	..	WRIG22
WRIGHT Philip	SJ		EX	Y	#	1665	1684	1693	1737	WRIG24
WRIGHT Richard	S		LN	V	#†	1568	..	1604	..	WRIG26
WRIGHT Richard	SJ					..	..	..	..	WRIG28
WRIGHT Robert	SJ					..	1683	..	1688	WRIG30
WRIGHT Stephen	SJ	L	EX	R	#	1620	1653	1645	1680	WRIG32
WRIGHT Thomas	S				4	..	..	..	1635	WRIG34
WRIGHT Thomas	S		NK	P		..	..	1767	1799	WRIG36
WRIGHT William	SJ	M	YO	R	13	1562	1581	1592	1639	WRIG38
WRIGLY see RIDGLEY										
WYBURNE Henry	OSB	L	KT	E		..	1723	..	1769	WYBU02
WYCHCOTT see WHICHCOTT										
WYCHE George	S			L	3	..	..	1697	..	WYCH04
WYCHE Joseph	OSB		MX	X		1672	1690	..	1727	WYCH06
WYKE James	S		MX	D		1728	..	1752	1799	WYKE02
WYNDHAM Philip Bernard	S	L	IT	R		1732	..	1756	1825	WYND02
WYNDHAM see also WENDON										
WYNNE Griffeth Charles	S			D	*3	1669	..	1694	1713	WYNN02
WYNNE Peter	S	W	CN	R	#	1637	..	1660	..	WYNN04
WYNNE William	S	W	DB	V	3	..	..	1676	..	WYNN06
WYNTER see WINTER										
WYSE see WISE										
WYTHIE see WITHY										
WYVILL Christopher (Peter)	OP	M	NT	N		1694	1712	1719	1725	WYVI02
YATES Bernard	OFM	N		F	234	..	1726	1737	1778	YATE00
YATE see YATES										
YATES (Daniel of S.John)	OFM		WR	F	12	1603	1632	..	1659	YATE02
YATES Edward (Bede)	ODC				1	1705	..	..	..	YATE03
YATES John	SJ		BK		#4	1550	1574	1581	1593	YATE04
YATE Thomas	CRT					..	..	..	1743	YATE06
YATES John	S		ST	Q	*	1549	..	1591	1624	YATE12
YATES John	S		LA	D	#	..	..	1598	..	YATE14
YATES John	S			D	3	..	..	1762	..	YATE16
YATES John	S	N	LA	D		1765	..	1795	1827	YATE18
YATES Richard	S			L	3	..	..	1674	..	YATE20
YATES Thomas	CRT			C		..	..	..	1743	YATE22
YAXLEY John	S				3	..	..	1624	..	YAXL02
YAXLEY John	S	N		D	*3	..	..	1679	1731	YAXL04
YAXLEY Richard VEN.	S	M	LN	Q	#+	..	..	1585	1589	YAXL06
YEATS see YATES										
YEKE Nicholas	S	M	ST	Q	#‡1	1557	..	1579	..	YEKE02
YELVERTON Charles	SJ		NK	R	#†	1575	1608	1604	1612	YELV02
YEMS see IMMES										
YEOMANS William	S		SM	Q	‡1	1553	..	1584	..	YEOM02
YORK John	S		YO	R	#	1654	..	1678	..	YORK02
YORK William or Thomas	SJ		GL	S	4	1581	1618	1604	1628	YORK04
YORK William (Lawrence) BP.	OSB	W	MX	G	*	1686	1705	1711	1770	YORK06
YOUNG (Anthony of S.Francis)	OFM	L	BK	F	123	1641	1662	1666	1712	YOUN02
YOUNG Daniel (Bernard)	OSB	W	LA	X		1741	1760	..	1801	YOUN04

125

Name	Reg	D	Co	T	Notes	Born	Prof	Ordn	Died	Code
YOUNG Francis	SJ	M	WR	R	‡	1570	1600	1599	1633	YOUN06
YOUNG John	S	N	YO	D	1	1605	..	1632	1671	YOUN08
YOUNG John	CRT			C		..	1641	..	1677	YOUN09
YOUNG Robert	S	L	YO	D		..	..	1602	..	YOUN10
YOUNG Thomas	S	L	YO	D		..	..	1595	..	YOUN12
YOUNG Thomas	S	N	LA	L	#	..	..	1681	1714	YOUN14
YOUNGER James	S	L	DH	R	#	1563	..	1587	..	YOUN16
(Zachary of Saluzzo)	CAP		ES		*7	..	..	..	..	ZACH02
ZOUCH see SOUCH										

The bold lines mark the boundaries of the
Northern, Western, Midland and London
Ecclesiastical Districts (pre 1840).

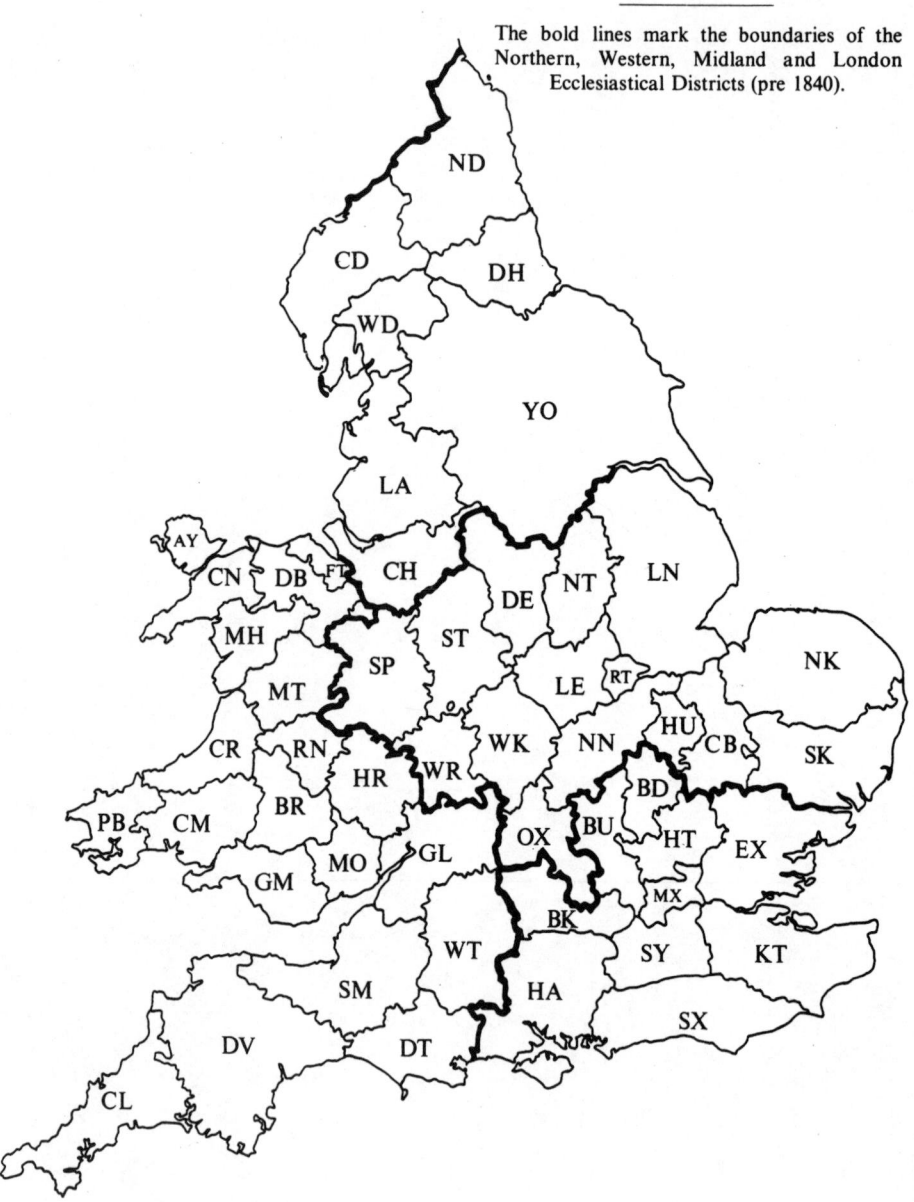

GEOGRAPHICAL LIST OF PRIESTS

Name	Reg	D	Co	T	Notes	Born	Prof	Ordn	Died	Code
					AY—ANGLESEY					
FLOYD Charles	SJ		AY	R	24	1562	1611	1596	1620	FLOY02
FLOYD Owen	S		AY	D	‡1	1545	..	1578	1591	FLOY18
LEWIS Owen BP.	S		AY		*‡	1533	..	..	1595	LEWI19
OWEN Hugh or John	SJ	W	AY	R	#§	1615	1648	1641	1689	OWEN02
ROBERTS Thomas	SJ	W	AY	Y	3	1673	1696	1705	1727	ROBE18
					BD—BEDFORDSHIRE					
HUNT Edward	S	L	BD	D	#3	..	..	1679	1726	HUNT02
KING Richard	OSB	W	BD	E	#	..	1639	1639	1664	KING02
PICKERING Robert	SJ		BD	Y		1606	1622	1132	1636	PICK06
PRINCE James	S	L	BD	D	#	1602	..	1628	..	PRIN02
RICHARDSON Francis or Richard	S	W	BD	R	1	1644	..	1669	..	RICH14
WOODFORD Gabriel	SJ		BD	Y		1599	1629	..	1663	WOOD26
					BK—BERKSHIRE					
BATTIN (Adam of S.Michael)	OFM		BK	F	12	1623	1642	..	1675	BATT08
BLANDY (Boniface)	OSB		BK		*	..	1606	..	1634	BLAN02
BLOUNT Richard (Godric)	OSB		BK	G		1617	1649	..	1667	BLOU12
BRICKNELL Gaspar George	S	M	BK	V		1768	..	1793	1833	BRIC04
BRUNING Francis	OSB	M	BK	X		1675	1699	..	1748	BRUN16
BUSBY Thomas	SJ	M	BK	Y	#	1656	1675	1683	1750	BUSB12
BUSBY William	SJ	M	BK	Y		1646	1667	1675	1692	BUSB14
CASEMORE William (Ignatius)	OFM		BK	F	3	1751	1777	1779	1824	CASE10
CHESTERMAN James	S	L	BK	R	#	1698	..	1724	1777	CHES02
CLAMPET Philip	S	L	BK	D		..	..	1624	1665	CLAM02
COLE Edmund	S	L	BK	V	#‡	..	..	1624	..	COLE02
CURRE John (Maurus)	OSB		BK	G		..	1614	..	1635	CURR02
CURRE (Nicholas)	OSB	M	BK	W	2	..	1615	..	1649	CURR04
DARELL William	SJ		BK	Y	3	1651	1671	1680	1721	DARE08
DORMER Charles, 6th Ld.	SJ		BK	Y	3	1690	1709	1718	1761	DORM02
DORMER Robert, Hon.	SJ	W	BK	Y	3	1726	1743	1751	1792	DORM08
ENGLEFIELD Charles (Felix)	OFM	W	BK	F	23	..	1731	1731	1767	ENGL02
ENGLEFIELD (Felix of S.Mary)	OFM		BK	F	12	1669	1689	1697	1703	ENGL04
ENGLEFIELD John	SJ	W	BK	Y	#3	1676	1696	1705	1733	ENGL06
EYSTON (Basil)	OSB		BK	G		1711	1733	..	1785	EYST02
EYSTON Charles (Jn.Capistran)	OFM	L	BK	F	123	1675	1693	1700	1732	EYST03
EYSTON George	SJ		BK	Y	13	1667	1688	1710	1745	EYST04
EYSTON John (Bernardine)	OFM		BK	F	123	1627	1644	1651	1709	EYST06
EYSTON Robeet	S		BK	S	13	1590	..	1612	..	EYST10
EYSTON Robert	SJ.	L	BK	Y	1	1729	1751	1757	1766	EYST12
EYSTON William (Joseph)	OP	L	BK	F	*	1674	1729	1697	1758	EYST14
FETTIPLACE Edward	CRT		BK	D	#3	1607	1646	1634	1659	FETT02
GIFFARD Thomas	S		BK	R	#§1	1600	..	1631	1632	GIFF22
GREEN Charles (Dominic)	OSB		BK	E	§	1665	1688	..	1699	GREE06
HORNBY Francis	S		BK	R	#	1633	..	1659	..	HORN04
HYDE Charles	S	L	BK	R		1683	..	1707	1745	HYDE02
HYDE Humphrey	S	L	BK	R	#	1579	..	1604	..	HYDE04
HYDE Leonard	S		BK	D		1550	..	1577	1608	HYDE05
HYDE Richard	SJ		BK	R	°12	1628	1646	..	1662	HYDE06
HYDE Richard	SJ		BK	Y	3	1687	1706	1715	1744	HYDE08

Name	Reg	D	Co	T	Notes	Born	Prof	Ordn	Died	Code
MEARA George	SJ		BK	Y	#	1675	1694	1703	1730	MEAR02
MEARA John	S	L	BK	R	#	1676	..	1703	1733	MEAR04
MEARA William	SJ		BK	Y	#3	1677	1698	1707	1728	MEAR06
MOORE James (Augustine)	OSB		BK	G		1722	1740	..	1775	MOOR04
MOORE John (Francis)	OSB	L	BK	E	°	..	1698	1711	1741	MOOR06
PERKINS Christopher, Kt.	SJ		BK	R	°1	1547	1566	..	1622	PERK02
PHILIPSON John	OSB		BK	G	1	1658	1676	..	1739	PHIL38
PHILIPSON William	OSB	N	BK	E		..	1684	..	1720	PHIL40
PLATT Francis	S		BK	R	#	1599	..	1623	..	PLAT04
PLATT Lawrence	S	L	BK	D	#	..	..	1626	1663	PLAT06
ROBERTS (Gregory of S.Jn.Bpt)	OFM		BK	F	123	1683	1700	1707	1710	ROBE04
RUSSELL Richard BP.	S		BK	D	*	1629	..	1653	1693	RUSS12
SADLER Albert	SJ		BK	Y		1590	1616	..	1672	SADL04
SCROGGS (Placid)	OSB	L	BK	G	#1	1615	1634	..	1692	SCRO04
SMITH Gregory	S		BK	R	#§	1600	..	1625	1629	SMIT21
STAFFERTON Francis	S	N	BK	Q		..	..	1584	..	STAF02
STAFFERTON William	S	N	BK	R	#‡4	1557	..	1584	1594	STAF04
TEMPEST Nicholas	S		BK	D	#3	..	..	1652	..	TEMP14
THOROLD Edmund	SJ	W	BK	Y		1657	1677	1686	1715	THOR16
THOROLD George	SJ	N	BK	Y		1670	1691	1698	1742	THOR22
TURBERVILLE John	SJ	L	BK	Y	#	1663	1683	1691	1735	TURB10
WHITE Philip	S		BK	L		1748	..	1772	1777	WHIT42
WINCHCOMBE William (Anthony)	OSB	L	BK	G	#	..	1614	..	1618	WINC02
WINCHCOMBE William (Benedict)	OSB	L	BK	W		1643	1662	..	1672	WINC04
YATES John	SJ		BK		#4	1550	1574	1581	1593	YATE04
YOUNG (Anthony of S.Francis)	OFM	L	BK	F	123	1641	1662	1666	1712	YOUN02

BR—BRECKNOCKSHIRE

Name	Reg	D	Co	T	Notes	Born	Prof	Ordn	Died	Code
BEVANS Francis (Ambrose)	OFM		BR	F	14	1620	..	..	1686	BEVA04
BRYCHAN Eleyson (Benedict)	OSB	L	BR	G	#	1610	1625	..	1676	BRYC02
EVANS John	S		BR	D	#3	1629	..	1658	1669	EVAN14
HAVARD Louis	S	L	BR	T		1774	..	1800	1858	HAVA02
JONES John (Leander)	OSB	L	BR	Z	#*‡	1575	1600	..	1635	JONE28
LLOYD John ST.	S	W	BR	V	+	..	..	1653	1679	LLOY04
POWELL David (Gregory)	OFM	W	BR	F		..	..	..	1781	POWE04
POWELL Roger (Philip) BL.	OSB	W	BR	N	#+=13	1594	1620	1618	1646	POWE20
VAUGHAN William	SJ	W	BR	Y		1644	1672	1677	1687	VAUG20
WILLIAMS John	S		BR	L		1696	..	1723	1763	WILL30
WINTER Andrew	OP		BR	N		1691	1712	1715	1754	WINT00
WINTER (Jerome)	OFM		BR	F	123	1677	1695	1701	1742	WINT01

BU—BUCKINGHAMSHIRE

Name	Reg	D	Co	T	Notes	Born	Prof	Ordn	Died	Code
ALCOCK John	SJ	M	BU	Y	#1	1615	1635	..	1703	ALCO02
BENSON (Thomas of S.Anne)	OFM	L	BU	F	123	1622	1652	1655	1705	BENS04
DRURY Robert VEN.	S	L	BU	V	+3	1567	..	1592	1607	DRUR04
EAST George	S		BU	Q		..	..	1581	..	EAST02
ELLIS Philip (Michael) BP.	OSB	L	BU	G	*§	1653	1670	..	1726	ELLI10
ELLIS William	SJ	N	BU		#1	1590	..	..	1640	ELLI14
FARMER Thomas	SJ	L	BU	R	#1	1594	1621	1620	1683	FARM04
FORTESCUE Adrian	SJ		BU	R	#124	1601	1624	..	1653	FORT04
GASCOIGNE Henry	SJ	M	BU	Y	1	1595	1617	..	1676	GASC04
GREENWAY Anthony	SJ	N	BU	R	#‡	1575	1611	1608	1644	GREE68
HARTWELL Bernard	SJ		BU	Y		1607	1626	..	1646	HART36
HITCHCOCK William	OSB		BU	R	#	1625	1654	1649	1711	HITC02
HOUSE William	S	L	BU	S	1	1573	..	1595	..	HOUS04
KEEL Thomas	SJ		BU			1577	1617	..	1651	KEEL02
KNIGHT John	S		BU	D	#	..	..	1601	..	KNIG10
LANE Thomas	S	M	BU	V	#‡3	1582	..	1609	..	LANE10
LEE Roger	SJ		BU		#	1568	1600	..	1615	LEEA22
LONGUEVILLE Thomas	S	L	BU	R		1598	..	1622	..	LONG12
MAYNE Henry	S		BU	R	#	1609	..	1636	1689	MAYN04
PECKHAM Robert	SJ	M	BU	V	#3	1586	1613	1608	1621	PECK02
PHILIPS Thomas	SJ	M	BU			1708	1726	..	1774	PHIL22
POULTON Ferdinand	SJ	L	BU	R	#§1	1584	1615	..	..	POUL06

Name	Reg	D	Co	T	Notes	Born	Prof	Ordn	Died	Code
POULTON Ferdinand John	SJ		BU	R	#12	1600	1621	..	1641	POUL10
POULTON Thomas	SJ		BU	R	#§	1577	1613	1617	1637	POUL28
RISLEY William	S	N	BU	V	=§	1594	..	1637	..	RISL04

CB—CAMBRIDGESHIRE

Name	Reg	D	Co	T	Notes	Born	Prof	Ordn	Died	Code
ARTON William	S	M	CB	V	§4	1576	..	1603	1610	ARTO02
ATKINS William	SJ	M	CB	S	x23	1601	1635	1628	1681	ATKI02
BALLARD John	S	L	CB	Q	#*†	..	..	1581	1586	BALL12
BARKER Thomas	OSB	M	CB	G	§3	1768	1790	1797	1798	BARK10
BUCK Robert	SJ		CB	D		1573	1612	1600	1648	BUCK04
CARLETON Philip	SJ	M	CB	Y	#	1606	1625	..	1658	CARL03
CARLETON Thomas	SJ		CB	V	#	1592	1617	1617	1666	CARL05
FINCH Richard	S		CB	R	#4	1635	..	1660	1689	FINC06
FLOYD Henry	SJ	L	CB	V	#13	1563	1599	1592	1641	FLOY08
FLOYD John	SJ		CB	R	#	1572	1592	..	1649	FLOY16
HARRIS William	S		CB	D	#3	1647	..	1676	..	HARR22
HEATH Henry (Paul) VEN.	OFM		CB	F	+†2	1600	1625	..	1643	HEAT04
HUDDLESTON John	S	M	CB	R		1693	..	1717	1773	HUDD08
HUDDLESTON William (Denis)	OSB	N	CB	X	°	1684	1701	..	1743	HUDD16
MATTHEW John	S		CB	V	#†3	1572	..	1603	..	MATT02
MORE Thomas	SJ		CB	R		1586	1611	1609	1623	MORE14
PRANCE Charles	S		CB	D	#	1646	..	1672	..	PRAN02
PRANCE Thomas	S	M	CB	V	#	..	..	1655	..	PRAN04
ROGERS Thomas	SJ	N	CB	R	#x§1	1596	1620	1620	1657	ROGE16
ST GEORGE William	S	N	CB	D	#†	1585	..	1614	..	SAIN02
TAYLOR William (Maurus)	OSB		CB	R	#‡†4	1576	1603	1602	1612	TAYL50
TEMPEST William	S	N	CB	D	3	1683	..	1710	1766	TEMP22
WITHY Edward	SJ		CB	Y	3	1689	1707	1721	1769	WITH20
WITHY John (Edward)	OSB	L	CB	G		1691	1708	1716	1743	WITH22

CD—CUMBERLAND

Name	Reg	D	Co	T	Notes	Born	Prof	Ordn	Died	Code
HILTON Thomas (Placid)	OSB	L	CD	D	#	1583	1610	1609	1626	HILT02
HOWARD John (Placid)	OSB	L	CD	G		1698	1719	..	1766	HOWA14
HOWARD Rbt.(Louis of Naz'eth)	OFM		CD	F	3	1597	..	1634	1676	HOWA19
HOWARD Thomas (Augustine)	OSB	L	CD	G		1644	1662	1668	1718	HOWA24
HOWARD William (Joseph)	OSB	M	CD	G		..	1712	..	1733	HOWA28
HUDDLESTON Brian	S		CD	S	6	..	..	..	..	HUDD03
MONK Richard (Gregory)	OSB	N	CD	D	#*2	..	1622	1633	1655	MONK04
PORTER George (Alban)	OSB	N	CD	X		..	1664	..	1693	PORT06
PORTER (Jerome)	OSB		CD	G	#	..	1622	..	1632	PORT10
ROBINSON Christopher VEN.	S	N	CD	Q	+	..	..	1592	1597	ROBI06
ROBINSON Christopher	SJ	N	CD	R	§	1586	1616	1610	1677	ROBI08
ROBINSON John	SJ		CD			1588	1628	..	1669	ROBI26
SALKELD George (Bernard)	OSB		CD	G	2	..	1650	..	1658	SALK04
SALKELD John	S		CD	S	°3	..	..	1608	1659	SALK08
SKELTON James	S	N	CD	L	1	1690	..	1714	1760	SKEL02
SKELTON John (Elphege)	OSB	N	CD	X		..	1688	..	1705	SKEL04
SKELTON John (Gregory)	OSB	N	CD	G		..	1681	1686	1721	SKEL06
SKELTON Nicholas	S	N	CD	D		1691	..	1718	1766	SKEL08
SKELTON Simon	S	N	CD	D		..	..	1620	..	SKEL10
SMEATON John (Basil)	OSB	N	CD	X		..	1664	..	1705	SMEA02
TAYLOR Richard	S	N	CD	D	3	1565	..	1594	..	TAYL34
WARCOP Thomas	SJ		CD	R	§	1560	1587	1584	1589	WARC02
WARWICK Thomas (Basil)	OSB	N	CD	G		..	1698	..	1732	WARW04

CH—CHESHIRE

Name	Reg	D	Co	T	Notes	Born	Prof	Ordn	Died	Code
ANTROBUS Ralph (Francis)	OSB	M	CH	Z	*‡	1576	1606	..	1626	ANTR02
ANTROBUS Richard	S	L	CH	D	#	1735	..	1773	1800	ANTR04
ASHTON Charles	S		CH	L	3	..	..	1792	1797	ASHT04
BENTLEY Hugh	S		CH	V	‡3	..	..	1593	..	BENT13
BENTNEY William	SJ		CH	Y	#x2	1609	1630	..	1692	BENT16
BERRY Thomas	S		CH	D		1635	..	1661	1684	BERR12
BRITTAIN Thomas (Louis)	OP	W	CH	N	§3	1745	1767	1771	1827	BRIT02

Name	Reg	D	Co	T	Notes	Born	Prof	Ordn	Died	Code
CHANTRELL William	S	N	CH	R		1708	..	1731	1753	CHAN06
COXIE William	S		CH	Q	#	..	..	1587	..	COX102
CROCKETT Ralph BL.	S	L	CH	Q	+†‡	1552	..	1585	1588	CROC02
DAMFORD John	S		CH	V		1576	..	1600	1601	DAMF02
DAVENPORT (Ignatius of Magd.)	OFM		CH	F	12	1626	1652	..	1679	DAVE04
DAVIES William	S		CH	D	1	1556	..	1604	..	DAV122
EGERTON John	S		CH	D	#	..	..	1613	..	EGER02
EVANS William	S		CH	R	#§	1679	..	1712	..	EVAN28
FLOYD Henry	SJ	M	CH	Y	#	1621	1643	..	1687	FLOY10
GARDINER John	S		CH	R	#	1606	..	1632	..	GARD12
GRADWELL John	S	N	CH	D		..	..	1617	..	GRAD04
GRIFFITH Thomas	S	N	CH	D	#3	1665	..	1690	..	GRIF28
HOLFORD Peter	S		CH	L	#§1	1690	..	1712	1722	HOLF02
HOLFORD Thomas BL.	S	L	CH	Q	#+§	1541	..	1583	1588	HOLF04
HOLLAND Henry	SJ	N	CH	R		1577	1609	1603	1656	HOLL10
HOUGHTON Henry	SJ	L	CH	V	#	1710	1733	1733	1750	HOUG04
HUXLEY George	S		CH	V	34	1581	..	1607	1607	HUXL02
JUMP Richard	SJ		CH	Y	#3	1714	1736	1743	1755	JUMP04
KINGSLEY Ignatius George	SJ		CH	R	#3	1701	1720	1735	1787	KING12
KINGSLEY Owen Joseph	SJ	M	CH	Y	13	1697	1716	1725	1739	KING14
KINGSLEY Thomas	SJ	L	CH	Y	3	1705	1723	1732	1781	KING18
LEIGH Edward	S		CH	R	3	1553	..	1595	..	LEIG06
MADDOCK John	S		CH	S	3	..	..	1610	..	MADD04
MAINWARING Thomas Lionel	S	M	CH	R	#§°	1681	..	1710	1740	MAIN10
MASSEY Edward ╱	S		CH	D	#	..	..	1611	..	MASS04
MINSHULL Randal	S	N	CH	R	#§	..	..	1634	1685	MINS02
MINSHULL Thomas	OSB	W	CH	D	2	..	1609	1608	1617	MINS04
PARSONS John	S		CH	R		1639	..	1664	..	PARS06
PRICE John	SJ	M	CH	S		1576	1601	..	1645	PRIC10
PRICE Thomas	SJ		CH	V		1571	1601	1599	1625	PRIC16
PROBIN Edward	S	M	CH	D	#	..	..	1616	..	PROB06
SAVAGE John 5th Visc.	S	N	CH	D	#*3	1665	..	1700	1737	SAVA02
SHERT John BL.	S	L	CH	R	#+‡3	..	..	1578	1582	SHER24
STANLEY Henry	SJ	N	CH	Y		1713	1732	1739	1786	STAN26
STANLEY-MASSEY Thomas	SJ	W	CH	Y	#3	1716	1732	1746	1805	STAN30
STARKEY Henry (Hugh)	OSB	L	CH	L	#	1612	1649	1638	1688	STAR02
STARKEY John	S		CH	R	#§	1570	..	1602	..	STAR04
STOCKTON Edward	S		CH	R	#§	..	..	1677	..	STOC04
WARREN Bernard	OSB		CH	E		..	1648	1649	1650	WARR10
WHITMORE Richard	SJ		CH	Y	#2	1577	1614	..	1649	WHIT84
WILCOX Robert BL.	S	L	CH	Q	+	1558	..	1585	1588	WILC12
WILLIAMS Francis	SJ		CH	Y	#†1	1622	1659	1664	1681	WILL18

CL—CORNWALL

Name	Reg	D	Co	T	Notes	Born	Prof	Ordn	Died	Code
BALDWIN William	SJ		CL	R	.	1563	1590	1588	1632	BALD08
BRUSHFORD John	S		CL	R	x	1559	..	1584	1593	BRUS02
CASTELL John	SJ		CL		=	..	1574	..	1580	CAST02
CHAMPION John	SJ	M	CL	Y	3	1695	1713	1723	1776	CHAM26
CORNELIUS John BL.	S	W	CL	R	#*+‡1	1554	..	1583	1594	CORN08
COUCHE John	SJ	L	CL	Y	3	1744	1762	1770	1813	COUC02
CURRY John	SJ	L	CL	D	#124	1550	1583	1577	1598	CURR06
HAMBLEY John VEN.	S	W	CL	Q	#+§	..	..	1584	1587	HAMB02
HANNE Charles	SJ	N	CL	Y		1711	1731	1739	1799	HANN02
HAYMAN Richard	SJ	W	CL	Y	#1	1668	1687	1696	1756	HAYM02
HUMPHREY Richard	S		CL	S		1578	..	..	..	HUMP04
KEMP David	OSS		CL	Q	#2	..	1588	1581	1615	KEMP02
MUNDAY Francis	S		CL	R	#‡	1628	..	1655	1657	MUND02
NEALE John or Cornelius	S		CL	R	‡	1532	..	1579	..	NEAL10
PEARCE Martin	S	W	CL	R	#4	1654	..	1679	1716	PEAR04
PENKEVELL Mark	SJ		CL	R	°4	1571	1600	1599	1621	PENK14
PENTRETH Richard	S		CL	V		1579	..	1600	..	PENT02
PICKFORD Edward	S		CL	D	#	1601	..	1627	1657	PICK10
PICKFORD John (Jerome)	OFM		CL	D	#24	1588	1619	1618	1665	PICK12
PICKFORD Thomas	SJ	M	CL	Y	#1	1608	1629	..	1676	PICK14
PRICE John	SJ	N	CL	Y		1739	1758	1765	1813	PRIC13

Name	Reg	D	Co	T	Notes	Born	Prof	Ordn	Died	Code
SMALL Christopher	S	N	CL	Q	‡4	..	..	1579	1593	SMAL02
STEPHENS Francis	SJ		CL	R	#§	1597	1624	1621	1648	STEP04
TIPPET John	CRT		CL	R	§	1560	..	1584	1593	TIPP04
VICTOR Francis	S	W	CL	L	#	1612	..	1636	1683	VICT04
VIVIAN John	OSS		CL	Q	‡2	..	1587	1579	1624	VIVI04
WORTHINALL Richard	S		CL	D	#	..	..	1615	1615	WORT02

CM—CARMARTHENSHIRE

Name	Reg	D	Co	T	Notes	Born	Prof	Ordn	Died	Code
LLOYD John or Nicholas	S		CM	L	#	1682	..	1707	1724	LLOY06
LLOYD William	S		CM	L	x	1614	..	1639	1679	LLOY14
PRICE William (Louis)	ODC		CM		2	1657	1682	..	..	PRIC28

CN—CAERNARVONSHIRE

Name	Reg	D	Co	T	Notes	Born	Prof	Ordn	Died	Code
CLENNOCK Morgan	S	W	CN	R		1558	..	1582	1620	CLEN02
EVANS Charles	SJ	L	CN	Y	3	1640	1661	1672	1680	EVAN02
EVANS Humphrey	SJ	W	CN	R	#‡	1599	1625	1623	1679	EVAN10
EVANS John	S		CN	S		1576	..	..	..	EVAN12
EVANS Thomas	S		CN	V	‡1	1570	..	1599	..	EVAN24
EVANS William	S		CN	V	#	1578	..	1603	..	EVAN26
FLOYD Griffin or Griffith	SJ		CN	R	°	1569	1593	1593	..	FLOY06
GLYN Cadwallador or John	S		CN	R	1	1660	..	1690	..	GLYN02
GRIFFETH Louis	S	W	CN	S		1571	..	1595	..	GRIF08
GWYN Charles	SJ	W	CN	R	#§	1582	1620	1613	1647	GWYN02
GWYN Robert	S	W	CN	D	‡	..	..	1575	..	GWYN04
GWYN Roger	S	W	CN	V		1577	..	1602	..	GWYN06
GWYN Thomas	S		CN	R		1604	..	1631	..	GWYN08
JEFFREY Owen	SJ	W	CN	S	#†	1591	1620	1617	1654	JEFF08
JONES Jn (Godfrey Maurice) ST	OFM	L	CN		#*+	1559	1591	..	1598	JONE26
LLOYD David	S		CN	R	#§14	1601	..	1626	1650	LLOY02
OWEN Robert	S		CN	D	3	..	..	1570	..	OWEN10
PUGH John	S		CN	R	#	1621	..	1645	1645	PUGH04
PUGH Robert	S		CN	V	*x1	1610	..	1633	1679	PUGH10
PUGH William	S	W	CN	V		..	..	1676	..	PUGH12
ROBERTS Thomas or Roderick	SJ	W	CN	Y	1	1642	1666	1670	1721	ROBE16
ROBINS William	S		CN	V	1	1574	..	1602	..	ROBI02
WALFRID Thomas	S		CN	V	#†	..	..	1624	..	WALF02
WHITE William	SJ	W	CN	R	#1	1631	1658	1657	1688	WHIT66
WILLIAMS John	SJ	W	CN	Y	1	1656	1678	1693	..	WILL26
WYNNE Peter	S	W	CN	R	#	1637	..	1660	..	WYNN04

DB—DENBIGHSHIRE

Name	Reg	D	Co	T	Notes	Born	Prof	Ordn	Died	Code
BOSTOCK George	S		DB	R	#	1664	..	1688	1727	BOST04
EDMUNDS Robert	S	L	DB	V	*x134	1583	..	1609	1615	EDMU10
EDWARDS Francis	S	L	DB	Q	‡°	1557	..	1584	..	EDWA06
EDWARDS Robert	S	W	DB	L	§	..	..	1664	1677	EDWA19
GOODEN Richard	S		DB	D		1668	..	..	..	GOOD12
GOODMAN John VEN.	S	L	DB	D	†x4	1592	..	1631	1645	GOOD16
HUGHES Humphrey	S	W	DB	R	#4	1572	..	1599	1652	HUGH08
JONES Robert	SJ	W	DB	R	#	1564	1583	..	1615	JONE42
PARRY John	S		DB	L	4	1622	..	1646	1694	PARR14
PARRY Pierce	S	M	DB	L	#	1716	..	1742	1792	PARR18
PUGH John	S	W	DB	L	3	1641	..	1666	1673	PUGH06
ROGERS Edward (Dunstan)	OSB	N	DB	E		..	1714	..	1746	ROGE06
ROGERS Philip	SJ	N	DB	Y	#3	1691	1717	1727	1761	ROGE14
TREVORS William	S		DB	D		..	..	1603	..	TREV04
VAUGHAN John	OFM		DB	F	#	..	1601	..	..	VAUG06
WHITE William (Claude)	OSB		DB	Z	#*23	1583	1605	1609	1655	WHIT68
WYNNE William	S	W	DB	V	3	..	..	1676	..	WYNN06

DE—DERBYSHIRE

Name	Reg	D	Co	T	Notes	Born	Prof	Ordn	Died	Code
BEAUMONT Edward	S	M	DE	D		1732	..	1757	1820	BEAU06
BELL Henry	SJ		DE		24	1563	1596	1589	1597	BELL06

Name	Reg	D	Co	T	Notes	Born	Prof	Ordn	Died	Code
BENTLEY Edward	SJ	W	DE	R	#1	1588	1609	..	1656	BENT 08
BENTLEY Henry	SJ		DE	R	#14	1583	1610	1609	1628	BENT 12
BENTLEY John	SJ		DE	R	#12	1590	1611	..	1663	BENT 14
BEVERIDGE Thomas	S		DE	R		1619	..	1644	..	BEVE 02
BEVERIDGE John	SJ		DE	Y		1615	1636	1646	1646	BEVE 06
BEVERIDGE Thomas	SJ		DE	Y	#12	1583	1604	..	1658	BEVE 08
BUXTON Christopher BL.	S		DE	R	+§	1562	..	1586	1588	BUXT 02
CLAYTON Francis	S	N	DE	R		1565	..	1589	1596	CLAY 08
CROSS (Nicholas of Hly Cross)	OFM	L	DE	F	1234	1615	1639	1640	1698	CROS 26
EATON William	SJ		DE	Q	24		1583	1582	1614	EATO 04
EYRE Edward	S	M	DE	D		1745	..	1772	1834	EYRE 04
EYRE John	S		DE	V	#*	1582	..	1607	..	EYRE 06
EYRE John	S	N	DE	P		1747	..	1772	1790	EYRE 08
EYRE Thomas	S	N	DE	D	3	1748	..	1772	1810	EYRE 12
FITZHERBERT Anthony	S		DE	R		1649	..	..	..	FITZ 02
FITZHERBERT (Francis)	CAP		DE		7	..	..	..	..	FITZ 03
FITZHERBERT Francis	SJ		DE	Y	#	1613	1634	..	1687	FITZ 04
FITZHERBERT John	S	M	DE	R	#1	1607	..	1632	1673	FITZ 06
FITZHERBERT Robert	S	M	DE	L	#	1629	..	1652	1701	FITZ 08
GARLICK Nicholas VEN.	S	M	DE	Q	+‡1	1554	..	1582	1588	GARL 02
GARNET Henry	SJ		DE	R	#*§3	1555	1575	1582	1606	GARN 08
GREEN Paul	S		DE	S	#3	..	..	1602	..	GREE 32
HALLAM Andrew	S	M	DE	D		..	..	1617	..	HALL 28
HARRISON James VEN.	S	N	DE	Q	+	..	..	1583	1602	HARR 34
HARTLEY William BL.	S	M	DE	Q	+‡	1551	..	1580	1588	HART 32
HEATHCOTE John	SJ		DE	R	#§	1590	1615	1614	1657	HEAT 06
HEWETT Martin	SJ	M	DE	Y	#	1606	1627	..	1661	HEWE 04
HOWARD Bernard	S	M	DE	D		1711	..	1735	1745	HOWA 02
HOWARD Charles	S	L	DE	P		1717	..	1742	1792	HOWA 04
HOWARD Thomas	S		DE	D		..	..	1743	1746	HOWA 22
JAMES Edward BL.	S	L	DE	R	+‡1	1559	..	1583	1588	JAME 04
LAYTON Thomas	SJ		DE	Y	#1	1592	1614	..	1661	LAYT 08
LUDLAM Robert VEN.	S	M	DE	Q	+‡1	1551	..	1581	1588	LUDL 02
MARSHALL Peter	SJ	M	DE	S	#2	1591	1620	..	1655	MARS 27
MIDDLETON William	OSB		DE	Z	#*x24	..	1604	..	1644	MIDD 30
NEEDHAM Oswald	S		DE	D		..	..	1597	..	NEED 14
PAGE Alexander	SJ	L	DE	Y		1609	1631	..	1662	PAGE 02
PEGGE Henry (Dominic)	OP		DE	R		1657	1677	1680	1691	PEGG 02
PEGGE William	S	M	DE	D	#3	1637	..	1666	1711	PEGG 04
POLE Anthony	SJ		DE	R	12	1627	1658	1658	1692	POLE 04
POLE Francis	SJ	M	DE	V		1624	1653	1649	1684	POLE 10
POLE George	SJ	N	DE	V		1628	1656	1653	1669	POLE 14
POLE Germain	SJ	M	DE	S	23	1578	1619	1608	1648	POLE 16
POLE Gervase	SJ	M	DE	R		1572	1608	1598	1641	POLE 18
POLE Henry	S	N	DE	R		1670	..	1694	..	POLE 20
POLE John	SJ		DE		4	1574	1598	..	1604	POLE 24
SHERWIN Ralph ST.	S	L	DE	R	+‡	1549	..	1577	1581	SHER 26
SKINNER John	SJ	N	DE	Y	3	1662	1679	1690	1708	SKIN 14
SLACK Richard or William	S		DE	Q		..	..	1579	..	SLAC 02
STAMP Thomas	S	L	DE	N	3	..	..	1575	..	STAM 04
STEPHENSON John	SJ	N	DE	Y		1641	1663	1672	1692	STEP 20
SWINBURNE John	SJ	N	DE	Y	#3	1660	1680	1688	1716	SWIN 04
THOMPSON Richard	SJ	M	DE	Y	#14	1600	1621	..	1644	THOM 32
WHITEHALL Andrew	S	M	DE	D	#3	..	..	1653	1682	WHIT 72
WINSTANLEY Edmund	S		DE	L		1772	..	1796	1852	WINS 04

DH—DURHAM

Name	Reg	D	Co	T	Notes	Born	Prof	Ordn	Died	Code
ADDY Bartholomew (Bede)	OSB	N	DH	X		..	1655	..	1705	ADDY 02
AISLEY Edward (Onuphrius)	ODC	L	DH		2	1661	1682	..	1711	AISL 01
ANDERSON William	S	N	DH	V	*1	1710	..	1733	1759	ANDE 13
APEDAILE George	S	M	DH	D	3	1738	..	1762	1799	APED 02
ASHMALL Ferdinand	S	N	DH	R		1650	..	1674	1712	ASHM 01
ASHMALL Ferdinand	S	N	DH	L		1696	..	1720	1798	ASHM 02
ASHMALL John	S	N	DH	R	4	1653	..	1676	1706	ASHM 06
BALES Christopher BL.	S	L	DH	Q	#+1	1564	..	1587	1590	BALE 02

Name	Reg	D	Co	T	Notes	Born	Prof	Ordn	Died	Code
BARRASS Nicholas	OSS		DH	Q		..	1585	1584	1621	BARR 10
BIRKBECK William	S		DH	Q	†	..	..	1581	..	BIRK 06
BIRKET George	S	L	DH	D	#	1549	..	1577	1614	BIRK 08
BLACKISTON Francis	OSB		DH	G		..	1626	..	1650	BLAC 13
BLACKISTON Francis	SJ		DH	Y	3	1617	1637	1646	1693	BLAC 14
BLACKISTON Michael	OSB		DH	G		..	1625	..	1632	BLAC 17
BOLNEY Robert	S		DH	L	3	1679	..	1705	1716	BOLN 02
BRADSHAW Bernard (Anselm)	OSB	N	DH	X		1742	1760	..	1799	BRAD 26
BRADSHAW Francis (Basil)	OSB		DH	X		..	1762	..	1770	BRAD 28
BROWN Francis	SJ	L	DH	Y	4	1590	1623	..	1625	BROW 10
BYERLEY William	S		DH	R		1669	..	1702	..	BYER 04
CALDWELL John BL.	SJ	L	DH	Y	#+§	168	1656	1664	1679	CALD 04
CLARK Henry	SJ	L	DH	Y	1	1669	1690	1699	1729	CLAR 18
CLAXTON Ralph	S		DH	D	#	..	..	1612	..	CLAX 04
COLLINGWOOD George	S		DH	R		1676	..	1698	1734	COLL 14
COLLINGWOOD Thomas	SJ	N	DH	Y	#	1651	1676	1685	1725	COLL 26
COLSTON Nicholas	OSB		DH	X		..	1673	..	1702	COLS 02
CORBY Ambrose	SJ		DH	Y	#	1604	1627	..	1649	CORB 14
COSIN John	S	L	DH	R	#†	1633	..	1658	1675	COSI 02
COXON Thomas	SJ	L	DH	Y		1654	1676	1687	1735	COXO 04
DEBORD John	S	N	DH	D	#	1715	..	1739	1774	DEBO 02
EDEN James (John)	CRT		DH	R	#*	1663	1698	1690	1707	EDEN 02
ELLERRER Thomas	SJ	N	DH	Y	3	1738	1755	1762	1795	ELLE 02
FORCER Francis	SJ	N	DH		1	1583	1604	..	1655	FORC 02
FORCER John	SJ	N	DH	R	#	1580	1605	1604	1630	FORC 04
GARGRAVE George	S	N	DH	V	§13	1598	..	1628	..	GARG 02
GREENWELL Thomas	S	N	DH	L		..	..	1735	1753	GREE 76
HARTBURN John or Rbt.(Placid)	OSB	N	DH	D	#	..	1617	1609	1655	HART 20
HARTBURN Martin (Cuthbert)	OSB	N	DH	G	#4	..	1614	..	1646	HART 22
HILDRETH William	S		DH	V	#§	1585	..	..	..	HILD 06
HODGSON Edmund	S		DH	R	#1	1608	..	1636	..	HODG 10
HODGSON John	S	N	DH	D	#14	1603	..	1631	1649	HODG 22
HODGSON Stephen	OSB	N	DH	W		1763	1784	1788	1816	HODG 34
HOUSEMAN Christopher	SJ		DH	Y	#1	1726	1744	1751	1769	HOUS 06
HUDD John	SJ	M	DH		x2	1571	1620	..	1649	HUDD 02
HUTTON Thomas (Placid)	OSB	N	DH	X		..	1714	1720	1755	HUTT 10
HUTTON William (Bede)	OSB	N	DH	X		..	1713	1720	1756	HUTT 12
HUTTON William (Cuthbert)	OSB	N	DH	G	#	..	1685	..	1702	HUTT 14
JACKSON Robert	S	L	DH	R		1741	..	1766	1814	JACK 28
JENISON Augustine	S	N	DH	D	#	1674	..	1701	..	JENI 04
JENISON Augustine	SJ	W	DH	Y	#34	1735	1755	1762	1794	JENI 06
JENISON James	SJ	W	DH	Y	3	1737	1755	1765	1799	JENI 08
JENISON John	SJ	W	DH	Y	#	1729	1745	1756	1793	JENI 10
JENISON Michael	S		DH	R	#	1628	..	1653	..	JENI 14
JENISON Michael	SJ	L	DH	Y	#1	1655	1675	1683	1735	JENI 16
JENISON Ralph	SJ	N	DH	Y	#1	1635	1656	1669	1719	JENI 18
JENISON Robert	SJ		DH	Y	#2	1590	1617	..	1656	JENI 20
JENISON Thomas	S		DH	R	#	1603	..	1637	..	JENI 22
JENISON Thomas	SJ		DH		#	1643	1664	1674	1701	JENI 26
JENISON William	SJ		DH	Y	3	1653	1675	1680	1683	JENI 30
JOHNSON Cuthbert	S	N	DH	Q	#	..	..	1583	..	JOHN 05
JOHNSON Robert	S	N	DH	D	3	1724	..	1753	1799	JOHN 30
JOHNSON Robert	OSB	L	DH	Z	#1	1580	1600	..	1663	JOHN 38
JOHNSON William	S	N	DH	V	°3	..	..	1603	..	JOHN 39
KENNET Brian	S	L	DH	D	#3	..	..	1680	1724	KENN 06
KENNET Charles	SJ	L	DH	Y	1	1660	1681	1689	1728	KENN 08
KENNET Henry	S	N	DH	D	3	1667	..	1691	1743	KENN 12
LIDDELL Thomas	S	N	DH	L	3	..	..	1698	1724	LIDD 02
LUCAS Anthony	SJ		DH			1633	1662	..	1693	LUCA 02
MAIRE Christopher	SJ		DH	Y	3	1697	1715	1727	1767	MAIR 02
MAIRE Edward	SJ		DH	Y	#3	1725	1742	1749	1797	MAIR 04
MAIRE George	SJ	M	DH	Y	3	1738	1754	1762	1796	MAIR 06
MAIRE Henry	S	N	DH	D		1714	..	1738	1775	MAIR 08
MAIRE James	SJ	M	DH	Y		1705	1726	1733	1746	MAIR 10
MAIRE Peter	SJ	N	DH	Y	3	1707	1726	1734	1763	MAIR 12
MAIRE Thomas	SJ		DH	Y	3	1703	1720	1729	1752	MAIR 14

Name	Reg	D	Co	T	Notes	Born	Prof	Ordn	Died	Code
MAIRE William	S	N	DH	D	#3	1659	..	1687	1740	MAIR 15
MAIRE William	S	N	DH	D		1699	..	1723	1733	MAIR 16
MARLEY John	S	N	DH	R		1574	..	1598	..	MARL 02
MASON Francis	SJ	N	DH	R	#1	1593	1623	1619	1681	MASO 02
MATHER James	S	N	DH	P	4	1718	..	1746	1801	MATH 06
MERRIMAN Michael	S	N	DH	D	#	..	..	1631	1673	MERR 02
MERRIMAN Thomas (Bede)	OSB		DH	W	#1	1585	1610	..	1614	MERR 04
METCALFE Nicholas	S	N	DH	L	#3	1648	..	1674	1695	METC 16
PERCY John	SJ	L	DH	R	#§	1568	1594	1593	1641	PERC 08
PINKNEY Miles	S		DH	D	#§	1599	..	1625	1674	PINK 02
PORTER Francis	OSB	N	DH	X		..	1658	..	1689	PORT 04
PORTER John (Peter)	OP		DH			1725	1744	1749	1759	PORT 14
READING Thomas	S	N	DH	R	#§	1597	..	1638	1672	READ 08
RICHARDSON William	SJ	N	DH	Y	#	1652	1674	1679	1689	RICH 38
RICHMOND William	S	N	DH	Q	#	..	..	1581	..	RICH 40
SALKELD Francis	S	N	DH	R	#	1625	..	1652	1671	SALK 02
SALKELD John	S		DH	R	#	1620	..	1647	1648	SALK 10
SALKELD Thomas	S	N	DH	R	#	1624	..	1652	1691	SALK 12
SALVIN Peter	OSB	W	DH	G		1605	1632	..	1675	SALV 02
SALVIN Ralph	SJ		DH	R	#	1600	1625	1624	1627	SALV 04
SELBY Richard (Wilfrid)	OSB		DH	G	#	..	1620	..	1659	SELB 10
SHAFTOE (Placid)	OSB	N	DH	X		1634	1655	1659	1681	SHAF 06
SIMPSON Joseph	SJ		DH	Y	3	1629	1656	1665	1667	SIMP 08
SMAITHWAITE William	S		DH	R		1682	..	1705	..	SMAI 02
SMITH George	SJ		DH	Y		1611	1631	..	1671	SMIT 18
SMITH Thomas	SJ		DH	Y	#3	1674	1691	1700	1721	SMIT 69
SMITH Thomas BP.	S	N	DH	D	*	1763	..	1787	1831	SMIT 72
SOUTHERN William VEN.	S	N	DH	D	+3	1579	..	1601	1618	SOUT 14
STELLING Robert (Augustine)	OSB		DH	E		..	1676	..	1727	STEL 02
STEPHENSON Thomas Richard	SJ		DH	Q	#	1552	1585	1581	1624	STEP 24
SWINBURNE Godric (Joachim)	OSB		DH	X		1754	1776	..	1797	SWIN 02
TAYLOR Thomas	S	N	DH	D	3	1765	..	1788	1818	TAYL 48
TEMPEST Edward	S		DH	Q		1568	..	1594	..	TEMP 04
TEMPEST Robert	S		DH	Q	14	1542	..	1584	1625	TEMP 18
TEMPEST Robert	SJ	L	DH	Q		1566	1624	1591	1640	TEMP 20
THIRKELD Richard BL.	S	N	DH	D	+‡	..	..	1579	1583	THIR 02
THOMPSON Lancelot	S		DH	P	#3	1677	..	1701	1729	THOM 28
THOMPSON Richard (Leander)	OSB		DH	G	#	..	1635	..	1669	THOM 36
THURSBY Charles	SJ	N	DH	D	2	1573	1606	1603	1639	THUR 04
TOCKETS Alexius	SJ	N	DH	V	#	1665	1689	1689	1731	TOCK 02
TODD Anthony	S		DH	D	#13	1648	..	1676	1698	TODD 02
TODD Anthony	S		DH	D	#	1671	..	1703	1746	TODD 04
TODD Christopher	S	N	DH	D	#3	1683	..	1709	1713	TODD 06
TROLLOPE Cuthbert	S	N	DH	R	#	1573	..	1596	..	TROL 02
WAKE John (Hilarion)	OSB		DH	G	#	..	1639	..	1657	WAKE 02
WARD Robert	S	N	DH	V	13	1660	..	1684	..	WARD 08
WATSON William	S	L	DH	Q	#‡=1	1558	..	1586	1603	WATS 08
WHITFIELD Thomas Hugh John	SJ		DH	Y		1615	1639	..	1686	WHIT 76
WILSON John (Benedict)	OSB	N	DH	G		..	1678	..	1725	WILS 12
WILSON Ralph (Maurus)	OSB	M	DH	X		..	1688	..	1723	WILS 24
WILSON William (Willibrord)	OSB		DH	X		..	1684	..	1692	WILS 42
WINTER William	S	N	DH	R		1738	..	1763	1796	WINT 02
WITHAM George	S		DH	D	3	1750	..	1774	1829	WITH 08
YOUNGER James	S	L	DH	R	#	1563	..	1587	..	YOUN 16

DT—DORSET

Name	Reg	D	Co	T	Notes	Born	Prof	Ordn	Died	Code
ADAMS John VEN.	S	W	DT	Q	#+‡1	1546	..	1580	1586	ADAM 02
BARNES John (Lawrence)	OSB	N	DT	G		1748	1768	..	1803	BARN 18
BIDDLECOMB Martin	S	W	DT	L	#	..	..	1633	1678	BIDD 02
BONVILLE Anthony	SJ		DT	R	#§	1621	1647	1647	1676	BONV 02
BONVILLE Francis	S		DT	L	3	..	..	1682	..	BONV 04
BOSGRAVE James	SJ		DT	R	1	1547	1564	1572	1623	BOSG 02
BULLY John	S	L	DT	R	#	1627	..	1654	1687	BULL 14
CASE William	S	L	DT	V	#	1585	..	1613	..	CASE 06
CHAPMAN Edward	S	L	DT	D		1539	..	1595	..	CHAP 16

Name	Reg	D	Co	T	Notes	Born	Prof	Ordn	Died	Code
DIGBY John, Hon.	S		DT		*	1617	..	..	1664	DIGB04
DIRDO James	S		DT	D	3	..	..	1660	..	DIRD02
FAULKNER John	SJ	W	DT	R	#‡	1577	1604	1603	1657	FAUL02
FLEET John (Bernardine)	OFM	M	DT	F	1	1740	1759	..	1815	FLEE02
GARDINER John	SJ		DT	Y		1588	1618	..	1652	GARD10
GERARD William	S		DT	D		1754	..	..	1830	GERA38
GILDON John	S	L	DT	L	#1	1637	..	1661	1700	GILD04
GILDON Robert	S		DT	D	#3	..	..	1656	1667	GILD08
GILDON William	S	W	DT	D	#3	1680	..	1703	1743	GILD10
HAYES John or Timothy	SJ	N	DT	D	#	1584	1617	1609	1646	HAYE02
HEMERFORD Thomas BL.	S		DT	R	+‡	1554	..	1583	1584	HEME02
HEYLIN John Francis	S	L	DT	D	#	1715	..	1739	1753	HEYL02
HOLMES Matthew	S	W	DT	S	7	..	..	..	..	HOLM14
HUSSEY Edward	OSB	W	DT	G		1712	1731	..	1786	HUSS02
HUSSEY Thomas	S		DT	R	#	1697	..	1729	1739	HUSS06
LEGATT (Amatus)	OSB		DT	G	4	..	1625	..	1633	LEGA06
LOCKETT John	S		DT	R	§1	1640	..	1666	..	LOCK04
MANGER Thomas	S	W	DT	Q	4	1566	..	1592	1643	MANG02
MARTIN Anthony (Athanasius)	OSB		DT	R	#‡4	1565	1594	1591	1626	MART04
MARTIN Thomas	S		DT	D	§34	1610	..	1633	1691	MART30
MARTIN Thomas	S		DT	D	‡4	1570	..	1594	1643	MART32
MUNDEN John BL.	S		DT	R	+‡	1543	..	1582	1584	MUND04
PENNY (Francis of S.Mary)	OFM		DT	F		1643	..	..	1672	PENN20
PITTS Robert	S		DT	D	#3	1620	..	1650	1682	PITT10
RICHARDS Henry	S	L	DT	R		1649	..	1676	1682	RICH06
SMITH John	S	L	DT	L	#3	..	..	1681	1714	SMIT38
SMITH Robert	S		DT	L	#	..	..	1681	1729	SMIT63
SNOD Peter	S	W	DT	D		1595	..	1622	..	SNOD02
STANNEY Thomas	SJ	L	DT	R		1558	1597	1585	1617	STAN32
TOUCHET George (Anselm), Hon.	OSB	L	DT	G	4	..	1643	..	1689	TOUC02
TRESHAM Thomas	SJ		DT	Y	23	1637	1663	1670	1671	TRES04
TRIM John	S	L	DT	D		..	..	1597	..	TRIM02
TRIM Richard	S		DT	S	#	1590	..	1613	..	TRIM04
WARHAM George	S	W	DT	D	#	1586	..	1612	1676	WARH02
WARHAM George	S		DT	D	#	1607	..	1633	..	WARH04
WARHAM John	S	W	DT	D	#	1582	..	1610	..	WARH08
WARMINGTON William	S		DT	Q	#	1556	..	1580	..	WARM02

DV—DEVONSHIRE

Name	Reg	D	Co	T	Notes	Born	Prof	Ordn	Died	Code
BALLYMAN John (Gregory)	OSB		DV	X	§	1734	1754	..	1811	BALL16
BALLYMAN Thomas	OSB	M	DV	X	§	1737	1756	..	1795	BALL18
BEAR Matthew	S		DV	P		1688	..	1721	1743	BEAR02
BOLT John	S		DV	D	#§	1563	..	1605	1640	BOLT06
BROOKE Thomas	S		DV	L	§	1727	..	1751	1756	BROO18
CARY Francis	SJ		DV	S		1610	1647	..	1665	CARY06
COFFIN Edward	SJ		DV	R	§	1570	1598	1593	1626	COFF02
COLLINS John	S		DV	D	#	..	..	1601	..	COLL28
COLUMB John	SJ		DV	N	‡1	1546	1572	..	1582	COLU02
DUNSCOMBE Simon (Augustine)	OSB		DV	X		1702	1722	..	1736	DUNS02
FORD Thomas BL.	S	L	DV	D	+‡	..	..	1573	1582	FORD02
FURSDON John (Cuthbert)	OSB	L	DV	G	#1	1604	1620	..	1638	FURS02
FURSDON (Cuthbert)	OSB		DV	W		1585	1620	..	1677	FURS04
GIBBONS John	S		DV	R	#§	1652	..	1677	..	GIBB08
GREENWAY John	S	W	DV	V		1752	..	1777	1800	GREE70
HART William	SJ	L	DV	Y	#34	1594	1616	1620	1624	HART16
HILL Robert	S	W	DV	R	#§4	1635	..	1661	1709	HILL10
HONNACOTT Abraham	SJ		DV	R	#*	1585	1612	1610	1612	HONN02
HUGHES Edward	S	L	DV	R	#	1601	..	1631	1672	HUGH06
HULL (Francis of S.Mary)	OSB		DV	W	2	..	1616	..	1645	HULL02
KENDALL Thomas	SJ		DV	Y		1612	1635	..	1672	KEND16
LOCK Richard	S		DV	L	‡	1695	..	1725	..	LOCK02
MARK John	OSS		DV	Y	*	1621	1663	..	1697	MARK02
MAYNE Cuthbert ST.	S	W	DV	D	+‡	1544	..	1575	1577	MAYN02
NANCONAN Peter	S		DV	D	#	..	..	1609	..	NANC02
PALMER Christopher	S		DV	R		..	..	1612	..	PALM02

Name	Reg	D	Co	T	Notes	Born	Prof	Ordn	Died	Code
PEARCE Philip	S		DV	R	#	1613	..	1637	..	PEAR06
PEARCE Thomas	SJ		DV			1607	1639	..	1685	PEAR08
POYNTZ John	SJ	L	DV	Y	#3	1709	1732	1739	1789	POYN08
REYNOLDS William	S		DV	D	‡	1543	..	1580	1594	REYN07
RICHARDS John	S		DV	R		1561	..	1587	..	RICH08
RISDON Thomas	SJ	W	DV	Y	#3	1662	1682	1694	1744	RISD02
RISDON Thomas (Cuthbert)	OSB		DV	E		..	1640	..	1652	RISD04
RISDON William	SJ		DV			..	..	..	1644	RISD06
RUDGE William (Constantine)	ODC		DV	R	#	1623	1649	1647	1664	RUDG02
SALISBURY Edward	OSB	W	DV	X	1	1685	1703	..	1725	SALI02
SCOBLE John	S		DV	R	#	1600	..	1624	1626	SCOB02
SHIMELL Charles	S	W	DV	D	3	1735	..	1763	1764	SHIM02
SOUTHCOTE Robert (Amandus)	OSB	W	DV	G		..	1624	..	1653	SOUT10
STUKELEY Augustine	S		DV	S	1	1575	..	..	..	STUK02
SWEET John	SJ		DV	R		1570	1609	1608	1632	SWEE02
TRAVERS George (Lucian)	ODC	L	DV	Z	*x§	1642	..	..	1691	TRAV02
TRAVERS John	SJ		DV	S	#§°23	1616	1645	1642	..	TRAV04
TRAVERS Walter Joseph (Bede)	ODC	L	DV	R		1619	1648	..	1696	TRAV06
TURNER Robert	S		DV	D		..	..	1574	1599	TURN30
VENNER Robert (Amandus)	OSB		DV	D	#	..	1614	1609	1628	VENN02
WAY William BL.	S	L	DV	Q	#+	1565	..	1586	1588	WAYA02
WOODRUFFE Robert	S		DV	R	#	1579	..	1606	..	WOOD34

ES—SPAIN

Name	Reg	D	Co	T	Notes	Born	Prof	Ordn	Died	Code
BAKER John	SJ		ES	Y	1	1644	1670	1678	1719	BAKE12
BROWN Peter	S	L	ES	D	13	1730	..	1754	1794	BROW26
COPLEY Thomas	SJ	L	ES	Y	#14	1595	1616	..	1652	COPL08
DEAN Thomas	SJ		ES	Y	#	1693	1709	1719	1719	DEAN03
FUENTE Diego de la	OP	L	ES		*	..	1601	..	1630	FUEN02
GAVIN Antonio	S		ES		*°8	..	..	..	..	GAVI02
HORMASA Raymond	SJ	N	ES		#	1741	1756	..	1789	HORM02
MAGUIRE (Dominic) ARCHBP.	OP	L	ES	Z	*	..	..	..	1708	MAGU02
PORTER Nicholas	SJ		ES	Y	3	1724	1741	1748	1802	PORT18
RAYMOND Charles	SJ		ES	V	3	1665	1686	1694	1725	RAYM04
WHITE John	S		ES	V	#3	..	..	1648	..	WHIT34
WRIGHT Matthew	SJ		ES	Y	#	1647	1668	1678	1711	WRIG18
(Zachary of Saluzzo)	CAP		ES		*7	..	..	..	..	ZACH02

EX—ESSEX

Name	Reg	D	Co	T	Notes	Born	Prof	Ordn	Died	Code
ANGEL James	S	L	EX	R		1720	..	1745	1775	ANGE02
APPLETON ?Roger (Lawrence)	OSB		EX	G	4	..	1635	..	1661	APPL16
BARKER John	SJ	M	EX	Y	1	1640	1662	1670	1705	BARK08
BERINGTON Charles BP.	S	M	EX	P	*	1748	..	1775	1798	BERI02
BERINGTON Thomas	S	L	EX	D	3	1740	..	1768	1805	BERI16
BETENSON Edward (Placid)	OSB		EX	G		1630	1649	..	1689	BETE02
BROWN George	OSB		EX	Z	#*2	..	1604	..	1628	BROW13
CANNON Edmund	S		EX	S	x34	1578	..	1602	1649	CANN08
CHAPLIN Roch	S	L	EX	R	1	1558	..	1584	..	CHAP13
CLARK John	SJ		EX	S	3	1604	1632	1630	1672	CLAR21
DEBENHAM Samuel (Jn. Francis)	MIN		EX		†1	1565	1586	..	1613	DEBE02
DRURY Robert	SJ	L	EX	R	#1	1587	1608	..	1623	DRUR06
DRURY William	S		EX	R	#	1584	..	1610	..	DRUR08
EVANS Thomas	SJ		EX	R		1558	1585	1585	1587	EVAN20
FITCH William (Benet)	CAP		EX	P	#§	1561	1588	..	1611	FITC02
FOX Nicholas	S	M	EX	Q	x‡	1533	..	1581	1592	FOXA02
FRERE Joseph	OSB		EX	G		1598	1620	1629	1694	FRER02
FRERE (Placid)	OSB		EX	G	1	1602	1624	1631	1632	FRER04
GERARD Thomas	SJ	L	EX	R	#=	1605	1629	1631	1665	GERA22
GLOSTER Edward	OSB		EX	E	#	..	1640	..	1652	GLOS02
GREEN Richard	S		EX	R		..	..	1582	1590	GREE34
GREENWOOD Christopher	SJ	L	EX	Y	1	1584	1605	..	1651	GREE78
GREENWOOD Henry (Paulinus)	OSB		EX	G	#	1586	1612	..	1645	GREE82
GRIME John Edward (Cuthbert)	OSB		EX	G		1743	1764	1784	1786	GRIM12
HAYNES Joseph	S		EX	V	#†3	1581	..	1609	1629	HAYN02

Name	Reg	D	Co	T	Notes	Born	Prof	Ordn	Died	Code
HOLMES John (Edward of Cross)	OFM		EX	F	°1	1733	1758	..	..	HOLM13
HUDDLESTON John	SJ	L	EX		#3	1636	1656	1669	1700	HUDD10
ITHELL Ralph	S	L	EX	R	*†°3	1547	..	1577	1618	ITHE04
JENNINGS Charles	S		EX	D	#	1628	..	1654	1677	JENN04
JENNINGS Jerome	S	,	M	EX	L	4	1621	..	1649	1681	JENN06
JENNINGS John	S	L	EX	S	#3	..	..	1637	1678	JENN10
JENNINGS Richard	SJ	M	EX	S	#3	1613	1637	1636	1643	JENN15
KIGHLEY Thomas	S	L	EX	V	#=3	1577	..	1611	..	KIGH02
LAURENSON John	SJ	N	EX	Y	3	1760	1803	1788	1834	LAUR06
MAYLER Henry	S	L	EX		#13	1576	..	1612	..	MAYL02
MICO Edward VEN.	SJ	L	EX	Y	#x1	1628	1650	1657	1678	MICO02
MORE Henry	SJ	L	EX		#	1586	1607	..	1661	MORE05
PETRE Benjamin BP.	S	L	EX	D	#*3	1672	..	1697	1758	PETR02
PETRE Francis	S		EX	L		..	..	1689	1699	PETR08
PETRE Francis BP.	S	N	EX	D	#*	1692	..	1720	1775	PETR10
PETRE John	SJ	M	EX	Y	#	1661	1680	1689	1738	PETR12
PETRE Philip	S		EX	D	3	1668	..	1693	..	PETR14
PETRE Richard	SJ		EX	Y	#	1634	1654	1661	1692	PETR16
PETRE Robert	SJ	L	EX	Y	#	1632	1654	1663	1713	PETR18
PETRE Robert	SJ		EX	Y	#13	1667	..	1695	1727	PETR20
PETRE Robert	SJ	N	EX	Y	3	1700	1719	1727	1766	PETR22
PETRE Thomas	SJ	N	EX	Y	13	1662	1679	1688	1729	PETR24
POWELL Francis	SJ	L	EX	Y	#1	1658	1677	1689	1733	POWE06
POWELL Richard	SJ	M	EX	Y	1	1610	1629	..	1653	POWE18
ROSS Edward	SJ		EX	V	§	1585	1618	..	1665	ROSS02
SADLER William	SJ		EX	Y		1609	1630	..	1674	SADL18
SCOTT Clement	S	L	EX	D		1692	..	1717	1731	SCOT02
SCOTT William (Maurus) BL.	OSB	L	EX		#*+†1	1578	1605	1610	1612	SCOT16
SHERBURN Edward	OSB	N	EX	E		..	1699	..	1745	SHER06
SIMPSON Thomas	S		EX	Q	#°1	1548	..	1585	..	SIMP16
SMITH Benjamin	S		EX	L		1769	..	1794	1795	SMIT05
SMITH Francis	S	M	EX	R	#1	1608	..	1632	1672	SMIT15
SOUTHCOTE Edward	SJ	L	EX	Y	3	1697	1719	1727	1780	SOUT02
SOUTHCOTE Francis (Augustine)	OSB	L	EX	G		1691	1708	..	1774	SOUT04
SOUTHCOTE John	S	L	EX	R	#	1587	..	1612	1637	SOUT06
SOUTHCOTE John (Augustine)	OSB		EX	E		..	1689	..	1730	SOUT08
SOUTHCOTE Thomas	OSB	L	EX	G		1670	1688	..	1748	SOUT12
THOROUGHGOOD James	S	L	EX	R	#	1607	..	1631	1671	THOR28
TILLINGHAM Charles	S	L	EX	L	#4	1653	..	..	1719	TILL04
TYAS George	CRT	L	EX	D	#	1604	..	1628	1668	TYAS04
TYRRELL Anthony	S		EX	R	3	1552	..	1580	1615	TYRR02
WALDEGRAVE Charles	SJ		EX	Y	#	1592	1616	..	1655	WALD02
WALDEGRAVE William	OSB	M	EX	V	#§	1588	1650	1618	1665	WALD10
WHITBREAD Thomas BL.	SJ	M	EX	Y	#+	1618	1635	..	1679	WHIT14
WHITE Jerome	S	M	EX	D	#3	..	..	1628	..	WHIT32
WHITE Thomas	S	L	EX	D	#	1593	..	1617	1676	WHIT54
WHITLEY Richard	SJ		EX	V	12	1583	1611	1611	1651	WHIT82
WISEMAN Francis Ignatius	S		EX	R	#	1602	..	1637	..	WISE04
WRIGHT Charles	SJ	N	EX	Y	3	1752	1769	1775	1827	WRIG04
WRIGHT Peter	S		EX	R		1669	..	1693	..	WRIG22
WRIGHT Philip	SJ		EX	Y	#	1665	1684	1693	1737	WRIG24
WRIGHT Stephen	SJ	L	EX	R	#	1620	1653	1645	1680	WRIG32

FR—FRANCE

Name	Reg	D	Co	T	Notes	Born	Prof	Ordn	Died	Code
ABATHELL Nicholas	S		FR	N	†3	..	..	1571	..	ABAT02
(Aimé of Beauvais)	CAP	L	FR		2	..	1612	..	1652	AIME01
ANDRE Philip	OFM		FR	F		..	..	1728	1772	ANDR01
(Angelus of Raconisio)	CAP	L	FR		2	..	1595	..	1637	ANGE04
(Angelus of Soissons)	CAP	L	FR		2	..	1615	..	1646	ANGE06
(Apollinaris of Paris)	CAP	L	FR			..	..	1665	ANGE06	APOL02
(Archangelus of Beauvais)	CAP	L	FR		2	..	1655	..	1706	ARCH01
AUBEIL Francis, or Marcus d'	SJ	L	FR		*7	..	..	..	..	AUBE02
(Basil of Rheims)	CAP		FR		2	..	1612	..	1655	BASI02
(Basil of Soissons)	CAP	L	FR		2	..	1634	..	1698	BASI04
BAZIER Matthieu	SJ		FR		#x12	1608	1633	..	1650	BAZI02

Name	Reg	D	Co	T	Notes	Born	Prof	Ordn	Died	Code
BERMINGHAM William	SJ		FR	Y	#1	1692	1711	1721	..	BERM04
BERULLE Pierre de CARD.	ORA	L	FR	P	*2	1575	1611	1599	1629	BERU02
BEVAN John	SJ		FR	Y	1	1702	1726	1724	1728	BEVA02
BOOTH Charles	SJ	W	FR	Y	#3	1707	1724	1731	1797	BOOT02
BOOTH Francis	S	L	FR	V		..	..	1733	..	BOOT06
BOOTH Ralph	SJ		FR	Y	#3	1721	1737	1747	1780	BOOT10
BOURGEOIS James Philip	SJ	W	FR	Y	#3	1738	1760	1767	1811	BOUR02
BREVAL Francis Durant de	CAP	L	FR		°	..	..	..	1707	BREV02
BRUNEAU Joseph	SJ		FR	P	4	1704	1721	..	1774	BRUN04
BULSTRODE James	S		FR	R		1724	..	1748	..	BULS02
(Charles of Beauvais)	CAP	L	FR		2	..	1616	..	1669	CHAR00
(Charles Francis Abbeville)	CAP	L	FR			..	..	..	1665	CHAR01
(Cherubimus of Amiens)	CAP	L	FR		2	..	1609	..	1653	CHER08
COFFIN Peter	S		FR	V	3	1583	..	1607	..	COFF04
COLGRAVE Andrew	SJ	M	FR		1	1717	1734	..	1768	COLG02
COPLEY Henry	S		FR	R		1705	..	1728	..	COPL02
(Cyprien of Gamaches)	CAP	L	FR		2	..	1620	..	1679	CYPR02
DALLAS Ignatius	SJ		FR	Y	#4	1733	1761	1761	1773	DALL02
(Damian of Touraine)	CAR	L	FR		*8	..	..	..	..	DAMI02
DEAN Michael	SJ		FR	Y	13	1695	1714	1724	1760	DEAN02
DEVOIS (Theodoric of S.René)	CAR	L	FR			1665	1681	..	1728	DEVO02
DONZE Francis	SJ		FR			..	1761	..	..	DONZ02
DUCLOS Anthony	SJ	L	FR		4	..	..	..	1764	DUCL02
DUPERRON Jacques BP.	S	L	FR		*	..	..	..	1649	DUPE02
DURET Pierre (Remigius)	ODC	L	FR			1661	1683	..	1728	DURE02
ECCOP Charles	SJ	L	FR	Y	3	1697	1715	1724	1735	ECCO02
FLEURY Charles	SJ	W	FR		#	1739	1756	..	1825	FLEU02
FLEUTOT (Maurus)	OSB		FR	W		1610	1630	..	1669	FLEU04
FONTAINE John Baptist de la	SJ		FR	Y	3	1739	1757	1767	1821	FONT02
(Francis Mary of Paris)	CAP		FR		2	..	1621	..	1652	FRAN05
GAGNIER John	CRL		FR	P	*°1	1670	..	..	1740	GAGN02
GAULTIER Francois	S		FR		*8	..	..	..	..	GAUL02
GICOU Francis	OSB		FR	E		1585	1617	..	1648	GICO02
GONEUTTE James	SJ		FR			1653	1688	..	1698	GONE02
GOUGH John Baptist	S		FR	D	3	..	..	1730	..	GOUG02
GROSSIER William (Romanus)	OSB		FR	E	*	..	1620	..	..	GROS03
GUILICK Nicholas	SJ		FR	Y	12	1647	1668	1674	1694	GUIL04
HAMEL Maurice de	SJ	L	FR		*7	..	..	..	..	HAME01
HARLAY Achille de BP.	ORA	L	FR		*	1581	..	..	1646	HARL02
HARRISON John	SJ	L	FR	Y	#	1690	1708	1718	1725	HARR44
HENRION Nicholas(Constantius)	OFM		FR	F	3	1733	1766	1779	1824	HENR02
JACOBSON William	SJ		FR	Y		1692	1714	1721	1764	JACO02
(John Mary of Trelon)	CAP		FR		2	..	1620	..	1647	JOHN02
JOSSAER Bernard	SJ	N	FR	Y	#	1712	1731	1739	1775	JOSS02
JOSSAER Michael	SJ		FR	Y	13	1708	1727	1736	1759	JOSS04
JOYEUSE Henri (Angelus) de	CAP		FR	P	*	1563	1587	..	1608	JOYE02
KIRBY Henry	S	M	FR	R		1712	..	1735	1767	KIRB04
LABROSSE Joseph (Angelus)	ODC	L	FR	Y	23	1636	1655	1660	1697	LABR02
LA COLOMBIERE Claude de BL.	SJ	L	FR	P	3	1641	1659	1670	1682	LACO02
LA CROIX Stephen	SJ		FR		4	1706	..	..	1761	LACR02
LALART John Bapt.	SJ	L	FR	Y	#3	1693	1715	1723	1743	LALA02
(Lambert of Fliscour)	CAP	L	FR		2	..	1619	..	1654	LAMB03
LA MOTTE DU PLESSIS Daniel BP	S	L	FR		*	..	..	..	1628	LAMO02
L'AUNAY Alambert	SJ		FR			..	..	..	1789	LAUN02
LE BRETON (Germain)	CAR	L	FR			1645	1664	..	..	LEBR02
LE COURAYER Pierre Francois	S	L	FR		*3	1681	..	1706	1776	LECO02
LE MAITRE Charles	SJ	L	FR	Y	#1	1672	1693	1702	1737	LEMA02
(Leonard of Paris)	CAP	L	FR		2	..	1586	..	1641	LEON04
LUYNES (Archangelus) de	CAP		FR			..	..	..	1649	LUYN02
(Matthew of S.Quentin)	CAP	L	FR		2	..	1640	..	1675	MATT01
MELLIERE (Alexis) de la	CAR	L	FR		8	..	..	..	..	MELL01
MOLIEN Edward	SJ		FR	N	3	1701	1720	1728	1761	MOLI02
MOLIEN Jean Baptiste	SJ	L	FR	N	4	1703	1721	1730	1775	MOLI04
MORIN Jean	ORA	L	FR	P	§	1591	1618	1619	1659	MORI02
NEIL John	SJ	W	FR	V	#3	1716	1740	1739	1760	NEIL02
NEIL William	SJ		FR	Y	#3	1714	1732	1739	1770	NEIL04

Name	Reg	D	Co	T	Notes	Born	Prof	Ordn	Died	Code
ORGAIN (Benedict of S.John)d'	OSB		FR	W	2	..	1611	..	1636	ORGA02
PAGES (Modestus of B.Trinity)	CAR		FR	Z	1	1650	1667	..	..	PAGE10
PATOUILLET Nicolas	SJ	L	FR			1622	..	..	1710	PATO02
PAZZI MANDIN (James) de	CAR		FR		1	1656	1674	..	..	PAZZ02
QUIMPER (Ant'y of Corisopito)	CAP	L	FR		2	..	1655	..	1688	QUIM02
RENOULT Romanus	SJ		FR			1703	1722	..	1776	RENO02
RIBERTIERRE Bernard	OSB		FR	G	*	..	1621	..	1664	RIBE04
(Robert of Paris)	CAP	L	FR		2	..	1640	..	1683	ROBE01
ROY Pierre (Placid) du	ODC	L	FR		14	1682	1701	..	1739	ROYA01
SACHMORTER Philip	SJ	L	FR	N	#3	1720	1738	1745	1795	SACH04
ST PAUL (Joseph) de	CAP	L	FR		2	..	1621	..	1662	SAIN05
SANDERSON (Bernard)	OSB		FR	X		..	1663	..	1669	SAND16
(Sebastian of Bar sur Seine)	CAP		FR		2	..	1619	..	1667	SEBA02
(Seraphinus of Compiègne)	CAP		FR			..	1613	..	1655	SERA02
SMITHERS William	SJ		FR	Y		1656	1675	1682	1685	SMIT82
SUFFREN Jean	SJ	L	FR			1571	1586	..	..	SUFF04
THOMPSON Edward	S		FR	V		1586	..	..	..	THOM18
TURNER Francis	S		FR	D		1646	..	..	1675	TURN12
VANTELET Robert de	CAP	L	FR		2	..	1611	..	1659	VANT02
(Victor of Paris)	CAP	L	FR		2	..	1622	..	1652	VICT06
(Victor of S.Cecily)	CAR	L	FR			..	..	..	1723	VICT08
VIETTE	ORA		FR		*7	..	..	..	..	VIET02
(Vincent of Beauvais)	CAP	L	FR		2	..	1597	..	1652	VINC06
WALSH Edward	SJ	N	FR	Y		1739	1756	1767	1822	WALS02
WALSH Thomas	S		FR	D		1752	..	1777	1817	WALS08

FT—FLINTSHIRE

Name	Reg	D	Co	T	Notes	Born	Prof	Ordn	Died	Code
BENNET Edward	S	L	FT	R	#	1569	..	1594	1637	BENN04
BENNET John	SJ	W	FT	D	#1	1548	1586	1578	1625	BENN06
BENNET John	S	W	FT	V	#13	1570	..	1597	1623	BENN08
CONWAY William	SJ		FT	Y	#3	1659	1679	1688	1689	CONW02
CONWAY William	SJ		FT	Y	#3	1683	1702	1710	1741	CONW04
DAVIES Miles	S	M	FT	R	#1	1662	..	1688	..	DAVI10
DAVIES William (Maurus)	OSB	N	FT	E	#	..	1642	..	1663	DAVI36
FOWLER Francis (William)	OP	M	FT		#2	1591	1610	..	1662	FOWL05
GRIFFITH George	SJ	W	FT	Y	13	1668	1688	165	1718	GRIF20
HACKET James	S		FT	L		1692	..	1715	1718	HACK01
HANMER Humphre	S	W	FT	Q	=	1546	..	1584	..	HANM04
JONES Robert	S	L	FT	D	#	1646	..	1672	1714	JONE44
MORGAN Edward VEN.	S		FT	Z	#*+§	1584	..	1618	1642	MORG04
MORGAN William	SJ	W	FT	R	†	1623	1651	1657	1689	MORG38
MOSTYN Andrew	SJ		FT	P		1663	1691	1692	1709	MOST02
MOSTYN John	SJ	N	FT	Y	#	1657	1693	..	1721	MOST04
MOSTYN Piers, Bt.	SJ	N	FT	Y	3	1687	1707	1715	1735	MOST06
PARRY Hugh	S	W	FT	L	#	..	..	1640	..	PARR08
PENNANT George	S	W	FT	D	3	..	..	1665	..	PENN02
PENNANT Thomas	SJ	W	FT	R	#§	1579	1613	1608	1638	PENN04
PENNANT Thomas	S	W	FT	D	#	1599	..	1625	..	PENN06
PUGH Henry	S		FT	R	*	..	..	1591	1592	PUGH02
PUGH William (Charles)	OSB	W	FT	E	#	..	1660	..	1680	PUGH14
ROBERTS John	S	W	FT	R		1673	..	1708	1753	ROBE12
WILLIAMS Edward	S	W	FT	R		1707	..	1731	1776	WILL14
WILLIAMS John	SJ	M	FT	Y	#3	1730	1750	1755	1801	WILL34
WILLIAMS John Morgan	S	W	FT	D	3	1761	..	1788	1816	WILL36
WILLIAMS Joseph (Francis)	CRT	M	FT	C		1729	1759	1760	1797	WILL38
WILLIAMS Peter	SJ	L	FT	Y	3	1689	1710	1719	1755	WILL50
WILLIAMS Peter	SJ	N	FT	Y	3	1717	1736	1744	1753	WILL52

GL—GLOUCESTERSHIRE

Name	Reg	D	Co	T	Notes	Born	Prof	Ordn	Died	Code
ALFIELD Thomas BL.	S	L	GL	D	#+†	1552	..	1581	1585	ALFI02
FOWLER Andrew	MIN		GL	Q		..	1587	1581	1594	FOWL02
HALL Henry	S		GL	R		1672	..	1700	1748	HALL06
HANSLEPP Roger	S	W	GL	D	#3	1642	..	1675	..	HANS08
HAWKINS James	OSB		GL	X		..	1705	..	1752	HAWK12

Name	Reg	D	Co	T	Notes	Born	Prof	Ordn	Died	Code
HEYDON Robert	S	L	GL	P	#	1683	..	1708	1718	HEYD02
KINN Edward	S	M	GL	D	#§	1625	..	1653	1711	KINN02
KINN John	S	M	GL	D	#§	..	..	1643	1683	KINN04
MARSHALL Joseph	SJ	W	GL	N		1683	1708	1715	1739	MARS22
MIDDLETON Charles	SJ		GL	Y	#§3	1660	1687	1692	1743	MIDD12
MORGAN Richard	SJ	N	GL	Y		1746	1766	1770	1814	MORG30
PEACH Edward	S	M	GL	T		1770	..	1795	1839	PEAC02
PEACH Henry	S	L	GL	D	3	1732	..	1759	1781	PEAC04
POYNTZ John	SJ		GL		#	1602	1625	..	1671	POYN06
RASTELL John	SJ		GL	N	13	1533	1568	1566	..	RAST02
SERGEANT Richard VEN.	S		GL	Q	#+‡	..	..	1583	1586	SERG08
SILVER Ferdinand	S	M	GL	P	3	1668	..	1696	1728	SILV02
SOMERSET Charles	S		GL	D	3	..	..	1655	..	SOME04
SOMERSET Thomas, Hon.	S		GL	R	34	..	..	1645	1670	SOME08
SOMERSET Thomas	S		GL	D	#4	..	..	1659	1670	SOME10
STANTON Henry Anthony or John	SJ		GL	R	#‡	1586	1616	1611	1635	STAN36
STOREY Richard	SJ		GL		2	..	1574	..	1600	STOR06
STRANGE Thomas	SJ		GL	R	#§123	1577	1600	1603	1639	STRA04
STRATFORD Arthur	S		GL	R		1557	..	1586	..	STRA14
WAKEMAN Edward	S		GL	R	#	1628	..	1660	..	WAKE06
WAKEMAN Joseph	SJ		GL	Y		1647	1665	1675	1720	WAKE10
WEBB Thomas	SJ	W	GL	Y		1575	1619	..	1658	WEBB10
WILLIAMS Thomas	S		GL	V	3	1577	..	1610	..	WILL58
YORK William or Thomas	SJ		GL	S	4	1581	1618	1604	1628	YORK04

GM—GLAMORGANSHIRE

Name	Reg	D	Co	T	Notes	Born	Prof	Ordn	Died	Code
CARNE Charles	S		GM	D	§3	1639	..	1663	1712	CARN04
MORGAN Roland	S		GM	Q	‡°	..	..	1583	..	MORG32
OWEN John	S	W	GM	R	+	1676	..	1711	1760	OWEN06
REES William	S		GM	R	#§	1605	..	1630	..	REES02
SEYES Roger	OFM		GM	R	#§2	1599	1623	1622	..	SEYE02
THOMAS John	S	N	GM	R	#	1702	..	1730	1754	THOM06
TURBERVILLE Anthony	OSB		GM	E		..	1664	..	1721	TURB02
TURBERVILLE Humphrey (Anselm)	OSB	W	GM	Z	#*2	1579	1604	..	1645	TURB08
WILLIAMS John	S	W	GM	L	§	1712	..	1735	1793	WILL32

GS—GERMAN STATES

Name	Reg	D	Co	T	Notes	Born	Prof	Ordn	Died	Code
COX Conrad	SJ		GS			1597	1619	..	1636	COXA03
FLORECKEN (Benedict)	OSB	L	GS	Z	*	..	..	..	1697	FLOR02
FRAMBACK Augustine	SJ		GS			1723	1744	..	1795	FRAM02
GEISSLER Luke	SJ		GS			1737	1755	..	1786	GEIS02
HORNE William	SJ		GS	Y	3	1736	1753	1762	1799	HORN12
KEMPER Herman	SJ	N	GS	Y		1745	1766	1774	1811	KEMP12
LATHAM Frederick (Alexius)	OSB		GS	X		..	1743	..	1761	LATH04
LEONARD Frederic or Ferdinand	SJ		GS			1728	1747	..	1764	LEON02
MASSER Nicholas	SJ		GS			1583	1619	..	..	MASS02
PELLENTZ James	SJ		GS			1727	1744	..	1800	PELL02
SCHNEIDER Theodore	SJ		GS			1703	1721	..	1764	SCHN02
SITTENSPERGER Matthias	SJ		GS		#	1719	1737	..	1775	SITT02
STEYNMEYER Ferdinand	SJ		GS		#	1720	1743	..	1786	STEY02
TURCK Augustus (Lawrence)	OSB		GS	X		..	1751	..	1769	TURC02
WAPPELER Wilhelm	SJ	N	GS			1711	1728	1739	1781	WAPP02

HA—HAMPSHIRE

Name	Reg	D	Co	T	Notes	Born	Prof	Ordn	Died	Code
AKERS James	S	L	HA	L	#°	1763	..	1788	1820	AKER02
BARLOW John	S	N	HA	R		1687	..	1712	1748	BARL10
BARR Thomas (Bernard)	OSB	M	HA	G		1740	1757	..	1823	BARR04
BELFIELD Henry	SJ	L	HA	R	#§	1578	1613	1608	1632	BELF02
BELFIELD John	S	L	HA	D	#§	..	..	1603	..	BELF04
BERRY Robert	S	L	HA	R	#	1686	..	1711	1736	BERR10
BETTS John (Philip)	S	L	HA	D		..	..	1726	1770	BETT08
BICKLEY Ralph	SJ		HA	R	‡1	1557	1597	1580	1619	BICK02
BLACKWELL William	SJ		HA	Y	1	1613	1640	..	1699	BLAC22

Name	Reg	D	Co	T	Notes	Born	Prof	Ordn	Died	Code
BRUNING Anthony	SJ	L	HA	Y	#	1636	1660	1668	1704	BRUN 08
BRUNING Anthony	SJ	L	HA	Y	3	1716	1733	1741	1776	BRUN 10
BRUNING Francis	SJ	M	HA	Y	#1	1620	1641	..	1680	BRUN 12
BRUNING Francis	SJ	N	HA	Y	#	1648	1670	1678	1714	BRUN 14
BRUNING George	SJ	L	HA	Y	3	1738	1756	1763	1802	BRUN 18
BRUNING Richard (Placid)	OSB	W	HA	E		..	1663	..	1719	BRUN 20
BRUNING Thomas	OSB	W	HA	E		1674	1696	..	1719	BRUN 22
CAREW (Henry of S.Mary)	OFM		HA	F	12	1640	1661	..	1683	CARE 02
CHADDERTON Henry	S	L	HA	R	#	1552	..	1601	..	CHAD 02
CHENEY Charles	S	L	HA	R	#1	1604	..	1636	..	CHEN 02
CHURCHER John	S	L	HA	V	34	..	..	1647	1692	CHUR 04
COOPER John	SJ		HA	Y		1610	1630	..	1646	COOP 12
COTTON Francis VEN.	SJ	W	HA	Y	#x	1595	1616	..	1679	COTT 16
CUFFAUD Alexander	SJ	W	HA	Y	#12	1602	1624	..	1674	CUFF 02
CUFFAUD Edward	SJ	L	HA	Y		1620	1641	..	1695	CUFF 04
CUFFAUD Godfrey	SJ	M	HA	R	#14	1608	1639	1633	1676	CUFF 06
CUFFAUD John	SJ	N	HA	Y	#	1668	1688	1697	1716	CUFF 10
CURTIS John	SJ	N	HA	D		1573	1612	1605	1651	CURT 02
CURTIS Peter	S	L	HA	R	#§	1595	..	1625	1673	CURT 04
CURTIS Peter	S	L	HA	D	3	1655	..	1681	1729	CURT 06
CURTIS Thomas	SJ	L	HA	D	#	1576	1605	1600	1657	CURT 08
DORMER Francis, Hon.	SJ	W	HA	Y	3	1717	1734	1743	1770	DORM 04
DORMER John Baptist, Hon.	SJ		HA	Y	3	1716	1734	1741	1743	DORM 06
DORMER William, Hon.	SJ	W	HA	Y		1696	1714	1723	1758	DORM 10
FISHWICK Richard	S	M	HA	D		1736	..	1773	1803	FISH 28
FIXER John	S		HA	Q	‡	1562	..	1587	..	FIXE 02
GIFFORD Wm.(Gabriel) ARCHBP.	OSB		HA	R	*‡	1558	1608	1581	1629	GIFF 26
GOLDSMITH Peter	S		HA	D	#	..	..	1609	..	GOLD 12
GOTHER John	S	L	HA	L	#1	1654	..	1676	1704	GOTH 02
HARRIS Francis	S	L	HA	D	°	1601	..	1625	..	HARR 12
HARRIS Richard (Swithun)	OSB	L	HA	E		1731	1755	..	1810	HARR 16
HEATH (Augustine)	OSB		HA	W	2	..	1620	..	1631	HEAT 02
HEWLETT William	OSB	N	HA	E		..	1699	..	1747	HEWL 02
HILL (Augustine of S.Monica)	OFM		HA	F	#123	1635	1652	1657	1702	HILL 02
HOOKER Thomas	S		HA	V	#	1572	..	1609	..	HOOK 02
HOUNSHILL (Martin)	S	L	HA	L		1720	..	1742	1783	HOUN 02
JONES John (Albert)	OFM		HA	F	123	1747	1764	1772	1793	JONE 27
KNAPP Joseph	S	L	HA	D		1747	..	1775	1817	KNAP 02
KNOWLES Gilbert	OSB	N	HA	G		1667	1692	1700	1734	KNOW 02
LAMB Anthony	SJ		HA	R	#	1592	1617	1617	1668	LAMB 01
LANE Bonaventure	SJ	N	HA	Y	13	1684	1706	1717	1750	LANE 02
LEGGE William	S	L	HA	Q	#	1561	..	1587	..	LEGG 02
LEWIS Theodore	SJ	L	HA	Y	#§13	1633	1654	1663	1707	LEWI 26
LINGARD John	S	N	HA	D		1771	..	1795	1851	LING 02
LISTER William	OP		HA	R	#	1561	1595	..	..	LIST 08
LOBB Emmanuel	SJ	L	HA	Y	#1	1593	1619	..	1671	LOBB 02
MANNOCK John	SJ	L	HA	R	#=34	1588	1624	1621	1651	MANN 18
MARTIN Francis	S		HA	D	#	1589	..	1614	..	MART 10
MASTERS John	S		HA	L	#§	1680	..	1702	1755	MAST 02
MATTHEWS Edward	S		HA	R	#§4	1704	..	1730	1782	MATT 06
MATTHEWS John	S	L	HA	D	#3	1659	..	1685	1744	MATT 12
MATTHEWS William	S	L	HA	D	3	1629	..	1663	1695	MATT 20
MIDDLETON Peter	SJ	M	HA	S	#4	1601	1629	1629	1665	MIDD 20
MILES Edward (of S.Anthony)	OFM		HA	F	13	1721	1738	1744	1751	MILE 01
MILES Thomas	S		HA	S	3	..	..	1603	..	MILE 08
MORLEY George	SJ		HA			1585	1610	..	1665	MORL 02
NICHOLS John (Thomas)	OP		HA	N		1754	1772	1775	1785	NICH 08
NORTON Benjamin	S	L	HA	R	4	1567	..	1591	1643	NORT 12
OWEN Thomas	SJ		HA		1	1557	1579	..	1618	OWEN 14
OXENBRIDGE Henry	SJ	L	HA	R	#=	1575	1605	1604	..	OXEN 02
PANSFORD John	SJ		HA	V	#3	1592	1621	1620	1668	PANS 02
PARKINS Francis	S	L	HA	D	3	1667	..	1693	1760	PARK 30
PITTS John	S		HA	R	‡	1560	..	1586	1616	PITT 06
PITTS William	S		HA	Q		..	..	1585	..	PITT 14
POTTINGER Simon	S		HA	D	#‡	..	..	1599	..	POTT 02
POUND John	S		HA		=3	..	..	1574	..	POUN 02

Name	Reg	D	Co	T	Notes	Born	Prof	Ordn	Died	Code
POYNTER William BP.	S	L	HA	D	*	1762	..	1786	1827	POYN02
PRICE Thomas	S		HA	R	#§	1603	..	1634	1635	PRIC18
READ Thomas	S	L	HA	D	‡	1606	..	1649	1669	READ06
RICHARDSON Edward	S		HA	V	#	1601		1627	..	RICH10
ROUGHT Walter	S	L	HA	D	#‡3	1608	..	1664	1688	ROUG02
SMITH Anthony	S	L	HA	L	#13	1620	..	1644	1685	SMIT03
SMITH James BP.	S	N	HA	D	#*	1645	..	1677	1711	SMIT26
SOUTHWELL John	SJ		HA	Y		1631	1649	..	..	SOUT18
TASBURGH Richard	SJ	M	HA	Y	3	1693	1710	1723	1735	TASB04
TICHBORNE Francis	S	L	HA	V	3	1584	..	1608	..	TICH02
TICHBORNE Henry	SJ		HA		1	1570	1587	..	1606	TICH04
TICHBORNE John	SJ	L	HA	Y	3	1694	1712	1725	1772	TICH06
TICHBORNE John Hermengild,Bt.	SJ	L	HA	R	#	1679	1700	1711	1748	TICH08
TICHBORNE Michael	SJ	N	HA	Y		1692	1712	1720	1751	TICH10
TICHBORNE Michael	S	L	HA	R		1725	..	1759	1767	TICH12
TICHBORNE Thomas VEN.	S	L	HA	R	+	1567	..	1592	1602	TICH14
WALL John (Alexius)	OSB		HA	X			1715	..	1730	WALL02
WARNFORD Peter	S.		HA	V	#*3	1582	..	1610	1657	WARN08
WELLS Charles	SJ	L	HA	Y		1702	1720	1733	1757	WELL04
WELLS Gilbert	SJ		HA	Y	#1	1713	1731	1739	1777	WELL08
WHEELER James	S	N	HA	P	3	1765	..	1789	1838	WHEE02
WHITE Richard	S	L	HA	Q		..	..	1587	..	WHIT46
WHITE Richard	S		HA	D	‡34	1539	..	1600	1612	WHIT48
WHITE Richard	S		HA	D	#	1603	..	1630	1687	WHIT50
WHITE Thomas	OP		HA	R	#	..	..	..	1694	WHIT58
WHITE William	S		HA			..	..	..	1640	WHIT64
WOODBERRY Gerard	S		HA	P	#	1715	..	1739	1783	WOOD14
WOODSON Leonard	SJ		HA	S	12	1591	1630	1612	1651	WOOD46

HR—HEREFORDSHIRE

Name	Reg	D	Co	T	Notes	Born	Prof	Ordn	Died	Code
ADDIS Joseph	S	L	HR	V		1742	..	1771	1821	ADDI02
BEDFORD William	S	W	HR	D	#3	1659	..	1694	1719	BEDF02
BERINGTON George	OSB	W	HR	V	12	1576	1600	..	1664	BERI04
BERINGTON John	SJ	N	HR	Y	#3	1673	1691	1699	1743	BERI06
BERINGTON John (Bernard)	OSB		HR	S	23	..	1607	1593	1639	BERI08
BERINGTON Joseph	S	L	HR	D		1743	..	1770	1827	BERI10
BERINGTON Simon	S	L	HR	D	#3	1680	..	1706	1755	BERI12
BLOUNT Francis	S		HR	R	#§	1612	..	1639	..	BLOU04
BODENHAM John	SJ	W	HR	Y	#13	1689	1709	1714	1750	BODE04
BODENHAM William	S		HR	L	#3	1630	..	1654	..	BODE06
BRETT John Bede	ODC		HR		1	1667	..	..	1711	BRET01
BRIDGES Richard	S	L	HR	R	#	1608	..	1632	1685	BRID04
BROME John	S		HR	Q		..	..	1584	..	BROM02
CADWALLADOR Roger VEN.	S	W	HR	V	#+1	1567	..	1593	1610	CADW04
CARPENTER William	S		HR	R	#°	1604	..	1630	..	CARP10
CASE Henry	S		HR	R	#	1609	..	1632	1633	CASE02
CASSEY (Anselm)	OSB	W	HR	G		1610	1626	..	1671	CASS04
CLARK Christopher	S	W	HR	V	#1	1607	..	1642	1677	CLAR10
CLARK Edward	S		HR	R	#	1606	..	1633	..	CLAR12
CLARK John (Anthony of S.Jn.)	OFM		HR	F	12	1593	1618	..	1673	CLAR23
ELLIOT William	S	W	HR	R	#	1610	..	1636	1678	ELLI06
HALL John	S	W	HR	R	#§	1636	..	1662	..	HALL14
HALSEY George	S	L	HR	R		1751	..	1775	1834	HALS04
HARPER William	S		HR	D	#	1572	..	1604	..	HARP04
HOSKINS Anthony	SJ		HR			1568	1593	..	1615	HOSK02
INGRAM John BL.	S	N	HR	R	#+	1565	..	1589	1594	INGR08
KEMBLE Francis (Simon Stock)	ODC		HR	R	13	1652	1671	1676	1720	KEMB02
KEMBLE George (Francis)	ODC		HR	R	1	1633	1652	..	1711	KEMB04
KEMBLE John ST.	S	W	HR	D	#+	1599	..	1625	1679	KEMB06
KEMBLE Roger (John Joseph)	ODC		HR		°	1640	1659	..	..	KEMB08
KEMBLE Walter (William)	OSB	W	HR	G		..	1620	..	1633	KEMB10
KEMBLE William (Augustine)	OFM	M	HR	F	13	1745	1761	1770	1801	KEMB12
LECHMERE Edmund	S		HR	D	#‡1	1586	..	1622	1640	LECH02
LEWIS Michael George	OSB	N	HR	G	°14	1735	1752	..	1804	LEWI18
LOCKHART Thomas	SJ		HR	Y		1672	1693	1702	1744	LOCK06

Name	Reg	D	Co	T	Notes	Born	Prof	Ordn	Died	Code
LOOP George (Edmund)	ODC	L	HR	R		1648	1667	..	1716	LOOP02
MILBURN James	S		HR	D	3	1641	..	1667	..	MILB02
MONINGTON Thomas	OSB	W	HR	G		..	1610	..	1642	MONI02
PARLOR John (Leo of M.Magdn.)	OFM		HR	F	123	1664	1684	1688	1692	PARL02
PHILIPS (Aldhelm)	OSB		HR	W		..	1620	..	1636	PHIL02
PHILIPS William	S		HR	D	#°	..	..	1610	..	PHIL28
POWELL John	S	W	HR	D	#	1614	..	..	1667	POWE12
PRICE James	S	L	HR	D	3	..	..	1667	1697	PRIC06
PRICE John	S	N	HR	R		1681	..	1708	1738	PRIC12
PRICE Philip (Pacificus)	OFM		HR	F	123	1643	1663	1671	1706	PRIC14
PRICE Thomas	S	M	HR	V		1763	..	1787	1831	PRIC20
PRICHARD William	S		HR	L	3	..	..	1734	1734	PRIC46
PROBERT Hugh or John	S		HR	R		1546	..	1581	..	PROB04
PROSSER Philip	S	L	HR	R	#	1635	..	1670	..	PROS02
RAVENHILL John	S	W	HR	R	#1	1625	..	1652	..	RAVE02
RAVENHILL Richard (Angelus)	OFM		HR	F	134	1726	1743	1752	1791	RAVE04
ROBERTS Francis	SJ		HR	Y		1611	1637	..	1652	ROBE02
ROSS John	S	L	HR	R		1647	..	1680	1689	ROSS06
SCRIVENER Hugh	SJ		HR		4	..	..	..	1593	SCRI04
SCUDAMORE Benedict	S	M	HR	D	#	1599	..	1624	..	SCUD02
SCUDAMORE John	S		HR	R	°1	1563	..	1592	..	SCUD06
SEBORNE William	S		HR	Q	=	..	..	1583	..	SEBO02
SLAUGHTER Edward	SJ		HR	Y		1655	1673	1682	1729	SLAU02
SLAUGHTER George	S		HR	L		..	..	1689	1741	SLAU04
SLAUGHTER James	S	M	HR	D		1712	..	1741	1781	SLAU06
SMITH Richard	S		HR	D	#§	..	..	1624	..	SMIT57
SOMERSET Henry	S		HR	D	#3	1671	..	1697	..	SOME06
STANDISH George	S	W	HR	V	#3	..	..	1661	..	STAN02
STREET Thomas	S	W	HR	D	#	1599	..	1624	1670	STRE04
TAYLOR Augustine	S	L	HR	R		1644	..	1669	1694	TAYL08
VAUGHAN Thomas	SJ	W	HR	D	x	1606	1632	1627	1675	VAUG12
WIGMORE Richard	SJ	W	HR	Y	#1	1593	1617	..	1677	WIGM02
WIGMORE William	SJ		HR	Y	#	1599	1624	..	1665	WIGM04
WILLIAMS (Pacificus of S.Fra)	OFM	W	HR	F	123	1618	1638	1642	1705	WILL46
WILLIAMS (Pacificus of S.Jn)	OFM		HR	F	12	1658	1676	..	1706	WILL48
WOODFEN Nicholas VEN.	S	L	HR	Q	#+	..	..	1581	1586	WOOD22
WOODBURN John	S		HR	R	#§	1607	..	1634	..	WOOD30

HT—HERTFORDSHIRE

Name	Reg	D	Co	T	Notes	Born	Prof	Ordn	Died	Code
EAST Alban	S		HT	V	#3	1595	..	1618	1671	EAST00
EAST Francis	SJ		HT	Y	#	1606	1626	..	1658	EAST01
EAST Richard	S		HT	D	#	1605	..	1631	..	EAST08
FORSTER John	SJ		HT	Y		1618	1637	..	1693	FORS08
HINDE George	S		HT	D	#3	1684	..	1710	1752	HIND06
KEIGHTLEY William	S		HT	D	3	1667	..	1692	1696	KEIG02
POTIER John	S	L	HT	D	#	1758	..	1783	1823	POTI02

HU—HUNTINGDONSHIRE

Name	Reg	D	Co	T	Notes	Born	Prof	Ordn	Died	Code
BLOODSWORTH Thomas	S	N	HU	V		1757	..	1781	1815	BLOO02
BROUGHTON Richard	S	M	HU	Q	#†	1561	..	1592	1635	BROU02
LE HUNT John	SJ	N	HU	Y	#	1675	1693	1703	1759	LEHU04
LLEWELLYN Edward (Augustine)	OSB	W	HU	E	†1	1621	1658	..	1711	LLEW02
SWINBURNE Robert	S		HU	Q	†	..	..	1583	..	SWIN08
VINTER Robert	S	N	HU	D	#†134	1637	..	1674	1706	VINT02
WAFERER Andrew	S	L	HU	V	#x§=4	1576	..	1603	1648	WAFE02
WINTER William (Benedict)	OSB		HU	G		..	1692	1707	1736	WINT04

IR—IRELAND

Name	Reg	D	Co	T	Notes	Born	Prof	Ordn	Died	Code
(Anselm of S.Simon Stock)	CAR	L	IR		*8	..	..	..	..	ANSE02
ARCHBOLD Richard	SJ		IR	Y	°23	1713	1731	1739	..	ARCH02
ARMOUR (Luke)	OP	L	IR		*	..	..	..	1764	ARMO02
ARTHUR (James)	OP	L	IR		*7	..	..	..	..	ARTH02
ASHTON John	SJ		IR	Y	3	1742	1759	1765	1815	ASHT08

Name	Reg	D	Co	T	Notes	Born	Prof	Ordn	Died	Code
(Augustine of Dublin)	CAP		IR		4	..	..	..	1748	AUGU02
BAKER Bernard	SJ	L	IR	Y	#34	1698	1721	1734	1773	BAKE08
BARNEWALL Anthony	S		IR			..	..	..	1778	BARN27
BARNEWALL John	S	L	IR			..	..	..	1782	BARN28
BARNEWALL Patrick	SJ	N	IR	Z		1709	..	..	1762	BARN32
BERMINGHAM Nicholas	SJ		IR		#	1721	1740	..	..	BERM02
(Bernard of S.Matthew)	CAR	L	IR	Z		..	..	..	1661	BERN01
BRADSHAIGH Edward (Elias)	ODC	L	IR	B	#	..	1619	1621	1652	BRAD12
BRENNAN John ? (James)	OP	L	IR		#*	..	..	..	1748	BREN00
BRENNAN Luke	S		IR	S		..	..	1772	..	BREN01
BRENNAN Thomas	SJ	M	IR	R	1	1708	1726	..	1773	BREN02
BROWN Christopher	S		IR		8	..	..	..	..	BROW08
BROWN (Francis Joseph)	CAP	L	IR			..	..	..	1675	BROW12
BROWN Ignatius	SJ		IR			..	..	..	1679	BROW18
BROWN (Mark)	OFM		IR		*7	..	..	..	..	BROW25
BRULLAGHAN Patrick BP.	OP	L	IR	R	#*13	1705	..	1730	1760	BRUL02
BURKE Jeffrey MacHugho	S	L	IR		*8	..	..	..	..	BURK04
BURKE (Theobald)	OFM	L	IR		*7	..	..	..	..	BURK06
BURKE William	SJ		IR	Y	3	1711	1731	1739	1746	BURK08
BUTLER (James)	OP	L	IR		*8	..	..	..	..	BUTL07
BUTLER John, Ld. Caher	SJ	W	IR	Y	#*3	1727	1745	1753	1786	BUTL13
BYRNE Denis	OFM	W	IR	N		..	..	1743	1779	BYRN02
BYRNE Edmund	OSA		IR		*7	..	..	..	..	BYRN04
CAHILL John	S	L	IR	Z	*8	..	..	..	..	CAHI02
CALLAGHAN Richard	SJ		IR	S	1	1728	..	..	1807	CALL02
CALLANAN (Hugh)	OP	L	IR		*7	..	..	..	..	CALL04
CARON Redmond or Raymond	OFM		IR	N		1605	..	..	1666	CARO04
CARROLL Anthony	SJ		IR	Y		1722	1744	1754	1794	CARR02
CARROLL James	SJ		IR	Y	3	1717	1741	1747	1756	CARR04
CARROLL William	OSA		IR		*7	..	..	..	..	CARR08
CARY Henry (Placid), Hon.	OSB		IR	E	*°13	1618	1641	1643	1653	CARY08
CASEY Matthew	S	L	IR			1732	..	..	1808	CASE12
CAVERLEY (James)	OFM	M	IR		*7	..	..	..	..	CAVE02
CLARK John	SJ		IR	Y	1	1662	1681	1689	1723	CLAR22
CLAY (Daniel of S.Francis)	OFM	L	IR		*4	..	..	..	1681	CLAY02
COEN Michael	S	L	IR	P		..	..	..	1810	COEN02
COLE (Anthony)	OFM	L	IR		#*7	..	..	..	..	COLE01
COLEMAN (Columbanus)	ODC		IR		4	..	..	..	1755	COLE14
COLEMAN Nicholas	ODC		IR		8	..	..	..	..	COLE16
COLLINS William	OP	L	IR		2	1622	1649	..	1699	COLL34
COMBERFORD Gerard	SJ	M	IR	Y		1632	1651	1657	..	COMB02
CONNELL Michael	SJ		IR	Y	3	1688	1707	1715	1726	CONN02
CONRY (Maurice)	OFM		IR	R	*4	..	..	..	1669	CONR02
CORBY Ralph BL.	SJ	N	IR	V	#+	1598	1625	..	1644	CORB18
CORBY Robert	SJ		IR	S	#3	1596	1626	1624	1637	CORB20
DELANEY (Dominic)	OP	L	IR		*	..	..	..	1763	DELA01
DELANEY James	S	L	IR	T	1	1768	..	1798	1847	DELA02
DEVEREUX John	S	L	IR	T	1	1764	..	1796	1838	DEVE02
DILLON (George) Hon.	OFM	L	IR		*7	..	..	..	..	DILL01
DILLON Gerald (Vincent)	OP	N	IR		x	..	..	..	1651	DILL02
DILLON (James)	OP	L	IR		*8	..	..	..	..	DILL03
DILLON Richard	S	L	IR	S		..	..	1742	1780	DILL04
DONELLAN Patrick	OP	L	IR			..	..	..	1794	DONE02
DORNAN (Hugh)	OFM		IR		*7	..	..	..	..	DORN02
DOWDALL (James)	OP	L	IR		*8	..	..	..	..	DOWD01
DOWDALL (Jn.Bp.of Glaspistle)	CAP	L	IR		x12	1625	1648	..	1710	DOWD02
DOWDALL John	OSA		IR		*	..	..	..	1739	DOWD03
DOWSE (Francis Dominic)	OP		IR		23	1688	1708	1713	1755	DOWS02
DOYLE William	SJ	N	IR		12	1716	1734	..	1785	DOYL04
DUFF (Matthew)	OFM		IR		#*7	..	..	..	..	DUFF01
DUNGAN Joseph	S	L	IR		3	1748	..	1772	1797	DUNG02
DUNN Lawrence	S	L	IR		8	..	..	..	..	DUNN08
EUSTACE John Chetwode	S	M	IR	Z	*13	1764	..	1795	1815	EUST02
EVERARD (Bernardine)	CAP		IR		8	..	..	..	..	EVER02
EVERARD John (Bernardine)	OFM	L	IR		*7	..	..	..	..	EVER09
EVERARD Patrick ARCHBP.	S	N	IR	Z	*	1753	..	1783	1820	EVER12

Name	Reg	D	Co	T	Notes	Born	Prof	Ordn	Died	Code
FALLON Thomas (James)	OP	L	IR		1	1752	..	..	1800	FALL02
FARRELL (Patrick)	OP	L	IR		*	..	..	..	1764	FARR05
FINGLAS Robert	SJ	N	IR		#	1606	1647	..	1663	FING02
FINN (James)	CAR	L	IR		*8	..	..	..	..	FINN01
FINN John	S		IR	S		..	..	1744	..	FINN02
FITZGERALD (Francis)	OFM		IR		*4	..	..	..	1666	FITZ00
FITZGERALD (John)	OFM	L	IR		*7	..	..	..	..	FITZ01
FITZMORRIS (James S.Joseph)	CAR	L	IR	Z	8	..	..	..	..	FITZ15
FITZMORRIS (Thomas S.Elias)	CAR	L	IR	Z	8	..	..	..	..	FITZ16
FITZSIMON Henry	SJ		IR	N	‡34	1566	1592	1597	1645	FITZ17
FLYNN Thomas	S	M	IR		1	1720	..	..	1797	FLYN02
FLYNN Thomas	OFM	W	IR		8	..	..	..	..	FLYN04
FRENCH James (Thomas)	OP	L	IR		*8	..	..	..	..	FREN04
FURLONG Pierce	OP		IR		*7	..	..	..	..	FURL02
GAFFEY Daniel	OFM	L	IR	N		..	..	1773	1815	GAFF02
GAHAN William	OSA		IR	N		1732	1748	1755	1804	GAHA02
GEARNON (Anthony)	OFM	L	IR		*7	..	..	..	..	GEAR01
GIBBON Henry	OSA	L	IR		*7	..	..	..	..	GIBB03
GORMLEY Patrick	OP		IR		4	..	..	..	1722	GORM02
GRACE Patrick	S	L	IR	S	#	..	..	1722	1778	GRAC02
GREEN Christopher	SJ		IR	R		1629	1658	1653	1697	GREE08
GREEN Martin	SJ		IR	Y		1616	1637	..	1667	GREE31
GRIMSHAW John	S	L	IR		*8	..	..	..	..	GRIM14
HOLYWOOD Christopher	SJ		IR		2	1559	1582	..	1626	HOLY02
HUSSEY Thomas BP.	S	L	IR	Z	*1	1745	..	1769	1803	HUSS08
(John of S.Augustine)	OSA		IR		*7	..	..	..	..	JOHN03
KEARNEY (Christopher Cashel)	CAP		IR			1582	..	..	1656	KEAR01
KEARNEY Francis	OFM		IR	N	12	1667	1689	1694	1747	KEAR02
KELLY (Dominic)	OP	L	IR		*7	..	..	..	..	KELL11
KELLY Francis	OSA		IR		*7	..	..	..	..	KELL14
KELLY John Joseph	SJ	N	IR	Y	#°3	1743	1762	1769	1808	KELL16
KENNEDY William (Joseph), Bt.	OSB		IR	E	§	1661	1692	1694	1738	KENN04
KIRWAN Walter Black	S	L	IR	N	*°	..	..	1775	1805	KIRW02
LYNCH (William)	OFM	L	IR		*7	..	..	..	..	LYNC04
MacCARTHY Daniel	S	L	IR		7	..	..	..	..	MACC06
MacCARTHY James	OSA	L	IR		*7	..	..	..	..	MACC07
McCORRY (Cyprian of Armagh)	CAP		IR		8	..	..	..	..	MACC08
MacDONELL Charles (Francis)	OFM	L	IR	F	1234	1770	1790	1800	1843	MACD06
MacGEOGHEGAN Arthur	OP	L	IR		+3	..	..	1624	1633	MACG02
MacGEOGHEGAN (Peter)	OFM	L	IR		*7	..	..	..	..	MACG03
MADDEN John	OSA		IR		7*	..	..	..	..	MADD01
MAGEE David	SJ	W	IR	Y	#3	1737	1755	1762	1768	MAGE02
MAGINN Patrick	S	L	IR		*7	..	..	..	..	MAGI02
MAGRUAIRK (Francis)	OFM		IR	R	°4	..	..	..	1665	MAGR02
MAHON Thomas	OFM	L	IR		8	..	..	..	..	MAHO02
MALONE John Baptist	S	L	IR		8	..	..	..	..	MALO02
MANSELL (Michael)	OFM		IR	R	*7	..	..	..	..	MANS01
MARTIN Francis	OSA		IR			1652	..	..	1722	MART11
MATTHEWS (Patrick)	OP		IR		*7	..	..	..	..	MATT13
MEEHAN Charles VEN.	OFM		IR		#+1	1639	..	..	1679	MEEH02
MOLONEY John Baptist	S	L	IR		8	..	..	..	..	MOLO02
MOORE Thomas	OP	L	IR			..	..	..	1778	MOOR12
MORAN (James)	OP	L	IR		*8	..	..	..	..	MORA02
MORRIS (Andrew)	OP		IR		*8	..	..	..	..	MORR01
MORRIS James	SJ	L	IR	Y	#	1674	1699	1708	1715	MORR10
NARY Cornelius	S		IR		*	1660	..	1682	1738	NARY02
NASH (Anthony)	OFM		IR		*7	..	..	..	..	NASH02
NOLAN James	S	L	IR	P	1	1723	..	..	1779	NOLA02
NUGENT Lavalin (Francis)	CAP		IR			1569	1592	1595	1635	NUGE06
NUGENT (Luke of Meath)	CAP		IR			..	..	..	1724	NUGE10
NUGENT (Peter of Meath)	CAP		IR			..	..	..	1691	NUGE12
O'BRIEN Peter	SJ		IR	Y	3	1735	1754	1759	1807	OBRI02
O'CONNELL (Terence)	OP	L	IR		*	..	..	..	1668	OCON01
O'CONOR Charles	S	L	IR	R	3	1764	..	1791	1828	OCON04
O'DALY Daniel (Chris'er) ABP.	OP	L	IR		*3	1595	..	1627	1662	ODAL02
O'FARRELL (Bernardine)	CAP		IR			..	..	..	1669	OFAR02

Name	Reg	D	Co	T	Notes	Born	Prof	Ordn	Died	Code
O'FARREL (Lawrence)	OP		IR		*8	..	..	..	..	OFAR04
O'GRADY (Patrick of Cork)	CAP	L	IR			..	..	..	1691	OGRA02
O'HEYN (Cornelius)	OP	L	IR	R	4	..	..	..	1686	OHEY02
O'LEARY Arthur	CAP	L	IR	Z	*3	1729	..	1756	1802	OLEA02
O'PHELAN James	OP	L	IR		*	..	..	..	1705	OPHE02
OSTE (Augustine)	OSA		IR		*7	..	..	..	..	OSTE02
O'SULLIVAN (John Baptist)	OP	L	IR		*7	..	..	..	..	OSUL02
(Patrick of S.Brigit)	ODC	L	IR		*7	..	..	..	..	PATR02
(Patrick of S.Columba)	ODC	L	IR			..	..	..	1657	PATR04
(Patrick of St Columba)	OFM	L	IR		*1	1606	..	..	..	PATR06
PHELAN William	S		IR	D		..	..	1779	..	PHEL02
PLUNKETT Oliver ARCHBP. ST.	S	L	IR	R	*+	1629	..	1654	1681	PLUN02
PLUNKETT (Oliver of Dublin)	CAP	L	IR			..	..	..	1748	PLUN03
POWELL (Mansuetus)	OSB		IR	Z	*	..	1621	..	1664	POWE16
POWER Edmund	SJ	M	IR	Y	34	1736	1754	1761	1779	POWE28
POWER James	SJ	L	IR		2	1725	1741	..	1788	POWE30
PRENDERGAST Peter	S	L	IR			..	..	..	1792	PREN02
RIDER Nicholas (Joseph)	ODC		IR		12	1600	1631	..	1682	RIDE02
ROBINSON Gerard	S	L	IR	S		1729	..	1754	1799	ROBI20
ROBSON Christopher	SJ		IR	Y	#	1619	1647	1657	1685	ROBS02
ROCHE (Philip)	OFM	L	IR		*7	..	..	..	..	ROCH02
SALE Joseph	S		IR	D	#	1706	..	1736	1750	SALE08
SALL (Nicholas)	OFM	L	IR		*7	..	..	..	..	SALL01
SHAW Gerard	S	L	IR	S		..	..	..	1780	SHAW06
SHAW Patrick	S	L	IR			..	..	..	1742	SHAW14
SKERRETT John	OSA	L	IR		14	1620	..	..	1688	SKER02
SLINGSBY Francis	SJ		IR	R	#‡	1612	1641	1641	1642	SLIN02
SMITH Gregory	OSA		IR		*7	..	..	..	..	SMIT22
STAFFORD Bernard	SJ	M	IR	Y	#13	1713	1735	1741	1788	STAF06
TALBOT Peter, ARCHBP.	S	N	IR	R	*x	1620	..	..	1680	TALB22
TALBOT (Thomas)	OFM	L	IR		*7	..	..	..	..	TALB27
TAYLOR Stephen (Joseph)	OP	L	IR		*8	..	..	..	..	TAYL41
TRENT (Henry of S.Teresa)	CAR	L	IR		°4	1652	1669	..	1701	TREN01
VANDERBERG	CAR	L	IR		7	..	..	..	..	VAND02
WAFER (Simon)	OFM	L	IR		*7	..	..	..	..	WAFE01
WALSH John	SJ	N	IR	Y	3	1700	1720	1728	1773	WALS04
WALSH (Peter)	OFM	L	IR	N	13	1614	..	1639	1688	WALS06
WARHAM Philip	S		IR	D		1722	..	1747	1748	WARH10
WELDON Thomas	SJ	N	IR			1714	1731	..	1776	WELD10
WELDON Thomas	S	N	IR	D	°	1761	..	1788	..	WELD12
WHITE Francis	SJ	L	IR		2	1610	1630	..	1697	WHIT28

IT—ITALIAN STATES

Name	Reg	D	Co	T	Notes	Born	Prof	Ordn	Died	Code
AYROLI John Baptist	SJ		IT	Y	#3	1652	1670	1682	..	AYRO02
BALDI Angelus Dominic	SJ	L	IT	Y		..	..	1683	..	BALD02
BELASYSE Chas.Ld.Fauconberg	S	L	IT	P		1750	..	1775	1815	BELA02
BUSINO Orazio	S	L	IT		*7	..	..	..	..	BUSI02
FERMOR Henry	S		IT	R		1756	..	..	1825	FERM04
FERMOR James	OP		IT	R		1757	1780	..	1833	FERM06
GALLI Anthony	SJ	L	IT		#12	1623	1645	..	1703	GALL02
GATTI	S	L	IT		*7	..	..	..	..	GATT02
LYCETT Francis	S	M	IT	T		1776	..	1800	1853	LYCE02
PIAZZA Hieronymo Bartolomeo	OP		IT		*°	..	..	..	1741	PIAZ02
PIAZZI Giuseppe	CRT		IT		*	1746	..	..	1826	PIAZ04
PORTER Joseph Thomas	S		IT	R	°	1772	..	1795	..	PORT16
RUGA Bartholomew	SJ	L	IT		#2	1634	1650	..	1715	RUGA02
STUART Henry Benedict CARD.	S		IT	R	*	1725	..	1748	1807	STUA01
VALENTINE Joseph	S	M	IT	R		1713	..	1736	1761	VALE02
VEZZOSI James	S		IT	R	#	1717	..	1740	1774	VEZZ02
VEZZOSI Joseph	SJ		IT	R	#	1720	1743	1743	1772	VEZZ04
VEZZOSI Stephen	S	L	IT	R	#	1716	..	1744	1781	VEZZ06
VISCONTI Hermes Mary	SJ		IT	Y		1650	1665	1678	..	VISC02
WYNDHAM Philip Bernard	S	L	IT	R		1732	..	1756	1825	WYND02

Name	Reg	D	Co	T	Notes	Born	Prof	Ordn	Died	Code
			KT—KENT							
APPLETON Thomas	SJ	L	KT	R	#	1596	1622	1622	1662	APPL18
BEAKE John	S	L	KT	D	*§	..	..	1587	..	BEAK02
BIX (John Ev of S.Hubert)	OFM		KT	F	1234	1658	1676	1685	1703	BIXA04
BOSVILLE John	S		KT	V	#134	1567	..	1592	1631	BOSV02
BRAMSTON Thomas	S		KT	Q	‡	1540	..	1585	1606	BRAM06
BROWN Peter	S		KT	P		1730	..	1757	..	BROW28
BUSBY John	S	L	KT	D	°	1762	..	1786	..	BUSB08
CHAPMAN John	SJ	L	KT	Y	#	1670	1692	1703	1729	CHAP22
CLARK Gabriel	S		KT	R	#4	1610	..	1635	1644	CLAR17
CLARK Thomas	S		KT	Q	°4	1555	..	1590	1610	CLAR28
COKE William	S		KT	R	#	1600	..	1624	..	COKE04
COLLIER Edward William	S		KT	D	°	..	..	1606	..	COLL04
COLLINS William	SJ	M	KT	Y		1650	1669	1678	1704	COLL36
CONYERS Christopher	SJ	L	KT	Y		1669	1688	1697	1730	CONY04
CONYERS George	SJ	L	KT	Y	1	1644	1665	1676	1711	CONY08
CONYERS John	SJ		KT	R	#134	1675	1694	1708	1724	CONY10
CONYERS Leonard or Louis	SJ	L	KT	Y	1	1671	1690	1699	1745	CONY12
CONYERS Thomas	SJ		KT	Y	#13	1664	1685	1694	1721	CONY18
DARELL James	SJ	L	KT	Y	3	1707	1723	1731	1785	DARE02
DARELL John	SJ	N	KT	Y	3	1705	1722	1731	1768	DARE04
DOBSON Robert (Elphege)	OSB		KT	X		..	1709	..	1750	DOBS04
DRYLAND Christopher	SJ		KT	D	#2	..	1603	1582	..	DRYL02
DUKE Edmund VEN.	S	N	KT	R	+§	1563	..	1589	1590	DUKE02
EDMUNDS (Bernard)	OSB		KT	W		..	1614	..	1636	EDMU06
FAULKNER Stephen	SJ	N	KT	S	3	1621	1650	1647	1670	FAUL08
FILCOCK Roger VEN.	SJ		KT	V	#+3	..	1600	1597	1601	FILC02
FINCH Thomas	S		KT	S	°3	..	..	1605	..	FINC04
GIBBON (Benedict)	OSB	L	KT	X		..	1673	..	1723	GIBB02
GREEN Thomas	SJ		KT	Y		1608	1627	..	1636	GREE46
HART John	S	M	KT	R	#§	1627	..	1654	1695	HART06
HART Nicholas	SJ	W	KT	R	#‡=12	1579	1604	1603	1650	HART12
HAWKINS John (Augustine)	OSB		KT	G	°	1745	1761	..	1804	HAWK14
INGHAM Walter	S		KT	Q		..	..	1591	..	INGH06
JENKIN (John)	OP		KT		§	1637	1660	1662	1663	JENK02
KENNET Samuel (Bartholomew)	OSB		KT	R	#§4	1563	1603	1589	1635	KENN14
KINGSLEY Thomas	SJ	L	KT	Y	#‡4	1650	1676	1684	1696	KING16
KNATCHBULL John	SJ		KT	S	#34	1571	1618	1602	1631	KNAT02
LEE John	SJ	W	KT	Y		1657	1678	1686	1687	LEEA12
LONE John	OSB		KT	G		1599	1620	..	1641	LONE02
LOVELACE Thomas	S		KT	R		1561	..	1586	1589	LOVE02
MOLYNEUX (Thomas)	OP		KT			1630	1658	1661	1708	MOLY18
NICHOLS Richard	S	L	KT	P	†	..	..	1650	..	NICH10
NORRIS Augustine (Ignatius)	CRT		KT	C		1740	1766	1767	1783	NORR04
PETIT Cyriac or Charles	SJ		KT	Y	#3	1672	1697	1704	1710	PETI02
PETT Henry	S		KT	R	#‡1	1570	..	1598	..	PETT02
PETT Robert	S		KT	R		..	..	1601	..	PETT04
PORDAGE William	SJ	M	KT	Y	#1	1651	1671	1680	1736	PORD02
RICH Francis	OSB	N	KT	G		1670	1692	1698	1740	RICH02
ROPER Thomas	SJ	M	KT	Y		1655	1673	1683	1716	ROPE02
STRANSHAM George	S		KT	Q	#†=	..	..	1585	..	STRA10
THOMPSON John	SJ		KT	V		..	1598	1598	1616	THOM24
THOMPSON Thomas	SJ		KT	Y	#	1614	1632	..	1680	THOM44
THUNDER Henry	SJ		KT	R	12	1575	1599	..	1638	THUN02
TILSEN Thomas	S	L	KT	L	#†	1622	..	1649	1688	TILD02
TODD Henry	SJ	W	KT	Y	13	1666	1687	1696	1712	TODD08
VINCENT William	S		KT	V	§1	1576	..	1602	1660	VINC04
WARREN Henry	SJ	M	KT	Y	#	1635	1652	1661	1702	WARR12
WARREN William	S		KT	R	#§	1631	..	1656	1701	WARR20
WATSON Walter	S		KT	R	#	1621	..	1649	..	WATS06
WESTBROOKE William (Maurus)	OSB		KT	X	#	..	1726	..	1774	WEST06
WESTON William	SJ	L	KT	R	#‡	1550	1575	..	1615	WEST22
WHETENHALL Henry	SJ		KT	Y	3	1694	1713	1722	1745	WHET02
WHETENHALL James	S		KT	R		1702	..	1726	1773	WHET04

Name	Reg	D	Co	T	Notes	Born	Prof	Ordn	Died	Code
WINDSOR John	S	L	KT	R		1590	..	1616	..	WIND06
WREST Thomas (Louis of S.Aug)	OFM		KT	F	12	1596	1631	..	1669	WRES02
WYBURNE Henry	OSB	L	KT	E		..	1723	..	1769	WYBU02

LA—LANCASHIRE

Name	Reg	D	Co	T	Notes	Born	Prof	Ordn	Died	Code
ADAMSON John	S	N	LA	V	3	1580	..	1604	..	ADAM11
AINSCOUGH Edward	S		LA	R	1	1675	..	1701	..	AINS06
AINSWORTH (Ralph)	OSB	W	LA	W		1763	1784	1788	1814	AINS08
ALBIN Robert or Richard	SJ		LA	Y		1630	1651	1660	1667	ALBI02
ALCOCK William (Jerome)	OSB		LA	X		1775	1792	..	1817	ALCO04
ALLEN William CARD.	S		LA	N	‡*	1532	..	1565	1594	ALLE12
ALLERTON Matthew (Denis)	OSB	N	LA	X		1754	1771	..	1829	ALLE16
ALMOND James	S	N	LA	R		1646	..	1669	1719	ALMO02
ALMOND John ST.	S	L	LA	R	#+	1567	..	1601	1612	ALMO06
ANDERTON Beuno	S	N	LA	R	#	1643	..	1668	1723	ANDE14
ANDERTON Christopher	OSB		LA	G	#	1607	1624	..	1653	ANDE18
ANDERTON Christopher	SJ		LA	Y		1615	1636	1645	1695	ANDE19
ANDERTON Edward	S	N	LA	R	#	1623	..	1648	1683	ANDE22
ANDERTON Francis	SJ	N	LA	R	3	1665	1685	1694	1723	ANDE22
ANDERTON Francis (Bede)	OSB	M	LA	G		1740	1757	..	1779	ANDE24
ANDERTON James	OSB	N	LA	G	4	1600	1623	..	1646	ANDE28
ANDERTON John	S		LA	R	#	1618	..	1642	..	ANDE32
ANDERTON John (Michael)	OSB		LA	X	°	1690	1709	1715	1742	ANDE33
ANDERTON Lawrence	SJ	N	LA	R	#†	1577	1604	..	1643	ANDE34
ANDERTON Robert	S	L	LA	R	#	1625	..	1651	1685	ANDE40
ANDERTON Robert (Celestine)	OSB	N	LA	D	2	1619	1650	1646	1697	ANDE44
ANDERTON Robert (Placid)	OSB		LA	E	#4	..	1635	1639	1677	ANDE47
ANDERTON Roger	S		LA	R	#	1621	..	1645	1696	ANDE48
ANDERTON Thomas	OSB	N	LA	E		1611	1630	1636	1671	ANDE52
ANDERTON Thomas	S	N	LA	R		1675	..	1702	1741	ANDE54
ANDERTON Thurstan	S	N	LA		3	..	..	1678	1697	ANDE56
ANDERTON William	S	L	LA	V	x	..	..	1637	..	ANDE58
ANDERTON William	SJ	W	LA	Y		1754	1806	1780	1823	ANDE60
ANDERTON William (Placid)	OSB	M	LA	E		1673	1696	..	1718	ANDE62
ANDERTON (William of S.Ant'y)	OFM	N	LA	F	12	1601	1628	1634	1672	ANDE64
APPLETON Thomas (Anselm)	OSB	N	LA	W		1766	1788	1790	1842	APPL19
ARROWSMITH Edmund	S		LA	Q	4	1563	..	1587	1601	ARRO01
ARROWSMITH Edmund Brian ST.	SJ	N	LA	D	#+	1585	1624	1612	1628	ARRO02
ASHTON Arthur (Alban)	OSB		LA	E		1680	1699	..	1748	ASHT02
ASHTON Richard (Joseph)	OSB		LA	G		1667	1688	..	1700	ASHT12
ASHTON Richard or Jn (Placid)	OSB	M	LA	E		1708	1725	..	1761	ASHT14
ASPINALL Edward	SJ	M	LA	Y	#°3	1678	1696	1705	1732	ASP102
ASPINALL Henry	SJ	M	LA	Y	#3	1715	1734	1747	1784	ASP104
ASPINALL Joseph	SJ		LA	Y	#3	1726	1745	1752	1763	ASP106
ASPINALL Thomas	SJ		LA	Y	#3	1719	1740	1747	1773	ASP108
ATHERTON Thomas	S	M	LA	D	#	1706	..	1732	1758	ATHE04
ATKINSON John	OSB	N	LA	E		1759	1781	..	1822	ATK112
ATKINSON William	S	L	LA	V	°3	..	..	1596	..	ATK122
BAINES John	S		LA	R		1626	..	1662	..	BAIN04
BAINES John	S	N	LA	R	#	1653	..	1678	1727	BAIN06
BALL Edward	S	L	LA	D	#	1717	..	1741	1789	BALL02
BALL George	S	N	LA	R		1678	..	1704	1734	BALL06
BALL George	S	N	LA	D	#	1704	..	1729	1748	BALL08
BALL John	S	M	LA	D	#	1723	..	1746	1781	BALL10
BAMBER Edward VEN.	S	N	LA	S	#+1	1602	..	1626	1646	BAMB02
BAMBER John	S	N	LA	D		1712	..	1740	1780	BAMB04
BAMBER William	S	M	LA	D	#4	1604	..	1628	1636	BAMB06
BANISTER Henry	S	N	LA	D	#3	1755	..	1781	1838	BAN104
BANISTER Robert	S	N	LA	D		1725	..	1750	1812	BAN108
BANISTER William	OSB	W	LA	G		..	1688	..	1726	BAN110
BARCROFT Thomas	S	N	LA	R		1566	..	1589	..	BARC02
BARKER Alexader	S	N	LA	D	#	1606	..	1631	1665	BARK01
BARLOW Edward (Ambrose) ST.	OSB	N	LA	G	#+	1585	1616	1617	1641	BARL04
BARLOW Edward	S	N	LA	D	#	1694	..	1721	1736	BARL08
BARLOW William (Rudesind)	OSB		LA		#*	1584	1606	1608	1656	BARL16

150

Name	Reg	D	Co	T	Notes	Born	Prof	Ordn	Died	Code
BARNARD Martin (Adrian)	OSB		LA	X		..	1690	..	1699	BARN10
BARON John	SJ		LA	R	#2	1605	1632	1630	1638	BARO02
BARRARD Richard	SJ		LA	Y	#	1661	1690	1698	1740	BARR06
BARRETT Edward	S	N	LA	D	3	1741	..	1765	1829	BARR24
BARRETT Richard (Maurus)	OSB	W	LA	W		1736	1751	..	1794	BARR28
BARROW Edward	SJ		LA	Y	#3	1660	1683	1690	1721	BARR34
BARROW James	S	N	LA	R		1726	..	1751	1800	BARR36
BARROW John	S	N	LA	R		1735	..	1766	1811	BARR38
BARROW John	S	N	LA	D		1751	..	1777	1811	BARR40
BARROW Joseph	SJ	N	LA	Y		1740	1758	1765	1813	BARR42
BARROW Richard	SJ	N	LA	Y	3	1738	1755	1763	1799	BARR44
BARROW Thomas	SJ	N	LA	Y	3	1747	1764	1772	1814	BARR46
BARROW William BL.	SJ	L	LA	Y	#+	1608	1632	..	1679	BARR48
BARTON John	S		LA	R	#°	1679	..	1703	..	BART18
BARTON Richard (Bede)	OSB		LA	E		1739	1757	..	1790	BART22
BARTON William	S	N	LA	R	#	1649	..	1673	1728	BART24
BATES Reginald	S	M	LA	R	#	1569	..	1594	..	BATE04
BEECH Robert (Anselm)	OSB		LA	Q	*14	1568	1596	1594	1634	BEEC02
BEESLEY George VEN.	S	L	LA	Q	#+	1562	..	1587	1591	BEES04
BEESLEY John	S	N	LA	D	#3	1609	..	1634	1674	BEES08
BEESLEY Richard	S	N	LA	Q		1570	..	1595	..	BEES10
BENNET John (Placid)	OSB	N	LA	W		1741	1758	..	1795	BENN10
BENNET Thomas	S	L	LA	R	#1	1656	..	1681	..	BENN14
BENNET Thomas (Bede)	OSB	L	LA	G		1723	1741	..	1800	BENN16
BENYON Thomas	S		LA	R		1715	..	1739	1756	BENY02
BERRY John (Jerome)	OSB		LA	W	#	1714	1731	..	1792	BERR08
BERRY Thomas	S	N	LA	D		1766	..	1797	1851	BERR14
BESWICK Francis	OSB		LA	G	x	1765	1786	..	1793	BESW04
BILLINGE Charles	SJ	M	LA	Y	°3	1735	1753	1763	1805	BILL02
BILLINGE Richard	SJ	N	LA	Y	1	1674	1698	1706	1733	BILL04
BILLINGE Richard Lawrence	SJ	L	LA	V	#	1713	1739	1739	1769	BILL06
BILLINGE Thomas	S	L	LA	R	#	1654	..	1682	1740	BILL08
BILLINGTON John	S	N	LA	L	3	1763	..	1784	1845	BILL10
BILLINGTON Richard	S	N	LA	D	3	1757	..	1781	1830	BILL12
BILLINGTON William	S	N	LA	V		1747	..	1775	1811	BILL14
BIRTWISTLE John	S	N	LA	V	*3	..	..	1600	1620	BIRT04
BIRTWISTLE Richard	S	N	LA	L	#	1713	..	1737	1743	BIRT08
BLACKBURN Edward	S	N	LA	R	#	1634	..	1661	1709	BLAC04
BLACKBURN John	S	N	LA	R		1654	..	1679	1728	BLAC06
BLACOE Joseph	S	L	LA	L	#3	..	..	1697	1740	BLAC24
BLACOE Robert	S	N	LA	D		1767	..	1794	1823	BLAC26
BLACOE William	S	N	LA	R		1732	..	1756	1815	BLAC28
BLEVIN (Aloysius)	CRT		LA	C		..	1730	..	1761	BLEV01
BLUNDELL Francis	S	N	LA	D		1753	..	1779	1792	BLUN02
BLUNDELL James	S	N	LA	L	3	1768	..	1792	1839	BLUN06
BLUNDELL Joseph	SJ	N	LA	Y		1686	1703	1712	1759	BLUN12
BLUNDELL Nicholas	SJ		LA	Y	3	1640	1662	1670	1680	BLUN14
BLUNDELL Robert Francis	SJ	N	LA	N	3	1717	1738	1745	1779	BLUN16
BLUNDELL Thomas	SJ	N	LA	Y		1648	1667	1678	1702	BLUN18
BLUNDELL William	S		LA	R		1568	..	1594	1596	BLUN20
BOLTON John	S		LA	R	4	1560	..	1584	1630	BOLT10
BOLTON John (Anselm)	OSB	N	LA	W		1736	1751	..	1805	BOLT14
BOLTON Joseph	S	L	LA	D	3	1736	..	1764	1783	BOLT16
BOOTH Edward	S	N	LA	L	#	1638	..	1663	1719	BOOT04
BORDLEY Simon George	S	N	LA	D	§	1709	..	1734	1799	BORD02
BOSTOCK George	S	N	LA	R	#	1672	..	1700	1728	BOST06
BRADILL Edward	S	N	LA	Q	#	..	..	1587	..	BRAD06
BRADLEY Richard	SJ	N	LA	Y	x2	1605	1622	..	1645	BRAD10
BRADSHAIGH Edward	S		LA	R	#4	1603	..	1628	1681	BRAD14
BRADSHAIGH Peter	SJ	N	LA	Y	#	1609	1631	..	1676	BRAD16
BRADSHAIGH Richard	SJ		LA	R	#	1601	1625	..	1669	BRAD18
BRADSHAIGH Robert	SJ		LA	S	#3	1589	1614	1612	1617	BRAD20
BRADSHAIGH Thomas	SJ	L	LA	R	#	1606	1631	1631	1663	BRAD22
BRADSHAW John	S	N	LA	R	1	1742	..	1766	1790	BRAD32
BRADSHAW Robert	S		LA	D	#†4	1572	..	1602	1610	BRAD34
BREERS Lawrence	S	L	LA	D	13	1667	..	1691	1744	BREE02

Name	Reg	D	Co	T	Notes	Born	Prof	Ordn	Died	Code
BREERS William	S	N	LA	L	#1	1690	..	1725	1741	BREE06
BREWER John	SJ	W	LA	Y	3	1732	1752	1761	1797	BREW04
BREWER John (Bede)	OSB	N	LA	W		1742	1758	..	1822	BREW06
BREWER Thomas	SJ	W	LA	Y	3	1743	1761	1771	1787	BREW08
BRINDLE John (Basil)	OSB	W	LA	W		1746	1765	..	1802	BRIN02
BROCKHOLES Charles	SJ	N	LA	Y	3	1684	1705	1713	1759	BROC02
BROCKHOLES Roger	S	N	LA	L	3	1658	..	1684	1700	BROC04
BROCKHOLES Roger	S	N	LA	R	1	1682	..	1708	1742	BROC06
BROCKHOLES Thomas	S	N	LA	D	3	1655	..	1680	1738	BROC08
BROCKHOLES Thomas	S	M	LA	D		1683	..	1706	1758	BROC10
BROMLEY Thomas (Anselm)	OSB		LA	W		1749	1766	..	1779	BROM07
BROWN George	SJ	N	LA	Y	#	1670	1688	1696	1735	BROW14
BULLEN Robert	S	N	LA	R		1740	..	1764	1792	BULL04
BULLER John	SJ	N	LA	Y	3	1746	1768	1771	1811	BULL06
BURGESS James (Bede)	OSB	N	LA	W		1768	1789	1792	1837	BURG02
BURSCOUGH Richard	S	N	LA	R	#	1651	..	1677	1731	BURS02
BURSCOUGH Richard	S		LA	V	3	..	..	1700	..	BURS04
BUTLER John	S		LA	D	#4	..	..	1625	1672	BUTL10
BUTLER Philip	S	N	LA	D		1724	..	1750	1777	BUTL14
BUTLER Richard (Bernard)	OSB	N	LA	G		1748	1776	..	1825	BUTL16
BUTLER Thomas, Hon.	SJ	M	LA	Y	#3	1718	1739	1746	1779	BUTL22
BUTLER Thomas	S	N	LA	D		1734	..	۱1761	1795	BUTL24
CALDERBANK (James)	OSB	W	LA	W		1770	1792	1793	1821	CALD02
CALDWELL William (Augustine)	OSB	L	LA	G	#	1735	1757	..	1815	CALD08
CALVERT Charles	SJ		LA	R	#	1620	1647	1644	1657	CALV04
CANSFIELD Brian VEN.	SJ		LA	R	#+x§	1580	1604	..	1645	CANS02
CANSFIELD Charles	S	L	LA	R	#	1613	..	1643	1693	CANS04
CARDWELL John	S	N	LA	R		1675	..	1701	1728	CARD06
CARTER Henry	S	N	LA	D	3	1761	..	1785	1826	CART04
CARTER James	S	N	LA	D	#3	1736	..	1762	1814	CART06
CARTER John	S	N	LA	L		1711	..	1736	1789	CART08
CARTER John	S	M	LA	D		1750	..	1776	1803	CART10
CASE James	SJ		LA	Y	3	1691	1712	1721	1731	CASE04
CASE William	SJ	M	LA	Y	#13	1689	1711	1720	1747	CASE08
CATON Thomas	S	N	LA	L		1756	..	1780	1826	CATO02
CATON William	S	N	LA	R		1675	..	1699	1749	CATO04
CATTERALL Alexander (Bene'ct)	OSB	N	LA	E		1725	1743	..	1791	CATT04
CATTERALL Edward (Bernard)	OSB	N	LA	W		..	1725	..	1781	CATT06
CAWSER Thomas (Benedict)	OSB		LA	E	x	1747	1764	..	1795	CAWS02
CHADDOCK William	S		LA	R	1	1561	..	1586	..	CHAD04
CHADWICK John	S	N	LA		4	..	..	..	1645	CHAD05
CHADWICK John	S	N	LA	D		1728	..	1752	1802	CHAD06
CHALLONER Henry	SJ		LA	Y	#1	1639	1660	..	1673	CHAL02
CHALLONER John	S	N	LA	D		..	..	1605	..	CHAL04
CHALLONER William	SJ		LA	V	#	..	1659	1656	1665	CHAL08
CHAMBERLAIN James	SJ		LA	Y	3	1739	1759	1765	1779	CHAM06
CHAMBERLAIN John Joseph	SJ	N	LA	R		1727	1752	1751	1796	CHAM08
CHARNLEY James	S	N	LA	D	#	1668	..	1695	..	CHAR04
CHARNOCK John	SJ	N	LA	Y	#	1744	1763	..	1804	CHAR06
CHARNOCK Robert	S	N	LA	L	#	1615	..	1639	1671	CHAR10
CHEW William (Alexius)	OSB	N	LA	W		1771	1792	1795	1832	CHEW02
CHORLEY Edward (John)	OSB	N	LA	G		..	1698	1704	1718	CHOR02
CHORLEY Thomas	SJ		LA	Y		1688	1705	1713	1718	CHOR04
CLARKSON Edward (Alban)	OSB	N	LA	X		1766	1787	..	1815	CLAR42
CLARKSON George	SJ	N	LA	Y	3	1738	1758	1765	1813	CLAR44
CLARKSON James (Augustine)	OFM	M	LA	F	134	1723	1746	1752	1776	CLAR45
CLARKSON John	S	L	LA	T	*	1773	..	1798	1823	CLAR48
CLAYTON John	SJ		LA	Y		1611	1629	..	1663	CLAY14
CLIFFE Francis Adam	S	N	LA	D		1728	..	1756	1799	CLIF02
CLIFFORD Thomas	SJ	N	LA	Y		1614	1635	..	1692	CLIF06
CLIFTON Cuthbert	SJ	N	LA	Y	#	1611	1630	..	1675	CLIF10
CLIFTON Francis	S	N	LA	R	‡	1682	..	1706	..	CLIF14
CLIFTON James	SJ	N	LA	Y	3	1698	1719	1728	1750	CLIF18
CLIFTON (Lambert)	OSB	N	LA		*4	..	..	..	1631	CLIF22
CLIFTON Thomas	SJ	M	LA	Y		1700	1718	1730	1777	CLIF28
CLIFTON William	SJ	N	LA	Y		1678	1699	1708	1749	CLIF30

Name	Reg	D	Co	T	Notes	Born	Prof	Ordn	Died	Code
COOPER John	S		LA	V	3	..	..	1676	..	COOP10
COOPER Louis (Francis)	OSB		LA	W		1771	1792	1795	1850	COOP14
COPELAND John	S	N	LA	D	#	..	..	1648	..	COPE04
CORBISHLEY Samuel	S	M	LA	L		1759	..	1789	1830	CORB10
CORNTHWAITE Richard	S	M	LA	D	3	1736	..	1765	1803	CORN16
COTTAM Thomas BL.	S		LA	D	*+‡3	1549	..	1580	1582	COTT06
COUPE Abraham (Maurus)	OSB		LA	E		..	1731	..	1753	COUP02
COUPE Thomas Jerome	OSB	N	LA	W		1754	1775	..	1827	COUP06
COWBAN John	S	N	LA	D	#	1701	..	1728	1777	COWB02
COWBAN William	S		LA	R	#	1611	..	1636	..	COWB04
COWLEY John	S		LA	R	#	..	..	1634	1662	COWL02
COWLEY John	S	N	LA	R	#	1643	..	1666	..	COWL04
COWLEY Thomas	S		LA	R	#	..	..	1631	1663	COWL06
COWLEY William (Gregory)	OSB	N	LA	W		1732	1749	..	1799	COWL10
COWLING John	S	N	LA	R		1712	..	1736	1768	COWL12
CRAVEN Vincent	OSB		LA	W		..	1686	..	1704	CRAV02
CRICHLOW Oliver	S	N	LA	R	#	1607	..	1634	1671	CRIC02
CRICHLOW Richard	S	N	LA	R	#1	1610	..	1634	..	CRIC04
CRICHLOW William	S	N	LA	R	#1	1600	..	1631	1669	CRIC06
CROOK George	S	N	LA	D		..	..	1661	1709	CROO02
CROOK George (James)	OSB		LA	E		..	1739	..	1770	CROO04
CROOK George (Joseph)	OSB	N	LA	X	#	1753	1771	..	1800	CROO06
CROSBY George	S		LA	D	#	1703	..	1729	1729	CROS02
CROSKELL William	S	N	LA	D	1	1767	..	1795	1838	CROS10
CROSS John	S	M	LA	Y		1767	..	..	1835	CROS22
CROSS Joseph	SJ		LA	Y	#	1766	1803	1791	1843	CROS24
CROSS Richard	S		LA	R	‡	..	..	1648	..	CROS28
CROSS Robert	S		LA	D	7	..	..	..	..	CROS30
CROSS Thomas	SJ	M	LA	Y	3	1739	1758	1765	1813	CROS32
CUERDON John (Hyacinth)	ODC		LA			1696	1715	1720	1761	CUER02
CUERDON Thomas	SJ	N	LA	Y	3	1718	1737	1745	1793	CUER04
CULCHETH Charles	SJ		LA	Y	#	1631	1652	1665	1667	CULC02
CULCHETH Thomas	SJ	L	LA	Y	#3	1654	1674	1686	1730	CULC04
CULCHETH Thomas	SJ	W	LA	Y	3	1741	1763	1765	1809	CULC06
CULCHETH William	SJ	M	LA	Y	#	1637	..	..	1684	CULC08
CULSHAW John	OSB		LA	G	°	1767	1788	..	..	CULS02
DANIEL Edward	S	N	LA	D	#	1709	..	1733	1765	DANI02
DANIEL Edward	S	N	LA	D		1749	..	1775	1819	DANI04
DANIEL John	S		LA	D	3	1745	..	1771	1823	DANI08
DANIEL John	S	N	LA	D		1755	..	1779	1802	DANI10
DANIEL Richard	S		LA	R		1687	..	1710	1753	DANI12
DANIEL Robert	OSB	N	LA	W		1717	1735	..	1781	DANI14
DANIEL Thomas	S	N	LA	D		1714	..	1739	1770	DANI16
DANIEL William	S		LA	D		1713	..	1741	1761	DANI20
DANIEL William	S	N	LA	D	#	1725	..	1750	1777	DANI22
DANSON William	S	N	LA	R	#	1730	..	1754	1806	DANS02
DARRAGH William	S	M	LA	V		1759	..	1783	1816	DARR02
DAWBER John	OSB	M	LA	W		1769	1791	..	1810	DAWB04
DAWNEY Obed (Alban)	OSB		LA	X	§	1654	1683	..	1737	DAWN02
DENNEN Henry	S	N	LA	D	3	1754	..	1780	1803	DENN02
DENNETT James	SJ	M	LA	Y	3	1702	1720	1728	1789	DENN04
DENNETT James	S	N	LA	L		1767	..	1794	1850	DENN06
DICCONSON Edward BP.	S	N	LA	D	#*	1670	..	1701	1752	DICC02
DICCONSON Thomas	SJ	N	LA	Y		1651	1672	1681	1704	DICC06
DICHFIELD Edward	S	N	LA	D		..	..	1618	..	DICH02
DIXON James	S	N	LA	D		1720	..	1745	1759	DIXO06
DUCKETT George (Edmund)	OSB		LA	E		1741	1760	..	1792	DUCK00
DUCKETT Henry	S	N	LA	R		1729	..	1754	1755	DUCK02
DUNN John	S	L	LA	D		1718	..	1743	1778	DUNN06
DUTTON Edmund	CRT		LA	D	#§	..	1649	1627	1652	DUTT02
EARPE Joseph	SJ	N	LA		#	1746	1764	1771	1827	EARP02
EASTHAM Evan (Anselm)	OSB	N	LA	E		1703	1731	..	1774	EAST14
EAVES (Oswald)	OSB	N	LA	W		1738	1753	..	1793	EAVE02
EAVES Thomas	OSB		LA	W		1659	1688	..	1747	EAVE04
ECCLES Edward (Thos of S.Edw)	OFM	W	LA	F	3	..	1740	1746	1767	ECCL02
ECCLESTON Thomas	SJ	N	LA	Y	#	1643	1668	1677	1698	ECCL04

Name	Reg	D	Co	T	Notes	Born	Prof	Ordn	Died	Code
ECCLESTON Thomas	S	N	LA	D	3	..	..	1661	1700	ECCL06
ECCLESTON Thomas	SJ	N	LA	Y	#3	1659	1697	1703	1743	ECCL08
EDISFORD John	SJ	W	LA	Y	#3	1738	1760	1767	1789	EDIS08
EDMONDSON Henry	S	N	LA	D		1723	..	1747	1785	EDMO02
EDMONDSON Hugh	S	N	LA	D		1715	..	1743	1755	EDMO04
EDMONDSON Richard	S	N	LA	D	3	1754	..	1779	1812	EDMO06
FARNWORTH John (Jerome)	OSB	N	LA	E		..	1696	..	1711	FARN02
FARNWORTH Ralph (Cuthbert)	OSB	N	LA	W	#	1680	1700	..	1754	FARN04
FARRAR James	SJ	N	LA	Y	3	1707	1725	1734	1763	FARR02
FARRINGTON John	SJ		LA	Y		1615	1637	..	1656	FARR06
FARRINGTON Thomas	SJ	N	LA	Y		1611	1631	..	1678	FARR08
FAULKNER Thomas	SJ	M	LA	Z	*§	1707	1732	..	1784	FAUL10
FAZAKERLEY Thomas	S	N	LA	R	#	1611	..	1635	1665	FAZA02
FINCH James (Bruno)	CRT	N	LA	C		1748	1770	1772	1821	FINC02
FISHER John	OSB	N	LA	W		1710	1726	..	1793	FISH10
FISHER Richard (Edward)	OSB	N	LA	W		1748	1766	1772	1824	FISH16
FISHER William	S	N	LA	L		..	..	1760	1813	FISH26
FITZWILLIAMS George	OSB	N	LA	G		..	1695	..	1725	FITZ26
FLETCHER John	S	L	LA	D		1766	..	1795	1845	FLET04
FLETCHER Richard	S	N	LA	D	#3	..	..	1650	1701	FLET09
FLETCHER Robert	S		LA	D	#	1609	..	..	..	FLET10
FLETCHER William	S	N	LA	D	#	1722	..	1746	1803	FLET14
FLETCHER William	S	N	LA	D		1752	..	1776	1812	FLET16
FORMBY (Macarius)	CRT		LA	C		..	1734	..	1771	FORM02
FORSHAW John (Lawrence)	OSB	N	LA	X	3	1769	1788	1795	1815	FORS04
FORTH James	S	N	LA	Q	#	..	..	1584	..	FORT10
FOSTER James	S	M	LA	R	#	1635	..	1661	..	FOST12
FOSTER James	S	N	LA	D		1747	..	1775	1824	FOST14
FOSTER Richard	SJ	N	LA	Y		1672	1692	1701	1707	FOST22
FOSTER William	S	N	LA	D	4	1707	..	1730	1754	FOST30
GARDINER James	S	N	LA	Q		..	..	1582	..	GARD06
GARDINER John	SJ	M	LA	Y		1659	1680	1687	1727	GARD16
GARDINER William	SJ	N	LA	Y	#	1651	1673	1681	1725	GARD22
GARNER Thomas (Benedict)	OSB		LA	X		1736	1758	..	1796	GARN02
GARNET Edmund	S		LA	V		..	..	1674	..	GARN06
GARNET Richard	S		LA	R	#†	1580	..	1606	..	GARN18
GARSTANG William (Dunstan)	OSB	L	LA	E		1736	1753	..	1814	GARS02
GAUNT James	S		LA	R	#	1580	..	1607	..	GAUN02
GAUNT James	S	N	LA	D		..	..	..	1734	GAUN04
GAUNT Thomas	S	N	LA	R	#	1587	..	1613	..	GAUN06
GAUNT William	S	N	LA	D	1	1721	..	1747	1773	GAUN08
GERARD Alexander	S	N	LA	Q	#	..	..	1586	..	GERA02
GERARD Caryl or Charles	S		LA	R	#	1695	..	1720	1779	GERA04
GERARD Gilbert	SJ	L	LA	R	1	1569	1602	1593	1606	GERA06
GERARD Gilbert	SJ		LA	R	#	1614	1642	1640	1645	GERA08
GERARD James	S	N	LA	R	x4	1677	..	1702	1715	GERA10
GERARD John	SJ		LA	R	#‡	1564	1588	1588	1637	GERA12
GERARD Miles BL.	S		LA	Q	#+	1549	..	1583	1590	GERA16
GERARD Ralph	S		LA	D	#3	1669	..	1698	1699	GERA20
GERARD Thomas	SJ	N	LA	Y	#3	1640	1675	1678	1682	GERA24
GERARD Thomas	SJ	N	LA	Y	#	1667	1686	1696	1715	GERA26
GERARD Thomas	SJ	M	LA	Y	13	1692	1714	1724	1761	GERA28
GERARD William	S	N	LA	V	1	1613	..	..	1673	GERA32
GERARD William	SJ		LA	Y	3	1687	1707	1716	1731	GERA36
GILLIBRAND Richard	SJ		LA	Y	3	1717	1735	1744	1774	GILL02
GILLIBRAND William	SJ	N	LA	Y	#3	1662	1682	1690	1722	GILL04
GILLIBRAND William	SJ	N	LA	Y	3	1716	1735	1743	1779	GILL06
GILLOW John	S	N	LA	D		1753	..	1779	1828	GILL10
GILLOW Thomas	S	N	LA	U	*	1769	..	1797	1857	GILL12
GIRLINGTON John	OSB	N	LA	E	#	..	1653	..	..	GIRL04
GLOVER Joseph	S		LA	L		1739	..	1764	1818	GLOV02
GOLDEN Richard	S		LA	R	#	1568	..	1597	..	GOLD02
GOODEN Peter	S	N	LA	L	3	1643	..	1670	1694	GOOD10
GORSUCH George	S		LA	V	#3	1580	..	1624	..	GORS02
GORSUCH James	S	N	LA	D	#3	1683	..	1710	1739	GORS04
GOULDING Fortescue	S		LA	V	#	..	..	..	1676	GOUL02

Name	Reg	D	Co	T	Notes	Born	Prof	Ordn	Died	Code
GRADWELL Christopher	S	N	LA	D		1709	..	1734	1758	GRAD02
GRADWELL Thomas	S	N	LA	D	#	..	..	1646	1672	GRAD06
GRAY George	SJ	M	LA	Y	1	1608	1629	..	1686	GRAY02
GREEN Francis	SJ	M	LA	Y	1	1744	1764	1772	1775	GREE16
GREEN John (Joseph)	OP	N	LA	P	#1	1702	1721	..	1750	GREE29
GREGSON (Augustine)	OSB		LA	W		..	1728	..	1779	GREG04
GREGSON Richard (Vincent)	OSB	N	LA	W		1721	1741	..	1800	GREG06
GREGSON William (Bernard)	OSB	L	LA	W		1650	1668	..	1711	GREG08
GREGSON William (Gregory)	OSB	L	LA	E		1728	1751	..	1800	GREG10
GRIMBALDSTONE Joseph (Paul)	OSB		LA	X		1756	1777	..	1807	GRIM00
GRIMBALDSTONE Thomas Emir	S	N	LA	D		1715	..	1739	1786	GRIM02
GRIMBALDSTONE William	S	N	LA	D		1708	..	1735	1770	GRIM08
GRIMBALDSTONE Wm. (Clement)	OSB	N	LA	X		1752	1774	..	1824	GRIM10
HALL Roger (Boniface)	OSB	W	LA	X		1737	1756	..	1803	HALL20
HALLOWELL Oliver	S		LA	R	4	1556	..	1582	1600	HALL30
HALSALL George	SJ	M	LA	R	1	1714	1739	1738	1744	HALS02
HANSON William (Ildephonsus)	OSB	N	LA	S	#	..	1615	..	1644	HANS12
HARGRAVE James	S	N	LA	V	§	1585	..	1609	..	HARG02
HARGRAVE William	S		LA	R	#	1597	..	1622	1661	HARG06
HARRISON Edmund	SJ	L	LA	Y	1	1727	1746	1755	1801	HARR28
HARRISON Henry	SJ		LA	Y	#3	1676	1698	1704	1739	HARR33
HARRISON John	S	N	LA	D		1714	..	1741	1780	HARR46
HARRISON Matthew or Matthias	S	N	LA	R		1638	..	1665	..	HARR51
HARSNIP Thomas (Placid)	OSB		LA	X		1753	1770	1777	1807	HARS02
HART Joseph (John)	OFM		LA	F	13	1760	1782	1784	1803	HART08
HAUGHTON Edward	SJ		LA	V	#	1602	1641	1629	1651	HAUG02
HAUGHTON William	S		LA	D	#	1597	..	1623	..	HAUG06
HAWARDEN Charles	S		LA	D	#	1677	..	..	..	HAWA02
HAWARDEN Edward	S		LA	D	#	1662	..	1686	1735	HAWA04
HAWARDEN Edward	S	N	LA	D		1732	..	1758	1793	HAWA06
HAWARDEN John	S	N	LA	D		1724	..	1749	1770	HAWA08
HAWARDEN Joseph (Bernard)	OSB	W	LA	G	°3	1771	1792	1800	1851	HAWA10
HAWARDEN Thomas	S	N	LA	D		1693	..	1719	1746	HAWA12
HAWARDEN William	S	N	LA	D	#3	1666	..	1693	1727	HAWA14
HAWETT Edmund	OSB	N	LA	E		..	1683	..	1688	HAWE02
HAWORTH Joseph (of S.Mary)	OSB		LA	W		..	1609	..	1624	HAWO02
HAYDOCK Cuthbert	S	M	LA	D	3	1684	..	1710	1763	HAYD02
HAYDOCK Ewan or Evan	S	N	LA	D		..	..	1575	1581	HAYD04
HAYDOCK George VEN.	S	L	LA	Q	+1	1556	..	1581	1584	HAYD06
HAYDOCK George Leo	S	N	LA	U		1774	..	1798	1849	HAYD08
HAYDOCK Gilbert	S		LA	D	3	1682	..	1709	1749	HAYD10
HAYDOCK (James)	OFM		LA	F	12	1671	1689	1697	1718	HAYD12
HAYDOCK James	S	N	LA	D		1765	..	1792	1809	HAYD13
HAYDOCK Richard	S	N	LA	D	1	1551	..	1577	1605	HAYD14
HAYDOCK Robert	OSB	N	LA	V	#1	1582	1603	..	1650	HAYD16
HAYES Thomas	SJ	N	LA	Y		1746	1765	1772	1774	HAYE03
HEATLEY Hugh (Jerome)	OSB	W	LA	X		1757	1777	..	1792	HEAT08
HEATLEY James	SJ	N	LA	Y		1715	1735	1744	1782	HEAT10
HEATLEY John (Louis)	OSB		LA	X		1752	1776	..	1805	HEAT12
HEATLEY William (Maurus)	OSB	L	LA	X		1722	1740	1746	1802	HEAT14
HEATON Henry or John	SJ	M	LA	R	#§1	1601	1626	1625	1683	HEAT16
HELME (Gregory)	OSB	N	LA	W		..	1686	..	1696	HELM02
HELME Hugh (Bede)	OSB	N	LA	Z	#*1	1580	1604	..	1636	HELM04
HELME Richard	OSB	N	LA	G		..	1676	..	1717	HELM06
HELME Thomas (Wilfrid)	OSB	N	LA	E		..	1699	..	1742	HELM08
HELMES Edward	S	N	LA	D		1725	..	1748	1773	HELM10
HESKETH Bartholomew (Gregory)	OSB	N	LA	W		..	1653	..	1695	HESK02
HESKETH George	S		LA	R	#§1	1598	..	1626	..	HESK04
HESKETH George	S		LA	L		1641	..	1665	1666	HESK06
HESKETH (Mellitus)	OSB	N	LA	W	2	1644	1664	..	1674	HESK12
HESKETH Nicholas	OSB	N	LA	W		..	1668	..	1688	HESK14
HESKETH Roger	S		LA	L	3	1643	..	1667	1715	HESK16
HESKETH (Jerome)	OSB		LA	G	#	..	1643	..	1693	HESK18
HESKETH Roger (Joseph)	OSB		LA	G		..	1681	..	1703	HESK20
HESKETH Thomas	S		LA		#3	..	..	1591	..	HESK22
HESKETH Thomas	OSB		LA	E		1655	1673	..	1694	HESK24

Name	Reg	D	Co	T	Notes	Born	Prof	Ordn	Died	Code
HESKETH Thomas	SJ		LA	Y	13	1668	..	1701	1712	HESK 26
HESKETH Thomas	S		LA	L		1696	..	1720	1730	HESK 28
HIGGINSON James	OSB	N	LA	G		1764	1785	..	1835	HIGG 10
HIGGINSON Joseph	S	N	LA	D		1758	..	1783	1846	HIGG 12
HITCHMOUTH Richard	S		LA	R	#°4	1676	..	1702	1727	HITC 04
HODGKINSON Charles	SJ	N	LA	R	#	1700	1729	1726	1770	HODG 04
HODGSON Charles	SJ		LA	Y		1742	1760	1771	1805	HODG 06
HODGSON John	SJ	N	LA	Y	13	1750	1769	1776	1807	HODG 24
HODSON Christopher	S		LA	R		..	..	1583	..	HODS 04
HOLDEN Henry	S		LA	D	#4	1597	..	1622	1662	HOLD 02
HOLDEN Henry	S	N	LA	D		..	..	..	1688	HOLD 04
HOLDEN Joseph	S	N	LA	P		..	..	1728	1767	HOLD 08
HOLLAND Alexander	SJ	N	LA	V		1623	1651	1649	1677	HOLL 02
HOLLAND Joseph or Richard	SJ	W	LA	Y	1	1676	1697	1709	1740	HOLL 14
HOLLAND Thomas BL.	SJ	L	LA	Y	#+13	1601	1620	1624	1642	HOLL 16
HOLME Edward	SJ	N	LA	Y	#3	1740	1759	1767	1809	HOLM 02
HOLME Francis	SJ	N	LA	Y	#	1724	1740	1752	1802	HOLM 04
HOLME John	SJ		LA	Y	#3	1718	1737	1750	1783	HOLM 06
HOLME John	S	M	LA	Y	#	1764	..	..	1826	HOLM 08
HOLME Richard	S	N	LA	R	#§	1604	..	1630	1634	HOLM 10
HOLMES (Germain)	OFM	N	LA	F	x123	1711	1728	1735	1746	HOLM 12
HOLMES Thomas	S	N	LA	S	§	1577	..	..	..	HOLM 18
HOLT Alexander	S	L	LA	R	#	1629	..	1656	1680	HOLT 02
HOLT Gilbert	SJ		LA	Y	13	1688	1710	1718	1725	HOLT 04
HOLT William	SJ		LA	D	#‡	1548	1578	1576	1599	HOLT 06
HORNBY Robert	SJ	L	LA	Y	3	1646	1668	1676	1694	HORN 06
HORRABIN Thomas	S	L	LA	V		1747	..	..	1801	HORR 02
HOTHERSALL George	OSB	N	LA	V	#234	1560	1614	1593	1633	HOTH 02
HOTHERSALL William	SJ	M	LA	Y	3	1725	1742	1751	1803	HOTH 04
HOUGHTON Charles	S	N	LA	D	3	1749	..	1775	1797	HOUG 02
HOUGHTON Richard (Bede)	OSB	N	LA	E	#	..	1642	1644	1687	HOUG 06
HOUGHTON Robert (Edward)	OSB	N	LA	W		..	1710	1720	1751	HOUG 07
HOUGHTON William (Hyacinth)	OP	N	LA	N		1736	1754	1760	1823	HOUG 08
HOWARD Charles	S	N	LA	P	#	1740	..	1765	1821	HOWA 06
HOWARD William	SJ		LA	V	#	1687	1713	1713	1770	HOWA 26
HOWES John	S	N	LA	L	34	..	..	1674	1704	HOWE 10
HUDDLESTON John (Denis)	OSB	L	LA	R	#2	1608	1653	1637	1698	HUDD 11
HUDDLESTON Richard	OSB	N	LA	D	#2	1583	1612	1607	1655	HUDD 12
HUDDLESTON William	S	N	LA	S	3	1578	..	1602	..	HUDD 14
HUDSON John (Augustine)	OSB	M	LA	W		..	1686	..	1732	HUDS 04
HULL William	S	N	LA	D	3	1751	..	1779	1835	HULL 04
HUNTER (Thomas)	OP	L	LA	N	12	1679	1700	..	1723	HUNT 28
HURST John	S	M	LA	D	3	1735	..	1761	1792	HURS 02
HURST Thomas	S		LA	L	3	1774	..	1798	1855	HURS 04
HURST William	S		LA	D	x	1737	..	1762	1793	HURS 06
HURST William	S	L	LA	L		1776	..	1800	1823	HURS 08
IRELAND Alexander	SJ	N	LA	R	#‡	1604	1638	1632	1652	IREL 02
IRELAND Lawrence	SJ	N	LA	Y	#	1634	1664	1672	1673	IREL 06
IRVING William	S	N	LA	V	#	1776	..	1800	1822	IRVI 02
ISHERWOOD John (Richard)	OSB	W	LA	X	#	..	1685	..	1745	ISHE 02
JACKSON (Michael)	OFM	N	LA	F	123	1653	1670	1677	1709	JACK 26
JAMESON Richard	S	N	LA	D	#3	..	..	1695	1734	JAME 08
JAMESON Thomas	S		LA	D		1667	..	1696	..	JAME 10
JANION George	SJ	N	LA	Y	#	1646	1668	1677	1698	JANI 02
JANION William	SJ		LA	Y		1652	1672	1678	1685	JANI 04
JENISON Michael	SJ		LA	Y	#	1603	1622	..	1648	JENI 12
JENKINSON Christopher	S	N	LA	L	3	..	..	1701	1723	JENK 10
JOHNSON James	S	N	LA	D	3	1745	..	1771	1790	JOHN 12
JOHNSON Lawrence BL.	S	N	LA	D	#+‡	..	..	1577	1582	JOHN 20
JOHNSON Robert	SJ	N	LA	Y		1745	1764	1771	1823	JOHN 32
JOHNSTON James (Oswald)	OSB	N	LA	X		1750	1772	..	1818	JOHN 44
JONES John	S	N	LA	D	13	1733	..	1760	1786	JONE 20
JUMP Gilbert	CRT		LA	C		1705	1726	..	1772	JUMP 02
KAYE James (Ambrose)	OSB	N	LA	W		1717	1735	..	1777	KAYE 02
KELLET Henry	S	N	LA	V		1763	..	1787	1808	KELL 06
KELLET Robert (Augustine)	OSB		LA	E		1731	1751	..	1809	KELL 08

156

Name	Reg	D	Co	T	Notes	Born	Prof	Ordn	Died	Code
KENDALL George	S	N	LA	D		1698	..	1722	1766	KEND02
KENDALL Henry	S	N	LA	D		1689	..	1716	1752	KEND04
KENDALL Hugh	S	M	LA	D		1708	..	1736	1781	KEND06
KENDALL Richard	S	L	LA	D		1709	..	1735	1780	KEND08
KENDALL Richard	S	L	LA	D	3	1685	..	1710	1748	KEND10
KENDALL Robert	S	N	LA	D		1700	..	1724	1746	KEND14
KENYON Edward	S	W	LA	V	3		..	1599	..	KENY02
KENYON Edward	S	N	LA	D		1761	..	1789	1837	KENY04
KENYON Thomas (Anselm)	OSB	M	LA	X		1770	1787	1794	1850	KENY06
KEYS Peter	S		LA	L	3	..	..	1693	..	KEYS02
KIRBY Lawrence	OSB	N	LA	W		..	1715	..	1743	KIRB06
KIRKHAM Richard	SJ		LA	Y	#	1671	1691	1700	1708	KIRK12
KITCHEN Edward	S	N	LA	D	#3	..	..	1675	..	KITC01
KITCHEN Edward	S		LA	D	1	1705	..	1731	1732	KITC02
KITCHEN Edward	S	N	LA	D	#	1747	..	1771	1793	KITC04
KITCHEN John	S	N	LA	D	3	1741	..	1770	1793	KITC06
LAITHWAIT Edward	SJ	W	LA	R	#§	1584	1615	1612	1643	LAIT02
LAITHWAIT Francis	SJ		LA		#24	1589	1607	..	1624	LAIT04
LAITHWAIT Thomas	SJ	L	LA	S	#3	1577	1607	1604	1655	LAIT06
LAMBERT John	S		LA	R	#	1600	..	1628	1631	LAMB06
LANCASTER Francis (Anthony)	OFM		LA	F	13	1728	1746	1751	1758	LANC03
LANCASTER George (Oswald)	OFM		LA	F	134	1734	1760	1767	1784	LANC06
LANCASTER James	S	N	LA	D		1768	..	1793	1827	LANC08
LANCASTER Oswald	S		LA	D		1715	..	1741	1753	LANC10
LANCASTER Thomas	S	N	LA	R		1690	..	1717	1752	LANC14
LANGDALE Marmaduke	SJ	N	LA	Y		1748	1766	1776	1786	LANG04
LANGTON John (Bonaventure)	OFM		LA	F	1234	1602	1630	1633	1634	LANG19
LANGTON Thomas	S		LA	R	#	1642	..	1669	1710	LANG20
LANGWORTH Anthony (Bern'dine)	OFM	N	LA	F	123	1643	1666	1671	1702	LANG23
LATHAM (Gabriel)	OSB		LA	E		..	1622	1627	1635	LATH06
LATHAM George (Joseph)	OSB	W	LA	D		..	1617	1615	1646	LATH08
LATHAM Henry (Augustine)	OSB	L	LA	E		1619	1640	1642	1677	LATH10
LATHAM Thomas (Torquatus)	OSB		LA	Z	*	..	1606	..	1624	LATH14
LATHAM (Vincent)	OSB	N	LA	G		..	1622	..	1640	LATH16
LATHAM William (Swithbert)	OSB	N	LA	D		..	1614	1612	1640	LATH18
LATHOT Henry	S		LA	R	#3	1626	..	1650	..	LATH20
LAURENSON James	S	N	LA	D	3	1752	..	1780	1828	LAUR04
LAYFIELD Christopher	S	M	LA	D		1713	..	1742	1761	LAYF02
LAYFIELD James	S	M	LA	R		1701	..	1726	1756	LAYF04
LECKONBY Richard	SJ	N	LA	Y	3	1699	1720	1729	1771	LECK02
LECKONBY Thomas	SJ		LA	Y	3	1707	1721	1730	1734	LECK04
LECKONBY Thomas	SJ	N	LA	Y	3	1717	1736	1744	1778	LECK06
LEIGH Alexander	SJ	N	LA	Y	#	1681	1700	1710	1748	LEIG02
LEIGH John	SJ		LA	Y	#3	1639	1660	1671	1703	LEIG08
LEIGH Philip	SJ	N	LA	R	#1	1650	1678	1675	1717	LEIG10
LEIGH Roger	SJ	N	LA	Y		1708	1728	1753	1781	LEIG14
LE MOTTE James	SJ		LA	R	#3	1712	1734	1735	1772	LEMO04
LEYBURN George	S	M	LA	D	3	1673	..	1699	1737	LEYB04
LEYBURN Nicholas	S	N	LA	P		1674	..	1700	1739	LEYB10
LIDIATE William	SJ	N	LA	Y		1650	1673	1681	1690	LIDI02
LINDOW John	S	L	LA	D	3	1729	..	1764	1806	LIND04
LISTER Christopher	S	M	LA	S	3	..	..	1605	..	LIST02
LISTER John	S	N	LA	Q		..	..	1584	..	LIST04
LISTER Thomas	SJ		LA		#	1559	1583	..	1628	LIST06
LIVESEY Thomas	S	N	LA	D	#	1764	..	1789	1857	LIVE04
LONG Henry	S	N	LA	R	#	1637	..	1663	1677	LONG02
LONSDALE John	S	N	LA	D	3	1736	..	1765	1802	LONS02
LOWE John	S	N	LA	Q		..	..	1579	..	LOWE03
LUND Anthony	S	N	LA	D	1	1734	..	1760	1811	LUND02
LUND John	S	N	LA	D		1733	..	1759	1812	LUND04
LUPTON Thomas	S	N	LA	U		1776	..	1800	1843	LUPT02
MADGEWORTH Christopher	SJ	N	LA	Y	#1	1658	1679	1685	1692	MADG02
MAINI Dominic Joseph	S	N	LA	U	13	1775	..	1798	1854	MAIN02
MAINWARING Edward	SJ	N	LA	R	#3	1604	1628	1628	1664	MAIN04
MALONE John (Columban)	OSB		LA	G		..	1609	..	1623	MALO04
MARKLAND Alexander	S		LA	Q		1561	..	1584	..	MARK06

157

Name	Reg	D	Co	T	Notes	Born	Prof	Ordn	Died	Code
MARSDEN William BL.	S		LA	Q	+‡13	1560	..	1585	1586	MARS02
MARSH James	S	N	LA	V		1762	..	1787	1811	MARS08
MARSH Richard	OSB	N	LA	W		1762	1783	1786	1843	MARS12
MARSH Thomas (Jerome)	OSB	N	LA	W		1743	1761	..	1798	MARS14
MARSH William or John	SJ	M	LA	Y		1637	1658	1666	1681	MARS18
MARSHALL Nicholas	S		LA	R		1649	..	1673	..	MARS26
MARSLAND John	S	L	LA	D		1738	..	1763	1817	MARS32
MARTINDALE John	SJ		LA	Y	#	1666	1690	1698	1734	MART38
MASHTER Francis	SJ	M	LA	Y	13	1678	1701	1711	1723	MASH02
MASON Thomas	S	N	LA	L		1719	..	1745	1751	MASO06
MASSEY (Masseus of S.Barbara)	OFM	L	LA	F	123	1628	1653	1658	1702	MASS12
MASSEY Thomas	S	L	LA	R	#	1622	..	1647	1676	MASS14
MATHER (Augustine)	OSB	N	LA	W		..	1666	..	1687	MATH02
MATHER James	OSB	L	LA	W		..	1668	..	1724	MATH04
MATHER James (Cyril)	OSB		LA	X		1769	1790	..	1812	MATH08
MAWDESLEY Henry	S	W	LA	L	34	..	..	1680	1698	MAWD02
MAWDESLEY Richard	S		LA	L	34	..	..	1680	1686	MAWD04
MAWDESLEY William	S		LA	L	4	..	..	1696	1733	MAWD06
MELLING Edward	S	N	LA	D	3	1683	..	1708	1733	MELL02
MELLING John	S	N	LA	D	#	..	..	1612	1633	MELL06
MELLING John	S		LA	D		1689	..	1713	1745	MELL08
MELLING Ralph	S	N	LA	D	1	1601	..	1629	1660	MELL10
MERCER William	SJ		LA	Y	1	1738	1755	1763	1777	MERC02
METCALFE William	SJ		LA	S	34	..	1599	1597	1604	METC26
MIDDLEHURST James	SJ		LA	V	#3	1714	1739	1738	1767	MIDD02
MIDDLEHURST Thomas	S	N	LA	R	#	1732	..	1754	1817	MIDD04
MILLINGTON George (Bernard)	OSB	W	LA	W		1627	1651	..	1667	MILL06
MOLYNEUX Edward	S	N	LA	D	#13	1640	..	1666	1704	MOLY02
MOLYNEUX Edward	S	N	LA	D	#	1700	..	1727	1739	MOLY04
MOLYNEUX Joseph	SJ		LA	Y	#	1732	1752	1763	1778	MOLY08
MOLYNEUX Robert	SJ		LA	Y	3	1738	1757	1767	1808	MOLY16
MOLYNEUX William, Visc., Bt.	SJ	N	LA	Y	3	1685	1704	1713	1759	MOLY20
MOLYNEUX William	SJ		LA	Y		1726	1748	1756	1789	MOLY22
MORE John	S	N	LA	D	1	1703	..	1731	1783	MORE10
MORLEY Henry	S	L	LA	R	#§4	1602	..	1626	1684	MORL04
MORRIS John	S	M	LA	Y	3	1770	..	1797	1830	MORR12
MOSSOCK Richard	S	N	LA	D	#	1626	..	..	1674	MOSS02
NAYLOR John (Ambrose)	OSB	N	LA	G		1739	1757	1764	1821	NAYL06
NAYLOR John (Placid)	OSB	L	LA	W		1724	1741	..	1795	NAYL08
NAYLOR William (Placid)	OSB	N	LA	W		..	1711	..	1772	NAYL10
NEEDHAM Daniel	SJ	M	LA	Y	#	1721	1741	1749	1783	NEED06
NELSON Henry (Anselm)	OSB	N	LA	E		..	1683	..	1717	NELS07
NELSON John	SJ		LA	R	#	1562	..	1588	1596	NELS10
NELSON (Maurus)	OSB		LA	E		..	1681	..	1690	NELS16
NELSON Ralph (James)	OSB		LA	E		1638	1660	..	1707	NELS18
NELSON Richard (Placid)	OSB		LA	E		..	1679	..	1742	NELS20
NELSON Thomas	OSB		LA	G		1684	1703	1707	1738	NELS24
NELSON William	S		LA	Q	‡	..	..	1587	1588	NELS26
NELSON William (Benedict)	OSB		LA	E		1618	1640	..	1699	NELS28
NEWBY Augustine	SJ	L	LA	Y		1616	1637	..	1669	NEWB02
NEWSHAM Andrew	S	N	LA	D	#	1597	..	1625	1647	NEWS02
NEWSHAM James	S	L	LA	D		1743	..	1767	1825	NEWS04
NIGHTINGALE James	S		LA	Q		..	..	1584	..	NIGH02
NIXON Thomas	SJ	N	LA	Y	3	1735	1756	1761	1793	NIXO04
NORRIS Andrew	SJ	M	LA	R	#3	1654	1676	1685	1722	NORR02
NORRIS Charles	SJ	L	LA	R		1646	1682	1670	1690	NORR06
NORRIS Richard	SJ		LA		#3	1658	1680	1686	1717	NORR14
NORRIS Sebastian	S	W	LA	R	#	1722	..	1746	1757	NORR18
NORTH John	S	N	LA	D	#	1603	..	1631	1669	NORT04
NUTTER John BL.	S		LA	Q	+†	..	..	1582	1584	NUTT08
NUTTER Robert VEN.	OP		LA	Q	#+‡12	1556	1587	1581	1600	NUTT10
ORRELL Brian	S	N	LA	D	#13	1664	..	1692	1739	ORRE02
ORRELL John	S	N	LA	D		1745	..	1770	1810	ORRE04
ORRELL Joseph	S	N	LA	D		1747	..	1773	1820	ORRE06
OSBALDESTON Edward VEN.	S	N	LA	Q	+	..	..	1585	1594	OSBA02
OSBALDESTON John	SJ	N	LA	Y		1655	1674	1683	1690	OSBA04

Name	Reg	D	Co	T	Notes	Born	Prof	Ordn	Died	Code
PARKER (Cuthbert)	OSB	L	LA	E		..	1673	..	1705	PARK06
PARKER Francis	SJ		LA	Y		1606	1626	..	1679	PARK08
PARKER Henry	OSB		LA	E		1752	1773	..	1817	PARK14
PARKER James	SJ	N	LA	S		1597	1623	1620	1657	PARK16
PARKER James	SJ	W	LA	Y	3	1747	1766	1771	1822	PARK18
PARKER Thomas	SJ	M	LA	V	#3	1739	1763	1763	1820	PARK28
PARKINSON Cuthbert	S		LA	D	3	1680	..	1710	1711	PARK38
PARKINSON Edward	S	N	LA	D	#13	1664	..	1688	1735	PARK42
PARKINSON Henry	S	N	LA	L		1772	..	1795	1832	PARK46
PARKINSON James	S	N	LA	D	#	1716	..	1740	1766	PARK48
PARKINSON James	S	N	LA	L		..	..	1758	1766	PARK50
PARKINSON Thomas	S	N	LA	D	#	1713	..	1740	1751	PARK58
PARKINSON Thomas or James	S	N	LA	L		1741	..	1768	1821	PARK60
PATERSON James	S	N	LA	R	#1	1600	..	1627	..	PATE07
PATTEN Thomas	OSB	N	LA	G		1727	1746	..	1787	PATT02
PEMBERTON John William	SJ	N	LA	V	#13	1705	1733	1733	1763	PEMB02
PENKETH Charles	S	N	LA	S	#3	..	..	1684	..	PENK02
PENKETH John	SJ	N	LA	R	#1	1627	1663	1656	1701	PENK04
PENKETH John	S		LA	R	#*	1681	..	1710	..	PENK06
PENKETH John	S	L	LA	D	13	1732	..	1761	1813	PENK08
PENKETH Richard	S	N	LA	V	#3	1647	..	1677	1721	PENK10
PENKETH William	S	N	LA	R	#	1679	..	1704	1762	PENK12
PENNINGTON (Alan)	OP		LA			1670	1695	1696	1728	PENN08
PENNINGTON (Edmund)	OSB	N	LA	W	3	1757	1778	1782	1794	PENN10
PENNINGTON William	SJ		LA	Y	3	1661	1681	1689	1736	PENN16
PENNINGTON William	S	N	LA	D		1718	..	1744	1793	PENN18
PENSWICK Thomas	S	N	LA	R		1717	..	1743	1791	PENS02
PENSWICK Thomas BP.	S	N	LA	U	*	1772	..	1797	1836	PENS04
PERCY George	S		LA	Q		..	..	1587	..	PERC06
PHILIPS John	S	N	LA	R	#	1678	..	1703	1738	PHIL12
PIERPOINT William	S	L	LA	D	#	1753	..	1779	1828	PIER08
PILKINGTON Robert	S		LA	Q		..	..	1583	..	PILK02
PILLING John (Bonaventure)	OFM		LA	F	1	1736	1752	1759	1801	PILL02
PILLING William (Leo S.Bonre)	OFM		LA	F	1	1746	1764	..	1801	PILL04
PLATT Ralph	S	N	LA	D	3	1758	..	1786	1837	PLAT08
PLEASINGTON John or Wm ST.	S	N	LA	V	#+1	1637	..	1662	1679	PLEA02
PLEASINGTON Joseph	SJ	N	LA	Y	#	1715	1737	1742	1781	PLEA04
POLE Francis	SJ	M	LA	Y		1711	1728	1736	1767	POLE12
POPE Edward (Alexius)	OSB	W	LA	W	#	1732	1749	..	1777	POPE02
POPE James (Alexius)	OSB	N	LA	W		1755	1776	..	1837	POPE04
POPE Richard	OSB	N	LA	W		1760	1781	..	1828	POPE06
POSTLETHWAITE James	S	N	LA	D		1723	..	1748	1781	POST06
POSTLETHWAITE John	S	N	LA	D	3	1727	..	1754	1785	POST08
POSTLETHWAITE Thomas	S		LA	L		..	..	1763	1776	POST10
PRESTON Henry	S	L	LA	L	3	..	..	1692	1733	PRES08
PRICE James (Bernard)	OSB	N	LA	W		1719	1737	..	1766	PRIC08
PRISTOE James (Angelus)	OFM		LA	F		1622	1641	..	1662	PRIS02
PROBERT Edward	S	L	LA	D	#	..	..	1612	..	PROB02
RADCLIFFE Fortunatus (Felix)	OFM		LA	F	124	1632	1658	..	1673	RADC01
RATHBONE William	S		LA	D		..	..	1607	1626	RATH02
REDMAN John	S	N	LA	R		1567	..	1591	1645	REDM02
RICHARDSON John	SJ	N	LA	Y	#	1662	1684	1691	1728	RICH20
RICHARDSON John	SJ	N	LA	Y	3	1734	1755	1762	1782	RICH22
RICHARDSON John (Nicholas)	OSB		LA	W		1715	1737	..	1762	RICH26
RICHARDSON Richard	SJ	N	LA	Y	1	1669	1690	1699	1738	RICH30
RICHARDSON Sylvester	S	N	LA	D	3	1741	..	1768	1776	RICH34
RIGBY James	S		LA	D	#3	1671	..	1699	1731	RIGB04
RIGBY James	S	M	LA	R		1705	..	1730	1751	RIGB06
RIGBY John	SJ	N	LA	Y	3	1712	1732	1738	1758	RIGB10
RIGBY John	SJ		LA	Y	1	1737	1758	1765	1767	RIGB12
RIGBY John	S	N	LA	P		1733	..	1782	1818	RIGB14
RIGBY John (Bede)	OSB		LA	X		1774	1798	..	1837	RIGB16
RIGBY John (Placid)	OSB		LA	W		..	1728	..	1764	RIGB18
RIGBY Lawrence	S	N	LA	D		1675	..	1703	1731	RIGB20
RIGBY Roger	SJ		LA	Y	#	1608	1629	1639	1646	RIGB22
RIGBY Thomas	S	L	LA	P		1747	..	1776	1815	RIGB24

Name	Reg	D	Co	T	Notes	Born	Prof	Ordn	Died	Code
RIGMAIDEN John	SJ	N	LA	Y	#	1710	1732	1739	1782	RIGM02
RIGMAIDEN John (Maurus)	OSB	M	LA	W	#	1672	1695	..	1759	RIGM04
RIGMAIDEN Simeon (Benedict)	OSB	W	LA	W	#	..	1708	..	1749	RIGM06
RIMMER Richard	S	N	LA	D		1754	..	1779	1828	RIMM02
RISHTON Edward	S	L	LA	D	‡	1550	..	1577	1585	RISH02
RISHTON Edward	S		LA	R	#	1614	..	1639	..	RISH04
RISHTON Ralph	S		LA	R	#	1612		1637	..	RISH06
ROBEY James	S	N	LA	D	3	1762	..	1788	1841	ROBE24
ROBINSON John	S	N	LA	L	1	1615	..	1640	1676	ROBI30
ROBINSON John (Bernard)	OSB	N	LA	W		1767	1788	1791	1851	ROBI34
ROBINSON Richard	S	N	LA	D		..	..	1612	1634	ROBI44
ROBINSON Thomas	S	N	LA	R	#	1651	..	1677	..	ROBI52
ROGERSON (James)	OFM		LA	F	3	..	1738	1746	1790	ROGE18
RYDING Andrew (Bernard)	OSB	N	LA	G		1752	1769	1776	1841	RYDI02
SAGER Stephen	S	N	LA	P	#1	1601	..	1625	..	SAGE02
SALE Edmund	SJ		LA	Y	#124	1604	1626	..	1648	SALE02
SALE John	S	N	LA	D	#4	1601	..	1625	1664	SALE04
SALE John	SJ	N	LA	Y		1722	1741	1748	1791	SALE06
SALE Richard	S	N	LA	R	#4	..	..	1668	1700	SALE10
SANDERSON John	S		LA	R	†3	..	..	1580	1602	SAND20
SANDERSON Nicholas	S	N	LA	R	#	1648	..	1670	..	SAND24
SANDERSON Nicholas	SJ	N	LA	Y	#	1731	1750	1756	1790	SAND26
SANDERSON Robert	SJ	N	LA	Y	3	1715	1738	1747	1781	SAND28
SANDERSON Thomas	S	N	LA	D	3	1761	..	1790	1826	SAND30
SANDYS John VEN.	S	W	LA	Q	+‡4	..	..	1584	1586	SAND36
SANKEY Francis	SJ	M	LA	Y		1604	1633	..	1663	SANK02
SANKEY Lawrence	SJ		LA	Y	1	1606	1636	..	1657	SANK04
SANKEY William	SJ	L	LA	Y	#1	1609	1628	..	1680	SANK06
SCARISBRICK Edward	SJ	N	LA	Y	#	1639	1659	1672	1709	SCAR02
SCARISBRICK Edward	SJ		LA	Y	#3	1664	1682	1690	1735	SCAR04
SCARISBRICK Edward	SJ		LA	Y	#3	1698	1716	1725	1778	SCAR06
SCARISBRICK Francis	SJ		LA	Y	#	1643	1663	1676	1713	SCAR08
SCARISBRICK Francis	SJ		LA	Y	#	1703	1722	1735	1789	SCAR10
SCARISBRICK Henry	SJ	N	LA	Y	#3	1641	1661	1670	1701	SCAR12
SCARISBRICK Joseph or Thomas	SJ		LA	Y	#3	1673	1692	1701	1729	SCAR16
SCARISBRICK Thomas	SJ	N	LA	Y	#13	1642	1663	1672	1673	SCAR18
SEEL Peter (Mary of S.Teresa)	ODC	N	LA	Z	#	1705	..	..	1752	SEEL02
SEFTON Thomas	SJ		LA	Y	#	1719	1738	1745	1748	SEFT04
SERGEANT John	S	N	LA	D		1715	..	1744	1795	SERG06
SHACKLETON William	SJ	N	LA	R	#‡1	1584	1612	1610	1655	SHAC02
SHARROCK James (Jerome)	OSB	M	LA	G		1750	1768	..	1808	SHAR12
SHARROCK John (Dunstan)	OSB	N	LA	W		1754	1775	..	1831	SHAR14
SHARROCK William (Gregory) BP	OSB	W	LA	G	*	1742	1758	1766	1809	SHAR16
SHAW John	SJ	N	LA	Y	3	1739	1759	1765	1808	SHAW12
SHEPHERD John	S	L	LA	L	3	1678	..	1706	1761	SHEP02
SHEPHERD John (Wm of S.Mary)	OFM	N	LA	F	12	1624	1657	..	1679	SHEP06
SHEPHERD Joseph	S		LA	D		1738	..	1764	1796	SHEP08
SHEPHERD Joseph	S	N	LA	V	#	1767	..	1791	1825	SHEP10
SHEPHERD Thomas	S	N	LA	D		1720	..	1745	1774	SHEP12
SHERBURN Charles	SJ		LA	Y		1684	1702	1715	1745	SHER04
SHERBURN Joseph	OSB		LA	E		1628	1652	..	1697	SHER08
SHERBURN Matthew	S	N	LA	D	#	1600	..	1623	1668	SHER10
SHERBURN Richard	S	N	LA	D	#	..	..	1622	..	SHER12
SHERBURN Thomas (James)	OSB	N	LA	G	#4	1594	1614	..	1657	SHER14
SHERRAT Henry	S		LA	S		1558	..	1593	1602	SHER20
SHIRLEY Andrew	OSB	N	LA	V		1577	1604	1603	1609	SHIR04
SHUTTLEWORTH Edmund (Wolstan)	OSB	N	LA	E	#	..	1640	..	1677	SHUT02
SHUTTLEWORTH John	SJ	M	LA	Y	#3	1708	1730	1743	1765	SHUT08
SHUTTLEWORTH John	S	N	LA	D	3	1756	..	1784	1839	SHUT10
SIMPSON John (Benedict)	OSB		LA	W	#	1713	1736	..	1775	SIMP04
SIMPSON John (Cuthbert)	OSB	M	LA	E		1725	1746	..	1785	SIMP06
SIMPSON Richard (Benedict)	OSB	N	LA	W		1728	1751	..	1801	SIMP14
SIMPSON Thomas	OSB	N	LA	W		1718	1737	..	1764	SIMP18
SINGLETON Michael William	S		LA	R		1741	..	1767	1783	SING04
SINGLETON Richard	SJ		LA	Y	2	1566	1584	..	1602	SING06
SINGLETON Robert	S		LA	D	#13	1612	..	1636	..	SING08

Name	Reg	D	Co	T	Notes	Born	Prof	Ordn	Died	Code
SLATER Edward (Bede) BP.	OSB	N	LA	W	*	1774	1794	1798	1832	SLAT02
SLATER John (Bernard)	OSB	N	LA	W		1744	1761	..	1810	SLAT04
SLATER Thomas (Benet)	OSB	N	LA	W		1756	1777	..	1801	SLAT06
SMITH Edmund (Augustine)	OSB		LA	R	†	1565	1592	1591	..	SMIT13
SMITH Edward (Benedict)	OSB		LA	S	#3	1585	1617	1616	1637	SMIT14
SMITH Henry	S		LA	R	#	1608	..	1632	..	SMIT23
SMITH James	S	N	LA	V		1775	..	1800	1827	SMIT28
SMITH John	SJ	N	LA	Y	#	1615	1637	..	1650	SMIT33
SMITH Thomas	SJ	N	LA	V	1	1631	1662	1659	1681	SMIT67
SMITH Thomas	S	N	LA	D	3	1674	..	1701	1755	SMIT68
SMITH Thomas (Bernardine)	OFM		LA	F	124	1613	1634	..	1666	SMIT73
SOUTHWORTH Christopher	S		LA	R	#	1556	..	1583	..	SOUT24
SOUTHWORTH John ST.	S	L	LA	D	#+1	1592	..	1618	1654	SOUT26
SOUTHWORTH Ralph	S	W	LA	D		1747	..	1771	1810	SOUT28
SOUTHWORTH Richard	S	L	LA	D	#	1743	..	1768	1817	SOUT30
SOUTHWORTH Thomas	S	M	LA	D	#	1749	..	1776	1816	SOUT32
SOUTHWORTH William	S	M	LA	D	#	1752	..	1777	1814	SOUT34
SPENCER Daniel	OSB	N	LA	E		1767	1788	..	1794	SPEN04
STANDISH James	S	L	LA	Q	‡4	..	..	1588	1621	STAN04
STANDISH Lawrence	SJ	M	LA	Y	#14	1604	1626	..	1671	STAN06
STANLEY Henry	SJ		LA	Y	#3	1688	1706	1714	1753	STAN24
STRANGUISH Philip	S		LA	Q	#x	..	..	1583	1598	STRA06
SUMNER Richard (Anthony)	OFM		LA	R		1775	1791	1799	1822	SUMN02
SUMNER James (Leo)	OFM	M	LA	R		1775	1791	1799	1822	SUMN04
SWARBRICK James	S	N	LA	R	#x	1654	..	1678	1716	SWAR02
SWARBRICK John	S	N	LA	R		1679	..	1703	1729	SWAR04
SWARBRICK Joseph	S		LA	V		1775	..	1800	1804	SWAR06
SWARBRICK Robert	S	N	LA	R	#	1675	..	1700	1737	SWAR08
SWARBRICK Robert	S	N	LA	D		1746	..	1776	1815	SWAR10
SYRES Joseph	S	L	LA	D		1738	..	1762	1807	SYRE02
TALBOT James (Oswald)	OSB	N	LA	W		1768	1789	1792	1847	TALB10
TALBOT John	SJ	N	LA	Y	#3	1708	1728	1739	1799	TALB16
TALBOT John	SJ		LA	Y	3	1737	1757	1764	1801	TALB20
TALBOT Richard	S	N	LA	R		1738	..	1762	1823	TALB24
TALBOT Thomas	SJ		LA	R		1572	1598	1597	1652	TALB26
TALBOT Thomas	SJ	L	LA	Y	#3	1717	1735	1750	1799	TALB28
TALBOT Thomas	S		LA	R		1736	..	1762	1818	TALB30
TALBOT William	SJ		LA	N	12	1596	1618	..	1660	TALB34
TARLETON William (Dunstan)	OSB	N	LA	W		1772	1794	..	1816	TARL04
TATLOCK Henry	SJ	N	LA	Y	#	1709	1729	1736	1771	TATL02
TATLOCK John	S	N	LA	Z	#3	..	..	1649	..	TATL06
TAYLOR Alexander	S	M	LA	P	°	..	..	1749	..	TAYL06
TAYLOR Charles (Boniface)	OSB	N	LA	X		1752	1772	..	1812	TAYL12
TAYLOR John (Boniface)	OSB		LA	X		1775	1792	..	1805	TAYL30
TAYLOR Richard	S	N	LA	L	#3	1657	..	1685	1726	TAYL36
TAYLOR Robert	S		LA	L		1743	..	1768	1769	TAYL40
TAYLOR Thomas	SJ	L	LA	R		1674	1702	1701	1726	TAYL44
TEMPEST Nicholas	SJ	N	LA	Y	x1	1631	1652	1661	1679	TEMP16
THOMPSON Richard	S	N	LA	U		1772	..	1797	1841	THOM34
THOMPSON William VEN.	S	L	LA	Q	#+	..	..	1584	1586	THOM46
THORNTON James	SJ		LA	Y	#13	1678	1700	1711	1752	THOR08
THULES Christopher	S		LA	R	#	1560	..	1584	..	THUL02
THULES John VEN.	S	N	LA	R	+	1568	..	1592	1616	THUL04
THULES Robert	S		LA	V	3	1572	..	1599	1602	THUL06
TOMLINSON James	S		LA	R	#	1673	..	1697	..	TOML02
TOOTELL Christopher	S	N	LA	L	#3	..	..	1686	1727	TOOT04
TOOTELL Hugh	S	M	LA	D	#	1671	..	1698	1743	TOOT06
TOWNELEY Richard (Columban)	CRT		LA	C		1664	1700	..	1729	TOWN02
TOWNELEY Thomas	S	N	LA	P	3	..	..	1694	1737	TOWN04
TOWNSON John	OSB	N	LA	X		..	1674	..	1718	TOWN08
TOWNSON Thomas (Augustine)	OSB	N	LA	X		..	1688	..	1722	TOWN10
TRAFFORD Henry	S	N	LA	D	#3	1633	..	1658	1664	TRAF02
TRISTRAM Joseph	SJ		LA	Y	#	1766	1803	1791	1843	TRIS02
TURNER George	OSB		LA	G		1770	1790	1800	1851	TURN14
TURNER John	OSB	N	LA	E		1765	1786	1790	1844	TURN22
TURNER John (Thomas)	OSB	N	LA	W		1743	1759	..	1802	TURN24

Name	Reg	D	Co	T	Notes	Born	Prof	Ordn	Died	Code
TURNER Robert	SJ		LA	Y	#	1677	1701	1712	1734	TURN 32
TURNER Robert (Augustine)	OSB	N	LA	X		1721	1740	..	1757	TURN 34
TYLDESLEY (Anthony)	OFM	M	LA	F	123	1686	1703	1710	1718	TYLD02
TYRER James	S	N	LA	D		1741	..	1766	1784	TYRE02
TYRER Joseph	SJ	W	LA	Y	3	1734	1753	1762	1798	TYRE04
URMESTON John	S	N	LA	S	7	..	..	..	..	URME02
VEAL Edward	OSS		LA	V		..	..	1635	..	VEAL02
WADDINGTON John	S	L	LA	D	#	..	..	1645	1689	WADD02
WAGSTAFFE James	S	N	LA	L		1762	..	1788	1847	WAGS02
WALKER George (Augustine)	OSB	N	LA	E	x	1721	1743	..	1794	WALK06
WALL John (Joachim) ST.	OFM	M	LA	R	#+	1620	1651	1645	1679	WALL04
WALL William (Cuthbert)	OSB	L	LA	R	#	1625	1668	1649	1704	WALL06
WALMESLEY Charles BP.	OSB	W	LA	E	*	1722	1739		1797	WALM02
WALMESLEY Christopher	SJ		LA	V	#3	1684	1708	1707	1734	WALM04
WALMESLEY Francis	OSB		LA	W		1718	1735	..	1747	WALM06
WALMESLEY (Mellitus)	OSB		LA	W		..	1679	..	1689	WALM08
WALMESLEY Richard	S	N	LA	V	#3	1709	..	1733	1744	WALM10
WALMESLEY Richard (Anselm)	OSB	N	LA	W		..	1709	..	1735	WALM12
WALMESLEY Richard (Peter)	OSB		LA	G	#	1717	1736	..	1790	WALM14
WALMESLEY Thomas	SJ		LA	Y	3	1716	1737	1744	1792	WALM16
WALMESLEY William	S	M	LA	D	#	..	..	1644	..	WALM18
WALMESLEY William	SJ	M	LA	Y	3	1712	1732	1740	1769	WALM20
WALTON James	S	N	LA	R	#	1609	..	1633	1671	WALT04
WALTON James	SJ		LA	Y	3	1736	1757	1765	1803	WALT06
WALTON John	SJ		LA	Y	#	1624	1642	..	1677	WALT08
WALTON Thomas	SJ	M	LA	Y	3	1740	1757	1765	1797	WALT10
WALTON William	SJ		LA	Y	3	1651	1671	1684	1706	WALT12
WALTON William BP.	S	N	LA	D	*	1715	..	1741	1780	WALT14
WARING (Ambrose)	OSB	N	LA	W		1734	1761	..	1776	WARI06
WARING John (Henry)	OFM		LA	F	34	1745	1763	1770	1816	WARI10
WARING Peter	S		LA	D	°	1712	..	1740	1773	WARI12
WARING Robert (Bruno)	OFM		LA	F	13	1726	1746	1755	1779	WARI13
WATMOUGH Arthur (Francis)	OSB		LA	W		1665	1684	..	1733	WATM02
WEARDEN John (Vincent)	OSB	N	LA	X		1769	1787	..	1801	WEAR02
WEATHERBY Peter	S	N	LA	D	#	1600	..	1624	1667	WEAT02
WELCH Thomas	OSB	N	LA	E		1726	1744	..	1790	WELC02
WELLS Edward	OSS		LA	V	#	..	1637	1635	1647	WELL06
WESTBY (Anthony of S.Francis)	OFM		LA	F	123	1670	1697	1703	1713	WEST08
WESTBY Peter	SJ		LA	Y	#	1727	1749	1757	1788	WEST10
WESTBY Thomas	SJ	L	LA	Y	3	1703	1724	1733	1736	WEST12
WHALLEY Richard (Alexius)	OFM		LA	F	#13	1739	1757	1764	1811	WHAL20
WHALLEY Thomas	S	M	LA	R	#	1675	..	1701	1730	WHAL22
WHITAKER Humphrey	S		LA	R	#	1613	..	1638	1653	WHIT04
WHITAKER Nicholas	S		LA	V	4	..	..	1646	1653	WHIT06
WHITAKER Thomas VEN.	S	N	LA	V	#+	1611	..	1638	1646	WHIT08
WHITE John	S	N	LA	R	#	1710	..	1733	1778	WHIT36
WHITE John	SJ	L	LA	Y	3	1744	1768	1769	1771	WHIT38
WHITE Luke	S	N	LA	R	#	1708	..	1731	1765	WHIT40
WILCOCK Charles (Peter Alcan)	OFM	N	LA	F	1	1749	1767	1773	1802	WILC02
WILCOCK Peter	OSB		LA	W		1715	1737	..	1776	WILC04
WILKINSON John Paul	S		LA	D		1703	..	..	1771	WILK14
WILKINSON Thomas	SJ	N	LA	V	#x	1638	1667	1662	1681	WILK16
WILLACY James	S	L	LA	D	3	1738	..	1761	1805	WILL02
WILLIAMSON Edward	SJ	L	LA	R		1580	1617	1605	1649	WILL68
WILSON James	S	N	LA	D	#	1726	..	1753	1808	WILS04
WILSON Thomas	S	M	LA	R		1690	..	1713	1766	WILS34
WINCKLEY Thomas	S		LA	D	#	1699	..	1727	1741	WINC06
WINCKLEY William	S	N	LA	R		1677	..	1704	1742	WINC08
WINDER Peter	S	N	LA	L	#3	1615	..	1642	..	WIND02
WINSTANLEY Edmund	S	M	LA	D	3	1735	..	1758	1783	WINS02
WOLFALL John	SJ		LA	Y	#	1682	1702	1711	1742	WOLF02
WOLFALL Thomas	S	N	LA	R	#	1675	..	1699	1720	WOLF04
WOLSTONHOLME Richard	S		LA	D	§	1539	..	1603	..	WOLS06
WOODCOCK John (Martin) VEN.	OFM	N	LA	R	#+1	1602	1631	1637	1646	WOOD16
WOODCOCK John	S	N	LA	D		1766	..	1793	1837	WOOD18
WOODCOCK William	SJ		LA	Y	#13	1659	1682	1690	1717	WOOD20

Name	Reg	D	Co	T	Notes	Born	Prof	Ordn	Died	Code
WOODRUFFE Robert	S	N	LA	R		1552	..	1581	..	WOOD32
WOODWARD (Joseph of S.Mary)	OFM		LA	F	1234	1657	1676	1681	1701	WOOD52
WOODWARD (Matthias)	OFM		LA	F	123	1672	1693	1697	1720	WOOD56
WORSLEY Edward	SJ		LA	Y	‡1	1605	1626	..	1676	WORS02
WORSLEY Thomas	S		LA	S	#3	1572	..	1595	..	WORS06
WORSWICK James	S	N	LA	D		1771	..	1795	1843	WORS12
WORSWICK John	S	N	LA	D		1761	..	1786	1809	WORS14
WORSWICK John (Dunstan)	OSB		LA	W		1743	1758	..	1770	WORS16
WORSWICK Robert	S	N	LA	P	#	1714	..	1744	1752	WORS18
WORSWICK Thomas	S		LA	D	#	1716	..	1740	1748	WORS20
WORTHINGTON James	S		LA	R		1587	..	1610	..	WORT04
WORTHINGTON John	SJ	N	LA	R		1573	1598	1597	1652	WORT06
WORTHINGTON John	S	N	LA	D		..	..	1609	1622	WORT08
WORTHINGTON John	SJ	N	LA	Y	#3	1713	1735	1742	1777	WORT12
WORTHINGTON Lawrence	SJ		LA	Y	#124	1575	1598	..	1637	WORT14
WORTHINGTON Peter	SJ		LA	R		1581	1602	..	1613	WORT16
WORTHINGTON Thomas	S		LA	D	*‡14	1548	..	1577	1626	WORT20
WORTHINGTON Thomas	S		LA	D		..	..	1625	..	WORT22
WORTHINGTON Thomas	OP	N	LA	R		1671	1692	1695	1754	WORT26
WORTHINGTON William	SJ		LA	D	4	1584	..	1609	1621	WORT28
YATES John	S		LA	D	#	..	..	1598	..	YATE14
YATES John	S	N	LA	D		1765	..	1795	1827	YATE18
YOUNG Daniel (Bernard)	OSB	W	LA	X		1741	1760	..	1801	YOUN04
YOUNG Thomas	S	N	LA	L	#	..	..	1681	1714	YOUN14

LC—LOW COUNTRIES

Name	Reg	D	Co	T	Notes	Born	Prof	Ordn	Died	Code
AERTS Philip	OP	L	LC		*7	..	..	..	..	AERT02
BABTHORPE Albert	SJ	N	LC	Y	1	1646	1664	1674	1720	BABT02
BOELMANS Lambert	SJ	L	LC	Y		1649	1672	1678	1690	BOEL02
BUSBY George	SJ		LC	Y	#	1638	1656	1667	1695	BUSB01
BUSBY John	S		LC	V	1	1640	..	..	..	BUSB04
BUSCA John James (Charles)	ODC	L	LC			1632	1652	..	1688	BUSC01
CAESTRYCK Charles (Benedict)	OP	M	LC	Z	*	1762	1785	..	1844	CAES02
CARPENTER Hermengild	SJ	M	LC	Y		1703	1721	1729	1770	CARP02
CHAMBERLAIN George BP.	S		LC	R	*	1576	..	1600	1634	CHAM04
CHENEY Philip	S	L	LC		7	..	..	..	..	CHEN04
CLEMENT Caesar	S		LC	R		1561	..	1586	1626	CLEM02
CLOSETTE Joseph	SJ	W	LC	Y		1752	1771	1776	1781	CLOS02
COPLEY John	S	L	LC	R	#° 1	1577	..	1602	1662	COPL04
CORBUSIER John	SJ	L	LC	Y	#	1707	1726	1738	1765	CORB12
CORHAM Robert	OSB		LC	G		..	1643	..	1665	CORH02
CORNELISON James	SJ		LC	Y	1	1644	1664	1672	..	CORN07
DENTIERS Philip	SJ		LC		4	1580	1598	..	1621	DENT02
DONCKER John Bapt de (Gaspar)	ODC		LC			1633	1657	..	1694	DONC02
GAGE Charles	SJ	M	LC	Y	#° 1	1655	1675	1683	..	GAGE02
GOVAERDT Christian	OSB		LC	G		..	1624	..	..	GOVA02
HARRISON Henry	SJ		LC	Y		1652	1673	1682	1701	HARR32
HARVEY George	SJ		LC		7	..	..	..	..	HARV02
HEIGHAM John	S		LC	R	#1	1617	..	1646	..	HEIG02
JULIAENS Peter (Charles)	OFM	L	LC	F	3	1735	1757	1764	1807	JULI02
KELLAM (Joachim)	OFM		LC	F	123	1657	1676	1686	1703	KELL02
KEMELE (Peter of S.Joseph)	OFM		LC	F	124	1624	1648	..	1653	KEME02
LANSANCH (Peter John) de	OFM		LC	F	12	1644	1675	..	1691	LANS02
L'EAU Louis de	OFM		LC	F	123	1685	1706	1722	1757	LEAU02
LE GRAND (Anthony of Padua)	OFM	M	LC	F	123	1628	1648	1653	1699	LEGR02
LEMANS (Martial)	OFM		LC		14	1717	1744	..	1776	LEMA04
LEONARD (Leonard of S.Fr'cis)	OFM		LC	F	123	1663	1687	1691	1699	LEON06
LOWE John	S	L	LC	D		..	..	1604	..	LOWE06
LOWE Nicholas	S		LC	D		1584	..	1606	1624	LOWE10
LOWE William	S	L	LC	D		..	..	1616	..	LOWE12
MALTON Thomas	S	M	LC	D	#	..	..	1642	1684	MALT02
MANNING Robert	S	L	LC	P	3	1655	..	1690	1732	MANN10
MARSH William	SJ	L	LC	Y	1	1615	1632	1641	1688	MARS16
MATAGON Francis	SJ	L	LC	Y	#12	1614	1632	..	1667	MATA02
MIDDLETON William	SJ		LC	A		..	1622	1619	1625	MIDD28

Name	Reg	D	Co	T	Notes	Born	Prof	Ordn	Died	Code
MORE Henry or Francis	SJ	L	LC	Y	#	1666	1684	1691	1730	MORE06
MOTET Ferdinand	SJ		LC	V	3	1658	1684	1684	1691	MOTE02
MURPHY Cornelius	SJ		LC	Y		1696	1711	1720	1766	MURP02
MURPHY John	SJ	N	LC	Y		1657	1678	1687	..	MURP04
MURPHY Melchior	SJ		LC	Y	1	1664	1684	1693	1736	MURP06
NELSON Francis	SJ	L	LC	Y	1	1632	1650	1660	1675	NELS06
NIFFO (Augustine)	OFM		LC		123	1605	1633	1635	1665	NIFF02
OGNATE John (Joseph) d'	OSB	N	LC	E		..	1700	..	1740	OGNA02
OUDART (William of S.B'vent)	OFM		LC	F	123	1623	1649	1650	1665	OUDA02
PAGE Francis BL.	S	L	LC	D	#*+2	..	1602	1600	1602	PAGE06
(Peter of the Mother of God)	ODC		LC		12	1635	1652	..	1705	PETE02
PLOTHO Delphine	SJ		LC	Y	1	1668	1687	1693	1747	PLOT02
POLE Charles de la	SJ	L	LC	Y		1669	1688	1697	1740	POLE06
POLE Toussaint de la	SJ		LC	Y		1673	1694	1703	1710	POLE32
PORA (Charles)	OFM		LC	F	#123	1629	1649	1653	1693	PORA02
PORTER James	SJ		LC	Y	3	1733	1752	1759	1810	PORT08
REVELL (Hyacinth)	OP		LC	N	4	..	..	..	1668	REVE02
ROUSSE Charles	SJ		LC	Y	#3	1690	1710	1718	1764	ROUS08
ROUSSE Louis	SJ		LC	Y	#3	1732	1753	1761	1794	ROUS10
SCHONDONCK Giles	SJ		LC	Y	#	1556	1576	..	1617	SCHO02
SELOSSE Anthony	SJ		LC			1621	1658	..	1687	SELO02
SELOSSE Anthony	SJ	L	LC	Y		1653	1671	1680	1696	SELO04
SHERWOOD (Joseph)	OSB		LC	X		..	1653	..	1690	SHER34
SIES Jerome (Benedict)	OSB		LC	X		..	1689	..	1697	SIES02
SOM Henry del	SJ		LC			..	..	..	1613	SOMA02
STEEN (Elijah Mt.Cml.) van de	CAR	L	LC			1656	1674	1680	1701	STEE04
STEPHENS Henry Robert	SJ		LC	Y	3	1665	1683	1688	1723	STEP06
STOCKER Thomas (Augustine)	OSB		LC	G	#	1598	1621	..	1668	STOC02
TANGHE (Urban)	OFM	M	LC		7	..	..	..	..	TANG02
TAYLOR Henry	S		LC		3	1602	..	1639	..	TAYL18
TAYLOR Thomas	S	L	LC	R		1604	..	1628	1635	TAYL42
TEVERS Peter	S		LC	R		..	..	1634	..	TEVE02
THOMPSON Peter (Antoninus)	OP	N	LC	N		1675	1696	1702	1760	THOM30
THROCKMORTON Fer'nd(Aemilian)	OSB		LC	E		..	1623	1627	1656	THRO02
TOULOTT Matthew	SJ	L	LC	Y	3	1639	1660	1666	1677	TOUL02
TYFFE Lambert de	SJ		LC		1	1603	1634	..	1672	TYFF02
VAN ERP Cornelius (Sigismund)	ODC	L	LC			1646	1669	..	1721	VANE04
VAN ERP James (Luke)	ODC	L	LC			1643	1666	..	1721	VANE06
VANSTRATER Paschasius	SJ		LC		4	1587	1612	..	1621	VANS02
VAN VALCKENISSE Peter(Crucis)	ODC	L	LC			1603	1624	..	1671	VANV02
WAKE Richard	S		LC	R		1607	..	1634	..	WAKE04
WALKER Thomas	S	N	LC	R	#	1598	..	1621	..	WALK14
WALLIS John (of S.Mary)	OFM		LC	F	12	1605	1638	..	1647	WALL26
WAMBEKE Adrian van	SJ		LC			1630	1666	..	1687	WAMB02
WIART (Gregory of S.Mary)	OFM		LC	F	1234	1625	1648	1652	1692	WIAR02
WILLEMART James	OSA	L	LC	D	*2	1626	1644	..	..	WILL05
WISE George	SJ	L	LC	V	#3	1643	1670	1670	1704	WISE02
WORSLEY Thomas	SJ	L	LC	Y	#	1597	1614	..	1671	WORS08
WORSLEY William	S		LC	V	#	1594	..	1618	..	WORS10
WORTHINGTON Richard	S	L	LC	R		1606	..	1631	1667	WORT18
WORTHINGTON Thomas	SJ	L	LC	Y	#	1616	1633	..	1670	WORT24

LE—LEICESTERSHIRE

Name	Reg	D	Co	T	Notes	Born	Prof	Ordn	Died	Code
BEAUMONT Henry	SJ	.	LE	Y	#1	1610	1630	..	1673	BEAU08
BLOUNT Richard	SJ		LE	R	#‡	1563	1596	1589	1638	BLOU11
BYERLEY Charles	SJ		LE	Y	3	1718	1738	1744	1796	BYER02
BYERLEY William (Ildephonsus)	OSB	M	LE	G	4	..	1708	1711	1753	BYER06
CANES Thomas (Jn Bpt Vincent)	OFM	L	LE	F	#†1	1609	..	..	1672	CANE02
CHAMBERS Sabine	SJ	L	LE		‡1	1560	1587	..	1633	CHAM22
DAKINS John	OSB	W	LE	E		1668	1688	1695	1710	DAKI04
EBERSON Thomas	SJ		LE	Y	#3	1660	1679	1689	1733	EBER02
EDWARDS Joseph	OP	L	LE	N	#§	1725	1754	..	1781	EDWA14
EYRE Thomas	SJ		LE	Y	1	1669	1687	1696	1715	EYRE10
EYRE William	SJ	N	LE	Y	#	1638	1658	1667	1675	EYRE16
FAUNT Lawrence Arthur	SJ		LE	R	‡	1554	1570	..	1591	FAUN02

Name	Reg	D	Co	T	Notes	Born	Prof	Ordn	Died	Code
FREEMAN Thomas	S		LE	Q		..	..	1581	..	FREE 08
HANDS Edward	S		LE	D	#4	..	..	1612	1625	HAND 04
HANMER Francis	SJ	L	LE	Y	12	1593	1610	..	1666	HANM 02
HARCOURT Henry	SJ		LE	Y	#1	1610	1630	..	1673	HARC 04
HOLLAND John	S		LE	R		1569	..	1603	..	HOLL 12
MABBS James (Lawrence)	OSB	L	LE	G	x†	1589	1620	..	1641	MACZ 01
MANNERS Oliver, Hon.,Kt.	S		LE	R	†=1	1580	..	1611	1613	MANN 06
NEVILLE Charles	SJ	W	LE	Y	#3	1746	1763	1771	1792	NEVI 02
SACHEVERELL John (William)	OP		LE	R	°	1568	..	1590	1625	SACH 02
SATERFORD John	S		LE	D		1566	..	1595	..	SATE 02
SMITH John	S		LE	R	#‡	1580	..	1604	1604	SMIT 29
SMITH Joseph	SJ	N	LE	Y	3	1725	1746	1760	1768	SMIT 46
THWAITES Francis	S	L	LE	R	#	..	..	1664	1723	THWA 02
TURNER Anthony BL.	SJ	M	LE	R	#+†1	1628	1653	..	1679	TURN 02
TURNER Edward	SJ		LE	Y	#x†3	1625	1658	1658	1681	TURN 08
TURVILLE Charles	SJ		LE	Y	#3	1681	1700	1708	1757	TURV 02
TURVILLE Henry	SJ		LE	Y		1674	1693	1701	1714	TURV 04
TURVILLE William	S	W	LE	R		1692	..	1719	1765	TURV 06

LN—LINCOLNSHIRE

Name	Reg	D	Co	T	Notes	Born	Prof	Ordn	Died	Code
ALLOT William	S	M	LN	N	†13	1540	..	1570	1587	ALLO 02
ANDERSON Lionel (Albert)	OP	L	LN		#§13	1620	1659	1665	1710	ANDE 08
ANDERSON William	SJ	M	LN	Y	#3	1689	1721	1729	1764	ANDE 12
BARKWORTH Mark BL.	OSB	L	LN	V	#+*‡	1572	1601	1599	1601	BARK 18
BEESTON George	S	M	LN	D	3	1737	..	1762	1797	BEES 12
BEESTON Peter	S	M	LN	D	3	1727	..	1752	1767	BEES 14
BEESTON Robert	SJ		LN	Y	#3	1659	1680	1688	1732	BEES 15
BEESTON Robert	S	M	LN	D	3	1743	..	1768	1832	BEES 16
BENTLEY Christopher	S	M	LN	V	3	..	..	1683	1694	BENT 04
BERESFORD William	SJ	M	LN	Y	#	1670	1692	1697	1726	BERE 02
BERTIE Jerome	SJ		LN	Y		1673	1693	1701	1739	BERT 02
BILCLIFFE Peter	S		LN	V	#	..	..	..	1632	BILC 02
BLACKISTON Francis	SJ	M	LN	Y	#12	1635	1657	1667	1701	BLAC 16
BREWSTER Francis Willoughby	ODC	M	LN			1770	..	..	1849	BREW 10
BURNELL Francis	SJ		LN	Y	x14	1656	1676	1685	1689	BURN 02
CALEY James (Anthony S.Jo'ph)	OFM	M	LN	F	13	1756	1776	1779	1800	CALE 02
CATER Francis	SJ	M	LN	Y	#	1598	1621	..	1656	CATE 02
CLIFFORD William Ld.Cumberld.	S		LN	V	#*3	1594	..	1619	1670	CLIF 08
COMPTON Richard	S	L	LN	R	†	1651	..	1701	1726	COMP 06
CONSTABLE John	S		LN	D	#	1605	..	1631	..	CONS 14
CONSTABLE John	SJ	M	LN	Y	#13	1676	1695	1704	1743	CONS 15
CONSTABLE Marmaduke or Joseph	SJ		LN	Y	1	1672	1690	1699	1750	CONS 18
CONSTABLE Thomas (Augustine)	OSB	L	LN	G		..	1649	..	1712	CONS 30
COOPER James	S		LN	V		1579	..	1603	..	COOP 04
COXON John	S		LN	R	#4	1639	..	1670	1688	COXO 02
DALYSON (Gregory)	OSB	L	LN	X		..	1670	..	1710	DALY 02
DALYSON (Nicholas of S.Mary)	OFM		LN	F	123	1639	1675	1677	i707	DALY 04
DAWSON Thomas (Simon Stock)	ODC	L	LN	R	#1	1574	1613	1610	1652	DAWS 06
DICCONSON Ignatius	SJ	M	LN	Y	°1	1663	1685	1693	..	DICC 03
DICCONSON Robert	SJ	M	LN	Y		1642	1663	1672	1693	DICC 04
DICKENSON Roger BL.	S		LN	Q	#+	..	..	1583	1591	DICK 06
EURE Thomas	SJ	M	LN	Y	#	1607	1630	..	1645	EURE 04
EURE William	SJ	M	LN	Y	#	1648	1669	1678	1698	EURE 06
FISHER Thomas	S		LN	D	#	1578	..	1603	1667	FISH 22
FITZWILLIAM George	S	N	LN	R		1649	..	1673	1678	FITZ 20
FITZWILLIAM John	SJ		LN	Y	#	1635	1654	1663	1665	FITZ 21
GREEN Thomas	S		LN	Q	†=	..	..	..	1591	GREE 50
HINDE Francis	S	M	LN	P	1	1716	..	1749	1810	HIND 04
HOLLAND Guy	SJ	M	LN	V	#†	1587	1615	1613	1660	HOLL 06
HUNT Thomas	SJ	M	LN		=24	1552	1582	..	1628	HUNT 16
IRELAND William BL.	SJ	L	LN	Y	#+	1636	1655	1667	1679	IREL 10
KENT Robert	S		LN	R	#§	1643	..	1667	1687	KENT 02
KNIGHT Francis (Benedict)	OSB		LN	X		1716	1733	..	1743	KNIG 04
KNIGHT James (Dunstan)	OSB	M	LN	X		1714	1732	..	1787	KNIG 08
KNIGHT Richard	SJ	M	LN	Y	#3	1720	1739	1746	1793	KNIG 16

Name	Reg	D	Co	T	Notes	Born	Prof	Ordn	Died	Code
LANGWORTH Basil	SJ		LN	V	#	1632	1661	1657	1683	LANG 24
MADDISON Edward	S		LN	D	#*	1589	..	1615	..	MADD 02
METCALFE John (Gregory)	OSB		LN	X		1724	1740	..	1752	METC 12
METCALFE William (Placid)	OSB	L	LN	X		1723	1740	..	1780	METC 28
MONSON Richard (Angelus)	OFM		LN	F	1234	1665	1686	1689	1713	MONS 01
MONSON (George)	OFM		LN	F	123	1678	1696	1705	1718	MONS 02
MOSELEY Joseph	SJ		LN	Y	3	1731	1748	1755	1787	MOSE 02
MOSELEY Michael	SJ	W	LN	Y	#3	1720	1739	1746	1777	MOSE 04
MOTTRAM John	S		LN	S	†°	..	..	..	1713	MOTT 02
NEALE Robert	SJ	M	LN	S	#3	1600	1629	1626	1688	NEAL 14
NEWTON Edward John Bapt.	SJ	M	LN	Y	#3	1720	1737	1746	1788	NEWT 02
NEWTON Robert	S	M	LN	L	#	1723	..	1747	1800	NEWT 08
NEWTON William	SJ	L	LN	Y	#13	1683	1702	1712	1756	NEWT 10
NEWTON William	SJ	M	LN	Y	3	1718	1736	1744	1755	NEWT 12
OVERTON Edward	S		LN	V	#§	1580	..	1608	..	OVER 02
PAYTON Thomas	SJ		LN	Y		1607	1630	..	1660	PAYT 02
PORMORT Thomas VEN.	S	L	LN	R	#+†	..	..	1587	1592	PORM 02
RAVENSCROFT James	S	M	LN	D		1635	..	1659	1703	RAVE 08
RISHWORTH William	S		LN	D	#	..	..	1615	1637	RISH 08
RIVERS Richard	SJ	M	LN	Y		1607	1648	..	1679	RIVE 06
ROBINSON Thomas	SJ		LN	D	4	..	1575	1573	1593	ROBI 50
SCOTT William	S		LN	D	#	1696	..	1730	1770	SCOT 14
SCRIMSHAW William	S	W	LN	R	#1	1711	..	1734	1800	SCRI 02
SERGEANT John	S	L	LN	L	#†	1623	..	1649	1707	SERG 04
SIMPSON Charles (Benedict)	OFM		LN	F	34	..	1764	1776	1784	SIMP 02
SMITH Richard BP.	S	L	LN	R	#‡*	1567	..	1592	1655	SMIT 56
SMITH Thomas	S	L	LN	D	#	1603	..	1629	1656	SMIT 66
SPENCER John	SJ	M	LN	Y	#†2	1601	1627	1632	1671	SPEN 06
STAPLETON Thomas	SJ		LN	Y		1632	1651	1664	1685	STAP 12
THIMELBY Edward	S		LN	R	#	1615	..	..	1676	THIM 02
THIMELBY John	S	L	LN	R		1675	..	1699	..	THIM 04
THIMELBY Richard	SJ	M	LN	Y	#	1614	1632	..	1680	THIM 08
THOMPSON Thomas	S	M	LN		7	..	..	..	..	THOM 40
THOROLD Alexander	SJ	M	LN	Y		1631	1655	1663	1681	THOR 14
THOROLD Edmund Epiphanius	SJ	M	LN	Y	#13	1669	1687	1695	1732	THOR 18
THOROLD Francis	OSS		LN	D	#	..	1646	..	..	THOR 20
THOROLD Thomas	SJ	L	LN	R	#	1600	1633	1633	1664	THOR 24
TORRE Vincent	OP	L	LN			1631	1652	1654	1687	TORR 02
VINCENT Nicholas	OP		LN	R	#24	1596	..	..	1616	VINC 02
WHICHCOTT William	SJ		LN	Y	#12	1580	1606	..	1654	WHIC 02
WHITE Eustace ST.	S	W	LN	R	+1	1560	..	1588	1591	WHIT 26
WILLIAMSON Richard	SJ	L	LN	Y	12	1605	1626	..	1649	WILL 72
WRIGHT John	S	M	LN	D		1754	..	1781	1797	WRIG 14
WRIGHT Richard	S		LN	V	#†	1568	..	1604	..	WRIG 26
YAXLEY Richard VEN.	S	M	LN	Q	#+	..	..	1585	1589	YAXL 06

MD—MARYLAND

Name	Reg	D	Co	T	Notes	Born	Prof	Ordn	Died	Code
BOARMAN John	SJ		MD	Y		1743	1762	1769	1797	BOAR 02
BOARMAN Sylvester	SJ		MD	Y	4	1746	1765	1772	1812	BOAR 04
BOON Edward	SJ	N	MD	Y	3	1734	1756	1764	1785	BOON 04
BOON John	SJ	N	MD	Y	3	1735	1756	1762	1795	BOON 06
BOON Joseph	SJ		MD	Y		..	..	..	1779	BOON 08
BROOKE Charles (Joseph)	CRT		MD	C		1735	1769	..	1784	BROO 05
BROOKE Ignatius	SJ		MD	V		1671	1699	1696	1751	BROO 08
BROOKE Ignatius	SJ		MD	Y	4	1751	1770	..	1815	BROO 09
BROOKE Leonard	SJ	W	MD	Y		1750	1769	..	1813	BROO 10
BROOKE Matthew	SJ		MD	V		1672	1699	1697	1702	BROO 12
BROOKE Robert	SJ		MD	Y	3	1663	1684	1692	1714	BROO 14
CARROLL John ARCHBP.	SJ	W	MD	Y	*	1735	1753	1761	1815	CARR 06
CHANDLER Richard (Paul)	OSB		MD	G		1685	1705	1710	1712	CHAN 04
COLE Henry	S		MD	V	3	..	..	1763	1763	COLE 06
COLE Joseph	SJ		MD	Y	3	1727	1747	1762	1763	COLE 08
COLE Robert	SJ	L	MD	Y	3	1732	1752	1760	1812	COLE 10
DIGGES Francis	SJ	N	MD	Y	3	1712	1733	1741	1781	DIGG 02
DIGGES John	SJ	N	MD	Y	3	1712	1734	1741	1746	DIGG 04

Name	Reg	D	Co	T	Notes	Born	Prof	Ordn	Died	Code
DIGGES John Dudley	S		MD	R	#	1689	..	1715	1771	DIGG 06
DIGGES Thomas	SJ		MD	Y	3	1711	1729	1737	1805	DIGG 10
DOYNE Joseph	SJ	N	MD	Y	3	1734	1758	1764	1803	DOYN 02
FAULKNER Ralph	S	L	MD	R		1736	..	1761	..	FAUL 06
FENWICK Edward (Dominic) BP.	OP	L	MD		*	1768	1790	1792	1832	FENW 02
FENWICK John (Ceslaus)	OP	L	MD		1	1759	1783	1785	1815	FENW 06
HOSKINS Ralph	SJ	N	MD	Y	3	1729	1749	1764	1794	HOSK 04
JENKINS (Augustine)	SJ		MD	Y	3	1742	1766	1773	1800	JENK 04
KNATCHBULL Robert	SJ	N	MD	Y		1716	1735	1742	1782	KNAT 04
LIVERS Arnold	SJ		MD	Y	3	1705	1724	1733	1767	LIVE 02
MATTHEWS Ignatius	SJ		MD	V	3	1730	1763	1763	1790	MATT 08
MATTINGLEY John	SJ		MD	Y		1745	1766	1770	1807	MATT 22
NEALE Benedict	SJ		MD	Y	3	1709	1728	1741	1787	NEAL 02
NEALE Charles	SJ		MD	Y		1751	1771	..	1823	NEAL 04
NEALE Henry	SJ		MD	Y		1702	1724	1738	1748	NEAL 08
NEALE Leonard ARCHBP.	SJ		MD	Y	*	1747	1767	1773	1817	NEAL 12
NEALE William	SJ	N	MD	Y	3	1743	1760	1767	1799	NEAL 16
PILE Henry	SJ	N	MD	Y	3	1743	1761	1768	1814	PILE 02
SEMMES Joseph	SJ	N	MD	Y	3	1743	1761	1767	1809	SEMM 02
SEWALL Charles	SJ		MD	Y	3	1744	1764	1771	1806	SEWA 02
SEWALL Nicholas	SJ	N	MD	Y		1745	1766	1772	1834	SEWA 04
THOMPSON Charles	SJ		MD	Y	#	1746	1766	1771	1795	THOM 14
WHARTON Charles	SJ	M	MD	Y	°3	1748	1766	1772	1833	WHAR 04

MH—MERIONETHSHIRE

Name	Reg	D	Co	T	Notes	Born	Prof	Ordn	Died	Code
MORGAN John	S	W	MH	D	#3	1660	..	1690	1719	MORG 20
ROBERTS John ST.	OSB	L	MH	V	+‡=1	1576	1600	1602	1610	ROBE 10

MI—ISLE OF MAN

Name	Reg	D	Co	T	Notes	Born	Prof	Ordn	Died	Code
ANDERTON Robert BL.	S		MI	Q	+‡	1560	..	1584	1586	ANDE 38
CANNELL James	SJ	N	MI	Y		1649	1671	1678	1722	CANN 02
OWEN Hugh	S	M	MI	R		1669	..	1692	1741	OWEN 03

MO—MONMOUTHSHIRE

Name	Reg	D	Co	T	Notes	Born	Prof	Ordn	Died	Code
ADAMS (Pacificus of S.Giles)	OFM		MO	F	123	1669	1686	1691	1701	ADAM 04
ANDREWS William (Bernardine)	OFM		MO	F	123	1636	1658	1663	1679	ANDR 02
ARCHER John	SJ	W	MO	Y	#12	1627	1650	1657	1674	ARCH 12
ARCHER Philip	S		MO	R	#4	1624	..	1650	1651	ARCH 14
AYLWORTH Matthew	S		MO	L	#	..	..	1641	..	AYLW 05
AYLWORTH William	SJ	M	MO	Y	#	1625	1641	..	1679	AYLW 06
BAKER David (Augustine)	OSB	L	MO		‡=	1575	1607	1613	1641	BAKE 10
BARBER Francis	S		MO	D	14	1593	..	1618	1633	BARB 10
BEAUMONT Francis	SJ	N	MO	Y	#	1682	1702	1711	1738	BEAU 07
BLUETT Thomas	S		MO	D	§°4	1539	..	1578	1604	BLUE 06
BOSVILLE Jhn	S	W	MO	D	#	1716	..	1743	1779	BOSV 04
COX James (Boniface)	OFM		MO	F	13	1736	1752	1761	1764	COXA 11
COX Thomas (Felix)	OFM	L	MO	F	13	1726	1742	1749	1788	COXA 16
DAVIES William VEN.	S	W	MO	Q	+‡1	1558	..	1585	1593	DAVI 18
DAVIES William	S	W	MO	D	3	1767	..	1794	1814	DAVI 34
EVANS Francis	SJ	W	MO	Y	#	1659	1679	1688	1727	EVAN 08
EVANS Philip ST.	SJ	W	MO	Y	+	1645	1665	1674	1679	EVAN 18
GOOD Thomas	S	M	MO	L		..	..	1689	1732	GOOD 06
GREEN Francis (Leander)	OSB	N	MO	X		..	1660	..	1704	GREE 18
GUILLIAM David	OSB		MO	E		..	1652	..	1669	GUIL 08
GUNTER William BL.	S	L	MO	Q	+1	1560	..	1587	1588	GUNT 02
GWYN William	S	W	MO	R	‡	1576	..	1602	1640	GWYN 10
HARRIS Thomas or John	SJ	W	MO	Y	14	1595	1619	...	1676	HARR 18
JONES Edward	S	W	MO	D	3	1747	..	1774	1799	JONE 06
JONES George	S		MO	D	#1	1657	..	..	..	JONE 08
JONES John	SJ	L	MO	Y	3	1721	1739	1752	1803	JONE 18
JONES Philip	S	W	MO	D	#	1722	..	1746	1800	JONE 40
JONES Walter	S		MO	V	3	..	..	1647	..	JONE 45
KEMYS David (Joseph)	OP	L	MO	R	x	..	..	..	1680	KEMY 01

Name	Reg	D	Co	T	Notes	Born	Prof	Ordn	Died	Code
LEWIS David ST.	SJ	W	MO	R	#+§=	1616	1645	1642	1679	LEWI02
LEWIS David	SJ		MO	R	#34	1671	1691	1705	1741	LEWI04
LEWIS John	SJ	W	MO	Y	#	1610	1631	..	1648	LEWI12
LEWIS Philip	S	M	MO		*	..	..	..	1710	LEWI22
LEWIS Philip	S		MO	R		1688	..	1713	..	LEWI24
LORYMER Francis	S	W	MO	R		1708	..	1733	1765	LORY02
LORYMER Michael (Anselm)	OSB	L	MO	G		1751	1768	..	1832	LORY04
MORGAN (David of S.Wilfrid)	OFM		MO	F	123	1637	1657	1663	1702	MORG01
MORGAN Francis	S		MO		7	..	..	..	..	MORG09
MORGAN George	SJ		MO		#124	1584	1609	..	1620	MORG10
MORGAN James	S		MO	D	#3	1647	..	1676	..	MORG14
MORGAN John	S	M	MO	D	3	1639	..	1663	..	MORG18
MORGAN Walter	SJ		MO	S	2	..	1607	..	..	MORG36
MORGAN William	SJ	L	MO	Y	#	1648	1669	1678	1710	MORG40
MORRIS David	S		MO	R	#	1630	..	1654	1710	MORR04
NEEDHAM Charles	S	W	MO	D		1716	..	1741	1802	NEED04
NEEDHAM Sebastian	SJ	L	MO	Y	#1	1671	1691	1700	1743	NEED16
PARRY (Jerome of S.James)	OFM		MO	F	#1234	1653	1670	1677	1714	PARR10
PARRY Philip	S	W	MO	L	#1	1605	..	1638	1678	PARR16
PERKINS Richard	S	W	MO	D	#	1602	..	1627	1672	PERK06
PHILIPS William	S	W	MO	V	#	1597	..	1622	1655	PHIL30
POWELL George	S		MO	R	#	1609	..	1632	..	POWE08
POWELL Thomas	S	W	MO	L	#	1615	..	1639	1700	POWE22
PRICHARD Charles	SJ	W	MO			1637	1662	..	1680	PRIC30
PRICHARD James	S		MO	D	3	1639	..	1663	1697	PRIC34
PRICHARD James	S		MO	R	#	1651	..	1677	..	PRIC35
PRICHARD (Leander)	OSB		MO	G	4	..	1623	..	1685	PRIC38
PRICHARD Matthew BP.	OFM	W	MO	F	*123	1669	1687	1693	1750	PRIC40
PRICHARD Nicholas (Maurus)	OSB		MO	G		1602	1620	..	1657	PRIC42
PRICHARD William	S		MO	R	#	1662	..	1687	..	PRIC44
ROBERTS William (Augustine)	OFM		MO	F	1	1763	1785	1789	1827	ROBE20
SALISBURY John	SJ	W	MO	V	#§	1575	1604	1600	1625	SALI04
SCUDAMORE John	SJ	W	MO	Y	#3	1696	1718	1727	1778	SCUD08
THOMAS Hugh	S	W	MO	D		..	..	1605	..	THOM02
TURNER John	SJ		MO	Y	#12	1640	1662	..	1672	TURN18
VAUGHAN Richard	SJ		MO	Y		1675	1690	1699	1727	VAUG08
VAUGHAN Walter (Dominic)	OFM		MO	F	123	1624	1647	1653	1661	VAUG14
VAUGHAN Walter	S		MO	R		1662	..	1696	1696	VAUG16
WATKINS Lawrence	S	W	MO	R	#4	1627	..	1653	1679	WATK04
WATKINS Walter (Gregory)	OFM	W	MO	F	13	1739	..	1770	1810	WATK06
WILLIAMS Charles	S		MO	L		1627	..	1651	1667	WILL10
WILLIAMS Edward (Dominic)	OP	L	MO	A		1643	1665	..	1688	WILL16
WILLIAMS John	S		MO	L	#	..	..	1653	1674	WILL24
WILLIAMS John	SJ	W	MO	Y	13	1691	1712	1723	1761	WILL28
WILLIAMS Louis	S	W	MO	D	§	1585	..	1610	1661	WILL40
WILLIAMS Nicholas	S		MO	D	#3	1665	..	1693	1737	WILL44
WILLIAMS Reginald	S	W	MO	R	#	1658	..	1682	1737	WILL54
WILLIAMS Thomas (Dominic) BP.	OP	N	MO	Z	*	1668	1686	1692	1740	WILL62

MT—MONTGOMERYSHIRE

Name	Reg	D	Co	T	Notes	Born	Prof	Ordn	Died	Code
BABE James (Bruno)	OFM		MT	F	#13	1716	1737	1743	1784	BABE02
CADWALLADOR Charles	S	W	MT	D	#‡	1591	..	1628	1650	CADW02
CROWTHER Arthur (Anselm)	OSB	L	MT	G	#	1588	1611	..	1666	CROW04
DAVIES Charles or Samuel	S	W	MT	R		1679	..	1704	1761	DAVI02
DAVIES James	S		MT	R		1667	..	1694	..	DAVI04
FOURNIERS Nicholas	SJ	N	MT	Y	#	1708	1725	1733	1779	FOUR02
HILL John	SJ	L	MT	Y		1683	1704	1712	1751	HILL06
KEMYS John	S	W	MT	R	#	1635	..	1658	1709	KEMY02
PRICE Humphrey	S	W	MT	L	#	1611	..	1636	..	PRIC03
ROBERTS James	S		MT	R		1687	..	1709	1709	ROBE06

MX—MIDDLESEX

Name	Reg	D	Co	T	Notes	Born	Prof	Ordn	Died	Code
ABBOT John Austin	OSS	L	MX	D	#*‡24	1588	1614	1612	1650	ABBO02

Name	Reg	D	Co	T	Notes	Born	Prof	Ordn	Died	Code
ABERCROMBIE John	S	L	MX	R	#3	1742	..	1770	1779	ABER 02
ACTON Francis (Augustine)	OSB	N	MX	G		1660	1681	..	1695	ACTO 02
ACTON John (Placid)	OSB	N	MX	G	1	1667	1685	..	1727	ACTO 04
AIERY James (Alban S.Agatha)	OFM		MX	F	123	1649	1667	1673	1705	AIER 02
AINSWORTH John	S	L	MX	D	#†	1577	..	1603	..	AINS 07
ALBERONI John (Francis)	OSB		MX	Z	*	..	1652	..	1693	ALBE 02
ALBERY William	S	L	MX	D	#		..	1624	1675	ALBE 04
ALLAM William (Ambrose)	OSB	M	MX	G	2	1749	1768	..	1812	ALLA 02
ALLEN Jerome	S	L	MX	L		1730	..	1756	1815	ALLE 05
ALLEN John	OSB		MX	G		..	1624	..	1635	ALLE 06
ALLEN Peter	S	L	MX	D	§13	1635	..	1666	..	ALLE 08
ALLEN Ralph	SJ		MX	D		..	1577	1574	1587	ALLE 10
ANDERTON Robert (John Ev.)	OFM	L	MX	F	1	1725	1746	1752	1795	ANDE 46
ANGIER Robert (Hyacinth)	OP	M	MX	N		1762	1787	1788	1850	ANGI 02
ANSON Joseph	S	L	MX	D	3	1753	..	1780	1827	ANSO 02
ANSTEAD William	S	L	MX	R		1737	..	1762	1791	ANST 02
APPLEBY James	S	L	MX	V			..	1790	1799	APPL 01
APRICE (Joseph)	OSB	L	MX	W		1650	1667	..	1703	APRI 02
APRICE Thomas (Ildephonsus)	OSB	L	MX	W		..	1668	..	1712	APRI 04
ARCHDEACON Robert	S	L	MX	R	#	1746	..	1769	1814	ARCH 04
ARCHER James	S	L	MX	D		1751	..	1780	1834	ARCH 08
ASHE Edward	OSB	L	MX		*	..	1605	..	1629	ASHE 02
ASKEW George	S		MX	R	‡	1575	..	1600	..	ASKE 02
ASTLEY Edward	SJ		MX	R	#§1	1584	1608	..	1646	ASTL 02
ASTON Philip (Placid)	OFM	W	MX	F	*23	1709	1726	1735	1755	ASTO 02
ASTON William	SJ		MX	Y		1735	1751	..	1800	ASTO 06
BANKS Richard	SJ		MX	R	#1	1569	1597	1592	1643	BANK 06
BARBER Christopher (Maurus)	OSB	N	MX	G		..	1683	..	1728	BARB 06
BARKER Edward (Bernard)	OFM		MX	F	134	1728	1746	1755	1776	BARK 07
BARKER Thomas (Giles S.Ambr.)	OFM		MX	F	12	1602	1625	..	1660	BARK 13
BARNABY Thomas	S	M	MX	D	#3	1727	..	1752	1783	BARN 04
BARNARD James	S	L	MX	S	§	1733	..	1757	1803	BARN 06
BARNES Louis (John)	OSB	L	MX	E		1731	1746	..	1775	BARN 22
BARNEWALL John (Cyprian)	OSB		MX	X		1761	1783	..	1788	BARN 29
BATESON George (Richard)	ODC	L	MX		1	1657	..	..	1694	BATE 06
BATESON John (Ildephonsus)	ODC		MX		24	1669	1686	..	1746	BATE 08
BAYAERT William	S		MX	D	#‡	1597	..	1625	1651	BAYA 02
BEAUCHAMP William	S	L	MX	T		..	..	1795	1812	BEAU 02
BENNET John	SJ		MX	Y	#	1692	1710	1719	1751	BENN 09
BESWICK Edward	SJ	M	MX	Y	#1	1615	1639	..	1680	BESW 02
BETTS James (Joseph)	CRT		MX	D	1	1665	1711	1691	1729	BETT 04
BETTS John	S		MX	L		..	..	1676	..	BETT 06
BEW John	S	M	MX	P		1755	..	1784	1829	BEWA 02
BIRD Christopher	S		MX	L	#34	..	..	1689	1710	BIRD 02
BIX (Angelus of S.Agnes)	OFM	L	MX	F	1234	1646	1666	1672	1695	BIXA 02
BLACKWELL George	S		MX	D	x‡	1547	..	1575	1612	BLAC 20
BLAIR James	SJ		MX	Y	3	1693	1713	1722	1759	BLAI 02
BLEVIN James	S		MX	L		1732	..	..	..	BLEV 02
BLEVIN William	S	L	MX	D	3	1735	..	1762	1788	BLEV 04
BLUNDEVILLE James	S		MX	D	#1	1603	..	1630	1658	BLUN 26
BOUCHER Richard	SJ	W	MX	Y	3	1696	1713	1727	1760	BOUC 02
BOUCHER Robert (Ambrose)	OSB		MX	X		1726	1744	..	1766	BOUC 04
BRAND John	S	M	MX	D	#3	1675	..	1706	1750	BRAN 02
BREWSTER William	SJ	M	MX	Y		1700	1724	1730	1758	BREW 12
BRODERICK Richard	S	L	MX	T		1771	..	1798	1831	BROD 02
BROOKE Adam	SJ		MX	R	‡	1542	1564	..	1605	BROO 02
BROWN James or Joseph	S	N	MX	D		1707	..	1740	..	BROW 20
BROWN Thomas Lont (Hyacinth)	OP		MX	N	#3	1754	1779	1779	1826	BROW 36
BRUNETTI Joseph	SJ		MX	Y		1671	1689	1698	1715	BRUN 06
BUCK John	SJ	N	MX	Y	#3	1715	1736	1741	1770	BUCK 02
BUCKLEY James	OSB	L	MX	E		..	1708	..	1749	BUCK 10
BUCKLEY James BP.	S	L	MX	L	*	1770	..	1794	1828	BUCK 12
BULMER John (Denis)	OSB		MX	X		..	1732	1736	1741	BULM 06
BURGESS Matthew	S		MX	D		1752	..	1777	1786	BURG 04
BURKE Charles	SJ	L	MX	Y	#3	1713	1733	1747	1787	BURK 02
CAMPION Edmund ST.	SJ		MX	D	#+‡	1540	1573	1578	1581	CAMP 04

Name	Reg	D	Co	T	Notes	Born	Prof	Ordn	Died	Code
CAPE (Peter of S. Augustine)	OFM		MX	F	12	1607	1628	..	1668	CAPE09
CARPUE Joseph Francis	S	L	MX	D	3	1766	..	1791	1849	CARP12
CARTERET Edward	SJ		MX	Y	#13	1689	1709	1719	1753	CART14
CARTERET Francis (Joseph)	OSB	L	MX	G		..	1723	..	1783	CART16
CARTERET Jean Frederick Cyr	S		MX		*8	..	..	..	..	CART18
CARTERET Philip	SJ	M	MX	Y	3	1694	1709	1721	1756	CART20
CATCHER Edward	SJ		MX	R	#§123	1584	1609	1619	1624	CATC02
CHAMBERS Matthew	S	N	MX	D	†	1623	..	1653	1698	CHAM12
CHAMBERS Robert	S	N	MX	D	†	1624	..	1653	1689	CHAM20
CHAMPNEY William (Lawrence)	OSB	N	MX	W		1667	1684	..	1732	CHAM32
CHAPLIN Michael (Anselm)	OSB	N	MX	X		1754	1771	..	1784	CHAP12
CHAPMAN James	SJ		MX	Y	#°3	1694	1711	1720	..	CHAP19
CHAPPELL Henry (Francis X.)	OP	M	MX	N		1749	1775	1776	1825	CHAP30
CHARNOCK Robert	S	L	MX	R	‡=13	1561	..	1586	..	CHAR08
CHURCHILL Thomas	S	L	MX	D	#	1628	..	1653	1705	CHUR06
CLARK James (Francis)	OFM		MX	F	13	1750	1767	1776	1782	CLAR20
CLARK Robert	S	L	MX	R	#	1628	..	1653	1685	CLAR24
CLARK William	SJ	W	MX	Y	3	1669	1687	1696	1734	CLAR40
CLIFFE Henry (Ildephonsus)	OSB		MX	R	#*	1585	1615	1609	1657	CLIF04
COCKETT (Constantine)	OSB		MX		*	..	1634	..	..	COCK06
COFFIN Thomas	SJ		MX	Y	4	..	..	..	1628	COFF08
COGHLAN James (Peter)	OFM		MX	F	1	1761	1783	1785	1798	COGH02
COGHLAN William Augustine	S	N	MX	V		1768	..	1791	1836	COGH04
COKE Thomas	SJ		MX	R	#§	1589	1614	1614	1670	COKE02
COLLINS William	SJ	M	MX	Y	13	1683	1704	1713	1745	COLL38
COLLINS William (Joseph)	OSB	N	MX	X		1758	1783	..	1803	COLL40
COLSTON William	S	L	MX	L		..	..	1678	1695	COLS04
CORBETT Christopher	S	L	MX	R	#	1674	..	1706	..	CORB06
CORDELL Charles	S	N	MX	D		1720	..	1744	1791	CORD02
COTTON George	SJ	L	MX	R	#	1636	1653	..	1697	COTT18
COTTON Richard	SJ	M	MX	Y	#	1665	1681	1693	1740	COTT22
COX David (Edmund)	OSB		MX	E		1662	1698	..	1748	COXA04
CRESWELL Arthur	SJ		MX	R	14	1556	1583	..	1588	CRES06
CRESWELL Joseph	SJ		MX	R	#4	1557	1583	..	1622	CRES08
CROSBY James	S	L	MX	V		1757	..	1781	1819	CROS04
DAVIES John (Bernard)	OSB		MX	X	#	1714	1733	1738	1789	DAVI08
DAVIES John (Leander)	OSB	L	MX	X		1670	1689	..	1734	DAVI09
DAVIES Peter	SJ		MX	Y	13	1690	1711	1720	1759	DAVI11
DAVIES Robert (Ambrose)	OSB	N	MX	E		..	1688	1697	1654	DAVI13
DAVIES Rowland	S	M	MX	D	§	1740	..	1772	1797	DAVI16
DAWSON Edward	SJ		MX		124	1576	1606	..	1624	DAWS02
DAY William	S		MX	D	#	1608	..	1636	1639	DAYA04
DELATTRE Anthony (Charles)	OSB		MX	X		1683	1711	1715	1731	DELA10
DELATTRE Edward (Augustine)	OSB		MX	R		1676	1706	1701	1733	DELA12
DIAS SANTOS Emanuel Thomas	S	L	MX	L	*	1765	..	1799	1834	DIAS02
DIGBY William (Jerome)	OSB	N	MX	G		1744	1761	..	1825	DIGB08
DORMER William	SJ	L	MX	Y	#°13	1710	1728	1736	..	DORM12
DRURY John	SJ		MX	Y	12	1600	1626	..	1663	DRUR02
DUCKETT John	CRT		MX	D		1588	1629	1615	1647	DUCK06
DUDDELL William (Odo)	OSB		MX	X		1670	1689	..	1738	DUDD02
DUPUY Louis	S		MX	R		1721	..	1743	1743	DUPU02
DUVIVIERS James (Placid)	OSB	W	MX	G	#	1740	1757	..	1808	DUVI02
EARLE John	S	L	MX	D		1749	..	1779	1818	EARL02
EDNER Louis (Justus)	OSB	M	MX	V	#2	1585	1604	..	1635	EDNE02
ELRINGTON Edward	S		MX	D	#3	1638	..	1661	1713	ELRI03
EMERSON Ralph	SJ	N	MX	S	3	1609	1635	1633	1684	EMER02
EMMOTT Joseph	SJ	N	MX	Y	3	1734	1753	1761	1816	EMMO02
EVANS John	S		MX	R	#	1688	..	1718	..	EVAN16
EVISON John Alexander	SJ	L	MX	Y	#1	1577	1599	..	1651	EVIS02
FAIRCLOUGH Alexander	SJ	M	MX	V	#23	1575	1605	1602	1645	FAIR04
FANNING Dominic	SJ	L	MX	Y	#3	1742	1762	1773	1812	FANN02
FECK Thomas	SJ		MX	R		1573	1601	1601	1647	FECK02
FENWICK Francis	OSB	L	MX	E		1645	1664	..	1694	FENW04
FISHER Daniel	S	L	MX	L	§3	1646	..	1670	1686	FISH04
FITZSIMON Patrick Lawrence	S	L	MX	S		..	..	1735	..	FITZ18
FITZWILLIAMS Charles	S	M	MX	R	#	1700	..	1729	1750	FITZ24

Name	Reg	D	Co	T	Notes	Born	Prof	Ordn	Died	Code
FLECKNOE Richard	S	L	MX	Y	§4	1600	..	1636	1678	FLEC02
FLEETWOOD Francis or Jn Waltr	SJ	L	MX	V	#3	1699	1735	1724	1774	FLEE04
FLEETWOOD John	SJ	N	MX	Y	3	1703	1723	1728	1734	FLEE06
FOOTHEAD John	S		MX	R		1763	..		1788	FOOT04
FORSTER Charles	SJ		MX	Y		1623	1643	..	1680	FORS07
FOSTER Francis	SJ	M	MX	V	2	1601	1622	..	1653	FOST04
FOWLER Francis	SJ	M	MX	Y	12	1609	1631	..	1659	FOWL04
FRAINE George	S		MX	D	#	1768	..	1792	1805	FRAI02
FRANCIS Alban (Placid)	OSB	M	MX	X		..	1670	..	1715	FRAN02
FULLER John	S	L	MX	D	3	1729	..	1754	1792	FULL06
FULWOOD Thomas (Damasus)	CAR	L	MX		#§° 12	1654	1674	..	..	FULW04
GABB Thomas	S	L	MX	D	#	1742	..	1772	1817	GABB02
GADBURY John	SJ	L	MX	Y	#12	1599	1620	..	1668	GADB02
GAGE Francis	S	M	MX	P	#	1621	..	1646	1682	GAGE04
GAGE John	S		MX	D	#	1619	..	1646	..	GAGE12
GAGE William	SJ	M	MX	Y	#	1599	1619	..	1683	GAGE20
GALLOWAY Edward	SJ	L	MX	Y		1706	1724	1735	1799	GALL06
GAWEN Henry	SJ		MX	Y	3	1668	1685	1693	1701	GAWE04
GAWEN John BL.	SJ	M	MX	R	#+	1640	1660	1670	1679	GAWE06
GAWEN Thomas	SJ	M	MX	Y	13	1646	1668	1677	1712	GAWE08
GAWEN William (Ambrose)	OSB	N	MX	X		..	1690	..	1737	GAWE10
GEARY John (Anselm)	OSB	L	MX	X		1714	1732	1739	1795	GEAR02
GIFFARD John	SJ	N	MX	Y	13	1683	1705	1713	1757	GIFF14
GIFFORD Maurice	OP	L	MX		2	..	1659	..	1699	GIFF24
GILDART George Thomas	S	W	MX	V		1764	..	1787	1827	GILD02
GOOD John	S		MX	L	#3	..	..	1698		GOOD04
GOODYEAR George (Hugh)	OFM		MX	F	12	1643	1664	..	1677	GOOD22
GOOLDE Robert	OSB	L	MX	E		1734	1755	..	1798	GOOL02
GREATON James or Joseph	SJ		MX	V	3	1679	1708	1708	1753	GREA02
GREEN Edward	SJ	L	MX	Y	#3	1647	1668	1678	1727	GREE12
GREEN Hugh BL.	S	W	MX	D	#+†1	1585	..	1612	1642	GREE22
GREEN James	S		MX	D	#	1725	..	1749	1803	GREE24
GREEN Stanislaus	SJ	N	MX	Y		1662	1682	1691	1720	GREE40
GREENHAM John	S	L	MX	V		1752	..	1775	1817	GREE66
GREENWELL John Baptist	S	L	MX	D		1750	..	1777	1802	GREE74
GRIFFETH John	S	L	MX	D		1753	..	1779	1815	GRIF06
GRIFFITH Michael	SJ	M	MX	N	#	1587	1607	..	1652	GRIF24
GUNSTON John	S	L	MX	R	#†	1693	..	1719	1736	GUNS02
GURNAL Thomas (Adrian)	OSB	N	MX	X		1724	1763	1767	1811	GURN02
HACKSHOTT John	S		MX	D	#	1601	..	1625	1663	HACK02
HADLEY John (Edmund)	OSB	N	MX	G		1744	1761	..	1807	HADL02
HADLEY Joseph (Lawrence)	OSB	N	MX	G		1739	1757	..	1805	HADL04
HALFORD John	S	W	MX	D	3	1753	..	1788	1806	HALF02
HALL Francis	S		MX	R	#	1662	..	1685	1728	HALL04
HALL John	SJ		MX	Y		1664	1683	1691	1703	HALL12
HALL Thomas	S		MX	D	1	1660	..	1689	1719	HALL24
HALL William	CRT	L	MX	L	3	1658	1693	1684	1718	HALL26
HARDESTY William (Lawrence)	OSB	N	MX	X		1714	1732	1738	1787	HARD16
HARDING James	S		MX	V	#	..	..	1621	..	HARD20
HARRIS William	S	M	MX	R		..	..	1795	1823	HARR24
HART William	SJ		MX	Y	#1	1640	1660	1667	1667	HART18
HARTLEY John Evangelist	SJ		MX	V	3	1716	1739	1739	1760	HART28
HARWOOD Edmund	SJ		MX	R		1554	1578	..	1597	HARW02
HASKETT Richard	S	L	MX	R	#	1694	..	1719	1774	HASK02
HAUGHTON Robert	CRT		MX	D	#2	1603	1631	1628	1675	HAUG04
HAWKER John	SJ	M	MX	Y	#3	1687	1704	1713	1764	HAWK04
HAWKINS Francis	SJ		MX	Y		1628	1649	..	1681	HAWK08
HAWKINS Henry	SJ	L	MX	R	#	1577	1615	1614	1646	HAWK10
HAYDON John	SJ	L	MX	Y		1603	1629	..	1663	HAYD18
HAYES William	S	M	MX	V		1775	..	1799	1855	HAYE04
HAZLE John	SJ		MX	Y	#	1621	1636	..	1649	HAZL02
HEALEY Richard (Bonaventure)	OFM	L	MX	F	#3	1726	1744	1749	1777	HEAL02
HEBB Edward	S	L	MX	R	1	1668	..	1692	1741	HEBB02
HICCOCKS John (Bede)	ODC	L	MX	N	#§	1588	1612	..	1647	HICC02
HIGGINS Adam	SJ		MX		4	..	..	..	1615	HIGG04
HIGGINS Isaac	S		MX	Q	°	1560	..	1584	..	HIGG09

171

Name	Reg	D	Co	T	Notes	Born	Prof	Ordn	Died	Code
HIGGS Charles	S	W	MX	L	3	1675	..	1702	1736	HIGG16
HILDYARD Thomas	SJ	W	MX	Y	3	1690	1707	1716	1746	HILD10
HILL John	S	L	MX	L	3	..	..	1703	1723	HILL04
HILLS Robert	S	L	MX	D	#	1671	..	..	1746	HILL18
HODGSON Joseph	S	L	MX	D		1756	..	..	1821	HODG26
HOLLAR John	SJ		MX	Y		1674	1696	1708	1712	HOLL18
HORNE Henry	S	L	MX	R	#	1732	..	1755	1769	HORN08
HORNE James	S	L	MX	R	#	1725	..	1750	1802	HORN10
HOUSE Joseph (James S.N'olas)	OFM	M	MX	F	13	1747	1763	1773	1822	HOUS02
HOWARD Philip (Thomas) CARD.	OP	L	MX	Z	*	1629	1646	1652	1694	HOWA16
HUDDLESTON John	SJ	M	MX	R	#	1597	1624	1621	1661	HUDD04
HUDSON Joseph Augustine	S		MX	V	3	1775	..	1797	..	HUDS06
HUGHES John	SJ	N	MX	Y		1754	1770	1778	1828	HUGH12
HUNT Joseph	S	L	MX	D	3	1765	..	1792	1841	HUNT08
IRELAND Richard	S		MX	P	‡	1571	..	1612	1637	IREL08
JACKSON John	SJ		MX	Y	#3	1698	1719	1728	1752	JACK22
JEFFREY Thomas	SJ		MX	Y	#3	1703	1721	1730	1730	JEFF10
JENNINGS John (Bruno)	OSB		MX	G	#	..	1668	..	1701	JENN12
JERNINGHAM Francis	SJ		MX	Y	3	1721	1738	1745	1752	JERN04
JERNINGHAM Hugh (Jo'ph S.Mgt)	OFM		MX	F	1	1730	1750	..	1793	JERN06
JOHNSON Edward	OSB		MX	R	#	1623	1663	1650	1683	JOHN06
JONES James Augustine	S		MX	R	§	1690	..	1719	1737	JONE14
JONES John	S		MX	D	§3	1760	..	1787	1840	JONE22
JONES John (Alexius)	OSB	M	MX	G		1679	1699	1705	1755	JONE24
JONES John (Francis Mary)	CAP		MX		1	1724	..	..	1799	JONE25
JONES Joseph	S		MX	R		1714	..	1740	1760	JONE30
JONES William (Benedict)	OSB	L	MX	D	#§2	..	1604	1598	1639	JONE48
JORIS Henry John	SJ	W	MX		#	1733	1752	..	1796	JOR102
JORIS Peter Andrew	SJ		MX			1735	1753	..	..	JOR104
KEARNEY George	S		MX	R		1676	..	1701	..	KEAR04
KELLY John (Louis S.Dominic)	OFM	M	MX	F	13	1748	1766	1779	1808	KELL18
KEMP Francis (Boniface)	OSB	N	MX	Z	*4	1578	1604	..	1644	KEMP06
KEMP George	S	L	MX	R	#	1626	..	1651	1698	KEMP08
KENNEDY Francis	S		MX	D		1723	..	1748	1791	KENN02
KEYNES Maximilian	SJ		MX	Y	#	1652	1674	1683	1720	KEYN18
KINGDON Abraham	SJ		MX	Y	3	1718	1737	1745	1782	KING08
KINGSLEY William	SJ	N	MX	Y	3	1696	1713	1721	1734	KING20
KINSMAN Bernard	SJ	M	MX	Y		1611	1626	..	1668	KINS02
KINSMAN Edward	S		MX	D		..	..	1627	..	KINS04
KINSMAN Michael	SJ		MX	Y		1614	1631	..	1694	KINS06
KIRBY George	S	L	MX	R		1739	..	1763	1784	KIRB02
LACEY Francis	S	L	MX	R	#3	1686	..	1712	1774	LACE01
LAMB John Augustine	S	M	MX	R	#	1742	..	1765	1809	LAMB02
LANGHORN Charles	S	L	MX	V	#	1660	..	1683	1723	LANG12
LANGHORN Francis	S	L	MX	V	#	..	..	1682	1709	LANG14
LANGTON John (Ambrose)	OSB		MX	W	24	..	1615	..	1620	LANG18
LAYTON William	S	N	MX	L	#	1638	..	1661	1689	LAYT10
LEE Benjamin Charles	CRT		MX	D	#	1674	1714	1716	1740	LEEA04
LEE John	S	L	MX	D		1768	..	1793	1839	LEEA16
LEE Joseph	S	W	MX	D		1765	..	1789	1840	LEEA18
LEE William	S		MX	R	#	1671	..	1696	..	LEEA28
LE GRAND James (Joseph)	OSB	N	MX	R	#§	1711	1737	1734	1772	LEGR04
LE HUNT William	S	L	MX	R		1668	..	1696	..	LEHU06
LEIGH Richard BL.	S	L	MX	R	#+	1561	..	1586	1588	LEIG12
LEWIS James	SJ		MX	Y		1731	1748	1756	1776	LEWI10
LEWKNER Edmund	OSB		MX	G	#	..	1680	..	1714	LEWK04
LINE Francis	SJ	L	MX	Y	#	1595	1623	1628	1675	LINE02
LOADER (Placid)	OSB		MX	G	#	..	1620	1624	1646	LOAD02
LOLLI James	S		MX	D	#*x°	1728	..	1754	1779	LOLL02
LOTHBURY Jasper	S		MX	D		1564	..	1599	..	LOTH02
LOWE Anthony	S		MX	R		1734	..	1758	1794	LOWE02
LOWE John VEN.	S	L	MX	R	+	1553	..	1582	1586	LOWE04
LOWE William	SJ		MX	Y	3	1704	1722	1731	1744	LOWE14
LUSHER Edward	S		MX	R	#	1628	..	1659	..	LUSH04
LUSHER Nicholas	SJ		MX		2	1589	1624	..	1653	LUSH06
LYNCH Francis (Anselm)	OSB		MX	G		1693	1714	..	1777	LYNC02

Name	Reg	D	Co	T	Notes	Born	Prof	Ordn	Died	Code
MacCARLY James or Charles	S	L	MX	R	°1	1698	..	1724	1742	MACC02
MacCARTHY Charles	S	L	MX	D		1751	..	1776	1799	MACC04
MACKWORTH Thomas	S	M	MX	R		1692	..	1716	1734	MACZ08
MANNERS John	SJ		MX	Y	#1	1609	1631	..	1695	MANN04
MANNING John	S	M	MX	R		1731	..	1756	1783	MANN08
MANNOCK Francis	SJ	N	MX	R	#	1670	1686	1696	1748	MANN12
MARTIN Joseph	OSB	L	MX	G	2	..	1652	..	1662	MART24
MARTINASH John	SJ		MX	Y	#3	1679	1699	1707	1725	MART36
MASSEY John	SJ	W	MX	Y	#3	1698	1717	1725	1760	MASS10
MATTHEWS John	SJ		MX	Y		1658	1677	1685	1695	MATT10
MATTHEWS Peter	SJ	N	MX	Y	#3	1692	1711	1722	1752	MATT14
MAXEY John	S	L	MX	L	x§	..	..	..	1617	MAXE02
MEADE John	SJ		MX		#	1572	1592	1602	1653	MEAD02
MENDOZA Christopher de	SJ	N	MX		#	1641	1657	..	..	MEND02
MEREDITH Richard	SJ		MX	D	#	1696	1716	1725	1754	MERE04
MILES Francis	SJ	L	MX	R	§2	1590	1619	1616	1653	MILE02
MILES Francis	SJ	M	MX	Y	1	1650	1672	1682	1693	MILE04
MILNER John BP.	S	M	MX	D	*	1752	..	1776	1826	MILN04
MOLYNEUX Henry	SJ	L	MX	Y	3	1693	1713	1722	1771	MOLY06
MOLYNEUX Richard	SJ	W	MX	Y	3	1696	1715	1723	1766	MOLY12
MOND Charles	S	N	MX	R	#§	1627	..	1655	1680	MOND02
MONTAGU Walter, Hon.	S	L	MX	R	*§1	1603	..	1636	1677	MONT02
MOORE Benjamin (Bede)	OSB		MX	E		..	1681	..	1735	MOOR02
MORDAUNT George (Ben'dct) Hon	OSB		MX	X	°1	1676	1696	..	1728	MORD02
MORGAN John	S		MX	D	#x	1627	..	1654	1680	MORG16
MOYLEN William	SJ		MX	Y	14	1746	1767	..	1800	MOYL02
MUDDLE (Angelus)	CAP	L	MX		1	1585	..	..	1638	MUDD02
MUMFORD William	SJ		MX	Y	1	1628	1647	..	1712	MUMF06
MURPHY Richard	SJ	W	MX	Y	#3	1716	1734	1741	1799	MURP10
MUSSON John	SJ	L	MX	Y		1680	1699	1708	1755	MUSS02
MUSSON Samuel	SJ		MX	Y	#3	1686	1705	1713	1769	MUSS04
NAYLOR George	S		MX	V	#§	..	..	1603	..	NAYL02
NECHILLS William (Bernard)	OSB		MX	E		1712	1729	..	1792	NECH02
NEEDHAM John Turberville	S	L	MX	D		1713	..	1738	1781	NEED08
NEWTON James	SJ		MX	Y	#3	1736	1754	1763	1803	NEWT04
NICHOLAS James	S	L	MX	D	3	1740	..	1766	1777	NICH02
NIXON Edward or Edmund	SJ	N	MX	Y	#	1675	1694	1703	1728	NIXO02
NORRIS John	SJ	L	MX	R	13	1671	1692	1706	1754	NORR08
NOTTLE (Joseph)	OP		MX	Z	#*	1654	1682	..	1696	NOTT02
O'BRIEN (Francis of S.B'nard)	OFM		MX	F	13	1681	..	1702	1711	OBRI01
ORME John	S	L	MX	R		1719	..	1744	1792	ORME02
OWEN John Francis	S		MX	D	3	1649	..	1676	..	OWEN07
PAGE Anthony VEN.	S	N	MX	Q	+‡	..	..	1591	1593	PAGE04
PAINE Thos.(Anselm S.Anthony)	OFM		MX	F	13	1736	1754	1761	1782	PAIN07
PALMER George	SJ	N	MX	Y	3	1692	1713	1722	1758	PALM06
PANTING John	SJ	W	MX	Y		1732	1749	1757	1783	PANT02
PARSONS Richard	SJ		MX	Y	23	1597	1627	1636	..	PARS08
PATERSON Thomas	SJ		MX			1625	1646	..	1699	PATE10
(Paul of London)	OP		MX		*3	..	..	1597	..	PAUL01
PELCON Peter	SJ		MX	Y	#§13	1631	1656	1663	1669	PELC02
PEMBRIDGE Michael (Benedict)	OSB	W	MX	G		1724	1741	..	1806	PEMB04
PENNINGTON John	SJ		MX	Y		1647	1665	1674	1685	PENN14
PETRE Charles	SJ	L	MX	Y	#	1646	1667	1673	1712	PETR04
PETRE Edward, Bt.	SJ	L	MX	Y	*	1633	1653	1662	1699	PETR06
PETRE (Francis of S.John)	OFM		MX	F	1234	1638	1677	1679	1694	PETR11
PIGOTT Adam	SJ		MX	Y	#1	1673	1694	1702	1751	PIGO02
PIGOTT Christopher	S	L	MX	R		1675	..	1697	1735	PIGO04
PIGOTT Francis (Dunstan)	OSB		MX	G		1704	1727	..	1751	PIGO08
PINCKARD Robert	S	L	MX	D	#1	1704	..	1727	1766	PINC02
PIPPARD Luke	SJ		MX	Y	#3	1716	1733	1742	1761	PIPP02
PLASDEN Polydore ST.	S	L	MX	R	#+	1563	..	1586	1591	PLAS02
PLUMMERDEN Robert	S		MX	R	#	1664	..	1688	1751	PLUM02
PLUMMERDEN Thomas	S		MX	D	#°3	1674	..	1703	..	PLUM04
PLUNKETT Gerard (Albert)	OP	N	MX	N	#1	1744	1762	1769	1814	PLUN01
PLUNKETT Richard	S	L	MX	R	#	1743	..	1768	1808	PLUN04
PLUNKETT Robert	SJ		MX	D	*	1752	1769	1779	1815	PLUN06

Name	Reg	D	Co	T	Notes	Born	Prof	Ordn	Died	Code
PLUNKETT Thomas (Anthony)	OP	N	MX	N		1750	1767	1774	1810	PLUN 08
POLE Anthony	SJ		MX	Y	#§° 13	1593	1614	1621	..	POLE 02
PORTMAN John	S	N	MX	R	#§°	1651	..	1675	..	PORT 24
POTIER Peter Philip (Pius)	OP	L	MX	N		1756	1782	1782	1846	POTI 04
POYNTZ Newdigate	S		MX	R	*	1680	..	1706	1723	POYN 10
PRESTON John	S		MX	L	§	1712	..	1736	1780	PRES 10
QUIN James	SJ		MX	Y	3	1698	1717	1725	1745	QUIN 04
QUINTIN George	S	L	MX	R	#	1619	..	1647	1685	QUIN 06
QUYNEO (Bernard)	OSB		MX	W		..	1693	..	1731	QUYN 02
RADFORD Joseph	SJ		MX	Y	°1	1646	1677	1685	..	RADF 04
RAFFA Anthony (Leander)	OSB	N	MX	G		..	1733	..	1758	RAFF 02
RAGWAY Thomas	S		MX	R		1674	..	1696	1698	RAGW 02
READ Robert	S	L	MX	R	§	1744	..	1768	1770	READ 04
REEVE John Austin	S	M	MX	D		1758	..	1783	1813	REEV 02
REYNOLDSON John	SJ		MX	Y	3	1655	1673	1681	1686	REYN 10
RICE Joseph	S	L	MX	R		1744	..	1768	1810	RICE 02
RICHARDSON John	S		MX	R	#14	1639	..	1664	1667	RICH 18
RICHARDSON Robert	SJ		MX	Y	#3	1671	1688	1698	1737	RICH 32
RIDGLEY John (John Baptist)	ODC		MX	R	#§2	1587	1634	1612	1669	RIDG 02
ROABES (Gabriel of S.Mary)	OFM		MX	F	12	1616	1639	..	1678	ROAB 02
ROBINSON Edward	SJ		MX	R	#	1592	1621	1618	1636	ROBI 12
ROBINSON George (Robert)	OSB		MX	X		..	1722	..	1762	ROBI 18
ROBINSON John	SJ	N	MX	Y	#3	1699	1718	1727	1742	ROBI 32
ROGE Joseph	SJ		MX	Y	#	1681	1704	1712	1763	ROGE 02
ROKEBY George (Joseph)	OSB		MX	X		1688	1703	..	1761	ROKE 02
ROUSE John	OSB		MX	W		..	1711	..	1720	ROUS 02
RYCAUT Andrew	OSB		MX	E		..	1664	..	..	RYCA 02
SABRAN Louis de	SJ	L	MX	Y	#	1652	1670	1679	1732	SABR 02
SADLER Edward	SJ	L	MX	Y	1	1663	1690	1699	1751	SADL 06
SADLER John	SJ	M	MX	Y	1	1664	1683	1691	1699	SADL 08
SCUDAMORE John (Placid)	OSB	L	MX	X		1659	1695	..	1704	SCUD 10
SCUPHOLME John	S	N	MX	R	#†1	1643	..	1670	..	SCUP 02
SEISON John	S		MX	D	#	1683	..	1712	1749	SEIS 02
SERGEANT Francis	S		MX	R	§	1651	..	1678	..	SERG 02
SHARP James (Vincent)	OP	M	MX	N		1752	1772	1775	1801	SHAR 04
SHAW James	S	L	MX	R	#	1710	..	1733	..	SHAW 10
SHELLEY Waltyer	SJ		MX	Y	3	1701	1717	1725	1750	SHEL 32
SHEPHERD John	S	L	MX	L	3	1714	..	1737	1789	SHEP 04
SHERIFF Thomas	S	L	MX	R		1720	..	1745	1758	SHER 16
SHERWOOD Henry	S	L	MX	Q		..	..	1588	..	SHER 28
SHERWOOD John	S		MX	Q		..	..	1583	1593	SHER 30
SHERWOOD Richard	S		MX	Q	#	..	..	1584	..	SHER 38
SHIRLEY Henry	S		MX	S	#3	..	..	1630	..	SHIR 08
SHUTTLEWORTH Thomas (Benedct)	OSB	N	MX	X		..	1723	..	1774	SHUT 14
SICKLEMORE Humphrey	S	N	MX	R		1570	..	1596	..	SICK 02
SIMEON Edward	SJ		MX	Y	#	1632	1656	1661	1701	SIME 02
SIMONS Nicholas	S	M	MX	L	#3	1675	..	1702	1714	SIMO 04
SINGLETON John	S	L	MX	V		1775	..	1800	1839	SING 02
SMITH (Maurus)	OSB		MX	G		..	1625	..	1633	SMIT 49
SMITH Nicholas	SJ	L	MX	Q	#*2	1558	1578	1583	1630	SMIT 52
SMITH Richard	S	L	MX	R		1725	..	1750	1808	SMIT 59
SMITHERS (Oswald)	OSB	M	MX	X		..	1694	..	1725	SMIT 79
SMYTHE Charles	OSB		MX	G		1727	1746	..	1780	SMYT 02
SOVIGO Octavian	S		MX	R	3	..	..	1592	..	SOVI 02
SQUIBB Francis	S		MX	D	#	1691	..	1716	1762	SQUI 02
STANLEY John	S	W	MX	V		1759	..	1785	1828	STAN 29
STARKEY Joseph	OSB		MX	G	#	1676	1703	..	1754	STAR 06
STEARE Robert (Benedict)	OSB	N	MX	G		1702	1720	..	1780	STEA 02
STEPHENSON Cyprian	S		MX	R	#	1600	..	1624	1626	STEP 18
STRICKLAND John	S		MX	D	#	1723	..	1747	1802	STRI 102
STRICKLAND Joseph	S	M	MX	P		1724	..	1748	1790	STRI 104
STRUTT John (Wilfrid)	OSB	W	MX	R	#	1713	1743	1738	1782	STRU 02
STUART William	SJ	N	MX	R	#	..	1640	..	1677	STUA 02
STUART d'AUBIGNY Ludovick,Dke	S		MX	P	*	1619	..	1652	1665	STUA 04
STUTTARD Richard	S		MX	L	#3°	1769	..	1795	..	STUT 02
SWINDALL Stephen	SJ		MX	Y	#3	1677	1695	1703	1758	SWIN 16

Name	Reg	D	Co	T	Notes	Born	Prof	Ordn	Died	Code
TAPRELL John	S	M	MX	D	°	1718	..	1748	..	TAPR 02
TAYLOR Edmund	OSB		MX	G		..	1680	..	1714	TAYL 16
TAYLOR James	S	L	MX	D	3	1761	..	1788	1806	TAYL 26
TAYLOR Ralph	SJ	N	MX	R	#	1678	1706	1704	1727	TAYL 32
TAYLOR Thomas	S	L	MX	V		1763	..	1787	1808	TAYL 46
TEMPEST Michael (Edward)	OSB		MX	X		..	1719	..	1773	TEMP 12
THOMAS Hugh Benedict	S	L	MX	R	#§	1704	..	1736	1770	THOM 04
THOMAS Richard	SJ	N	MX	Y	#3	1685	1704	1713	1735	THOM 10
THOMPSON Charles	SJ		MX	Y	#12	1607	1625	..	1673	THOM 12
THORPE Andrew	SJ	N	MX	Y	3	1741	1758	1765	1799	THOR 32
TIMINGS Charles	S	W	MX	V		1757	..	1781	1832	TIM 102
TOMMINS Robert	S	L	MX	R		1741	..	1764	1810	TOMM 02
TOWERS Francis	S	L	MX	R	#4	1645	..	1668	1733	TOWE 02
TREVENNIAN Charles	SJ	L	MX	Y	#13	1667	1685	1694	1737	TREV 02
TUITE Francis	S	L	MX	D	3	1768	..	1791	1838	TUIT 02
TUITE William (Raymund)	OP	L	MX	N		1766	1790	1792	1833	TUIT 04
TYRWHIT Henry	SJ		MX	Z	#*	1672	1692	1702	1742	TYRW 02
VARDER John	S	L	MX	R	#	1580	..	1606	..	VARD 02
VAUGHAN Arthur	S	M	MX	D		1725	..	1749	1792	VAUG 02
VERE Henry (Joseph)	OP		MX	D		..	1661	1653	1683	VERE 02
VERHUYCK John	S	L	MX	R	#	1688	..	1715	1738	VERH 02
WAFERER Francis	SJ		MX	Q	=1	1540	1585	1585	1588	WAFE 04
WALKEDEN John	SJ		MX	R	#3	1663	1682	1694	1718	WALK 02
WALKER (George)	CAR	L	MX		4	..	..	..	1720	WALK 05
WALLET Louis Albert	S	L	MX	D	3	1735	..	1759	1812	WALL 18
WAREHAM John (Denis)	OSB		MX	X	#	..	1744	..	1763	WARE 02
WARREN Thomas	S	N	MX	R	#§	1631	..	1658	..	WARR 18
WARRILOW William	SJ	N	MX	Y	3	1738	1760	1766	1807	WARR 24
WATERSON Edward BL.	S	N	MX	Q	+§	..	..	1592	1593	WATE 04
WATKINSON John (Gregory)	OSB	N	MX	G		1727	1746	..	1792	WATK 10
WATKINSON Matthias	S		MX	L		1634	..	1658	1710	WATK 12
WATSON Ignatius	SJ	W	MX	R	#4	1586	1615	1612	1625	WATS 02
WEBB George	SJ		MX	Y		1653	1672	1681	1725	WEBB 04
WEBB James	S	L	MX	D	3	1726	..	1754	1781	WEBB 06
WEBB Michael	SJ	N	MX	Y		1623	1642	..	1665	WEBB 08
WEBSTER Thomas	S	L	MX	L		1757	..	1783	1828	WEBS 02
WELLS Ambrose	S		MX	V	#*3	..	..	1724	..	WELL 02
WESTHEAD Henry	S		MX	R	#	1698	..	1723	1772	WEST 14
WESTON Edward	S	N	MX	R	‡4	1565	..	1589	1635	WEST 16
WHARTON Charles (Christopher)	ODC	L	MX		2	1663	1686	..	..	WHAR 02
WHITAKER Thomas	S	L	MX	R	#§	1702	..	1729	1778	WHIT 10
WHITE Andrew	SJ		MX	S	3	1579	1607	1606	1656	WHIT 20
WHITE Henry	SJ	L	MX	Y	#	1662	1680	1689	1693	WHIT 30
WHITE James (Anselm)	OFM	M	MX	F	134	1712	1740	1746	1778	WHIT 31
WHITE Thomas	S	L	MX	D	3	1764	..	1791	1826	WHIT 60
WHITTELL Roger (Joseph)	OSB		MX	E		1707	1726	..	1786	WHIT 90
WIGGS William	S		MX	R	‡4	..	..	1582	1602	WIGG 02
WIGNAL Francis	SJ		MX	Y	#1	1678	1697	1706	1728	WIGN 02
WILFORD Humphrey	S		MX	V	#3	..	..	1604	..	WILF 04
WILFORD Peter (Boniface)	OSB	L	MX	V	#x	1584	1609	1607	1646	WILF 06
WILKINSON Charles	SJ		MX	Y	#	1622	1643	..	1686	WILK 08
WILLIS Thomas	S		MX	R		1722	..	1746	1768	WILL 76
WILLIUGHBY Edward	ODC	M	MX		#°2	1766	1783	..	..	WILL 82
WILSON Charles	SJ		MX	Y	1	1660	1680	1689	1730	WILS 02
WINTON James	OSB		MX	X	#	1672	1690	..	1712	WINT 10
WOODS John (Ambrose)	OP		MX	N		1766	1790	1792	1842	WOOD 38
WOOLS Thomas	S	L	MX	R		1744	..	1769	1788	WOOL 12
WORTLEY Francis	S		MX	L		..	..	1691	..	WORT 30
WRENCH Bernard	S	L	MX	D	#	1602	..	1627	1629	WREN 04
WYCHE Joseph	OSB		MX	X		1672	1690	..	1727	WYCH 06
WYKE James	S		MX	D		1728	..	1752	1799	WYKE 02
YORK William (Lawrence) BP.	OSB	W	MX	G	*	1686	1705	1711	1770	YORK 06

ND—NORTHUMBERLAND

Name	Reg	D	Co	T	Notes	Born	Prof	Ordn	Died	Code
ARMSTRONG John	SJ	N	ND	R	#	1591	1621	1616	1660	ARMS 08

Name	Reg	D	Co	T	Notes	Born	Prof	Ordn	Died	Code
ARMSTRONG Robert	OP	N	ND	R	#	1603	1626	..	1663	ARMS 12
ARMSTRONG Thomas	OP	N	ND	R	#	1607	1632	..	1662	ARMS 14
BEADNALL James	SJ		ND	Y	#3	1718	1739	1746	1772	BEAD04
BERRY James (Augustine)	OSB	N	ND	E		1758	1779	..	1786	BERR06
BERTRAM William (Michael)	OP	N	ND	Z	*13	1643	1666	1675	1691	BERT04
BLACKISTON William John	SJ		ND	V	#3	1698	1723	1723	1768	BLAC18
BLAKEY Philip	OSB		ND	X		..	1690	..	1707	BLAK08
BLAKEY William (Anselm)	OSB	L	ND	X	4	..	1682	..	1723	BLAK10
CATTERALL John (Stephen)	OP	N	ND	Z	*	1702	1719	1726	1765	CATT10
CHARLTON John	OSB	N	ND	G		1717	1736	..	1786	CHAR02
CHILTON Philip Jos.(Vincent)	OP		ND	R	3	1664	1682	1688	1722	CHIL02
CLAVERING Nicholas Matthew	S	N	ND	D	#	1728	..	1752	1805	CLAV02
CLAVERING Ralph	S		ND	R	4	1655	..	1686	1718	CLAV04
CLAVERING Thomas	S		ND	R	#§14	1628	..	1654	1695	CLAV06
COATES John	S	N	ND	D		1700	..	1725	1794	COAT02
COLLINGWOOD Charles	SJ	M	ND	Y		1664	1688	1691	1719	COLL12
COLLINGWOOD Robert	SJ	M	ND	Y		1657	1677	1686	1741	COLL18
COLLINGWOOD Roger (Anselm)	OSB	N	ND	X	x	..	1663	..	1679	COLL20
COLLINGWOOD Thomas	S	N	ND	V	3	..	..	1631	..	COLL22
COLLINGWOOD Thomas	SJ	N	ND	Y	#1	1631	1652	1661	1680	COLL24
DICKENSON Matthew	OFM	M	ND	F	134	1725	1741	1749	1767	DICK05
DUNN Francis	S	L	ND	D		1722	..	1748	1757	DUNN02
DUNN John	S	N	ND	D	#	1692	..	1717	1741	DUNN04
ERRINGTON Anthony	S		ND		4	..	..	..	1719	ERR102
FENWICK Louis (Lawrence)	OSB	L	ND	G		..	1685	..	1746	FENW08
FENWICK William (Augustine)	OSB	N	ND	G		..	1693	1694	1726	FENW10
FERLAMAN James	OP		ND	N	3	1740	1759	1762	1796	FERL02
GARDINER James	S	N	ND	D	#3	1669	..	1699	1750	GARD08
GARDINER Luke	S	N	ND	P	#	1683	..	1713	1740	GARD18
GIBSON George	S	N	ND	D		1726	..	1750	1778	GIBS06
GIBSON George (Thomas)	OP	N	ND			..	1673	..	1696	GIBS08
GIBSON Matthew BP.	S	N	ND	D	*3	1734	..	1758	1790	GIBS14
GIBSON Richard	S	M	ND	D	3	1739	..	1763	1801	GIBS16
GIBSON Thomas	S	N	ND	D	#3	1688	..	1716	1765	GIBS18
GIBSON William BP.	S	N	ND	D	*3	1738	..	1765	1821	GIBS20
GIBSON William (Thomas)	OP	N	ND	R		1668	1687	1692	1724	GIBS22
GRAY (Philip of S.Clare)	OFM		ND	F		1616	1636	1642	1698	GRAY08
GRAY Robert	S		ND	R	#°	1562	..	1586	..	GRAY10
GREAVES Joseph (Bernard)	OSB	N	ND	G		..	1676	..	1720	GREA08
HAGGERSTON (Francis S.Clare)	OFM		ND	F	12	1665	1686	..	1704	HAGG03
HAGGERSTON Francis (Placid)	OSB		ND	G		1680	1701	1708	1716	HAGG04
HAGGERSTON Henry	SJ	N	ND	Y	#3	1658	1679	1688	1714	HAGG06
HAGGERSTON John	SJ	N	ND	Y	#	1661	1680	1689	1726	HAGG08
HALSALL Arthur (Bede)	OSB		ND	G		..	1687	..	1739	HALS01
HANKIN John	S	N	ND	D		1706	..	1731	1782	HANK02
HILDRETH John	SJ		ND	Y	1	1654	1677	1690	1702	HILD04
HUNTER George	CRT		ND	V		..	1694	..	1727	HUNT22
HUNTER George	SJ		ND	Y	3	1713	1730	1744	1779	HUNT24
HUNTER Thomas	SJ	N	ND	Y	3	1666	1684	1696	1725	HUNT26
HUNTER Thomas	SJ	N	ND	Y	#3	1718	1735	1744	1773	HUNT30
HUTCHINSON Joseph (Wilfrid)	OSB	N	ND	X		..	1679	..	1717	HUTC06
HUTCHINSON Matthew (Dunstan)	OSB		ND	X		..	1685	..	1730	HUTC08
JEFFERSON Philip	OSB	N	ND	E		1732	1750	..	1776	JEFF02
JENISON Thomas	SJ	M	ND	Y	#x§3	1643	1663	1672	1679	JENI24
KIRSOPP William (Peter)	OP		ND	R		1670	1687	1694	1705	KIRS02
LAWSON Henry	SJ	N	ND	Y	#x§	1628	1656	1662	1679	LAWS06
LEADBITTER Edward	OP	N	ND	N	#	1747	1770	..	1788	LEAD02
LEADBITTER Jasper (Dalmatius)	OP	N	ND	N	3	1749	1772	1775	1830	LEAD04
LEADBITTER (John)	OP	N	ND	N	3	1740	1767	1769	1811	LEAD06
LEADBITTER (Matthew)	OP		ND	N		1702	1724	1726	1735	LEAD08
LEADBITTER Nicholas(Hyacinth)	OP	N	ND	N		1722	1743	1745	1768	LEAD10
LORRAINE (Lawrence of S.Mary)	OFM	N	ND	F	123	1651	1670	1676	1718	LORR02
MACKAY John (Gregory)	OSB	N	ND	G		1704	1724	..	1778	MACZ06
MITFORD Roger	S	N	ND	D		..	..	..	1697	MITF02
MORRISON William	S		ND	R	#	1674	..	1697	..	MORR20
NEWTON Lancelot (Bede)	OSB	N	ND	X		1714	1732	1737	1777	NEWT06

Name	Reg	D	Co	T	Notes	Born	Prof	Ordn	Died	Code
OGLE William	S	N	ND	Q		..	..	1598	..	OGLE 02
OGLE William	S		ND	L	#3	..	..	1644	..	OGLE 04
ORD Ralph (Anthony)	OSB	N	ND	G		..	1685	..	1725	ORDA 02
PHILIPS (Dominic)	OP	N	ND	N		1742	1759	1764	1783	PHIL 08
POTTS Henry Joseph	S		ND	L		1772	..	..	1800	POTT 06
POTTS John (Bede)	OSB	N	ND	X		1674	1691	..	1744	POTT 08
POTTS Luke	S	N	ND	D	#	1717	..	1744	1787	POTT 10
RADCLIFFE Francis (Ildeph'us)	OSB		ND	X		..	1669	..	1689	RADC 02
READ Francis	S		ND	R		1628	..	1652	..	READ 02
RIDDELL Edward (Joseph)	OSB		ND	X		..	1719	..	1736	RIDD 02
RIDDELL George (Gregory)	OSB	L	ND	X		..	1688	..	1730	RIDD 04
RIDDELL Peter	SJ		ND	Y	4	1636	1656	1664	1668	RIDD 06
RIDDELL Robert	S	N	ND	R	#4	1644	..	1668	1702	RIDD 08
RIDDELL Robert (Thomas)	OSB		ND	X		1698	1715	..	1740	RIDD 10
RIDDELL William	SJ	N	ND	Y	13	1669	1687	1695	1711	RIDD 12
SANDERSON (Denis)	OSB		ND	X		..	1664	..	1670	SAND 18
SCOTT Joseph (Dunstan)	OSB	M	ND	X		1741	1760	..	1826	SCOT 06
SCOTT Robert (Bede)	OSB		ND	X		1743	1763	..	1789	SCOT 12
SELBY (Daniel of S.Francis)	OFM		ND	F	123	1650	1669	1674	1715	SELB 02
SELBY Edward (Gregory)	OSB	N	ND	X		..	1726	..	1759	SELB 04
SELBY John	S	N	ND			1627	..	..	..	SELB 06
SELBY John	S	L	ND			1757	..	..	1821	SELB 08
SHAFTOE (Celestine)	OSB	W	ND	X		..	1672	..	1722	SHAF 02
SHAFTOE John	S		ND	Q	#3	..	..	1582	..	SHAF 04
SHAFTOE William (Benedict)	OSB		ND	E		..	1715	..	1742	SHAF 08
SHAW Ralph (Maurus)	OSB		ND	E		1729	1757	..	1814	SHAW 16
SMITH Henry	SJ	N	ND	V	3	1699	1724	1724	1756	SMIT 25
STOREY Arthur	S	N	ND	P		1742	..	1767	1825	STOR 02
STOREY John (Joseph)	OSB	N	ND	X		..	1751	..	1799	STOR 04
STOREY Thomas	S	N	ND	D	3	1738	..	1766	1795	STOR 10
STRANGE Richard	SJ		ND	Y		1611	1631	..	1682	STRA 02
SWINBURNE Joseph	S	N	ND	U		1774	..	1800	1845	SWIN 06
SWINBURNE Thomas	OSB		ND	G		1607	1625	..	1667	SWIN 12
SWINBURNE William	SJ		ND	Y		1617	1636	..	1669	SWIN 14
TALBOT Gilbert	S	N	ND	R		1681	..	1711	1748	TALB 08
TESIMOND Oswald	SJ	M	ND	R	#1	1563	1584	..	1635	TESI 02
THOMPSON Robert	S		ND	R	#1	1613	..	1638	..	THOM 38
THORNTON William (Bede)	OSB		ND	G	#	..	1634	..	1694	THOR 12
TIDYMAN Michael	S	N	ND	V		1762	..	1785	1832	TIDY 02
TINDALL Robert	S		ND	R		1740	..	1767	1811	TIND 04
WALKER Robert	S		ND	R		..	..	1601	..	WALK 12
WALSINGHAM Francis	SJ	M	ND	R	#‡=	1576	1609	1608	1647	WALS 10
WELDON Charles or James	SJ		ND	V	#34	1716	1739	1738	1803	WELD 04
WELDON Thomas or Fenwick	SJ	N	ND	Y	#3	1705	1723	1731	1786	WELD 08
WELDON William	SJ	N	ND	Y	#3	1711	1732	1739	1761	WELD 14
WHITE Robert	SJ		ND	Y	#4	1622	1641	..	1678	WHIT 52
WHITFIELD Andrew	OSB		ND	G		..	1638	..	1688	WHIT 74
WIDDRINGTON Henry (Paul)	OFM		ND	F	12	1627	1646	..	1685	WIDD 04
WIDDRINGTON Henry, Hon.	SJ	N	ND	Y		1667	1687	1696	1729	WIDD 06
WIDDRINGTON Robert, Hon.	SJ	N	ND	Y	#34	1660	1679	1688	1742	WIDD 08
WILLIAMSON (Ambrose)	OFM		ND	F	123	1663	1684	1688	1701	WILL 66
WILSON Matthew or Edward	SJ		ND	R	#§	1581	1606	1606	1656	WILS 16

NK—NORFOLK

Name	Reg	D	Co	T	Notes	Born	Prof	Ordn	Died	Code
ALDRED Thomas	S		NK	R	#1	1670	..	1694	..	ALDR 06
ANGIER Thomas	SJ	M	NK	Y		1730	1752	1760	1788	ANGI 04
ANGIER Thomas	SJ	M	NK	Y		1754	1772	1780	1837	ANGI 06
APPLETON James	S	M	NK	D	#3	1742	..	1769	1813	APPL 10
ATKINS William (Maurus)	OSB		NK	G		..	1614	..	1635	ATKI 04
BACON George (Gregory)	OSB	M	NK	V	#2	1594	1622	1618	1663	BACO 02
BACON John	SJ		NK	Y	#°	1597	..	..	1667	BACO 04
BACON Nathaniel	SJ		NK	R	#	1599	..	1622	1676	BACO 06
BACON Thomas	SJ		NK	R	#	1592	1613	..	1647	BACO 08
BAKER Alexander	SJ	L	NK	S	2	1582	1610	..	1638	BAKE 04
BARDWELL James	SJ		NK	Y	#†=12	1583	1610	..	1633	BARD 02

Name	Reg	D	Co	T	Notes	Born	Prof	Ordn	Died	Code
BARNES John	OSB		NK	V	†1	1581	1605	1608	1661	BARN16
BASTARD Robert	SJ		NK	D		1571	1608	1602	1633	BAST02
BEDINGFELD Chas.(Bonaventure)	OFM		NK	F	§23	1698	1725	1731	1782	BEDI06
BEDINGFELD Edmund	S		NK	S		1615	..	1644	1680	BEDI08
BENSON Robert	S		NK	R	#	1571	..	1597	..	BENS02
BENSTEAD Thomas VEN.	S	M	NK	S	#+	1574	..	..	1600	BENS06
BLOOMER Edward (Lawrence)	OFM		NK	F	12	1602	1626	..	1672	BLOO03
BOLT Clement	S		NK	R	#†	1659	..	1692	..	BOLT02
BRADDOCK Edmund	S		NK	R		..	..	1583	..	BRAD02
BRADDOCK Henry	S		NK	Q		..	..	1583	..	BRAD04
BROWN Levinius	SJ		NK	R		1671	1698	1696	1764	BROW24
CARLETON John	S	M	NK	R	#1	1595	..	1618	1671	CARL02
CHAMBERLAIN George	S	L	NK	D	†	1739	..	1783	1815	CHAM05
CHAPLIN James (Maurus)	OSB	N	NK	X		1745	1763	..	1808	CHAP10
CLARK Francis	S		NK	V	#§3	1576	..	1600	..	CLAR14
COCKETT Thomas	CRL		NK	R		..	1626	..	..	COCK08
CORNWALLIS Richard	S		NK	R	†	1568	..	1599	..	CORN20
CORNWALLIS William	S		NK	Q	14	1527	..	1580	1600	CORN22
COTTON John	SJ	W	NK	Y	#23	1724	1741	1749	1769	COTT20
COWPER Thomas (Vincent Hyac.)	OP		NK	R	†	1629	1667	1659	1690	COWP02
CRANE William	SJ	L	NK	R	#	1650	1676	1674	1709	CRAN04
DEDAY James (Benedict)	OSB	M	NK	G		1773	1794	1800	1845	DEDA02
DOWNES Edmund	SJ		NK	R	#	1578	1625	1621	1637	DOWN02
DOWNES Thomas VEN.	SJ	L	NK	Y	#x1	1617	1639	..	1678	DOWN04
DRURY William	S		NK	R	1	1645	..	1670	..	DRUR10
DYMOCK James	S	L	NK		4	..	..	..	1718	DYMO04
EASTGATE William	S		NK	D	#3	1646	..	1671	1687	EAST12
FULLER Henry	S	L	NK	L	3	..	..	1690	1713	FULL04
FULLER Zachary (Alban)	OSB		NK	W		..	1674	..	1691	FULL08
GARDINER Bernard	S	L	NK	R		1563	..	1592	..	GARD04
GREEN Thomas	S	L	NK	V	#1	1600	..	..	1657	GREE48
GROSSE John	SJ	M	NK	R	#†	1580	1610	1606	1645	GROS02
HACON Hubert	SJ		NK	Y	#3	1677	1698	1707	1751	HACO02
HANSOM John (Anselm)	ODC	L	NK		1	1603	1625	..	1679	HANS10
HATTON Clare (Augustine)	OSB		NK	X		1738	1758	..	1823	HATT04
HAVERS John (Bartholomew)	OSB		NK	G		..	1729	..	1735	HAVE04
HAVERS Thomas	SJ		NK	Y	1	1668	1688	1696	1737	HAVE06
HODGSON James	S	M	NK	D		1709	..	1736	1750	HODG18
HUMBERSTON Edward	SJ	L	NK	R	#1	1635	1667	1663	1707	HUMB02
HUMBERSTON Henry	SJ	M	NK	Y	#	1638	1658	1669	1708	HUMB04
JERNINGHAM Francis	SJ	M	NK	Y	3	1688	1707	1714	1739	JERN02
LANE William	SJ	L	NK	V	1	1671	1699	1696	1752	LANE12
LUSHER Edward	SJ	L	NK	Y	#	..	..	..	1665	LUSH02
LUSHER Thomas	S		NK	V		1575	..	1599	..	LUSH08
LYNN Richard	S		NK	D		..	..	1607	..	LYNN02
MONTFORT Francis	S	M	NK	R		1566	..	1591	..	MONT08
MONTFORT Thomas	S	M	NK	S	3	1577	..	1600	..	MONT14
MOORE (John of the Hly Cross)	OFM		NK	F	#123	1629	1647	1653	1689	MOOR05
MORSE Henry ST.	SJ	L	NK	R	#+†=3	1595	1625	1620	1645	MORS02
MORSE William	SJ		NK	D	#§2	1591	1620	1617	1649	MORS04
MUMFORD James	SJ	M	NK	Y		1606	1626	..	1666	MUMF04
MUMFORD John	OSB		NK	G	#	..	1614	..	1646	MUMF05
PALGRAVE (Augustine of S.Ann)	OFM		NK	F	12	1608	1630	..	1679	PALG02
PASTON Clement	OSB		NK	E		1663	1683	..	1724	PAST02
PASTON Edward	S		NK	D	#	1641	..	1666	1714	PAST04
PITCHFORD Thomas Edward	S	N	NK	T		..	..	1800	1808	PITC02
ROGERS Francis	SJ		NK	Y		1599	1623	..	1660	ROGE08
RUFFET John	S		NK	V	#3	1567	..	1597	..	RUFF02
SMITH Clement	SJ	N	NK	Y		1657	1678	1687	1696	SMIT08
SMITH John	S	M	NK	R	#	1656	..	1681	..	SMIT39
SMITH John	S	L	NK	R	§	1739	..	1766	1817	SMIT44
SOUTHWELL Robert ST.	SJ	L	NK	R	#+	1561	1578	1584	1595	SOUT22
STEPHENS John	S	W	NK	R	#	1578	..	1602	..	STEP08
TASBURGH Thomas	SJ	L	NK	Y	#1	1672	1691	1700	1727	TASB08
THOMPSON William	S	M	NK	D	#13	1667	..	1712	1726	THOM50
WALDEGRAVE Charles	S	M	NK	L	#3	1627	..	1650	..	WALD04

Name	Reg	D	Co	T	Notes	Born	Prof	Ordn	Died	Code
WALDEGRAVE Nicholas	S		NK	L	1	1666	..	1689	1734	WALD08
WALPOLE Christopher	SJ		NK	R	†	1568	1592	..	1606	WALP02
WALPOLE Christopher	SJ		NK	R	#2	1598	1624	1622	1664	WALP04
WALPOLE Edward	SJ		NK	R	#†1	1560	1593	1592	1637	WALP06
WALPOLE Henry ST.	SJ	N	NK	R	+†=	1558	1584	1588	1595	WALP08
WALPOLE Michael	SJ		NK	R	#4	1570	1593	..	1620	WALP10
WALPOLE Richard	SJ		NK	R	#†2	1564	1593	1589	1607	WALP12
WARMOLL John (Bernard)	OSB	M	NK	G		1719	1737	..	1807	WARM04
WHALL Charles	S		NK	D	3	1639	..	1663	..	WHAL06
WHALL Edward	S		NK	D	#	1612	..	1653	..	WHAL10
WHALL George	OSB		NK	W		..	1666	..	1709	WHAL12
WHALL Thomas	S		NK	D	#	..	..	1632	..	WHAL14
WHALL William	S		NK	D	#14	1608	..	..	1640	WHAL16
WHALL William	S	M	NK	D	#	..	..	1659	1671	WHAL18
WILSON William	SJ	N	NK	Y		1615	1635	..	1679	WILS40
WRIGHT Thomas	S		NK	P		..	..	1767	1799	WRIG36
YELVERTON Charles	SJ		NK	R	#†	1575	1608	1604	1612	YELV02

NN—NORTHAMPTONSHIRE

Name	Reg	D	Co	T	Notes	Born	Prof	Ordn	Died	Code
BOWKER Alexander	S		NN	D	#§*°	..	..	1608	1618	BOWK02
BRAMSTON James Yorke BP.	S	L	NN	L	*§=	1763	..	1799	1836	BRAM04
BUTLER Alban	S		NN	D	#	1709	..	1734	1773	BUTL02
BUXTON George	S		NN	R	#§1	1686	..	1713	1759	BUXT04
CARPENTER Richard Francis	S		NN	R	#*§°	1606	..	1635	1670	CARP06
DARCY Arthur	S		NN	R	#	1605	..	1630	..	DARC04
EVERARD John	SJ		NN		#†	1584	..	..	1649	EVER08
FARMER John	S	L	NN	D		..	..	1605	1660	FARM02
FISHER George	S	L	NN	R	#§1	1580	..	1606	1645	FISH06
FONTAINE Wm. (Placid) de la	OSB		NN	G		..	1731	..	1780	FONT04
GARTER John	OSB		NN	E		..	1639	1643	1650	GART02
HANSE Everard BL.	S	L	NN	Q	+†	..	..	1581	1581	HANS04
HANSE William	S	M	NN	Q	#	..	..	1579	..	HANS06
HOLLAND Henry	S		NN	Q	‡	1550	..	1580	1625	HOLL08
JENNINGS Michael	S	M	NN	R	*	1597	..	1628	1667	JENN14
KELLISON Matthew	S		NN	R	#	1561	..	1587	1641	KELL10
LEWIS John	SJ	L	NN	Y	#3	1721	1740	1747	1788	LEWI14
LOVETT George	SJ	L	NN		#12	1576	1611	..	1640	LOVE14
MANBY Thomas	SJ		NN	R	#§14	1588	1611	..	1620	MANB02
MULSHO John	SJ		NN	D	#§4	1584	1616	1608	1661	MULS02
NEWPORT Charles	S		NN	D	#	..	..	1601	..	NEWP02
NEWPORT Richard BL.	S		NN	R	#+§	1572	..	1599	1612	NEWP04
OSBORNE Edward	S	L	NN	Q	†4	1555	..	1581	1600	OSBO02
PAGE Richard	S	L	NN	D	#	..	..	1610	1653	PAGE08
PAINE John ST.	S	L	NN	D	+§	..	..	1576	1582	PAIN04
POULTON Andrew	SJ	L	NN	Y		1654	1674	1685	1710	POUL02
POULTON Charles	SJ		NN	Y	#x	1616	1637	..	1690	POUL04
POULTON Ferdinand	SJ	N	NN		#	1605	1625	..	1666	POUL08
POULTON George	SJ		NN	Y	3	1689	1707	1732	1739	POUL12
POULTON Giles	SJ		NN	Y	#1	1600	1622	..	1666	POUL14
POULTON Giles	SJ		NN	R	#	1694	1721	1719	1752	POUL16
POULTON Henry	SJ		NN	V	3	1583	..	1612	..	POUL18
POULTON Henry	SJ		NN	Y	#	1679	1700	..	1712	POUL20
POULTON John	SJ		NN	R	#	1610	1650	1636	1656	POUL22
POULTON John (Joseph of Jn.B)	OFM	L	NN	F	3	1682	1701	1707	1748	POUL26
POULTON Thomas	SJ		NN	Y	3	1668	1685	1694	1725	POUL30
POULTON Thomas	SJ		NN	Y	3	1697	1717	1724	1749	POUL32
POULTON William	SJ		NN		4	..	..	..	1596	POUL34
POULTON William	S	L	NN	R	#	1616	..	1655	1672	POUL36
POYNTZ Francis (James)	OSB	L	NN	E	§	1661	1688	..	1718	POYN04
PRATT Henry (Felix)	OSB		NN	D	#	..	1614	1606	1634	PRAT06
PRESTON William	SJ	L	NN	R	#	1637	1662	1661	1702	PRES14
ROBERTS John	S		NN	R	†	1560	..	1587	..	ROBE08
SWEETMAN John	SJ		NN	V	#	1579	1606	1606	1622	SWEE04
TIMCOCK Anthony (Francis)	OSB		NN	V	#†3	1581	1609	1609	1668	TIMC02
TRESHAM Francis	OFM		NN	G	*3	1592	1649	1643	1660	TRES02

Name	Reg	D	Co	T	Notes	Born	Prof	Ordn	Died	Code
WILKINSON Henry	SJ		NN	Y	1	1594	1617	..	1673	WILK10
WILLIAMSON William	SJ	M	NN	R	#‡	1577	1617	1611	1626	WILL74
WOODWARD Thomas	S		NN	D	#	..	..	1624	1662	WOOD60
WRIGHT Peter BL.	SJ		NN	Y	#+§1	1603	1629	..	1651	WRIG20

NT—NOTTINGHAMSHIRE

Name	Reg	D	Co	T	Notes	Born	Prof	Ordn	Died	Code
ARMSTRONG Daniel	SJ	N	NT	V	#3	1643	1675	1667	1684	ARMS06
BLUNDESTON Daniel or Robert	S	N	NT	D	#4	1596	..	1622	1657	BLUN22
BLUNDESTON Lawrence	S		NT	R	#§	1592	..	1620	..	BLUN24
BOWER William	S		NT	D	3	1735	..	1766	1773	BOWE04
CARTWRIGHT (Gervase of S.Fra)	OFM		NT	F	123	1628	1647	1651	1691	CART22
CLIFTON Francis	SJ		NT	Y	3	1702	1719	1732	1757	CLIF16
FAIRBURN George	S	L	NT	S	x3	..	..	1608	1615	FAIR01
GOLDING (Edward of S.Anne)	OFM	L	NT	F	123	1627	1653	1657	1688	GOLD06
GOLDING (George of S.Barbara)	OFM		NT	F	123	1630	1650	1656	1701	GOLD08
HARDING Robert, Jn or Richard	SJ		NT	Y	3	1701	1722	1731	1772	HARD22
HASELHURST Peter	S		NT	R	#†	1585	..	1615	..	HASE02
HASELWOOD James	S		NT	D	#4	1602	..	1625	1679	HASE04
HOWARD Henry, Hon.	S	L	NT	D	*	1684	..	1709	1720	HOWA10
HOWARD Richard, Hon.	S		NT	R	3	1687	..	1708	1722	HOWA18
KINDER (Augustine)	OSB	W	NT	G		1596	1621	..	1676	KIND02
LANE George	S		NT	D	34	1669	..	1702	1702	LANE04
MUMFORD Gervase	SJ		NT	Y		1635	1658	1669	1684	MUMF02
NEEDHAM Nicholas	S		NT	D	#	..	..	1600	..	NEED12
PEDLY (Henry of S.Mary)	OFM		NT	F	123	1630	1651	1655	1693	PEDL02
SHUTTLEWORTH George	S	M	NT	D	#	1718	..	1744	1791	SHUT04
SHUTTLEWORTH John	S	M	NT	D	#3	1680	..	1711	1739	SHUT06
STANLEY John	S		NT	D		1720	..	1744	1770	STAN28
STRUTT Richard	S		NT	V	§3	1577	..	1608	1608	STRU04
SUDBURY Henry (Peter of Alc.)	OFM		NT	F	123	1600	1624	1624	1676	SUDB02
WYVILL Christopher (Peter)	OP	M	NT	N		1694	1712	1719	1725	WYVI02

OX—OXFORD

Name	Reg	D	Co	T	Notes	Born	Prof	Ordn	Died	Code
ALLOWAY John James	SJ	N	OX	R		1743	1766	1769	1808	ALLO04
ALMOND Oliver	S	M	OX	R	#‡	1561	..	1587	..	ALMO08
ANSLEY Henry	S		OX	R		..	..	1584	..	ANSL02
APPLETREE John	S	L	OX	Q	#‡1	1555	..	1579	..	APPL20
ARCHER Giles	S		OX	Q		..	..	1587	1602	ARCH06
BERE Anthony	S		OX	R	#§	1624	..	1648	..	BEER02
BISHOP Bartholomew (Denis)	OSB	L	OX	X		..	1682	..	1725	BISH02
BLOUNT Henry Tichborne	S	M	OX	D	#	1723	..	1748	1810	BLOU08
BROWN (Anselm)	OSB		OX	W		..	1688	..	1706	BROW04
BUSBY John	SJ	W	OX	Y	#	1679	1699	1708	1743	BUSB02
BUSTARD John	SJ		OX		‡12	1550	1570	..	1576	BUST02
CARLETON William	SJ		OX			1577	1617	..	1622	CARL06
CHERITON (Basil)	OSB		OX	E		..	1651	..	1662	CHER04
CHERITON Matthew	OSB	N	OX	W		..	1656	..	1670	CHER06
CLEMENTS Charles	S	M	OX	V		1765	..	1790	1797	CLEM04
CLINCH Henry	S	M	OX	Q		..	..	1581	..	CLIN02
CLINCH John	S	N	OX	Q		..	..	1590	..	CLIN04
COLLINGRIDGE Peter(Ber'dn) BP	OFM	W	OX	F	*3	1757	1780	1784	1829	COLL08
COLLINGRIDGE Thomas	S	N	OX	Y		1771	..	..	1854	COLL10
CURZON Peter, Bt.	SJ	L	OX	Y	#13	1686	1705	1715	1766	CURZ02
DAY John (Nicholas)	OFM	M	OX		12	1575	1601	..	1655	DAYA02
FERMOR Henry	SJ	M	OX	Y	#3	1637	1656	1665	1680	FERM02
FERMOR Thomas	SJ	L	OX	Y		1649	1667	1676	1710	FERM08
FILBY John	S	M	OX	D	#‡	..	..	1578	..	FILB02
FILBY William BL.	S	L	OX	Q	+‡1	1555	..	1581	1582	FILB04
FLECKNOE William	SJ	W	OX	D	#2	1575	1611	1600	1632	FLEC04
FLETCHER Owen	S		OX	Q	‡	..	..	1592	..	FLET06
GARDINER Michael	S		OX	D		..	..	1603	..	GARD20
GREEN Thomas BL.	S	L	OX	S	#+	1579	..	1602	1642	GREE52
GREENWOOD (Gabriel)	OFM		OX	F	4	1669	1699	1706	1709	GREE79
GREENWOOD (Gregory)	OSB	M	OX	G		1670	1688	..	1744	GREE80

Name	Reg	D	Co	T	Notes	Born	Prof	Ordn	Died	Code
GRIMSTON John	SJ	W	OX	Y	#	1576	1620	..	1649	GRIM18
HARRISON Philip	SJ		OX			..	..		1578	HARR53
HART John	SJ		OX	D		..	1583	1578	1586	HART02
HARTLEY George	S	M	OX	L		1769	..	1794	1806	HART26
HAWKER John	S		OX	R	#	1650	..	1673	1707	HAWK02
HAYWARD (Gregory)	OSB		OX	G	1	1602	1621	1628	1632	HAYW02
HAYWOOD John	S		OX	Q		..	..	1586	..	HAYW04
HILDESLEY Francis	SJ	M	OX	Y	1	1655	1675	1683	1719	HILD02
HODGSON Matthew Francis(Bede)	ODC		OX	R	#	1630	1656	1654	1667	HODG28
HUMPHREY John	S		OX	D		..	..	1597	..	HUMP02
KIMBER Thomas	SJ	W	OX	Y		1688	1706	1716	1742	KIMB02
LAZENBY John	SJ	L	OX	Y	#	1655	1675	1683	1724	LAZE02
LOVELL George	SJ		OX	Y		1650	1669	1678	1720	LOVE08
LOVELL John	SJ	M	OX	Y	1	1604	1629	..	1683	LOVE10
MANSELL Thomas	SJ		OX	Y	#3	1668	1686	1695	1724	MANS02
MANSELL William	SJ		OX	Y	#13	1669	1686	1694	1720	MANS04
MILDMAY Francis	OSB	W	OX	X		..	1674	..	1720	MILD02
MILDMAY George	OP		OX			1638	1663	1665	1668	MILD04
MILDMAY Matthew	SJ	W	OX	Y	#13	1640	1664	1672	1713	MILD06
NAPPER Charles (Francis)	OFM		OX	F	12	1623	1653	..	1679	NAPP01
NAPPER George BL.	S	M	OX	D	+‡	1550	..	1596	1610	NAPP02
NAPPER William (Marianus)	OFM		OX	F	#123	1615	1639	1648	1693	NAPP04
NICHOLS George VEN.	S	M	OX	Q	+‡	..	..	1583	1589	NICH04
OWEN John	S	L	OX	Q	#‡°	1560	..	1584	..	OWEN04
OWEN John	S	W	OX	S	#	1593	..	..	..	OWEN05
OWEN Walter	S		OX	Q	3	..	..	1591	1591	OWEN24
PIERPOINT Thomas	S		OX	Q	3	..	..	1591	1591	PIER06
PIGOTT Edward (Gregory)	OSB		OX	G		1692	1711	..	1749	PIGO06
PITTS Arthur	S	M	OX	R	‡4	1557	..	1580	1635	PITT02
PITTS Robert	S	M	OX	D	‡4	1576	..	1576	1592	PITT08
PITTS Thomas (Walter)	CRT		OX	C	2	..	1575	..	1611	PITT12
PLOWDEN Francis	SJ		OX	Y	#1	1661	1682	1689	1736	PLOW06
PLOWDEN George	S		OX	R	*	1651	..	1676	1694	PLOW10
PLOWDEN Joseph	SJ		OX	Y		1655	1676	1685	1692	PLOW12
PLOWDEN Thomas	SJ	L	OX	Y	#	1594	1617	..	1664	PLOW20
POSTGATE Ralph	SJ	M	OX	R		1648	1674	1674	1718	POST04
PRINCE Richard	SJ		OX	Y	#x	1648	1668	1677	1680	PRIN04
RAND Thomas	SJ	M	OX		124	1577	1600	..	1657	RAND02
RAWLINS Alexander BL.	S	N	OX	Q	#+‡	1560	..	1590	1595	RAWL02
REYNOLDS William	S	M	OX	L	3	1648	..	1675	1718	REYN08
RIDLEY Roger (Bartholomew)	OSB		OX	D	‡124	1563	1610	1600	1616	RIDL02
RIGBY John	S		OX	D	#	1600	..	1632	1684	RIGB08
ROOK Henry	S		OX	Q		..	..	1589	..	ROOK02
ROWSHAM Stephen VEN.	S	M	OX	Q	#+‡	..	..	1581	1587	ROWS02
SAVORY John (Robert)	OSB	M	OX	G		..	1687	..	1726	SAVO02
SHELDON Henry	SJ		OX	Y		1652	1670	1679	1714	SHEL08
SHELDON Ralph	SJ		OX	Y	#3	1681	1700	1709	1741	SHEL14
SHIRLEY Anthony	S		OX	Q	‡	..	..	1583	..	SHIR06
SKINNER John	S	M	OX	L	#	1611	..	1636	1674	SKIN10
SMITH Edmund	S		OX	R	#‡	1577	..	1603	1605	SMIT09
STONOR Christopher	S	M	OX	P		1716	..	1743	1795	STON12
STONOR John	S	M	OX	D	#	1738	..	1764	1765	STON15
STONOR John Talbot BP.	S	M	OX	P	*	1678	..	1711	1746	STON16
STRANSHAM Edward BL.	S	L	OX	Q	#+‡	1555	..	1580	1586	STRA08
STRANSHAM Thomas	S		OX	D		..	..	1578	..	STRA12
TALBOT James Robert, BP.	S	L	OX	D	*	1726	..	1750	1790	TALB12
TALBOT John	S		OX	D		1724	..	1749	1751	TALB18
TALBOT Thomas Joseph, BP.	S	M	OX	D	*	1727	..	1752	1795	TALB32
TEMPEST William (Bartholomew)	OFM		OX	F	12	1620	1637	..	1647	TEMP24
THOMPSON Francis	SJ	W	OX	R	#	1577	1606	1603	1614	THOM20
TODKILL Richard	S	M	OX	D	#4	1607	..	1632	1657	TODK02
TURNER Francis	SJ	M	OX	Y		1612	1635	..	1659	TURN10
TURNER John	SJ		OX	Y		1604	1623	1635	1681	TURN16
VINES Henry	S		OX	R	#§	1587	..	1613	..	VINE02
WEEDON William	S		OX	V	#°	..	..	1698	..	WEED08
WHITE Richard	S	M	OX	Q		..	..	1581	..	WHIT44

Name	Reg	D	Co	T	Notes	Born	Prof	Ordn	Died	Code
WILLIAMS Thomas	SJ		OX	R	‡	1539	1557	..	1613	WILL 56
WRIGHT Francis	S		OX	D	#1	1593	..	1621	..	WRIG 10

PB—PEMBROKESHIRE

Name	Reg	D	Co	T	Notes	Born	Prof	Ordn	Died	Code
BARLOW Louis	S	M	PB	D	*=1	1550	..	1574	1610	BARL 12
BARLOW William (Archangelus)	CAP	L	PB	P		..	1587	..	1632	BARL 14
MORGAN David	S	L	PB	L		1721	..	1742	1758	MORG 02
PHILIPS John (Columban)	OSB		PB	E		1613	1632	1639	1699	PHIL 14
SANDERS Erasmus	S		PB	R	*	1575	..	1600	..	SAND 04
TANKE John (Stanislaus)	OSB		PB	G		..	1625	..	1639	TANK 02
TANKE Thomas	OSB		PB	G	4	..	1623	..	1668	TANK 04

PL—PORTUGAL

Name	Reg	D	Co	T	Notes	Born	Prof	Ordn	Died	Code
ALMEIDA Paul d'		L	PL		*7	..	..	..	..	ALME 02
DIAZ Emmanuel		L	PL		*7	..	..	..	..	DIAZ 02
FEREIRA James	S	L	PL		*8	..	..	..	..	FERE 02
FERNANDEZ Antonio	SJ	L	PL			..	..	..	1674	FERN 02
FERREYRA James Roiz	OSB	L	PL	W		..	1676	..	1712	FERR 04
HEREDIA Martin de (Gratian)	ODC	L	PL		1	1610	1641	..	1667	HERE 02
LAURENZO Augustine	SJ	L	PL		7	..	..	..	..	LAUR 08
LEMOS Benedict de	SJ	L	PL		7	..	..	..	..	LEMO 02
MACEDO (Francis of S.Aug'ine)	OFM	L	PL		*7	..	..	..	..	MACZ 02
MACHADO (Antonio of S.B'dine)	OFM	L	PL		*7	..	..	..	..	MACZ 03
MAGELLAN Jean Hyacinthe de	OSA	L	PL		*°2	1723	1755	..	1790	MAGE 06
MANRIQUE Sebastiano	OSA	L	PL		*1	1595	..	..	1669	MANR 02
MELLO Emmanuel de		L	PL		*7	..	..	..	..	MELL 16
MEPNESYN Biemigro dos		L	PL		*7	..	..	..	..	MEPN 02
MILES John	S		PL	P	3	..	..	1645	..	MILE 06
NASSAU John	S	L	PL	N		1767	..	..	1807	NASS 02
(Paulino de la Estrella)	OFM	L	PL		*7	..	..	..	..	PAUL 04
PEREIRA Manoel		L	PL		*7	..	..	..	..	PERE 02
(Salvador of the Holy Spirit)	OFM	L	PL		*7	..	..	..	..	SALV 01
WRIGHT Joseph	SJ		PL	Y	13	1698	1720	1727	1760	WRIG 16

RN—RADNORSHIRE

Name	Reg	D	Co	T	Notes	Born	Prof	Ordn	Died	Code
BASKERVILLE (Bonavent.S.Mary)	OFM		RN	F	123	1666	1682	1691	1705	BASK 02
BASKERVILLE William (Bernard)	OFM	W	RN	F	234	1655	1671	1679	1727	BASK 04
LINGEN (Francis of the Cross)	OFM		RN	F	123	1665	1681	1689	1693	LING 04

RT—RUTLAND

Name	Reg	D	Co	T	Notes	Born	Prof	Ordn	Died	Code
DIGBY Joseph	S		RT	D	13	1662	..	1693	1708	DIGB 06
DURAND Thomas	SJ		RT	Y	12	1597	1620	..	1633	DURA 02
HOWLETT John	SJ		RT	D	#‡	1545	1571	..	1589	HOWL 02
LE HUNT Edward	S	M	RT	R	#	1641	..	1667	..	LEHU 02

SC—SCOTLAND

Name	Reg	D	Co	T	Notes	Born	Prof	Ordn	Died	Code
ABERCROMBIE Robert	SJ	L	SC		#1	1532	..	..	1613	ABER 04
ANDERSON Patrick	SJ	L	SC	R		1575	1597	..	1624	ANDE 10
ASLOAN Audomarus John	OSB	N	SC	J	12	1595	1624	..	1661	ASLO 02
ASLOAN George (Benedict)	OSB	N	SC	R	34	..	1639	1619	1661	ASLO 04
BAILLIE William (Placid)	OSB		SC	J	#3	1633	..	1660	1674	BAIL 06
BALLENDEN William	S		SC	R	*3	1616	..	1641	1661	BALL 14
BOWER Archibald	SJ		SC	R	°	1686	1706	..	1766	BOWE 02
BROWN Alexander (Bernardine)	OFM	M	SC	D	#13	1723	1745	1746	1757	BROW 01
BROWN Alexander (Macarius)	OSB	N	SC	J		1639	1660	..	1697	BROW 02
BROWN (John)	MIN	L	SC		12	1568	1595	..	1643	BROW 23
CAMERON Alexander	SJ		SC		x	1701	1734	..	1746	CAME 02
COMPTON George	S		SC	D	3	..	..	1662	..	COMP 02
DALRYMPLE George (Robert)	CAP		SC			1567	..	..	1603	DALR 02
DANIEL Thomas	SJ	N	SC	Y	#13	1716	1751	1757	1779	DANI 18
DUNN Roland (William)	OSB	N	SC	J	4	1644	1660	..	1678	DUNN 12

Name	Reg	D	Co	T	Notes	Born	Prof	Ordn	Died	Code
DURHAM John	SJ	N	SC			1616	..	..	1674	DURH02
FLEMING (Bruno)	CRT	N	SC	C		..	1732	..	1761	FLEM02
FORBES John, Ld.(Archangelus)	CAP		SC		§	1570	1593	..	1606	FORB04
FORBES Wm. (Archangelus) Hon.	CAP		SC			1563	1589	..	1592	FORB06
FORSYTE	OP	L	SC	R	*°7	..	..	..	..	FORS16
GARDEN James	SJ		SC		1	1718	..	..	1793	GARD02
GEDDES Alexander	S	L	SC	P		1737	..	1764	1802	GEDD02
GORDON (Andrew)	OSB	L	SC	J		..	1755	..	..	GORD02
GORDON James (Mary of S.Mrgt)	ODC	M	SC			1702	..	..	..	GORD04
GORDON Rbt. (Peter Alcantara)	OFM		SC	F	1234	1668	1696	1700	1748	GORD06
GORDON William	OSB	N	SC	J	12	1560	1609	..	1638	GORD08
GRANT James	SJ		SC			1721	1743	1752	1769	GRAN12
GRANT William (Killian)	OSB		SC	J		1700	1726	1724	1765	GRAN16
HAMILTON James (Placid)	OSB	L	SC	J	1	1699	1719	..	1786	HAMI02
HAY Alexander	S		SC	D		..	..	1603	..	HAYA02
HAY Richard (Augustine)	CRL	L	SC		*§4	1661	1678	1685	1736	HAYA06
HISLOP (Clement of S.Andrew)	OFM		SC	F	12	1670	1698	1703	1723	HISL02
(John Chrysostom II)	CAP		SC			..	..	..	1688	JOHN00
JOHNSTON (Dominic Thomas)	OP		SC		*3	..	1670	1645	1685	JOHN42
(Julian of Garneston)	CAP		SC			..	..	..	1641	JULI04
LE FEVRE George	SJ	L	SC		#	..	..	..	1703	LEFE02
LEITH Gall (Robert)	OSB	W	SC	J		1706	1726	..	1775	LEIT02
LESLIE Alexander, Hon.	SJ	L	SC			1693	1712	..	1760	LESL02
LESLIE Charles, Hon.	SJ	M	SC	Y	#1	1745	1764	..	1806	LESL04
LESLIE George (Archangelus)	CAP		SC	R	1	1587	..	1608	1637	LESL05
LESLIE James, Hon.	SJ	M	SC			1741	1760	..	1816	LESL06
LINDSAY (Epiphanius)	CAP		SC		6	..	..	..	..	LIND06
LUMSDEN Alexander	OP	L	SC		4	1622	..	..	1700	LUMS02
MacCALL Adam	OSB	N	SC	J		..	..	..	1640	MACC01
MacDONALD Archibald(Benedict)	OSB	N	SC	G		1739	1757	..	1814	MACD02
MacDONELL Alexander BP.	S	L	SC	V	*	1760	..	1787	1840	MACD04
MacKENZIE Alexander	SJ	W	SC	Y	#	1730	1749	1758	1800	MACK04
MAITLAND John (Francis)	MIN	L	SC		#4	1597	..	..	1642	MAIT02
MAMBRECHT John	SJ	L	SC		#	..	..	..	1679	MAMB02
MAXWELL Albert or Herbert	SJ		SC		1	1653	1675	..	1729	MAXW02
MAXWELL James	S	M	SC	D	#1	1700	..	1722	1778	MAXW04
MONTEITH William	SJ	L	SC	Y		1619	1637	..	1663	MONT04
OLIVER Andrew	S	M	SC			..	..	..	1823	OLIV02
PATERSON George	SJ	L	SC		#	1621	1641	..	1703	PATE06
PENDRYCK William (Eliseus)	ODC	L	SC	R	§	1583	1613	..	1650	PEND04
PHILIPS Robert	ORA	L	SC		13	1585	..	1612	1647	PHIL20
RUSSELL Alexander	SJ		SC		#	1669	1691	..	1742	RUSS01
SEMPLE Hugh	SJ		SC		3	1701	1717	1728	..	SEMP04
STUART Charles	OFM	L	SC	F	#134	1724	1744	1752	1800	STUA00
THOMPSON William	CON	L	SC	R	3	..	..	1602	..	THOM48

SK—SUFFOLK

Name	Reg	D	Co	T	Notes	Born	Prof	Ordn	Died	Code
BARRETT Thomas	S	L	SK	V	#†3	..	..	1613	1631	BARR29
BEDINGFELD Anthony	SJ		SK	Y	3	1697	1714	1723	1752	BEDI04
BEDINGFELD Edward	SJ	M	SK	Y	#1	1595	1617	..	1659	BEDI10
BEDINGFELD Henry	SJ	L	SK	R	1	1582	1602	..	1659	BEDI12
BEDINGFELD Thomas	SJ		SK	S	#34	1612	1635	1635	1649	BEDI16
BRIANT Henry	SJ	M	SK		1	1599	..	..	1658	BRIA10
BURTON Christopher	SJ	N	SK	Y	13	1671	1693	1703	1744	BURT04
CARY Edward	S	W	SK	R		..	..	1651	1711	CARY04
CARY John	SJ		SK	Y		1618	..	..	1682	CARY10
CARY Thomas	SJ		SK	Y		1621	1639	..	1672	CARY16
CATTAWAY Henry	SJ	M	SK	Y		1675	1693	1701	1718	CATT02
CHRISTMAS John	S		SK	D	†3	..	..	1693	1743	CHRI08
COOK Thomas	S		SK	R	#	..	..	1631	..	COOK04
COPPINGER Henry	SJ	M	SK	R	#†2	1580	1615	1613	1652	COPP02
DANVERS William (Romuald)	OSB		SK	D	†	..	1620	1619	1634	DANV02
ENGLISH Robert	S	M	SK	Q	†#	..	..	1580	..	ENGL10
EVERARD (Dunstan)	OSB	L	SK	G		..	1616	..	1650	EVER04
EVERARD Thomas	SJ	L	SK	Q	†	1560	1593	1592	1633	EVER14

Name	Reg	D	Co	T	Notes	Born	Prof	Ordn	Died	Code
EVERARD William	S		SK	S	#§3	1590	..	1615	..	EVER 20
FLACK William	SJ		SK	V	†	1561	1585	1591	1637	FLAC02
FOSTER Bartholomew	SJ		SK	R	#12	1592	1616	1616	1617	FOST02
FOSTER Michael	SJ		SK	Y	#3	1642	1660	1667	1684	FOST 20
FOSTER Robert	SJ	L	SK	Z	#*	1588	1609	..	1641	FOST 23
FOSTER William	SJ		SK		#§1	1588	1609	..	1657	FOST 28
GAGE James (Ambrose)	OP	L	SK	N		1723	1745	1747	1796	GAGE 10
GAGE John	SJ	M	SK	Y	#	1651	1670	1679	1728	GAGE 14
GAGE John	SJ	M	SK	Y	3	1720	1740	1744	1790	GAGE 16
GODFREY Arthur (Michael)	OSB		SK	Z	#*4	..	1611	..	1626	GODF02
GOLDING Edward, Bt.	CAP		SK		124	1599	1655	..	1666	GOLD04
GOLTY Samuel	S	L	SK	L	#†3	..	..	1689	1725	GOLT02
GOOCH Thomas	S	L	SK	V	#†	1578	..	1603	..	GOOC02
HAREWELL William	S	L	SK	D	#4	..	..	1615	1640	HARE02
HARVEY Monox	S		SK	R	#§	1699	..	1728	1756	HARV06
JETTER George	S	L	SK	Q	4	..	..	1581	1609	JETT02
LAND Thomas	SJ		SK	Y	12	1582	1612	..	1632	LAND02
LANMAN Henry	SJ		SK	R	#§	1573	1606	1603	1614	LANM02
LOMAX John	S	M	SK	V		..	..	1697	1732	LOMA04
MANNOCK George, Bt.	SJ	M	SK	Y	3	1724	1741	1749	1787	MANN 14
MANNOCK Henry	S	M	SK	D	#1	1587	..	1612	..	MANN 16
MANNOCK John (Anselm)	OSB	M	SK	G	1	1677	1700	..	1764	MANN 20
MANNOCK William	S		SK	D	#§	1580	..	1605	..	MANN 22
MANNOCK William	S		SK	R	3	1677	..	1700	1749	MANN 24
MARTIN Edward	OP		SK			1673	1695	1697	1753	MART06
MARTIN Henry	SJ	L	SK	Y		1642	1662	1672	1672	MART 16
MARTIN John	SJ		SK	Y		1645	1667	1672	1717	MART 18
MARTIN John	OP	M	SK	N		1677	1697	1700	1761	MART 20
MARTIN Joseph	S	M	SK	D	#	1688	..	1716	1729	MART 26
NORMANTON Thomas (Leander)	OSB		SK	G	#§	1615	1649	..	1665	NORM02
NUTTAL Edward (Constantius)	OSB	M	SK	W	#2	..	1610	..	1659	NUTT04
PELHAM William	SJ		SK	Y	1	1623	1643	..	1671	PELH02
ROE Bartholomew (Alban) ST.	OSB	L	SK	W	#+†	1583	1612	1615	1642	ROEA02
ROE James (Maurus)	OSB		SK	W	#§	..	1626	..	1657	ROEA04
ROOKWOOD Francis	OSB	M	SK	G		1660	1680	..	1750	ROOK04
ROOKWOOD Henry	SJ	M	SK	Y	13	1658	1681	1690	1730	ROOK06
ROOKWOOD Robert	S	L	SK	R	#	1582	..	1604	..	ROOK 12
ROOKWOOD Robert	S		SK	R	#	1588	..	1621	1668	ROOK 14
ROSIER James	S		SK	R	#†	1576	..	1609	1609	ROSI02
ROUSE Anthony	S		SK	D	§=	..	..	1592	..	ROUS01
SAYER Robert (Gregory)	OSB		SK	R	†	1560	1589	1585	1602	SAYE06
SCOTT Montford VEN.	S	M	SK	D	+†	..	..	1577	1591	SCOT08
SHORT Francis	SJ	L	SK	Y	#13	1718	1737	1746	1755	SHOR02
SHORT John (Jordan)	OP		SK	N		1685	1719	1721	1754	SHOR04
SHORT Thomas	S		SK	L	#†	1616	..	1641	..	SHOR06
SHORT William (Benedict)	OP	L	SK	N	3	1723	1741	1746	1800	SHOR08
SMITH John	SJ		SK	Y		1620	1640	..	1661	SMIT 34
STAFFORD Charles	SJ		SK	Y	#	1653	1676	1684	1732	STAF08
STAFFORD Nathaniel	SJ	M	SK	Y	#13	1634	1656	1665	1697	STAF 16
SULYARD Andrew	SJ	M	SK	Y	#	1605	1628	..	1673	SULY02
SULYARD Francis (Augustine)	OSB		SK	W		1686	1709	..	1768	SULY04
SULYARD John	S	M	SK	R	3	1634	..	1658	..	SULY06
TASBURGH Henry	SJ	N	SK	Y	#1	1641	1664	1671	1718	TASB02
TASBURGH Richard (Felix)	OSB	L	SK	E	1	1660	1682	..	1731	TASB06
TIDDER Edward	SJ		SK	Y	#	1630	1652	1661	1699	TIDD02
TIMPERLEY Henry (Gregory)	OSB	M	SK	E		1631	1677	..	1709	TIMP02
WARNER John, Bt.	SJ		SK	Y	#§	1640	1665	1670	1705	WARN04
WEBB Edward	SJ		SK	R	§	1575	1609	1605	1622	WEBB02
WESTON John	SJ	M	SK		#1	1589	1620	..	1649	WEST 18
WOODWARD Lionel	S		SK	Q	4	..	..	1592	1609	WOOD54
WOODWARD Philip	S	L	SK	R	†	1558	..	1583	1610	WOOD58

		SM	**SOMERSET**							
ATKINSON John	S	W	SM	R	§	1709	..	1746	1750	ATKI11
BALDWIN George	S	W	SM	V		1749	..	1775	1818	BALD03

Name	Reg	D	Co	T	Notes	Born	Prof	Ordn	Died	Code
BEAUMONT John (Baptist)	OFM	W	SM	F	13	1697	..	1725	1774	BEAU 14
BEAUMONT Joseph	SJ	N	SM	Y	3	1702	1723	1730	1773	EAU 16
BEAUMONT William	SJ	W	SM	Y	3	1697	1718	1727	1764	BEAU 24
BERRIMAN (Alban)	OSB	L	SM	E		..	1661	..	1715	BERR 02
BERRIMAN Joseph	OSB	W	SM	G		..	1654	..	1715	BERR 04
BOURNE Jonas	S	N	SM	R	#3	1690	..	1715	1738	BOUR 04
BRETT Robert	SJ	W	SM	Y	3	1636	1657	1667	1678	BRET 04
BRETT Robert (Gabriel)	OSB	L	SM	Z	1*	1597	1615	1627	1665	BRET 06
BRIANT Alexander ST.	SJ	W	SM	D	*+‡	1556	1581	1578	1581	BRIA 06
BUCKLAND Ralph	S	W	SM	R	‡	1564	..	1588	1611	BUCK 06
BURT William	S		SM	D	#	..	..	1603	..	BURT 02
BYFLEET John (Edward)	OSB	W	SM	G	#	1607	1624	..	1701	BYFL 02
BYFLEET Robert	S		SM	D	#	1616	..	1642	..	BYFL 04
BYFLEET William	S	W	SM	D	#3	1613	..	1640	1703	BYFL 06
CAPES John (Augustine)	OSB		SM	R	#§	1585	..	1612	1628	CAPE 10
CARNE Francis	SJ	N	SM	Y	3	1686	1704	1713	1715	CARN 06
CLAYBROOK William	S		SM		#*‡	1603	..	..	..	CLAY 04
COLLETON John	S	L	SM	D	#‡	1548	..	1576	1635	COLL 02
COMPTON Philip	S	W	SM	D		1734	..	1763	1803	COMP 04
COOMBES William	S	W	SM	D	3	1743	..	1777	1822	COOM 02
COOMBES William Henry	S	W	SM	D		1767	..	1791	1850	COOM 04
COPLEY Peter	SJ		SM	Q		..	1586	1581	1587	COPL 06
COTTAM John	S	N	SM	D	3	1646	..	1670	..	COTT 02
EWEN Maurice	SJ	L	SM	R	#	1611	1636	1634	1687	EWEN 02
FATHERS Thomas	S	L	SM	D	#	1591	..	1622	1663	FATH 02
FENN James BL.	S	W	SM	Q	+‡1	1540	..	1580	1584	FENN 02
FENN John	S		SM	L	‡3	1535	..	1574	1614	FENN 04
FENN Robert	S		SM		‡1	1536	..	..	1587	FENN 06
FITZJAMES Nicholas	OSB	W	SM	D	‡1	1564	1608	1601	1652	FITZ 12
FITZJAMES Thomas	S		SM	R	3	1668	..	1694	..	FITZ 14
FRYER Charles	S		SM	D	#	1738	..	1771	1811	FRYE 04
FRYER William	S		SM	D		1739	..	1770	1805	FRYE 06
FRYER William Victor	S	L	SM	L		1768	..	..	1844	FRYE 08
GIBBONS Andrew	S		SM	R		..	..	1581	1583	GIBB 04
GIBBONS John	SJ		SM	R	‡3	1544	1578	1576	1589	GIBB 06
GIBBONS Richard	SJ		SM		3	1549	1572	1575	1632	GIBB 10
GILBERT William	SJ	M	SM	Y		1607	1627	..	1677	GILB 02
GILDON Joseph	S	L	SM	L	3	..	..	1707	1736	GILD 06
GLEWE Henry	S		SM	D	‡	..	..	1643	..	GLEW 02
GODSALF George	S	M	SM		‡4	..	..	1576	1592	GODS 02
GODSALF John	S		SM		‡	1553	..	1584	..	GODS 04
GOODWIN James (Ignatius)	SJ	L	SM	V	#12	1601	1623	..	1667	GOOD 20
GREAVES John	SJ		SM	R	‡	1574	1601	1599	1652	GREA 06
GREENWAY Robert	S		SM	R	#	1655	..	1690	1694	GREE 72
HART William BL.	S	N	SM	R	+‡	1558	..	1581	1583	HART 14
HILL Thomas (of S.Gregory)	OSB	L	SM	R	#	1564	1613	1594	1644	HILL 12
HUNT Joseph	S	W	SM	D	#	1762	..	1790	1838	HUNT 07
ISHAM William	S		SM	V		1578	..	1602	..	ISHA 02
JEANES Robert	S	W	SM	D		..	..	1606	..	JEAN 02
KEMYS Thomas	OSB		SM	R	#‡2	1575	1612	1603	..	KEMY 04
KENDALL Richard (Peter)	OSB	M	SM	G		1758	1779	1782	1814	KEND 12
KEYNES Alexander	SJ		SM	R	#	1642	1669	1665	1713	KEYN 02
KEYNES Charles	SJ		SM		#3	..	1663	1671	1673	KEYN 04
KEYNES Edward	SJ	N	SM	Y	12	1608	1627	..	1665	KEYN 06
KEYNES George	SJ		SM		‡	1553	1593	..	1611	KEYN 08
KEYNES George	SJ		SM	R	#	1628	1649	1654	1659	KEYN 10
KEYNES John	SJ	L	SM		1	1624	1645	..	1697	KEYN 12
KEYNES Maurice	SJ		SM		1	1591	1616	..	1654	KEYN 16
KINGDON John	SJ		SM	Y		1716	1735	1743	1761	KING 10
KNIGHT George	SJ	W	SM	Y		1733	1754	1761	1790	KNIG 06
KNIGHT William (Nicholas)	OFM		SM	F	3	1730	1750	1758	1806	KNIG 18
LANCASTER Roger	S		SM	Q		..	..	1584	1598	LANC 12
LANGDON William	S		SM	Q		..	..	1582	..	LANG 08
MARTIN William (John)	OSB		SM	G	3	..	1661	1672	1672	MART 34
MASSEY John	S		SM	D	‡	1655	..	1693	1715	MASS 08
MEREDITH Jonas	S		SM	D	#‡	1547	..	1576	..	MERE 02

185

Name	Reg	D	Co	T	Notes	Born	Prof	Ordn	Died	Code
MICO Walter	SJ		SM	R	#§	1594	1620	1620	1647	MICO04
MORE Francis	SJ		SM	Y		1698	1718	1727	1727	MORE03
MUTTLEBURY Francis	OSB	L	SM	D	#1	1610	1658	1635	1697	MUTT02
MUTTLEBURY John (Placid)	OSB	W	SM	D	#12	1563	1610	1601	1632	MUTT04
NORRIS Richard	S	L	SM	Q	‡	..	..	1579	1590	NORR10
NORRIS Robert or John	S		SM	D	°3	1764	..	1786	..	NORR16
NORRIS Silvester	SJ		SM	R	#12	1570	1606	1595	1630	NORR20
PARSONS John	CRT		SM	V	2	..	1615	1594	1639	PARS04
PARSONS Robert	SJ		SM	R	‡	1546	1575	1578	1610	PARS10
PARSONS Robert	SJ	W	SM	R	#§3	1588	1628	1619	1658	PARS12
PEARCE James	SJ		SM	Y	#°	1692	1713	1720	..	PEAR02
PHILIPS William	SJ		SM		1	1544	1569	1574	1584	PHIL26
PRATER Joseph	OSB		SM	S		..	1600	1603	1631	PRAT02
PRATER Richard	S		SM	D		..	..	1604	..	PRAT04
RICHARDSON John (Augustine)	OSB		SM	G	4	..	1618	..	1626	RICH24
ROGERS John	SJ	L	SM	R	#‡	1585	1611	1610	1657	ROGE10
SHERWOOD Robert	OSB	M	SM	G	#	1588	1613	..	1665	SHER40
SHERWOOD Thomas	S		SM	R	#*§=	1583	..	1610	1610	SHER42
SHERWOOD William (Elphege)	OSB		SM	W		..	1626	..	1663	SHER44
TIPPET John	S		SM	D		..	..	1577	..	TIPP02
TUCKER James	SJ		SM	Y	#3	1710	1728	1735	..	TUCK02
WARFORD William	SJ		SM	R	#‡	1560	1594	1584	1608	WARF02
WILCOX Hugh	S		SM	Q		..	..	1582	..	WILC08
WORSLEY Lawrence	SJ		SM	Y		1613	1633	..	1676	WORS04
YEOMANS William	S		SM	Q	‡1	1553	..	1584	..	YEOM02

SP—SHROPSHIRE

Name	Reg	D	Co	T	Notes	Born	Prof	Ordn	Died	Code
BERINGTON Thomas	S	L	SP	D	3	1673	..	1698	1755	BERI14
BLOUNT Gilbert	S		SP	L		1621	..	1645	..	BLOU06
BLOUNT Thomas	S	M	SP	L	x1	1616	..	1641	1647	BLOU14
BOLAS Bernard (Benedict)	OSB	N	SP	X		..	1744	..	1773	BOLA02
BOLAS Thomas (Anselm)	OSB	N	SP	X		1732	1751	..	1797	BOLA04
BRADSHAW Anselm (Bernard)	OSB		SP	X	#	..	1723	..	1774	BRAD24
BROWN William	S		SP	R	4	1609	..	1632	1663	BROW38
BRUERTON John	SJ		SP	Y	#	1633	1651	..	1684	BRUE02
CLAYTON Ralph	S	L	SP	D	#3	..	..	1686	1743	CLAY16
CLAYTON Thomas	S	M	SP	D	#	1672	..	1699	1746	CLAY20
CLOUGH Anthony	S	M	SP	D		1729	..	1753	1793	CLOU02
CLOUGH Richard	SJ	M	SP	Y	#3	1728	1744	1757	1777	CLOU04
COOK Thomas	S		SP	D	3	..	..	1690	..	COOK06
CROWTHER John (Mark)	OSB	W	SP	V	#3	1584	1609	1608	1658	CROW06
CROWTHER Thomas	S		SP	D	x‡1	1546	..	1575	1585	CROW08
DAVIES William	S		SP	V	3	1538	..	1595	..	DAVI20
DORRINGTON Andrew	S	M	SP	R	#3	1567	..	1597	..	DORR04
DORRINGTON Francis	S		SP	R	#	1608	..	1638	..	DORR06
EDWARDS Gerard or Edward BL.	S		SP	Q	#+‡1	1552	..	1587	1588	EDWA08
ELLIOT Edward (Ambrose)	OSB	M	SP	G		1699	1719	..	1773	ELLI02
ELLIOT Nathaniel	SJ	M	SP	Y	#3	1705	1723	1736	1780	ELLI04
FOSTER Francis (Thomas)	OSB	M	SP	D	#2	1572	1611	1598	1631	FOST06
FOXE James	SJ	N	SP	Y		1729	1749	1755	1795	FOXE02
GIFFARD Peter	S	N	SP	L		1629	..	1653	1689	GIFF20
GRAVENOR John	S		SP	D	#	..	..	1606	..	GRAV04
GRAVENOR Walter	S		SP	V	1	1576	..	1602	..	GRAV06
HANMER John	SJ	L	SP	Y	#1	1663	1691	1697	1716	HANM06
HARNAGE Henry	S	M	SP	L		1650	..	..	1737	HARN02
HARNAGE Thomas	S	L	SP	D	#	1664	..	..	1719	HARN04
HASSALL William	S	M	SP	D		1706	..	1730	1741	HASS02
HOWE Joseph	SJ	N	SP	Y	#3	1711	1729	1737	1792	HOWE04
HOWE William	SJ	M	SP	Y	#3	1701	1722	1731	1746	HOWE06
JOHNSON Emmanuel	S		SP	R	#	1559	..	1603	..	JOHN08
JOHNSON Robert BL.	S	L	SP	D	*+	..	..	1576	1582	JOHN28
JUKES John	SJ	M	SP	R	#°23	1580	1624	1616	..	JUKE02
KIRK John	S	M	SP	R		1760	..	1784	1851	KIRK06
KYNASTON Roger	S	W	SP	R		1649	..	1675	1712	KYNA02
LACON Edward	S	L	SP	R	#	1615	..	1641	1679	LACO04

Name	Reg	D	Co	T	Notes	Born	Prof	Ordn	Died	Code
LACON John	S		SP	R	#	1610	..	1635	..	LACO06
LACON Richard	S		SP	R		1640	..	1666	..	LACO08
LACON Rowland (Michael)	OSB	N	SP	G		1744	1761	..	1807	LACO10
LEECH Humphrey	SJ	N	SP	R	#‡	1571	1618	1612	1629	LEEC02
LEWIS Francis	S		SP	R	#§	1608	..	1634	1641	LEWI08
LUTLEY Humphrey	S	M	SP		1	1599	..	..	..	LUTL02
LUTLEY Philip	S	M	SP	R	#	1601	..	1624	1684	LUTL04
MIDDLEMORE Humphrey	SJ		SP	R	#2	1594	1624	1619	1629	MIDD06
MOLYNEUX Mathias or Matthew	S	M	SP	R		1689	..	1712	1759	MOLY10
MORRIS-NANNY David	S		SP	V	#§3	1580	..	1613	..	MORR18
NORTHALL John	OSB		SP	G	#	..	1626	..	1666	NORT06
NORTHALL Richard (Clement)	OSB	L	SP	G	#	..	1645	..	1686	NORT08
PENDRIL Richard	SJ		SP	Y	#*°	1710	1730	1738	..	PEND01
PENDRIL William	SJ	N	SP	V	#	1682	1708	1708	1748	PEND02
PERCY Thomas	SJ		SP	Y	3	1648	1667	1677	1685	PERC16
PERCY Walter	SJ		SP	Y	*	1651	1674	1682	..	PERC18
PICKERING Thomas	ODC	M	SP		1	1703	..	..	1789	PICK08
PLOWDEN Charles	SJ	N	SP	R	#	1743	1759	1770	1821	PLOW02
PLOWDEN Francis	S		SP	P	3	..	..	1732	1788	PLOW08
PLOWDEN Robert	SJ	W	SP	Y	3	1740	1756	1764	1823	PLOW18
PRESTON Roland (Thomas)	OSB	L	SP	R	x	1566	1592	1590	1647	PRES12
PURCELL Philip	S	L	SP	L	3	..	..	1699	..	PURC02
PURCELL Walter Chetwynd	S	M	SP	D	13	1654	..	1680	1720	PURC06
RONE Jerome	S	M	SP	R	#	1614	..	1639	..	RONE02
SANDFORD Matthew	OSB		SP	D	2	1588	1614	..	1644	SAND32
SANDFORD Michael	CRT		SP	D	#	1589	..	1613	..	SAND34
SHIMELL Richard	S	W	SP	L	#§	1692	..	1716	1763	SHIM04
SHIMELL Thomas	S		SP	D		1716	..	1741	1779	SHIM06
SLADE William	S		SP	D	‡*	..	1582	1578	..	SLAD04
SPARCHFORD John	S		SP	S		1567	..	1593	..	SPAR02
TURNER Richard	S		SP	L		..	..	1696	1744	TURN28
WOOLFE (Lawrence)	OSB		SP	E		1632	1656	..	1697	WOOL04

ST—STAFFORDSHIRE

Name	Reg	D	Co	T	Notes	Born	Prof	Ordn	Died	Code
ADAMS John	S	L	ST	R		1709	..	1735	1737	ADAM03
ADAMS Thomas	S	M	ST			..	..	..	1733	ADAM09
ARNOLD Richard	S		ST	R	#	1586	..	1610	..	ARNO08
ASHTON Nicholas	S		ST	V	#34	..	..	1595	1605	ASHT10
BACKHOUSE Richard	S	M	ST	D	#	1589	..	1615	..	BACK02
BADDULEY Robert	SJ		ST		#1	1598	1618	..	1642	BADD02
BADDULEY William	SJ		ST	V	1	1597	1622	..	..	BADD04
BAGSHAWE Christopher	S	L	ST	Q	‡4	1552	..	1583	1625	BAGS02
BAGSHAWE Robert (Sigebert)	OSB		ST	Q		..	1613	1586	1633	BAGS04
BAGSHAWE Thomas	S	N	ST	D	#	..	..	1616	..	BAGS06
BARKER Charles	OSB	M	ST	W		..	1688	..	1703	BARK02
BECKET Nicholas	OSB	M	ST		*2	1583	1604	..	1618	BECK04
BETHAM James	SJ	L	ST	Y	1	1604	1624	..	1669	BETH01
BIDDULPH Andrew	S		ST	V	#3	1605	..	1629	1661	BIDD04
BIDDULPH Francis	SJ		ST	Y	#1	1595	1615	..	1673	BIDD06
BIDDULPH Peter	S		ST	R	#	1602	..	1625	1657	BIDD08
BISHOP John	S		ST	D	#‡	1580	..	1602	..	BISH12
BLOUNT James Walter (Jerome)	OSS		ST	L	#	1622	..	1649	1694	BLOU10
BLUETT John	SJ	L	ST	Y	#	1602	1628	..	1678	BLUE04
BODENHAM Hugh	S		ST	R		1645	..	1676	..	BODE02
BOLBET Roger	SJ.		ST		2	..	1559	..	1572	BOLB02
BOURNE Samuel	S		ST	D	#§3	1682	..	1711	1711	BOUR06
BROMWICH Andrew	S	M	ST	L	3	..	..	1672	1702	BROM08
BUTTON Richard	S		ST	R	#4	..	..	1594	1643	BUTT04
CALDWELL William	SJ		ST	R	#‡4	1580	1609	1606	1609	CALD06
CARLOS William	SJ	L	ST	Y	#3	1631	1656	1667	1679	CARL08
CHETWIN Ralph	SJ		ST	Y	#	1641	1665	1673	1719	CHET02
CLARK William	S		ST	R	*1	1568	..	1592	1603	CLAR34
CLOUGH Robert	S	M	ST	R	#	1616	..	1641	..	CLOU08
COLEMAN Walter (Christopher)	OFM	L	ST	F	#x123	1600	1626	1634	1645	COLE20
COLLINS John	S		ST	V	#3	1601	..	1627	1678	COLL30

187

Name	Reg	D	Co	T	Notes	Born	Prof	Ordn	Died	Code
CORNE Charles	S		ST	D	§3	1716	..	1757	1777	CORN02
CORNE James	S	M	ST	D	3	1745	..	1773	1817	CORN04
CORNE John	S	M	ST	D		1749	..	1776	1816	CORN06
CORNFORTH Thomas	S	W	ST	D	3	1679	..	1708	1748	CORN15
COYNEY Edward	S	M	ST	D	#3	1646	..	1670	1722	COYN02
CUMBERLEGE John (Benedict)	OSB		ST	X		..	1703	..	1730	CUMB02
DODD Francis	S		ST	L	3	..	..	1698	1734	DODD02
DODD James	S	L	ST	V	#	..	..	1683	1738	DODD06
FISHER Thomas (Wilfrid)	OSB	N	ST	X	3	1767	1787	1791	1847	FISH24
FITTER Daniel	S	M	ST	L	#	1628	..	1651	1700	FITT02
FITTER Francis	S	M	ST	L	#	1622	..	1645	1710	FITT04
FITZHERBERT Thomas	SJ		ST	R	‡	1552	1613	1602	1640	FITZ10
FLEETWOOD John (Ignatius)	ODC	M	ST	Z	1	1662	1681	..	1733	FLEE08
FOWLER John	S		ST	R	#‡3	1569	..	1610	..	FOWL06
FROST James (Peter)	OFM	M	ST	F	3	1731	1749	1755	1785	FROS02
FULWOOD Hugh	S		ST	R	#	1602	..	1627	..	FULW02
GENNINGS Edmund ST.	S	L	ST	Q	#+§	1567	..	1590	1591	GENN02
GENNINGS John (Thomas)	OFM		ST	R	§2	1576	1616	1600	1660	GENN04
GERARD Philip, 7th Ld.	SJ	W	ST	Y	#	1665	1684	1693	1733	GERA18
GERARD William	SJ		ST	Y	#3	1662	1683	1688	1706	GERA34
GERVASE John	S		ST	V		..	..	1599	1599	GERV04
GIFFARD Andrew	S	L	ST	D	#*13	1646	..	1674	1714	GIFF02
GIFFARD Augustine	S	M	ST			..	..	..	1721	GIFF04
GIFFARD Bonaventure BP.	S	L	ST	D	#*13	1643	..	1667	1734	GIFF06
GIFFARD Edward	SJ	N	ST	R	#1	1598	1621	..	1640	GIFF10
GIFFARD Joseph	SJ	M	ST	Y	#	1620	1640	..	1673	GIFF16
GIFFARD Peter or Richard	SJ	L	ST	Y	#	1613	1633	1642	1697	GIFF18
GREEN John	S		ST	Q		1561	..	1585	..	GREE26
GREEN William	S	L	ST	L		..	..	..	1727	GREE58
GROSVENOR Richard	S		ST	D	#3	1646	..	1675	1726	GROS04
HARCOURT Francis	S		ST	R	#	1632	..	1657	1657	HARC02
HARCOURT Valentine	S	M	ST	R	#4	1611	..	1633	1691	HARC06
HASSELS Walter	S		ST	D		1574	..	1599	..	HASS04
HEMISS John	S		ST	D	#1	1579	..	1621	..	HEMI02
HEVENINGHAM John	SJ		ST	Y	#	1642	1667	1673	1708	HEVE02
HINDE Brian	S	M	ST	D	#3	..	..	1682	1724	HIND02
HODGSON Thomas	SJ	N	ST	R	‡	1562	1601	1601	1646	HODG36
HODGSON Thomas	S		ST	V	#§3	1601	..	1628	..	HODG38
HOWE George	S	M	ST	L		1771	..	1795	1837	HOWE02
HOWELL John	S	W	ST	V		1765	..	1789	1810	HOWE08
JAKEMAN Francis	S	M	ST	R	#§	1698	..	1725	1778	JAKE02
JAKEMAN George	S	M	ST	R	#§3	1700	..	1730	1740	JAKE04
JONES Edward	S		ST	L		1669	..	1691	1738	JONE04
KEELING Thomas	S		ST	D	#	..	..	1601	..	KEEL04
KNOWLES John	SJ		ST	Y		1607	1624	..	1637	KNOW04
LEE Francis	S	L	ST	D		1759	..	1785	1830	LEEA08
LEE Stephen	S	M	ST	D	#	1622	..	1622	1671	LEEA24
LEEK Thomas	S	L	ST	V	#‡	1565	..	1596	1638	LEEK04
LEIGH William	SJ		ST			1598	1621	..	..	LEIG16
LEVESON Edward	SJ	M	ST	R		1642	1669	1667	1720	LEVE04
LEVESON Francis (Ignatius) VEN	OFM		ST	F	x1234	1646	1664	1674	1680	LEVE06
LEVESON Richard	SJ		ST	Y		1649	1670	1679	1715	LEVE08
LEVESON William (John Bapt)	OFM		ST	F	123	1648	1666	1673	1709	LEVE10
MALLET Francis	S		ST	S	3	..	..	1619	..	MALL04
MAXFIELD Thomas BL.	S	L	ST	D	#+1	1585	..	1614	1616	MAXF02
NEWMAN William	S		ST	S	#	1577	..	1606	1640	NEWM02
ONION Thomas	S	M	ST	R	#	1740	..	1766	1814	ONIO02
PALIN Richard	S	M	ST	D	3	1670	..	1698	1751	PALI02
PALIN Vincent	OSB		ST	W		..	1711	..	1735	PALI04
PARKER John	SJ	W	ST	Y		1611	1630	..	1684	PARK20
PERRY John Placidus	S	M	ST	D	3	1741	..	1770	1819	PERR06
PERRY Philip Mark	S	M	ST	P		1720	..	1751	1774	PERR08
PHILMOT Philip	SJ	M	ST	Y	1	1652	1674	1683	1725	PHIL42
PLOTTS John	SJ		ST	Y	#	1614	1634	..	1688	PLOT04
POTTS Thomas	S	M	ST	D		1754	..	1778	1819	POTT12
PURCELL John	SJ	L	ST	R	#	1633	1653	1666	1701	PURC01

Name	Reg	D	Co	T	Notes	Born	Prof	Ordn	Died	Code
PURCELL Walter	S	M	ST	R	#	1627	..	1651	1679	PURC04
RIDER Francis	S	M	ST	D	1	1622	..	1650	..	RIDE01
RIDER Simon	S	L	ST	P	3	1668	..	1693	1730	RIDE04
ROCK Samuel	S	M	ST	D	3	1762	..	1787	1839	ROCK02
ROTTON Roger (Serenus)	OSB		ST	G		..	1679	..	1697	ROTT02
SHELDON Richard	S		ST	R	°	1570	..	1593	..	SHEL16
SHELDON William	S		ST	R	‡	1564	..	1591	..	SHEL18
SHELLEY Thomasd	S	M	ST	D	3	1737	..	1763	1807	SHEL30
SOUTHERN William	SJ	M	ST	V	#3	1594	1625	1625	1658	SOUT16
STAFFORD Henry	SJ		ST	Y		1606	1624	1632	1657	STAF10
STAFFORD Ignatius	SJ		ST	Y	#	1599	1618	..	1642	STAF11
STAFFORD Ignatius	SJ		ST	Y	#	1652	1672	1682	1720	STAF12
STAFFORD John	SJ	M	ST	Y	1	1603	1623	..	1667	STAF14
STANFORD Robert	SJ		ST	R	#	1593	1617	1617	1659	STAN16
STANLEY Edward	SJ		ST	R	12	1564	1619	1611	1639	STAN20
STITCH James	S	M	ST	L	#	1720	..	1744	1764	STIT02
STONE Benjamin	S	M	ST	D	3	1742	..	1770	1819	STON02
STONE Marmaduke	SJ	N	ST	Y		1748	1767	1775	1834	STON06
STONE Thomas	S	M	ST	D		1746	..	1770	1797	STON08
SUGAR John VEN.	S	M	ST	D	#+‡	1562	..	1601	1604	SUGA02
SUTTON Abraham	S	N	ST	D	‡	1551	..	1578	..	SUTT02
SUTTON Robert VEN.	S	M	ST	D	+‡	1544	..	1578	1588	SUTT04
SUTTON John	SJ	L	ST	D	‡	..	1582	1577	1590	SUTT14
TALBOT Gilbert, Earl of S'bry	SJ		ST	Y	#*1	1672	1694	1700	1743	TALB06
TATLOCK John	SJ	L	ST	Y	#3	1709	1729	1736	1756	TATL08
TRENTHAM Roger	S		ST	D	#3	..	..	1686	1742	TREN02
TURBERVILLE Henry	S		ST	D	#13	1607	..	1635	1678	TURB06
UNDERHILL James	S		ST	L	#3	..	..	1681	..	UNDE02
WAKEMAN John	S		ST	R	#	1594	..	1620	..	WAKE08
WAKEMAN Thomas	SJ		ST	R	#	1599	1632	1630	1636	WAKE14
WARD William	SJ	M	ST	Y	°	1708	1727	1735	..	WARD12
WARRILOW Joseph	S	L	ST	D	#1	1675	..	1712	1765	WARR22
WHITGREAVE James Abel	SJ	M	ST	Y	13	1689	1715	1724	1750	WHIT78
WHITGREAVE Thomas	SJ	M	ST	Y	1	1696	1718	1726	1757	WHIT80
WHITTINGHAM Thomas	S	M	ST	P		1738	..	1763	1783	WHIT92
WILSON John	S		ST	R		1576	..	1605	..	WILS08
WILSON Simon	SJ		ST	R	1	1623	1692	1649	1695	WILS28
WILSON Thomas	S	M	ST	D	#	1712	..	1737	1779	WILS36
WOLSELEY Edward	OSB	M	ST	G		..	1632	..	1669	WOLS02
WOLSELEY John	S		ST	Q		..	..	1586	..	WOLS04
WOOD Edward	SJ		ST	Y	4	1663	1683	1695	1726	WOOD04
WOODRUFFE Robert	S	M	ST	L		..	..	1680	..	WOOD36
YATES John	S		ST	Q	*	1549	..	1591	1624	YATE12
YEKE Nicholas	S	M	ST	Q	#‡1	1557	..	1579	..	YEKE02

SX—SUSSEX

Name	Reg	D	Co	T	Notes	Born	Prof	Ordn	Died	Code
ARDEN Henry	S		SX	R	#14	1578	..	1602	1602	ARDE04
ARDEN Robert	SJ		SX			..	1567	..	..	ARDE06
BLACKFAN John	SJ		SX	V	#†3	1560	1594	1593	1641	BLAC10
BLACKFAN Thomas	SJ	W	SX	Y	#4	1601	1624	..	1663	BLAC12
BOWES Robert	S	W	SX	D	#3	1673	..	1697	1735	BOWE06
BOWES Stanislaus	S		SX	R		1680	..	1709	1710	BOWE08
BOWES Stephen	S		SX	D		1676	..	..	1713	BOWE10
BROOKE Thomas	SJ	M	SX	V	13	1678	1701	1701	1761	BROO16
BRYON Francis	SJ		SX	Y	#°3	1725	1742	1749	..	BRYO02
BULLAKER Thomas (Jn Bp.) VEN.	OFM	L	SX	V	+123	1604	1624	1628	1642	BULL02
CAPE (Francis)	OSB		SX	G		1608	1620	..	1668	CAPE02
CAPE Joseph (Anth'y of S.Jos)	OFM		SX	F	124	1600	1620	..	1669	CAPE04
CAPE Luke (Benedict)	OSB		SX	G	4	..	1615	..	1620	CAPE06
CAPE (Michael)	OSB	N	SX	E		1609	1628	1638	1668	CAPE08
CARYLL Charles	SJ	W	SX	Y	#3	1685	1704	1713	1745	CARY18
CARYLL Peter (Alexius)	OSB	L	SX	G		1631	1654	..	1686	CARY20
CARYLL Richard, Hon.	SJ	W	SX	Y	#3	1692	1711	1720	1751	CARY22
CHALLONER Richard BP.	S	L	SX	D	#*	1691	..	1716	1781	CHAL06
COPLEY (Richard)	OFM		SX	F	123	1666	1684	1690	1702	COPL07

Name	Reg	D	Co	T	Notes	Born	Prof	Ordn	Died	Code
CORBY Henry	SJ		SX	Y	3	1700	1722	1730	1765	CORB16
CROUCHER Christopher	S		SX	L		1713	..	1757	1765	CROU02
CRUMP John	S		SX	D	*3	1654	..	1688	..	CRUM02
DARELL John	S		SX	V	#3	1586	..	1610	..	DARE03
DARELL Richard	SJ		SX	Y	#	1596	1616	..	1628	DARE06
DARREL John	S		SX	V	#3	1586	..	1610	..	DARR04
DOWNING John	S		SX	D	3	..	..	1646	..	DOWN06
FENNELL Simon	S	L	SX	Q	‡	..	..	1583	..	FENN10
FILIALL John	S		SX	D	7	..	..	..	..	FILI02
FLETCHER Thomas	S	L	SX	R	#	1590	..	1616	..	FLET12
FRANCIS John	S		SX	D	#	1672	..	1706	1729	FRAN04
GAGE George	S		SX		*	..	..	1614	..	GAGE06
GERVASE George BL.	OSB		SX	D	*+2	1569	1608	1603	1608	GERV02
GOUGH Stephen	ORA		SX	P	3	1605	1652	1652	1682	GOUG04
GUILDFORD Henry	SJ	L	SX	Y	#13	1603	1625	1630	1638	GUIL02
HAMELYN John	S		SX	S	#1	1619	..	1644	..	HAME02
HAWKINS Thomas	SJ	M	SX	R	#	1722	1747	1747	1785	HAWK16
KEMP Henry	SJ	M	SX	Y	#	1672	1692	1700	1737	KEMP10
LANE Richard	S	L	SX	V	#3	1585	..	1608	1656	LANE08
LEEDES Edward	SJ	L	SX	R	#1	1598	1621	..	1677	LEED02
LEEDES Thomas	SJ		SX	R	#‡	1594	1618	1618	1668	LEED04
LEWKNER Edmund	S		SX	Q	†	..	..	1580	..	LEWK02
MARTIN Gregory	S		SX	D	‡	..	..	1573	1582	MART12
MOREY Blaise	S	M	SX	V		..	1744	..	1775	1823	MORE20
NORTON John	OSB		SX	G		..	1624	..	1631	NORT16
PILCHARD Thomas VEN.	S		SX	Q	#+‡1	1557	..	1583	1587	PILC02
ROOTES John	S	W	SX	D	#	..	..	1661	..	ROOT04
SCOTT Nicholas	S	M	SX	V	#3	1599	..	1624	..	SCOT10
SCROGGS John (Maurus)	OSB	W	SX	G		1617	1634	..	1672	SCRO02
SHELLEY Anthony	S	L	SX	D		1601	..	1628	..	SHEL20
SHELLEY Cyrpian	S		SX	R	4	1592	..	1616	1624	SHEL22
SHELLEY Edward	S		SX	D	#§	1588	..	1612	..	SHEL24
SHELLEY Owen	SJ		SX	R	#	1585	1615	1610	1666	SHEL26
SHELLEY Thomas	SJ		SX	R	13	1586	1620	1610	1651	SHEL28
SHELLEY William	S	L	SX	V	34	1583	..	1606	1643	SHEL34
SMITH George	S		SX	V	‡	1602	..	1645	..	SMIT19
SMITH John, Hon.	SJ		SX	Y	#1	1632	1663	1671	1689	SMIT37
SMITH Richard	SJ		SX	Y	#13	1660	1680	1687	1735	SMIT58
STAPLETON Thomas	S		SX	N		..	..	1563	1598	STAP11
SUMPNER Charles	OSB		SX	G	§	1645	1672	..	1702	SUMP02
THREEL Maurice	S		SX	D	#	..	..	1655	..	THRE02
TINDALL Edmund	S		SX	D	#	1584	..	1608	..	TIND02
TRAPPES Nicholas	S	L	SX	R	#	1647	..	1675	..	TRAP04
TRAPPES (Richard)	OFM		SX	F	123	1654	1670	1678	1694	TRAP06
TURNER Bernard	S	L	SX	D	#	1693	..	1720	1735	TURN04
VAUDREY John	SJ		SX	Y	#3	1658	1677	1686	1725	VAUD02
WARD Francis	S		SX	R	4	1597	..	1621	1623	WARD02
WHITEHAIR Anthony	S	M	SX	V	#4	1594	..	1620	1672	WHIT70

SY—SURREY

Name	Reg	D	Co	T	Notes	Born	Prof	Ordn	Died	Code
BAYNHAM George (Athanasius)	OFM	L	SY	F	13	1738	1754	1761	1803	BAYN08
CLARK Anthony	S	L	SY	D	3	..	..	1687	..	CLAR08
COPLEY William	SJ	M	SY	Y	13	1668	1686	1695	1727	COPL10
FROMOND Gregory	S		SY	V	#	1592	..	1618	..	FROM02
GAGE George	S		SY	D	#x	..	..	1626	1652	GAGE08
GAGE Thomas	OP		SY		°14	1604	..	..	1656	GAGE18
GARNET Thomas ST.	SJ	M	SY	V	#+3	1574	1604	1599	1608	GARN22
GREGG John	S	L	SY	D		1760	..	1784	1811	GREG02
GRIFFITH Robert	SJ		SY	R	#§	1582	1611	1607	1640	GRIF27
JENKINS Peter	SJ	M	SY	Y	3	1735	1753	1762	1818	JENK08
LEE Augustine	OSB	L	SY	S	#3	..	1624	1603	1640	LEEA02
SANDER Nicholas	S		SY	R	‡=3	1530	..	1560	1581	SAND01
WALLIS Francis	SJ		SY	Y		1589	1613	..	1656	WALL24
WOOD William	SJ		SY	Y	#	1671	1689	1698	1720	WOOD12
WRIGHT Edward	SJ	W	SY	Y	3	1752	1768	1776	1826	WRIG08

Name	Reg	D	Co	T	Notes	Born	Prof	Ordn	Died	Code

WD—WESTMORLAND

Name	Reg	D	Co	T	Notes	Born	Prof	Ordn	Died	Code
BENLOS Peter	SJ		WD	R	#†	1568	1613	..	1636	BENL02
BIRKBECK Edward	SJ		WD	Y	#	1667	1690	1699	1722	BIRK02
BIRKBECK Gervase	S		WD	R	#1	1671	..	1710	1733	BIRK04
BLENKINSOP Francis	S		WD	D		..	..	1612	..	BLEN02
BOSTE John ST.	S	N	WD	Q	#‡+1	1543	..	1581	1594	BOST02
BRAITHWAITE (Richard of Magd)	OFM		WD	F		1626	1653	1655	1695	BRAI06
BRAITHWAITE Robert	S		WD	D	#1	1623	..	1650	..	BRAI08
BROWN William (Ambrose)	OSB		WD	G		1670	1700	1706	1755	BROW42
DUCKETT Robert	S		WD	D	#	1598	..	1627	1656	DUCK12
DUDLEY Richard	S	N	WD	R	#=	1563	..	1588	..	DUDL02
FLETCHER Anthony	SJ	L	WD	R	#	1564	1612	1610	1624	FLET02
GANDY James	S	N	WD	D	#3	1698	..	1726	1761	GAND02
GILPIN Arthur	CRT		WD	D	#	..	..	1612	1630	GILP02
LEYBURN George	S	L	WD	D	#	1600	..	1625	1677	LEYB02
LEYBURN John BP.	S	L	WD	P	*	1620	..	1646	1702	LEYB06
LEYBURN Nicholas	S		WD	D	#1	1626	..	1661	1701	LEYB08
LEYBURN Roger	S		WD	D	#3	1641	..	1668	..	LEYB12
LEYBURN William	S		WD	D	#3	1644	..	1668	..	LEYB14
MACHELL George	S		WD	D	#	1587	..	1618	..	MACZ04
PICKERING Lancelot	S	N	WD	R		1681	..	1706	1763	PICK04
SALKELD Henry	S		WD	S	°3	1584	..	1610	..	SALK06
SOMERS Thomas BL.	S	L	WD	D	#+	..	..	1606	1610	SOME02
SPROTT Thomas VEN.	S	M	WD	D	#+	1571	..	1596	1600	SPRO02
STRICKLAND Nicholas	S		WD	D	#34	1609	..	1634	1645	STRI06
STRICKLAND Roger	S	N	WD	D	4	..	..	1595	1643	STRI08
STRICKLAND Thomas John F BP.	S		WD	P	*13	1679	..	1712	1740	STRI12
STRICKLAND William	SJ	L	WD	Y		1731	1748	1756	1819	STRI14
THORNBURGH William	S	N	WD	D		1701	..	1724	1750	THOR04
TUNSTALL Thomas BL.	S	M	WD	D	#*+	..	..	1609	1616	TUNS10
WARINER Richard	S		WD	D	3	..	..	1607	..	WARI02
WEBSTER William BL.	S	L	WD	D	#+1	1565	..	1608	1641	WEBS04
WHARTON Michael	S	N	WD	L		1733	..	1760	1809	WHAR08
WILKINSON John	S	N	WD	R	#	1670	..	1698	1734	WILK12

WK—WARWICKSHIRE

Name	Reg	D	Co	T	Notes	Born	Prof	Ordn	Died	Code
APPLETON John (Henry)	OFM	M	WK	F	#3	..	1738	1746	1766	APPL13
ARNOLD Richard (Joachim)	OFM	N	WK	F	134	1724	1743	1749	1778	ARNO10
ATWOOD John (Peter)	OP	L	WK	N	#	1643	1664	1669	1712	ATWO02
BAMFIELD George	SJ		WK	Y	#1	1589	1613	..	1657	BAMF02
BARRETT George	S	M	WK	L	#	1638	..	1661	1699	BARR26
BARRETT Richard	S		WK	R	#‡	1544	..	1580	1599	BARR27
BETHAM John	S		WK	D	#3	1642	..	1667	1709	BETH02
BETHAM William	S		WK	D	#1	1597	..	1628	..	BETH04
BISHOP George	S	M	WK	P	3	1695	..	1723	1768	BISH06
BISHOP Henry	OFM	M	WK	F	3	1726	1749	1755	1811	BISH08
BISHOP William BP.	S	L	WK	R	*‡3	1553	..	1581	1624	BISH18
BOLT Henry	SJ		WK	Y	#3	1670	1691	1699	1743	BOLT05
BUTLER George	S		WK	Q	#	1553	..	1592	..	BUTL06
CANNING John	OP		WK	N	1	1641	1658	1665	1676	CANN04
CANNING William	S		WK	D	#	..	..	1643	..	CANN06
CHAPMAN Francis (Athanasius)	OFM		WK	F	3	1704	1728	1729	1749	CHAP18
CLAYTON John	S	M	WK		#4	..	..	..	1656	CLAY12
CLAYTON Thomas	S		WK	R	#	1616	..	1641	..	CLAY18
CLOPTON Cuthbert	S	L	WK	R	#	1607	..	1636	1644	CLOP02
COTTRELL Benjamin (Thomas)	OFM		WK	F	134	1739	1759	1767	1817	COTT26
COX Robert	SJ	M	WK	Y	1	1579	1623	..	1648	COXA12
DAVENPORT Christophr(Francis)	OFM	L	WK	F	#§1	1590	1618	1620	1680	DAVE02
DIBDALE Robert VEN.	S	L	WK	Q	#+	..	..	1584	1586	DIBD02
FERRERS Joseph	ODC	L	WK			1725	1745	1749	1797	FERR02
FLINT Thomas	SJ	M	WK	R		1576	1621	1600	1638	FLIN02
FRANCIS Thomas (Leo)	OFM		WK	F	13	1726	1742	1749	1774	FRAN06
FREEMAN John	S		WK	R	#	1594	..	1620	..	FREE02
GIBSON Francis	SJ	M	WK	Y	13	1668	1687	1695	1738	GIBS04

Name	Reg	D	Co	T	Notes	Born	Prof	Ordn	Died	Code
GIBSON Isaac	SJ	M	WK	Y	2	1674	1693	1702	1738	GIBS10
GOOD John	S		WK	R	#†	1584	..	1612	..	GOOD02
GRAFTON Thomas (Stephen)	OFM	W	WK	F	3	1764	1780	1788	1847	GRAF02
GRAVENOR John	SJ		WK		#	1589	1623	..	1640	GRAV02
GREEN Adam	S	M	WK	Q	‡	..	..	1591	..	GREE02
GRIFFIN George	OSS		WK	L	1	1621	..	..	1695	GRIF12
GRIFFIN Nicholas	SJ	M	WK	Y	4	1672	1691	1700	1720	GRIF14
GRISOLD George	S		WK	V	3	1579	..	1602	..	GRIS02
HARTLEY Thomas	S	M	WK	R		1740	..	1764	1781	HART30
HARTLEY William	S	M	WK	R		1742	..	1766	1794	HART34
HAWLEY James (Lawrence S.Jn.)	OFM	M	WK	F	13	1752	1769	1779	1833	HAWL04
HICHIN Philip	S	M	WK	R		1670	..	1696	1736	HICH02
HICHIN William	S	M	WK	R		1635	..	1675	..	HICH04
HIGGINSON Thomas	S		WK	R		1667	..	1690	..	HIGG14
INGRAM John (Angelus)	OFM		WK	F	134	1742	1761	1767	1794	INGR09
INGRAM Thomas (Joachim)	OFM		WK	F	134	1737	1755	1761	1803	INGR10
JOHNSON George	OSB	M	WK	G		1748	1768	..	1803	JOHN10
KINGTON Thomas (Pacificus)	OFM	W	WK	F	13	1754	1770	1779	1827	KING22
KNIGHT John	S		WK	R	#‡	1633	..	1657	1657	KNIG12
KNIGHTLEY Andrew	S	L	WK			..	..	..	1660	KNIG20
KNIGHTLEY John (Maurus)	OSB	L	WK	X		..	1670	..	1708	KNIG22
MOORE Richard	SJ		WK	Y		1672	1693	1702	1753	MOOR10
MORGAN Francis	OSB	L	WK	G		1602	1623	..	1669	MORG08
NEVILLE Fulke	S		WK	D	#§	..	..	1600	..	NEVI06
NUTT John (Pacificus)	OFM	M	WK	F	13	1738	1754	1761	1799	NUTT02
PETO Humphrey (Placid)	OSB		WK	Z	#*x24	..	1604	..	1643	PETO02
PITTS Henry	SJ	M	WK	Y	1	1638	1659	1668	1690	PITT04
POLE Edward	S	L	WK	Q	x	..	..	1580	1584	POLE08
PORTER Simon	S		WK	D	#	..	..	1612	..	PORT20
RANDOLPH (Leo of St M.Magd.)	OFM	M	WK	F	1234	1631	1652	1656	1700	RAND04
REEVE Joseph	SJ	W	WK	Y	#3	1733	1752	1765	1820	REEV04
REEVE Richard	SJ	N	WK	Y	#3	1740	1757	1765	1816	REEV06
RICHARDSON Joseph	SJ	M	WK	Y		1606	1637	..	1670	RICH28
SADLER Thomas Vinc. (Faustus)	OSB	L	WK	W		1604	1622	..	1681	SADL14
SADLER Walter Robt (Vincent)	OSB	L	WK	Q	§1	1563	1607	1592	1621	SADL16
SANDERS Charles	S	N	WK	R	#	1686	..	1712	1737	SAND02
SANDERS Thomas	SJ	M	WK	Y	3	1724	1744	1751	1790	SAND10
SHELDON Edward	OSB		WK	G		1624	1644	..	1685	SHEL04
SHELDON Edward	SJ		WK	Y	°3	1716	1733	1741	..	SHEL06
SHEPHERD Thomas (Alexius)	OSB		WK	G		..	1721	..	1755	SHEP14
SKINNER Andrew	S		WK	D	#1	1610	..	1648	1672	SKIN02
SKINNER James	S	L	WK	D	#3	1608	..	1634	..	SKIN06
SKINNER John	S	M	WK	L	#3	..	..	1658	1685	SKIN12
SKINNER William	S	W	WK	D	#3	..	..	1661	1694	SKIN16
SMITH Edmund	SJ	N	WK	Y	#	1666	1690	1698	1727	SMIT12
SMITH Francis	S	W	WK	L	3	..	..	1692	1748	SMIT16
SMITH John	SJ	L	WK	Y	3	1669	1688	1695	1754	SMIT42
SMITH William	S	L	WK	R	#	1648	..	1672	1722	SMIT76
STANFORD Edmund (of S.Martin)	ODC	L	WK	B		..	..	..	1635	STAN10
STANFORD John	S	M	WK	R		1654	..	1677	1737	STAN14
WALTERS Thomas	SJ	M	WK	Y		1619	1640	..	1647	WALT02
WARING Humphrey	S	L	WK	L		1605	..	1635	1676	WAR108
WARING William	S	M	WK	L	#	1604	..	1633	1652	WARI14
WARNER John	SJ	L	WK	D		1628	1662	1653	1692	WARN02
WATTS John	S	L	WK	D	#‡	1616	..	1653	1675	WATT02
WEBB William Henry (Dunstan)	OSB	N	WK	X		1764	1784	1789	1848	WEBB14
WEETMAN Edward (Andrew)	OFM	W	WK	F	3	1765	..	1790	1843	WEET02
WEETMAN Francis (Andrew)	OFM	W	WK	F	13	1742	1759	1767	1795	WEET04
WILKS Joseph (Cuthbert)	OSB		WK	E		1748	1764	1772	1829	WILK18

WR—WORCESTERSHIRE

Name	Reg	D	Co	T	Notes	Born	Prof	Ordn	Died	Code
ACTON Thomas	SJ		WR	Y	#	1640	1662	1675	1721	ACTO05
ATWOOD Peter	SJ		WR	Y	3	1682	1703	1711	1734	ATWO04
BARNSLEY Henry	S	M	WR	D	#4	1604	..	1628	1678	BARN40
BARTLETT Edward	S	M	WR	D		1702	..	1727	1782	BART04

192

Name	Reg	D	Co	T	Notes	Born	Prof	Ordn	Died	Code
BARTLETT Felix	SJ	M	WR	Y		1708	1726	1734	1777	BART06
BARTLETT Richard	S	M	WR	D	#3	1684	..	1709	1734	BART10
BARTLETT Richard	SJ		WR	R	#	1577	1616	1612	1645	BART12
BARTLETT Richard (Bernard)	OSB	N	WR	G		1669	1692	..	1735	BART13
BAYNHAM John	SJ	M	WR	Y	#3	1720	1740	1746	1796	BAYN10
BELL Arthur (Francis) VEN.	OFM		WR	V	+	1591	1619	1618	1643	BELL02
BISHOP Francis	S	M	WR	D		1757	..	1783	1821	BISH04
BLOUNT Charles	S	M	WR	D	3	1735	..	1761	1810	BLOU02
BRACEY Edmund	SJ	M	WR	Y	4	1709	1730	1738	1783	BRAC02
BRADSHAW Thomas (Augustine)	OSB	M	WR	V	#	1576	1600	1600	1618	BRAD36
BRENT Richard (George)	OSB		WR	X		..	1696	..	1716	BREN10
BRISTOW Richard	S	L	WR	D	‡x	1538	..	1573	1581	BRIS04
CARTER George (Anselm)	OSB	N	WR	G	1	1648	1670	..	1727	CART02
CECIL John	S		WR	R	#‡	1558	..	1584	1626	CECI02
COFFIN Thomas	S	N	WR	R	#	1568	..	1591	..	COFF06
COLE Thomas	S	L	WR	R	#§	1596	..	1620	..	COLE12
CROSBY John	SJ	N	WR	Y	#13	1637	1664	1672	1709	CROS06
CROSBY Roland (Wulstan)	OSB		WR	R	#	1640	1660	1666	1713	CROS08
DIXON Henry (Thomas)	OFM		WR	F	134	1729	1746	1755	1776	DIXO05
ELMER Felix (Jocelin)	OSB		WR	W	23		1613	1617	1651	ELME02
FARLEY Elliot	SJ		WR	R	#‡1	1600	1632	1629	1650	FARL02
FOLLIOT John	S		WR	D	#	..	..	1607	..	FOLL02
FORTESCUE (Angelus of S.Mary)	OFM		WR	F	123	1658	1675	1683	1718	FORT06
GREEN Richard	S	L	WR	L		1683	..	..	1750	GREE38
GREEN Thomas	S		WR	R	#‡	1639	..	1665	1666	GREE54
GRIFFITH James	S	M	WR	L	3	..	..	1688	1735	GRIF22
HARDING Anthony	S		WR	V	#	..	..	1621	..	HARD18
HARRISON John	SJ		WR	Y		1615	1636	1645	1678	HARR42
HIGGINS (Augustine)	OFM		WR	F	123	1660	1678	1685	1707	HIGG06
HORNYOLD John Joseph BP.	S	M	WR	D	*	1706	..	1736	1778	HORN18
HORNYOLD Ralph	SJ	N	WR	Y	#	1674	1693	1702	1740	HORN20
HORNYOLD Thomas	S		WR	D		1664	..	..	..	HORN22
HUGFORD Henry	S	M	WR	D	4	1666	..	..	1739	HUGF02
HUTTON Robert	SJ		WR	R	#13	1628	1656	1653	1692	HUTT08
INGRAM Christopher	S		WR	Q	†4	..	..	1582	1594	INGR04
JENKS Silvester	S	L	WR	D	#*	1656	..	1684	1714	JENK12
JONES James	SJ		WR	D	#	1573	1623	1612	1636	JONE12
LANE James	SJ	M	WR	Y		1737	1758	1769	1821	LANE06
LUCAS Simon	S	L	WR	V		1745	..	1775	1801	LUCA06
LUDDINGTON Walter (Gervase)	ODC	M	WR	N	#‡1	1600	1630	..	1658	LUDD02
MARSHALL John	S		WR	N	‡3	..	..	1570	1597	MARS20
MEALS John	S		WR	D	#3	1687	..	1712	1756	MEAL02
MERYING Robert (Benedict)	OSB		WR	X	14	1598	1658	..	1666	MERY02
METCALFE Joseph	SJ	N	WR	Y	#1	1670	1692	1701	1703	METC15
MILWARD Isaac (Anselm)	OFM		WR	F	12	1757	1778	1782	1813	MILW02
MORGAN George	SJ	L	WR	Y	3	1636	1657	1671	1674	MORG12
OAKLEY Francis	SJ	N	WR	Y	#3	1694	1715	1729	1755	OAKL02
PARKER Francis	S	M	WR	P		1738	..	1763	1779	PARK10
PENNINGTON Francis	SJ		WR	Y		1644	1664	1674	1699	PENN12
PENRICE Charles	S	M	WR	L	3	..	..	1679	..	PENR02
PERROTT (George of S.William)	OFM		WR	F	12	1601	1623	..	1670	PERR02
PERROTT John	S	L	WR	L	#1	1629	..	1653	1714	PERR04
PHILIPS Peter	S	N	WR			1710	..	..	1761	PHIL18
PHILIPS Vincent	SJ		WR	Y	#3	1698	1717	1726	1760	PHIL24
PHILIPS William	OSB	L	WR	G	#	..	1682	..	1739	PHIL34
POULTON William	S.	M	WR	R		1676	..	1703	1726	POUL38
RAWLINS Henry	S		WR	R		1659	..	1686	..	RAWL04
RAYMENT Benedict	S	N	WR	D		1764	..	1788	1842	RAYM02
REEVE Thomas	SJ	L	WR	Y	#	1752	1770	..	1826	REEV08
RUSSELL (Martin)	OP	M	WR			1632	1657	1658	1711	RUSS08
RUSSELL Thomas	SJ	M	WR	Y	4	1655	1676	1685	1724	RUSS14
SALWAY Thomas	S		WR	Q		..	..	1588	..	SALW02
SANDERS Francis	SJ		WR	R	#	1648	1674	1672	1710	SAND06
SHELDON Henry	SJ		WR	Y	3	1686	1705	1718	1756	SHEL10
SHELDON Lionel	OSB	L	WR	G		1633	1653	1657	1678	SHEL12
WEEDON Thomas	S	N	WR	R	#4	1637	..	1661	1719	WEED06

Name	Reg	D	Co	T	Notes	Born	Prof	Ordn	Died	Code
WHEELER John	S	M	WR	R		..	..	1696	..	WHEE04
WHITE Edward	S	L	WR	D	1	1731	..	1759	1762	WHIT24
WHITE Thomas	S		WR	R	†	1643	..	1666	1670	WHIT56
WOODHOPE (Thomas)	OSB	M	WR	G	#4	..	1622	..	1654	WOOD31
WOODWARD Humphrey	SJ		WR	R	1	1552	1577	..	1587	WOOD48
WOOLFE John	S		WR	L	#	..	..	1674	1735	WOOL02
YATES (Daniel of S.John)	OFM		WR	F	12	1603	1632	..	1659	YATE02
YOUNG Francis	SJ	M	WR	R	‡	1570	1600	1599	1633	YOUN06

WT—WILTSHIRE

Name	Reg	D	Co	T	Notes	Born	Prof	Ordn	Died	Code
ADELHAM John (Placid)	OSB	L	WT	E	x§	..	1652	..	1679	ADEL01
BARNES William	S	M	WT	R	13	1764	..	1793	1845	BARN26
BATT William	S	W	WT	D	#	..	..	1604	..	BATT04
BATT William (Anthony)	OSB		WT	W		..	1616	..	1651	BATT06
CLARE John	SJ	W	WT	V	#1	1581	1605	1603	1628	CLAR02
CODRINGTON (Anthony)	OFM		WT	F	123	1693	1711	1719	1729	CODR02
CODRINGTON (Bonaventure)	S	L	WT	D		..	..	..	1727	CODR04
CODRINGTON Thomas	S		WT	D	#	..	..	1676	1694	CODR06
COMPTON James (Bernard)	OSB		WT	Y	*°3	1748	1775	1773	..	COMP03
ERRINGTON William	S	L	WT	D		1716	..	1747	1768	ERRI10
EVERARD Thomas	S		WT	R	#‡=	1570	..	1601	..	EVER16
FAULKNER John	S		WT	R	§3	1600	..	1623	1664	FAUL04
GILMORE Robert (Paul)	OSB	N	WT	X		..	1685	..	1748	GILM02
IPSLEY Thomas	SJ		WT		#	1580	1603	..	1642	IPSL02
KNIPE William	S		WT	D	3	1643	..	1667	..	KNIP02
LEGATT John	SJ		WT	Y	#	1615	1635	..	1672	LEGA08
MASON Richard (Angelus)	OFM	W	WT		123	1599	1630	1624	1678	MASO04
MATHEW Tobie, Kt.	S		WT		*§	1577	..	1614	1655	MATH10
MAYHEW Cuthbert	S		WT	V	3	1580	..	1603	..	MAYH02
MAYHEW Edward	OSB		WT	R		1569	1607	1594	1625	MAYH04
MAYHEW Henry	S		WT	V	3	..	..	1592	1616	MAYH06
SCAMELL John	SJ	M	WT	S	3	1585	1610	1610	1624	SCAM02
STEPHENS Richard	S		WT	R	§	1631	..	1655	1657	STEP10
STOURTON John, Hon.	OSB	N	WT	G		1674	1693	1699	1748	STOU02
STOURTON Thomas, Hon.	OSB		WT	G		..	1645	..	1684	STOU04
TUCHINER Anthony	S	M	WT	D	‡4	..	..	1600	1643	TUCH02
WALDEGRAVE Francis	SJ	N	WT	R	#	1626	1655	1651	1701	WALD06
WHEBLE James	SJ	W	WT	Y	#3	1725	1743	1750	1788	WHEB02
WHITE William	SJ	N	WT	S	3	1584	1617	1609	1624	WHIT62
WOODSON Felix	SJ		WT	Y		1584	1612	..	..	WOOD42
WOODWARD John	S	N	WT	D	#3	..	..	1641	1677	WOOD50

YO—YORKSHIRE

Name	Reg	D	Co	T	Notes	Born	Prof	Ordn	Died	Code
ADDISON Thomas ?John	SJ	N	YO	V	#x3	1634	1668	1660	1685	ADDI03
ADDISON William	S	N	YO	D	#13	1662	..	1690	1736	ADDI04
ALLANSON Matthew (Paul)	OSB	M	YO	X	1	1692	1713	..	1768	ALLA06
ALLEN Henry	S	N	YO	D		1681	..	1704	1733	ALLE04
ALLEN William	SJ	L	YO	Y	#13	1732	1750	1757	1814	ALLE14
ALLIBON Job	S	L	YO	D	#§13	1638	..	1661	1709	ALLI02
AMIAS John BL.	S	N	YO	Q	#+	..	..	1581	1589	AMIA02
ANDLEBY William BL.	S	N	YO	D	+†1	1552	..	1577	1597	ANDL02
ANNE George	SJ	N	YO	R	x	1595	1623	1620	1660	ANNE02
APPLEBY Robert (Paulinus)	OSB	N	YO		#*2	1580	1604	..	1645	APPL02
APPLEBY William	SJ	L	YO	S	#3	1591	1629	1629	1671	APPL04
ASKEW Robert	S		YO	D	#	..	..	1602	..	ASKE06
ASPINALL John	OSB	L	YO	E		..	1714	..	1762	ASP105
ATKINSON Matthew (Paul)	OFM	L	YO	F	x13	1655	1673	1679	1729	ATKI14
ATKINSON (Peter of S.Ber'dne)	OFM	N	YO	F	123	1654	1672	1680	1686	ATKI16
ATKINSON Thomas VEN.	S	N	YO	Q	+1	1546	..	1588	1616	ATKI18
ATKINSON Thomas	S		YO	D		1700	..	1724	1728	ATKI19
ATKINSON William	S	N	YO		3	..	..	1570	..	ATKI20
BABTHORPE Ralph	SJ	N	YO	N	#124	1594	1615	..	1628	BABT04
BABTHORPE Richard	SJ	M	YO	R	1	1618	1651	1645	1681	BABT06
BABTHORPE Robert (Mellitus)	OSB	N	YO	W	#1	1584	1609	..	1654	BABT08

Name	Reg	D	Co	T	Notes	Born	Prof	Ordn	Died	Code
BABTHORPE Thomas	SJ		YO	R	#12	1598	1618	..	1656	BABT 10
BABTHORPE Thomas	SJ		YO	R	#1	1613	1635	..	1655	BABT 12
BABTHORPE William	S		YO		#	1613	..	..	..	BABT 14
BAILEY Andrew (Gabriel)	OP	L	YO	R	°24	..	1592	..	1610	BAIL 02
BANKS Christopher	S	N	YO	R	#†1	1615	..	1647	1678	BANK 02
BARKER William	S		YO	R	‡	1562	..	1588	..	BARK 14
BARNABY Francis	S	L	YO	R	‡=°	1573	..	1598	..	BARN 02
BARRASS (Bernardine)	OFM		YO	F	4	1659	1686	1687	1696	BARR 08
BATCHELOR William (Edmund)	OSB	L	YO	E		1709	1726	..	1737	BATC 02
BEESLEY John	SJ	M	YO	S	#	1593	1622	1620	1670	BEES 06
BELL John	S	N	YO	D		1767	..	1794	1854	BELL 10
BELL Thomas	S	N	YO	R	§°3	1551	..	1579	..	BELL 12
BERNEY (Robert of S.Francis)	OFM		YO	F	12	1593	1634	..	1659	BERN 06
BESTUNICUS Nicholas	S		YO	D	*	..	..	1618	..	BEST 06
BILCLIFFE Peter	CRT		YO	C		..	1661		1693	BILC 04
BING John	S	N	YO	Q		..	..	1594	..	BING 04
BLYDE Ignatius	SJ		YO	Y	13	1720	1756	1762	1788	BLYD 02
BOOTH John	S	N	YO	L		..	..	1696	1722	BOOT 08
BOWLAND James	S	N	YO	R		1564	..	1586	..	BOWL 01
BOYCE George	S	N	YO	D	#§	1590	..	1615	..	BOYC 02
BRAMLY George	S	N	YO	D	#	..	..	1577	..	BRAM 02
BRIGHAM Henry (Augustine)	OSB		YOG		..	1731	..	1738		BRIG 02
BRISCOE Thomas	S		YO	V	‡3	1553	..	1594	..	BRIS 02
BRITTON Matthew	S	N	YO	R	#4	1564	..	1590	1643	BRIT 04
BRITTON Richard	S		YO	S	3	..	..	1610	..	BRIT 06
BROOMHEAD Roland	S	N	YO	R		1751	..	1775	1820	BROO 22
BROWN Thomas	S	L	YO	D	#3	1662	..	1686	1728	BROW 31
BUCKLEY John (Maurus)	OSB	N	YO	G		..	1714	..	1729	BUCK 16
BULLOCK Charles	OP		YO	N	13	1752	1769	1777	1794	BULL 08
BULLOCK John (Raymund)	OP	L	YO	N		1750	1767	1773	1819	BULL 10
BULMER Bertram (Edward)	OSB	N	YO	X		..	1685	..	1745	BULM 02
BULMER Bertram (Maurus)	OSB	N	YO	W		1704	1724	..	1788	BULM 04
BURDEN Edward VEN.	S		YO	Q	+‡	..	..	1584	1588	BURD 02
BURDETT Anthony	SJ	N	YO	D	1	1610	1642	..	1657	BURD 06
BURNETT Thomas	SJ	N	YO	Y	1	1659	1681	1689	1727	BURN 04
BURTON (Augustine of Bern'dn)	OFM		YO	F	123	1679	1696	1705	1706	BURT 03
BUSBY Richard	SJ	N	YO	Y		1595	1623	1627	1648	BUSB 10
CALVERLEY Edmund	S		YO	R	1	1563	..	1585	..	CALV 02
CALVERT William	S	N	YO	V		..	..	1689	1735	CALV 06
CASSE (Lawrence)	OSB	N	YO	E		..	1689	..	1732	CASS 02
CATTERICK Edmund BL.	S	N	YO	D	#+3	1605	..	1630	1642	CATT 14
CATTERICK George	S	N	YO	D	#1	1595	..	1621	1667	CATT 16
CHAMBERS Oswald	S	N	YO	Q		..	..	1579	..	CHAM 14
CHAMPNEY Anthony	S	L	YO	R	#	1569	..	1596	1644	CHAM 28
CHAMPNEY (William)	OSB	N	YO	W	4	..	1712	..	1740	CHAM 30
CLARGENET William	S		YO	Q		..	..	1585	..	CLAR 04
CLARK Anthony	S		YO	Q	°3	1565	..	1590	..	CLAR 06
CLARKSON Thomas	S	N	YO	D		..	..	1600	..	CLAR 50
CLAXTON James BL.	S		YO	Q	#+	..	..	1582	1588	CLAX 02
CLAYTON James	S	M	YO	Q	§	..	..	1584	1589	CLAY 10
CLITHEROW Henry	OP		YO	R		1572	..	..	..	CLIT 02
CLITHEROW William	CRT		YO	Q		1542	1589	1582	..	CLIT 04
CLITHEROW William	S	N	YO	D	1	1563	..	1608	1636	CLIT 06
CONSTABLE David (Benedict)	OSB	N	YO	X	x	..	1669	..	1683	CONS 04
CONSTABLE Henry	S		YO	R	#†1	1587	..	1618	1623	CONS 10
CONSTABLE John (Philip)	OSB	N	YO	G		..	1660	..	..	CONS 16
CONSTABLE Michael	SJ		YO	Y	1	1648	1668	1681	1707	CONS 20
CONSTABLE Philip (Wilfrid)	OSB	M	YO	E		1707	1725	..	1764	CONS 22
CONSTABLE Robert	SJ		YO	R	#	1597	1619	..	1678	CONS 24
CONSTABLE Robert	SJ		YO	Y	13	1673	1711	1716	1739	CONS 26
CONSTABLE Robert	SJ	W	YO	R		1705	1729	1728	1770	CONS 28
CONYERS (Augustine)	OSB		YO	G	4	..	1638	..	1682	CONY 02
CONYERS George	SJ	N	YO	R	1	1575	1604	1602	1652	CONY 06
CONYERS Samuel	S		YO	Q		..	..	1582	1587	CONY 14
CONYERS Thomas	SJ		YO		1	1562	1584	..	1639	CONY 16
CORKER James (Maurus)	OSB	L	YO	X	§	1636	1656	..	1715	CORK 02

Name	Reg	D	Co	T	Notes	Born	Prof	Ordn	Died	Code
CORNFORTH Thomas	S	N	YO	D	134	1648	..	1672	1720	CORN14
COWLING Richard	SJ		YO	R	#	1562	1588	1587	1617	COWL14
COWLING William	S		YO	R		1557	..	1582	1592	COWL16
CRATHORNE Francis	OSB	M	YO	G	*	1575	1621	..	1667	CRAT02
CRATHORNE Francis	S	N	YO	V		1762	..	1787	1822	CRAT04
CRATHORNE John	SJ	M	YO	Y		1590	1611	..	1656	CRAT06
CRATHORNE Ralph	S		YO	P	3	1667	..	1693	1698	CRAT08
CRATHORNE Thomas (Anselm)	OSB		YO	X		..	1703	..	1746	CRAT10
CRATHORNE William	S	L	YO	D	#	1670	..	1697	1740	CRAT12
CRESSY Hugh P'linus (Serenus)	OSB	L	YO	G	#‡13	1605	1649	1651	1674	CRES04
CROSLAND Charles	SJ		YO	Y	3	1655	1677	1686	1724	CROS14
CROSLAND George	S	N	YO	R		1667	..	1705	1731	CROS16
CROSLAND Henry (Thomas)	OP	N	YO			1670	1692	1693	1719	CROS18
CROW Alexander VEN.	S	N	YO	Q	+1	1551	..	1583	1587	CROW02
CUDWORTH (Anthony of S.Mary)	OFM		YO	F	12	1624	1653	..	1681	CUDW02
DAKINS Edward	S		YO	Q	#†	1554	..	1582	..	DAKI02
DALBY Robert BL.	S	N	YO	Q	+§	..	..	1588	1589	DALB02
DALTON James	S	N	YO	R	#	1597	..	1631	1672	DALT02
DALTON Marmaduke	S	N	YO	D	#†3	1637	..	1670	1695	DALT04
DANBY John	S	N	YO	L	†1	1661	..	1689	1719	DANB02
DANBY Thomas (George)	OFM		YO	F	12	1645	1665	..	1673	DANB04
DAWSON Miles	S		YO	V	†1	1566	..	1594	..	DAWS04
DEAN William BL.	S	L	YO	Q	+†1	1557	..	1581	1588	DEAN04
DENTON William	S	L	YO	Q	1	1530	..	1581	..	DENT04
DICKENSON Francis BL.	S		YO	Q	#+	1565	..	1589	1590	DICK02
DINMORE William	S	N	YO	R	§4	1650	..	1676	1716	DINM02
DODSWORTH Christopher	S	L	YO	D	4	..	..	1612	1613	DODS02
DOLMAN Robert	S	N	YO	R	1	1634	..	1658	..	DOLM04
DOUGLASS John BP.	S	L	YO	D	*3	1743	..	1768	1812	DOUG02
DUCKETT John BL.	S	N	YO	D	#+§	1614	..	1639	1644	DUCK08
DUFFIELD Thomas	S	N	YO	D	#	..	..	1646	..	DUFF02
DUNN William	S	N	YO	P	#1	1749	..	1780	1805	DUNN14
EDISFORD John	SJ		YO	Y		1656	1675	1684	1720	EDIS04
EDISFORD John	SJ		YO	Y	#3	1700	1720	1729	1750	EDIS06
EDISFORD William	S	N	YO	R	4	1673	..	1697	1700	EDIS10
ELRINGTON Edward	S	M	YO	V	#†3	1599	..	1624	1652	ELRI02
ELRINGTON Henry	S		YO	D	3	1637	..	1667	..	ELRI04
EMERSON Thomas	OSB		YO		#*§1	1579	1604	..	1630	EMER04
ERRINGTON Charles	S		YO	R	#	1640	..	1664	1666	ERRI04
ERRINGTON William	S	N	YO	L		..	..	1693	1733	ERRI08
EURE Francis	SJ	M	YO	Y	#	1630	1647	..	1698	EURE02
EXLEY John	S	L	YO	D	#	1716	..	1748	1778	EXLE02
FAIRFAX Thomas	SJ		YO	Y	#1	1655	1675	1683	1716	FAIR08
FERBY Thomas	S	N	YO	R		1740	..	1763	1823	FERB02
FINGLEY John BL.	S	N	YO	Q	+†	1553	..	1581	1586	FING04
FIRTH Anthony (Richard)	ODC		YO			1719	1738	..	1792	FIRT02
FISHER Clement	S	L	YO	V		1743	..	1775	..	FISH02
FISHER John	SJ	M	YO	Y	1	1608	1628	..	1654	FISH08
FISHER Ralph	S		YO	D		..	..	1598	..	FISH14
FLATHERS Matthew or Major VEN	S	N	YO	D	+‡1	1560	..	1606	1608	FLAT02
FOSTER (Joseph)	OSB		YO	W		..	1630	..	1636	FOST16
FOSTER Matthew	S	N	YO	D	#	1658	..	..	1723	FOST18
FOSTER Seth	OSS		YO	R		1557	1584	1581	1628	FOST24
FOSTER Thomas	SJ	M	YO	R	#	1590	1617	1614	1648	FOST26
FOXE James	SJ		YO	Y	#3	1685	1707	1715	1760	FOXE01
FRANKLAND Hugh	OSB	N	YO	G		1671	1700	1705	1755	FRAN08
FRANKS Richard	S	N	YO	V	#3	1601	..	1632	..	FRAN12
FRANKS Richard	S	N	YO	V		1630	..	1655	1696	FRAN14
FREEMAN John	SJ		YO	V		..	1632	..	..	FREE04
FREEMAN Michael	SJ	N	YO	R		1578	1608	1603	1642	FREE06
FREEMAN William BL.	S	M	YO	Q	#+‡	..	..	1587	1595	FREE10
GAILE (Bede)	OSB	N	YO	G	#	..	1620	..	1629	GAIL02
GASCOIGNE Francis	S	N	YO	D	#3	1605	..	1636	1676	GASC02
GASCOIGNE John (Placid)	OSB	N	YO	W	#2	1599	1615	1623	1681	GASC06
GASCOIGNE Michael	OSB	N	YO	G		..	1622	..	1657	GASC08
GASCOIGNE Thomas	SJ	N	YO	Y		1605	1630	..	1669	GASC10

Name	Reg	D	Co	T	Notes	Born	Prof	Ordn	Died	Code
GASCOIGNE William	CRT		YO	B	1	1557	1579	..	1588	GASC12
GASCOIGNE William	S	N	YO	D	#3	1631	..	1655	1690	GASC14
GATENBY Richard	S	N	YO	V	#	..	..	1645	1677	GATE02
GIBSON (Dunstan)	OSB		YO	E		..	1629	1634	..	GIBS02
GILPIN Thomas	S	N	YO	D	#	1646	..	1668	1717	GILP06
GIRLINGTON John	S	N	YO	L	13	1657	..	1684	1729	GIRL02
GOODRICK Thomas	S	N	YO	D	4	1600	..	1630	1678	GOOD18
GOWER John	S		YO	R	#	1547	..	1580	..	GOWE06
GRANGE George (Gregory)	OSB	N	YO	G	#	1598	1624	..	1673	GRAN02
GRANGE Gregory	S		YO	D	#13	1658	..	1688	1736	GRAN04
GRANGE Thomas	S	L	YO	D	#3	1648	..	1676	1722	GRAN06
GRANGE William (Gregory)	OSB	L	YO	V	#§2	1579	1603	..	1619	GRAN08
GRANT Robert	SJ		YO	Y	#14	1594	1618	..	1655	GRAN14
GREAVES Francis	S	L	YO	D	#	..	..	1611	1673	GREA04
GREEN Edmund	S	M	YO	D	#	1606	..	1633	1685	GREE10
GREEN Henry	S	N	YO	D		1584	..	1628	..	GREE20
GRIMSTON (Martin of St Chas.)	OFM		YO	F	123	1657	1675	1682	1729	GRIM20
GROSVENOR Robert	SJ	M	YO	R	#=	1582	1620	1616	1668	GROS06
HALDENBY Francis	S	M	YO	L		1654	..	1678	..	HALD02
HAMERTON Gervase	SJ	N	YO	Y	23	1668	1686	1695	1708	HAME04
HAMERTON Henry	SJ		YO	Y	3	1644	1669	1678	1718	HAME06
HAMERTON Peter	SJ	M	YO	Y	#13	1637	1661	1669	1714	HAME08
HANSBIE Morgan (Joseph)	OP	L	YO	N		1663	1696	1698	1750	HANS02
HARDCASTLE Robert (John)	OSB	L	YO	W		..	1692	..	1741	HARD02
HARDESTY John	SJ		YO	Y	#	1681	1699	1711	1752	HARD10
HARDESTY Thomas (Adrian)	OSB		YO	X	#	1686	1703	..	1761	HARD12
HARDESTY William	S		YO	R	°	1559	..	1586	..	HARD14
HARDWICK Francis (Jn Bened't)	CAM	L	YO	R	#*2	1644	1679	1669	..	HARD26
HARDWICK William (Francis)	OFM		YO	F	123	1649	1671	1677	1705	HARD34
HARRINGTON Mark	S	L	YO	D	#	1592	..	1616	1657	HARR02
HARRINGTON William BL.	S	L	YO	Q	+	1566	..	1592	1594	HARR06
HARRISON John (Augustine)	OSB		YO	G		1773	1792	1800	1846	HARR48
HARRISON Richard (Maurus)	OSB	N	YO	G		..	1701	1707	1717	HARR56
HAWKESWORTH Robert	S		YO	R	°	1567	..	1593	..	HAWK06
HEIGHINGTON William	S		YO	R		1563	..	1585	..	HEIG04
HEMSWORTH John	S	N	YO	Q		..	..	1579	..	HEMS04
HEWETT John BL.	S		YO	Q	#+†	..	..	1585	1588	HEWE02
HILDRETH William	S	N	YO	D	§	..	..	1691	1736	HILD08
HILL Richard VEN.	S	N	YO	Q	+	..	..	1589	1590	HILL08
HIMSWORTH Robert	S	N	YO	D	3	1761	..	1788	1811	HIMS02
HIRD (Paulinus)	OSB	N	YO	G	#	..	1631	..	1645	HIRD02
HODGSON Christopher	S	N	YO	L		1729	..	1753	1765	HODG08
HODGSON Francis	S		YO	D	#3	1682	..	1707	1733	HODG14
HODGSON George	S	N	YO	D	14	1632	..	..	1679	HODG16
HODGSON (Richard of S.John)	OSB		YO	G	4	..	1614	..	1624	HODG30
HODGSON Samuel	S	L	YO	L		..	..	1760	1766	HODG32
HODGSON Thomas	SJ		YO	Y		1682	1703	1711	1726	HODG40
HODSON Thomas	S		YO	Q		..	..	1578	..	HODS08
HODSON Thomas	S		YO	V		1566	..	1597	..	HODS10
HOGG Gregory	S		YO	D		1631	..	..	..	HOGG02
HOGG John VEN.	S	N	YO	Q	+	..	..	1589	1590	HOGG04
HOLDSWORTH Daniel	S		YO	R		1558	..	1583	1596	HOLD14
HOLIDAY Richard or John VEN.	S	N	YO	Q	+	..	..	1589	1590	HOLI02
HOLTBY George	SJ		YO	R	#	1591	1617	1616	1669	HOLT08
HOLTBY Richard	SJ	N	YO	D	#†‡	1552	1583	1578	1640	HOLT12
HOLTBY Robert	S	L	YO	R	#4	1596	..	1621	1659	HOLT14
HORNER Richard VEN.	S	N	YO	D	+	..	..	1595	1598	HORN14
HORSMAN James (Adrian)	OSB		YO	X		1765	1787	..	1799	HORS04
HUNGATE Robert (Gregory)	OSB	N	YO	G		..	1610	..	1657	HUNG02
HUNGATE (Augustine)	OSB	N	YO	Z	*12	1584	1607	..	1672	HUNG04
HUNT Gilbert	SJ	M	YO	D	2	1576	1622	1605	1647	HUNT06
HUNT Thurstan VEN.	S	N	YO	Q	#+	..	..	1585	1601	HUNT14
HUNT William	S	N	YO	L	3	..	..	1707	1733	HUNT18
HUNTER Anthony	SJ	L	YO		#x13	1606	1649	1649	1684	HUNT20
HUSBAND William	S	N	YO	D	3	1743	..	1768	1779	HUSB04
HUTCHINSON Anthony (Cuthbert)	OSB	N	YO	G		..	1723	..	1760	HUTC02

Name	Reg	D	Co	T	Notes	Born	Prof	Ordn	Died	Code
HUTTON Thomas (John)	OSB	N	YO	S	3	1573	1600	1598	1642	HUTT09
INGLEBY Augustine	SJ	L	YO	Y		1602	1624	..	1657	INGL02
INGLEBY Charles	S	N	YO	R		1694	..	1718	1743	INGL04
INGLEBY Francis VEN.	S	N	YO	Q	+‡=	..	..	1583	1586	INGL06
INGLEBY Robert	OSB		YO	W		..	1626	..	1636	INGL12
INGLEBY Thomas	S		YO	V	=	1595	..	1636	..	INGL14
INGLEBY Thomas	S	N	YO	D	3	1635	..	1664	..	INGL16
INGLEBY Thomas	SJ	W	YO	Y		1684	1703	1712	1729	INGL18
INGLETON John	S		YO	P	3	1658	..	1688	1739	INGL20
JACKSON Ambrose	SJ	N	YO	Y	#	1685	1704	1712	1746	JACK02
JACKSON Anthony	S	N	YO	D	1	1666	..	..	1741	ACK04
JACKSON Bernard	S		YO	D		..	..	1604	..	JACK06
JACKSON Francis	SJ	N	YO	D	#	1579	1608	1605	1645	JACK14
JEFFERSON Robert	S	N	YO	D	3	167	..	1695	1735	JEFF04
JOHNSON John	S	M	YO	D	3	1657	..	1689	1739	JOHN16
JOHNSON (Placid)	OSB		YO	W		..	1652	..	1668	JOHN24
JOHNSON Richard	S		YO	D	#§	1562	..	1603	..	JOHN26
JOHNSTON Henry (Joseph)	OSB	L	YO	E	§	..	1675	..	1723	JOHN43
JOWSEY Andrew	S	N	YO	D	1	1646	..	1674	..	JOWS02
JOWSEY John	S	N	YO	D		..	..	1647	1678	JOWS04
KAYE Thomas	S	N	YO	L	3	1768	..	1795	1838	KAYE06
KILLINGBECK Robert	OSB	N	YO	X		1630	1653	..	1710	KILL02
KIRBY Luke ST.	S		YO	D	+	1548	..	1577	1582	KIRB08
KIRKMAN Richard BL.	S	N	YO	Q	+	..	..	1579	1582	KIRK14
KNARESBOROUGH Ch'pher or Rchd	S	L	YO	S	3	..	..	1603	..	KNAR02
KNARESBOROUGH John	S	N	YO	D	3	1672	..	1699	1722	KNAR04
LACEY William BL.	S	N	YO	R	+1	1531	..	1581	1582	LACE02
LAMBERT (Alexander)	OFM		YO	F	1234	1658	1670	1682	1707	LAMB04
LAMBERT (Anthony of S.Marg't)	OFM		YO	F	12	1671	1688	1697	1714	LAMB05
LAMBTON Joseph VEN.	S	N	YO	R	+	1568	..	1592	1592	LAMB08
LANGDALE Jordan (Maurus)	OSB		YO	G		1733	1751	..	1760	LANG02
LASCELLES Christopher	S	N	YO	Q		..	..	1588	..	LASC02
LASCELLES John	S	N	YO	D	#4	1600	..	1625	1663	LASC04
LASCELLES Ralph	S		YO	D	#3	1612	..	1641	..	LASC06
LASCELLES Riichard	S		YO	D	#	1603	..	1632	1668	LASC08
LASCELLES Thomas	S	N	YO	D	#	1599	..	1624	..	LASC10
LAWSON Francis	OSB	N	YO	G		..	1650	..	1712	LAWS04
LAWSON Henry	OSB	N	YO	G		1763	1785	1788	1829	LAWS07
LAWSON Thomas	SJ	N	YO	Y	#	1666	1684	1691	1750	LAWS10
LAWSON Thomas	SJ	L	YO	Y	3	1720	1736	1744	1807	LAWS12
LAWSON Thomas (Augustine)	OSB	N	YO	G		1758	1779	1783	1830	LAWS14
LAWSON William (Benedict)	OSB		YO	X		..	1685	..	1737	LAWS16
LAYTON John	SJ	N	YO	R	#1	1588	1614	1611	1624	LAYT02
LEWIS Thomas	SJ		YO	Y		1613	1628	1638	1644	LEWI28
LIDDELL Thomas	S		YO	L		1718	..	1743	1775	LIDD04
LINDLEY (Ambrose)	OSB		YO	X		..	1670	..	1699	LIND02
LOCKWOOD Francis	S		YO	Q	4	..	..	1587	1632	LOCK10
LOCKWOOD John BL.	S	N	YO	R	#+	1561	..	1597	1642	LOCK12
LOCKWOOD Thomas	S	N	YO	D	#3	..	..	1676	1686	LOCK14
LODGE John	S	N	YO	D	#34	1648	..	1676	1731	LODG02
LODGE John	S	N	YO	D	3	1681	..	1706	1741	LODG04
LODGE John	S	N	YO	D		1722	..	1746	1795	LODG06
LODGE Miles	S	N	YO	D	13	1653	..	1680	1749	LODG08
LODGE Thomas	SJ	W	YO	Y	3	1726	1744	1751	1764	LODG10
LONGSTAFF Robert	S	N	YO	D	#3	1736	..	1763	1798	LONG14
LONGSTAFF Valentine or M'duke	S	N	YO	D	#	1731	..	1758	1823	LONG16
LOWICK (Lawrence)	OSB	M	YO	W		..	1620	..	1633	LOWI02
LOWICK Henry (Bernard)	OSB	L	YO	E		..	1673	..	1720	LOWI04
LUMLEY John	OSB		YO	W		..	1656	..	1703	LUML02
MAIRE William BP.	S	N	YO	D	*	1704	..	1730	1769	MAIR18
MALLET John (Gregory)	OSB	M	YO	W	#	1604	1625	1627	1681	MALL08
MANN Wm Theodore (Augustine)	CRT		YO	C	*§	1735	1759	1760	1809	MANN02
MARTIN John	S	L	YO	D		1734	..	1772	1788	MART22
MAY John	S	N	YO	V	#	..	..	1649	..	MAYA02
MAYES Lawrence	S		YO	D		1673	..	1697	1749	MAYE02
MESSENGER John	SJ	N	YO	Y	1	1688	1708	1716	1752	MESS02

Name	Reg	D	Co	T	Notes	Born	Prof	Ordn	Died	Code
METCALFE John	S	N	YO	R	#	1615	..	1641	1673	METC08
METCALFE John	S	L	YO	R	#	1663	..	1687	1729	METC10
METCALFE Joseph	S	N	YO	D	#	1633	..	1661	1695	METC14
METCALFE Peter	S	L	YO	L	#	1603	..	1633	1671	METC18
METCALFE Thomas	S		YO	D	#3	1586	..	1613	1651	METC20
METCALFE William	OSB	N	YO	G		1672	1690	1698	1738	METC24
METHAM Anthony	S	N	YO	D	#3	1642	..	1670	1694	METH02
METHAM Francis	SJ		YO	Y	#	..	1645	..	1681	METH04
METHAM Philip (Sylvester)	OSB	N	YO	G		..	1683	..	1715	METH06
METHAM Thomas	SJ		YO	N	x‡	1532	1579	..	1592	METH08
MEYNELL James	S	N	YO	D	14	1685	..	..	1731	MEYN04
MEYNELL James	SJ	N	YO	Y		1689	1708	1713	1746	MEYN06
MEYNELL Robert	S		YO	R	#§	1608	..	1640	..	MEYN08
MEYNELL Thomas	SJ	L	YO	Y	3	1737	1756	1762	1804	MEYN10
MEYNELL William	S	N	YO	D	#	1618	..	1645	1683	MEYN12
MEYNELL William	SJ	N	YO	Y	3	1744	1761	1773	1826	MEYN14
MIDDLETON Anthony BL.	S	L	YO	Q	+	..	..	1586	1590	MIDD10
MIDDLETON Robert BL.	S	N	YO	R	*+§	1570	..	1598	1601	MIDD22
MIDDLETON Thomas (Cuthbert)	OSB		YO	G		..	1643	..	1678	MIDD26
MILESON Richard	SJ	M	YO	Y	#†	1607	1643	..	1668	MILE10
MORE Christopher	SJ		YO	Y	3	1729	1746	1754	1781	MORE02
MORE Thomas	S	L	YO	R	#3	1565	..	1591	1625	MORE12
MORE Thomas	SJ	L	YO	Y	3	1722	1752	1760	1795	MORE16
MORTON Robert BL.	S	L	YO	Q	+	1548	..	1587	1588	MORT04
NANDYKE Thomas	SJ	N	YO	Y		1726	1745	1752	1793	NAND02
NELSON John BL.	S		YO	D	+	1534	..	1576	1578	NELS08
NELSON Martin	S	W	YO	D		..	..	1574	1625	NELS14
NELSON Thomas	S		YO	D	†	..	..	1577	1625	NELS22
NESFIELD John	S	L	YO	D		1726	..	1751	1777	NESF02
NEVILLE Edmund	SJ	N	YO	R	#	1563	1609	1608	1646	NEVI04
NICHOLSON Richard	S		YO	D	13	1650	..	1676	..	NICH12
NIGHTINGALE Richard	S		YO	R	#†°4	1585	..	1610	1641	NIGH04
NORTON Basil or John	S	L	YO	D	#	1595	..	1621	1662	NORT10
NORTON Matthew (Thomas)	OP	M	YO	N	§	1732	1754	1757	1800	NORT18
OGLE (Ambrose)	OFM		YO	F	123	1675	1695	1699	1728	OGLE01
OLDCORNE Edward BL.	SJ	M	YO	R	#+2	1561	1588	1587	1606	OLDC02
PALASER Thomas VEN.	S	N	YO	V	+3	..	..	1595	1600	PALA02
PALMER Ralph	SJ	M	YO	Y		1610	1638	..	1649	PALM08
PALMES George	SJ	N	YO	D	#2	1576	1608	1607	1621	PALM14
PALMES George (Bernard)	OSB		YO	S	#3	1618	1643	1642	1663	PALM15
PALMES William	SJ	N	YO	R	#	1595	1618	1618	1670	PALM16
PARK Archibald	S		YO	R		1688	..	1718	..	PARK02
PARKER Richard	S	N	YO	D	#*	..	..	1577	..	PARK26
PARKINSON Richard	SJ		YO	R		1681	1704	..	1748	PARK52
PAVIER Francis	S		YO	L	#	1602	..	1633	1644	PAVI02
PEARSON John	S	N	YO	L		..	..	1689	..	PEAR10
PEARSON William	S	N	YO	R	#4	1632	..	1656	1669	PEAR14
PERCY Charles	SJ	M	YO	Y	3	1665	1685	1694	1735	PERC02
PERCY Philip	SJ	N	YO	Y	13	1660	1683	1694	1724	PERC12
PERCY Robert	SJ	M	YO	Y	#1	1652	1674	1682	1715	PERC14
PERCY William	S		YO	D		..	..	1578	..	PERC20
PERISON William	SJ		YO	Y		1611	1631	..	1666	PER102
PIATT John	SJ	N	YO	Y	13	1686	1706	1715	1743	PIAT02
PIBUSH John BL.	S	L	YO	Q	#+	1557	..	1587	1601	PIBU02
POLE John	SJ	N	YO	V		1621	1660	1647	1666	POLE26
POLE Michael	SJ	W	YO	Y	3	1687	1707	1716	1748	POLE28
POSTGATE Nicholas VEN.	S	N	YO	D	#+1	1598	..	1628	1679	POST02
PRACID Jeremiah or John	SJ	N	YO	R	#§	1639	1675	1665	1686	PRAC02
PUDSEY Stephen	S		YO	D	#34	1610	..	1636	1649	PUDS02
PULLEYN Joshua	SJ	L	YO	D		1543	1594	1578	1607	PULL02
PULLEYN Michael	OSB		YO	G		1653	1672	..	1723	PULL04
PULLEYN William	S		YO	Q	‡	..	..	1583	..	PULL06
QUATERMAIN William	S	W	YO	V	#3	..	..	1676	1720	QUAT02
REDMAN William	S		YO	D		1581	..	1610	..	REDM06
REVELL Thomas	S		YO	L	3	..	..	1697	..	REVE04
REYNER Clement (Lawrence)	OSB		YO	D	#	1587	1609	..	1664	REYN04

Name	Reg	D	Co	T	Notes	Born	Prof	Ordn	Died	Code
REYNER Wilfrid (Clement)	OSB		YO	D	#	..	1610	1602	1651	REYN05
RICHARDSON William BL.	S	L	YO	S	#+3	1572	..	1600	1603	RICH36
RICKABY John	S	N	YO	U		..	..	1798	1821	RICK02
RIDDELL Thomas	S	N	YO	D	#	..	..	1608	..	RIDD11
RILEY John	SJ	N	YO	R	#§	1610	1640	1635	1667	RILE02
ROBINSON Andrew	SJ	M	YO	Y	3	1741	1763	1769	1826	ROBI04
ROBINSON Francis	S	N	YO	R		1569	..	1597	..	ROBI14
ROBINSON George (Placid)	OSB		YO	X	#	..	1701	..	1739	ROBI16
ROBINSON John BL.	S	M	YO	Q	+	..	..	1585	1588	ROBI24
ROBINSON John	SJ	N	YO		#1	1598	1620	..	1675	ROBI28
ROBINSON (Maurus)	OSB		YO	E		..	1653	..	1662	ROBI38
ROBINSON Michael	S	N	YO	D	#	1598	..	1624	..	ROBI40
ROCKLEY Francis	SJ		YO	Y	#4	1656	1675	1683	1725	ROCK04
ROLSTON Francis	S	N	YO	D	1	1588	..	..	..	ROLS02
ROWNTREE Leonard	S		YO	D	§°	..	..	1611	..	ROWN02
ROYDON Thomas	S	N	YO	D	#14	1630	..	1653	1700	ROYD02
ROYDON Thomas	S	N	YO	D	#3	1662	..	1686	1741	ROYD04
ROYDON Thomas	S	N	YO	D		1705	..	1730	1764	ROYD06
RUSSELL George	S		YO	D		..	..	1644	..	RUSS04
RYTHER Thomas	SJ		YO	Y		1663	1683	1691	1733	RYTH02
SALTHOUSE Arthur	S	N	YO	D	#§13	1604	..	1637	..	SALT02
SALTMARSH Edward	SJ		YO	Y	#	1656	1678	1687	1737	SALT04
SALTMARSH Gerard	S		YO	R	#§	1652	..	1676	1733	SALT06
SALTMARSH Peter	S	L	YO	R	#1	1658	..	1686	1725	SALT08
SAMPSON Christopher	SJ	N	YO	R	#	1605	1634	1629	1674	SAMP02
SANDERS William	SJ	N	YO	Y	3	1638	1657	1662	1676	SAND12
SAUL Charles	S	N	YO	U		1767	..	1794	1813	SAUL02
SAYLES Samuel	S	N	YO	R	3	1752	..	1776	1818	SAYL02
SCOREY Thomas	SJ	N	YO	Y		1681	1703	1710	1720	SCOR02
SHARP James	SJ	M	YO	V	#‡	1578	1607	1604	1630	SHAR02
SHARP Matthew	S	N	YO	D	3	1756	..	1784	1826	SHAR06
SHERSON Martin	S	L	YO	Q	x‡	1563	..	1586	1588	SHER22
SHERWOOD Philip	S	N	YO		3	..	..	1570	..	SHER36
SIMPSON Richard VEN.	S	N	YO	D	+‡	..	..	1577	1588	SIMP12
SIMPSON William (Andrew)	OSB		YO	E	#1	1612	1642	..	1652	SIMP20
SIMPSON William	S	N	YO	V	14	1690	..	1713	1730	SIMP22
SKINNER Anthony (Basil)	OSB	N	YO	G	4	..	1657	..	1685	SKIN04
SKINNER James (Placid)	OSB		YO	G		..	1662	..	1697	SKIN08
SMARTHWAITE Cuthbert	S		YO	D		..	..	1601	..	SMAR02
SMARTHWAITE Thomas	S		YO	Q		..	..	1582	..	SMAR04
SMITH Christopher	S	N	YO	V	#3	1602	..	1628	..	SMIT07
SMITH John	SJ	N	YO		#x§3	..	1622	1622	1651	SMIT32
SMITH John	S		YO	D	3	1735	..	1759	1764	SMIT43
SMITH Joseph (Augustine)	OP	N	YO		4	1760	1784	1785	1811	SMIT47
SMITH William	S	N	YO	R	#	1556	..	1581	..	SMIT74
SMITH William	OSS		YO			1597	..	..	1647	SMIT75
SMITHSON Augustine	S	N	YO	D		..	..	1656	1717	SMIT83
SMITHSON John	S		YO	V	1	1567	..	1594	1596	SMIT84
SMITHSON John	SJ	N	YO	Y		1612	1637	..	1684	SMIT85
SMITHSON John (Alphonsus)	OFM		YO	F	12	1623	1644	..	1672	SMIT86
SNOW Peter VEN.	S	N	YO	Q	+	..	..	1591	1598	SNOW02
SPENCER William VEN.	S	N	YO	Q	+‡	..	..	1583	1589	SPEN08
STANFIELD Robert	SJ		YO	Y	3	1668	1687	1695	1751	STAN08
STAPLETON Gregory BP.	S	L	YO	D	*3	1748	..	1771	1802	STAP06
STAPLETON Gregory (Benedict)	OSB	L	YO	G		1623	1643	1647	1680	STAP08
STAPLETON Thomas	S	L	YO	D	1	1713	..	1736	1754	STAP14
STEEL William	S		YO	D		1715	..	1739	1764	STEE02
STEPHENSON Paul	S	N	YO	D	13	1648	..	1673	..	STEP22
STILLLINGTON Thomas	S		YO	R		1558	..	1582	1597	STIL04
STILLINGTON William	SJ	N	YO	Y	12	1596	1622	..	1654	STIL06
STONEHOUSE Andrew	SJ	N	YO	R	#	1597	1634	1631	1663	STON10
STRICKLAND Simon James	S	N	YO	D	#	1739	..	..	1782	STRI10
SUTCLIFF (Thomas)	OFM		YO	F	#1234	1647	1672	1675	1721	SUTC02
SUTTON Robert	S	N	YO	L	#	1641	..	1662	1675	SUTT06
SUTTON Thomas	S	L	YO	L	#3	1643	..	1670	1674	SUTT10
SUTTON William	OSS		YO	L	#	1632	..	1655	1690	SUTT16

Name	Reg	D	Co	T	Notes	Born	Prof	Ordn	Died	Code
SWALE Lawrence	OSB		YO	X		..	1670	..	1718	SWAL02
SWINBURNE Simon	SJ		YO	R		1561	1586	1586	1638	SWIN10
SYKES Edmund VEN.	S	N	YO	Q	+	..	..	1581	1587	SYKE02
TALBOT George Trentham	S	L	YO	R		1685	..	1712	1752	TALB02
TANCARD Charles	SJ		YO	Z		1563	1584	..	1599	TANC02
TANCARD Richard	SJ		YO	Z	#12	1556	1578	..	1596	TANC04
TATE John (Joseph)	OFM		YO	F	13	1747	1774	1779	1815	TATE02
TATHAM James (Cuthbert)	OSB		YO	G		..	1678	..	1718	TATH02
TATHAM John (Bede)	OSB		YO	G	#°	1642	1657	..	1700	TATH04
TAYLOR Christopher	S	L	YO	R	#	1730	..	1760	1812	TAYL14
TAYLOR James	S	N	YO	R		1730	..	1758	1774	TAYL24
TEMPEST Charles	SJ		YO	V		1699	1724	1724	1768	TEMP02
TEMPEST Francis (Augustine)	OSB	N	YO	X		..	1664	..	1729	TEMP06
TEMPEST John	OSB		YO	X		1639	1661	..	1711	TEMP08
TEMPEST John	SJ	L	YO	R		1694	1712	1727	1737	TEMP10
THIMELBY Matthew	S		YO	R	#	..	..	1643	..	THIM06
THOMPSON James BL.	S	N	YO	Q	#+	..	..	1581	1582	THOM22
THOMPSON John	S	N	YO		#x	..	..	..	1642	THOM26
THORNTON Robert	SJ		YO	Y	#	1658	1678	1683	1704	THOR10
THORPE John	SJ		YO	R	3	1726	1747	1759	1792	THOR34
THORPE Robert VEN.	S	N	YO	Q	#+	..	..	1585	1591	THOR36
THURSBY Thomas	S		YO	D		..	..	1600	..	THUR06
THWING Edward VEN.	S	N	YO	Q	+	1565	..	1590	1600	THWI02
THWING Ralph	S	N	YO	D	#4	1644	..	..	1691	THWI04
THWING Robert	SJ		YO	R	#§	1606	1627	..	1658	THWI06
THWING Thomas	S	N	YO	R	#	1609	..	1634	..	THWI08
THWING Thomas BL.	S	N	YO	D	+	1635	..	1665	1680	THWI10
TILLETSON Francis	S		YO	Q	°	..	..	1585	..	TILL02
TINDALL William	S		YO	S	3	..	..	1614	..	TIND06
TORBET John	S	N	YO	V	#13	1663	..	1684	1727	TORB02
TUNSTALL Peter Brian	S	N	YO	D	#3	1673	..	1696	1742	TUNS06
TUNSTALL Thomas	SJ		YO	Y		1635	1655	1664	1665	TUNS12
TUNSTALL William	SJ		YO	Y	1	1611	1631	..	1681	TUNS14
TYAS George	S	L	YO	D		..	..	1597	..	TYAS02
VAVASOUR Francis	OFM	N	YO	F	124	1607	1626	..	1652	VAVA02
VAVASOUR Henry	S		YO	D	#	1597	..	1625	1660	VAVA04
VAVASOUR James	S		YO	R		1561	..	1586	1593	VAVA06
VAVASOUR Walter, Bt.	SJ	N	YO	Y		1662	1681	1689	1740	VAVA08
VAVASOUR William	SJ		YO	Y	#3	1618	1665	1668	1683	VAVA10
WAITE James	SJ	N	YO	Y		1617	1640	..	1679	WAIT02
WALKER Robert	S	N	YO	D	1	1585	..	1620	..	WALK10
WALKER Thomas	ODC		YO		2	..	1736	..	..	WALK16
WARD George	SJ		YO	Y	#1	1596	1619	..	1654	WARD04
WARD Lawrence	S		YO	D	#	1677	..	..	1741	WARD06
WARD William	S	L	YO	R	#4	1592	..	1618	1645	WARD10
WARWICK George	S	N	YO	Z	#	1585	..	1609	1658	WARW02
WATERHOUSE George	S	N	YO	R	#	1712	..	1735	1778	WATE02
WATERTON Charles	SJ		YO	Y		1744	1762	1771	1773	WATE06
WATERTON Thomas	SJ	N	YO	Y	3	1701	1721	1729	1766	WATE08
WATKINSON Robert BL.	S	L	YO	D	#+	1579	..	1602	1602	WATK14
WATSON James	S	N	YO	R	#‡	1699	..	1723	1772	WATS04
WHARTON Christopher VEN.	S	N	YO	Q	+‡	..	..	1584	1600	WHAR06
WHITTINGHAM William Edward	SJ	L	YO	Y	#	1590	1611	..	1620	WHIT94
WILKES John	S		YO		#x	..	..	..	1642	WILK02
WILKINSON Anthony	S		YO	Q		..	..	1580	..	WILK06
WILLIAMSON George	SJ	L	YO	Y	3	1695	1718	1725	1741	WILL70
WILSON John	SJ		YO	Y	3	1637	1658	1663	1666	WILS10
WILSON John (Jerome)	OSB		YO	G		..	1685	..	1700	WILS14
WILSON Ralph	SJ	M	YO	Y		1743	1763	1770	1770	WILS20
WILSON Ralph (Jerome)	OSB	N	YO	G		1652	1668	1677	1719	WILS22
WILSON Thomas	OSB		YO	G		1667	..	..	1712	WILS30
WILTON John	S	N	YO	Q		..	..	1591	..	WILT02
WITHAM Anthony	S	M	YO	P	3	..	..	1709	1763	WITH02
WITHAM Christopher	S	N	YO	D	#3	1659	..	1683	1734	WITH04
WITHAM George BP.	S		YO	P	#*3	1655	..	1688	1725	WITH06
WITHAM James (Wilfrid)	OSB	N	YO	X		..	1715	..	1764	WITH10

Name	Reg	D	Co	T	Notes	Born	Prof	Ordn	Died	Code
WITHAM Robert	S	N	YO	D	#3	1667	..	1691	1738	WITH 12
WITHAM Roger (Michael)	OSB		YO	G		..	1636	..	1657	WITH 14
WITHAM Thomas	S	N	YO	P		..	..	..	1727	WITH 16
WITHAM Thomas	OSB	N	YO	G		..	1685	..	1729	WITH 18
WIVELL Henry	S	N	YO	D	#	1603	..	1634	..	WIVE 02
WOLFE William	SJ	M	YO	Y	#‡	1587	1611	..	1673	WOLF 08
WRIGHT William	SJ	M	YO	R	13	1562	1581	1592	1639	WRIG 38
YORK John	S		YO	R	#	1654	..	1678	..	YORK 02
YOUNG John	S	N	YO	D	1	1605	..	1632	1671	YOUN 08
YOUNG Robert	S	L	YO	D		..	..	1602	..	YOUN 10
YOUNG Thomas	S	L	YO	D		..	..	1595	..	YOUN 12

GENERAL NOTES

Many of the notes that follow specify a place of origin. A distinction is made between a county of origin, shown by two upper case letters (see Abbreviations p 30) and a diocese of origin, shown by an upper and a lower case letter (see Technical Introduction p 20). For references (in brackets) see Bibliography p 249. AI to AIV indicates Anstruther's *Seminary Priests* and TL indicated the Trappes-Lomax Card Index.

ABBO 02   Entered SJ 3 Aug 1612. Expelled, c.1621. Entered OSS, c.1623. Died in prison London, c.1650 (AII,1-2)
ADAM 00   East Anglia (CRS 70,17)
ADAM 08   Possibly of family of Marston-Montgomery, DE (TL)
AERT 02   In household of the Ambassador of Archduke Albert of Austria, Governor of the Netherlands, 1609-1621 (TL)
ALBE 02   OSB Monte Cassino, Professor of Philosophy, Pisa (TL)
ALDI 02   Wr or YO (AII,4)
ALDR 04   MX or NK (CRS 70,18)
ALLE 11   Sa (AI,4)
ALLE 12   Cardinal,1587. Archbp of Malines, 1589 (AI,5)
ALME 02   Chaplain to Catherine of Braganza, c.1671. Possibly OFM. (CRS 38,31)
AMBL 02   Yo (AI,7)
ANDE 13   Assumed, apparently without proper claim, the baronetcy of Anderson of Penley (TL)
ANSE 02   In London, c.1700. Perhaps Anselm *Jackson* (Smet,285)
ANTR 02   Professed S.Benito, Sahagun,, Spain (Lunn,235)
APPL 02   Professed S.Salvador, Onia, Spain (Moore)
ARAY 02   Ce (AI,10)
ARMO 02   Working at Venetian Embassy Chapel, London, at time of death (Mould,241)
ARTH 02   Chapel Royal, Somerset House, 1665-1671 (Mould,241)
ASHE 02   Professed S.Maria, Obarenes, Spain (Lunn,235)
ASHT 16   LA or MX (CRS 70,21)
ASKE 04   Ln (AI,12)
ASTO 02   Doubtful claimant to barony of Forfar (TL)
ATHE 02   Lo (AI,13)
ATKI 01   Born Bombay of British parentage. Educated in Brazil. Possibly not ordained (CRS 70,22)
ATKI 10   LA or WR (CRS 70,22)
AUBE 02   French Chapel, London, 1680-1687 (CRS 70,23)
AUGU 04   In London, 1702 (Zimmerman,364)
AYLW 04   Chaplain, Syon Abbey, Lisbon c.1783 (TL)
BALD 04   Yo (AI,18)
BALF 02   In England, 1625-1626, in service of Henrietta Maria (TL)
BALL 12   Executed following the Babington Plot (AI,20)
BALL 14   Arrested on landing at Rye, SX, c.1656. Spent two years in English prison before banishment (TL)
BARK 04   Nr (AII,15)
BARK 18   He became friendly with the Benedictines at Valladolid and was granted permission 'to profess himself' in danger of death. At his martyrdom he wore a habit. He was never formally professed (AI,21-22)
BARL 12   The first Seminary Priest to arrive in England, 1574 (AI,22)
BARL 16   Professed S.Salvador, Cellanova, Spain (Lunn,235)
BARN 14   Wi (AI,24)
BARN 20   Ce (AIV,20)
BARN 24   Sb (AI,24)
BARR 50   Wi (AII,18)
BARW 01   Er (AI,25)
BARW 02   Lo (AI,25)

BAVA02   Ch. Died in prison (TL)
BEAK02   M.A. of one of the universities (AI,27)
BECK04   Professed S.Benito, Sahagun, Spain (Lunn,235)
BEEC02   Professed S.Giustina, Padua, Italy (Lunn,234)
BELL14   Ch (AIV,28)
BENN12   Sa (AI,32)
BERI02   Cons Bp of Hierocaesarea, 1 Aug 1786. Coadj to Bp Thomas Talbot, Midland Dist, 1786. Succeeded as V.A. Midland Dist, 1795.
BERT04   Priestly studies at Rennes, France (Gumbley,40)
BERU02   In England with Henrietta Maria, 1625. Founded French Oratory, 1611. Cardinal, 1627 (TL)
BEST06   Lat)n form of English name ? (AII,23) Possibly Beeston (ed)
BEWE02   Ce (AII,24)
BEWL02   Ce (AII,24)
BIAR02   Ln (AI,34)
BIRT04   Possibly OSB late in life (Lunn,227)
BISH18   Cons Bp of Chalcedon, 4 Jun 1623. V.A. of England, 1623.
BLAC08   Yo (AI,39)
BLAN02   Professed S.Benito, Sahagun, Spain (Lunn, 235)
BLAY02   Lo (AIII,18)
BLIN02   Ce (AI,41)
BOLT04   Nr (AI,43)
BOOT14   Wi (AIII,20)
BOWK02   Executed for coining (AII,23)
BOWL02   Lo (AIV,44)
BRAM04   Cons Bp of Usulae, 29 Jun 1823. Coadj to Bp William Poynter, London Dist, 1823. Succeeded as V.A. London ist, 1827.
BREN00   In England, c.1723-1748 (Mould,241-2)
BRET06   Professed S.Malo (Birt,44)
BRIA02   Bs (AI,49)
BRIA04   Sa (AIII,23)
BRIA06   Perhaps Er or DT. Admitted SJ in prison (AI,50-51)
BROO20   Lh (AI,54)
BROW09   Born Antigua, W.Indies (CRS 70,44)
BROW13   Professed S.Maria, Obarenes, Spain (Lunn 235)
BROW25   Stated in 1666 that he had engaged in theological debates with non-catholics at Oxford and had converted one of them. Did pastoral work in England (Millett,546)
BROW29   An Englishman educated probably in Italy, but in England after 1731 (Smet,287)
BROW30   Lh (AI,56)
BROW32   Sa (AIII,28)
BRUL02   Bp of Derry, 1751-1752 (Gumbley,69)
BUCK12   V.A. of the West Indies, 1819-1828 (AIV,50)
BUFF02   Officiated at marriages in London, 1722-1729 (CRS 38,173)
BURK04   Portuguese Chapel, London, 1751-1754 (CRS 38,171)
BURK06   In London, c.1662 (Millett,434)
BURY02   Clothed OSB, 1614, at St Gregory's, but left same year. (AII,38)
BUSB06   Pb (AIV,51)
BUSI02   Chaplain to Venetian Embassy, London, 1617-1618 (TL)
BUTL07   Portuguese Chapel, London, c.1721-1748 (Mould,242))
BUTL08   Ch (AI,59)
BUTL13   Nominated Bp of Limerick, Ireland, 1778, but declined. Baron Caher for a fortnight before his death. (CRS 30,50)
BUTL15   Priestly studies at Louvain and S.Maria Novella, Florence (Gumbley,57)
BUTL18   Sb (AI,59)
BUTL20   Lh (AI,59)
BYFI02   Lo (AI,63) Professed Parma (Lunn,235)
BYRN04   In England, c.1694 (de Mejer,136)
CABL02   Sb (AI,61)
CAES02   Professed Dominican House, Ypres (Gumbley,95)
CAHI02   Educ. at a French college (CRS 49,3) In charge of a newly opened chapel at Portsmouth, c.1800 (TL)
CALL04   Served Catherine of Braganza's Chapel, London, 1671-1672 (Mould,242)
CARN02   Ce (AIII,32),
CARP06   Educ. Trinity, Oxford and King's, Cambridge. Tried OFM and OSB before entering English College, Rome (AII,45)
CARP08   Er (AI,63)
CARR06   Bp of Baltimore, 1789. Archbp 1808 (CRS 70,53)
CARR08   In England, c.1693 (de Mejer,136)
CART18   Canon of St Peter's, Lille. Chaplain to the Young Pretender, 1742 (TL)
CARY08   Son of Henry, 1st Visc. Falkland. Possibly born OX (Simpson,126)

CATR 02 Lo (AIV,58)
CATT 10 Priestly studies at Louvain and Civitavecchia, Italy (Gumbley,72)
CAVE 02 Worked in England, c.1669, residing near Coventry at the house of Mr Sadler (Millett,545)
CHAL 06 Cons Bp of Debra, 29 Jan 1741. Coadj. to Bp Francis Petre, London Dist, 1741. Succeeded as V.A. London Dist, 1758.
CHAM 04 Bp of Ypres, 1628 (AI,69)
CHAM 16 Lo. After apostacy was executed for felony (AII,51)
CHAM 18 Yo (AI,70)
CHAM 24 Lo or Sb (AI,72)
CHAP 14 Lo or Sb (AI,72)
CHAP 20 Sb(AI,73)
CHAP 24 Sb (AI,73)
CHRI 06 Nr (AIII,34)
CHUR 02 CL or MX (CRS 70,58)
CLAR 15 SX or WT (Foley VII,132)
CLAR 34 Executed folowing the Bye-Plot (AI,77)
CLAR 48 Confused by Zimmerman (p.385) with CLAR 54.
CLAY 02 An Irishman incorporated into English OFM Province, 1655 (Millett,543)
CLAY 04 Possibly not a priest, but his various ecclesiastical sinecures suggest orders. (AII,61)
CLIB 02 Ch (AI,80)
CLIF 04 Professed S.Malo (AII,62)
CLIF 08 Inherited Barony of Cumberland but did not use the title. (AII,63)
CLIF 22 Professed S.Benito, Sahagun, Spain (Moore)
CLIF 24 Ca (AI,80)
COCK 06 Professed Monte Cassino, Italy (TL)
CODN 02 Professed Ravenna, Italy (Lunn,234)
COLE 01 In London, 1661-c.1670 (Millett,546)
COLE 04 Lo (AI,82)
COLL 08 Cons Bp of Thespiae, 11 Oct 1807. Coadj. to Bp Wm Gregory Sharrock, Western Dist, 1807. Succeeded as V.A., 1809.
COLL 16 Ln (AIV,69)
COLL 42 Ch (AI,85)
COMP 03 Admitted SJ, 1765. Professed OSB, St Edmund's, Paris, 1775 (CRS 70,65; Scott)
CONR 02 On English Mission, c.1652-1655. In prison 1655-1658. On mission again later (Millett,544)
CONS 12 YO or NK (CRS 70,67)
CONY 20 KT or MX (CRS 70,66)
COOK 03 Lh (AI,86)
COOP 02 Ch (AI,86)
COOP 06 Lo (AI,86)
COOP 16 Ch (AI,87)
COOP 18 Lo. (AII,70)
COPE 02 Lo. Canon of S.Peter's, Rome. No record of ordination (AI,67)
CORN 08 Admitted SJ on scaffold (AI,88)
CORN 10 Dh (AI,89)
COTT 06 SJ 1579, but left. Possibly re-admitted in prison (AI,90-91)
COTT 08 Ch (AI,91)
COUL 02 An English Augustinian. In England, c1686 (de Mejer,132)
COWL 08 Ch (AIII,41)
CRAT 02 SJ c.1618-1621 (AII,75)
CRAY 02 Dh(AI,92)
CROS 02 Born Teneriffe, Canary Is. (CRS 70,73)
CRUM 02 Possibly identical to MILL 02 (AIII,44)
DAMI 02 Departed from England, c 1701 (Smet,285)
DARB 04 Ch (AI,97)
DARC 06 Served Bavarian and Portugese Chapels, London (CRS 38,172)
DAVI 12 HR or WR (AI,97)
DAVI 14 Lf (AI,98)
DAWB 02 Nr (AI,99)
DEAK 02 Perhaps two priests of this name, one a Carthusian, the other a Secular, native of Pb (AI,100)
DELA 01 Austrian Chapel, London, c1728. Later at the Portugese Chapel. Died in London. (Mould,242)
DIAS 02 OP 1792-1796 (AIV,233)
DIAZ 02 In London, c1683-1687. Possibly OFM (CRS 38,175)
DICC 02 Cons Bp of Mallus, 19 March 1741. Vicar Apostolic, Northern Dist, 1741.
DIDE 02 Born Luxembourg (CRS 70,79)
DIGB 04 Second son of John, 1st Earl of Bristol (AII,85)
DILL 01 Son of Theobald, 1st Viscount Dillon. In London,c1662 (Millett,434)
DILL 03 Neapolitan Chapel, London, 1759. Portugese Chapel, 1763. Returned to Ireland, 1769 (Mould,242)
DOBS 02 Dh (AI,103)

DOMI02	Born in modern Yugoslavia, left SJ to become Archbp of Spalato (Split) in Dalmatia. On apostacy received various benefices from the Church of England including the deanery of Windsor. Reconciled to church but died accused of heresy in Roman prison (Patterson)
DORN02	Requested missionary faculties for the English Mission, 1656 (Millett,543)
DOUG02	Cons Bp of Centuriae, 19 December 1790. Vicar Apostolic, London District, 1790.
DOWD01	Spanish Chapel, London, 1724-1727 (Mould,242)
DOWD03	In England, 1688, and after (de Mejer,134)
DOYL06	Lo (AIII,51)
DUCK04	Lo (AII,89)
DUFF01	Requested missionary faculties for the English Mission, 1656 (Millett,543)
DUPE02	In England, 1632-1640, as Royal chaplain. Bp of Angouleme, 1636, and afterwards of Evreux (Gallia Christiana)
EATO02	LN or Ch(AI,107-108)
EDEN02	SJ 1692-1696 (CRS 70,85)
EDMU08	Professed S.Martin, Compostella, Spain. (Lunn,235)
EDMU10	Has often been confused with EDMU08 (AII,93)
ELLI10	Cons Bp of Aureliopolis, 6 May 1688. Non-resident Vicar Apostolic Western District, 1688-1708. Bp of Segni, Italy, 1708
ELLI12	Yo (AI,109)
ELYA02	Hr (AI,110)
EMER04	Professed S.Benito, Sahagun, Spain (Lunn,235)
ENGH02	Ca (AI,110)
ENGL12	Sb. Alumnus of German College, Rome (AI,111)
EUST02	Ordained Maynooth, Ireland, c.1795 (TL)
EVAN06	A Welshman educated at Scots College, Douai (AIII,57)
EVER09	'In England had recently (c1657) converted more than eighty heretics by his devotional and very learned sermons as well as by his exemplary life and conversation' (Millett,544)
EVER12	Educated at Irish College, Salamanca. Many years in North of England. Coadj to Archbp of Cashel 1815-1820. Archbp 1820
EYRE06	Late in career became Augustinian at Antwerp. Sometime SJ (AII,97)
EYRE18	LE or NK (CRS 70,89)
EYST14	Entered OFM Douai 1696 as Br Bonaventure. Later OP (Gumbley, 68)
FAIR02	MO, or MT, or MX (CRS 70,90)
FARR05	Venetian Embassy Chapel, London, 1761 (Mould,242)
FAUL10	SJ Paraguy Province (CRS 70,91)
FEAT06	CD or LA (CRS 70,92)
FELT02	Lo (AI, 113)
FENW02	First Bp of Cincinnati,U.S.A., 13 Jan 1822 (Gumbley,92)
FERE02	St James's Palace, London, 1676 (TL)
FIDD02	Priestly studies at Leitmeritz, Bohemia (Gumbley,35)
FIEL02	Lh (AI,116)
FINN01	Educated in Touraine (France) Province. Came to England 1695 (Smet,284)
FITT06	Ch (AI,117)
FITZ00	In London, c.1665, as agent of Irish Franciscan Province (Millett,63,546)
FITZ01	In London during 1670's (Millett,548)
FLET08	Yo (AI,119)
FLOR02	Monk of Marienmünster, Germany. Possibly in London,1687-1692 (TL)
FLOR04	Dh. Student at Perugia (AI,119-120)
FLOY20	Sa (AI,121)
FORS06	Professed St Malo (Moore)
FORS16	Spanish Embassy Chapel, London, c.1620 (Anstuther 1958, 109)
FOST08	Dh (Gumbley, 29)
FOST23	Studied Theology in Lithuania (Foley 7, 276)
FOUL02	NN or WK (Foley 7, 278)
FRAN07	Yo (AI,124)
FREN04	In London, c.1773-1782 (Mould,242)
FUEN02	Spanish Embassy Chapel, London, c.1614. (Gumbley,6)
FURL02	In prison , England, c.1700 (Coleman,29)
GAGE06	Not at an English seminary but was secretly ordained by St Robert Bellamine in Rome, 20 May 1614, together with Sir Tobie Mathew (AII,120)
GAGN02	Canon Regular of St Geneviève, Paris. Probably never exercised his ministry in England (TL)
GARD14	Ch (AIII,62)
GARN08	Executed for supposed complicity in Gunpowder Plot (Foley 7,288)
GARN20	Ch (AI,127)
GART06	Dh (AI,128)
GATT02	Chaplain, Venetian Ambassador, London, c.1619 (TL)
GAUL02	Chaplain, Imperial Ambassador, London, c.1702-c1714 (TL)
GAVI02	Licenced to officiate by Anglican Bp of London, 1716 (TL)

GEAR01	In London, c.1662 (Millett,434)
GERV02	Clothed, and perhaps professed OSB *in articulo mortis* (AII,129)
GIBB03	In London, c1662 (Millett,434)
GIBB12	Born Tangiers, North Africa, of Irish parents (AIII,65)
GIBL02	Lo or Wi (AI,131)
GIBS14	Cons Bp of Comana 3 Sept 1780. Vicar Apostolic, Northern District, 1780.
GIBS20	Cons Bp of Acanthus, 5 December 1790. Vicar Apostolic, Northern District, 1790.
GIFF02	Bp of Centuriae *Elect* and Vicar Apostolic Western District *Designate*, 1705, but declined.
GIFF06	Cons Bp of Madaura, 22 April 1687. Vicar Apostolic, Midland District 1688-1703. President of Magdalen College, Oxford, 1688. Vicar Apostolic, London District, 1703.
GIFF23	Lh (AI,132)
GIFF26	Archbp of Rheims, 1621-1629.
GILL12	Appointed Vicar Apostolic, West Indies, 1818, but declined.
GILP04	Yo (AIII,77)
GODF02	Professed, Monte Cassino, Italy (Lunn,234)
GOOD08	DB or DE (CRS 70,104)
GOOD14	Studied at Berg-Saint-Wiroc, Low Countries (Gumbley,37)
GOWE02	Ch (AII,135)
GRAI02	Lo (TL)
GRAN18	Chaplain, Portuguese Embassy, London, 1724-1740 (Zimmerman,374)
GRAY04	Professed, Italy, 1611 (Lunn,234)
GRAY06	MX or Yo (CRS 70, 105)
GREE30	Studied at Naples (Gumbley,59)
GREE44	Professed, S.Benito, Valladolid, Spain (Lunn,235)
GRIF04	Bg or Sa (AI,139)
GRIF16	Wr (AI,139)
GRIF26	Bg (Foley 7, 321)
GRIM14	Moorfields, London, c.1791 (TL)
GRIS04	Lh (AI,140)
GROS03	Professed St Edmund's, Paris, for St Malo (Birt, 30)
GRYM02	Studied at Rennes, France (Gumbley, 52)
GUIL06	Born Wales. Professed St Malo (Birt,12)
HABE02	Hr (AI,142)
HALE02	Lo (AII,142)
HALL10	Nr (AI,143)
HALL22	Yo (AI,144)
HAME01	Preacher, French Embassy Chapel, London, 1673 (CRS 70,109)
HAMM04	Lh (AI,145)
HAND06	LE or Yo or Lh (AII,143)
HARD26	Entered Camaldolese, 1678. General, 1685 (AIII,92)
HARD28	Lh (AIV,128)
HARD30	Yo (AI,148)
HARG04	Ch or Yo (AI,148)
HARL02	In London, 1625-1626. Bp of S.Malo, 1631 (TL)
HARL04	Wr (AI,149)
HARP02	Professed S.Millan, Spain (Lunn,235)
HARR14	Lo. Alumnus of German College, Rome (AI,150)
HARR20	Ln (AI,150)
HARR30	Yo (AII,149)
HARR36	Ln (AI,151)
HARR40	Pb (AI,151)
HARR50	Yo. Perhaps a martyr (AI,152)
HARR58	ST or WK (AI,152)
HARR60	Sa (AI,153)
HART24	Ch (AI,155)
HARV04	MX or YO (CRS 70,113)
HARV10	MX or YO (CRS 70,113)
HATH02	Lh (AIII,93)
HATH04	MD or MX (CRS 70,113)
HAYA06	Canon Regular, S.Geneviève, Paris. In England 1686, perhaps in an attempt to establish the Canons Regular in England and Scotland (TL)
HEBB04	Dh (AI,160)
HEDD02	Yo (AIV,136)
HELM04	Professed Montserrat, Spain (Lunn,235)
HODG02	Educated somewhere in Portugal but not at English College, Lisbon (AIV,138)
HODG12	Yo (AIII,103)
HODS06	Yo (AI,168)
HODS12	Yo (AI,169)

HOLM 16 Ce (AI,174)
HONN 02 SJ on deathbed (AII,162)
HOPE 02 Born Chios, Greece (CRS 70,121)
HORN 16 Ln (AI,175)
HORN 18 Cons Bp of Philomenlia, 10 Feb 1752. Coadj to Bp John Talbot Stonor, Midland Dist,1752. Succeeded as V.A., 1756.
HOWA 10 Bp elect of Utica and Coadj designate to Bp Giffard, London Dist. at time of death.
HOWA 16 Studied at Rennes, France. Cardinal, 1675, Cardinal Protector of England and Scotland, 1684.
HOWA 30 Lh (AIV,146)
HUGH 02 Ch (AI,176)
HUGH 04 Sa (AI,176)
HUGH 10 Sa or SP or 'born near Bristol' (AI,178-9)
HUGH 14 Lf (AI,179)
HUGH 16 Sa (AII,165)
HUNG 04 Professed Montserrat, Spain (Lunn,235)
HUNT 32 ND or YO (CRS 70,126)
HUSB 02 Yo (AIII,109)
HUSS 04 Born W.Indies (Foley 7,386)
HUSS 08 Educated Salamanca. Bp of Waterford, 1794
INGL 10 Born LN or YO (CRS 70,127)
ITHE 02 Lf (AI,184)
ITHE 04 SJ 1564-c.1572 (AI,184)
JACK 12 Possibly identical with HARR36 (AI,187)
JACK 18 Yo (AI,186)
JACK 30 Yo (AI,187)
JENK 12 V.A. elect Northern Dist at time of death
JENN 08 Hr (AII,171)
JENN 14 Possibly two contemporary priests of this name (AII,172)
JOHN 03 In England, c.1688 (de Majer,134)
JOHN 28 Ch (?) (AI,191)
JOHN 36 Ch (AI,192)
JOHN 42 Ordained as a secular. OSB at Ratisbon (Dom Ninian) before entering OP (Gumbley,37)
JONE 02 Sa (AI,192)
JONE 16 GL or WR (CRS 70,134)
JONE 26 Entered OFM at Pontoise, France, probably already ordained as secular. Professed at Ara Coeli, Rome (Farmer,222)
JONE 28 Professed S.Martin's, Compostella, Spain. Ordained and took DD at Salamanca (Birt,17)
JONE 46 Sa (AII,174)
JONE 50 Lo (AIV,157)
JOYA 02 DT or WT (CRS 70,135)
JOYE 02 Possibly in England, c.1589 (TL)
KEAT 02 A 'Cordelier', ie OFM. In London, 1723 (CRS 38,72)
KELL 11 Portuguese Chapel, London, 1676 (Mould,242)
KELL 14 England c.1693 (de Mejer,136)
KEMP 04 Er (AI,195)
KEMP 06 Professed Montserrat, Spain (Lunn,235)
KEOG 02 Perhaps Royal Chaplain, London, 1669 (Mould,242)
KIER 02 Perhaps identical with a *Francis* Kiernan, at Spanish Chapel, London, 1738 (AIV,162)
KIRK 08 DE or NT (CRS 70,139)
KIRK 10 Yo (AI,198)
KIRW 02 Chaplain at Neapolitan Embassy, London, 1778 - c.1787 (Duffy 1976,19) Name in religion Bonaventure (Jennings, Irish Names)
KNIG 02 Ce (AI,200)
KNIG 14 Ce (AI,201)
KORS 02 Born and educated in Russia (CRS 70,141)
LAMO 02 In England, c.1625. Bp of Mende, France, 1625 (Gallia Christiana; TL)
LANG 10 Ln (AI,266)
LATH 14 Professes S.Salvador, Cellanova, Spain (Lunn,235)
LAWA 04 Lo (AIV,167)
LECO 02 An advocate for the validity of Anglican Orders. Lived in lodgings in Holborn. Buried at Westminster Abbey. (TL)
LEEA 14 Ln (AIV,169)
LEEA 26 Lo (AII,188)
LEIG 04 OX or SX (Zimmerman,108)
LEVE 02 Lo (AI,208)
LEWG 02 No evidence of an ordination date or college but seems to have been a priest (AII,189-190)
LEWI 19 Bp of Cassano, Naples, 1588
LEWI 22 Fellow and Dean of Divinity, Magdalen College, Oxford, 1688 (AIII,132)

LEWI30 Lf (AI,210)
LEYB06 Cons Bp of Adrumetum, 9 Sep 1685. V.A. of England, 1685-1688. V.A. London Dist, 1688
LIBB02 Ca (AI,210)
LINE04 Lo (AIII,135)
LOLL02 Died King's Bench Debtors Prison, London (AIV,175)
LOMA02 Ch (AI,212)
LONG06 Er, Gl or Ba (AI,213)
LOPE02 Sb (AI,213)
LOUI02 In England, c.1635. Possibly really Louis Leicester (Anstruther 1958,149)
LYNC04 In London, c.1662 (Millett,434)
MACC07 In London, c.1667 (de Mejer,118)
MACD04 Travelled in England as chaplain to the Glengarry Regt. after 1794, first RC Chaplain in the British Army
        since the Reformation. Negotiated Canadian immigration in London. First Bp of Kingston, Canada, 1820
        (TL)
MACG03 In London, 1662 (Millett,434)
MACZ02 Published several books in London, 1653-54, and probably resident there (Clancy,59)
MACZ03 One of Catherine of Braganza's Chaplains (Info. from Dr D.Rogers)
MADD01 England c.1686-1688 (de Mejer,132)
MADD02 Perhaps later joined OSB in Spain (AII,207)
MAGE06 Abandoned religious life before coming to England in 1764 and probably formally apostasised soon after
        arrival (TL)
MAGI02 In London, c.1669-1675 (TL)
MAGU02 Chaplain, Spanish Ambassador, London, c.1678. Archbp of Armagh, 1681
MAIR18 Cons Bp of Cinna, 29 May 1768. Coadj to Bp Francis Petre, Northern Dist., 1768
MAJO02 Lo (AI,216)
MALL12 Perhaps later OP in Ireland (AII,208)
MANN02 Exclaustrated, 1773 (Hendriks,333)
MANR02 Murdered in London, 1669, when on a Papal mission (TL)
MANS01 In London c.1664-1669 (Millett,63)
MANS06 BU or SY (CRS 70,158)
MANS08 Confessor to Duke of York, c.1685, living probably at St James's (TL)
MARK02 SJ 1641, OSS c.1663 (AI,488)
MARS09 Ey or Yo (AI,219) MARS30 Yo (AI,220)
MART28 Lo (AI,221)
MASO05 In London after 1698 (Smet,285)
MATH10 Ordained by St Robert Bellarmine in Rome. Possibly SJ in secret (AII,120)
MATT13 In England, 1676 (Mould,242)
MAXF04 Yo (AI,220)
MELL04 Ch (AIV,189)
MELL12 Ch (AII,213)
MELL16 Somerset House, 1683-84 (CRS 38,173)
MEPN02 In London, 1674. Possibly OFM (CRS 38,175)
METC04 Yo (AII,217)
METC22 Yo (AII,219)
MICH02 Yo (AI,229)
MIDD16 Yo (AI,229)
MIDD22 Admitted SJ in prison (AI,231)
MIDD30 Professed S.Martin, Compostella, Spain (Lunn,235)
MILL02 Perhaps SX and educated Douai (AIII,149)
MILL04 Lo (AI,231)
MILL08 Lo (AIV,190)
MILN02 Lo (AIV,190)
MILN04 Cons Bp of Castabala, 22 May 1803. V.A. Midland Dist, 1803
MOLI06 Lo (AIII,151)
MOLY14 SP or ST (CRS 70,167)
MONK02 Ce (AI,232)
MONK04 Birt (p.35) identifies D.Gregory Moore or Monke as a secular priest and says he was professed on the mission,
        1622. I have identified him with Richard Monke (AII,223) assuming Birt's profession date is wrong.
MONT02 *Titular* Abbot of S.Martin, Pontoise, France from 1635, but was probably not professed OSB.
MONT10 Portuguese Embassy Chapel, London, 1748-1751 (Zimmerman,375)
MORA02 London c.1737-1754 (Mould,242)
MORC02 Lh (AI,233)
MORE18 LE or MO (Foley 7,521)
MORG04 Educated Salamanca, Spain (AII,224)
MORG22 Wr (AIII,153)
MORR01 In England, 1758-1759 (Mould,242)
MORR06 Lf (AI,237)
MORR08 Bs (AII,226)

MORR16 Ch (AI,238)
MORT02 Yo (AI,238)
MURP08 Born Montserrat, West Indies (CRS 70,134)
MUSH02 Ch (AI,240)
MUSH04 Ch (AI,242)
NARY02 In London, c.1696-c.1702, as tutor to Randal McDonnel, 4th Earl of Antrim (TL)
NASH02 In England, 1660 (Millett, 545-6)
NAYL04 Lo (AI,243)
NEAL12 Coadj to Archbp John Carroll of Baltimore, 1800. Archbp of Baltimore, 1815
NELS04 Ch (AIII,154)
NEWM01 Pb (AII,230)
NICH16 Ch (AI,252)
NIHI02 Born Antigua, W.Indies (CRS 70,179)
NIHI04 Born Antigua, W.Indies (CRS 70,179)
NORD02 Lo (AI,252)
NORM04 Pb (AI,254)
NOTT02 Educated Naples (Gumbley,44)
NUTS02 Ch (AI,258)
NUTT06 Ch (AI,258)
OCON01 In 1669 said to have been 28 years in London (Mould,242)
ODAL02 Chaplain to Catherine of Braganza. Archbp of Braga and Bp of Coimbra, Portugal, but never consecrated
         (Anstruther 1958,157)
OFAR04 In England, c.1700 (Coleman,59)
OLEA02 Ordained Capuchin House, S.Malo (TL)
OPHE02 In prison, London, for about 2 years, c.1700 (Coleman,29)
OSTC02 Yo (AI,262)
OSTE02 In England, c.1686 (de Mejer,132)
OSUL02 Chapel Royal, London, 1685 (Mould,142)
OTWA02 Ce. Possibly a Marian priest (AI,262-3)
OWEN08 Sa (AI,263)
OWEN12 Sa (AII,235)
OWEN26 Bg (AI,264)
PAGE06 Entered SJ in prison (AI,265)
PALM10 Professed in Cassinese Congregation, house unknown (Lunn,234)
PARK24 Ln (AI,268)
PARK26 Perhaps SJ 1608 but not in Foley (AI,269)
PARK54 Ln (AI,269)
PARR22 Sb (AI,269)
PARS02 Yo (AIII,159)
PARS14 NK or SK (CRS 70,185)
PATE02 Dh (AI,270)
PATE04 Dh (AI,270)
PATR02 In London c.1663 (Zimmerman,123-4)
PATR06 Began work in England, 1641 (Millett,543)
PAUL01 In Lisbon, 1616 (Gumbley,31)
PAUL04 Published a book in London 1667 (Info from Dr D.Rogers)
PEAR12 DH or YO (CRS 70,186)
PEEL02 Wi (AI,271)
PEND01 MX or ST (CRS 70,187)
PENK06 SJ 1702-1704 (CRS 70,188)
PENS04 Cons Bp of Europus, 29 June 1824. Coadj to Bp Thomas Smith, V.A. Northern Dist. Succeeded as V.A.,
         1831.
PERC18 Left SJ 1685 to become a Carthusian (CRS 70,190)
PERE02 Chaplain to Catherine of Braganza, 1671. Possibly OFM (CRS 38,xxxi)
PETE04 Lo (AIV,211)
PETE06 Lo (AIV,211)
PETO02 Professed S.Benito, Sahagun, Spain (Lunn,235)
PETR02 Cons Bp of Prusa, 11 Nov 1721. Coadj to Bp Bonaventure Giffard, London Dist., 1721. Suceeded as V.A.,
         1734.
PETR06 Clerk of the Closet, 1685. Privy Councillor, 1687 (Foley 7,592)
PETR10 Cons Bp of Amorium 27 Jul 1751. Coadj to Bp Edward Dicconson, Northern Dist, 1751. Succeeded as V.A.,
         1752.
PETR26 MX or SK (CRS 70,193)
PETT06 Possibly two Pettingers, one secular the other OSB (Ed)
PHIL01 Confessor to Henrietta Maria (Dockery 1960,67n)
PHIL10 Lf (AI,274)
PHIL16 Composer of music who held various ecclesiastical offices in the Low Countries (Petti)
PIAZ02 Left Italy for England, probably already an apostate, and settled in Cambridge (TL)
PIAZ04 An astronomer. In England c.1790 (TL)

PICK 02   Yo (AI,276)
PLOW 04   MX or OX (CRS 70,196)
PLOW 10   Perhaps SJ (CRS 70,196)
PLOW 14   MX or OX. Also known as Joseph or Peter or Thomas (CRS 70,197)
PLOW 16   MX or OX (CRS 70,197)
PLUN 02   Archbp of Armagh, 1669. Martyred in London.
PLUN 06   SJ 1769. Possibly readmitted SJ before death (CRS 70,198)
PORT 12   Wr (AII,249)
POWE 02   OX or ST (CRS 70,203)
POWE 10   Lf (AI,281)
POWE 16   Professed S.Malo (Birt,42)
POWE 26   Sa (Foley 7,627)
POYN 02   Cons Bp of Halia 29 May 1803. Coadj to Bp John Douglass V.A. London Dist, 1803. Succeeded as V.A.,
           1812
POYN 10   Perhaps SJ on deathbed (CRS 70,204)
PRES 02   Lo (AIV,223)
PRES 04   Professed Monte Cassino, Italy (TL)
PRET 02   Wr (AII,255)
PRET 04   Wr (AII,255)
PRIC 26   Sa (AII,256)
PRIC 40   Cons Bp of Myra, 9 Jun 1715. V.A. Western Dist, 1715.
PUGH 02   SJ on deathbed (AI,283)
PUGH 10   SJ 1633-45 (AII,258)
QUIN 08   Lo (AII,260)
RADF 02   Lh (AI,284)
RAVE 06   Admitted OFM tertiary at Douai, 1666. Later ordained priest in Ireland and worked on the English Mission
           (Thaddeus, 294)
RAWD 02   Yo (AI,285)
RAWL 06   Yo (AII,261)
RAYN 06   Dh (AI,286)
REDF 02   Born FR or MX (CRS 70,207)
REDM 04   Ch (AI,287)
REYN 06   Ln (AI,286)
RIBE 04   Professed S.Gregory's, Douai, for S.Malo (Birt,42)
RICH 16   DH or ND (CRS 70,209)
RIDE 00   Ce or Ch (AI,289-290)
RIGB 02   Ch (TL)
ROBI 42   Ch (AI,294)
ROCH 02   In London, c.1662 (Millett,434)
ROEA 06   Ch (AIV,231)
ROLL 02   Yo (AII,270)
ROOT 06   Wi (AIII,190)
ROWL 02   Lh (AI,296)
ROYA 02   Born Pennsylvania, N.America (CRS 70,216)
RUSS 06   Possibly joined Trinitarian order (AIII,192)
RUSS 12   Bp of Portallegro, Portugal, 1671. Translated to Vizen, Portugal, 1682.
SAIN 04   In London, 1673-1675, as preacher to Duchess of York (CRS 70,217)
SALL 01   In London, c.1662 (Millett,434)
SALV 01   In London, 1665 (Info provided by Dr D.Rogers)
SAND 04   Sd. Admitted SJ on deathbed (AI,300)
SAVA 02   Fifth Viscount Savage, Fifth Earl Rivers (AIII,196)
SCOT 16   Professed S.Benito, Sahagun, Spain (Lunn,235
SEWE 02   Dh (AI,305)
SEWE 04   Ce (AI,306)
SHAR 16   Cons Bp of Telmessus, 12 Aug 1780. Coadj to Bp Charles Walmesley, V.A. Western Dist, 1780. Succeeded as
           V.A., 1797.
SHAW 04   Ch (AI,306)
SHAW 08   Ch (AI,307)
SHAW 18   Ch (AII,290)
SHEL 02   Wi (AI,307)
SHEP 22   Sb (AI,308)
SHER 18   'Perhaps the only known bogus Elizabethan priest' (AI,310)
SHER 42   SJ on deathbed (AII,294)
SHEW 02   Lh (AI,314)
SHEW 04   Ce (AI,314)
SIDG 02   Ch (TL)
SING 12   Ch. M.A. of one of the universties (AI,318))
SLAD 04   SJ 1582-c.1589 (AI,319)
SLAT 02   Bp of Ruspa and V.A. of Mauritius, 1818.

SMIT 17	Dh (AI,320)
SMIT 22	In England, c.1686 (de Mejer,132)
SMIT 26	Cons Bp of Callipolis, 13 May 1688. V.A. Northern Dist, 1688.
SMIT 52	Readmitted to SJ after leaving 1582 and 1592/3 (AI,320-1)
SMIT 53	Wr (AI,321)
SMIT 54	Lo (AI,321)
SMIT 55	Ce (AI,321)
SMIT 56	Cons Bp of Chalcedon, 12 Jan 1625. V.A. of England, 1625.
SMIT 62	Sb (AI,322)
SMIT 65	Ln (AI,323)
SMIT 72	Cons Bp of Bolina, 11 Mar 1810. Coadj to Bp William Gibson, Northern Dist. Succeeded as V.A., 1821.
SMIT 77	Educated at a seminary in Naples (AIV,251)
SNAP 02	Ln (AI,324)
SPEN 02	Yo (AI,328)
STAM 02	Lo (AI,330)
STAP 02	Yo (AI,332)
STAP 04	Yo (AI,333)
STAP 06	Cons Bp of Hierocaesarea, 8 Mar 1801. V.A. Midland Dist, 1801.
STEP 12	Sb. First English SJ to go to the E.Indies. Died at Goa (Foley 7,738)
STEP 16	Yo (AI,336)
STOK 04	Lo (AI,336)
STON 13	Monk—order not stated (Info from Hon.G.Stonor)
STON 14	Priest at Louvain (Info from Hon.G.Stonor)
STON 16	Cons Bp of Thespiae, Aug 1716. V.A. Midland Dist, 1716.
STOR 03	Lf (AI,336)
STOR 08	Ln (AI,336)
STOU 06	Yo (AIV,263)
STRE 02	Nr (AIII,213)
STRI 12	Bp of Namur, Low Countries, 1727.
STUA 01	Cardinal, 1747. Archbp of Corinth *i.p.i.*, 1758. Bp of Frascati, 1761.Taken by some Stuart supporters to have been King Henry IX of England.
STUA 04	Youngest son of 3rd Duke of Lennox. Succeeded his brother George, 1642. Died at Paris on way to Rome to be made Cardinal (AII,313)
SUDA 02	Ch (AI,340)
SUDA 04	Ch (AIV,266)
TALB 06	Thirteenth Earl of Shrewsbury. (CRS 70,240)
TALB 12	Cons Bp of Birtha, 24 Aug 1759. Coadj to Bp Richard Challoner, V.A. London Dist, 1759. Succeeded as V.A., 1781.
TALB 22	Worked for some time in England. SJ until c.1650. Archbp of Dublin, 1669 (Foley 7,757)
TALB 27	Brother of Archbp Talbot. In London 1658 (Millett,546)
TALB 32	Cons Bp of Acone, Mar 1766. Coadj to Bp John Hornyold, V.A. Midland Dist, 1766.Succeeded as V.A., 1778.
TASK 02	Lo (AIV,271)
TAYL 20	Dh (AI,345)
TAYL 22	Dh or Wr (AI,345)
TAYL 28	Ch (AIV,274)
TAYL 38	Dh (AI,346)
TAYL 41	Neapolitan Embassy, London, 1770 (Mould,242)
TEDD 02	Wr (AI,347)
THOM 08	Sd (AI,350)
THOM 16	Lo (AI,350)
THOR 02	Lo (AI,351)
THOR 06	Sb (AI,352)
TOOL 02	In England c.1689 (de Mejer,1357). He was an Englishman but this could be a name in religion (St Lawrence O'Toole) (Ed.)
TOTT 02	Ch (AI,363)
TRAV 02	Studied at Lille (Zimmerman,312)
TRES 02	OSB S.Gregory's, Douai. Left to join OFM, 1649 or 1650 (TL)
TUNS 10	Received OSB habit on the mission (Birt,4-5)
TURB 08	Professed Montserrat, Spain (Lunn,235)
TURN 20	Lf or Sd (AIII,235)
TWYF 02	Lo (AI,365)
TYRW 02	Studied theology in Naples (CRS 70,252)
TYRW 04	Ln (AI,365)
UNDE 04	Lo (AIV,283)
VALE 04	Died at Palermo, Italy. He came from a 'noble' English family (Zimmerman,145)
VANC 02	Lo (AIV,284)
VARL 02	Ch (AIV,284)

VAUX02	Ce. Student at Louvain and Valenciennes, France (AI,366)
VENI02	Ordained in Durham Cathedral, 25 Mar 1559, according to the rites of the Catholic Church (AI,366)
VIET02	In England, 1625, with Henrietta Maria (TL)
WAFE01	In London, c.1662 (Millett,434)
WAKE12	Wr (AI,368)
WALL20	Ch (AI,369)
WALM02	Cons Bp of Ramatha, 21 Dec 1756. Coadj to Bp William Lawrence York, V.A. Western Dist, 1756. Succeeded as V.A., 1770.
WALT14	Cons Bp of Trachonitis, Dec 1770. Coadj to Bp Francis Petre, V.A. Northern Dist, 1770. Succeeded as V.A., 1775.
WARH06	Lo (AIV,290)
WARN08	Clothed OSB but not professed (AII,339)
WATS01	In London, 1623 (Anstruther 1958,129)
WATT04	Sd (AI,374)
WELD06	Lo (AIV,294)
WELL02	Later OFM in Spain (AIV,294)
WEND02	Nr (AI,375)
WESL02	At Portuguese Chapel, London (CRS 38,170)
WEST04	Yo (AI,375)
WEST20	Lo (AII,345)
WHIT12	Lo (AII,347)
WHIT68	Professed S.Claudio, Leon, Spain (Lunn,235)
WHIT86	Ch (AI,380)
WIDD02	DH or LN (CRS 70,265)
WILC10	Professed S.Benito, Valladolid (Lunn,235)
WILD02	Lo (AIV,301)
WILL05	In London, 1685 (de Mejer,123)
WILL06	A monk of Cluny aggregated to English Congregation (Birt,62)
WILL08	Lf (AIII,248)
WILL20	Lf (AI,381)
WILL22	Sa (AI,382)
WILL42	Lf (AI,382)
WILL62	Educated Naples. Cons Bp of Tiberiopolis, 30 Dec 1725. V.A. Northern Dist, 1725.
WILS38	Ch (AI,383)
WITH06	Cons Bp of Marcopolis, 15 Apr 1703. V.A. Midland Dist, 1703. Translated to Northern Dist, 1715.
WOLF06	BK, SP or ST (CRS 70,270)
WOLL02	Ch (AI,384)
WOOD08	Ln (AI,384)
WORT20	Perhaps later joined ORA or SJ (AI,388)
WOTT02	Lo (AI,389)
WREN02	Ch (AI,389)
WYNN02	Bg (AIII,256)
YATE12	SJ on deathbed (AI,389)
YAXL04	Nr (AIII,257)
YORK06	Cons Bp of Nisibis, 10 Aug 1741. Coadj to Bp Matthew Prichard, V.A. Western Dist, 1741. Succeeded as V.A., 1750. Resigned, 1763.
ZACH02	On English Mission, c.1633 (Dockery 1960,41)

ALPHABETICAL INDEX OF ALIASES

Alias	Code	Alias	Code	Alias	Code
BEAUMONT	POYN08	BLAKE	CLOU08	BRIDGES	STRE04
BEAUMONT	MUTT02	BLAKISTON	ROLL02	BRINCKBORNE	DRYL02
BEAUMONT	HARC04	BLAKISTON	COSI02	BRINKHURST	MEAR06
BEAUMONT	HUNT07	BLANCO	WHIT34	BRINKHURST	MEAR02
BEAUMONT	JENI20	BLAXTON	PLAS02	BRINKHURST	MEAR04
BEAUMONT	TESI02	BLAXTON	ROLL02	BROOKE	QUIN06
BEBRIDGE	HAZL02	BLECHINGTON	LIBB02	BROOKE	HAWK10
BECKETT	FAIR08	BLEWITT	RIVE02	BROOKE	GERA12
BECKWITH	LOCK14	BLOFIELD	IPSL02	BROOKES	POUL06
BEDFORD	DRUR06	BLOND	BLOU11	BROOKES	GREE22
BEDFORD	DRUR08	BLOUNT	COTT18	BROOKES	POUL10
BEDINGFELD	IPSL02	BLOUNT	DAVI10	BROOKES	YOUN14
BEDINGFELD	MILD06	BLUET	COLL30	BROOKES	POUL28
BEDINGFELD	DOWN04	BLUET	RISD02	BROOKESBY	MORE18
BEESTON	BOUR02	BLUET	WILL24	BROUGHTON	CROW06
BELLOT	STOC04	BLUNDELL	PEMB02	BROUGHTON	CROW04
BENISON	RICH15	BLUNDELL	CALV04	BROUGHTON	NOTT02
BENNET	THOM04	BLUNDELL	RICH18	BROWN	ASKE06
BENNET	DANI02	BLUNT	GUNS02	BROWN	BOOT02
BENNET	WHIT68	BODNAM	LAZE02	BROWN	BUTL06
BENNET	THOM50	BODWELL	GWYN02	BROWN	JACK30
BENNET	DAVI36	BODWELL	WYNN04	BROWN	GWYN02
BENNET	BENT16	BODWILL	CANE02	BROWN	LLOY02
BENNET	BLAC12	BODYCOAT	GOOD04	BROWN	WORS06
BENSON	THOR20	BOLD	LASC08	BROWN	MUSS04
BENSON	HAYD16	BOLD	LASC10	BROWN	BREN00
BENSON	CANS02	BOLD	LASC04	BROWN	BOOT14
BENTLEY	SKIN06	BOLD	LASC06	BROWN	BUSB01
BENTLEY	SKIN02	BOLDROP	GOOC02	BROWN	GREE22
BERINGTON	LIVE04	BONHAM	EVIS02	BROWN	LEMA02
BERINGTON	CLAY12	BONVILLE	TURB06	BROWN	BUSB02
BERINGTON	CLAY18	BOOTH	YATE14	BROWN	HEAT16
BERNARD	HUSB02	BOOTH	DALT04	BROWN	MANN18
BERRY	CATE02	BORDE	BLUN26	BROWN	MAXW04
BERRY	FOST18	BOUCHER	BOWK02	BROWN	WOOL02
BETHAM	MOLI06	BOWEN	LLOY06	BROWN	EVAN10
BETTS	GOTH02	BOYER	SCUD02	BROWNING	COPP02
BEVERIDGE	EBER02	BRADLEY	BRUL02	BRUNCHARD	WHIT30
BIANCHI	WHIT58	BRADLEY	LEYB02	BUCKLAND	HILL12
BIANCHI	WHIT66	BRADLEY	WIND02	BUCKLEY	GWYN02
BIESLEY	NELS10	BRADSHAW	ARRO02	BUCKLEY	JONE26
BIGGS	SIMO04	BRAITHWAITE	TRAP06	BUDD	PETO02
BIGGS	VANC02	BRAITHWAITE	GILP04	BUDD	PICK14
BILLINGSLY	BEDF02	BRAMHALL	BAKE08	BUDE	HOLF04
BILTON	CORN10	BRAMLEY	BRAM02	BULMER	GIBS18
BIRCH	PEAR06	BRAND	PRAC02	BULMER	RICH38
BIRCH	PEND02	BRAYLSFORD	NEWT10	BUN	BOND02
BIRKHEAD	BIRK08	BREADNALL	BEAD04	BURCHARD	PARK28
BIRTWISTLE	HAWA04	BREATHER	BATT04	BURDETT	MAIR04
BIRTWISTLE	HAWA02	BRENT	ASPI06	BURDETT	HUSS06
BISHOP	PEAR04	BRENT	PRAC02	BURGES	RIDG02
BISHOP	VICT04	BRENT	ASPI08	BURGIS	LEAD02
BLACK	RUSS01	BRENT	ASPI04	BURNET	HARD04
BLACK	SAGE02	BRERETON	BARL04	BURRELL	WHIT52
BLACK	SMIT74	BRERETON	HOLT06	BURROUGHES	EATO02
BLACKBURN	THOM46	BRERETON	STAN20	BURTON	BARO02
BLACKBURN	TAYL36	BRETON	FURS02	BURTON	CATC02
BLACKLOW	TOOT04	BRETT	HOLT14	BURTON	HASE02
BLACKLOW	WHIT32	BRETT	KEYN10	BURTON	JUKE02
BLACKLOW	BAIN06	BREWER	BENN04	BUSTON	STEP12
BLACKLOW	WHIT54	BREWERTON	PROB06	BUTLER	BOWK02
BLACKNOLL	FLET02	BRIAN	CRAN04	BUTLER	BERR08
BLACKWELL	FLET02	BRIANT	PARS12	BUTLER	LIST06
BLACOE	TOOT04	BRIDGEMAN	STRU02	BUTLER	SEEL02
BLACON	BAIN06	BRIDGES	GRAT02	BUTLER	WORS20
BLAKE	SAGE02	BRIDGES	DUVA02	BUTLER	COWB02

Alias	Code	Alias	Code	Alias	Code
CROSS	BUTL02	DOUGELL	REYN05	ENGLISH	GREE22
CROSS	MOOR05	DOUGELL	REYN04	ERRINGTON	EXLE02
CROSS	MORR10	DOUGHTY	DAWS06	ERRINGTON	COLL24
CRUMP	MILL02	DOUGLAS	REYN04	ERRINGTON	GRAN02
CUFFAUD	LAMB01	DOUGLAS	REYN05	ESCHAM	DARB04
CULCHETH	STAN24	DOUTHWAITE	DANS02	ESDRAS	SIMP16
CULPEPER	TIMC02	DOVINGTON	CARL08	ESON	BLUN24
CUMMINGS	HART20	DOWGILL	REYN05	ESSEX	COTT16
CUMMINGS	HART22	DOWGILL	REYN04	ETON	JONE42
CURTIS	SHOR02	DOWNES	HASK02	EURE	SALT08
CURWEN	WILK12	DOWNHAM	CHUR06	EVANS	FAIR02
CUTHBERT	STON10	DOWNING	HAME02	EVANS	PHIL10
CUTHBERT	MORS02	DOWRICH	RUDG02	EVERARD	PAST04
DACRE	HILL02	DRAKE	GUIL02	EVERS	BALE02
DACRE	CARP06	DRAPER	METC15	EVERS	SALT08
DADE	MIDD24	DRAPER	JONE42	EVERY	EURE02
DAGGERS	BLOU11	DRAYCOTT	COYN02	EVERY	EURE06
DALTON	SHUT02	DRAYTON	HANS06	EVERY	EURE04
DAMAR	BURT06	DREW	KEMP08	EXTON	REDF02
DAMBENY	HARD18	DRUMMOND	TREV02	EYLES	JACK02
DAMFORD	WREN04	DRURY	HARR02	EYRE	FITZ06
DANBY	FARM01	DRURY	RUDG02	EYRE	FITZ08
DANBY	RILE02	DU PRE	MAMB02	EYSTON	LACE01
DANIEL	HARR22	DU PUY	ASHT16	FACEBY	ROYD02
DANIEL	MILE10	DUBOIS	FULW04	FAIRFAX	STON10
DANIEL	SIMP04	DUCKETT	HOLT12	FAIRFAX	CART14
DANIEL	PICK12	DUCKETT	JONE42	FAIRFAX	ROBI16
DANIEL	PICK10	DUCKETT	HOLT08	FAIRFAX	PERC08
DARBY	FITZ04	DUCKETT	HOLT14	FALLOWES	BISH12
DARCY	FOST02	DUGUID	LESL04	FARINGTON	FARN04
DARCY	BERM02	DUNN	EARP02	FARINGTON	BENN04
DARCY	THOM12	DUNNING	GRAN08	FARMABY	HOUG06
DARCY	FOST23	DURAND	LANG24	FARMER	SMIT21
DARCY	GARN08	DURANT	LEHU02	FARMER	MERE02
DARELL	WEST06	DURHAM	SMIT35	FARMER	STEY02
DARELL	TASB08	DURHAM	COLL26	FARMER	GARN08
DARELL	JOHN05	DUTTON	IREL02	FARMER	VENN02
DAVENPORT	WINT10	DYER	TUNS10	FARRAR	HARE02
DAVIES	TAVE02	EARPE	DUNN14	FARRINGTON	WOOD16
DAVIES	BENN08	EARTH	LEIG12	FAULKNER	PITT10
DAVIES	BARR34	EATON	DICC02	FAWCETT	NEWT08
DAVISON	DEBO02	EATON	EYRE06	FELL	UMFR02
DAWSON	DEBO02	ECCLES	LEEC02	FELTON	GROS02
DAY	MULS02	ECCLESFIELD	METC14	FENNELL	WALS10
DAY	CUFF02	ECCLESTON	GORS04	FENWICK	WARW02
DAY	BROW32	EDMUNDS	WEST22	FENWICK	CALD04
DE BOIS	KING16	EDWARDS	BRAD34	FERIMAN	RAWL02
DEACON	SMIT65	EDWARDS	ACTO05	FERMOR	TURB10
DEE	MORG04	EDWARDS	MONK04	FERMOR	VENN02
DENNY	BARD02	EDWARDS	EVEL02	FERRERS	IREL06
DESPERAMUS	HOPE02	EGERTON	BELF04	FETHERSTON	HOLT12
DEVEREUX	WOOD22	EGERTON	POTT02	FIELD	MAXF02
DILLON	NEVI02	ELLERKER	DALT02	FINCH	FRAI02
DINGLEY	YOUN16	ELLIOT	SHEL14	FINCH	HOLM16
DINGLEY	FAUL02	ELLIS	PRIN04	FINES	ROBS02
DINGLEY	MORG10	ELLIS	JUMP04	FISHER	COWL04
DITCHFIELD	SANK06	ELLIS	WARI14	FISHER	FITT04
DITCHLING	SANK06	ELLIS	ELRI02	FISHER	PERC08
DODD	TOOT06	ELLISON	BUTL10	FISHER	POPE02
DOMINGUEZ	DONI02	ELMER	CADW02	FISHER	GARN18
DOMINIC	CLAR02	ELMORE	CADW02	FISHER	STUT02
DONWALL	POWE08	ELSTON	WINC06	FISHER	STAN06
DONWELL	POWE08	ELSTON	CHAD02	FISHER	FITT02
DORMER	HUDD10	ELSTON	LACE01	FISHER	CHAL06
DORMER	SMIT37	ELSTON	PHIL12	FISHER	COPL08
DORMER	HUDD04	ELWICK	EMER04	FISHER	FLOY17

Alias	Code	Alias	Code	Alias	Code
FITTON	BIDD 04	GARNET	HEIG 02	GREEN	GAWE 02
FITTON	BIDD 08	GARTER	KENN 14	GREEN	SCOT 14
FITTON	BIDD 06	GARTH	LEIG 12	GREEN	SALE 08
FITZHERBERT	FETT 02	GASCOIGNE	GATE 02	GREEN	WHIT 70
FITZHERBERT	HALL 04	GAUNTLETT	STAN 36	GREEN	GAWE 06
FITZWILLIAMS	FING 02	GAWEN	HACO 02	GREEN	TOML 02
FLEMING	GRIF 26	GAZAIN	ROBI 32	GREEN	WAKE 08
FLETCHER	COTT 20	GAZIN	ROBI 32	GREEN	HORN 08
FLETCHER	PEND 01	GEFFRESON	SMIT 55	GREEN	FATH 02
FLICHON	FLEE 04	GELIBOURN	GILL 04	GREEN	GILP 02
FLISK	ELLI 14	GEOFFREY	FOWL 06	GREENLOW	HUNT 14
FLITUN	FLEE 04	GEORGE	JORI 02	GREENWALL	TESI 02
FLOWER	WALD 02	GERARD	BART 24	GREENWAY	TESI 02
FLOWER	WAYA 02	GERARD	CRIC 02	GREENWAYS	CADW 04
FLOWER	CORB 20	GERARD	JENI 14	GREGORY	GRAV 04
FLOWER	CORB 18	GERMIN	FERM 02	GREGSON	CROO 06
FLOYD	ROOT 04	GERVISON	SMIT 07	GRIFFETH	MORG 20
FLOYD	BENN 06	GIBBONS	WAKE 08	GRIFFIN	WOOD 30
FORD	ALLI 02	GIBBS	YORK 02	GRIFFIN	GRIF 26
FORD	HART 20	GIFFARD	PURC 04	GRIFFIN	PIGO 02
FORD	MUMF 05	GIFFARD	PEAR 04	GRIFFITH	JONE 26
FORD	GASC 06	GIFFARD	VAVA 10	GRIMES	BAZI 02
FORD	GUIL 02	GIFFARD	TRAP 04	GRIMSDITCH	BRUN 14
FORD	MORE 06	GIFFARD	WAKE 06	GROSVENOR	MANN 04
FORMBY	HOWA 06	GIFFARD	WHEB 02	GROVE	CARP 10
FORRESTER	CHAM 28	GIFFARD	WRIG 18	GROVE	ARCH 14
FORRESTER	FLEU 02	GILDRIDGE	KEMP 10	GROVE	ARCH 12
FORSTER	TATL 02	GILFORD	FITZ 06	GROYNE	HAUG 04
FORSTER	THOR 12	GILLING	GIRL 04	GUARDEFORD	WARF 02
FORSTER	DANI 22	GILLOW	CRIS 10	GULLICK	WOOD 12
FORTESCUE	GOUL 02	GILMET	SHIR 08	GULLICK	FOST 20
FORTESCUE	BALL 12	GIRLINGTON	DUCK 08	GUTTERIDGE	HARP 04
FOSTER	PIBU 02	GLASSCOCK	GLOS 02	GWILLIM	TYRW 02
FOSTER	CRIC 06	GLEGG	MASS 04	HABARD	HALI 02
FOSTER	CRIC 04	GODFREY	ROUG 02	HABERLEY	GREE 48
FOSTER	DANI 22	GOLD	GOWE 06	HACON	ADAM 00
FOSTER	CRIC 02	GOLDEN	PARK 58	HALES	LICH 02
FOSTER	PILC 02	GOLDING	GOOD 02	HALL	BIRK 08
FOUNTAIN	LEYB 02	GOLDSMITH	MIDD 20	HALL	DIGG 06
FOUQUANT	SCHO 02	GOODEN	TILD 02	HALL	LINE 02
FOURNIERS	CLOU 06	GOODRICK	HARP 04	HALL	LUCA 04
FOWLER	CLAR 24	GORSUCH	ECCL 08	HALL	OLDC 02
FOWLER	DARE 06	GOSLING	BENN 09	HALL	HUMB 02
FOWLER	ROBI 28	GOWER	HORN 20	HALL	LICH 02
FOX	PARK 42	GRACE	GRAY 06	HALL	HUMB 04
FOXLEY	GRAT 02	GRADELL	NEIL 04	HALLIWELL	BIRT 08
FOXWELL	FRYE 04	GRADWELL	NEIL 02	HAMERTON	WALM 18
FRANKLAND	WHIT 02	GRAFTON	HAUG 06	HAMMON	PETT 02
FREER	JONE 26	GRANT	LEYB 02	HAMMOND	JACK 18
FRENCH	WHIT 70	GRAVENOR	PIBU 02	HAMMOND	HOLL 16
FREVILLE	JENI 26	GRAY	JENI 22	HAMMOND	HACK 02
FREVILLE	JENI 20	GRAY	JENI 12	HAMMOND	HART 12
FREVILLE	JENI 16	GRAY	GREE 36	HAMPSHIRE	DARB 04
FREVILLE	JENI 18	GRAY	JENI 24	HANDFORD	BRAD 24
FRIAR	WAFE 02	GRAY	GRAN 14	HANFORD	PARR 10
FROST	THOM 32	GRAY	TATH 04	HANMER	CLAY 04
FYLDE	MAXF 02	GRAY	TALB 06	HANMER	STAR 06
GAGE	PLOW 04	GRAY	JENI 14	HANMER	BUXT 04
GAGE	ROOK 16	GRAY	HARE 02	HANMER	HAYE 02
GAGE	PETR 26	GREEN	WAKE 14	HANNAN	APPL 13
GAGE	ALCO 02	GREEN	DAKI 02	HANSOM	SMIT 66
GAMAGE	BRAD 34	GREEN	WARD 06	HANSON	HESK 10
GARBOT	RICH 32	GREEN	GREA 04	HARCOTT	WHIT 14
GARDINER	OWEN 04	GREEN	HORN 10	HARCOURT	BARR 48
GARDINER	STEP 04	GREEN	CLOP 02	HARCOURT	BEAU 08
GARNET	GARD 12	GREEN	JOSS 02	HARCOURT	AYLW 06

Alias	Code	Alias	Code	Alias	Code
HARCOURT	PURC01	HEIGHTON	CHAR04	HUNT	WEST22
HARCOURT	WHIT14	HELMES	BAMB02	HUNT	BENS06
HARDING	MANS02	HELMES	TUNS10	HUNTER	WELD08
HARDING	BARR50	HENRIQUE	ROOT02	HUNTER	HARD26
HARDING	MANS04	HERBERT	VANE02	HUNTER	WELD04
HARDING	LEEA04	HERBERT	JONE26	HUNTER	WELD14
HAREKLEY	BOST02	HERBERT	PHIL30	HUNTER	OLDC02
HARFORD	HARD20	HERBERT	TURN18	HUTTON	OLDC02
HARPER	BERI06	HERBERT	HART06	HUY	JONE42
HARPER	PORA02	HERNE	WAFE02	HYDE	BRUN08
HARPER	SMIT26	HESKETH	HANS12	HYDE	BAYA02
HARRINGTON	MOLY04	HESPER	WALD10	HYDE	BRUN14
HARRINGTON	HOOK02	HEWENS	EVAN16	HYDE	HILL18
HARRINGTON	SMIT23	HICKMAN	PAGE06	IBERIES	METH04
HARRIOTT	PAGE08	HIDALGO	PETT06	INGLEBY	WARD04
HARRIS	HORM02	HIDE	LAWS10	INGLEBY	TIDD02
HARRIS	PRET04	HIGHGATE	SIMP16	INGLEBY	WARD10
HARRIS	WALM04	HILDINGE	VINC02	IRELAND	THOR08
HARRIS	NEWP02	HILDRETH	ADD104	IRELAND	GROS06
HARRIS	PRET02	HILL	LAWS10	IRELAND	LOAD02
HARRIS	PRIC04	HILL	BEES15	IRELAND	ROCK04
HARRISON	SMIT33	HILL	HUTT08	IRELAND	SALT06
HARRISON	LANG20	HILL	OWEN05	IRELAND	DUTT02
HARRISON	GERA12	HILL	GREE54	IRELAND	MEYN12
HARRISON	PHIL30	HILL	STAF08	IREMONGER	IREL10
HARRISON	GERA20	HILLS	BERR10	IRONMONGER	GENN02
HARRISON	BARR48	HIND	HYDE04	IRONMONGER	IREL10
HARRISON	BREE06	HINSLEY	GOLD02	ISLES	JACK02
HART	HARG06	HOARD	GAGE08	JACKSON	EDIS06
HART	HATH02	HODGES	MASS10	JACKSON	HACK02
HART	EARP02	HOLCROFT	RICH20	JACKSON	FOST12
HART	KIRK10	HOLDCRAFT	HARG06	JACKSON	GOWE02
HART	OWEN12	HOLLAND	ECCL08	JACKSON	MALL08
HARVEY	WORS08	HOLLAND	MART38	JACKSON	THOM36
HARVEY	WORS10	HOLLAND	SERG04	JAKEMAN	WILD02
HARVEY	HAYN02	HOLLAND	KEMB06	JAMES	HEYL02
HARVEY	MICO04	HOLLAND	MORR18	JAMES	NEWP04
HARVEY	MALL06	HOLLAND	BARN40	JAMES	ROSI02
HARVEY	MICO02	HOLLAND	ECCL04	JAMESON	SACH04
HARWOOD	CANN06	HOLLAND	JONE42	JEFFREY	WARH08
HASKEY	REEV08	HOLME	HOWA26	JEFFREY	WARH02
HASKEY	REEV04	HOLT	HOLL06	JENISON	POTI02
HASKEY	REEV06	HORTON	WARR22	JENNINGS	POWE12
HASTINGS	PEGG04	HOSKINS	PERK06	JENNINGS	WOOD30
HASTINGS	HUDD04	HOUGHTON	GREE44	JENNINGS	TILL04
HASTINGS	CAMP04	HOWARD	HAGG06	JERMYN	HACO02
HATCLIFFE	SPEN06	HOWARD	GROS06	JERMYN	FERM02
HAUGHTON	BUTT04	HOWARD	HOLM04	JERNINGHAM	EAST08
HAVARD	BLOU04	HOWARD	HAGG08	JERNINGHAM	EAST00
HAVARD	ELYA02	HOWARD	GAGE20	JERSON	EVIS02
HAVELLAND	HAZL02	HOWARD	HOLM06	JOHNSON	BOLT06
HAWKINS	STIT02	HOWARD	HOLM02	JOHNSON	HAND06
HAWKSHEE	HACK02	HOWARD	HOLM08	JOHNSON	WATS06
HAWLEY	BRAN02	HOWE	MOLY14	JOHNSON	SOME10
HAY	JONE42	HOWELL	TRAF02	JOHNSON	LEEA02
HAYDOCK	SHUT04	HOWELL	LEVE02	JOHNSON	FREE02
HAYES	HARR33	HOWLING	HOWL02	JOHNSON	SAIN02
HAYES	HARR50	HUDDLESTON	CATT14	JOHNSON	WHIT50
HAYES	BYRO02	HUDDLESTON	CATT16	JOHNSON	BARW02
HEADLAM	WILL24	HUDSON	THOM22	JOHNSON	CLIF04
HEADLAM	BATE02	HUGHES	OWEN02	JOHNSON	JACK22
HEATH	HOTH02	HUNGERFORD	STRA04	JOHNSON	GASC02
HEATH	DORR04	HUNT	DAVE02	JOHNSON	COWB04
HEATHCOTE	MIDD30	HUNT	DAWS06	JOHNSON	FLEC04
HEATON	BANK02	HUNT	HOLF06	JOHNSON	HOLD02
HEIGHAM	KIRK10	HUNT	HANM06	JOHNSON	PHIL30

Alias	Code	Alias	Code	Alias	Code
JOHNSON	WALL04	LANTON	BRID04	LUCAS	GROV04
JOHNSON	DICK06	LARGE	BARR27	LUCAS	BURK02
JOHNSON	HAND04	LASCELLES	LOCK12	LUCY	GREE82
JOHNSON	JENI04	LATHAM	MAIN06	LUSTY	GREE36
JOHNSON	MAGE02	LATHAM	KIRK12	LUTTON	ELRI02
JOHNSON	MIDD04	LATHAM	ALMO06	LUTTON	ELRI03
JONES	AYLW05	LATHAM	MAIN04	LUTTRELL	COPL04
JONES	VANE02	LATHROPPE	DAVE02	LUTTRELL	LINE04
JONES	VARD02	LATON	HIRD02	LUTTRELL	KEYN18
JOSEPHSON	HUDD11	LAURENSON	BILL06	LUTTRELL	KEYN02
JOURNO	GAGE02	LAWRENCE	HALL25	LYNES	HUGH08
JUDOLI	GALL02	LAWRENCE	DICK02	LYNN	STEP08
JUSTINIANI	AYRO02	LAWSON	BRAI08	LYONS	DUFF01
KEIGHLEY	DICK02	LAYTON	HOUS06	MACCAUGHWELL	COLE01
KELHAM	GERA22	LAYTON	MALT02	MACINTOSH	BOLT05
KELLICK	WOOD12	LAYTON	LEIG02	MAHONY	MEEH02
KELLY	WOOD60	LAYTON	JOHN26	MAHUN	BIRD02
KELLY	CARY22	LAYTON	LEIG10	MAHUN	CORN08
KEMP	YELV02	LAYTON	LEIG08	MAINWARING	CODR06
KENDALL	SOUT34	LEA	SOUT06	MAIRE	HAWA14
KENDALL	SOUT32	LEA	SERG08	MALLETT	BALE02
KENDALL	BAIN06	LECKONBY	WHIT36	MALLETT	MUTT04
KENDALL	SOUT30	LECKONBY	WHIT40	MANDEVILLE	MIDD06
KENSINGTON	LAIT06	LEE	STAR02	MANLEY	CHAR10
KENSINGTON	LAIT04	LEE	RUDG02	MANLEY	MAST02
KENSINGTON	LAIT02	LEE	CLAY20	MANN	BLOU11
KENT	NEAL14	LEE	SOUT26	MANN	ANTR04
KEYNES	EWEN02	LEE	VINE02	MANNERS	VAVA04
KING	TREN02	LEE	STAF11	MANNERS	SITT02
KING	GREE24	LEE	BADD02	MANNERS	PELC02
KING	KNIG10	LEE	CLAY16	MANNOCK	PETR20
KINSON	DICK06	LEE	GERA12	MANNOCK	PETR12
KIRK	DAVI08	LEFEBURE	PATE06	MANNOCK	STRI02
KIRKHAM	HART16	LEGATT	LANG12	MANSELL	TALB16
KITCHEN	SMIT12	LEGATT	LANG14	MANSELL	TALB28
KNIGHT	MERE04	LEIGHTON	YOUN16	MANSELL	WATS02
KNIGHT	BAYN10	LENNY	LANE08	MANSELL	CLIF08
KNIVETON	WHIT72	LENS	LEEA22	MANSFIELD	TALB16
KNOTT	WILS16	LEPPARD	LEWI14	MANSFIELD	TALB28
KNOTT	WALS10	LESLEY	LIST08	MARBERY	MADD02
KNOWLES	RIGB22	LEVESON	GIFF06	MARCHANT	SHAW04
LACEY	DICK06	LEVESON	GIFF02	MARKHAM	HUGH06
LACEY	CONS15	LEVESON	GIFF10	MARKHAM	WITH06
LACEY	WOLF08	LEWIS	SALT04	MARLOW	MATT02
LACEY	GODF02	LEWIS	SMIT69	MARSDEN	KITC04
LACEY	PRIN04	LEWIS	GAGE14	MARSH	WALL06
LACON	HARN04	LEWIS	KEMY02	MARSH	COLE02
LAMBERT	LACO06	LEYBURN	GAND02	MARSH	WALL04
LAMBERT	BARK18	LIBANUS	PARR18	MARSHALL	SMIT57
LAMBERT	LACO04	LIDDELL	VERH02	MARSHALL	WALL06
LAMBERT	SEYE02	LINCOLN	AKER02	MARSON	MART26
LAMBTON	BIRK08	LINCOLN	ATKI13	MARTIN	ARAY02
LAMPTON	CUFF06	LINGEN	INGR08	MARTIN	WHIT10
LAMPTON	LAMB01	LISLE	LIST08	MARTIN	BARR26
LANCASTER	ALLE14	LLOYD	ROOT04	MARTIN	BIDD02
LANCASTER	NORT04	LLOYD	WILL44	MARTIN	COWL08
LANCASTER	LEMO04	LONG	SERG08	MARTIN	BART10
LANE	HARC02	LONG	GERA12	MARTIN	ORRE02
LANE	BOWE06	LONT de	BROW36	MARTIN	ONIO02
LANE	HARC06	LOSTOCK	HOLF02	MARTINEZ	SMIT03
LANE	MEND02	LOVE	MEND02	MASON	MUND02
LANE	HIND02	LOVELADY	JONE36	MASON	FREE10
LANE	GRIM18	LOVELL	SOUT06	MASON	JENN12
LANGLEY	HODG22	LOVELL	GOTH02	MASSEY	STAN30
LANGLEY	HODG10	LOWE	MEND02	MASSINGHAM	INGR08
LANGTON	BRID04	LUCAS	AYRO02	MATTHEWS	NUTT04

Alias	Code	Alias	Code	Alias	Code
MATTHEWS	SWIN 16	MOORE	WHIT 84	NEVILLE	SCAR 10
MATTHEWS	MATA 02	MORE	ALBE 04	NEVILLE	SCAR 04
MAUDSLEY	TURN 32	MORE	BOUR 04	NEVILLE	MEYN 08
MAURICE	PLUM 02	MORE	MOSS 02	NEVILLE	PALM 14
MAURIQUE	CRES 08	MORE	ENGL 10	NEVILLE	SCAR 08
MAWDESLEY	CART 06	MORE	VAUD 02	NEVILLE	SCAR 16
MAXFIELD	JAKE 02	MORE	HODG 38	NEWMAN	SCOT 10
MAXFIELD	DORR 06	MORE	WHIT 84	NEWMAN	NAYL 02
MAXFIELD	ARRO 02	MORE	APPL 10	NEWMAN	EVER 16
MAXFIELD	MELL 06	MORE	BELF 02	NEWPORT	KEYN 04
MAXFIELD	JAKE 04	MORE	LUSH 04	NEWPORT	JENN 04
MAYNARD	GADB 02	MORE	SAND 02	NEWPORT	JENN 15
MAYNARD	CUFF 10	MORE	HOUG 04	NEWPORT	KEYN 18
MAYNARD	MAYL 02	MORGAN	JONE 40	NEWPORT	JENN 10
MCCONNER	CORN 08	MORGAN	PRIC 44	NEWTON	NORR 20
MCMAHON	CORN 08	MORGAN	NEED 16	NICHOLS	POSS 02
MELDRUM	BAIL 06	MORGAN	CASE 06	NICHOLS	BOUR 04
MENDOZA	BEDI 16	MORGAN	PARR 22	NICHOLSON	MACZ 04
MENTISSE	NORT 08	MORGAN	POWE 20	NICHOLSON	TAYL 14
MENTISSE	NORT 06	MORGAN	POUL 06	NICHOLSON	SWEE 04
MERE	PORM 02	MORLAND	WILS 04	NORRIS	CLIF 10
MEREDITH	EVAN 26	MORLEY	MASO 02	NORRIS	READ 08
MERRIMAN	WAKE 02	MORLEY	WILS 04	NORRIS	TUCK 02
METCALFE	HEBB 04	MORNE	THOR 28	NORTH	HOLT 12
METCALFE	LEIG 10	MORRIS	PAGE 08	NORTH	JONE 42
METCALFE	JENK 12	MOSSON	MOST 04	NORTON	CLAR 17
METCALFE	RAWL 06	MOSTYN	PENN 06	NORTON	KNAT 02
METHAM	HARR 02	MOTHERSALL	WELL 02	NORWOOD	HANS 08
METHAM	CLAX 04	MOUNTFORD	ARMS 06	NOWELL	RISH 06
METHAM	GORS 04	MOYLAN	BARN 30	NUGENT	BERM 04
MEYNELL	BARL 08	MOYSES	WHIT 02	O'MAHONY	CORN 08
MEYNELL	GASC 14	MULLINS	BEES 08	OGLE	GREE 10
MEYNELL	TODD 04	MUMFORD	ARMS 06	OGLETHORPE	PAVI 02
MEYNELL	TODD 02	MUMFORD	DOWN 04	OKELEY	SAND 34
MEYNELL	TODD 06	MUMFORD	TANC 04	OLDCROFT	RICH 20
MIDDLEMERE	GOOD 20	MUNSON	ANDE 08	ORMES	CHAL 02
MIDDLETON	GRAD 06	MUNSON	MART 26	OSBALDSTONE	EGER 02
MIDDLETON	GOLD 12	MUSCOTE	FISH 06	OWEN	REES 02
MIDDLETON	MASS 14	MUSGRAVE	HILT 02	PALMER	THWI 08
MIDDLETON	THOR 10	MUSKET	FISH 06	PALMER	COOP 18
MIDDLETON	STRI 06	NAILER	FILC 02	PALMER	IPSL 02
MIDDLETON	METC 08	NANFAN	WILL 54	PALMER	POUL 08
MIDFORD	FORC 04	NATEBY	SALT 02	PALMER	POUL 22
MILBET	STOC 02	NAYLOR	HESK 18	PALMER	BOSV 02
MILBURN	HARP 04	NEALE	KENT 02	PALMER	POUL 04
MILDMAY	WALD 10	NEALE	RAWL 02	PALMER	THWI 06
MILDMAY	BLOU 11	NEEDHAM	HITC 02	PALMER	BETH 04
MILLS	SHAF 04	NELSON	GERA 12	PALMER	DIBD 02
MILWARD	MILL 02	NELSON	BEES 06	PALMER	POUL 16
MIN	DAYA 04	NELSON	JACK 18	PALMER	PLAS 02
MINSHALL	CONY 10	NELSON	METC 18	PALMER	POUL 14
MISSENDON	MADD 02	NELSON	NEIL 04	PALMER	LEGG 02
MITFORD	GARD 08	NELSON	NEVI 04	PALMER	POUL 20
MITFORD	GARD 18	NELSON	PORT 10	PALMER	PORT 12
MITFORD	FORC 04	NELSON	NEWT 04	PARKER	ALMO 08
MOHUN	CORN 08	NEVILLE	SALE 10	PARKER	OLDC 02
MOLLINS	BEES 08	NEVILLE	SCAR 12	PARKER	BUCK 02
MOLYNEUX	PANS 02	NEVILLE	APPL 18	PARKER	CULC 02
MOLYNEUX	WILK 16	NEVILLE	SALE 02	PARKER	WALD 04
MOLYNEUX	ALMO 06	NEVILLE	MATT 14	PARKER	APPL 02
MONINGTON	PROS 02	NEVILLE	SCAR 02	PARKER	SPRO 02
MONNINGTON	WILL 34	NEVILLE	COTT 16	PARKER	CULC 04
MONSON	ANDE 08	NEVILLE	SALE 04	PARKER	FLET 10
MONTFORD	DOWN 04	NEVILLE	SCAR 06	PARKER	THOM 14
MONTFORD	MILE 02	NEVILLE	SCAR 18	PARKER	CULC 08
MOORE	MONK 04	NEVILLE	HAWK 02	PARKER	HEAT 16

221

Alias	Code	Alias	Code	Alias	Code
PARKER	BEES08	PLAYLE	WALD10	RAWSON	BRIT04
PARKER	BURT02	PLOWDEN	BRYO02	READE	SELB10
PARKER	FULW02	PLOWDEN	DEAN03	READING	BAMB02
PARKINSON	HUDD12	POINES	NIXO02	REDIATE	WHIT94
PARR	BARK01	POLE	FOXE01	REILLY	PAIN06
PARR	MORE05	POLE	JEFF08	REMINGTON	CLAR14
PARRY	SALI04	POLE	ANDE48	REVEL	BROW30
PARRY	CONW02	POLE	WALF02	REYMIREZ	MART10
PARRY	HAYN02	POLEWHEEL	WARH04	REYNOLDS	GREE52
PARRY	ROGE02	POLLARD	GIBB08	REYNOLDS	BLOU11
PARRY	PRIC35	POLLARD	SHAR02	RICH	WALP06
PASSELAW	BEES04	POLLET	DAVI10	RICH	DIDE02
PATRICK	CAMP04	POOLE	FOXE01	RICHARDS	PLOW16
PAUL	CURR06	POOLE	PIER08	RICHARDSON	SHUT08
PAULET	THIM06	POOLE	BIRK04	RICHARDSON	GERA16
PAULET	CHEN02	POOLE	BIRK02	RICHARDSON	CAPE10
PAUPER	WALP06	PORT	LAYT08	RICHARDSON	JOHN20
PEARCE	HAYM02	PORT	LAYT02	RICHARDSON	BENS02
PEARSON	ATHE04	PORTER	CORB12	RICHARDSON	WATT02
PELHAM	WALD06	PORTER	WHAL22	RICHARDSON	PARS12
PELHAM	WARR12	POTTER	STRA10	RICHARDSON	SALE10
PELHAM	WARR20	POTTER	STAF12	RICHMOND	WAFE02
PELHAM	FAIR04	POTTER	STAF16	RIDDELL	NEVI06
PEMBERTON	KELL10	POULTON	MORG22	RIDING	BAMB02
PENDRILL	HOWE06	POWELL	CADW02	RIGBY	HOLT02
PENDRILL	HOWE04	POWELL	CLAR12	RIGBY	WALT08
PENDRILL	HEAL02	POYNTZ	NIXO02	RIGBY	ARRO02
PERCIVAL	PANS02	PRANNELL	QUIN08	RIGBY	MORL04
PERCY	INGL08	PRATT	ELLI12	RIGBY	BARR06
PERCY	JOHN06	PRESTON	EDWA10	RIGGE	EDNE02
PERCY	SLIN02	PRICE	EVAN14	RINGBY	STEP18
PEREGRINE	SHOR06	PRICE	JONE48	RISLEY	BEES06
PERKINS	OLDC02	PRICE	PUGH08	RISLEY	HAUG02
PERKINS	HAWK16	PRICE	SCUD08	RIVERS	BURS02
PERROTT	PLOW04	PRICE	POYN08	RIVERS	PENK12
PERROTT	PLOW06	PRICE	BENN06	RIVERS	PENK02
PESTEL	PHIL34	PRICE	BABE02	RIVERS	SAVA02
PETER	HOLT06	PRICE	BRIA04	RIVERS	ABBO02
PETERS	WARM02	PRICE	WARR16	RIVERS	PENK06
PETERS	COLL02	PRICE	PORT20	RIVERS	WHIT70
PETERS	LALA02	PRICHARD	LEWI12	RIVERS	FLOY08
PETERSON	HAME08	PRICHARD	JONE32	RIVERS	PENK04
PETERSON	CURT04	PRICHARD	PLUM04	RIVERS	PENK10
PETERSON	CHAM16	PROCTOR	SHAW18	RIVETT	HARV06
PETRE	SQUI02	PROCTOR	METC20	ROBECK	LEFE02
PHELPS	SMIT52	PROSSER	POWE20	ROBERTS	BOSV04
PHILIPS	LUTL04	PROSSER	HALL14	ROBERTS	BLUN22
PHILIPS	WATK04	PRYCE	PORM02	ROBERTS	RICH40
PHILIPS	PUGH14	PUDSEY	PEAR14	ROBERTS	ARMS12
PHILIPS	STAF16	PUGH	JONE44	ROBERTS	BUSB12
PHILIPS	GARN08	PURSHALL	PHIL18	ROBERTS	POUL04
PHILIPS	CLIF08	QUARLEYS	MART04	ROBERTS	SWIN16
PHILIPS	WORT02	QUASHET	MAIT02	ROBERTS	GARN08
PHILIPS	COTT22	QUINTIN	BOUR06	ROBINSON	WHAL10
PHILIPS	GOLT02	RADCLIFFE	SHEP10	ROBINSON	KIGH02
PHILIPS	PUGH04	RADCLIFFE	BARL16	ROBINSON	ROBS02
PHIPPS	SMIT52	RADCLIFFE	BARL04	ROBINSON	CONS10
PIETRO	GIFF23	RADCLIFFE	MUSH02	ROBINSON	VEZZ02
PINCKARD	THOM06	RAILTON	WILS06	ROBINSON	VEZZ06
PINNINGTON	ASPI02	RAINES	WATS04	ROBINSON	WHAL18
PIPPARD	BROW14	RAMIRER	MART10	ROBINSON	DOWN02
PITTS	ATWO02	RAND	WATS04	ROBINSON	RISH08
PLACE	CONS12	RANDALL	BLOU11	ROBINSON	VEZZ04
PLANTIN	PLAT06	RANDALL	LEWI08	ROBINSON	WHAL14
PLANTIN	PLAT04	RATHWELL	EXLE02	ROBINSON	WHAL16
PLATT	NEED06	RAWLEY	ROOK14	ROBINSON	LOVE14

222

Alias	Code	Alias	Code	Alias	Code
ROBINSON	ROOK 12	SAVAGE	TRAV 04	SIMONS	PLOW 04
ROBINSON	APPL 04	SAVAGE	GRAC 02	SIMONS	PLOW 06
ROBINSON	BEVE 08	SAVAGE	SWIN 04	SIMONS	NANC 02
ROBINSON	ABER 04	SAVILLE	WHIC 02	SIMONS	DAWS 06
ROCHESTER	ROGE 16	SAVILLE	HEWE 02	SIMONS	PLOW 02
RODNEY	ROBI 12	SAVILLE	SMIT 58	SIMPSON	HILD 06
ROE	NORR 14	SAVILLE	PLOW 16	SIMPSON	HODG 14
ROELS	ROUS 10	SAWYER	GARN 22	SIMPSON	SAMP 02
ROELS	ROUS 08	SAYER	GARN 22	SIMPSON	BENL 02
ROGERS	CADW 04	SCARGILL	TUNS 06	SIMPSON	KIRK 02
ROGERS	MANB 02	SCARISBRICK	COTT 16	SIMPSON	TORB 02
ROGERS	FLOY 08	SCARISBRICK	PLEA 02	SIMS	BOOT 10
ROGERS	POWE 22	SCOTT	LAIT 06	SINGLETON	WADD 02
ROLFE	ROEA 04	SCOTT	KING 02	SINGLETON	MORG 04
ROLFE	ROEA 02	SCRIMSHAW	SKIN 16	SINGLETON	SWAR 02
ROOKWOOD	GARN 22	SCRIMSHAW	SKIN 12	SINGLETON	SAND 24
ROPER	SCUD 04	SCROOP	ANDE 34	SKEVINGTON	AINS 07
ROPER	STON 15	SCROOP	HART 18	SKIDMORE	HILL 12
ROSE	ROOK 08	SCROOP	HART 04	SLAUGHTER	WEBS 04
ROSS	RISH 08	SCROOP	METC 20	SLYFIELD	NEWM 02
ROSS	ROEA 02	SCROPE	HART 04	SMALL	WILL 74
ROSS	ROEA 04	SCROPE	HART 18	SMALLEY	WILL 74
ROTHWELL	RIGM 02	SCUDADMORE	JONE 28	SMALLMAN	JOHN 08
ROUSE	BROU 02	SEABORN	CLAR 12	SMELT	ARCH 04
ROUSE	ROWS 02	SEABORN	CASE 02	SMITH	SKIN 10
ROWE	HAYE 02	SEABORN	CLAR 10	SMITH	FLOY 08
ROWLAND	CROS 06	SEATON	HOWA 30	SMITH	KITC 01
ROWLEY	NUTT 10	SEBASTIAN	NORR 18	SMITH	OWEN 04
ROYDON	BROW 31	SEDDON	JAME 08	SMITH	BRAD 06
RUDD	WIVE 02	SEFTON	WORT 24	SMITH	DARE 03
RUDDELL	NEVI 06	SEFTON	WORT 12	SMITH	NEWP 04
RUSSELL	BULL 14	SELBY	JANI 02	SMITH	SOUT 16
RUSSELL	NAPP 04	SELBY	PARS 02	SMITH	CALD 06
RUSSELL	LACE 01	SHARP	STUA 02	SMITH	LUDD 02
RUSSELL	RAVE 02	SHARP	GUNS 02	SMITH	PORT 22
RUTTER	BANI 04	SHAW	ROBI 52	SMITH	WINC 02
RYDER	WILL 80	SHAW	WOOD 20	SMITH	BABT 04
SACKEVERELL	POUL 36	SHEFFIELD	ANDE 12	SMITH	BABT 12
SACKVILLE	POUL 36	SHELDON	ELLI 04	SMITH	GERA 18
SALISBURY	PLOW 20	SHELLEY	BETH 02	SMITH	GR1F 28
SALISBURY	SUTT 10	SHELLEY	ANDE 20	SMITH	HOLM 10
SALISBURY	SUTT 06	SHELLEY	LEWI 26	SMITH	HUNT 20
SALISBURY	SUTT 16	SHELLEY	ANDE 32	SMITH	BEDF 02
SALISBURY	KEMY 02	SHEPHERD	PRAN 04	SMITH	BOLT 02
SALMAN	ALDR 06	SHEPHERD	CRAT 12	SMITH	PARK 26
SALVIN	BIRK 08	SHEPHERD	PRAN 02	SMITH	PROB 02
SALVIN	CONS 24	SHERBURN	ISHE 02	SMITH	SALV 04
SALVIN	HUTT 14	SHERBURN	WALM 14	SMITH	SIME 02
SAMFORD	DUCK 12	SHERBURN	TAYL 36	SMITH	TURV 02
SAMUEL	TURN 04	SHERBURN	IRVI 02	SMITH	BLAC 16
SANDERS	ABER 04	SHERRINGTON	SHER 40	SMITH	PERC 14
SANDERS	FROM 02	SHERRINGTON	SHER 42	SMITH	RIGM 06
SANDERS	BESW 02	SHIPMAN	CAPE 10	SMITH	PORT 24
SANDERSON	HOLL 16	SHIRLEY	HUDD 10	SMITH	SCUP 02
SANDERSON	POUL 04	SIDDLE	HODG 04	SMITH	BABT 10
SANDERSON	SHUT 06	SIDLEY	WISE 02	SMITH	EVER 08
SANDFORD	JENI 06	SIGLEY	WISE 04	SMITH	NORR 20
SANDFORD	HUDD 11	SILESDON	BEDI 10	SMITH	SERG 04
SANDFORD	SALE 04	SIMCOCKS	MANN 04	SMITH	THOR 10
SANDS	GAUN 06	SIMEON	PLOW 16	SMITH	THWA 02
SANDS	MADG 02	SIMEON	PLOW 02	SMITH	BABT 08
SANDS	GAUN 02	SIMEON	PLOW 06	SMITH	PORT 24
SANDYS	WIGN 02	SIMEON	LOBB 02	SMITH	POLE 02
SANMAN	LANM 02	SIMEON	BRUN 12	SMITH	RIGM 04
SAVAGE	CALD 06	SIMONDS	FLOY 08	SMITHSON	STUK 04
SAVAGE	CODN 02	SIMONS	JUKE 02	SMITHSON	JACK 14

Alias	Code	Alias	Code	Alias	Code
SNOWDEN	CECI02	STRANGE	ARMS08	THOMPSON	HAWK04
SOLMON	ALDR06	STRANGUISH	HART12	THOMPSON	JENI10
SOMMERWELL	HONN02	STRATFORD	LECH02	THOMPSON	BARN04
SOPHIA	WISE02	STREET	RIGB08	THOMPSON	BUTL22
SOUTHWELL	BACO02	STREET	COPE04	THOMPSON	CHEN02
SOUTHWELL	BACO06	STRODE	GREE72	THOMPSON	COXO02
SOUTHWELL	BACO08	STRONG	KELL10	THOMPSON	GERA12
SOUTHWELL	BACO04	STROUD	GREE72	THOMPSON	JOLL02
SOUTHWORTH	ARRO02	STUMER	NEED12	THOMPSON	PLOT04
SPENCE	WARW02	STYCKE	BRID06	THOMPSON	SAND26
SPENCER	POUL36	SUGAR	MORG16	THOMPSON	BUTL13
SPENCER	PETR04	SUTTON	SCRI02	THORNBOROUGH	GAUN06
SPENCER	HOLT12	SUTTON	SUTC02	THORNE	WALP12
SPENCER	BAGS06	SUTTON	COWL02	THORNTON	BLAC10
SPENCER	MAIN10	SUTTON	SULY02	THORNTON	FORS06
SPENCER	ADAM00	SUTVILL	EAST12	THORNTON	LEHU04
SPENCER	WARR18	SWARBRICK	EDIS08	THOROLD	KNIG16
SPENCER	CHAR06	SWEET	LANE10	THORPE	STAF12
SPENCER	PETR18	SWEET	MERI02	THORPE	MAST02
ST GEORGE	ROGE02	SWEET	SUGA02	THROCKMORTON	THOM44
ST LEGER	CHAP19	SWINBURNE	OGLE04	THWINGE	VAVA10
ST LEGER	CHAP22	SWINNERTON	STRA06	TICHBORNE	SHEL26
STAFFORD	BADD02	SYDALL	HODG04	TICHBORNE	BLOU08
STAFFORD	KELL16	SYMONS	LOBB02	TICHBORNE	TASB02
STAFFORD	STAN16	TALBOT	GORS02	TICKLE	MOLY08
STALIE	SHER24	TALBOT	KENN06	TILNEY	GREE68
STAMFORD	DALL02	TALBOT	EVER20	TIPPER	PINC02
STANDISH	GERA12	TALBOT	WATE02	TOLSON	BRAI08
STANFIELD	PIPP02	TALBOT	DAYA04	TOOTELL	WHAL20
STANFORD	DALL02	TALBOT	GROS04	TOVEY	WRIG10
STANFORD	ANDE40	TALBOT	FORT04	TOWN	STON10
STANHOPE	BANK06	TALMAN	MORE05	TOWNELEY	MADG02
STANLEY	SAYE04	TANFIELD	RADF02	TOWNSEND	PRAN02
STANLEY	BIDD02	TANKARD	YAXL06	TOWNSEND	ROOK12
STANLEY	MINS02	TANSFIELD	GERA12	TRAFFORD	SCOB02
STANLEY	PETI02	TAPPIN	HELM04	TRANSAM	TYAS04
STANLEY	SING08	TARLTON	SMIT26	TRAVAGAN	BLAC18
STANLEY	DRUR06	TAYLOR	WILF04	TRAVERS	HAUG02
STANLEY	KNIG12	TAYLOR	GARD22	TRAVIS	WEAT02
STANLEY	LAYT10	TAYLOR	HARR30	TREGWETHAN	HAMB02
STANLEY	LATH12	TAYLOR	LEWK04	TREMAIN	HARR54
STANLEY	BODE04	TAYLOR	ROBI40	TRISTRAM	CROS24
STANNOP	FORC04	TAYLOR	WILF06	TUFTON	STRU02
STANTER	STAN02	TAYLOR	JOHN34	TUNSTALL	SHER10
STANTON	SHAC02	TEMPE	SMIT65	TUNSTALL	SHER12
STAPLETON	FOWL05	TEMPEST	TODK02	TUNSTALL	ERRI04
STAPLETON	CLAV02	TEMPEST	HARD12	TUNSTALL	SHER14
STAPLETON	WALK14	TEMPEST	HARD10	TURNER	SHIM04
STARKEY	WHIT04	TEMPLE	THOM50	TURNER	THOR18
STARKEY	GERA12	TERRETT	BRAD38	TURNER	ALDR04
STARKEY	WHIT08	TERRETT	BABT12	TURNER	SMIT39
STAUNTON	GERA12	THIMELBY	THOM28	TURNER	MARS27
STAVELEY	BRAN02	THIRKILL	DUFF02	TURNER	WHIT12
STEPHENS	STUA00	THOMAS	BRYC02	TURNER	BALL12
STEPHENS	POYN06	THOMPSON	WILK02	TURNER	HILL10
STEPHENSON	GILP06	THOMPSON	WOOD50	TURNER	FARL02
STEPHENSON	LEEA24	THOMPSON	OVER02	TURNER	MURP10
STEPHENSON	LAYT10	THOMPSON	SMIT32	TURRET	BABT12
STILLINGTON	BILC02	THOMPSON	BALL12	TWEEDLE	METC16
STOKES	ENGL06	THOMPSON	KEMP02	TWISDEN	CHET02
STONE	STON10	THOMPSON	PRAT06	TWISDEN	EVIS02
STONE	COXI02	THOMPSON	SOUT24	TYLECOTE	EDWA14
STOURTON	COOK04	THOMPSON	GERA08	TYRELL	BONV02
STRANGE	ARMS14	THOMPSON	WOOD16	TYRWHITT	SPEN06
STRANGE	HART12	THOMPSON	CALD04	TYRWHITT	BABT12
STRANGE	ARMS12	THOMPSON	BUXT04	TYRWHITT	THOM21

Alias	Code	Alias	Code	Alias	Code
TYRWHITT	BABT 14	WARHAM	SMIT 63	WHITGIFT	PORM 02
UDALL	BLOU 11	WARING	BARR 48	WHITLEY	WRIG 24
UNDERHILL	POUL 28	WARNER	BEER 02	WHITMORE	POST 02
UNDERHILL	PLUN 01	WARNER	BRAB 02	WHITMORE	SABR 02
UNDERHILL	PLUN 04	WARNER	WALP 04	WILFORD	CLAR 10
UNDERWOOD	CORN 10	WARREN	SKIN 10	WILKES	HOLT 14
UPSALL	ROBI 28	WASHINGTON	GREE 32	WILKINS	SMIT 32
VANDERHAGEN	CROW 04	WATERS	STEP 24	WILKINSON	FLET 14
VAUGHAN	PRIC 03	WATERS	DUVI 02	WILKINSON	LIVE 04
VAUGHAN	SOME 06	WATKINS	JONE 08	WILKS	THOM 26
VAUGHAN	WATK 02	WATSON	POST 02	WILLARD	CHAL 06
VAUGHAN	HALL 14	WATSON	ADAM 10	WILLEC	STRA 08
VEALE	WELL 06	WATSON	WIDD 08	WILLIAMS	PETR 16
VENABLES	HEMI 02	WATSON	DANI 18	WILLIAMS	LEWK 06
VENABLES	GOTH 02	WATSON	GRIF 26	WILLIAMS	PETR 18
VERE	HODG 28	WATTS	GRAY 10	WILLIAMS	ROMS 02
VERNALTY	BARK 04	WEBB	WALL 04	WILLIAMS	VAUG 06
VERTUE	WEST 14	WEBB	SMIT 09	WILLIAMS	ABER 02
VILLIERS	FITZ 21	WEBB	THRE 02	WILLIAMS	GITT 02
VINCAM	PHIL 28	WEBB	PECK 02	WILLIAMS	MATT 12
VINCENT	PRES 14	WEBSTER	THOM 10	WILLIAMS	VICT 04
VINCENT	CARP 06	WEEDON	TURN 18	WILLIAMS	FLOY 10
VINCENT	OLDC 02	WEEDON	PLOW 20	WILLIAMS	WELL 08
VINCENT	YATE 04	WELBURY	TROL 02	WILLIAMS	HACO 02
WADE	YEKE 02	WELBY	DICK 06	WILLIAMS	BEAU 07
WAKE	MERR 02	WELDON	HUNT 30	WILLIAMS	WILL 82
WAKE	SMIT 56	WELDON	HEWE 02	WILLIAMS	FITZ 24
WAKE	MERR 04	WELLS	BARR 29	WILLIAMS	MATT 06
WAKELEY	BROW 13	WENHAM	WARE 02	WILLIAMSON	STAF 04
WAKEMAN	HIND 06	WENTWORTH	PETT 06	WILLIAMSON	WEED 06
WAKEMAN	JEFF 10	WEST	EAST 01	WILLIAMSON	BUTT 04
WALDEGRAVE	TIMC 02	EST	MORE 12	WILLIS	BENW 02
WALDEGRAVE	DUDL 02	WEST	BOST 04	WILLOUGHBY	LANC 02
WALGRAVE	TIMC 02	WEST	EAST 00	WILMOT	TEMP 14
WALKER	SWAR 08	WEST	WARN 08	WILMOT	QUAT 02
WALKER	WALK 02	WEST	DANI 18	WILSON	TATL 06
WALKER	GIFF 16	WEST	EAST 08	WILSON	FOST 23
WALKER	LAMB 06	WESTBROOK	SHAW 10	WILSON	LEGA 08
WALKER	BENT 12	WESTBY	BILL 08	WILSON	WATK 14
WALKER	BENT 14	WESTBY	GREE 29	WILSON	LONG 16
WALKER	GIFF 18	WESTCOTE	LITT 02	WILSON	MIDD 12
WALKER	PRAT 06	WETHERBY	BROW 31	WILSON	MORR 20
WALKER	WEST 10	WHARTON	STRI 10	WILSON	SOME 02
WALKER	BENT 08	WHARTON	FOST 26	WILSON	LONG 14
WALLER	WEBS 04	WHATLEY	BROW 13	WIMBUSH	NORT 10
WALLES	RICH 10	WHEATLEY	ARNO 08	WINDSOR	SCRO 04
WALLEY	MOLY 02	WHEELER	WOOD 22	WINN	PARR 08
WALLIS	RICH 10	WHITBY	SHEL 24	WINTER	LEYB 02
WALLIS	HARR 44	WHITE	BRAD 36	WINTER	MORG 40
WALLIS	CLAR 15	WHITE	PETR 02	WINTER	MILD 06
WALMESLEY	CALD 08	WHITE	PORM 02	WITMORE	SABR 02
WALMESLEY	PLEA 04	WHITE	GAGE 04	WOOD	HASE 04
WALMESLEY	INGH 04	WHITE	OXEN 02	WOOLRICH	BERI 12
WALSH	RICH 10	WHITE	FLOY 16	WORSLEY	GILD 08
WALTERS	BLOU 10	WHITE	GAGE 12	WORSLEY	BYFL 02
WALTON	BLAC 24	WHITE	WRIG 32	WORSLEY	BYFL 06
WALTON	DODD 06	WHITE	JACK 24	WORSLEY	GILD 04
WALWIN	ASHT 10	WHITE	RIGB 08	WORSLEY	VAUD 02
WANSFORD	YORK 02	WHITE	WHIT 14	WORSLEY	BYFL 04
WARBURTON	STAR 02	WHITE	WOOD 31	WORTH	HOLT 12
WARD	MORS 02	WHITE	MART 36	WORTH	WOOD 34
WARD	TATL 08	WHITE	GIFF 10	WORTHINGTON	NEWS 02
WARD	PARR 16	WHITE	JERN 10	WORTHINGTON	BALL 02
WARD	WEBS 04	WHITE	PRIC 36	WORTHINGTON	SEFT 04
WARD	ROGE 12	WHITELOCK	WHIT 70	WORTHINGTON	BALL 08
WARHAM	SMIT 38	WHITFIELD	LAWS 06	WORTHINGTON	BAMB 06

225

ALIAS INDEX BY CODE NUMBERS

Code	Alias	Code	Alias	Code	Alias
ABBO 02	ASHTON	ARMS 06	MOUNTFORD	BALE 02	MALLETT
ABBO 02	RIVERS	ARMS 06	MUMFORD	BALL 02	WORTHINGTON
ABER 02	WILLIAMS	ARMS 08	ALANSON	BALL 08	WORTHINGTON
ABER 04	SANDERS	ARMS 08	STRANGE	BALL 10	WORTHINGTON
ABER 04	ROBINSON	ARMS 12	STRANGE	BALL 12	THOMPSON
ACTO 05	EDWARDS	ARMS 12	ROBERTS	BALL 12	FORTESCUE
ADAM 00	SPENCER	ARMS 14	STRANGE	BALL 12	TURNER
ADAM 00	HACON	ARNO 08	WHEATLEY	BAMB 02	RIDING
ADAM 02	YOUNG	ARNO 08	AUDLEY	BAMB 02	HELMES
ADAM 10	WATSON	ARRO 02	SOUTHWORTH	BAMB 02	READING
ADDI 03	ALISON	ARRO 02	MAXFIELD	BAMB 06	WORTHINGTON
ADDI 03	ALANSON	ARRO 02	RIGBY	BAMF 02	BATES
ADDI 04	HILDRETH	ARRO 02	BRADSHAW	BANI 04	RUTTER
AINS 07	SKEVINGTON	ASHT 10	WALWIN	BANK 02	HEATON
AKER 02	LINCOLN	ASHT 16	DU PUY	BANK 06	STANHOPE
ALBE 04	MORE	ASKE 06	BROWN	BARD 02	DENNY
ALCO 02	GAGE	ASPI 02	PINNINGTON	BARK 01	PARR
ALDI 02	CARTRICK	ASPI 04	BRENT	BARK 04	VERNALTY
ALDI 02	CRACKMORE	ASPI 06	BRENT	BARK 18	LAMBERT
ALDR 04	TURNER	ASPI 08	BRENT	BARL 04	BRERETON
ALDR 06	SALMAN	ASTL 02	ALEGAMBE	BARL 04	RADCLIFFE
ALDR 06	SOLMON	ATHE 04	PEARSON	BARL 08	MEYNELL
ALFI 02	BADGER	ATKI 13	LINCOLN	BARL 16	RADCLIFFE
ALLE 14	LANCASTER	ATWO 02	PITTS	BARN 04	THOMPSON
ALLI 02	FORD	AYLW 05	JONES	BARN 30	COOLEY
ALMO 06	MOLYNEUX	AYLW 06	HARCOURT	BARN 30	MOYLAN
ALMO 06	LATHAM	AYRA 02	WRIGHT	BARN 40	HOLLAND
ALMO 08	PARKER	AYRO 02	JUSTINIANI	BARO 02	BURTON
ALMO 08	ANDREWS	AYRO 02	LUCAS	BARR 06	RIGBY
AMIA 02	ANNE	BABE 02	PRICE	BARR 26	MARTIN
ANDE 08	MONSON	BABT 04	SMITH	BARR 27	LARGE
ANDE 08	MUNSON	BABT 08	SMITH	BARR 29	WELLS
ANDE 12	SHEFFIELD	BABT 10	SMITH	BARR 34	DAVIES
ANDE 14	CARRINGTON	BABT 12	TYRWHITT	BARR 48	HARCOURT
ANDE 18	ASHLEY	BABT 12	SMITH	BARR 48	WARING
ANDE 20	SHELLEY	BABT 12	TURRET	BARR 48	HARRISON
ANDE 32	SHELLEY	BABT 12	TERRETT	BARR 50	HARDING
ANDE 34	SCROOP	BABT 14	TYRWHITT	BART 10	CHARNOCK
ANDE 40	STANFORD	BACK 02	BASSET	BART 10	MARTIN
ANDE 47	ASHTON	BACO 02	SOUTHWELL	BART 12	ANDREWS
ANDE 48	POLE	BACO 04	SOUTHWELL	BART 12	AUDREY
ANTR 04	MANN	BACO 06	SOUTHWELL	BART 18	BARVILLE
APPL 02	PARKER	BACO 08	SOUTHWELL	BART 24	GERARD
APPL 04	ROBINSON	BADD 02	STAFFORD	BARW 02	JOHNSON
APPL 10	MORE	BADD 02	COMBERFORD	BATE 02	HEADLAM
APPL 13	HANNAN	BADD 02	LEE	BATE 04	BATT
APPL 18	NEVILLE	BAGS 06	SPENCER	BATE 04	BATTY
APPL 20	YATES	BAIL 06	MELDRUM	BATT 04	BREATHER
ARAY 02	MARTIN	BAIN 06	BLACON	BAYA 02	HYDE
ARAY 02	COTTON	BAIN 06	BLACKLOW	BAYN 10	KNIGHT
ARCH 04	SMELT	BAIN 06	KENDALL	BAZI 02	GRIMES
ARCH 12	GROVE	BAKE 08	BRAMHALL	BEAD 04	BREADNALL
ARCH 14	GROVE	BAKE 08	BALL	BEAU 07	WILLIAMS
ARDE 04	COLE	BALE 02	EVERS	BEAU 08	HARCOURT

Code	Alias	Code	Alias	Code	Alias
BEDF02	SMITH	BLAC10	THORNTON	BREE06	HARRISON
BEDF02	BILLINGSLY	BLAC12	BENNET	BREN00	BROWN
BEDI10	SILESDON	BLAC16	SMITH	BRIA04	PRICE
BEDI16	MENDOZA	BLAC18	TRAVAGAN	BRID04	LANTON
BEER02	WARNER	BLAC24	WALTON	BRID04	LANGTON
BEES04	PASSELAW	BLAK02	CROSS	BRID06	STYCKE
BEES06	RISLEY	BLOU04	HAVARD	BRIT04	RAWSON
BEES06	NELSON	BLOU08	TICHBORNE	BROU02	CLAPHAM
BEES08	MULLINS	BLOU10	WALTERS	BROU02	ROUSE
BEES08	MOLLINS	BLOU11	RANDALL	BROW01	CARRUTHERS
BEES08	PARKER	BLOU11	MANN	BROW13	WHATLEY
BEES15	HILL	BLOU11	UDALL	BROW13	WAKELEY
BELF02	MORE	BLOU11	BLOND	BROW14	PIPPARD
BELF04	EGERTON	BLOU11	REYNOLDS	BROW30	REVEL
BENL02	SIMPSON	BLOU11	BASSET	BROW31	WETHERBY
BENN04	BREWER	BLOU11	MILDMAY	BROW31	ROYDON
BENN04	COOK	BLOU11	DAGGERS	BROW32	DAY
BENN04	FARINGTON	BLUE04	COLLINS	BROW36	LONT de
BENN06	PRICE	BLUN22	ROBERTS	BRUE02	ALANSON
BENN06	BAKER	BLUN22	CAMPION	BRUE02	ALISON
BENN06	FLOYD	BLUN24	CHONE	BRUL02	BRADLEY
BENN08	DAVIES	BLUN24	ESON	BRUN08	HYDE
BENN09	GOSLING	BLUN26	BORDE	BRUN12	SIMEON
BENN14	BAINES	BLYT01	COURTNEY	BRUN14	GRIMSDITCH
BENS02	RICHARDSON	BODE04	STANLEY	BRUN14	HYDE
BENS06	CANFIELD	BODE06	BASKERVILLE	BRYC02	THOMAS
BENS06	HUNT	BOLT02	SMITH	BRYO02	PLOWDEN
BENT08	WALKER	BOLT05	MACINTOSH	BUCK02	PARKER
BENT12	WALKER	BOLT06	JOHNSON	BULL14	RUSSELL
BENT14	WALKER	BOND02	BUN	BURK02	LUCAS
BENT16	BENNET	BONV02	TYRELL	BURS02	RIVERS
BENW02	WILLIS	BOOT02	BROWN	BURT02	PARKER
BERE02	CLOD	BOOT04	BARLOW	BURT06	DAMAR
BERI06	HARPER	BOOT10	SIMS	BUSB01	BROWN
BERI12	WOOLRICH	BOOT14	BROWN	BUSB02	BROWN
BERM02	DARCY	BOST02	HAREKLEY	BUSB12	ROBERTS
BERM04	NUGENT	BOST04	WEST	BUTL02	CROSS
BERR08	BUTLER	BOST06	BARON	BUTL06	BROWN
BERR10	HILLS	BOSV02	PALMER	BUTL08	BANISTER
BESW02	SANDERS	BOSV04	ROBERTS	BUTL10	ELLISON
BETH02	SHELLEY	BOUR02	BEESTON	BUTL13	THOMPSON
BETH04	PALMER	BOUR04	MORE	BUTL22	THOMPSON
BEVE08	ROBINSON	BOUR04	NICHOLS	BUTT04	HAUGHTON
BEWE02	ADAMS	BOUR06	QUINTIN	BUTT04	WILLIAMSON
BIDD02	STANLEY	BOWE06	LANE	BUXT04	THOMPSON
BIDD02	MARTIN	BOWK02	BUTLER	BUXT04	HANMER
BIDD02	COFFIN	BOWK02	BOUCHER	BYFL02	WORSLEY
BIDD04	FITTON	BOYC02	ARMSTRONG	BYFL04	WORSLEY
BIDD06	FITTON	BRAB02	WARNER	BYFL06	WORSLEY
BIDD08	FITTON	BRAD06	SMITH	BYRO02	HAYES
BILC02	STILLINGTON	BRAD12	BARWELL	CADW02	POWELL
BILL06	LAURENSON	BRAD14	BARTON	CADW02	ELMER
BILL08	WESTBY	BRAD16	BARTON	CADW02	ELMORE
BIRD02	MAHUN	BRAD18	BARTON	CADW04	ROGERS
BIRK02	POOLE	BRAD20	BARTON	CADW04	GREENWAYS
BIRK04	CATTERICK	BRAD22	BARTON	CALD04	FENWICK
BIRK04	POOLE	BRAD24	HANDFORD	CALD04	THOMPSON
BIRK08	HALL	BRAD34	EDWARDS	CALD06	SAVAGE
BIRK08	BIRKHEAD	BRAD34	GAMAGE	CALD06	SMITH
BIRK08	SALVIN	BRAD36	WHITE	CALD08	WALMESLEY
BIRK08	LAMBTON	BRAD38	TERRETT	CALV04	BAINES
BIRT02	CLAYTON	BRAI08	LAWSON	CALV04	BLUNDELL
BIRT08	HALLIWELL	BRAI08	TOLSON	CAMP04	PATRICK
BISH12	FALLOWES	BRAM02	BRAMLEY	CAMP04	CHARLTON
BISH14	CASELEY	BRAN02	HAWLEY	CAMP04	HASTINGS
BLAC04	CARY	BRAN02	STAVELEY	CANE02	BODWILL

Code	Alias	Code	Alias	Code	Alias
CANN06	HARWOOD	CLIF08	MANSELL	COWL02	BANISTER
CANS02	BARTON	CLIF10	NORRIS	COWL04	FISHER
CANS02	BENSON	CLOP02	GREEN	OWL06	BANISTER
CANS04	ASHTON	CLOU06	FOURNIERS	COWL08	MARTIN
CAPE10	SHIPMAN	CLOU08	BEALOT	COWL14	COLLINS
CAPE10	RICHARDSON	CLOU08	BLAKE	COWL14	COULINS
CARL02	COMPTON	CODN02	SAVAGE	COXI02	STONE
CARL03	COMPTON	CODR06	MAINWARING	COXO02	THOMPSON
CARL05	COMPTON	COFF06	BARNABY	COYN02	DRAYCOTT
CARL08	DOVINGTON	COKE02	COLFORD	CRAN04	BRIAN
CARL08	CHARLES	COKE04	COLFORD	CRAT12	YAXLEY
CARP06	VINCENT	COLE01	MACCAUGHWELL	CRAT12	SHEPHERD
CARP06	DACRE	COLE02	MARSH	CRES04	CLARK
CARP10	GROVE	COLE12	BUTLER	CRES08	MAURIQUE
CART06	MAWDESLEY	COLE20	COMBERFORD	CRIC02	GERARD
CART14	FAIRFAX	COLE20	COMBE	CRIC02	FOSTER
CARY18	CHARLTON	COLL02	COLLINGTON	CRIC04	FOSTER
CARY22	KELLY	COLL02	PETERS	CRIC06	FOSTER
CASE02	SEABORN	COLL24	ERRINGTON	CRIS02	CAREY
CASE06	MORGAN	COLL26	DURHAM	CRIS10	GILLOW
CASE08	BAXTER	COLL28	CLARK	CROO06	GREGSON
CATC02	BURTON	COLL30	BLUET	CROS02	ASCOUGH
CATE02	BERRY	COLL32	ASHTON	CROS02	ASQUITH
CATT14	HUDDLESTON	CONS10	ROBINSON	CROS06	ROWLAND
CATT16	HUDDLESTON	CONS12	PLACE	CROS08	BAINES
CECI02	SNOWDEN	CONS14	CATTERALL	CROS24	TRISTRAM
CHAD02	ELSTON	CONS15	LACEY	CROW04	BROUGHTON
CHAL02	ORMES	CONS24	SALVIN	CROW04	VANDERHAGEN
CHAL06	FISHER	CONW02	PARRY	CROW06	BROUGHTON
CHAL06	WILLARD	CONW04	WRIGHT	CUFF02	DAY
CHAL08	BASSET	CONY10	MINSHALL	CUFF06	LAMPTON
CHAM16	PETERSON	CONY18	BARRUM	CUFF06	COMPTON
CHAM28	FORRESTER	COOK04	STOURTON	CUFF10	MAYNARD
CHAP19	ST LEGER	COOP18	PALMER	CULC02	PARKER
CHAP22	ST LEGER	COPE04	STREET	CULC04	PARKER
CHAR04	HEIGHTON	COPL04	LUTTRELL	CULC08	PARKER
CHAR04	CHARLTON	COPL08	FISHER	CURR06	PAUL
CHAR06	SPENCER	COPP02	BROWNING	CURT04	PETERSON
CHAR10	MANLEY	CORB06	CRABAN	CURT08	COURTE de la
CHEN02	PAULET	CORB12	PORTER	CURZ02	CHILD
CHEN02	THOMPSON	CORB14	CARLINGTON	DAKI02	GREEN
CHES02	YATES	CORB14	CARLTON	DALL02	STANFORD
CHET02	TWISDEN	CORB18	CARLTON	DALL02	STAMFORD
CHUR06	DOWNHAM	CORB18	CARLINGTON	DALT02	ELLERKER
CLAR02	DOMINIC	CORB18	FLOWER	DALT04	BOOTH
CLAR10	SEABORN	CORB20	CARLINGTON	DANI02	BENNET
CLAR10	WILFORD	CORB20	FLOWER	DANI02	BARRET
CLAR12	SEABORN	CORB20	CARLTON	DANI18	WEST
CLAR12	POWELL	CORN08	O'MAHONY	DANI18	WATSON
CLAR14	REMINGTON	CORN08	MOHUN	DANI22	FOSTER
CLAR15	WALLIS	CORN08	MCMAHON	DANI22	FORSTER
CLAR17	NORTON	CORN08	MCCONNER	DANS02	DOUTHWAITE
CLAR24	FOWLER	CORN08	MAHUN	DARB04	ESCHAM
CLAV02	STAPLETON	CORN10	UNDERWOOD	DARB04	HAMPSHIRE
CLAV06	CONYERS	CORN10	BILTON	DARC04	ANGELINO
CLAX02	CLARKSON	COSI02	BAINES	DARE03	SMITH
CLAX04	METHAM	COSI02	BLAKISTON	DARE06	FOWLER
CLAY04	HANMER	COTT16	SCARISBRICK	DAVE02	HUNT
CLAY04	CHALLONER	COTT16	NEVILLE	DAVE02	COVENTRY
CLAY12	BERINGTON	COTT16	ESSEX	DAVE02	LATHROPPE
CLAY16	LEE	COTT18	BLOUNT	DAVI08	KIRK
CLAY18	BERINGTON	COTT20	FLETCHER	DAVI10	POLLET
CLAY20	LEE	COTT22	PHILIPS	DAVI10	BLOUNT
CLIF04	COWPER	COWB02	BUTLER	DAVI36	BENNET
CLIF04	JOHNSON	COWB04	JOHNSON	DAWS06	HUNT
CLIF08	PHILIPS	COWL02	SUTTON	DAWS06	DOUGHTY

Code	Alias	Code	Alias	Code	Alias
DAWS06	SIMONS	ELLI14	FLISK	FLEC04	JOHNSON
DAYA04	TALBOT	ELRI02	LUTTON	FLEE04	FLITUN
DAYA04	MIN	ELRI02	ELLIS	FLEE04	FLICHON
DEAN03	PLOWDEN	ELRI03	LUTTON	FLET02	BLACKNOLL
DEBO02	DAWSON	ELYA02	HAVARD	FLET02	BLACKWELL
DEBO02	DAVISON	EMER04	ELWICK	FLET09	BARTON
DIBD02	PALMER	ENGL06	STOKES	FLET10	PARKER
DICC02	EATON	ENGL10	MORE	FLET12	CARUS
DICK02	KEIGHLEY	ERRI04	TUNSTALL	FLET14	WILKINSON
DICK02	LAWRENCE	EURE02	EVERY	FLEU02	FORRESTER
DICK06	KINSON	EURE02	CLARE	FLOY08	SIMONDS
DICK06	LACEY	EURE04	EVERY	FLOY08	SMITH
DICK06	WELBY	EURE06	EVERY	FLOY08	RIVERS
DICK06	JOHNSON	EVAN08	ANDREWS	FLOY08	ROGERS
DIDE02	RICH	EVAN10	BROWN	FLOY10	WILLIAMS
DIGG06	HALL	EVAN14	PRICE	FLOY16	WHITE
DODD06	WALTON	EVAN16	HEWENS	FLOY17	FISHER
DONI02	DOMINGUEZ	EVAN26	MEREDITH	FOLL02	CHANCEY
DORM12	ANDERSON	EVAN28	BANKS	FORC04	STANNOP
DORR04	HEATH	EVEL02	EDWARDS	FORC04	MIDFORD
DORR06	MAXFIELD	EVER08	SMITH	FORC04	MITFORD
DOWN02	CORNELY	EVER16	NEWMAN	FORS06	THORNTON
DOWN02	ROBINSON	EVER20	TALBOT	FORT04	TALBOT
DOWN02	CLAPTON	EVER22	CATRICE	FORT10	BANKS
DOWN04	MUMFORD	EVIS02	TWISDEN	FOST02	DARCY
DOWN04	MONTFORD	EVIS02	JERSON	FOST06	CLARK
DOWN04	BEDINGFELD	EVIS02	BONHAM	FOST12	CHARNOCK
DRUR06	BEDFORD	EWEN02	KEYNES	FOST12	JACKSON
DRUR06	STANLEY	EXLE02	RATHWELL	FOST18	BERRY
DRUR08	BEDFORD	EXLE02	ERRINGTON	FOST20	GULLICK
DRYL02	BRINCKBORNE	EYRE06	EATON	FOST23	WILSON
DUCK08	GIRLINGTON	EYRE16	ALFORD	FOST23	DARCY
DUCK12	SAMFORD	FAIR02	EVANS	FOST26	WHARTON
DUDL02	WALDEGRAVE	FAIR04	PELHAM	FOST28	ANDERSON
DUFF01	LYONS	FAIR08	BECKETT	FOUR02	CLOUGH
DUFF02	THIRKILL	FANN02	CLIFTON	FOWL05	STAPLETON
DUNN04	CARR	FARL02	TURNER	FOWL06	GEOFFREY
DUNN14	EARPE	FARM01	DANBY	FOXE01	POLE
DUTT02	IRELAND	FARM04	BARKER	FOXE01	POOLE
DUVA02	BRIDGES	FARN04	FARINGTON	FRAI02	FINCH
DUVI02	WATERS	FATH02	GREEN	FRAN04	CAVE
EARP02	HART	FAUL02	DINGLEY	FRAN12	ARDINGTON
EARP02	DUNN	FAZA02	ASHTON	FREE02	JOHNSON
EAST00	WEST	FERM02	JERMYN	FREE10	MASON
EAST00	JERNINGHAM	FERM02	GERMIN	FROM02	SANDERS
EAST01	WEST	FETT02	FITZHERBERT	FRYE04	FOXWELL
EAST08	JERNINGHAM	FILB02	BYFOREST	FULW02	PARKER
EAST08	WEST	FILC02	NAILER	FULW04	DUBOIS
EAST12	SUTVILL	FILC02	ARTHUR	FURS02	BRETON
EATO02	BURROUGHES	FINC06	BARRET	GABB02	CLAYTON
EBER02	BEVERIDGE	FING02	FITZWILLIAMS	GADB02	MAYNARD
ECCL04	HOLLAND	FISH06	MUSCOTE	GAGE02	JOURNO
ECCL08	HOLLAND	FISH06	ASHTON	GAGE04	WHITE
ECCL08	GORSUCH	FISH06	MUSKET	GAGE08	HOARD
EDEN02	CLARE	FISH22	ASHTON	GAGE12	WHITE
EDIS06	JACKSON	FITT02	FISHER	GAGE14	LEWIS
EDIS08	SWARBRICK	FITT04	FISHER	GAGE20	HOWARD
EDNE02	COOK	FITT06	BATEMAN	GAIL02	BANISTER
EDNE02	RIGGE	FITZ04	DARBY	GALL02	JUDOLI
EDWA08	CAMPION	FITZ06	BAINES	GAND02	LEYBURN
EDWA10	PRESTON	FITZ06	GILFORD	GARD08	MITFORD
EDWA14	TYLECOTE	FITZ06	EYRE	GARD12	GARNET
EGER02	OSBALDSTONE	FITZ06	CLIFFORD	GARD18	CARNABY
ELLI04	SHELDON	FITZ08	EYRE	GARD18	MITFORD
ELLI06	CLIFFORD	FITZ21	VILLIERS	GARD22	TAYLOR
ELLI12	PRATT	FITZ24	WILLIAMS	GARN08	PHILIPS

Code	Alias	Code	Alias	Code	Alias
GARN 08	FARMER	GOOC 02	BOLDROP	GWYN 02	BODWELL
GARN 08	DARCY	GOOD 02	GOLDING	GWYN 02	BROWN
GARN 08	ROBERTS	GOOD 04	BODYCOAT	GWYN 02	BUCKLEY
GARN 18	FISHER	GOOD 20	MIDDLEMERE	HACK 02	JACKSON
GARN 22	SAWYER	GORS 02	TALBOT	HACK 02	HAMMOND
GARN 22	SAYER	GORS 02	ANDERTON	HACK 02	HAWKSHEE
GARN 22	ROOKWOOD	GORS 04	ECCLESTON	HACO 02	JERMYN
GASC 02	JOHNSON	GORS 04	METHAM	HACO 02	WILLIAMS
GASC 06	FORD	GOTH 02	BETTS	HACO 02	GAWEN
GASC 14	MEYNELL	GOTH 02	LOVELL	HAGG 06	HOWARD
GATE 02	GASCOIGNE	GOTH 02	VENABLES	HAGG 08	HOWARD
GAUN 02	SANDS	GOUL 02	FORTESCUE	HALI 02	HABARD
GAUN 06	SANDS	GOWE 02	JACKSON	HALL 04	FITZHERBERT
GAUN 06	THORNBOROUGH	GOWE 06	GOLD	HALL 14	PROSSER
GAWE 02	GREEN	GRAC 02	SAVAGE	HALL 14	VAUGHAN
GAWE 06	GREEN	GRAD 06	MIDDLETON	HALL 25	LAWRENCE
GENN 02	IRONMONGER	GRAN 02	CARNABY	HAMB 02	TREGWETHAN
GERA 02	ASHTON	GRAN 02	ERRINGTON	HAME 02	DOWNING
GERA 04	WRIGHT	GRAN 04	YAXLEY	HAME 08	PETERSON
GERA 08	THOMPSON	GRAN 06	YAXLEY	HAME 08	YOUNG
GERA 12	STAUNTON	GRAN 08	DUNNING	HAME 08	BARNES
GERA 12	HARRISON	GRAN 14	GRAY	HAND 04	JOHNSON
GERA 12	NELSON	GRAT 02	BRIDGES	HAND 06	JOHNSON
GERA 12	STARKEY	GRAT 02	FOXLEY	HANM 06	HUNT
GERA 12	THOMPSON	GRAV 02	ALTAM	HANS 06	DRAYTON
GERA 12	LONG	GRAV 04	GREGORY	HANS 08	NORWOOD
GERA 12	STANDISH	GRAY 06	GRACE	HANS 12	HESKETH
GERA 12	TANSFIELD	GRAY 10	WATTS	HARC 02	LANE
GERA 12	BROOKE	GREA 04	GREEN	HARC 04	BEAUMONT
GERA 12	LEE	GREE 10	OGLE	HARC 06	LANE
GERA 16	RICHARDSON	GREE 12	WRIGHT	HARD 04	BURNET
GERA 18	SMITH	GREE 22	BROOKES	HARD 10	TEMPEST
GERA 18	CLOVEL	GREE 22	BROWN	HARD 12	TEMPEST
GERA 20	HARRISON	GREE 22	ENGLISH	HARD 18	DAMBENY
GERA 22	KELHAM	GREE 22	CALLARD	HARD 20	HARFORD
GERA 24	CLOVEL	GREE 24	KING	HARD 26	HUNTER
GERA 26	CLOVEL	GREE 29	WESTBY	HARE 02	FARRAR
GERA 34	CLOVEL	GREE 32	WASHINGTON	HARE 02	GRAY
GIBB 08	POLLARD	GREE 36	GRAY	HARG 06	HOLDCRAFT
GIBS 18	BULMER	GREE 36	LUSTY	HARG 06	HART
GIFF 02	COLE	GREE 44	HOUGHTON	HARN 04	LACON
GIFF 02	LEVESON	GREE 48	HABERLEY	HARP 04	MILBURN
GIFF 06	LEVESON	GREE 52	REYNOLDS	HARP 04	GUTTERIDGE
GIFF 10	WHITE	GREE 54	HILL	HARP 04	GOODRICK
GIFF 10	LEVESON	GREE 68	TILNEY	HARR 02	METHAM
GIFF 16	WALKER	GREE 72	STROUD	HARR 02	DRURY
GIFF 18	WALKER	GREE 72	STRODE	HARR 22	DANIEL
GIFF 22	BARKER	GREE 82	LUCY	HARR 30	TAYLOR
GIFF 23	PIETRO	GRIF 24	ALFORD	HARR 33	HAYES
GIFF 23	COLERDIN	GRIF 26	FLEMING	HARR 44	WALLIS
GIFF 23	CORNELYS	GRIF 26	GRIFFIN	HARR 50	HAYES
GILD 04	WORSLEY	GRIF 26	WATSON	HARR 54	TREMAIN
GILD 04	BYFLEET	GRIF 27	ALFORD	HART 04	SCROPE
GILD 08	WORSLEY	GRIF 28	SMITH	HART 04	SCROOP
GILD 10	BYFLEET	GRIM 18	LANE	HART 06	HERBERT
GILL 04	GELIBOURN	GROS 02	FELTON	HART 12	STRANGUISH
GILP 02	GREEN	GROS 04	TALBOT	HART 12	STRANGE
GILP 04	BRAITHWAITE	GROS 06	HOWARD	HART 12	HAMMOND
GILP 06	STEPHENSON	GROS 06	IRELAND	HART 16	KIRKHAM
GIRL 04	GILLING	GROS 06	ARDEN	HART 18	SCROOP
GITT 02	WILLIAMS	GROV 02	CRAFFE	HART 18	SCROPE
GLOS 02	GLASSCOCK	GROV 04	LUCAS	HART 20	FORD
GODF 02	LACEY	GUIL 02	DRAKE	HART 20	CUMMINGS
GOLD 02	HINSLEY	GUIL 02	FORD	HART 22	CUMMINGS
GOLD 12	MIDDLETON	GUNS 02	SHARP	HARV 04	BARTON
GOLT 02	PHILIPS	GUNS 02	BLUNT	HARV 06	RIVETT

231

Code	Alias	Code	Alias	Code	Alias
HARV 10	BARTON	HODG 38	MORE	HUTC 04	CLARK
HASE 02	BURTON	HOLD 02	JOHNSON	HUTT 08	HILL
HASE 04	WOOD	HOLF 02	LOSTOCK	HUTT 14	SALVIN
HASK 02	DOWNES	HOLF 04	ACTON	HYDE 04	HIND
HATH 02	HART	HOLF 04	BUDE	INGH 04	WALMESLEY
HAUG 02	TRAVERS	HOLF 06	HUNT	INGL 08	PERCY
HAUG 02	RISLEY	HOLL 06	HOLT	INGR 08	LINGEN
HAUG 04	GROYNE	HOLL 16	SANDERSON	INGR 08	MASSINGHAM
HAUG 04	CLARK	HOLL 16	HAMMOND	IPSL 02	PALMER
HAUG 06	GRAFTON	HOLM 02	HOWARD	IPSL 02	BEDINGFELD
HAWA 02	BIRTWISTLE	HOLM 04	HOWARD	IPSL 02	BLOFIELD
HAWA 04	BIRTWISTLE	HOLM 06	HOWARD	IREL 02	DUTTON
HAWA 14	MAIRE	HOLM 08	HOWARD	IREL 06	FERRERS
HAWK 02	NEVILLE	HOLM 10	SMITH	IREL 10	IREMONGER
HAWK 04	THOMPSON	HOLM 16	FINCH	IREL 10	IRONMONGER
HAWK 10	BROOKE	HOLT 02	RIGBY	IRVI 02	SHERBURN
HAWK 16	PERKINS	HOLT 06	PETER	ISHE 02	SHERBURN
HAYD 16	BENSON	HOLT 06	BRERETON	JACK 02	ISLES
HAYE 02	ROWE	HOLT 08	DUCKETT	JACK 02	EYLES
HAYE 02	HANMER	HOLT 12	NORTH	JACK 14	SMITHSON
HAYM 02	PEARCE	HOLT 12	WORTH	JACK 18	HAMMOND
HAYN 02	HARVEY	HOLT 12	DUCKETT	JACK 18	NELSON
HAYN 02	PARRY	HOLT 12	SPENCER	JACK 22	JOHNSON
HAZL 02	HAVELLAND	HOLT 12	FETHERSTON	JACK 24	WHITE
HAZL 02	BEBRIDGE	HOLT 14	BRETT	JACK 30	BROWN
HEAD 02	BATES	HOLT 14	WILKES	JAKE 02	MAXFIELD
HEAL 02	PENDRILL	HOLT 14	DUCKETT	JAKE 04	MAXFIELD
HEAT 06	CRISP	HONN 02	SOMMERWELL	JAME 08	SEDDON
HEAT 06	CRIPPS	HOOK 02	HARRINGTON	JANI 02	SELBY
HEAT 16	PARKER	HOPE 02	DESPERAMUS	JEFF 08	POLE
HEAT 16	BROWN	HORM 02	HARRIS	JEFF 10	WAKEMAN
HEBB 04	METCALFE	HORN 04	BARTON	JENI 04	JOHNSON
HEIG 02	GARNET	HORN 08	GREEN	JENI 06	SANDFORD
HELM 04	TAPPIN	HORN 10	GREEN	JENI 10	THOMPSON
HEMI 02	VENABLES	HORN 20	GOWER	JENI 12	GRAY
HESK 04	ALLEN	HOTH 02	HEATH	JENI 14	GRAY
HESK 10	HANSON	HOUG 04	MORE	JENI 14	GERARD
HESK 18	NAYLOR	HOUG 06	FARMABY	JENI 16	FREVILLE
HESK 18	CARPENTER	HOUS 06	LAYTON	JENI 18	FREVILLE
HESK 18	BARKER	HOUS 06	CROFTS	JENI 20	FREVILLE
HESK 22	ALLEN	HOWA 06	FORMBY	JENI 20	BEAUMONT
HEVE 02	COOK	HOWA 26	HOLME	JENI 22	GRAY
HEWE 02	SAVILLE	HOWA 30	SEATON	JENI 24	GRAY
HEWE 02	WELDON	HOWE 04	PENDRILL	JENI 26	FREVILLE
HEWE 04	ALLOTT	HOWE 06	PENDRILL	JENK 12	METCALFE
HEYD 02	COLLINGTON	HOWL 02	HOWLING	JENN 04	NEWPORT
HEYL 02	JAMES	HUDD 04	HASTINGS	JENN 10	NEWPORT
HICC 02	BEADLE	HUDD 04	DORMER	JENN 12	MASON
HILD 06	SIMPSON	HUDD 10	SHIRLEY	JENN 15	NEWPORT
HILL 02	DACRE	HUDD 10	DORMER	JERN 10	WHITE
HILL 10	TURNER	HUDD 11	JOSEPHSON	JOHN 05	DARELL
HILL 12	BUCKLAND	HUDD 11	SANDFORD	JOHN 06	PERCY
HILL 12	SKIDMORE	HUDD 12	PARKINSON	JOHN 08	SMALLMAN
HILL 18	HYDE	HUGH 06	MARKHAM	JOHN 20	RICHARDSON
HILT 02	MUSGRAVE	HUGH 08	LYNES	JOHN 26	LAYTON
HIND 02	LANE	HUMB 02	HALL	JOHN 34	TAYLOR
HIND 06	WAKEMAN	HUMB 04	HALL	JOHN 38	CHAMBERS
HIRD 02	LATON	HUNT 02	COLEBECK	JOLL 02	THOMPSON
HITC 02	NEEDHAM	HUNT 07	BEAUMONT	JONE 08	WATKINS
HITC 04	BARKER	HUNT 14	GREENLOW	JONE 10	ANDREWS
HODG 04	SYDALL	HUNT 20	BAKER	JONE 12	ACTON
HODG 04	SIDDLE	HUNT 20	SMITH	JONE 26	BUCKLEY
HODG 10	LANGLEY	HUNT 30	WELDON	JONE 26	HERBERT
HODG 14	SIMPSON	HUSB 02	BERNARD	JONE 26	FREER
HODG 22	LANGLEY	HUSB 02	BARNARD	JONE 26	GRIFFITH
HODG 28	VERE	HUSS 06	BURDETT	JONE 28	SCUDADMORE

Code	Alias	Code	Alias	Code	Alias
JONE 32	PRICHARD	LAMB 06	WALKER	LEYB 14	CROFT
JONE 36	LOVELADY	LANC 02	WILLOUGHBY	LIBB 02	BLECHINGTON
JONE 40	MORGAN	LANE 08	LENNY	LICH 02	HALL
JONE 42	DRAPER	LANE 10	SWEET	LICH 02	HALES
JONE 42	HAY	LANG 12	LEGATT	LINE 02	HALL
JONE 42	DUCKETT	LANG 14	LEGATT	LINE 04	LUTTRELL
JONE 42	HUY	LANG 20	HARRISON	LIST 06	BUTLER
JONE 42	HOLLAND	LANG 24	DURAND	LIST 08	LESLEY
JONE 42	ETON	LANM 02	SANMAN	LIST 08	LISLE
JONE 42	NORTH	LANM 02	BUTLER	LITT 02	WESTCOTE
JONE 44	PUGH	LASC 04	BOLD	LIVE 04	BERINGTON
JONE 48	PRICE	LASC 06	BOLD	LIVE 04	WILKINSON
JONE 50	COLLINGTON	LASC 08	BOLD	LLOY 02	BROWN
JORI 02	GEORGE	LASC 10	BOLD	LLOY 06	BOWEN
JOSS 02	GREEN	LATH 12	STANLEY	LOAD 02	IRELAND
JUKE 02	SIMONS	LATH 20	ANDERSON	LOBB 02	SIMEON
JUKE 02	BURTON	LAWS 06	WHITFIELD	LOBB 02	SYMONS
JUMP 04	ELLIS	LAWS 10	HILL	LOCK 12	LASCELLES
KEEL 04	WRIGHT	LAWS 10	HIDE	LOCK 14	BECKWITH
KELL 10	PEMBERTON	LAYT 02	PORT	LODG 02	BATES
KELL 10	STRONG	LAYT 08	PORT	LOLL 02	CHESTER
KELL 16	STAFFORD	LAYT 10	STANLEY	LONG 02	CANSFIELD
KEMB 06	HOLLAND	LAYT 10	STEPHENSON	LONG 14	WILSON
KEMP 02	THOMPSON	LAZE 02	BODNAM	LONG 16	WILSON
KEMP 08	DREW	LAZE 02	BADNAM	LOVE 14	ROBINSON
KEMP 10	GILDRIDGE	LEAD 02	BURGIS	LUCA 04	HALL
KEMY 02	LEWIS	LECH 02	STRATFORD	LUDD 02	SMITH
KEMY 02	SALISBURY	LEEA 02	JOHNSON	LUSH 02	ARROW
KEMY 04	CLEMENS	LEEA 04	HARDING	LUSH 04	MORE
KENN 06	TALBOT	LEEA 22	LENS	LUTL 04	PHILIPS
KENN 14	GARTER	LEEA 24	STEPHENSON	MACK 04	CLINTON
KENT 02	NEALE	LEEA 28	CORNWALLIS	MACZ 04	NICHOLSON
KEYN 02	LUTTRELL	LEEC 02	ECCLES	MACZ 04	BAKER
KEYN 04	NEWPORT	LEED 02	COURTNEY	MADD 02	MARBERY
KEYN 10	BRETT	LEED 04	COURTNEY	MADD 02	MISSENDON
KEYN 18	NEWPORT	LEEK 02	ALLEN	MADG 02	SANDS
KEYN 18	LUTTRELL	LEFE 02	ROBECK	MADG 02	TOWNELEY
KIGH 02	ROBINSON	LEGA 08	WILSON	MAGE 02	JOHNSON
KING 02	SCOTT	LEGG 02	PALMER	MAIN 04	LATHAM
KING 12	CLAYTON	LEGR 04	ALLEN	MAIN 06	LATHAM
KING 16	DE BOIS	LEHU 02	DURANT	MAIN 10	SPENCER
KINN 02	COLLETON	LEHU 04	THORNTON	MAIR 04	BURDETT
KINN 04	COLLETON	LEIG 02	LAYTON	MAIR 15	CONYERS
KIRK 02	SIMPSON	LEIG 08	LAYTON	MAIT 02	QUASHET
KIRK 10	HEIGHAM	LEIG 10	METCALFE	MALL 06	HARVEY
KIRK 10	HART	LEIG 10	LAYTON	MALL 08	JACKSON
KIRK 12	LATHAM	LEIG 12	EARTH	MALT 02	LAYTON
KITC 01	SMITH	LEIG 12	GARTH	MAMB 02	DU PRE
KITC 04	MARSDEN	LEMA 02	BROWN	MANB 02	ROGERS
KNAT 02	NORTON	LEMO 04	LANCASTER	MANN 04	SIMCOCKS
KNIG 10	KING	LESL 04	DUGUID	MANN 04	GROSVENOR
KNIG 12	STANLEY	LEVE 02	HOWELL	MANN 12	ARTHUR
KNIG 16	THOROLD	LEWI 02	BAKER	MANN 16	YOUNG
LACE 01	EYSTON	LEWI 04	BAKER	MANN 18	BROWN
LACE 01	RUSSELL	LEWI 08	RANDALL	MANN 22	YOUNG
LACE 01	ELSTON	LEWI 12	PRICHARD	MANS 02	HARDING
LACO 04	LAMBERT	LEWI 14	LEPPARD	MANS 04	HARDING
LACO 06	LAMBERT	LEWI 26	SHELLEY	MARS 27	TURNER
LAIT 02	KENSINGTON	LEWK 04	TAYLOR	MART 04	QUARLEYS
LAIT 04	KENSINGTON	LEWK 06	WILLIAMS	MART 10	RAMIRER
LAIT 06	KENSINGTON	LEYB 02	FOUNTAIN	MART 10	REYMIREZ
LAIT 06	SCOTT	LEYB 02	WINTER	MART 26	MARSON
LALA 02	PETERS	LEYB 02	BRADLEY	MART 26	MUNSON
LAMB 01	LAMPTON	LEYB 02	GRANT	MART 36	WHITE
LAMB 01	CUFFAUD	LEYB 08	CROFT	MART 38	HOLLAND
LAMB 02	AUSTIN	LEYB 12	CROFT	MASO 02	MORLEY

233

Code	Alias	Code	Alias	Code	Alias
MASS04	GLEGG	MOLY08	TICKLE	NIXO02	POINES
MASS10	HODGES	MOLY14	HOWE	NORM02	CLIFTON
MASS14	MIDDLETON	MOND02	CLAYTON	NORR02	BAINES
MAST02	MANLEY	MONK04	MOORE	NORR14	ROE
MAST02	THORPE	MONK04	EDWARDS	NORR18	SEBASTIAN
MATA02	MATTHEWS	MOOR05	CROSS	NORR20	NEWTON
MATT02	MARLOW	MORE05	PARR	NORR20	SMITH
MATT06	WILLIAMS	MORE05	TALMAN	NORT04	LANCASTER
MATT12	WILLIAMS	MORE06	FORD	NORT06	MENTISSE
MATT14	NEVILLE	MORE12	WEST	NORT08	MENTISSE
MAXF02	FYLDE	MORE18	BROOKESBY	NORT10	WIMBUSH
MAXF02	FIELD	MORG04	SINGLETON	NOTT02	BROUGHTON
MAXF02	CLEATON	MORG04	DEE	NUTT04	MATTHEWS
MAXW04	BROWN	MORG10	DINGLEY	NUTT10	ASKEW
MAYA02	ACLAM	MORG14	CONYERS	NUTT10	ROWLEY
MAYL02	MAYNARD	MORG16	SUGAR	OAKL02	AUCKLAND
MAYN04	BAINES	MORG20	GRIFFETH	OGLE04	SWINBURNE
MEAD02	ALMEIDA	MORG22	POULTON	OLDC02	PARKER
MEAL02	CORNWALL	MORG40	WINTER	OLDC02	HALL
MEAR02	BRINKHURST	MORL04	RIGBY	OLDC02	HUTTON
MEAR04	BRINKHURST	MORR04	CAMPION	OLDC02	VINCENT
MEAR06	BRINKHURST	MORR10	CROSS	OLDC02	PERKINS
MEEH02	MAHONY	MORR18	HOLLAND	OLDC02	HUNTER
MELL06	MAXFIELD	MORR20	WILSON	ONIO02	MARTIN
MEND02	´ LANE	MORS02	CUTHBERT	ORRE02	MARTIN
MEND02	LOWE	MORS02	WARD	OVER02	THOMPSON
MEND02	LOVE	MORS02	CLAXTON	OWEN02	HUGHES
MERE02	FARMER	MORS04	COLLISON	OWEN04	SMITH
MERE04	KNIGHT	MOSE04	BYERS	OWEN04	GARDINER
MERI02	SWEET	MOSS02	MORE	OWEN05	HILL
MERR02	WAKE	MOST04	MOSSON	OWEN12	HART
MERR04	WAKE	MULS02	DAY	OXEN02	WHITE
METC08	MIDDLETON	MUMF05	FORD	PAGE06	HICKMAN
METC10	COLLINGWOOD	MUND02	MASON	PAGE08	MORRIS
METC14	ECCLESFIELD	MURP10	TURNER	PAGE08	HARRIOTT
METC15	DRAPER	MUSH02	RADCLIFFE	PAIN06	REILLY
METC16	TWEEDLE	MUSS04	BROWN	PALM14	NEVILLE
METC18	NELSON	MUTT02	BEAUMONT	PALM15	CONYERS
METC18	BANKS	MUTT04	MALLETT	PALM16	CONYERS
METC20	SCROOP	NANC02	SIMONS	PANS02	MOLYNEUX
METC20	PROCTOR	NAPP04	RUSSELL	PANS02	PERCIVAL
METC22	CARLETON	NAYL02	NEWMAN	PARK04	CROSS
METH02	BYON	NEAL14	KENT	PARK26	SMITH
METH04	IBERIES	NEED06	PLATT	PARK28	BURCHARD
MEYN08	NEVILLE	NEED12	STUMER	PARK42	FOX
MEYN12	IRELAND	NEED16	MORGAN	PARK48	COTTAM
MICO02	BAINES	NEIL02	GRADELL	PARK58	GOLDEN
MICO02	HARVEY	NEIL02	GRADWELL	PARR08	WINN
MICO04	HARVEY	NEIL04	NELSON	PARR10	HANFORD
MIDD02	ASHBY	NELS10	BIESLEY	PARR16	WARD
MIDD04	JOHNSON	NEVI02	DILLON	PARR18	LIBANUS
MIDD06	MANDEVILLE	NEVI04	NELSON	PARR22	MORGAN
MIDD12	WILSON	NEVI06	RIDDELL	PARS02	SELBY
MIDD20	GOLDSMITH	NEVI06	RUDDELL	PARS12	BRIANT
MIDD24	DADE	NEVI10	CARY	PARS12	RICHARDSON
MIDD30	HEATHCOTE	NEWM02	SLYFIELD	PAST04	EVERARD
MILD06	BEDINGFELD	NEWP02	HARRIS	PATE06	LEFEBURE
MILD06	WINTER	NEWP04	SMITH	PATE07	ARDEN
MILE02	MONTFORD	NEWP04	JAMES	PAVI02	OGLETHORPE
MILE10	DANIEL	NEWS02	WORTHINGTON	PEAR02	CHAMBERLAIN
MILL02	CRUMP	NEWT02	CLINQUEMAILLE	PEAR04	BISHOP
MILL02	MILWARD	NEWT04	NELSON	PEAR04	GIFFARD
MINS02	STANLEY	NEWT08	FAWCETT	PEAR06	BARKER
MOLI06	BETHAM	NEWT10	BRAYLSFORD	PEAR06	BIRCH
MOLY02	WALLEY	NIGH04	CARLISLE	PEAR14	PUDSEY
MOLY04	HARRINGTON	NIXO02	POYNTZ	PECK02	WEBB

Code	Alias	Code	Alias	Code	Alias
PEGG04	HASTINGS	PLOW04	PERROTT	PRAN02	SHEPHERD
PELC02	CATWELL	PLOW06	SIMONS	PRAN04	COLDHAM
PELC02	BARTON	PLOW06	SIMEON	PRAN04	SHEPHERD
PELC02	MANNERS	PLOW06	PERROTT	PRAT06	THOMPSON
PEMB02	BLUNDELL	PLOW16	SIMEON	PRAT06	WALKER
PEND01	FLETCHER	PLOW16	RICHARDS	PRES14	VINCENT
PEND02	BIRCH	PLOW16	SAVILLE	PRES14	BAINES
PENK02	RIVERS	PLOW20	SALISBURY	PRET02	HARRIS
PENK04	RIVERS	PLOW20	ACTON	PRET04	HARRIS
PENK06	RIVERS	PLOW20	WEEDON	PRIC03	VAUGHAN
PENK10	RIVERS	PLUM02	MAURICE	PRIC04	ANDREWS
PENK12	RIVERS	PLUM04	PRICHARD	PRIC04	HARRIS
PENN04	CONWAY	PLUN01	UNDERHILL	PRIC18	CAMPION
PENN06	MOSTYN	PLUN04	UNDERHILL	PRIC35	PARRY
PERC08	FISHER	POLE02	SMITH	PRIC36	WHITE
PERC08	FAIRFAX	POPE02	FISHER	PRIC44	MORGAN
PERC14	SMITH	PORA02	HARPER	PRIN02	COOK
PERK06	HOSKINS	PORD02	COLLINS	PRIN04	ELLIS
PERR04	BARNSLEY	PORM02	WHITE	PRIN04	LACEY
PETI02	STANLEY	PORM02	PRYCE	PROB02	SMITH
PETO02	BUDD	PORM02	WHITGIFT	PROB06	COLBECK
PETR02	WHITE	PORM02	MERE	PROB06	BREWERTON
PETR04	SPENCER	PORT10	NELSON	PROS02	MONINGTON
PETR10	ANDREWS	PORT12	PALMER	PUDS02	BANISTER
PETR12	MANNOCK	PORT20	PRICE	PUGH04	PHILIPS
PETR16	WILLIAMS	PORT22	SMITH	PUGH08	PRICE
PETR18	WILLIAMS	PORT24	SMITH	PUGH14	PHILIPS
PETR18	SPENCER	PORT24	SMITH	PURC01	HARCOURT
PETR20	MANNOCK	POSS02	NICHOLS	PURC04	GIFFARD
PETR26	GAGE	POST02	WATSON	QUAT02	WILMOT
PETT02	HAMMON	POST02	WHITMORE	QUIN06	BROOKE
PETT06	WENTWORTH	POTI02	JENISON	QUIN08	PRANNELL
PETT06	HIDALGO	POTT02	EGERTON	RADF02	TANFIELD
PHIL10	EVANS	POTT10	COOPER	RAVE02	RUSSELL
PHIL12	ELSTON	POUL04	PALMER	RAWL02	FERIMAN
PHIL18	PURSHALL	POUL04	SANDERSON	RAWL02	NEALE
PHIL24	ASTLEY	POUL04	ROBERTS	RAWL06	METCALFE
PHIL28	VINCAM	POUL06	BROOKES	READ08	NORRIS
PHIL30	HARRISON	POUL06	MORGAN	REDF02	EXTON
PHIL30	HERBERT	POUL08	PALMER	REES02	OWEN
PHIL30	JOHNSON	POUL10	BROOKES	REEV04	HASKEY
PHIL34	PESTEL	POUL14	PALMER	REEV06	HASKEY
PIBU02	FOSTER	POUL16	PALMER	REEV08	HASKEY
PIBU02	GRAVENOR	POUL20	PALMER	REYN04	DOUGLAS
PICK10	DANIEL	POUL22	PALMER	REYN04	DOUGELL
PICK12	DANIEL	POUL22	CONYERS	REYN04	DOWGILL
PICK14	BUDD	POUL28	UNDERHILL	REYN05	DOUGELL
PIER08	POOLE	POUL28	BROOKES	REYN05	DOWGILL
PIGO02	GRIFFIN	POUL36	SPENCER	REYN05	DOUGLAS
PILC02	FOSTER	POUL36	SACKEVERELL	RICH10	WALLIS
PINC02	TIPPER	POUL36	SACKVILLE	RICH10	WALLES
PINK02	CARR	POWE06	ASHTON	RICH10	WALSH
PIPP02	STANFIELD	POWE08	DONWALL	RICH15	BENISON
PITT10	FAULKNER	POWE08	DONWELL	RICH18	BLUNDELL
PLAS02	BLAXTON	POWE12	JENNINGS	RICH20	HOLCROFT
PLAS02	PALMER	POWE20	PROSSER	RICH20	OLDCROFT
PLAT04	PLANTIN	POWE20	MORGAN	RICH32	GARBOT
PLAT06	PLANTIN	POWE22	ROGERS	RICH36	ANDERSON
PLEA02	SCARISBRICK	POYN06	STEPHENS	RICH38	BULMER
PLEA04	CATESBY	POYN06	CAMPION	RICH40	ROBERTS
PLEA04	WALMESLEY	POYN08	BEAUMONT	RIDD08	CARY
PLOT04	THOMPSON	POYN08	PRICE	RIDD11	CARTER
PLOW02	SIMEON	PRAC02	CORNWALLIS	RIDG02	BURGES
PLOW02	SIMONS	PRAC02	BRENT	RIGB04	BARKER
PLOW04	GAGE	PRAC02	BRAND	RIGB08	STREET
PLOW04	SIMONS	PRAN02	TOWNSEND	RIGB08	WHITE

Code	Alias	Code	Alias	Code	Alias
RIGB22	KNOWLES	SALE04	NEVILLE	SHER12	TUNSTALL
RIGM02	ROTHWELL	SALE04	SANDFORD	SHER14	TUNSTALL
RIGM04	SMITH	SALE08	GREEN	SHER24	STALIE
RIGM06	SMITH	SALE10	NEVILLE	SHER38	CARLETON
RILE02	DANBY	SALE10	RICHARDSON	SHER40	SHERRINGTON
RISD02	BLUET	SALI04	PARRY	SHER42	SHERRINGTON
RISH04	ANDERTON	SALK02	ANDERTON	SHIM04	TURNER
RISH06	NOWELL	SALK10	ANDERTON	SHIR08	GILMET
RISH08	ROBINSON	SALK12	ANDERTON	SHOR02	CURTIS
RISH08	ROSS	SALT02	NATEBY	SHOR06	PEREGRINE
RIVE02	BLEWITT	SALT04	LEWIS	SHUT02	DALTON
ROBI12	RODNEY	SALT06	IRELAND	SHUT04	HAYDOCK
ROBI16	FAIRFAX	SALT08	EURE	SHUT06	SANDERSON
ROBI28	COLLINGWOOD	SALT08	EVERS	SHUT08	RICHARDSON
ROBI28	UPSALL	SALV04	SMITH	SIME02	SMITH
ROBI28	FOWLER	SAMP02	SIMPSON	SIMO04	BIGGS
ROBI32	GAZAIN	SAND02	MORE	SIMP04	DANIEL
ROBI32	GAZIN	SAND06	BAINES	SIMP16	ESDRAS
ROBI40	TAYLOR	SAND24	SINGLETON	SIMP16	HIGHGATE
ROBI52	SHAW	SAND26	THOMPSON	SIMP20	BAINES
ROBS02	ROBINSON	SAND34	OKELEY	SING08	STANLEY
ROBS02	FINES	SANK06	DITCHLING	SITT02	MANNERS
ROCK04	IRELAND	SANK06	DITCHFIELD	SKIN02	BENTLEY
ROEA02	ROLFE	SAVA02	RIVERS	SKIN06	BENTLEY
ROEA02	ROSS	SAYE04	STANLEY	SKIN10	SMITH
ROEA04	ROLFE	SCAR02	NEVILLE	SKIN10	WARREN
ROEA04	ROSS	SCAR04	NEVILLE	SKIN12	SCRIMSHAW
ROFF02	CARLTON	SCAR06	NEVILLE	SKIN16	SCRIMSHAW
ROGE02	ST GEORGE	SCAR08	NEVILLE	SLIN02	PERCY
ROGE02	PARRY	SCAR10	NEVILLE	SMIT03	MARTINEZ
ROGE10	BAMPFIELD	SCAR12	NEVILLE	SMIT07	GERVISON
ROGE12	WARD	SCAR16	NEVILLE	SMIT09	WEBB
ROGE14	ANSELM	SCAR18	NEVILLE	SMIT12	KITCHEN
ROGE16	ROCHESTER	SCHO02	FOUQUANT	SMIT14	ASPINALL
ROLL02	BLAKISTON	SCOB02	TRAFFORD	SMIT15	ANDERTON
ROLL02	BLAXTON	SCOT10	NEWMAN	SMIT21	FARMER
ROMS02	WILLIAMS	SCOT14	GREEN	SMIT23	HARRINGTON
RONE02	CROSLAND	SCOT16	CRAWFORD	SMIT26	HARPER
ROOK08	ROSE	SCRI02	SUTTON	SMIT26	TARLTON
ROOK12	ROBINSON	SCRO04	WINDSOR	SMIT29	CARRINGTON
ROOK12	TOWNSEND	SCUD02	BOYER	SMIT32	THOMPSON
ROOK14	RAWLEY	SCUD04	ROPER	SMIT32	WILKINS
ROOK16	GAGE	SCUD08	PRICE	SMIT33	HARRISON
ROOT02	HENRIQUE	SCUP02	SMITH	SMIT35	DURHAM
ROOT04	FLOYD	SEEL02	BUTLER	SMIT37	DORMER
ROOT04	LLOYD	SEFT04	WORTHINGTON	SMIT37	CARRINGTON
ROSI02	JAMES	SEIS02	BAXTER	SMIT38	WARHAM
ROUG02	GODFREY	SELB10	READE	SMIT39	TURNER
ROUS08	ROELS	SERG04	HOLLAND	SMIT52	PHELPS
ROUS10	ROELS	SERG04	SMITH	SMIT52	PHIPPS
ROWS02	ROUSE	SERG08	LEA	SMIT55	GEFFRESON
ROYD02	FACEBY	SERG08	LONG	SMIT56	BAKER
ROYD04	CORNFORTH	SEYE02	LAMBERT	SMIT56	CLARKSON
RUDG02	LEE	SHAC02	BANISTER	SMIT56	WAKE
RUDG02	DOWRICH	SHAC02	STANTON	SMIT57	MARSHALL
RUDG02	DRURY	SHAF04	MILLS	SMIT58	SAVILLE
RUFF02	ADAMS	SHAR02	POLLARD	SMIT63	WARHAM
RUGA02	BARTHOLOMEW	SHAW04	CORBET	SMIT65	TEMPE
RUSS01	BLACK	SHAW04	MARCHANT	SMIT65	DEACON
SABR02	WITMORE	SHAW10	WESTBROOK	SMIT66	HANSOM
SABR02	WHITMORE	SHAW18	PROCTOR	SMIT69	LEWIS
SACH04	JAMESON	SHEL14	ELLIOT	SMIT74	BLACK
SAGE02	BLAKE	SHEL24	WHITBY	SMIT76	CARRINGTON
SAGE02	BLACK	SHEL26	TICHBORNE	SOME02	WILSON
SAIN02	JOHNSON	SHEP10	RADCLIFFE	SOME06	VAUGHAN
SALE02	NEVILLE	SHER10	TUNSTALL	SOME10	JOHNSON

236

Code	Alias	Code	Alias	Code	Alias
SOUT06	LOVELL	SUGA02	SWEET	THOR36	CHURCH
SOUT06	LEA	SULY02	SUTTON	THRE02	WEBB
SOUT06	CLARK	SUTC02	SUTTON	THUL02	ASHTON
SOUT16	SMITH	SUTT06	SALISBURY	THWA02	SMITH
SOUT22	COOPER	SUTT10	SALISBURY	THWI04	CHAMPNEY
SOUT22	COTTON	SUTT16	SALISBURY	THWI06	PALMER
SOUT24	THOMPSON	SWAR02	SINGLETON	THWI08	PALMER
SOUT26	LEE	SWAR08	WALKER	TICH08	COTTON
SOUT30	KENDALL	SWEE04	NICHOLSON	TIDD02	INGLEBY
SOUT32	KENDALL	SWIN04	SAVAGE	TILD02	GOODEN
SOUT34	KENDALL	SWIN16	MATTHEWS	TILL04	JENNINGS
SPEN06	TYRWHITT	SWIN16	ROBERTS	TIMC02	WALGRAVE
SPEN06	HATCLIFFE	TALB06	GRAY	TIMC02	CULPEPER
SPRO02	PARKER	TALB16	MANSELL	TIMC02	WALDEGRAVE
SQUI02	PETRE	TALB16	MANSFIELD	TIND02	COBB
STAF04	WILLIAMSON	TALB28	MANSELL	TOCK02	YOUNG
STAF06	CASSIDY	TALB28	MANSFIELD	TOCK02	CONSTABLE
STAF08	HILL	TANC04	MUMFORD	TODD02	MEYNELL
STAF11	LEE	TASB02	TICHBORNE	TODD04	MEYNELL
STAF12	THORPE	TASB08	DARELL	TODD06	MEYNELL
STAF12	POTTER	TATH04	GRAY	TODK02	TEMPEST
STAF16	PHILIPS	TATL02	FORSTER	TOML02	GREEN
STAF16	POTTER	TATL06	WILSON	TOOT04	BLACKLOW
STAN02	STANTER	TATL08	WARD	TOOT04	BLACOE
STAN06	FISHER	TAVE02	DAVIES	TOOT06	DODD
STAN16	STAFFORD	TAVE02	BANISTER	TORB02	SIMPSON
STAN20	BRERETON	TAYL14	NICHOLSON	TOWE02	CARY
STAN24	CULCHETH	TAYL32	CAVENDISH	TRAF02	HOWELL
STAN30	MASSEY	TAYL32	CANDISH	TRAP04	GIFFARD
STAN36	GAUNTLETT	TAYL36	SHERBURN	TRAP06	BRAITHWAITE
STAR02	LEE	TAYL36	BLACKBURN	TRAV04	SAVAGE
STAR02	WARBURTON	TAYL50	ADAMS	TREN02	KING
STAR04	AMIANS	TAYL50	ADAM	TREV02	DRUMMOND
STAR06	HANMER	TEMP14	WILMOT	TRIM04	BARNES
STEP04	GARDINER	TESI02	GREENWAY	TRIS02	CROSS
STEP08	LYNN	TESI02	GREENWALL	TROL02	WELBURY
STEP12	BUSTON	TESI02	BEAUMONT	TUCK02	NORRIS
STEP18	RINGBY	THIM02	ASHBY	TUNS06	SCARGILL
STEP24	WATERS	THIM06	PAULET	TUNS10	HELMES
STEY02	FARMER	THIM08	ASHBY	TUNS10	DYER
STIT02	HAWKINS	THOM04	BENNET	TURB06	BONVILLE
STOC02	MILBET	THOM06	PINCKARD	TURB08	BARRET
STOC04	BELLOT	THOM10	WEBSTER	TURB10	FERMOR
STON10	CUTHBERT	THOM12	DARCY	TURN02	BAINES
STON10	STONE	THOM14	PARKER	TURN02	ASHBY
STON10	FAIRFAX	THOM20	YATES	TURN04	SAMUEL
STON10	TOWN	THOM21	TYRWHITT	TURN08	ASHBY
STON15	ROPER	THOM22	HUDSON	TURN18	WEEDON
STRA04	HUNGERFORD	THOM26	WILKS	TURN18	HERBERT
STRA04	ANDERTON	THOM28	THIMELBY	TURN32	MAUDSLEY
STRA06	SWINNERTON	THOM32	FROST	TURV02	SMITH
STRA08	WILLEC	THOM36	JACKSON	TYAS04	TRANSAM
STRA08	BARBER	THOM38	CARR	TYRW02	GWILLIM
STRA10	POTTER	THOM44	THROCKMORTON	UMFR02	FELL
STRE04	BRIDGES	THOM46	BLACKBURN	UNDE02	BARKER
STRI02	WRIGHT	THOM50	BENNET	VANC02	BIGGS
STRI02	MANNOCK	THOM50	TEMPLE	VANE02	JONES
STRI06	MIDDLETON	THOR08	IRELAND	VANE02	HERBER
STRI10	WHARTON	THOR10	MIDDLETON	VARD02	JONES
STRU02	TUFTON	THOR10	SMITH	VARD02	CHAMBERLAIN
STRU02	BRIDGEMAN	THOR12	FORSTER	VAUD02	MORE
STUA00	STEPHENS	THOR18	TURNER	VAUD02	WORSLEY
STUA02	SHARP	THOR20	BENSON	VAUG06	WILLIAMS
STUK04	SMITHSON	THOR24	CARVILL	VAVA04	MANNERS
STUT02	FISHER	THOR24	CARWELL	VAVA10	THWINGE
SUGA02	COX	THOR28	MORNE	VAVA10	GIFFARD

Code	Alias	Code	Alias	Code	Alias
VENN02	FERMOR	WARW02	SPENCE	WHIT84	MOORE
VENN02	FARMER	WATE02	TALBOT	WHIT94	REDIATE
VERH02	LIDDELL	WATK02	VAUGHAN	WIDD08	WATSON
VEZZ02	ROBINSON	WATK04	PHILIPS	WIGM02	CAMPION
VEZZ04	ROBINSON	WATK14	WILSON	WIGM04	CAMPION
VEZZ06	ROBINSON	WATS02	MANSELL	WIGN02	SANDYS
VICT04	WILLIAMS	WATS04	RAINES	WILD02	JAKEMAN
VICT04	BISHOP	WATS04	RAND	WILF04	TAYLOR
VINC02	HILDINGE	WATS06	JOHNSON	WILF06	TAYLOR
VINE02	LEE	WATS08	COLPEPPER	WILK02	THOMPSON
VINT02	COLSTON	WATT02	RICHARDSON	WILK08	CAMPION
WADD02	SINGLETON	WAYA02	FLOWER	WILK12	CURWEN
WAFE02	RICHMOND	WEAT02	TRAVIS	WILK16	MOLYNEUX
WAFE02	FRIAR	WEBS04	SLAUGHTER	WILL18	CRIMMES
WAFE02	HERNE	WEBS04	WALLER	WILL24	HEADLAM
WAKE02	MERRIMAN	WEBS04	WARD	WILL24	BLUET
WAKE06	GIFFARD	WEED06	WILLIAMSON	WILL34	MONNINGTON
WAKE08	GIBBONS	WEED08	ACTON	WILL44	LLOYD
WAKE08	GREEN	WELD04	HUNTER	WILL54	NANFAN
WAKE14	GREEN	WELD08	HUNTER	WILL74	SMALLEY
WALD02	FLOWER	WELD14	HUNTER	WILL74	SMALL
WALD04	PARKER	WELL02	MOTHERSALL	WILL80	RYDER
WALD06	PELHAM	WELL06	VEALE	WILL82	WILLIAMS
WALD10	MILDMAY	WELL08	WILLIAMS	WILL84	BARKER
WALD10	PLAYLE	WEST06	DARELL	WILS04	MORLAND
WALD10	HESPER	WEST10	WALKER	WILS04	MORLEY
WALF02	POLE	WEST14	VERTUE	WILS06	RAILTON
WALK02	WALKER	WEST18	WRIGHT	WILS16	KNOTT
WALK14	STAPLETON	WEST22	EDMUNDS	WILS36	CLARK
WALL04	WEBB	WEST22	HUNT	WINC02	SMITH
WALL04	MARSH	WHAL10	ROBINSON	WINC06	ELSTON
WALL04	JOHNSON	WHAL14	ROBINSON	WIND02	BRADLEY
WALL06	MARSH	WHAL16	ROBINSON	WINT10	DAVENPORT
WALL06	MARSHALL	WHAL18	ROBINSON	WISE02	SOPHIA
WALM04	HARRIS	WHAL20	TOOTELL	WISE04	SIDLEY
WALM10	COLGRAVE	WHAL22	PORTER	WISE04	SIGLEY
WALM14	SHERBURN	WHEB02	GIFFARD	WITH04	WYVILL
WALM18	HAMERTON	WHIC02	SAVILLE	WITH06	WYVILL
WALP04	WARNER	WHIT02	FRANKLAND	WITH06	MARKHAM
WALP06	RICH	WHIT02	MOYSES	WITH12	WYVILL
WALP06	PAUPER	WHIT04	CLAYTON	WIVE02	RUDD
WALP10	CHRISTOPHORSN	WHIT04	STARKEY	WOLF02	CARY
WALP12	THORNE	WHIT08	STARKEY	WOLF04	BUTLER
WALS10	FENNELL	WHIT10	MARTIN	WOLF08	LACEY
WALS10	KNOTT	WHIT12	TURNER	WOOD12	GULLICK
WALT04	COTTAM	WHIT14	HARCOTT	WOOD12	KELLICK
WALT08	RIGBY	WHIT14	WHITE	WOOD14	BARNARD
WARD04	INGLEBY	WHIT14	HARCOURT	WOOD16	THOMPSON
WARD06	GREEN	WHIT30	BRUNCHARD	WOOD16	FARRINGTON
WARD10	INGLEBY	WHIT32	BLACKLOW	WOOD20	SHAW
WARE02	WENHAM	WHIT34	BLANCO	WOOD22	WHEELER
WARF02	GUARDEFORD	WHIT36	LECKONBY	WOOD22	DEVEREUX
WARH02	JEFFREY	WHIT40	LECKONBY	WOOD30	GRIFFIN
WARH04	POLEWHEEL	WHIT50	JOHNSON	WOOD30	JENNINGS
WARH08	JEFFREY	WHIT52	BURRELL	WOOD31	WHITE
WARI14	ELLIS	WHIT54	BLACKLOW	WOOD34	WORTH
WARM02	PETERS	WHIT58	BIANCHI	WOOD50	THOMPSON
WARN04	CLARE	WHIT66	BIANCHI	WOOD60	KELLY
WARN08	WEST	WHIT68	BENNET	WOOD60	BARBER
WARR12	PELHAM	WHIT70	WHITELOCK	WOOL02	ALLEN
WARR16	PRICE	WHIT70	CHEEK	WOOL02	BROWN
WARR18	SPENCER	WHIT70	RIVERS	WORS06	BROWN
WARR20	PELHAM	WHIT70	GREEN	WORS08	HARVEY
WARR22	HORTON	WHIT70	FRENCH	WORS10	HARVEY
WARW02	FENWICK	WHIT72	KNIVETON	WORS18	BUTLER
WARW02	CHAMBERS	WHIT84	MORE	WORS20	BUTLER

Code	Alias	Code	Alias	Code	Alias
WORT 02	PHILIPS	WRIG 24	WHITLEY	YELV 02	KEMP
WORT 12	SEFTON	WRIG 26	YARWELL	YORK 02	WANSFORD
WORT 14	CHARNOCK	WRIG 32	WHITE	YORK 02	GIBBS
WORT 24	SEFTON	WYNN 04	BODWELL	YOUN 14	BROOKES
WREN 04	DAMFORD	YATE 04	VINCENT	YOUN 16	DINGLEY
WRIG 10	TOVEY	YATE 14	BOOTH	YOUN 16	CHRISTOPHER
WRIG 18	GIFFARD	YAXL 06	TANKARD	YOUN 16	LEIGHTON
WRIG 20	BEALE	YEKE 02	WADE		

APPENDIX I   OFFICIALS

The list of Vicars Apostolic includes only those who held authority, not those who were appointed but died before taking office. The title of defunct bishoprics, often in Asia Minor, *in partibus infidelium*, was bestowed on the Vicars Apostolic and their coadjutors. The list of the holders of these titular sees includes those who, although ordained before 1800, were not consecrated until later and those coadjutors who were consecrated but never served as Vicar Apostolic. Those who held foreign bishoprics, or who were consecrated as titular bishops, but did not work on the English Mission in an episcopal capacity, are not included here.

The list of Benedictine Presidents is taken from *Moore*, that of the Dominican Provincials from *Gumbley* and that of the Franciscan Provincials from *Thaddeus*. The list of Jesuit Provincials was provided by The Department of Historiography and Archives at Mount Street. Adjustments have been made where spellings and forms of names differed from those in the main list.

(i) THE GOVERNMENT OF THE MISSION

THE ARCHPRIESTS

George Blackwell, 1599-1608	BLAC 20
George Birket, 1603-1614	BIRK 08
William Harrison, 1615-1621	HARR 58

THE VICARS APOSTOLIC

All England and Wales

William Bishop, 1623-1624	BISH 18
Richard Smith, 1625-1655	SMIT 56
John Leyburn, 1685-1688	LEYB 06

The London District

John Leyburn, 1688-1702	LEYB 06
Bonaventure Giffard, 1703-1734	GIFF 06
Benjamin Petre, 1734-1758	PETR 02
Richard Challoner, 1758-1781	CHAL 06
James Robert Talbot, 1781-1790	TALB 12
John Douglass, 1790-1812	DOUG 02

The Midland District

Bonaventure Giffard, 1688-1703	GIFF 06
George Witham, 1703-1716	WITH 06
John Talbot Stonor, 1716-1756	STON 16
John Joseph Hornyold, 1756-1778	HORN 18
Thomas Joseph Talbot, 1778-1795	TALB 32
Charles Berington, 1795-1798	BERI 02

The Northern District

James Smith, 1688-1711	SMIT 26
George Witham, 1716-1725	WITH 06
Thomas Dominic Williams, 1726-1740	WILL 62
Edward Dicconson, 1740-1752	DICC 02
Francis Petre, 1752-1775	PETR 10
William Walton, 1775-1780	WALT 14
Matthew Gibson, 1780-1790	GIBS 14
William Gibson, 1790-1821	GIBS 20

The Western District

Philip Michael Ellis, 1688-1705	ELLI 10
Matthew Prichard, 1713-1750	PRIC 40
William Lawrence York, 1750-1763	YORK 06
Charles Walmesley, 1763-1797	WALM 02
William Gregory Sharrock, 1797-1809	SHAR 16

TITULAR SEES OF THE VICARS APOSTOLIC

Acanthus	William Gibson	GIBS 20
Acone	Thomas Joseph Talbot	TALB 32
Adrumetum	John Leyburn	LEYB 06
Amorium	Francis Petre	PETR 10
Aurelipolis	Philip Michael Ellis	ELLI 10
Birtha	James Robert Talbot	TALB 12
Bolina	Thomas Smith	SMIT 72
Callipolis	James Smith	SMIT 26
Castabala	John Milner	MILN 04
Centuriae	John Douglass	DOUG 02
Chalcedon	William Bishop	BISH 18
	Richard Smith	SMIT 56
Cinna	William Maire	MAIR 18
Comana	Matthew Gibson	GIBS 14
Debra	Richard Challoner	CHAL 06
Europus	Thomas Penswick	PENS 04
Halia	William Poynter	POYN 02
Hierocaesarea	Charles Berington	BERI 02
	Gregory Stapleton	STAP 06
Madaura	Bonaventure Giffard	GIFF 06
Mallus	Edward Dicconson	DICC 02

Marcopolis	George Witham	WITH 06
Myra	Matthew Prichard	PRIC 40
Nisibis	William Lawrence York	YORK 06
Philomenlia	John Joseph Hornyold	HORN 18
Prusa	Benjamin Petre	PETR 02
Ramatha	Charles Walmesley	WALM 02
Telmessus	William Gregory Sharrock	SHAR 16
Thespiae	John Talbot Stonor	STON 16
	Peter Bernardine Collingridge	COLL 08
Tiberiopolis	Thomas Dominic Williams	WILL 62
Trachonitis	William Walton	WALT 14
Usulae	James Yorke Bramston	BRAM 04

(ii) THE PRESIDENTS GENERAL OF THE ENGLISH BENEDICTINES

John Leander Jones, 1619-1621	JONE 28
William Rudesind Barlow, 1621-1629	BARL 16
Robert Sigebert Bagshawe, 1630-1633	BAGS 04
William Claude White, 1633	WHIT 68
John Leander Jones, 1633-1635	JONE 28
Wilfrid Clement Reyner, 1633-1641	REYN 05
Felix Jocelin Elmer, 1641-1645	ELME 02
Richard Wilfrid Selby, 1645-1649	SELB 10
John Placid Gascoigne, 1649-1653	GASC 06
William Claude White, 1653-1655	WHIT 68
Clement Lawrence Reyner, 1655-1657	REYN 04
Robert Paul Robinson, 1657-1659	ROBI 48
Thomas Cuthbert Horsley, 1659-1661	HORS 02
Augustine Hungate, 1661-1669	HUNG 04
Gregory Benedict Stapleton, 1669-1680	STAP 08
James Maurus Corker, 1680-1681	CORK 02
Joseph Sherburn, 1681-1697	SHER 08
Thomas Augustine Howard, 1697	HOWA 24
William Bernard Gregson, 1697-1701	GREG 08
Thomas Augustine Howard, 1701-1705	HOWA 24
William Bernard Gregson, 1705-1710	GREG 08
George Gregory Riddell, 1710-1713	RIDD 04
Arthur Francis Watmough, 1713-1717	WATM 02
Louis Lawrence Fenwick, 1717-1721	FENW 08
Thomas Southcote, 1721-1741	SOUT 12
Ralph Cuthbert Farnworth, 1741-1753	FARN 04
John Placid Howard, 1753-1766	HOWA 14
John Placid Naylor, 1766-1772	NAYL 08
John Fisher, 1772-1777	FISH 10
George Augustine Walker, 1777-1794	WALK 06
William Gregory Cowley, 1794-1799	COWL 10
John Bede Brewer, 1799-1822	BREW 06

(iii) THE PROVINCIALS OF THE ENGLISH DOMINICANS

Vincent Torre, 1685-1687	TORR 02
Edward Dominic Williams, 1687-1688	WILL 16
Thomas White, 1688-1694	WHIT 58
William Collins, Vicar General, 1694-1695	COLL 34
Edward Bing, 1695-1697	BING 02
Richard Ambrose Grymes,	
Vicar General 1698-1700, Provincial 1700-1708	GRYM 02
Thomas Worthington, 1708-1712	WORT 26
Thomas Dominic Williams, 1712-1716	WILL 62
John Raymund Green, 1716-1721	GREE 30
Morgan Joseph Hansbie, 1721-1725	HANS 02
Thomas Dominic Williams, 1725	WILL 62
Thomas Worthington, 1726-1730	WORT 26
Edward Ambrose Burgess, 1730-1734	BURG 01
Morgan Joseph Hansbie, 1734-1738	HANS 02
Richard Albert Lovett, 1738-1742	LOVE 16
Thomas Worthington, 1742-1746	WORT 26
Edward Ambrose Burgess, V.G. 1746-1747	BURG 01
Andrew Winter, Joint V.G. 1747-1748	WINT 00
Morgan Joseph Hansbie, Joint V.G. 1747-1748	HANS 02
Morgan Joseph Hansbie, 1748-1750	HANS 02
John Clarkson, Vicar General, 1750	CLAR 46
Edward Antoninus Hatton, 1754-1758	HATT 06
John Clarkson, 1758-1762	CLAR 46
John Stephen Catterall, 1762-1765	CATT 10
William Benedict Short, 1766-1770	SHOR 08
Edward Antoninus Hatton, 1770-1774	HATT 06
Joseph Edwards, 1774-1778	EDWA 14
William Benedict Short, 1778-1782	SHOR 08
Robert Peter Robson, 1782-1786	ROBS 04
William Benedict Short, 1786-1790	SHOR 08
John Raymund Bullock, 1790-1794	BULL 10
William Benedict Short, 1794-1798	SHOR 08
John Raymund Bullock, 1798-1802	BULL 10

(iv) THE PROVINCIALS OF THE ENGLISH FRANCISCAN RECOLLECTS

John Thomas Gennings, 1630	GENN 04
Christopher Francis Davenport, 1637	DAVE 02
George of St William Perrott, 1640	PERR 02
John Thomas Gennings, 1643	GENN 04
John Jerome Pickford, 1647	PICK 12
Christopher Francis Davenport, 1650	DAVE 02
Daniel of St John Yates, 1653	YATE 02
George of St William Perrott, 1656	PERR 02
Richard Angelus Mason, 1659	MASO 04

Nicholas of Holy Cross Cross, 1662	CROS 26
Christopher Francis Davenport, 1665	DAVE 02
Daniel of St Francis Clay, 1668	CLAY 02
Nicholas of Holy Cross Cross, 1671	CROS 26
John of Holy Cross Moore, 1674	MOOR 05
Daniel of St Francis Clay, 1677	CLAY 02
Nicholas of Holy Cross Cross, 1680	CROS 26
Gervase of St Francis Cartwright, 1683	CART 22
John of Holy Cross Moore, 1686	MOOR 05
Nicholas of Holy Cross Cross, 1689	CROS 26
Masseus of St Barbara Massey,	
Vicar Provincial, 1691, Provincial, 1692	MASS 12
Philip Pacificus Price, 1615	PRIC 14
Anthony of Padua Le Grand, 1698	LEGR 02
Masseus of St Barbara Massey, Vicar Provincial, 1699	MASS 12
Bonaventure of St Anne Parry, 1701	PARR 02
Philip Pacificus Price, 1704	PRIC 14
Louis Grimbaldstone, Vicar Provincial, 1706	GRIM 01
Martin of St Charles Grimston, 1707	GRIM 20
Angelus of St Mary Fortescue, 1710	FORT 06
Cuthbert Anthony Parkinson, 1713	PARK 40
Bernardine Smith, 1716	SMIT 06
William Bernard Baskerville, 1719	BASK 04
Cuthbert Anthony Parkinson, 1722	PARK 40
Thomas Philip of St Anne Sadler, 1725	SADL 12
John Joseph St John Baptist Poulton, 1728	POUL 26
Charles John Capistran Eyston, 1731	EYST 03
Thomas Philip of St Anne Sadler, Vicar Provincial, 1732	SADL 12
Bruno Cantrill, Vicar Provincial 1733, Provincial, 1734	CANT 02
John Joseph of St John Baptist Poulton, 1737	POUL 26
Thomas Holmes, 1740	HOLM 20
Bruno Cantrill, 1743	CANT 02
John Joseph of St John Baptist Poulton, 1746	POUL 26
Thomas Holmes, Vicar Provincial, 1748, Provincial, 1749	HOLM 20
Joseph Alexius Smallwood, 1752	SMAL 02
Charles Felix Englefield, 1755	ENGL 02
Thomas Holmes, 1758	HOLM 20
Arthur Pacificus Baker, 1761	BAKE 06
Philip André, 1764	ANDR 01
George Joachim Ingram, 1767	INGR 06
Arthur Pacificus Baker, 1770	BAKE 06
Richard Bonaventure Healey, 1773	HEAL 02
Joseph Needham, 1776	NEED 10
Romanus Chapman, 1779	CHAP 26
James Peter Frost, 1782	FROS 02
John Pacificus Nutt, 1785	NUTT 02
Romanus Chapman, 1788	CHAP 26

John Bonaventure Pilling, 1791	PILL 02
John Pacificus Nutt, 1794	NUTT 02
William Nicholas Knight,	
Vicar Provincial, 1799, Provincial 1800	KNIG 18

(v) THE PROVINCIALS OF THE ENGLISH JESUITS

Richard Blount, 1623	BLOU 11
Henry More, 1635	MORE 05
Matthew or Edward Wilson, 1641/2	WILS 16
Henry Bedingfeld, 1645/6	BEDI 12
Francis Foster, 1650	FOST 04
Matthew or Edward Wilson, 1653	WILS 16
Richard Bradshaigh, 1656	BRAD 18
Edward Leedes, 1660	LEED 02
John Clark, 1664	CLAR 21
Emmanuel Lobb, 1667	LOBB 02
George Gray, 1671	FRAY 02
Richard Strange, 1674	STRA 02
Thomas Whitbread, 1677/8	WHIT 14
John Warner, 1679	WARN 02
John Keynes, 1683	KEYN 12
William Morgan, 1688	MORG 38
John Warner, 1689	WARN 04
Anthony Lucas, 1693	LUCA 02
John Warner, 1693	WARN 04
William Mumford, 1694	MUMF 06
Henry Humberston, 1697	HUMB 04
James Blake, 1701	BLAK 02
Peter Hamerton, 1704	HAME 08
Louis de Sabran, 1709	SABR 02
Thomas Culcheth, 1712	CULC 04
Richard Plowden, 1716	PLOW 16
John Edisford, 1719	EDIS 04
Robert Beeston, 1721	BEES 15
Thomas Lawson, 1724	LAWS 10
John Turberville, 1725	TURB 10
Richard Richardson, 1731	RICH 30
Levinius Brown, 1733	BROW 24
Henry Bolt, 1739	BOLT 05
Charles Sherburn, 1740	SHER 04
Henry Sheldon, 1744	SHEL 10
Philip Carteret, 1751	CART 20
Henry Corby, 1756	CORB 16
James Dennett, 1762	DENN 04
Nathaniel Elliot, 1766	ELLI 04
Thomas More, 1769	MORE 16

APPENDIX II   STATISTICS

The reader is reminded, before reaching any conclusions from the tables of statistics, that for certain purposes a distorted impression might result from two elements in the compiler's policy for this work: the inclusion of priests of overseas and Scottish origin who worked on the English Mission and the inclusion of priests of English origin who either worked abroad or joined contemplative communities on the Continent. In general it may be said that the overwhelming majority of the clergy were English (or Welsh) of longstanding native stock as can be seen from a glance at the names on any page.

The following are the ten most common surnames and Christian names recorded in the work:

Smith (63); Green (31); Williams (29); Brown (27); Jones (26); White (26); Taylor (25); Anderton (24); Robinson (24); Thompson (22).

John (1007); Thomas (626); William (582); James (281); Richard (273); Robert (256); Francis (246); Edward (230); George (209); Henry (190).

1. ORDINATIONS OF PRIESTS PER QUARTER CENTURY

The following figures are necessarily imprecise but serve to show the general trend of clerical recruitment each quarter century. The figures are based on the records in this book with the exception of the 9 for whom no century has been determined. The operative date is that of ordination but where this is unknown other dates, in the following order of preference, have been used to estimate the date of ordination: a) birth, assuming ordination after 24 years; b) profession, assuming ordination after 4 years; c) death, assuming a ministry of 27 years in the 16th century, 32 years in the 17th century and 34 years in the 18th century.

	16th cent.	17th cent.	18th cent.
1st quarter	—	852	490
2nd quarter	—	734	526
3rd quarter	90	582	500
4th quarter	779	735	309
Quarter unknown	7	159	53
Sub-totals:	876	3062	1878

TOTAL as above	5816
add (century unknown)	9
GRAND TOTAL	5825

2A.   COUNTIES OF ORIGIN

	16th cent.	17th cent.	18th cent.	TOTAL
Lancashire	64	331	481	876
Yorkshire	107	281	106	494
Middlesex	31	192	236	459
Staffordshire	20	88	33	141
Durham	17	72	39	128
Northumberland	4	65	50	119
Hampshire	16	54	33	103
Oxford	34	47	18	99
Norfolk	18	58	18	94
Somerset	28	42	23	93
Lincolnshire	11	51	28	90
Warwickshire	9	49	29	87
Suffolk	9	57	13	79
Worcestershire	9	43	26	78
Essex	9	54	14	77
Monmouthshire	4	56	17	77
Herefordshire	11	48	13	72
Shropshire	9	39	22	70
Sussex	7	48	12	67
Kent	15	37	14	66
Berkshire	5	37	19	61
Derbyshire	16	33	8	57
Northamptonshire	10	30	10	50
Cheshire	11	24	14	49
Devon	9	29	10	48
Dorset	10	29	7	46
Westmorland	5	20	8	33
Wiltshire	3	23	5	31
Leicestershire	6	16	8	30
Flintshire	5	15	10	30
Gloucestershire	7	16	6	29
Cornwall	13	10	4	27
Caernarvon	8	18	0	26
Buckinghamshire	4	20	1	25
Nottinghamshire	1	14	10	25
Cambridgeshire	4	14	6	24
Cumberland	3	15	5	23
Denbighshire	3	11	3	17
Surrey	2	9	4	15
Brecknockshire	1	6	5	12
Montgomeryshire	0	5	6	11
Glamorganshire	1	5	3	9
Huntingdonshire	1	4	3	8
Hertfordshire	0	5	2	7
Pembrokeshire	3	3	1	7
Bedfordshire	0	6	0	6
Anglesey	3	1	1	5
Rutland	1	3	0	4
Carmarthenshire	0	2	1	3
Isle of Man	1	2	0	3
Radnorshire	0	3	0	3
Merionethshire	0	2	0	2

2B. OTHER COUNTRIES OF ORIGIN

Ireland	3	87	88	178
France	6	53	42	101
Low Countries	5	68	14	87
Scotland	7	29	24	60
Maryland	0	3	38	41
Italian States	0	7	13	20
Portugal	0	16	4	20
German States	0	2	14	16
Spain	0	7	6	13

3. SECULAR AND REGULAR CLERGY

	16th cent.	17th cent.	18th cent.	TOTAL
SECULARS (S)	614	1319	765	2698
JESUITS (SJ)	166	819	536	1521
BENEDICTINES (OSB)	27	420	269	716
REC. FRANCISCANS (OFM)	5	222	154	382
DOMINICANS (OP)	8	82	82	172
CARTHUSIANS (CRT)	30	44	21	95
DISC. CARMELITES (ODC)	0	46	28	74
CAP. FRANCISCANS (CAP)	13	47	11	71
CARMELITES (CAR)	0	13	9	22
BRIDGETTINES (OSS)	6	15	0	21
AUG. FRIARS (OSA)	1	16	3	20
ORATORIANS (ORA)	1	7	0	8
MINIMS (MIN)	4	1	0	5
AUG. CANONS (CRL)	0	3	0	3
CONV. FRANCISCAN (CON)	0	1	0	1
CAMALDOLESE (CAM)	0	1	0	1

BIBLIOGRAPHY

1. MSS AND UNPUBLISHED MATERIAL

DOWNSIDE ABBEY, BATH

(a) ARCHIVES

Fasti Gregoriani MS Biographies of the Monks of St Gregory's.

A.Allanson, *Biography of the English Benedictines* (MS biographies of all known E.B.C. monks to 1850). Annotated *Birt*.

A.Moore, *Historical Lists of the English Benedictine Congregation* (1980) (Typescript).

(b) RECUSANT STUDIES ROOM

G.Parmiter, *Elizabethan Members of the Inns of Court who became Priests* (1983) (Typescript).

G.Scott, *Alphabetical List of Late Seventeenth Century and Eighteenth Century English Benedictines* (1983) (Computer print-out).

W.V.Smith, *Corrections and Additions to Anstruther* 1-4 (1983) (Xerox of MS).

FOREST GATE FRANCISCAN FRIARY, LONDON, E.7

ARCHIVES OF THE ENGLISH PROVINCE O.F.M.

Clothing and Profession Book of St Bonaventure's Friary, Douai, 1737-1789 (Copy of transcript made from original in Douai Municipal Archives).

Nomina omnium FF. Defunctorum in Alma Nostra Provincia, 1618-1761 (MS original of item published in C.R.S.24).

Personal register 1755-1758 of Fr Felix Englefield, Minister Provincial. 'Residences of Our Gentlemen in 1758' (MS). Annotated *Thaddeus*.

114 MOUNT STREET, LONDON, W.1 (Society of Jesus)

(a) CATHOLIC RECORD SOCIETY COLLECTION

The Trappes-Lomax Card Index (13 boxes with over 5000 cards)

(b) ENGLISH PROVINCE S.J. ARCHVES

Annotated *Foley*.

WESTMINSTER, ARCHBISHOP'S HOUSE, LONDON, S.W.1

ARCHIVES OF THE ARCHBISHOP OF WESTMINSTER

Annotated *Anstruther* 1-4.

2. PRINTED

(a) STANDARD REFERENCE WORKS

Alumni Cantabrigienses (Venn).
Alumni Oxonienses (Foster).
The Catholic Directory.
The Dictionary of National Biography (DNB).
Dictionnaire d'Histoire et de Géographie Ecclésiastiques.
Dictionnaire de Spiritualité.
Gallia Christiana.
Hierarchia Catholica Medii et Recentioris Aevi.
The New Catholic Encyclopedia.
The Oxford Dictionary of the Christian Church (Cross).
The Oxford Dictionary of Saints (Farmer).

(b) OTHER PRINTED WORKS

Addington, R., *The Idea of the Oratory* (London, 1966).

Albion, G., *Charles I and the Court of Rome* (Louvain, 1935).

'The Old Chapter and Brotherhood, 1623-1973', *Clergy Review* 58 (1973), 679-688.

Alger, B., 'The Priest and Informer Hitchmough', *North West Catholic History* 1 (1969), 3-8, 83-94, 124-130.

Allison, A.F., 'The Later Life and Writings of Joseph Creswell, S.J. (1556-1623)', *Recusant History* 15 (1979), 79-144.

'Who was John Brereley? The Identity of a Seventeenth Century Controversialist', *Recusant History* 16 (1982), 17-41.

and Rogers, D.M., *A Catalogue of Catholic Books in English Printed Abroad or Secretly in England, 1558-1640* (Bognor Regis, 1956).

Anderson, W.J., 'William Thomson of Dundee, Friar Minor Conventual', *Innes Review* 18 (1967), 99-111.

Anstruther, G., *Vaux of Harrowden* (Newport, 1953).

A Hundred Homeless Years, English Dominicans 1558-1658 (London, 1958).

The Seminary Priests: 1. *Elizabethan 1558-1603* (Ware and Ushaw, 1968). 2. *Early Stuarts 1603-1659* (Great Wakering, 1975). 3. *1660-1715* (Great Wakering, 1976). 4. *1716-1800* (Great Wakering, 1977).

Antheunis, L., 'The Right Rev. George Chamberlain, Bishop of Ypres (1576-1634); *Recusant History* 2 (1953), 84-86.

Arundell of Wardour, *Notes by the 12th Lord Arundell of Wardour on the Family History* (London, 1916).

Attwater, D., *The Catholic Church in Modern Wales* (London, 1935).

Aveling, J.C.H., *Post-Reformation Catholicism in East Yorkshire* (York, 1960)

Catholic Recusancy in the West Riding 1558-1791 (Leeds, 1963)

Northern Catholics. Recusancy in the North Riding, 1558-1791 (London, 1966).

The Handle and the Axe. The Catholic Recusants in England from the Reformation to Emancipation (London, 1976).

The Jesuits (London, 1981).

'The Education of Eighteenth Century English Monks', *Downside Review* 79 (1961), 135-152.

Barnes, A.S., 'Catholic Chapels Royal under the Stuart Kings', *Downside Review* 19 (1900), 246-252; 20 (1901), 158-165, 232-249; 21 (1902), 39-55.

Basset, B., *The English Jesuits from Campion to Martindale* (London, 1967).

Beales, A.C.F., *Education under Penalty. English Catholic Education from the Reformation to the Fall of James II 1547-1689* (London, 1963).

Bellenger, D., 'The French Revolution and the Religious Orders. Three Communities 1789-1815', *Downside Review* 98 (1980), 25-41.

'The French Exiled Clergy in the North of England', *Archaeologia Aeliana* 10 (1982), 171-177.

'A Durham Priest in Counter Reformation Paris: Miles Pinkney (1599-1674)', *Northern Catholic History* 19 (1984), 13-17.

Berkeley, J., *Lulworth and the Welds* (Gillingham, 1971).

Birt, N.H., *Obit Book of the English Benedictines 1600-1912* (Edinburgh), 1913.

Blundell, F.O., *Old Catholic Lancashire*, 3 vols. (London, 1925-1941).

Bossy, J., *The English Catholic Community 1570-1850* (London, 1975).

'The Character of Elizabethan Catholicism', *Past and Present* 21 (1962), 39-59.

'Four Catholic Congregations in Rural Northumberland, 1750-1850', *Recusant History* 9 (1967), 88-119.

Buckingham, C., 'The Hawkins of Boughton-under-Blean', *London Recusant* 2 (1972), 1-11.

Burke, T., *Catholic History of Liverpool* (Liverpool, 1910).

Burke, W.P., *Irish Priests in the Penal Times 1660-1760* (Waterford, 1914).

Burton, E.H., *The Life and Times of Bishop Challoner, 1691-1781*, 2 vols. (London, 1909).

Butler, C., *Historical Memoirs of the English, Irish and Scottish Catholics since the Reformation*, 4 vols. (London, 1822).

Camm, R.B., *A Benedictine Martyr in England, Dom John Roberts* (London, 1897).

Forgotten Shrines (London, 1910).

Nine Martyr-Monks (London, 1931).

'Jesuits and Benedictines at Valladolid', *The Month* 92 (1898), 364-378.

Caraman, P., *John Gerard, the Autobiography of an Elizabethan* (London, 1951).

William Weston, the Autobiography of an Elizabethan (London, 1955).

Henry Morse, Priest of the Plague (London, 1957).

The Other Face, Catholic Life under Elizabeth I (London, 1960).

Henry Garnet, 1555-1606, and the Gunpowder Plot (London, 1964).

The Years of Siege. Catholic Life from James I to Cromwell (London, 1966).

Carrier, B. *A Missive to .... King James ....* (Reprinted Paris, 1649).

Castle, E. (ed.), *The Jerningham Letters, 1780-1843*, 2 vols.(London, 1896).

Catholic Record Society (CRS) Record Volumes.

1. (1905) Miscellanea.
2. (1906) Miscellanea.
3. (1906) Miscellanea.
4. (1907) Miscellanea.
5. (1908) Unpublished Documents relating to the English Martyrs 1, 1584-1603.

6. (1909) Miscellanea.
7. (1909) Miscellanea: Bedingfeld Papers, etc.
8. (1910) Diary of the Blue Nuns of the Immaculate Conception of Our Lady at Paris.
9. (1911) Miscellanea.
10-11. (1911) The Douay College Diaries, 1598-1654.
12. (1913) Obituaries and Catholic Memorial Inscriptions.
13. (1913) Miscellanea.
14. (1914) Miscellanea: Poor Clares Gravelines, etc.
15. (1913) Lancashire Registers 1: The Fylde 1.
16. (1914) Lancashire Registers 2: The Fylde 2.
17. (1915) Miscellanea: Liege C.R.S.S., Pontoise O.S.B., Registers, etc.
18. (1916) Recusants: Exchequer Roll, 1592-1593.
19. (1917) Miscellanea: Ghent Nuns O.S.B., Paris St Gregory's, 3 Registers O.S.F., and Lincolns Inn.
20. (1916) Lancashire Registers 3: North Part.
21. (1919) Ven.Philip Howard, Earl of Arundel, 1557-1595. English Martyrs 2.
22. (1921) Miscellanea: Early Recusants, Archpriest Controversy, Four Registers, Mawson Paper.
23. (1922) Lancashire Registers 4: Brindle, Samlesbury.
24. (1923) Franciscana: Annals of Nuns of Taunton. Obituary of Friars Minor.
25. (1925) Dominicana: Cardinal Howard, etc.
26. (1926) Miscellanea: Sanders Letters, Four Registers.
27. (1927) Miscellanea: Robert Graeme. Everingham Banquet. Three Registers.
28. (1928) Douay College Diaries. The Seventh Diary, 1715-1778.
29. (1929) The English College at Madrid, 1611-1767.
30. (1930) Registers of the English College at Valladolid, 1589-1862.
31. (1931) Lancashire Registers 5: Fernyhalgh, Goosnargh, Alston Lane.
32. (1932) Miscellanea: Francis Tregian, York Recusants 1735, Reports of Martyrs, Five Registers.
33. (1933) Memorials of Fr Augustine Baker (1571-1641) and Other Records relating to the English Benedictines.
34. (1934) London Sessions Records, 1605-1685.
35. (1936) Miscellanea: Registers of St Wilfrid's, York, Newcastle-upon-Tyne, Nuthill and Hedon.
36. (1936) Lancashire Registers 6: Chipping, Lee House, Ribchester, Dunkenhalgh.
37. (1940) Liber Ruber Venerabilis Collegii Anglorum de Urbe. Nomina Alumnorum, 1579-1630.
38. (1941) Registers of the Catholic Chapels Royal and of the Portugese Embassy Chapel, 1662-1829. 1. Marriages.
39. (1942) Letters and Memorials of Father Robert Persons 1. 1578-1588.
40. (1943) Liber Ruber ... 1631-1783.
41. (1948) Letters of Thomas Fitzherbert, 1608-1610.
42. (1949) Hampshire Registers 1.
43. (1949) Hampshire (and Dorset) Registers 2.
44. (1949) Hampshire Registers 3.
45-46. (1950, 1951) Archdeacon Nicholas Harpsfield's Canterbury Visitations, 1556-1558.
47-48. (1953, 1955) History of the English Persecution of Catholics and the Presbyterian Plot (1678-1685) by John Warner, S.J.
49. (1955) Hampshire Registers 4.
50. (1956) The Mawhood Diary, 1764-1790.
51. (1958) The Wisbech Stirs, 1595-1598.
52. (1959) Letters and Despatches of Richard Verstegan, c.1550-1640.
53. (1961) Miscellanea: Recusant Records.
54-55. (1962, 1963) Responsa Scholarum of the English College, Rome, 1598-1685.
56. (1964) Miscellanea: Meynell, Lambeth, Marnhull.
57. (1965) Recusant Roll 2 (1593-1594).
58. (1966) Letters of William Allen and Richard Barret, 1572-1598.
59. (1968) Isle of Wight Registers.
60. (1968) Recusant Documents from the Ellesmere Manuscripts, 1577-1715.
61. (1970) Recusant Rolls 3 (1594-1595) and 4 (1595-1596).
62. (1971) The Letter Book of Lewis Sabran, S.J., Rector of St Omer's College, October 1713 to October 1715.
63. (1972) Douai College Documents, 1639-1794.
64. (1973) Spain and the Jacobean Catholics 1.
65-66. (1975, 1976) Post-Reformation Catholicism in Bath.
67. (1981) Elizabethan Casuistry
68. (1978) Spain and the Jacobean Catholics 2.
69. (1979) St Omers and Bruges Colleges, 1593-1773. A Biographical Dictionary, by T.G.Holt.
70. (1984) The English Jesuits, 1650-1829. A Biographical Dictionary, by T.G.Holt.

Catholic Record Society (CRS) Monograph Series.
1. (1968) J.A.Williams, *Catholic Recusancy in Wiltshire, 1660-1791*
2. (1970) J.C.H.Aveling, *Catholic Recusancy in York, 1588-1791*
3. (1982) T.M.Blom, *The Post-Tridentine English Primer*

Catholic Record Society (CRS) Occasional Publications
1. (1980) Returns of Papists, 1767. Chester Diocese.

Chadwick, H., *St Omer's to Stonyhurst* (London,1962)

Challoner, R., *Memoirs of Missionary Priests*, ed.J.H.Pollen (London, 1924)

Champ, J.F., 'The Catholic Revival in Birmingham, c.1650-1850', *Worcestershire Recusant* 32 (1978), 3-12.

Charlton, L.E.O. (ed), *The Recollections of a Northumbrian Lady 1815-1866* (London, 1949).

Chaussy, Y., *Les Bénédictins Anglais Réfugiés en France au XVIIe siècle* (Paris, 1967).
    'New Evidence on the English Benedictines', *Downside Review* 88 (1970), 36-56.

Clancy, T.H., *English Catholic Books 1641-1700: A Bibliography* (Chicago, 1974).

Cleary, J.M., *The Catholic Recusancy of the Barlow Family of Slebech in Pembrokeshire in the Sixteenth and Seventeenth Centuries* (Cardiff, 1956).
    A Checklist of Welsh Students in the Seminaries 1568-1603 (Cardiff, 1958).

Coleman, A.(ed.), *The Irish Dominicans of the Seventeenth Century* (Dundalk, 1902).

Couve de Murville, M., and Jenkins, P., *Catholic Cambridge* (London, 1983).

Cuthbert, Father, *The Capuchins. A Contribution to the History of the Counter-Reformation* 2 vols. (London, 1928).

Dilworth, M., *The Scots in Franconia. A Century of Monastic Life* (Edinburgh, 1974).
    'Two Necrologies of Scottish Benedictine Abbeys in Germany', *Innes Review* 9 (1958), 173-203.
    'Three Scottish Benedictines', *Downside Review* 82 (1964), 233-245
    'Scottish Benedictines at Würzburg: A Supplement to the Necrology', *Innes Review* 15 (1964), 171-181.
    'The First Benedictine Mission to Scotland', *Downside Review* 83 (1965), 60-72, 159-168.
    'The First Scottish Monks in Ratisbon', *Innes Review* 16 (1965), 180-198.
    'The Würzburg Scots and the English Congregation', *Downside Review* 85 (1967), 39-61.
    'George and Audomarus John Asloan, Monks and Missionaries', *Innes Review* 22 (1971), 47-50.

Docherty, H., 'The Friars Minor in England: Their Historical Continuity'. *Clergy Review* 37 (1952), 332-351.

Dockery, J.B., *Collingridge. A Franciscan Contribution to Catholic Emancipation* (Newport, 1954).
    Christopher Davenport, Friar and Diplomat (London, 1960).

Duffy, E.,(ed.) *Challoner and his Church. A Catholic Bishop in Georgian England* (London, 1981).
    'Over the Wall': Converts from Popery in Eighteenth-Century England', *Downside Review* 94 (1976), 1-25.
    'Poor Protestant Flies': Conversions to Catholicism in Early Eighteenth-Century England', *Studies in Church History* 15 (1978), 289-304.
    'Richard Challoner and the English Salesian Tradition', *Clergy Review* 65 (1981), 449-453.
    — 'The English Secular Clergy and the Counter Reformation', *Journal of Ecclesiastical History* 34 (1983), 214-230.

Durkan, J., 'The Scottish Minims', *Innes Review* 2 (1951), 77-81.
    'John Francis Maitland, Minim', *Innes Review* 20 (1970), 163-164.
    'The Career of John Brown, Minim', *Innes Review* 20 (1970), 164-169.

Edwards, F.O.(ed), *The Elizabethan Jesuits* (London, 1981).

Ellis, T.P., *Welsh Benedictines of the Terror* (Newtown, 1936).

Emery, K., 'All and Nothing': Benet of Canfield's *Regle de Perfection*, *Downside Review* 92 (1974, 46-61.

Estcourt, E., and Payne, J.O., *English Catholic Non-Jurors 1715* (London, 1885).

Evans, N., 'The Tasburghs of South Elmham: the Rise and Fall of a Suffolk Gentry Family', *Suffolk Institute of Archaeology and History Proceedings* 34 (1980), 269-280.

Fenning, H., *Undoing of the Friars of Ireland* (Louvain, 1972).

Fletcher, J.R., *The Story of the English Bridgettines of Syon Abbey* (South Brent, 1933).

Foley, H.(ed.) *Records of the English Province of the Society of Jesus* 7 vols. (London, 1875-1883).

Foster, M., 'Walter Montague, Courtier, Diplomat and Abbot, 1603-1677', *Downside Review* 96 (1978), 85-102, 208-225.

Foster, S., *The Catholic Church in Ingatestone* (Ingatestone, 1982).

Fothergill, B., 'Behind the Grey Eminence: Benet of Canfield', *Pax* 55 (1965), 108-113.

Gaffney, W.J., *Elizabethan Students of the English College of St Alban, Valladolid* (Privately Printed, 1979).

Gamache, C.de, 'Memoirs', in *Court of Charles I*, Vol.2, ed.by R.F.Williams (London, 1848) 289-501.

Gell, J., 'The Return of the Cistercians to England', *Hallel* 10 (1982), 81-86.

Giblin, C., 'John Brown and John Francis Maitland, Scottish Minims', *Innes Review* 6 (1955), 145-148.

Gillespie,K., *Friends of Wales* (London, 1957).

Gillow, J., *A Bibliographical Dictionary of the English Catholics* 5 vols. (London, 1885-1902).
    The Haydock Papers. A Glimpse into English Catholic Life (London, 1888).

Grauwe, J.de, *Prosopographia Cartusiana Belgica (1314-1796)* (Salzburg, 1976).
    'Chartreuse de Sheen Anglorum à Nieuport', *Monasticon Belge (Province de Flandre Occidentale IV* 3 (1978), 1231-1262.

Green, B., *The English Benedictine Congregation. A Short History* (London, 1979).

Guilday, P., *The English Catholic Refugees on the Continent 1558-1795* (London, 1914).

Gumbley, W., *Obituary Notices of the English Dominicans 1555-1952* (London, 1955).

Haigh, C., *Reformation And Resistance in Tudor Lancashire* (Cambridge, 1975).

Harting, J.H., *London Catholic Missions* (London, 1905).

Havran, M.J., *The Catholics in Caroline England* (Stanford, California, 1962).

Hemphill, B., *Early Vicars Apostolic of England* (London, 1954).

Hendriks, L., *The London Charterhouse* (London, 1889).

Hicks, L., 'Father Persons and the Seminaries in Spain', *The Month* 177 (1931), 193-204, 410-417, 497-506; 178 (1931), 26-35, 143-152, 234-244.

Hilton, J.A., 'The Cumbrian Catholics', *Northern History* 16 (1980), 40-58.

Hinchcliffe, E., 'Hugh Sewell: The Identity of a Seminary Priest', *North Western Catholic History* 8 (1981), 1-2.

Hodgson, A.M., 'The Berkeley Family of Spetchley Park', *Worcestershire Recusant* 14 (1969), 22-33; 16 (1970), 22-34.
'The Chapel at Spetchley Park', *Worcestershire Recusant* 30 (1977), 9-16.

Holt, T.G., 'The Embassy Chapels in Eighteenth Century London'. *London Recusant* 2 (1972), 19-37.
'The English Province. The Ex-Jesuits and the Restoration (1773-1814)', *Archivum Historicum Societas Iesu* 42 (1973), 288-311.
'Long Melford and the Martin Family', *London Recusant* (1978), 2-8.
'Father Thomas West', *North West Catholic History* 5 (1978), 14-33.

Ingold, A.M.P., *Essai de Bibliographie Oratorienne* (Paris,1880-1882).

Jenkins, P., 'A Welsh Lancashire? Monmouthshire Catholics in the English Century, *Recusant History* 15 (1980), 176-188.

Jennings, B.(ed.), *Louvain Papers 1606-1827* (Dublin, 1968)
'Irish Names in the Malines Ordination Registers, 1602-1749', *Irish Ecclesiastical Record* 76-77 (1951-1952).

Jukes, J., *English Province of the Order of Friars Minor Conventual* (London, 1967).

Kirk, J., *Biographies of English Catholics in the Eighteenth Century*, ed. by J.H.Pollen and E.H.Burton (London, 1909).

Leherpeur, M., *L'Oratoire de France* (Paris, 1926).

Lekai, L.J., *The Cistercians. Ideals and Reality* (Kent State, 1977).

Lesouard, J.A., *Les Catholiques dans la Société Anglaise 1765-1865* (Lille and Paris, 1978).

Little, B., *Catholic Churches since 1623* (London, 1966).

Loomie, A.J., *The Spanish Elizabethans. The English Exiles at the Court of Philip II* (New York, 1963).

Lugano, P.T., *La Congregazione Camaldolese degli Eremiti di Montecorona* (Rome, 1908).

Lunn, D., *The English Benedictines 1540-1688* (London, 1980).

McCann, J., *English Benedictine Missions* (Privately Printed, 1940).

McGrath, P., *Papists and Puritans under Elizabeth I* (London, 1967).
'Winchester College and the Old Religion in the Sixteenth Century', *Winchester College Sixth-Centenary Essays*, ed.R.Custance (London, 1982), 229-280.

McGreal, W., 'Carmelites in London: A Penal Times Mission', *Aylesford Review* 7 (1965), 66-74.

McLoughlin, J., 'The Franciscans in Worcestershire', *Worcestershire Recusant* 19 (1972), 2-14.
'Baddesley Chapel - Two Eighteenth Century Lists', *Worcestershire Recusant* 23 (1974), 2-6.

Magee, B., *English Recusants* (London, 1938).

Martin, F.X., *Friar Nugent. A Study of Francis Lavalin Nugent, 1569-1635*, (London and Rome, 1962).
'The Irish Augustinians in Rome, 1656-1956', *The Irish Augustinians in Rome*, ed.J.F.Madden (Rome, 1956), 16-74.
'Obstinate' Skerrett, Missionary in Virginia, the West Indies and England, c.1674-c.1688', *Journal of the Galway Archaeological and Historical Society* 35 (1976), 12-51.

Martyrs of England and Wales, 1535-1680, A Chronological List (London, 1979).

Mathew, D., *Catholicism in England, 1535-1935* (London, 1936)
Sir Tobie Mathew (London, 1950).

Matthews, J.H., *The Vaughans of Courtfield* (London, 1912).

Mejer, A.de, 'The Attempt to Re-establish the English Augustinian Province under Queen Mary Tudor', *Analecta Augustiniana* 24 (1961), 5-29.
'James Willemart, O.S.A. at the Court of James II. The Fourth Attempt to Re-establish the English Augustinian Province', *Analecta Augustiniana* 41 (1978), 115-155.

Milburn, D., *History of Ushaw College* (Ushaw, 1964).

Miller, J., *Popery and Politics in England, 1660-1688* (Cambridge, 1973)

Millett, B., *The Irish Franciscans, 1651-1665* (Rome, 1964).

Minney, T.R., 'The Sheldons of Beoley', *Worcestershire Recusant* 5 (1965), 1-17.

Moorman,J.R.H., *The Franciscans in England* (London, 1974).

Morey, A., *The Catholic Subjects of Elizabeth I* (London, 1978).

Mould,D.D.C.P., *The Irish Dominicans* (Dublin, 1957).

O'Keefe, M.C., *Four Martyrs of South Wales and the Marches* (Cardiff, 1970).

Oliver, G., *Collections Illustrating the History of the Catholic Religion in the Counties of Cornwall, Devon, Dorset, Somerset, Wiltshire and Gloucestershire* (London, 1857).

Palmer, R., *Obituary Notices* (London, 1884).

Parmiter, G., *Elizabethan Popish Recusancy in the Inns of Court* (London, 1976).

Patterson, W.B., 'The Peregrinations of Marco Antonio de Dominis, 1616-1624', *Studies in Church History* 15 (1978), 241-257.

Payne, J.O., *Old English Catholic Missions* (London, 1889).

Petti, A.G., 'Peter Philips, Composer and Organist, 1561-1628' *Recusant History* 4 (1957), 48-60.

Price, W., 'Some Recusant Shropshire Families and their Worcestershire Connections', *Worcestershire Recusant* 11 (1968), 13-20.

'Provinciae Anglicae Ordinis Fratrum Minorum Conspectus, ejusdemque Ordinis Familiae Capuccinne Necrologium', *Capuchin Ordo* (Bristol, 1963), 52-62.

Reel, C., 'Father Constantine, O.F.M.Cap., 15? -1616', *Recusant History* 2 (1953), 23-36.

Reynolds, E.E., *The Roman Catholic Church in England and Wales: a Short History* (London, 1973).

'Secular Priests mentioned in the Mawhood Diary, 1764-1790', *Recusant History* 2 (1953), 167-182.

Roberti, G.M., *Disegno Storico dell Ordine de Minimi* 3 vols. (Rome, 1902-1922).

Robinson, J.M., *The Dukes of Norfolk - A Quincentennial History* (Oxford, 1982).

Rogers, D.M., 'John Abbott (1588?-1650)', *Recusant History* I (1951), 22-33, 245-250.

'An English Friar Minim in France', *Recusant History* 10 (1970), 273-291.

Scarisbrick, J.J., *The Reformation and the English People* (Oxford, 1984).

Scott, G., 'Fighting Old Battles: the English Benedictine Mission, 1689-1715', *Downside Review* 98 (1980), 9-24.

'A Berkshire Benedictine Mission in the Eighteenth Century', *South Western Catholic History* I (1983), 19-28.

Shanahan, D., 'Tyas of Leyton', *Essex Recusant* 6 (1964), 98-100.

Sharratt, M., 'Alban Butler, Newtonian in Part', *Downside Review* 96 (1978), 103-111.

'The Lisbon Collection at Ushaw', *Catholic Archives* 1 (1981), 36-39.

Sheppard, L.C., *The English Carmelites* (London, 1943).

Simpson, R.(ed.), *The Lady Falkland. Her Life. Also a Memoir of Father Francis Slingsby* (London, 1861).

Sitwell, G., 'The 1617 Constitutions of the English Benedictine Congregation', *Downside Review* 98 (1980), 291-297.

Smet, J., *History of the Carmelites* 3 (Darien, Illinois, 1982).

Smith, C., *The Catholics of Marnhull* (Marnhull, 1982).

'The Husseys of Marnhull' *South Western Catholic History* 2 (1984), 32-43.

Smith, W.V., 'The Riddell Family of Gateshead and Fenham as Recusants in the Seventeenth Century', *Northern Catholic History* 3 (1976), 10-16.

'St Mary's Parish, Stockton-on-Tees, to 1900, *Northern Catholic History* 9 (1979), 13-19.

'The Chaplains to the Radcliffe Family of Dilston Castle', *Northern Catholic History* 11 (1980),11-19.

Stapleton, B., *A History of the Post-Reformation Catholic Missions in Oxfordshire* (London, 1906).

Stewart, R.L., 'Thomas Stapleton, Student in Divinity', *Dublin Review* 240 (1966), 230-246.

Stonor, R.J., *Stonor. A Catholic Sanctuary in the Chilterns from the Fifth Century till Today* (Newport, 1951).

Strudwick, B., 'The Darells of Calehill', *Kent Recusant History* 4 (1980), 89-99.

Thaddeus, Father, *The Franciscans in England, 1600-1850* (London, 1898).

Trappes-Lomax, T.B., 'The Southcotes of Witham Place and their Contribution to the Survival of Catholicism in Essex', *Essex Recusant* 3 (1961), 105-115.

Tweedy, J.M., Popish Elvet: *The History of St Cuthbert's, Durham* I (Durham, 1981).

Walsh, E., 'The Spanish Chapel in the Eighteenth Century, 1713-1788', *London Recusant* 2 (1972), 72-84.

Walsh, T.J., *The Irish Continental College Movement* (Dublin and Cork, 1973).

Ward, B., *History of St Edmund's College, Old Hall* (London, 1893).

The Eve of Catholic Emancipation 3 Vols. (London, 1911-1912).

Whelan, B., *A Series of Lists relating to the English Benedictine Congregation* (Stanbrook1932).

Whitmore, P.J.S., *The Order of Minims in Seventeenth-Century France* (The Hague, 1967).

Williams, J.A., *Bath and Rome: the Living Link. Catholicism in Bath from 1559 to the Present Day* (Bath, 1963)

'Who was William Byfleet?', *Downside Review* 79 (1960/1961), 46-49.

'Sources for Recusant History (1559-1791) in English Official Archives', *Recusant History* 16 (1983), 331-451.

Williams, M.E., *The Venerable English College, Rome* (London, 1979).

Worrall, E.S., 'Beringtons of Herefordshire and Essex, *Essex Recusant* 9 (1967), 20-22.

Yeo, C.R., *The Structure and Content of Monastic Profession* (Rome, 1982).

Zimmerman, B., *Carmel in England* (London, 1899).